THE OXFORD
POPULAR
THESAURUS

THE OXFORD
POPULAR
THESAURUS

Prepared by

SARA HAWKER

Based on

The Oxford Minireference
Thesaurus

ALAN SPOONER

Based on The Oxford Minireference Thesaurus © Alan Spooner 1992.
This abridged edition published 1994 as The Oxford Popular Thesaurus
by Parragon Book Services and Magpie Books, an imprint of Robinson
Publishing Ltd., by arrangement with Oxford University Press.

Oxford is a trade mark of Oxford University Press

ISBN 1 85813 534 6

Typeset by Wyvern Typesetting Ltd.

Printed and bound in the United Kingdom by
HarperCollins Manufacturing

Contents

Using the thesaurus   vii

Abbreviations used   ix

THESAURUS   1

Using the Thesaurus

In this thesaurus you will find

Headwords

The words you want to look up are printed in bold and arranged in a single alphabetical sequence. In addition, there may be subheads in bold at the end of main entries for derived forms and phrases.

Synonyms

Synonyms are listed alphabetically, except that distinct senses of a headword are numbered and treated separately.

Under some headwords, in addition to the lists of synonyms given there, a cross-reference printed in SMALL CAPITALS takes you to another entry to provide an extended range of synonyms. These cross-references are marked by the arrowhead symbol ▷.

Antonyms

Cross-references printed in SMALL CAPITALS introduce you to lists of opposites. These cross-references are preceded by the abbreviation *Opp*.

Part-of-speech labels

Part-of-speech labels are given throughout. (See list of abbreviations.) Under each headword, synonyms for *adjective*, *adverb*, *noun*, and *verb* uses are separated by the symbol ●.

Illustrative phrases

Meanings of less obvious senses are indicated by illustrative phrases printed in *italic*.

Usage warnings

Usage markers in *italic* precede words which are normally only used in certain contexts—for example, slang, poetic, or jocular usage. (See list of abbreviations.)

Abbreviations used

Parts of speech

adj	adjective
adv	adverb
int	interjection
n	noun
prep	preposition
v	verb

Other abbreviations

derog	derogatory
inf	informal
joc	jocular
opp	opposite
pl	plural
poet	poetic
sl	slang
Amer	American usage
Fr	French
Lat	Latin
Scot	Scottish

A

abandon v 1 evacuate, leave, quit, vacate, withdraw from. 2 break with, desert, *inf* dump, forsake, jilt, leave behind, *inf* leave in the lurch, maroon, renounce, strand, *inf* throw over, *inf* wash your hands of. 3 *abandon a claim.* abdicate, cancel, cede, *inf* chuck in, discontinue, disown, *inf* ditch, drop, forfeit, forgo, give up, relinquish, resign, surrender, waive, yield.

abbey n cathedral, church, convent, friary, monastery, nunnery, priory.

abbreviate v abridge, compress, condense, cut, edit, précis, reduce, shorten, summarize, truncate. *Opp* LENGTHEN.

abdicate v renounce the throne, *inf* step down. ▷ ABANDON, RESIGN.

abduct v carry off, kidnap, *inf* make away with, seize.

abhor v detest, execrate, loathe, shudder at. ▷ HATE.

abhorrent adj abominable, detestable, execrable, loathsome, nauseating, obnoxious, repellent, revolting. ▷ HATEFUL. *Opp* ATTRACTIVE.

abide v 1 accept, bear, endure, put up with, stand, stomach, suffer, tolerate. 2 ▷ STAY. **abide by** ▷ OBEY.

ability n aptitude, bent, brains, capability, capacity, cleverness, competence, expertise, flair, genius, gift, intelligence, knack, *inf* know-how, knowledge, means, power, proficiency, prowess, resources, scope, skill, strength, talent, training, wit.

ablaze adj afire, aflame, aglow, alight, blazing, burning, flaming, lit up, on fire, raging.

able adj 1 accomplished, adept, capable, clever, competent, effective, efficient, experienced, expert, handy, intelligent, masterly, practised, proficient, skilful, skilled, talented. *Opp* INCOMPETENT. 2 allowed, at liberty, authorized, available, eligible, fit, free, permitted, willing. *Opp* UNABLE.

abnormal adj aberrant, anomalous, atypical, *inf* bent, bizarre, curious, deformed, deviant, distorted, eccentric, exceptional, extraordinary, freak, funny, idiosyncratic, irregular, *inf* kinky, malformed, odd, peculiar, perverted, queer, singular, strange, uncharacteristic, unnatural, unorthodox, unrepresentative, untypical, unusual, wayward, weird. *Opp* NORMAL.

abolish v abrogate, annul, delete, destroy, dispense with, do away with, eliminate, end, eradicate, finish, get rid of, liquidate, nullify, overturn, put an end to, quash, remove, suppress, terminate, withdraw. *Opp* CREATE.

abominable adj abhorrent, appalling, atrocious, awful, base, beastly, brutal, cruel, despicable, detestable, disgusting, dreadful, execrable, foul, hateful, heinous, horrible, inhuman, inhumane, loathsome, nasty, obnoxious, odious, repellent, repugnant, repulsive, revolting, terrible, vile. *Opp* PLEASANT.

abort *v* 1 be born prematurely, die, miscarry. 2 *abort take-off.* call off, end, halt, nullify, stop, terminate.

abortion *n* miscarriage, premature birth, termination of pregnancy.

abortive *adj* fruitless, futile, ineffective, pointless, stillborn, unfruitful, unsuccessful, vain. *Opp* SUCCESSFUL.

abound *v* be plentiful, flourish, prevail, swarm, teem, thrive.

abrasive *adj* biting, caustic, galling, grating, harsh, hurtful, irritating, rough, sharp. ▷ UNKIND. *Opp* KIND.

abridge *v* abbreviate, compress, condense, cut, edit, précis, reduce, shorten, summarize, truncate. *Opp* EXPAND.

abridged *adj* abbreviated, bowdlerized, censored, compact, concise, cut, edited, *inf* potted, shortened.

abrupt *adj* 1 hasty, headlong, hurried, precipitate, quick, rapid, sudden, unexpected, unforeseen. 2 *abrupt drop.* precipitous, sharp, sheer, steep. 3 *abrupt manner.* blunt, brisk, brusque, curt, discourteous, rude, snappy, terse, uncivil, ungracious. *Opp* GENTLE, GRADUAL.

absent *adj* 1 away, *sl* bunking off, gone, missing, off, out, playing truant, *sl* skiving. *Opp* PRESENT. 2 ▷ ABSENT-MINDED.

absent-minded *adj* absent, absorbed, abstracted, careless,

distracted, dreamy, forgetful, inattentive, oblivious, preoccupied, scatterbrained, unaware, unthinking, vague, withdrawn, wool-gathering. *Opp* ALERT.

absolute *adj* 1 categorical, certain, complete, conclusive, decided, definite, downright, genuine, implicit, inalienable, indubitable, out and out, perfect, positive, pure, sheer, sure, thorough, total, unadulterated, unambiguous, unconditional, unequivocal, unmitigated, unqualified, unreserved, unrestricted, utter. 2 *absolute ruler.* autocratic, despotic, dictatorial, omnipotent, totalitarian, tyrannical. 3 *absolute opposites. inf* dead, diametrical, exact.

absorb *v* 1 assimilate, consume, digest, drink in, hold, imbibe, incorporate, ingest, mop up, soak up, suck up, take in. *Opp* EMIT. 2 *absorb a blow.* cushion, deaden, lessen, soften. 3 *absorb a person.* captivate, engage, engross, enthral, fascinate, occupy, preoccupy. ▷ INTEREST. **absorbed** ▷ INTERESTED.

absorbent *adj* absorptive, permeable, pervious, porous, spongy. *Opp* IMPERVIOUS.

absorbing *adj* engrossing, fascinating, gripping, spellbinding. ▷ INTERESTING.

abstain *v* abstain from avoid, cease, deny yourself, desist from, eschew, forgo, give up, go without, refrain from, refuse, resist, shun, withhold from.

abstemious *adj* ascetic, frugal, moderate, restrained, self-denying, sparing, temperate. *Opp* SELF-INDULGENT.

abstract adj 1 academic, hypothetical, indefinite, intangible, intellectual, metaphysical, notional, philosophical, theoretical, unreal. *Opp* CONCRETE. 2 *abstract art*. non-pictorial, non-representational, symbolic. • *n* outline, précis, résumé, summary, synopsis.

abstruse adj complex, cryptic, deep, devious, difficult, enigmatic, esoteric, hard, incomprehensible, mysterious, obscure, perplexing, problematic, profound, unfathomable. *Opp* OBVIOUS.

absurd adj crazy, *inf* daft, eccentric, farcical, foolish, grotesque, illogical, incongruous, irrational, laughable, ludicrous, nonsensical, outlandish, paradoxical, preposterous, ridiculous, senseless, silly, stupid, surreal, unreasonable, zany. ▷ FUNNY, MAD. *Opp* RATIONAL.

abundant adj ample, bountiful, copious, excessive, flourishing, generous, lavish, liberal, luxuriant, overflowing, plentiful, profuse, rampant, rank, rich, well-supplied. *Opp* SCARCE.

abuse *n* 1 assault, ill-treatment, maltreatment, misappropriation, misuse, perversion. 2 *verbal abuse*. curse, execration, imprecation, insult, invective, obscenity, slander, vilification, vituperation. • *v* 1 damage, exploit, harm, hurt, ill-treat, injure, maltreat, misuse, molest, rape, spoil, treat roughly. 2 *abuse verbally*. affront, berate, be rude to, *inf* call names, castigate, curse, defame, denigrate, insult, inveigh against, libel, malign, revile, slander, smear, sneer at, swear at, vilify, vituperate, wrong.

abusive adj acrimonious, angry, censorious, critical, cruel, defamatory, denigrating, derogatory, disparaging, hurtful, impolite, injurious, insulting, libellous, offensive, opprobrious, pejorative, rude, scathing, scornful, scurrilous, slanderous, vituperative. *Opp* POLITE.

abysmal adj 1 bottomless, boundless, deep, immeasurable, incalculable, infinite, profound, vast. 2 ▷ BAD.

abyss *n inf* bottomless pit, chasm, crater, fissure, gap, gulf, hole, pit, rift, void.

academic adj 1 collegiate, educational, scholastic. 2 bookish, *inf* brainy, clever, erudite, highbrow, intelligent, learned, scholarly, studious. 3 *academic study*. abstract, conjectural, hypothetical, impractical, intellectual, speculative, theoretical. • *n inf* egghead, highbrow, intellectual, scholar, thinker.

accelerate *v* 1 *inf* get a move on, go faster, hasten, pick up speed, quicken, speed up. 2 bring on, expedite, spur on, step up, stimulate.

accent *n* 1 brogue, cadence, dialect, enunciation, intonation, pronunciation, speech pattern, tone. 2 accentuation, beat, emphasis, pulse, rhythm, stress.

accept *v* 1 get, *inf* jump at, receive, take, welcome. 2 acknowledge, admit, bear, put up with, reconcile yourself to, resign yourself to, submit to, suffer, tolerate, undertake. 3 *accept an argument*. abide by, accede to, acquiesce in, agree to, believe in, be reconciled to, con-

acceptable *adj* 1 agreeable, gratifying, pleasant, pleasing, worthwhile. 2 adequate, admissible, moderate, passable, satisfactory, suitable, tolerable. *Opp* UNACCEPTABLE.

acceptance *n* acquiescence, agreement, approval, consent. *Opp* REFUSAL.

accepted *adj* acknowledged, agreed, axiomatic, common, indisputable, recognized, standard, undisputed, unquestioned. *Opp* CONTROVERSIAL.

accessible *adj* approachable, at hand, attainable, available, close, convenient, handy, within reach. *Opp* INACCESSIBLE.

accessory *n* 1 addition, appendage, attachment, component, extra. 2 ▷ ACCOMPLICE.

accident *n* 1 blunder, chance, coincidence, fate, fluke, fortune, luck, misadventure, mischance, mishap, mistake, *inf* pot luck, serendipity. 2 catastrophe, collision, crash, disaster, *inf* pile-up, wreck.

accidental *adj* arbitrary, casual, chance, coincidental, *inf* fluky, fortuitous, fortunate, haphazard, inadvertent, lucky, random, unexpected, unforeseen, unintended, unintentional, unlucky, unplanned, unpremeditated. *Opp* INTENTIONAL.

acclaim *v* applaud, celebrate, cheer, clap, commend, extol, hail, honour, praise, salute, welcome.

accommodate *v* 1 assist, equip, fit, furnish, help, provide, serve, supply. 2 *accommodate guests.* billet, board, cater for, harbour, house, lodge, provide for, *inf* put up, quarter, shelter, take in. 3 *accommodate yourself to new surroundings.* accustom, adapt, reconcile. **accommodating** ▷ CONSIDERATE.

accommodation *n* board, *inf* digs, home, housing, lodgings, pied-à-terre, premises, rooms, shelter.

accompany *v* 1 attend, chaperon, conduct, escort, follow, go with, guard, guide, look after, partner, *inf* tag along with. 2 be associated with, be linked with, belong with, complement, occur with, supplement.

accompanying *adj* associated, attached, attendant, complementary, related.

accomplice *n* abettor, accessory, associate, collaborator, colleague, confederate, conspirator, helper, partner.

accomplish *v* achieve, attain, *inf* bring off, carry out, carry through, complete, consummate, discharge, do successfully, effect, finish, fulfil, realize, succeed in.

accomplished *adj* adept, expert, gifted, polished, proficient, skilful, talented.

accomplishment *n* ability, attainment, expertise, gift, skill, talent.

accord *n* agreement, concord, harmony, rapport, understanding.

account *n* 1 bill, calculation, check, computation, invoice, receipt, reckoning, *inf* score, statement. 2 commentary, description, diary, explanation, history, log, memoir, narrative, record, report, statement, story, tale, *inf* write-up. 3 *of no account.*

advantage, benefit, concern, consequence, importance, interest, significance, use, value, worth. **account for** ▷ EXPLAIN.

accumulate v accrue, aggregate, amass, assemble, bring together, build up, collect, come together, gather, grow, heap up, hoard, increase, multiply, pile up, stockpile, store up. *Opp* DISPERSE.

accumulation n inf build-up, collection, conglomeration, gathering, heap, hoard, mass, stockpile, store.

accurate adj authentic, careful, correct, exact, factual, faultless, meticulous, minute, nice, perfect, precise, reliable, scrupulous, sound, inf spot-on, true, truthful, unerring, veracious. *Opp* INACCURATE.

accusation n allegation, charge, citation, complaint, impeachment, indictment, summons.

accuse v attack, blame, bring charges against, censure, charge, condemn, denounce, impeach, impugn, indict, inf point the finger at, prosecute, summons, tax. *Opp* DEFEND.

accustomed adj common, customary, established, expected, familiar, habitual, normal, ordinary, prevailing, routine, traditional, usual. **get accustomed** ▷ ADAPT.

ache n anguish, discomfort, hurt, pain, pang, smart, soreness, throbbing, twinge. ● v 1 be painful, be sore, hurt, smart, sting, throb. 2 ▷ DESIRE.

achieve v 1 accomplish, attain, bring off, carry out, complete, conclude, do successfully, effect, engineer, execute, finish, fulfil, manage, succeed in. 2 *achieve*

fame. acquire, earn, gain, get, obtain, reach, win.

acid adj sharp, sour, stinging, tangy, tart, vinegary. *Opp* SWEET.

acknowledge v 1 accede, accept, acquiesce, admit, allow, concede, confess, confirm, endorse, grant, own up to, profess. *Opp* DENY. 2 *acknowledge a greeting.* answer, react to, reply to, respond to, return. 3 *acknowledge a friend.* greet, hail, recognize, inf say hello to. *Opp* IGNORE.

acme n apex, crown, height, highest point, peak, pinnacle, summit, top, zenith. *Opp* NADIR.

acquaint v announce, apprise, brief, enlighten, inform, make aware, make familiar, notify, reveal, tell.

acquaintance n 1 awareness, familiarity, knowledge, understanding. 2 ▷ FRIEND.

acquire v buy, come by, earn, get, obtain, procure, purchase.

acquisition n addition, inf buy, gain, possession, purchase.

acquit v absolve, clear, declare innocent, discharge, excuse, exonerate, find innocent, free, let off, release, reprieve, set free, vindicate. *Opp* CONDEMN. **acquit yourself** ▷ BEHAVE.

acrid adj bitter, caustic, pungent, sharp, unpleasant.

acrimonious adj abusive, acerbic, angry, bad-tempered, bitter, caustic, hostile, hot-tempered, ill-tempered, irascible, quarrelsome, rancorous, sarcastic, sharp, spiteful, tart, testy, venomous, virulent, waspish. *Opp* PEACEABLE.

act n **1** deed, exploit, feat, opera-tion, undertaking. ▷ ACTION. **2** act of parliament. bill [= draft act], decree, edict, law, regula-tion, statute. **3** stage act. perform-ance, routine, sketch, turn.
● v **1** behave, carry on, conduct yourself. **2** function, operate, serve, take effect, work. **3** Act now! do something, get involved, take steps. ▷ BEGIN. **4** act a role. appear (as), derog camp it up, characterize, dramatize, enact, derog ham it up, impersonate, mime, mimic, derog overact, per-form, personify, play, portray, pose as, represent. ▷ PRETEND.

acting adj deputy, interim, stand-by, stopgap, substitute, temporary, vice-.

action n **1** act, deed, enterprise, exploit, feat, measure, perform-ance, proceeding, step, undertak-ing, work. **2** activity, drama, energy, enterprise, excitement, exertion, liveliness, movement, vigour, vitality. **3** action of a play. events, happenings, story. **4** action of a watch. mechanism, operation, working, works. **5** military action. ▷ BATTLE.

activate v actuate, energize, excite, fire, galvanize, initiate, mobilize, rouse, set in motion, set off, start, stimulate, trigger.

active adj **1** animated, brisk, bustling, busy, dynamic, ener-getic, enthusiastic, functioning, hyperactive, live, lively, milit-ant, nimble, inf on the go, rest-less, sprightly, strenuous, vigor-ous, vivacious, working. **2** active support. committed, dedicated, devoted, diligent, hard-working, industrious, involved, occupied, sedulous, staunch, zealous. Opp INACTIVE.

activity n **1** action, animation, bustle, commotion, energy, hurly-burly, hustle, industry, life, movement, stir. **2** hobby, interest, job, occupation, pas-time, pursuit, task, venture. ▷ WORK.

actor, actress ns artist, artiste, lead, leading lady, performer, player, star, supporting actor. **actors** cast, company, troupe.

actual adj authentic, bona fide, confirmed, corporeal, definite, existing, factual, genuine, indis-putable, in existence, legitimate, living, material, real, tangible, true, verifiable. Opp IMAGINARY.

acute adj **1** narrow, pointed, sharp. **2** acute pain. excruciat-ing, exquisite, extreme, intense, keen, piercing, racking, severe, sharp, shooting, violent. **3** acute mind. alert, analytical, astute, inf cute, discerning, incisive, intelligent, keen, penetrating, perceptive, sharp, subtle. ▷ CLEVER. **4** acute problem. cru-cial, immediate, important, over-whelming, pressing, serious, urgent. **5** acute illness. critical, sudden. Opp CHRONIC, STUPID.

adapt v **1** acclimatize, accustom, adjust, attune, become condi-tioned, become hardened, fit, get accustomed (to), get used (to), habituate, reconcile, suit, tailor, turn. **2** adapt to a new use. alter, amend, change, convert, modify, process, rearrange, rebuild, reconstruct, refashion, remake, reorganize, transform. ▷ EDIT.

add v annex, append, attach, com-bine, integrate, join, inf tack on, unite. Opp DEDUCT. **add to** ▷ INCREASE. **add up (to)** ▷ TOTAL.

addict n 1 alcoholic, sl junkie, inf user. 2 ▷ ENTHUSIAST.

addiction n compulsion, craving, dependence, fixation, obsession.

addition n 1 adding up, calculation, computation, reckoning, totalling, inf totting up. 2 accessory, addendum, additive, adjunct, admixture, annexe, appendage, appendix, attachment, continuation, development, expansion, extension, extra, increase, increment, postscript, supplement.

additional adj added, extra, further, increased, more, new, other, spare, supplementary.

address n 1 directions, location, whereabouts. 2 deliver an address. discourse, harangue, homily, lecture, sermon, speech, talk. ● v 1 accost, approach, inf buttonhole, greet, hail, salute, speak to, talk to. 2 address an audience. give a speech to, harangue, lecture.
  address yourself to ▷ TACKLE.

adept adj clever, competent, gifted, practised, proficient. ▷ SKILFUL. Opp UNSKILFUL.

adequate adj acceptable, all right, average, competent, fair, fitting, middling, inf OK, passable, presentable, satisfactory, inf so-so, sufficient, tolerable. Opp INADEQUATE.

adhere v bind, bond, cement, cling, glue, gum, paste. ▷ STICK.

adherent n aficionado, devotee, fan, follower, inf hanger-on, supporter.

adhesive adj glued, gluey, gummed. ▷ STICKY.

adjoining adj abutting, adjacent, bordering, juxtaposed, neighbouring, next, touching. Opp DISTANT.

adjourn v break off, defer, discontinue, interrupt, postpone, put off, suspend.

adjournment n break, interruption, pause, postponement, recess, stay, suspension.

adjust v 1 adapt, alter, amend, balance, change, convert, correct, modify, put right, rectify, regulate, remake, remodel, reorganize, reshape, set, tailor, temper, tune. 2 acclimatize, accommodate, accustom, fit, habituate, reconcile yourself.

administer v 1 administrate, conduct affairs, control, direct, govern, lead, manage, organize, oversee, preside over, regulate, rule, run, supervise. 2 administer justice. carry out, execute, implement, prosecute. 3 administer medicine. dispense, distribute, give, hand out, measure out, mete out, provide, supply.

administrator n bureaucrat, civil servant, controller, director, executive, manager, derog mandarin, organizer. ▷ CHIEF.

admirable adj awe-inspiring, commendable, creditable, deserving, estimable, excellent, exemplary, great, honourable, laudable, marvellous, meritorious, pleasing, praiseworthy, wonderful, worthy. Opp CONTEMPTIBLE.

admiration n appreciation, awe, commendation, esteem, hero-worship, high regard, honour, praise, respect. Opp CONTEMPT.

admire v applaud, appreciate, approve of, be delighted by, commend, esteem, have a high opinion of, hero-worship, honour, idolize, laud, look up to, marvel at, praise, respect, revere, think highly of, value, venerate, wonder at. ▷ LOVE. **admiring** ▷ COMPLIMENTARY, RESPECTFUL.

admission n 1 access, admittance, entrance, entry. 2 acceptance, acknowledgement, affirmation, concession, confession, declaration, disclosure, revelation. *Opp* DENIAL.

admit v 1 accept, allow in, let in, provide a place (in), receive, take in. 2 *admit guilt.* accept, acknowledge, allow, concede, confess, declare, disclose, own up, recognize, reveal, say reluctantly. *Opp* DENY.

adolescence n boyhood, girlhood, growing up, puberty, *inf* teens, youth.

adolescent adj boyish, girlish, immature, juvenile, pubescent, teenage, youthful. ● n boy, girl, juvenile, minor, *inf* teenager, youngster, youth.

adopt v 1 appropriate, approve, back, choose, embrace, endorse, follow, *inf* go for, patronize, support, take on, take up. 2 befriend, foster, stand by, take in.

adore v dote on, glorify, honour, love, revere, venerate, worship. ▷ ADMIRE. *Opp* HATE.

adorn v beautify, decorate, embellish, garnish, ornament, trim.

adrift adj 1 afloat, anchorless, drifting, floating. 2 aimless, astray, directionless, lost, purposeless.

adult adj full-grown, full-size, grown-up, marriageable, mature, of age. *Opp* IMMATURE.

adulterate v alloy, contaminate, corrupt, debase, dilute, *inf* doctor, pollute, taint, weaken.

advance n development, evolution, forward movement, growth, headway, improvement, progress. ● v 1 approach, bear down, come near, forge ahead, gain ground, go forward, make headway, make progress, move forward, press on, progress, *inf* push on. *Opp* RETREAT. 2 *our knowledge will advance.* develop, evolve, improve, prosper, thrive. 3 *advance your career.* accelerate, assist, benefit, boost, further, help the progress of, promote. *Opp* HINDER. 4 *advance a theory.* adduce, give, present, propose, submit, suggest. 5 *advance money.* lend, offer, pay, provide, supply. *Opp* WITHHOLD.

advanced adj 1 latest, modern, sophisticated, up-to-date. 2 *advanced ideas.* avant-garde, contemporary, experimental, forward-looking, futuristic, imaginative, innovative, new, novel, original, pioneering, progressive, revolutionary, trend-setting, *inf* way-out. 3 *advanced maths.* complex, difficult, hard, higher. 4 *advanced for her age.* grown-up, mature, precocious, sophisticated. *Opp* BACKWARD, BASIC.

advantage n 1 aid, asset, assistance, benefit, boon, gain, help, profit, usefulness. 2 *have an advantage.* dominance, edge, *inf* head start, superiority. **take advantage of** ▷ EXPLOIT.

advantageous adj beneficial, favourable, helpful, positive, profitable, salutary, useful, valu-

able, worthwhile. ▷ GOOD.
Opp USELESS.

adventure n 1 chance, escapade, exploit, feat, gamble, occurrence, risk, undertaking, venture.
2 danger, excitement, hazard.

adventurous adj 1 audacious, bold, brave, courageous, daredevil, daring, *derog* foolhardy, intrepid, *derog* reckless, venturesome. 2 *adventurous trip*. challenging, dangerous, difficult, exciting, hazardous, risky.
Opp UNADVENTUROUS.

adversary n antagonist, attacker, enemy, foe, opponent.

adverse adj 1 attacking, censorious, critical, derogatory, hostile, hurtful, inimical, negative, uncomplimentary, unfavourable, unkind, unsympathetic. 2 *adverse conditions*. detrimental, disadvantageous, harmful, inappropriate, inauspicious, opposing, prejudicial, uncongenial, unpropitious.
Opp FAVOURABLE.

advertise v announce, broadcast, display, flaunt, make known, market, merchandise, *inf* plug, proclaim, promote, publicize, *inf* push, show off, tout.

advertisement n *inf* advert, bill, *inf* blurb, circular, commercial, leaflet, notice, placard, *inf* plug, poster, promotion, publicity, sign, *inf* small ad.

advice n 1 admonition, counsel, guidance, help, opinion, recommendation, tip, view, warning.
2 ▷ NEWS.

advisable adj expedient, judicious, politic, prudent, recommended, sensible. ▷ WISE.

advise v 1 admonish, caution, counsel, enjoin, exhort, guide,

instruct, recommend, suggest, urge, warn. 2 ▷ INFORM.

adviser n confidant(e), consultant, counsellor, guide, mentor.

advocate n 1 apologist, backer, champion, proponent, supporter. 2 ▷ LAWYER. ● v argue for, back, champion, favour, recommend, speak for, uphold.

aesthetic adj artistic, beautiful, cultivated, sensitive, tasteful.
Opp UGLY.

affair n 1 activity, business, concern, issue, interest, matter, project, subject, topic, undertaking. 2 circumstance, episode, event, happening, incident, occurrence, thing. 3 *love affair*. amour, attachment, intrigue, involvement, liaison, relationship, romance.

affect v 1 act on, agitate, alter, attack, change, concern, disturb, have an effect on, have an impact on, impinge on, impress, influence, move, perturb, relate to, stir, touch, trouble, upset. 2 *affect an accent*. adopt, assume, feign, *inf* put on. ▷ PRETEND.

affectation n artificiality, insincerity, mannerism, posturing.
▷ PRETENCE.

affected adj 1 artificial, contrived, insincere, *inf* put on, studied, unnatural. ▷ PRETENTIOUS. 2 *affected by disease*. afflicted, damaged, infected, injured, poisoned, stricken, troubled.

affection n attachment, fondness, friendliness, friendship, liking, partiality, *inf* soft spot, tenderness, warmth. ▷ LOVE.

affectionate adj caring, doting, fond, kind, tender. ▷ LOVING.
Opp ALOOF.

affinity n closeness, compatibility, kinship, like-mindedness, likeness, rapport, relationship, similarity, sympathy.

affirm v assert, avow, declare, maintain, state, swear, testify.

affirmation n assertion, avowal, declaration, oath, promise, statement, testimony.

affirmative adj agreeing, assenting, concurring, confirming, positive. Opp NEGATIVE.

afflict v affect, annoy, beset, bother, burden, cause suffering to, distress, harass, harm, hurt, oppress, pain, plague, torment, torture, trouble, try, worry, wound.

affluent adj 1 inf flush, sl loaded, moneyed, prosperous, rich, wealthy, inf well-heeled, well-off, well-to-do. 2 affluent life-style. expensive, gracious, lavish, opulent, self-indulgent, sumptuous. Opp POOR.

afford v 1 be rich enough, have the means, manage to give, sacrifice, inf stand. 2 ▷ PROVIDE.

afloat adj aboard, adrift, floating, on board ship, under sail.

afraid adj 1 aghast, agitated, alarmed, anxious, apprehensive, cowardly, cowed, daunted, diffident, faint-hearted, fearful, frightened, hesitant, horrified, intimidated, inf jittery, nervous, panicky, panic-stricken, reluctant, scared, terrified, timid, timorous, trembling, unheroic. Opp FEARLESS. 2 [inf] I'm afraid I'm late. apologetic, regretful, sorry. be afraid ▷ FEAR.

afterthought n addendum, addition, extra, postscript.

age n 1 advancing years, decrepitude, dotage, old age, senility.

2 bygone age. days, epoch, era, time. 3 [inf] ages ago. lifetime, long time. ● v degenerate, grow older, look older, mature, mellow, ripen. aged ▷ OLD.

agenda n list, plan, programme, schedule, timetable.

agent n broker, delegate, envoy, executor, functionary, go-between, intermediary, mediator, middleman, negotiator, proxy, representative, surrogate, trustee.

aggravate v 1 add to, augment, compound, exacerbate, exaggerate, increase, inflame, intensify, make worse, worsen. Opp ALLEVIATE. 2 ▷ ANNOY.

aggressive adj antagonistic, assertive, bellicose, belligerent, bullying, inf butch, hostile, inf macho, militant, offensive, pugnacious, inf pushy, quarrelsome, violent, warlike. Opp DEFENSIVE, PEACEABLE.

aggressor n assailant, attacker, instigator, invader.

agile adj acrobatic, adroit, deft, fleet, graceful, lissom, lithe, mobile, nimble, quick-moving, sprightly, spry, supple. Opp CLUMSY.

agitate v 1 beat, churn, froth up, ruffle, shake, stimulate, stir, toss, work up. 2 alarm, arouse, confuse, discomfit, disconcert, excite, fluster, incite, perturb, stir up, trouble, unsettle, upset, worry. Opp CALM. agitated ▷ EXCITED, NERVOUS.

agitator n firebrand, rabble-rouser, revolutionary, troublemaker.

agonize v hurt, labour, suffer, worry, wrestle.

agony n anguish, distress, suffering, torment, torture. ▷ PAIN.

agree v 1 accede, acquiesce, admit, allow, assent, be willing, concede, consent, grant, make a contract, pledge yourself, promise, undertake. 2 accord, be unanimous, be united, concur, correspond, fit, get on, harmonize, match, inf see eye to eye. Opp DISAGREE. **agree on** ▷ CHOOSE. **agree with** ▷ ENDORSE.

agreeable adj acceptable, delightful, enjoyable, nice. ▷ PLEASANT. Opp DISAGREEABLE.

agreement n 1 accord, compatibility, concord, conformity, consensus, consistency, correspondence, harmony, similarity, sympathy, unanimity, unity. 2 alliance, armistice, arrangement, bargain, compact, contract, convention, covenant, deal, entente, pact, settlement, treaty, truce, understanding. Opp DISAGREEMENT.

agricultural adj 1 agrarian, bucolic, pastoral, rural. 2 agricultural land. cultivated, farmed, productive, tilled.

agriculture n agronomy, crofting, cultivation, farming, husbandry, tilling.

aground adj beached, grounded, helpless, marooned, shipwrecked, stranded.

aid n assistance, avail, backing, benefit, cooperation, donation, funding, grant, guidance, help, loan, patronage, relief, sponsorship, subsidy, succour, support. ● v abet, assist, back, benefit, collaborate with, cooperate with, encourage, facilitate, help, inf lend a hand, promote, prop up, inf rally round, relieve, subsidize, succour, support.

ailing adj feeble, infirm, poorly, sick, unwell, weak. ▷ ILL.

ailment n affliction, disorder, infirmity, sickness. ▷ ILLNESS.

aim n ambition, cause, design, destination, direction, dream, focus, goal, hope, intent, intention, mark, object, objective, plan, purpose, wish. ● v 1 address, beam, direct, fire at, line up, point, sight, take aim, train, turn, zero in on. 2 aim to win. aspire, design, endeavour, essay, intend, plan, propose, resolve, strive, try, want, wish.

aimless adj chance, directionless, purposeless, rambling, random, undisciplined, unfocused. Opp PURPOSEFUL.

air n 1 airspace, atmosphere, ether, heavens, sky. 2 fresh air. breath, breeze, draught, wind. 3 air of authority. ambience, appearance, aspect, aura, bearing, character, demeanour, feeling, impression, look, manner, mood, style. ● v 1 aerate, dry off, freshen, ventilate. 2 air opinions. articulate, display, exhibit, express, give vent to, make known, make public, vent, voice.

aircraft n aeroplane, old use flying-machine, plane.

airman n old use aviator, flier, pilot.

airport n aerodrome, airfield, airstrip, heliport, landing strip.

airy adj breezy, draughty, fresh, open, ventilated. Opp STUFFY.

aisle n corridor, gangway, passage, passageway.

akin adj allied, related, similar.

alarm n 1 alert, signal, warning. 2 anxiety, consternation, dismay, fright, nervousness, panic, uneasiness. ▷ FEAR.
● v agitate, dismay, distress, panic, inf put the wind up, shock, startle, unnerve, worry. ▷ FRIGHTEN. Opp REASSURE.

alcohol n inf booze, drink, hard stuff, liquor, spirits.

alcoholic adj brewed, distilled, fermented, intoxicating, inf strong. ● n addict, dipsomaniac, drunkard, inebriate. Opp TEETOTALLER.

alert adj active, alive (to), attentive, awake, careful, eagle-eyed, heedful, lively, observant, on the lookout, on the watch, on your guard, on your toes, perceptive, ready, sensitive, sharp-eyed, vigilant, watchful, wide awake. Opp ABSENT-MINDED, INATTENTIVE. ● v advise, alarm, forewarn, make aware, notify, signal, tip off, warn.

alibi n excuse, explanation.

alien adj extra-terrestrial, foreign, outlandish, strange, unfamiliar. ● n foreigner, newcomer, outsider, stranger.

alight adj ablaze, aflame, blazing, burning, fiery, ignited, illuminated, lit up, live, on fire.
● v come down, come to rest, disembark, dismount, get down, get off, land, touch down.

align v 1 arrange in line, line up, straighten up. 2 align with the opposition. affiliate, ally, associate, join, side, sympathize.

alike adj analogous, cognate, comparable, equivalent, identical, indistinguishable, like, matching, parallel, resembling, similar, twin, uniform. Opp DISSIMILAR.

alive adj 1 animate, breathing, existing, extant, flourishing, in existence, live, living, old use quick. 2 alive to new ideas. ▷ ALERT. Opp DEAD.

allay v calm, check, diminish, ease, mollify, pacify, quell, quench, quieten, reduce, slake (thirst), subdue. ▷ ALLEVIATE. Opp STIMULATE.

allegation n accusation, assertion, charge, claim, declaration, statement, testimony.

allege v assert, attest, avow, claim, contend, declare, maintain, make a charge, plead, state.

allegiance n devotion, duty, faithfulness, fidelity, loyalty.

allergic adj antipathetic, averse, hostile, incompatible (with), opposed.

alleviate v abate, allay, ameliorate, assuage, diminish, ease, lessen, lighten, mitigate, moderate, quell, quench, reduce, relieve, slake (thirst), soften, subdue, temper. Opp AGGRAVATE.

alliance n affiliation, agreement, bloc, cartel, coalition, compact, concordat, confederation, connection, consortium, covenant, entente, federation, guild, marriage, pact, partnership, relationship, treaty, union.

allot v allocate, allow, assign, deal out, inf dish out, inf dole out, dispense, distribute, give out, grant, provide, ration, share out.

allow v 1 approve, authorize, consent to, enable, grant permission for, let, license, permit, sanction, stand, tolerate. Opp FORBID. 2 acknowledge, admit, concede, grant, own. 3 ▷ ALLOT. Opp DENY.

allowance n 1 allocation, measure, portion, quota, ration, share. 2 alimony, annuity, grant, payment, pension, pocket money. 3 *allowance on the full price*. deduction, discount, rebate, reduction. **make allowances for** ▷ TOLERATE.

alloy n admixture, aggregate, amalgam, blend, compound, fusion, mixture.

allude v allude to make an allusion to, mention, refer to, speak of, touch on.

allure v attract, beguile, cajole, charm, draw, entice, fascinate, lead on, lure, seduce, tempt.

allusion n mention, reference, suggestion.

ally n abettor, accessory, accomplice, associate, backer, collaborator, colleague, companion, comrade, friend, helper, *inf* mate, partner, supporter. Opp ENEMY.
• v affiliate, amalgamate, associate, collaborate, combine, cooperate, form an alliance, fraternize, join, join forces, league, *inf* link up, side, *inf* team up, unite.

almighty adj 1 all-powerful, omnipotent, supreme. 2 ▷ BIG.

almost adv about, all but, approximately, around, as good as, just about, nearly, not quite, practically, virtually.

alone adj apart, deserted, desolate, forlorn, friendless, isolated, lonely, on your own, separate, single, solitary, unaccompanied, unassisted.

aloof adj chilly, cold, cool, detached, disinterested, dispassionate, distant, formal, haughty, inaccessible, indifferent, remote, reserved, reticent, self-contained, standoffish,
supercilious, unapproachable, unconcerned, undemonstrative, unforthcoming, unfriendly, unresponsive, unsociable, unsympathetic. Opp FRIENDLY, SOCIABLE.

aloud adv audibly, clearly, distinctly, out loud.

also adv additionally, besides, furthermore, in addition, moreover, *joc* to boot, too.

alter v adapt, adjust, amend, change, convert, edit, modify, reconstruct, reform, remodel, reorganize, reshape, revise, transform, vary.

alteration n adjustment, amendment, change, difference, modification, reorganization, revision, transformation.

alternate v follow in turn, interchange, oscillate, rotate, *inf* see-saw, take turns.

alternative n 1 choice, option. 2 replacement, substitute.

altitude n elevation, height.

altogether adv absolutely, completely, entirely, fully, perfectly, quite, thoroughly, totally, utterly, wholly.

always adv consistently, constantly, continually, endlessly, eternally, evermore, forever, invariably, perpetually, persistently, regularly, repeatedly, unceasingly, unfailingly.

amalgamate v affiliate, ally, associate, band together, blend, coalesce, combine, come together, compound, form an alliance, fuse, integrate, join, join forces, *inf* link up, marry, merge, mix, synthesize, *inf* team up, unite. Opp SPLIT.

amateur adj inexperienced, lay, unpaid, unqualified.

▷ AMATEURISH. ● n dabbler,
dilettante, layman, non-
professional. *Opp* PROFESSIONAL.

amateurish *adj* clumsy, crude,
inf do-it-yourself, incompetent,
inept, *inf* rough-and-ready,
second-rate, shoddy, unprofessional, unskilful, untrained.
Opp SKILLED.

amaze *v* astonish, astound, awe,
bewilder, daze, dumbfound,
flabbergast, perplex, shock, stagger, startle, stun, stupefy, surprise. **amazed** ▷ SURPRISED.

amazing *adj* astonishing,
astounding, breathtaking, exceptional, exciting, extraordinary,
inf fantastic, incredible, miraculous, phenomenal, prodigious,
remarkable, *inf* sensational,
shocking, staggering, startling,
stunning, stupendous, wonderful. *Opp* ORDINARY.

ambassador *n* agent, attaché,
consul, delegate, diplomat, emissary, envoy, representative.

ambiguous *adj* ambivalent, confusing, enigmatic, indefinite,
indeterminate, puzzling,
unclear, vague, woolly.
▷ UNCERTAIN. *Opp* DEFINITE.

ambition *n* 1 commitment,
drive, energy, enterprise, enthusiasm, *inf* go, initiative, *inf* push,
thrust, zeal. 2 aim, aspiration,
desire, dream, goal, hope, ideal,
intention, object, objective,
target, wish.

ambitious *adj* 1 committed,
eager, enterprising, enthusiastic, go-ahead, *inf* go-getting,
keen, *inf* pushy, zealous.
2 *ambitious ideas*. *inf* big, far-
reaching, grand, grandiose,
unrealistic. *Opp* APATHETIC.

ambivalent *adj* ambiguous, contradictory, equivocal, hesitant,

indecisive, unclear, unresolved.
▷ UNCERTAIN.

ambush *n* attack, snare, surprise
attack, trap. ● *v* attack, ensnare,
intercept, lie in wait for, pounce
on, surprise, trap, waylay.

amenable *adj* accommodating,
acquiescent, adaptable, agreeable, complaisant, compliant,
cooperative, docile, open-
minded, persuadable, responsive, tractable, willing.
Opp OBSTINATE.

amend *v* adapt, adjust, alter,
ameliorate, change, correct, edit,
improve, mend, modify, put
right, rectify, reform, remedy,
revise, transform, vary.

amiable *adj* affable, agreeable,
amicable, friendly, genial, good-
natured, kind-hearted, kindly,
likeable, well-disposed.
Opp UNFRIENDLY.

ammunition *n* bullets, cart-
ridges, grenades, missiles,
rounds, shells, shrapnel.

amoral *adj* unethical, unprincipled, without standards.

amorous *adj* affectionate,
ardent, doting, enamoured, fond,
impassioned, loving, lustful, passionate, *sl* randy, sexy.
Opp COLD.

amount *n* aggregate, bulk, entir-
ety, extent, lot, mass, measure,
quantity, reckoning, size, sum,
supply, total, value, volume,
whole. ● *v* **amount to** add up to,
come to, equal, make, mean,
total.

ample *adj* abundant, bountiful,
broad, capacious, commodious,
considerable, copious, extensive,
generous, great, large, lavish, liberal, munificent, plentiful, profuse, roomy, spacious, substan-

tial, unstinting, voluminous.
Opp INSUFFICIENT.

amplify *v* 1 add to, augment,
broaden, develop, elaborate,
enlarge, expand, expatiate on,
extend, fill out, lengthen, make
fuller, supplement. 2 *amplify
sound.* boost, heighten, increase,
intensify, magnify, make louder.
Opp DECREASE.

amputate *v* chop off, cut off,
dock, lop off, remove, sever,
truncate. ▷ CUT.

amuse *v* absorb, cheer (up),
delight, divert, engross, entertain, interest, involve, make
laugh, occupy, please, *inf* tickle.
Opp BORE. **amusing**
▷ ENJOYABLE, FUNNY.

amusement *n* 1 delight, enjoyment, fun, hilarity, laughter,
mirth. ▷ MERRIMENT.
2 distraction, diversion, entertainment, game, hobby, interest,
leisure activity, pastime, play,
pleasure, recreation, sport.

anaemic *adj* bloodless, colourless, pale, pallid, pasty, sallow,
sickly, unhealthy, wan, weak.

analogy *n* comparison, likeness,
metaphor, parallel, resemblance,
similarity, simile.

analyse *v* break down, dissect,
evaluate, examine, interpret,
investigate, scrutinize, separate
out, test.

analysis *n* breakdown, critique,
dissection, enquiry, evaluation,
examination, interpretation,
investigation, *inf* post-mortem,
scrutiny, study, test.

analytical *adj* analytic, critical,
inf in-depth, inquiring, investigative, logical, methodical, penetrating, questioning, rational,
searching, systematic.

anarchy *n* bedlam, chaos, confusion, disorder, insurrection,
lawlessness, misrule, mutiny,
pandemonium, riot. *Opp* ORDER.

ancestor *n* antecedent, forebear,
forefather, forerunner, precursor, predecessor.

ancestry *n* blood, derivation, descent, extraction, family, genealogy, heredity, line, lineage,
origin, parentage, pedigree,
roots, stock, strain.

anchor *v* berth, make fast, moor,
secure, tie up. ▷ FASTEN.

anchorage *n* harbour, haven,
moorings, port, shelter.

ancient *adj* 1 aged, antediluvian,
antiquated, antique, archaic, fos-
silized, obsolete, old, old-
fashioned, out-of-date, passé,
superannuated, time-worn, venerable. 2 *ancient times.* bygone,
earlier, early, former, olden
(*days*), past, prehistoric, primitive, primordial, remote, *old use*
of yore. *Opp* MODERN.

angel *n* archangel, cherub,
divine messenger, seraph.

angelic *adj* 1 blessed, celestial,
cherubic, divine, ethereal, heavenly, holy, seraphic, spiritual.
2 *angelic behaviour.* exemplary,
saintly, virtuous. ▷ GOOD.
Opp DEVILISH.

anger *n* annoyance, antagonism,
bitterness, displeasure, exasperation, fury, hostility, indignation,
ire, irritation, outrage, passion,
rage, resentment, spleen, vexation, wrath. ● *v inf* aggravate,
antagonize, displease, *inf* drive
mad, enrage, exasperate,
incense, inflame, infuriate, irritate, madden, *inf* make someone's
blood boil, outrage, provoke,
vex. ▷ ANNOY. *Opp* PACIFY.

angle n **1** bend, corner, crook, nook. **2** *new angle*. approach, outlook, perspective, point of view, position, slant, standpoint, viewpoint. ● v bend, slant, turn, twist.

angry adj apoplectic, bad-tempered, bitter, *inf* bristling, choleric, crabby, cross, disgruntled, enraged, exasperated, fiery, fuming, furious, heated, hostile, *inf* hot under the collar, incensed, indignant, infuriated, *inf* in high dudgeon, irascible, irate, irritated, livid, mad, outraged, raging, *inf* ratty, raving, resentful, seething, smouldering, *inf* sore, *inf* steamed up, vexed, *inf* up in arms, wild, wrathful. ▷ ANNOYED. *Opp* CALM. **be angry, become angry** *inf* blow up, boil, bridle, bristle, flare up, *inf* fly off the handle, fulminate, fume, *inf* get steamed up, lose your temper, rage, rant, rave, *inf* see red, seethe, snap, storm. **make angry** ▷ ANGER.

anguish n agony, anxiety, distress, grief, heartache, misery, pain, sorrow, suffering, torment, torture, woe.

angular adj bent, crooked, jagged, sharp-cornered, zigzag. *Opp* STRAIGHT.

animal adj beastly, bestial, brutish, carnal, fleshly, inhuman, instinctive, physical, savage, sensual, subhuman, wild. ● n **1** beast, being, brute, creature, *pl* fauna, organism, *pl* wildlife. **2** amphibian, bird, fish, insect, invertebrate, mammal, reptile, vertebrate.

animate adj alive, breathing, conscious, feeling, live, living, sentient. ▷ ANIMATED. *Opp* INANIMATE. ● v activate,

arouse, brighten up, cheer up, encourage, energize, enliven, excite, fire, galvanize, incite, inspire, invigorate, kindle, move, *inf* pep up, quicken, revitalize, revive, rouse, spark, spur, stimulate, stir, urge.

animated adj active, alive, bright, brisk, bubbling, busy, eager, ebullient, energetic, enthusiastic, excited, exuberant, gay, impassioned, lively, passionate, quick, spirited, sprightly, vibrant, vigorous, vivacious. *Opp* LETHARGIC.

animation n activity, eagerness, ebullience, energy, enthusiasm, excitement, gaiety, high spirits, life, liveliness, *inf* pep, sparkle, spirit, verve, vigour, vitality, vivacity, zest. *Opp* LETHARGY.

animosity n acrimony, antagonism, antipathy, aversion, bad blood, bitterness, dislike, enmity, grudge, hate, hatred, hostility, ill will, loathing, malevolence, malice, odium, rancour, resentment, sourness, spite, unfriendliness, venom, vindictiveness, virulence. *Opp* FRIENDLINESS.

annex v acquire, appropriate, conquer, occupy, purloin, seize, take over, usurp.

annihilate v destroy, eliminate, eradicate, erase, exterminate, extinguish, extirpate, *inf* kill off, liquidate, obliterate, raze, slaughter, wipe out.

annotation n comment, commentary, elucidation, explanation, footnote, gloss, interpretation, note.

announce v **1** advertise, broadcast, declare, disclose, divulge, give notice of, make public, notify, proclaim, publicize, publish, put out, report, reveal, state. 2 *announce a speaker.* introduce, present.

announcement *n* advertisement, bulletin, communiqué, declaration, disclosure, notification, proclamation, publication, report, revelation, statement.

announcer *n* anchorman, broadcaster, commentator, compère, disc jockey, DJ, herald, master of ceremonies, *inf* MC, messenger, newscaster, newsreader, reporter.

annoy *v inf* aggravate, antagonize, badger, bother, *sl* bug, displease, drive mad, exasperate, fret, gall, *inf* get on your nerves, grate, harass, harry, infuriate, irk, irritate, jar, madden, make cross, molest, *inf* needle, *inf* nettle, offend, pester, pique, *inf* plague, provoke, put out, rankle, rile, *inf* rub up the wrong way, ruffle, tease, trouble, try (someone's patience), upset, vex, worry. ▷ ANGER. *Opp* PLEASE.

annoyance *n* 1 chagrin, displeasure, exasperation, irritation, pique, vexation. ▷ ANGER. 2 *Noise is an annoyance.* *inf* aggravation, bother, irritant, nuisance, *inf* pain in the neck, pest, provocation, worry.

annoyed *adj* chagrined, cross, displeased, exasperated, *inf* huffy, irritated, *inf* miffed, *inf* nettled, offended, *inf* peeved, piqued, put out, *inf* shirty, *inf* sore, upset, vexed. ▷ ANGRY. *Opp* PLEASED. **be annoyed** take offence, *inf* take umbrage.

annoying *adj inf* aggravating, displeasing, exasperating, galling, grating, inconvenient,

infuriating, irksome, irritating, maddening, offensive, provocative, tiresome, troublesome, trying, upsetting, vexatious, vexing, worrying.

anoint *v* 1 lubricate, oil, smear. 2 baptize, consecrate, sanctify.

anonymous *adj* 1 incognito, nameless, unidentified, unknown, unnamed, unspecified, unsung. 2 *anonymous letters.* unsigned. 3 *anonymous style.* characterless, impersonal, nondescript, unidentifiable, unrecognizable.

answer *n* 1 acknowledgement, *inf* comeback, reaction, rejoinder, reply, response, retort, riposte. 2 explanation, solution. 3 *answer to a charge.* countercharge, defence, plea, refutation, vindication. ● *v* 1 acknowledge, give an answer, react, reply, respond, retort, return. 2 explain, resolve, solve. 3 *answer a charge.* counter, defend yourself against, refute. 4 *answer a need.* correspond to, fit, meet, satisfy, serve, suffice, suit. **answer back** ▷ ARGUE.

antagonism *n* antipathy, enmity, friction, opposition, rivalry, strife. ▷ HOSTILITY.

antagonize *v* alienate, anger, annoy, irritate, make an enemy of, offend, provoke, upset.

anthem *n* canticle, chant, hymn, psalm.

anthology *n* collection, compendium, compilation, digest, miscellany, selection, treasury.

anticipate *v* 1 forestall, pre-empt, prevent. 2 ▷ FORESEE.

anticlimax *n* bathos, *inf* come-down, *inf* damp squib, disappointment, *inf* let-down.

antics pl n capers, clowning, escapades, inf larking-about, pranks, inf skylarking, tomfoolery, tricks.

antidote n antitoxin, corrective, countermeasure, cure, neutralizing agent, remedy.

antiquated adj anachronistic, ancient, antediluvian, archaic, dated, obsolete, old, old-fashioned, outmoded, out-of-date, passé, inf past it, inf prehistoric, primitive, quaint, superannuated, unfashionable. ▷ ANTIQUE. Opp NEW.

antique adj collectible, historic, traditional, veteran, vintage. ▷ ANTIQUATED. ● n collectible, collector's item, curio, curiosity, Fr objet d'art, rarity.

antiquity n classical times, days gone by, former times, olden days, the past.

antiseptic adj aseptic, clean, disinfectant, disinfected, germ free, germicidal, hygienic, medicated, sterile, sterilized, sterilizing.

antisocial adj alienated, disagreeable, disruptive, misanthropic, obnoxious, offensive, rebellious, rude, troublesome, uncooperative, unruly, unsociable. ▷ UNFRIENDLY. Opp SOCIABLE.

anxiety n 1 angst, apprehension, concern, disquiet, distress, doubt, dread, fear, foreboding, misgiving, nervousness, stress, tension, uncertainty, unease, worry. 2 anxiety to succeed. desire, eagerness, impatience, longing.

anxious adj 1 afraid, agitated, apprehensive, concerned, desperate, distraught, distressed, disturbed, edgy, fearful, inf fraught, fretful, inf jittery, nervous,

inf on edge, perturbed, restless, solicitous, tense, troubled, uneasy, upset, worried. 2 anxious to succeed. inf desperate, inf dying, eager, impatient, itching, keen, longing, yearning. be anxious ▷ WORRY.

apathetic adj casual, cool, dispassionate, half-hearted, impassive, indifferent, languid, lethargic, listless, passive, phlegmatic, sluggish, tepid, torpid, unambitious, uncommitted, unconcerned, unenthusiastic, uninterested, uninvolved, unresponsive. Opp ENTHUSIASTIC.

apathy n coolness, indifference, lassitude, lethargy, listlessness, passivity, torpor. Opp ENTHUSIASM.

apex n 1 crest, crown, head, peak, pinnacle, point, summit, tip, top. 2 apex of your career. acme, climax, crowning moment, culmination, height, high point, zenith. Opp NADIR.

aphrodisiac adj arousing, erotic, sexy, stimulating.

apologetic adj ashamed, conscience-stricken, contrite, penitent, regretful, remorseful, repentant, rueful, sorry. Opp UNREPENTANT.

apologize v be apologetic, express regret, make an apology, repent, say sorry.

apology n defence, excuse, explanation, justification, plea.

apostle n crusader, disciple, evangelist, follower, missionary, preacher, teacher.

appal v disgust, dismay, distress, horrify, nauseate, outrage, revolt, shock, sicken. ▷ FRIGHTEN. **appalling**

▷ ATROCIOUS, BAD, FRIGHTENING.

apparatus n appliance, contraption, device, equipment, gadget, inf gear, implement, instrument, machine, machinery, mechanism, system, tackle, tool, utensil.

apparent adj blatant, clear, conspicuous, discernible, evident, manifest, noticeable, obvious, ostensible, overt, patent, perceptible, recognizable, self-explanatory, unconcealed, unmistakable, visible. Opp HIDDEN.

apparition n chimera, ghost, hallucination, illusion, manifestation, phantasm, phantom, presence, shade, spectre, spirit, inf spook, vision, wraith.

appeal n 1 application, call, cry, entreaty, petition, plea, prayer, request, supplication. 2 allure, charisma, charm, inf pull, seductiveness. • v ask earnestly, beg, beseech, call, canvass, entreat, implore, invoke, petition, plead, pray, request, solicit, supplicate. **appeal to** ▷ ATTRACT.

appear v 1 arise, arrive, be published, be seen, inf bob up, come into view, come out, inf crop up, develop, emerge, inf heave into sight, loom, materialize, occur, show, spring up, surface, turn up. 2 I appear to be wrong. look, seem, transpire, turn out. 3 appear in a play. ▷ PERFORM.

appearance n 1 arrival, advent, presence. 2 smart appearance. air, aspect, bearing, demeanour, exterior, impression, likeness, look, mien, semblance.

appease v 1 assuage, calm, conciliate, humour, mollify, pacify, placate, quiet, reconcile, satisfy,

soothe, inf sweeten, win over. Opp ANGER.

appendix n addendum, addition, codicil, epilogue, postscript, rider, supplement.

appetite n craving, demand, desire, eagerness, greed, hankering, hunger, keenness, longing, lust, passion, predilection, relish, stomach, taste, thirst, urge, willingness, wish, yearning, inf yen, zest.

appetizing adj delicious, inf moreish, mouthwatering, tasty, tempting.

applaud v acclaim, approve, inf bring the house down, cheer, clap, commend, compliment, congratulate, eulogize, extol, give an ovation, laud, praise, salute. Opp CRITICIZE.

applause n acclaim, approval, cheering, clapping, ovation, plaudits. ▷ PRAISE.

appliance n apparatus, contraption, device, gadget, implement, instrument, machine, mechanism, tool, utensil.

applicant n candidate, competitor, entrant, interviewee.

apply v 1 administer, affix, put on, rub on, spread, stick. ▷ FASTEN. 2 rules apply to all. be relevant, have a bearing (on), pertain, refer, relate. 3 apply common sense. employ, exercise, implement, practise, use, utilize, wield. **apply for** ▷ REQUEST. **apply yourself** ▷ CONCENTRATE.

appoint v 1 arrange, decide on, determine, establish, fix, ordain, settle. 2 appoint you to do a job. assign, choose, delegate, depute, designate, detail, elect, name, nominate, inf plump for, select, settle on, vote for.

appointment n 1 arrangement, assignation, consultation, date, engagement, fixture, interview, meeting, rendezvous, session. 2 choice, choosing, election, naming, nomination, selection. 3 job, office, place, position, post, situation.

appreciate v 1 admire, approve of, be grateful for, cherish, commend, enjoy, esteem, find worthwhile, like, praise, prize, rate highly, respect, sympathize with, treasure, value, welcome. *I appreciate the facts.* acknowledge, comprehend, know, realize, recognize, see, understand. 3 *property value appreciates.* build up, escalate, go up, grow, improve, increase, inflate, mount, rise, soar. *Opp* DEPRECIATE, DESPISE, DISREGARD.

apprehensive adj afraid, concerned, disturbed, edgy, fearful, *inf* jittery, nervous, uneasy, worried. ▷ ANXIOUS. *Opp* FEARLESS.

apprentice n beginner, learner, novice, probationer, pupil, starter, trainee.

approach n 1 advance, advent, arrival, coming. 2 access, doorway, entrance, entry, road, way in. 3 attitude, method, mode, procedure, style, system, technique, way. 4 appeal, application, invitation, overture, overture, proposal, proposition. ● v 1 advance, bear down, catch up, draw near, gain (on), loom, move towards, near. *Opp* RETREAT. 2 *approach a task.* ▷ BEGIN. 3 *approach someone for help.* ▷ CONTACT.

approachable adj accessible, affable, informal, kind, open, relaxed, sympathetic, well-disposed. ▷ FRIENDLY. *Opp* ALOOF.

appropriate adj applicable, apposite, apt, befitting, compatible, correct, deserved, due, felicitous, fit, fitting, happy, just, opportune, pertinent, proper, relevant, right, seasonable, seemly, suitable, tactful, tasteful, timely, well-judged, well-timed. *Opp* INAPPROPRIATE. ● v annex, commandeer, confiscate, *inf* hijack, requisition, seize, take, take over, usurp. ▷ STEAL.

approval n 1 acclaim, acclamation, admiration, applause, appreciation, approbation, commendation, esteem, favour, liking, plaudits, praise, regard, respect, support. *Opp* DISAPPROVAL. 2 acceptance, acquiescence, agreement, assent, authorization, *inf* blessing, consent, endorsement, *inf* go-ahead, *inf* green light, *inf* OK, permission, ratification, sanction, seal, stamp, *inf* thumbs up. *Opp* REFUSAL.

approve v accede to, accept, agree to, allow, authorize, *inf* back, confirm, consent to, countenance, endorse, *inf* give your blessing to, pass, permit, ratify, *inf* rubber-stamp, sanction, sign, support, uphold. *Opp* REFUSE, VETO. **approve of** ▷ ADMIRE.

approximate adj estimated, imprecise, loose, rough. *Opp* EXACT. ● v **approximate to** approach, be similar to, come near to, equal roughly, resemble.

approximately adv about, approaching, around, close to, just about, more or less, nearly, *inf* nigh on, *inf* pushing, roughly, round about.

aptitude n ability, bent, capability, facility, fitness, flair, gift, suitability, talent. ▷ SKILL.

arbitrary adj 1 capricious, casual, chance, erratic, irrational, random, subjective, unpredictable, unreasonable, whimsical. Opp METHODICAL. 2 arbitrary rule. absolute, autocratic, despotic, dictatorial, high-handed, imperious, summary, tyrannical, uncompromising.

arbitrate v adjudicate, decide the outcome, intercede, judge, make peace, mediate, negotiate, referee, settle, umpire.

arbitration n adjudication, intercession, judgement, mediation, negotiation, settlement.

arbitrator n adjudicator, arbiter, go-between, intermediary, judge, mediator, middleman, negotiator, ombudsman, peacemaker, referee, umpire.

arch n arc, archway, bridge. ● v bend, bow. ▷ CURVE.

archetype n classic, example, ideal, model, original, paradigm, pattern, precursor, prototype, standard.

archives pl n annals, chronicles, documents, papers, records, registers.

ardent adj eager, enthusiastic, fervent, hot, impassioned, intense, keen, passionate, warm, zealous. Opp APATHETIC.

arduous adj demanding, exhausting, gruelling, herculean, laborious, onerous, punishing, rigorous, severe, strenuous, taxing, tiring, uphill. ▷ DIFFICULT. Opp EASY.

area n 1 acreage, breadth, expanse, extent, patch, sheet, space, stretch, surface, tract, width. 2 district, environment, environs, locality, neighbourhood, part, precinct, province, quarter, region, sector, terrain, territory, vicinity, zone. 3 area of study. field, sphere, subject.

argue v 1 answer back, inf bandy words, bicker, debate, demur, differ, disagree, discuss, dispute, dissent, fall out, fight, haggle, inf have words, quarrel, inf row, spar, squabble, wrangle. 2 argue a case. assert, claim, contend, demonstrate, hold, maintain, plead, prove, reason, show, suggest.

argument n 1 altercation, bickering, clash, conflict, controversy, difference (of opinion), disagreement, dispute, fight, quarrel, inf row, inf set-to, squabble, inf tiff, wrangle. 2 debate, deliberation, discussion. 3 argument of a lecture. case, contention, gist, hypothesis, idea, outline, reasoning, theme, thesis, view.

arid adj 1 barren, desert, dry, fruitless, infertile, lifeless, parched, sterile, unproductive, waste, waterless. Opp FRUITFUL. 2 ▷ BORING.

arise v come up, inf crop up, get up, rise. ▷ APPEAR.

aristocrat n grandee, lady, lord, nobleman, noblewoman, peer.

aristocratic adj inf blue-blooded, courtly, elite, lordly, noble, patrician, princely, royal, thoroughbred, titled, upper class.

arm n appendage, bough, branch, extension, limb, offshoot, projection. ● v equip, fortify, furnish, provide, supply. **arms** ▷ WEAPON(S).

armed services *pl n* air force, army, forces, militia, navy, troops.

armistice *n* agreement, ceasefire, peace, treaty, truce.

armoury *n* ammunition-dump, arsenal, magazine, stockpile.

aroma *n* bouquet, fragrance, odour, perfume, redolence, savour, scent, smell, whiff.

arouse *v* awaken, call forth, encourage, foment, foster, kindle, provoke, quicken, stimulate, stir up, whip up.
▷ CAUSE. *Opp* ALLAY.

arrange *v* 1 adjust, align, array, categorize, classify, collate, display, dispose, distribute, grade, group, lay out, marshal, order, organize, position, put in order, range, set out, sort (out), systematize, tabulate, tidy up.
2 *arrange a meeting.* bring about, contrive, coordinate, devise, organize, plan, prepare, see to, set up. 3 *arrange music.* adapt, orchestrate.

arrangement *n* 1 adjustment, alignment, design, distribution, grouping, layout, organization, planning, positioning, spacing, tabulation. ▷ ARRAY.
2 agreement, bargain, contract, deal, pact, scheme, settlement, terms, understanding. 3 *musical arrangement.* adaptation, orchestration, setting, version.

array *n* arrangement, assemblage, collection, display, exhibition, formation, *inf* line-up, panoply, parade, show. ● *v* 1 adorn, attire, clothe, deck, decorate, dress, equip, fit out, garb, robe, wrap. 2 ▷ ARRANGE.

arrest *n* capture, detention, seizure. ● *v* 1 bar, block, check, delay, end, halt, hinder, impede,

inhibit, interrupt, obstruct, prevent, restrain, retard, slow, stem, stop. 2 *arrest a suspect.* apprehend, capture, catch, *inf* collar, detain, have up, hold, *inf* nab, *inf* nick, seize, take into custody.

arrival *n* 1 advent, appearance, approach, entrance, homecoming, landing, return, touchdown. 2 *new arrival.* caller, newcomer, visitor.

arrive *v* 1 appear, come, disembark, enter, get in, land, make an entrance, *inf* roll up, show up, touch down, turn up.
2 ▷ SUCCEED. **arrive at**
▷ REACH.

arrogant *adj* boastful, brash, brazen, bumptious, cavalier, *inf* cocky, conceited, condescending, disdainful, egotistical, haughty, *inf* high and mighty, high-handed, imperious, lofty, overbearing, patronizing, pompous, presumptuous, proud, scornful, self-important, *inf* snooty, *inf* stuck-up, supercilious, superior, vain.
Opp MODEST.

arsonist *n* fire-raiser, incendiary, pyromaniac.

art *n* 1 aptitude, artistry, cleverness, craft, craftsmanship, dexterity, expertise, facility, knack, proficiency, skilfulness, skill, talent, technique, touch, trick. 2 artwork, craft, fine art.

artful *adj* astute, canny, clever, crafty, cunning, designing, devious, *inf* foxy, ingenious, scheming, shrewd, skilful, sly, smart, subtle, tricky, wily. *Opp* NAIVE.

article *n* 1 item, object, thing. 2 *magazine article.* feature, item, piece, story.

articulate *adj* clear, coherent, comprehensible, distinct, eloquent, expressive, fluent, *derog* glib, intelligible, lucid, understandable, vocal. *Opp* INARTICULATE. ● *v* ▷ SPEAK.

articulated *adj* bending, flexible, hinged, jointed.

artificial *adj* **1** fabricated, man-made, manufactured, synthetic, unnatural. **2** *artificial style*. affected, assumed, bogus, contrived, counterfeit, fake, false, feigned, forced, imitation, insincere, mock, *inf* phoney, pretended, *inf* pseudo, *inf* put on, sham, simulated, spurious, unreal. *Opp* NATURAL.

artist *n* craftsman, craftswoman, illustrator, painter, photographer, potter, sculptor, silversmith, weaver. ▷ ENTERTAINER, MUSICIAN, PERFORMER.

artistic *adj* aesthetic, attractive, beautiful, creative, cultured, decorative, imaginative, ornamental, tasteful.

ascend *v* climb, come up, fly, go up, lift off, make an ascent, mount, move up, rise, scale, soar, take off. *Opp* DESCEND.

ascent *n* climb, gradient, hill, incline, ramp, rise, slope. *Opp* DESCENT.

ascertain *v* confirm, determine, discover, establish, find out, identify, learn, make certain, make sure, verify.

ascetic *adj* abstemious, austere, celibate, chaste, frugal, harsh, hermit-like, plain, puritanical, restrained, rigorous, self-denying, severe, spartan, strict. *Opp* SELF-INDULGENT.

ash *n* burnt remains, cinders, embers.

ashamed *adj* **1** abashed, apologetic, chastened, conscience-stricken, contrite, guilty, humiliated, mortified, penitent, remorseful, repentant, rueful, shamefaced, sorry. **2** bashful, blushing, demure, diffident, embarrassed, modest, prudish, self-conscious, sheepish, shy. *Opp* SHAMELESS.

ask *v* appeal, apply, badger, beg, beseech, crave, demand, enquire, entreat, implore, importune, inquire, interrogate, invite, petition, plead, pray, press, query, question, quiz, request, require, seek, solicit, supplicate, seek for ▷ ATTRACT.

asleep *adj* comatose, *inf* dead to the world, dormant, dozing, hibernating, inactive, *inf* in the land of nod, napping, *inf* out like a light, resting, sleeping, slumbering, snoozing, unconscious. ▷ NUMB. *Opp* AWAKE.

aspect *n* **1** angle, characteristic, circumstance, detail, element, facet, feature, quality, side, standpoint, viewpoint. **2** air, appearance, attitude, bearing, countenance, demeanour, expression, face, look, manner, mien, visage. **3** *southern aspect*. direction, outlook, position, prospect, situation, view.

asperity *n* abrasiveness, acidity, astringency, bitterness, harshness, hostility, rancour, roughness, severity, sharpness, sourness, virulence. *Opp* MILDNESS.

aspiration *n* aim, ambition, craving, desire, dream, goal, hope, longing, objective, purpose, wish, yearning.

aspire *v* aspire to aim for, crave, desire, dream of, hope for, pursue, seek, set your sights on,

want, wish for. **aspiring**
▷ POTENTIAL.

assail v assault, bombard, pelt,
set on. ▷ ATTACK.

assault n battery, inf GBH, mugging, rape. ▷ ATTACK.
● v inf beat up, molest, pounce
on, rape, set about, set on, violate. ▷ ATTACK.

assemble v 1 come together, congregate, convene, converge,
crowd, flock, gather, group,
herd, join up, meet, rally round,
swarm. 2 accumulate, amass,
bring together, collect, get
together, marshal, mobilize,
muster, rally, round up. 3 build,
construct, erect, fabricate, make,
manufacture, piece together, produce, put together.
Opp DISMANTLE, DISPERSE.

assembly n conference, congregation, congress, convention,
convocation, council, gathering,
meeting, parliament, rally,
synod. ▷ CROWD.

assent n acceptance, accord,
acquiescence, agreement,
approbation, approval, consent,
inf go-ahead, permission, sanction, willingness. Opp REFUSAL.
● v accede, accept, acquiesce,
agree, approve, comply, concede,
consent, submit, yield.
Opp REFUSE.

assert v affirm, allege, argue,
attest, claim, contend, declare,
insist, maintain, proclaim, profess, protest, state, stress, swear,
testify. **assert yourself**
▷ INSIST.

assertive adj aggressive, authoritative, inf bossy, certain, confident, decided, definite, dogmatic, emphatic, firm, forceful,
insistent, derog opinionated, peremptory, positive, derog pushy,

self-assured, strong, strong-
willed. Opp SUBMISSIVE.

assess v appraise, calculate, compute, consider, determine, estimate, evaluate, fix, gauge, judge,
price, reckon, review, inf size
up, value, weigh up.

asset n advantage, aid, benefit,
blessing, boon, inf godsend,
good, help, profit, resource,
strength, support. **assets** capital,
effects, estate, funds, goods, holdings, means, money, possessions, property, resources,
savings, securities, valuables,
wealth, inf worldly goods.

assign v 1 allocate, allot, apportion, consign, dispense, distribute, give, hand over, share out.
2 appoint, authorize, delegate,
designate, nominate, prescribe,
select, specify. 3 assign my success to luck. ascribe, attribute,
credit.

assignment n chore, duty,
errand, job, mission, obligation,
post, project, task. ▷ WORK.

assist v abet, advance, aid, benefit, collaborate, cooperate, facilitate, further, help, inf lend a
hand, promote, reinforce,
relieve, second, serve, succour,
support, work with. Opp HINDER.

assistance n aid, backing, collaboration, contribution,
cooperation, encouragement,
help, patronage, relief, succour,
support. Opp HINDRANCE.

assistant n accessory, accomplice, aide, ally, associate,
backer, collaborator, colleague,
companion, comrade, deputy,
helper, inf henchman, mainstay,
derog minion, partner,
inf right-hand man, second,
second-in-command, stand-by,
subordinate, supporter.

associate n ▷ ASSISTANT, FRIEND. ● v 1 ally yourself, be friends, combine, consort, fraternize, inf gang up, inf hob nob (with), keep company, link up, mingle, mix, side, socialize. Opp DISSOCIATE. 2 associate snow with winter. connect, put together, relate, inf tie up.

association n affiliation, alliance, body, brotherhood, cartel, clique, club, coalition, combination, company, confederation, consortium, corporation, federation, fellowship, group, league, merger, organization, partnership, party, society, syndicate, union. ▷ FRIENDSHIP.

assorted adj different, diverse, mixed, various. ▷ MISCELLANEOUS.

assortment n array, choice, collection, diversity, jumble, medley, miscellany, inf mishmash, inf mixed bag, mixture, pot-pourri, range, selection, variety.

assume v 1 believe, deduce, expect, guess, imagine, infer, presume, suppose, surmise, suspect, take for granted. 2 assume duties. accept, take on, undertake. 3 assume a disguise, an attitude. acquire, adopt, affect, don, fake, feign, pretend, put on, simulate, try on.

assumption n belief, conjecture, expectation, guess, hypothesis, premise, premiss, supposition, surmise, theory.

assurance n guarantee, oath, pledge, promise, vow, undertaking, word (of honour).

assure v convince, guarantee, persuade, pledge, promise, reassure, swear, vow. **assured** ▷ CONFIDENT.

astonish v amaze, astound, baffle, bewilder, confound, daze, inf dazzle, dumbfound, flabbergast, leave speechless, nonplus, shock, stagger, startle, stun, stupefy, surprise, take by surprise. **astonishing** ▷ AMAZING.

astound v ▷ ASTONISH.

astray adv adrift, lost, off course, wide of the mark, wrong.

astute adj acute, artful, canny, clever, crafty, cunning, discerning, ingenious, intelligent, knowing, observant, perceptive, perspicacious, sharp, shrewd, sly, subtle, wily. Opp STUPID.

asylum n haven, refuge, retreat, safety, sanctuary, shelter.

asymmetrical adj awry, crooked, distorted, irregular, lop-sided, unbalanced, uneven, inf wonky. Opp SYMMETRICAL.

atheist n heathen, pagan, sceptic, unbeliever.

athletic adj acrobatic, active, energetic, fit, muscular, powerful, robust, sinewy, inf sporty, strong, vigorous, well-built, wiry.

athletics pl n field events, sports, track events.

atmosphere n 1 air, ether, heavens, sky, stratosphere. 2 ambience, aura, character, climate, environment, feeling, mood, spirit, tone.

atom n inf bit, crumb, grain, iota, jot, molecule, morsel, particle, scrap, speck, spot.

atone v compensate, do penance, expiate, make amends, make reparation, pay the penalty, pay the price, redeem yourself, redress.

atrocious adj abominable, appalling, barbaric, brutal, callous, cruel, diabolical, dreadful, evil, fiendish, frightful, grim, gruesome, heartless, heinous, hideous, horrendous, horrible, horrific, horrifying, inhuman, monstrous, nauseating, revolting, sadistic, savage, shocking, sickening, terrible, vicious, vile, villainous, wicked.

atrocity n crime, cruelty, enormity, offence, outrage. ▷ EVIL.

attach v 1 add, append, bind, combine, connect, fix, join, link, secure, stick, tie, unite. ▷ FASTEN. *Opp* DETACH. 2 ascribe, assign, associate, attribute, impute. **attached** ▷ LOVING.

attack n 1 ambush, assault, battery, blitz, bombardment, charge, foray, incursion, invasion, offensive, onset, onslaught, raid, rush, sortie, strike. 2 *verbal attack*. abuse, censure, criticism, diatribe, invective, outburst, tirade. 3 *attack of coughing*. bout, convulsion, fit, outbreak, paroxysm, seizure, spasm, *inf* turn. ● v 1 ambush, assail, assault, *inf* beat up, bombard, charge, counterattack, *inf* do over, fall on, fight, fly at, invade, jump on, lash out at, *inf* lay into, mob, mug, *inf* pitch into, pounce on, raid, set about, set on, storm, strike at, *inf* wade into. 2 *attack verbally*. abuse, censure, criticize, denounce, impugn, inveigh against, libel, malign, round on, slander, snipe at, vilify. *Opp* DEFEND. 3 *attack a task*. ▷ BEGIN.

attacker n aggressor, assailant, critic, detractor, enemy, fighter, intruder, invader, mugger, opponent, persecutor, raider, slanderer.

attain v accomplish, achieve, acquire, arrive at, complete, fulfil, gain, get, grasp, *inf* make, obtain, reach, realize, secure, touch, win.

attempt n bid, effort, endeavour, *inf* go, start, try. ● v aim, aspire, do your best, endeavour, *inf* have a go, make a bid, make an effort, put yourself out, seek, strive, tackle, try, undertake, venture.

attend v 1 be present, go (to), frequent, present yourself, *inf* put in an appearance, visit. 2 accompany, chaperon, conduct, escort, follow, guard, usher. 3 *attend carefully*. concentrate, hear, heed, listen, mark, mind, note, notice, observe, pay attention, watch. **attend to** assist, care for, help, look after, mind, nurse, see to, take care of, tend.

attendant n assistant, escort, helper, usher. ▷ SERVANT.

attention n 1 care, concentration, concern, diligence, heed, notice, thought, vigilance. 2 consideration, courtesy, good manners, kindness, politeness, regard, respect, thoughtfulness.

attentive adj 1 alert, awake, concentrating, intent, observant, watchful. *Opp* INATTENTIVE. 2 ▷ POLITE. *Opp* RUDE.

attire n apparel, array, clothes, clothing, costume, dress, finery, garb, garments, *inf* gear, outfit, wear. ● v ▷ DRESS.

attitude n 1 air, approach, bearing, behaviour, demeanour, disposition, frame of mind, manner, mien, mood, posture, stance. 2 *attitude towards politics*. belief, feeling, opinion, outlook, position, standpoint, thought, view, viewpoint.

attract v 1 allure, appeal to, beguile, bewitch, captivate, charm, enchant, entice, fascinate, interest, lure, seduce, tempt, *sl* turn someone on. 2 *a magnet attracts iron.* draw, pull. 3 *attract attention.* ask for, cause, court, generate, induce, invite, provoke, seek out, *inf* stir up. Opp REPEL.

attractive adj adorable, appealing, appetizing, becoming, bewitching, captivating, charming, *inf* cute, delightful, desirable, enchanting, endearing, engaging, enticing, fascinating, fetching, glamorous, good-looking, gorgeous, handsome, hypnotic, interesting, inviting, irresistible, lovable, lovely, magnetic, personable, pleasing, pretty, seductive, stunning, *inf* taking, tasteful, tempting, winning. ▷ BEAUTIFUL. Opp REPULSIVE.

attribute n characteristic, feature, property, quality, trait.
● v ascribe, assign, charge, credit, impute, put down, refer.

audacious adj adventurous, courageous, daring, fearless, *derog* foolhardy, intrepid, *derog* rash, *derog* reckless. ▷ BOLD. Opp TIMID.

audacity n boldness, cheek, effrontery, impertinence, impudence, presumptuousness, rashness, temerity. ▷ COURAGE.

audible adj clear, detectable, distinct, high, perceptible. Opp INAUDIBLE.

audience n assembly, congregation, crowd, gathering, listeners, meeting, onlookers, spectators, *inf* turn-out, viewers.

auditorium n assembly room, concert hall, hall, theatre.

augment v add to, amplify, boost, enlarge, expand, fill out, grow, increase, magnify, make larger, multiply, raise, reinforce, strengthen, supplement, swell. Opp DECREASE.

augur v bode, forebode, foreshadow, forewarn, give an omen, herald, portend, predict, promise, prophesy, signal.

augury n forecast, omen, portent, prophecy, sign, warning.

auspicious adj favourable, *inf* hopeful, lucky, promising, propitious. Opp OMINOUS.

austere adj 1 abstemious, ascetic, chaste, cold, forbidding, formal, frugal, grave, hard, harsh, hermit-like, parsimonious, puritanical, restrained, rigorous, self-denying, serious, severe, sober, spartan, stern, strict, thrifty. 2 *austere dress.* modest, plain, simple, unadorned. Opp LUXURIOUS, ORNATE.

authentic adj accurate, actual, bona fide, certain, factual, genuine, honest, legitimate, original, real, reliable, true, truthful, undisputed, valid.
▷ AUTHORITATIVE. Opp FALSE.

authenticate v certify, confirm, corroborate, endorse, substantiate, validate, verify.

author n 1 composer, dramatist, novelist, playwright, poet, scriptwriter, writer. 2 creator, designer, father, founder, initiator, inventor, maker, originator, prime mover.

authoritarian adj autocratic, *inf* bossy, despotic, dictatorial, dogmatic, domineering, strict, tyrannical.

authoritative *adj* definitive, dependable, official, recognized, sanctioned. ▷ AUTHENTIC.

authority *n* 1 approval, authorization, consent, permission, permit, sanction, warrant. 2 command, control, force, influence, jurisdiction, might, power, prerogative, right, sovereignty, supremacy, sway, weight. 3 *authority on wine*. *inf* buff, connoisseur, expert, specialist. **the authorities** government, management, officialdom, *inf* powers that be.

authorize *v* accede to, agree to, allow, approve, *inf* back, commission, consent to, empower, endorse, entitle, legalize, license, make official, *inf* OK, pass, permit, ratify, *inf* rubber-stamp, sanction, validate. **authorized** ▷ OFFICIAL.

automatic *adj* 1 conditioned, habitual, impulsive, instinctive, involuntary, reflex, spontaneous, unconscious, unthinking. 2 automated, computerized, mechanical, programmed, self-regulating, unmanned.

autonomous *adj* free, independent, self-determining, self-governing, sovereign.

auxiliary *adj* additional, backup, emergency, extra, reserve, secondary, spare, subordinate, subsidiary, substitute, supplementary, supporting.

available *adj* accessible, at hand, convenient, disposable, free, handy, obtainable, ready, to hand, uncommitted, usable. *Opp* INACCESSIBLE.

avaricious *adj* ▷ GREEDY.

avenge *v inf* get your own back, repay, take revenge.

average *adj* commonplace, everyday, mediocre, medium, middling, moderate, normal, regular, *inf* run-of-the-mill, typical, unexceptional, usual. ▷ ORDINARY. *Opp* EXCEPTIONAL. ● *n* mean, mid-point, norm, standard. ● *v* even out, standardize.

averse *adj* antipathetic, disinclined, hostile, opposed, reluctant, resistant, unwilling.

aversion *n* antagonism, antipathy, dislike, distaste, hostility, reluctance, unwillingness. ▷ HATRED.

avert *v* change the course of, deflect, fend off, parry, prevent, stave off, turn aside, ward off.

avoid *v* abstain from, *inf* beg the question, *inf* bypass, circumvent, dodge, *inf* duck, elude, escape, evade, fend off, find a way round, *inf* get round, *inf* give a wide berth to, ignore, keep away from, refrain from, shirk, shun, side-step, skirt round, steer clear of. *Opp* SEEK.

await *v* be ready for, expect, hope for, lie in wait for, look out for, wait for.

awake *adj* 1 aware, conscious, sleepless, *inf* tossing and turning, wakeful, wide awake. 2 ▷ ALERT. *Opp* ASLEEP.

awaken *v* alert, arouse, call, excite, kindle, revive, rouse, stimulate, stir up, wake.

award *n* cup, decoration, gift, grant, medal, prize, reward, trophy. ● *v* allot, assign, bestow, confer, endow, give, grant, hand over, present.

aware *adj* acquainted, alive (to), appreciative, attentive, conscious, familiar, heedful, informed, knowledgeable, mindful, observant, responsive, sensitive. Opp IGNORANT, INSENSITIVE.

awe n admiration, amazement, apprehension, dread, fear, respect, reverence, terror, veneration, wonder.

awe-inspiring adj awesome, breathtaking, dramatic, grand, imposing, impressive, magnificent, marvellous, overwhelming, solemn, inf stunning, stupendous, sublime. ▷ FRIGHTENING, WONDERFUL. Opp INSIGNIFICANT.

awful adj ▷ BAD.

awkward adj 1 blundering, bungling, clumsy, gauche, gawky, inf ham-fisted, inelegant, inept, maladroit, uncoordinated, ungainly, ungraceful, unskilful. 2 awkward load. bulky, cumbersome, unmanageable, unwieldy. 3 awkward problem. annoying, difficult, inconvenient, perplexing, inf thorny, ticklish, troublesome, trying, vexing. 4 awkward silence. embarrassing, touchy, tricky, uncomfortable, uneasy. 5 awkward children. inf bloody-minded, defiant, disobedient, exasperating, intractable, naughty, obstinate, perverse, rebellious, rude, stubborn, uncooperative, undisciplined, unruly, wayward. Opp COOPERATIVE, EASY, NEAT.

awning n canopy, screen, shade, shelter, tarpaulin.

axe n chopper, cleaver, hatchet.
● v cancel, cut, discontinue, dismiss, eliminate, get rid of, inf give the chop to, remove, sack, withdraw.

axle n rod, shaft, spindle.

B

baby n babe, child, infant, newborn, toddler.

babyish adj childish, immature, infantile, juvenile, puerile, simple. Opp MATURE.

back adj dorsal, end, hind, hindmost, last, rear, rearmost.
● n 1 end, hindquarters, posterior, rear, stern, tail, tail-end. 2 reverse, verso. Opp FRONT.
● v 1 back away, backtrack, inf beat a retreat, give way, move back, recede, recoil, retire, retreat, reverse. Opp ADVANCE. 2 ▷ SUPPORT. **back down** ▷ RETREAT. **back out** ▷ WITHDRAW.

backer n ▷ SPONSOR.

background n 1 circumstances, context, history, inf lead-up, setting, surroundings. 2 education, experience, tradition, training, upbringing.

backing n 1 aid, approval, assistance, encouragement, endorsement, funding, grant, help, investment, loan, patronage, sponsorship, subsidy, support. 2 musical backing. accompaniment, orchestration.

backward adj 1 retreating, retrograde, reverse. 2 bashful, coy, diffident, hesitant, inhibited, modest, reluctant, reserved, reticent, self-effacing, shy, timid, unassertive, unforthcoming. 3 backward pupil. disadvantaged, immature, late-starting, slow, undeveloped. Opp FORWARD.

bad adj 1 bad men, deeds. abhorrent, base, corrupt, criminal, cruel, dangerous, delinquent, deplorable, depraved, evil, guilty, immoral, infamous, malevolent, malicious, mean, mischievous, nasty, naughty, offensive, reprehensible, shameful, sinful, vicious, vile, villainous, wicked, wrong. 2 bad accident. appalling, awful, calamitous, dire, disastrous, dreadful, frightful, ghastly, grave, hair-raising, hideous, horrible, serious, severe, shocking, terrible, unfortunate, unpleasant, violent. 3 bad driving, work. abominable, abysmal, appalling, atrocious, awful, inf chronic, defective, diabolical, disgraceful, dreadful, faulty, feeble, hopeless, inadequate, incompetent, incorrect, inferior, inf lousy, pitiful, poor, shoddy, inf sorry, substandard, unsatisfactory, useless, weak, worthless. 4 bad conditions. adverse, detrimental, discouraging, inf frightful, harmful, harsh, hostile, inauspicious, prejudicial, uncongenial, unfavourable, unfortunate. 5 bad smell. decayed, decomposing, foul, loathsome, mildewed, mouldy, nauseating, noxious, obnoxious, odious, offensive, polluted, putrid, rancid, repulsive, revolting, sickening, rotten, sour. 6 I feel bad. ▷ ILL. Opp GOOD.

badge n chevron, crest, device, emblem, insignia, logo, mark, medal, sign, symbol, token.

bad-tempered adj angry, cantankerous, crabby, cross, crotchety, disgruntled, dyspeptic, gruff, grumpy, hostile, ill-humoured, irascible, irritable, moody, morose, peevish, petulant, quarrelsome, querulous, rude, short-tempered, shrewish, snappy, inf stroppy, sulky, sullen, truculent. Opp GOOD-TEMPERED.

baffle v 1 inf bamboozle, bemuse, bewilder, confound, confuse, inf floor, inf flummox, frustrate, mystify, perplex, puzzle, inf stump. **baffling** ▷ INEXPLICABLE.

bag n carrier, carrier bag, case, handbag, haversack, holdall, rucksack, sack, satchel, shopping bag. ▷ BAGGAGE. ● v capture, catch, ensnare, snare.

baggage n accoutrements, bags, belongings, inf gear, paraphernalia. ▷ LUGGAGE.

bait n attraction, bribe, inf carrot, decoy, inducement, lure, temptation. ● v annoy, goad, harass, hound, persecute, pester, provoke, tease, torment.

balance n 1 scales, weighing machine. 2 equilibrium, poise, stability, steadiness. 3 correspondence, equality, evenness, parity, symmetry. 4 spend a bit & save the balance. remainder, surplus. ● v 1 compensate for, counterbalance, equalize, even up, level, make steady, match, offset, stabilize. 2 keep balanced, poise, steady, support. **balanced** ▷ EVEN, IMPARTIAL, STABLE.

bald adj 1 bare, hairless, smooth, thin on top. 2 bald truth. direct, forthright, plain, simple, stark, unadorned, uncompromising.

bale n bunch, bundle, pack, package. ● v bale out eject, escape, jump out.

ball n 1 drop, globe, globule, orb, sphere. 2 dance, disco, party.

balloon n airship, dirigible, hot-air balloon. • v ▷ BILLOW.

ballot n election, plebiscite, poll, referendum, vote.

ban n boycott, embargo, moratorium, prohibition, veto.
• v banish, bar, debar, disallow, exclude, forbid, make illegal, ostracize, outlaw, prevent, prohibit, proscribe, restrict, stop, suppress, veto. Opp PERMIT.

banal adj boring, clichéd, commonplace, inf corny, dull, hackneyed, humdrum, obvious, over-used, pedestrian, platitudinous, stereotyped, trite, unimaginative, unoriginal.

band n 1 belt, border, hoop, line, loop, ribbon, ring, strip, stripe, swathe. 2 body, clique, club, company, crew, gang, horde, party, troop. ▷ GROUP. 3 [music] ensemble, group, orchestra.

bandage n dressing, gauze, lint, plaster.

bandit n brigand, buccaneer, desperado, gangster, gunman, highwayman, hijacker, marauder, outlaw, pirate, robber, thief.

bandy adj bandy-legged, bowed, bow-legged. • v bandy words. exchange, swap. ▷ ARGUE.

bang n 1 blow, bump, collision, knock, punch, smack, thump, sl wallop, inf whack. 2 blast, boom, clap, crash, explosion, shot.

banish v 1 deport, drive out, eject, evict, exile, expatriate, expel, ostracize, oust, outlaw, send away. 2 ban, bar, debar, eliminate, exclude, make illegal, prohibit, proscribe, put an embargo on, remove, suppress, veto.

bank n 1 declivity, dyke, earthwork, embankment, gradient, incline, mound, ramp, ridge, rise, slope. 2 river bank. brink, edge, margin, shore, side. 3 bank of controls. array, collection, display, group, panel, row, series.
• v 1 incline, lean, list, pitch, slope, tilt, tip. 2 bank money. deposit, save.

bankrupt adj inf broke, failed, sl gone bust, gone into liquidation, insolvent, ruined, wound up. ▷ POOR. Opp SOLVENT.

banner n colours, ensign, flag, pennant, pennon, standard, streamer.

banquet n inf binge, sl blow-out, dinner, feast, repast, inf spread.

banter n chaffing, joking, raillery, repartee, teasing, wordplay.

bar n 1 beam, girder, pole, rail, railing, rod, shaft, stake, stick, strut. 2 barrier, deterrent, impediment, obstacle, obstruction. 3 bar of colour. band, line, streak, strip, stripe. 4 bar of soap. block, cake, chunk, hunk, ingot, lump, nugget, piece, slab, wedge. 5 café, counter, wine bar. ▷ PUB. • v 1 ban, banish, debar, exclude, keep out, ostracize, outlaw, prohibit. 2 block, deter, halt, hinder, impede, obstruct, prevent, stop, thwart.

barbarian adj ▷ BARBARIC.
• n heathen, ignoramus, lout, pagan, philistine, savage, vandal, sl yob.

barbaric adj barbarous, brutal, brutish, crude, inhuman, primitive, rough, savage, uncivilized, wild. ▷ CRUEL. Opp CIVILIZED.

bare adj 1 bald, exposed, naked, nude, stark-naked, unclothed, uncovered, undressed. 2 bare *hills.* barren, bleak, desolate, open, treeless, unwooded, windswept. **3** *bare trees.* denuded, leafless, shorn, stripped. **4** *bare rooms.* austere, empty, plain, simple, unadorned, undecorated, unfurnished, vacant. **5** *bare walls.* blank, clean, unmarked. **6** *bare facts.* hard, literal, open, plain, straightforward, unconcealed, undisguised. **7** *the bare minimum.* basic, essential, just adequate, just sufficient, minimal. • *v* expose, lay bare, make known, reveal, show, uncover, undress, unmask, unveil.

bargain *n* **1** agreement, arrangement, contract, deal, negotiation, pact, promise, settlement, transaction, understanding. **2** *bargain in the sales.* *inf* give-away, good buy, *inf* snip, special offer. • *v* argue, barter, discuss terms, do a deal, haggle, negotiate. **bargain for** ▷ EXPECT.

bark *v* **1** growl, yap. **2** *bark your shin.* chafe, graze, rub, scrape, scratch.

barmaid, barman *ns* server, steward, stewardess, waiter, waitress.

barracks *pl n* billet, camp, garrison, lodging, quarters.

barrage *n* **1** ▷ BARRIER. **2** *barrage of gunfire.* assault, attack, battery, bombardment, cannonade, fusillade, onslaught, salvo, storm, volley.

barrel *n* butt, cask, churn, drum, keg, tank, tub, water-butt.

barren *adj* **1** arid, bare, desert, desolate, dried-up, dry, lifeless, treeless, uncultivated, unproductive, useless, waste. **2** infertile, sterile, unfruitful. *Opp* FERTILE.

barricade *n* ▷ BARRIER. • *v* bar, block off, defend, obstruct.

barrier *n* **1** bar, barrage, barricade, boom, bulwark, dam, embankment, fence, hurdle, obstacle, obstruction, palisade, railing, rampart, stockade, wall. **2** *barrier to progress.* handicap, hindrance, impediment, limitation, restriction, stumbling block.

barter *v* bargain, exchange, negotiate, trade.

base *adj* contemptible, cowardly, degrading, despicable, dishonourable, evil, ignoble, immoral, inferior, low, mean, selfish, shabby, shameful, sordid, undignified, unworthy, vulgar, vile. ▷ WICKED. • *n* **1** basis, bed, bedrock, bottom, core, essentials, foot, footing, foundation, fundamentals, groundwork, infrastructure, pedestal, rest, root, stand, substructure, support, underpinning. **2** camp, centre, headquarters, starting point, station. • *v* build, construct, establish, found, ground, locate, position, set up, station.

basement *n* cellar, crypt, vault.

bashful *adj* abashed, backward, blushing, coy, demure, diffident, embarrassed, inhibited, meek, modest, reserved, reticent, retiring, self-conscious, self-effacing, shamefaced, sheepish, shy, timid, unforthcoming. *Opp* ASSERTIVE.

basic *adj* central, chief, crucial, elementary, essential, fundamental, important, intrinsic, key, main, necessary, primary, principal, underlying, vital. *Opp* UNIMPORTANT.

basin *n* bath, bowl, container, dish, pool, sink.

basis n base, core, footing, foundation, ground, premise, principle, starting point, support.

bask v enjoy, glory, lie, lounge, luxuriate, relax, sunbathe, wallow.

basket n bag, hamper, pannier, punnet.

bastard n illegitimate child, *old use* love-child, natural child.

bat n club, racket, racquet.

bath n jacuzzi, pool, shower, *inf* soak, *inf* tub, wash.

bathe v 1 clean, cleanse, immerse, rinse, soak, steep, swill, wash. 2 go swimming, paddle, plunge, splash about, swim, *inf* take a dip.

bathos n anticlimax, *inf* come-down, disappointment, *inf* let-down. *Opp* CLIMAX.

baton n cane, bludgeon, cudgel, rod, staff, stick, truncheon.

batter v beat, bludgeon, cudgel, keep hitting, pound. ▷ HIT.

battery n 1 artillery unit, emplacement. 2 *electric battery.* accumulator, cell. 3 *assault and battery.* assault, attack, thrashing, violence.

battle n action, attack, blitz, campaign, clash, combat, conflict, contest, confrontation, crusade, encounter, engagement, fight, fray, hostilities, offensive, quarrel, *inf* shoot-out, siege, skirmish, strife, struggle, war, warfare. ● v ▷ FIGHT.

battlefield n arena, battleground, theatre of war.

bawdy adj earthy, erotic, lusty, *inf* naughty, racy, *inf* raunchy, ribald, sexy, *inf* spicy. [*derog*] blue, coarse, dirty, indecent, indelicate, lascivious, lewd, licentious, obscene, prurient, risqué, rude, smutty, suggestive, titillating, vulgar. *Opp* PROPER.

bawl v cry, roar, shout, thunder, wail, yell, yelp.

bay n 1 cove, creek, estuary, fjord, gulf, harbour, inlet, sound. 2 alcove, booth, compartment, opening, recess.

bazaar n auction, boot-sale, bring-and-buy, fair, fête, jumble sale, market, sale.

be v 1 be alive, breathe, endure, exist, live. 2 *be here all day.* continue, last, persist, remain, stay, survive. 3 *the next event will be at noon.* arise, happen, occur, take place. 4 *want to be a writer.* become.

beach n bank, coast, coastline, sand, sands, seashore, seaside, shore.

beacon n bonfire, fire, flare, light, lighthouse, signal.

bead n blob, drip, drop, droplet, globule, jewel, pearl.

beaker n cup, glass, goblet, jar, mug, tankard, tumbler.

beam n 1 bar, girder, joist, plank, post, rafter, spar, support, timber. 2 *beam of light.* gleam, ray, shaft, stream. ● v 1 aim, direct, emit, radiate, send out, shine, transmit. 2 beam happily. grin, laugh, look radiant, radiate happiness, smile.

bear v 1 carry, hold, shoulder, support, sustain, take. 2 *bear an inscription.* display, have, possess, show. 3 *bear gifts.* bring, carry, convey, deliver, take, transfer, transport. 4 *bear pain.* abide, accept, brook, cope with, endure, live with, put up with, stand, stomach, suffer, tolerate. 5 *bear young, fruit.* breed, develop, give birth to, produce, spawn, yield. **bear out** ▷ CONFIRM. **bear up** ▷ SURVIVE. **bear witness** ▷ TESTIFY.

bearable *adj* acceptable, endurable, supportable, tolerable.

bearing *n* 1 air, appearance, aspect, attitude, carriage, demeanour, deportment, look, manner, mien, posture, presence, stance, style. 2 *evidence had no bearing*. application, connection, pertinence, relationship, relevance, significance. **bearings** course, direction, orientation, position, sense of direction.

beast *n* brute, creature, monster, savage. ▷ ANIMAL.

beastly *adj* bestial, brutal, cruel, savage. ▷ VILE.

beat *n* 1 accent, pulse, rhythm, stress, tempo. 2 *policeman's beat*. course, itinerary, journey, path, rounds, route, way. ● *v* 1 batter, bludgeon, buffet, cane, clout, flog, hammer, knock about, lash, *inf* lay into, pound, punch, strike, *sl* tan, thrash, punch, *sl* wallop, *inf* whack, whip. ▷ HIT. 2 *beat eggs*. blend, mix, stir, whip, whisk. 3 *His heart beat faster*. palpitate, pound, pulsate, race, throb, thump. 4 *beat an opponent*. best, conquer, crush, defeat, get the better of, *inf* lick, outclass, outdistance, outdo, outwit, overcome, overpower, overthrow, overwhelm, rout, subdue, surpass, *inf* thrash, trounce, vanquish, worst. **beat up** ▷ ATTACK.

beautiful *adj* admirable, alluring, appealing, artistic, attractive, becoming, bewitching, brilliant, captivating, charming, old

use comely, decorative, delightful, elegant, exquisite, *old use* fair, fascinating, fetching, fine, good-looking, glamorous, glorious, gorgeous, graceful, handsome, lovely, magnificent, picturesque, pleasing, pretty, radiant, ravishing, scenic, seductive, spectacular, splendid, stunning, superb, tasteful, tempting. *Opp* UGLY.

beautify *v* adorn, deck, decorate, embellish, ornament, prettify. *Opp* DISFIGURE.

beauty *n* allure, appeal, attractiveness, bloom, charm, elegance, glamour, glory, grace, loveliness, magnificence, prettiness, radiance, splendour.

becalmed *adj* helpless, idle, motionless, still, unmoving.

beckon *v* gesture, motion, signal, summon, wave.

become *v* 1 change into, develop into, grow into, mature into, turn into. 2 *Red becomes you*. be becoming to, enhance, flatter, suit. **becoming** ▷ ATTRACTIVE, SUITABLE.

bed *n* 1 berth, bunk, cot, couch, divan, resting place. 2 *bed of concrete*. base, foundation, layer, substratum. 3 *river bed*. bottom, channel, course. 4 *flower bed*. border, garden, patch, plot.

bedclothes *pl n* bedding, bed linen, blankets, duvets, pillows, pillowcases, quilts, sheets.

bedraggled *adj* dishevelled, drenched, messy, *inf* scruffy, sodden, unkempt, untidy, wet. *Opp* SMART.

beer *n* ale, bitter, lager, mild, stout.

befall *v* ▷ HAPPEN.

before *adv* already, earlier, in advance, previously.

befriend *v* get to know, make friends with, make the acquaintance of, *inf* pal up with.

beg *v* 1 *inf* cadge, scrounge, sponge. 2 *beg a favour.* ask, beseech, crave, entreat, implore, importune, petition, plead, pray, request, supplicate.

beget *v* ▷ CREATE.

beggar *n* destitute person, down-and-out, homeless person, mendicant, pauper, scrounger, sponger, tramp, vagrant.

begin *v* 1 activate, approach, attack, commence, conceive, create, embark on, enter into, found, *inf* get going, inaugurate, initiate, instigate, introduce, launch, lay the foundations, lead off, move off, open, originate, pioneer, precipitate, provoke, set about, set in motion, set out, set up, *inf* spark off, start, *inf* take steps, take the initiative, take up, touch off, trigger off, undertake. 2 *Spring will begin soon.* appear, arise, come into existence, emerge, happen, materialize, originate. *Opp* END.

beginner *n* 1 creator, founder, initiator, instigator, originator, pioneer. 2 *only a beginner.* apprentice, inexperienced person, initiate, learner, novice, recruit, starter, trainee.

beginning *n* 1 birth, commencement, conception, creation, dawn, embryo, emergence, establishment, foundation, genesis, germ, inauguration, inception, initiation, instigation, introduction, launch, onset, opening, origin, outset, point of departure, rise, source, start, starting point, threshold. 2 *beginning of*

a book. preface, prelude, prologue. *Opp* END.

begrudge *v* be bitter about, covet, envy, grudge, mind, object to, resent.

behave *v* 1 acquit yourself, act, conduct yourself, function, operate, perform, react, respond, work. 2 *told to behave.* act properly, be good, be on best behaviour.

behaviour *n* actions, attitude, bearing, conduct, demeanour, deportment, manners, performance.

behead *v* decapitate, guillotine.

behold *v* descry, discern, espy, look at, note, notice, see, set eyes on, view.

being *n* 1 actuality, essence, existence, life, reality, substance. 2 animal, creature, individual, person, spirit, soul.

belated *adj* behindhand, delayed, last-minute, late, overdue, tardy, unpunctual.

belch *v* 1 *inf* burp. 2 *belch smoke.* discharge, emit, gush, send out, spew out.

belief *n* 1 acceptance, assent, assurance, certainty, confidence, credence, reliance, security, sureness, trust. 2 *religious belief.* conviction, creed, doctrine, dogma, ethos, faith, feeling, ideology, morality, notion, opinion, persuasion, principles, standards, tenets, theories, views. *Opp* SCEPTICISM.

believe *v* 1 accept, be certain of, credit, depend on, endorse, have faith in, rely on, subscribe to, *inf* swallow, swear by, trust. *Opp* DISBELIEVE. 2 assume, consider, *inf* dare say, gather, guess, imagine, judge, maintain, presume, speculate, suppose, take it for granted, think. **make believe** ▷ IMAGINE.

believer n adherent, devotee, disciple, follower, supporter, upholder. *Opp* ATHEIST.

belittle v criticize, decry, denigrate, deprecate, detract from, disparage, minimize, *inf* play down, slight, speak slightingly of, undervalue. *Opp* EXAGGERATE, FLATTER, PRAISE.

bell n alarm, chime, knell, peal, signal. ▷ RING.

belligerent adj aggressive, antagonistic, argumentative, bellicose, bullying, combative, contentious, defiant, disputatious, fierce, hawkish, hostile, jingoistic, martial, militant, militaristic, provocative, pugnacious, quarrelsome, violent, warlike, warmongering, warring.
▷ UNFRIENDLY. *Opp* PEACEABLE.

belong v 1 be owned (by), be the property of. 2 be at home, feel welcome, have a place. 3 *belong to a club*. be a member of, be connected with, *inf* be in with.

belongings pl n chattels, effects, *inf* gear, goods, possessions, property, things.

belt n 1 band, circle, loop. 2 *belt round the waist*. cummerbund, girdle, girth, sash, strap, waistband. 3 *green belt*. area, district, stretch, strip, swathe, tract, zone.

bemuse v befuddle, bewilder, confuse, muddle, perplex, puzzle.

bench n 1 form, pew, seat, settle. 2 counter, table, workbench, work table. 3 *He was up before the bench*. court, courtroom, judge, magistrate, tribunal.

bend n angle, arc, corner, crook, curve, loop, turn, turning, twist, zigzag. ● v 1 arch, be flexible, bow, buckle, coil, contort, curl, curve, distort, flex, fold, *inf* give, loop, turn, twist, warp, wind, yield. 2 *bend down before the queen*. bow, crouch, curtsy, genuflect, kneel, stoop.

benefactor n *inf* angel, backer, donor, *inf* fairy godmother, patron, philanthropist, promoter, sponsor, supporter, well-wisher.

beneficial adj advantageous, benign, constructive, favourable, good, health-giving, healthy, helpful, improving, nourishing, nutritious, profitable, salubrious, salutary, supportive, useful, valuable, wholesome.
Opp HARMFUL.

beneficiary n heir, heiress, inheritary, legatee, recipient, successor (*to title*).

benefit n 1 advantage, asset, blessing, convenience, gain, good thing, help, privilege, profit, service, use.
Opp DISADVANTAGE.
2 *unemployment benefit*. aid, allowance, assistance, *inf* dole, grant, handout, income support, payment, social security, welfare. ● v aid, assist, better, boost, do good to, enhance, further, help, improve, profit, promote, serve.

benevolent adj altruistic, benign, caring, charitable, compassionate, considerate, friendly, generous, helpful, humane, kind-hearted, kindly, merciful, philanthropic, sympathetic, unselfish, warmhearted. ▷ KIND. *Opp* UNKIND.

benign adj gentle, harmless, kind. ▷ BENEFICIAL, BENEVOLENT.

bent adj 1 arched, bowed, buckled, coiled, contorted, crooked, curved, distorted, hunched, twisted, warped. 2 [inf] *The dealer was bent.* corrupt, dishonest, immoral, untrustworthy, wicked. Opp HONEST, STRAIGHT. ● n ▷ APTITUDE, BIAS.

bequeath v endow, hand down, leave, make over, pass on, settle, will.

bequest n endowment, gift, inheritance, legacy, settlement.

bereavement n death, loss.

bereft adj deprived, devoid, lacking, wanting.

berserk adj inf beside yourself, crazy, demented, deranged, frantic, frenzied, furious, insane, mad, violent, wild. Opp CALM. **go berserk** ▷ RAGE, RAMPAGE.

berth n 1 bed, bunk. 2 *berth for ships.* anchorage, dock, harbour, haven, landing stage, moorings, pier, port, quay, wharf. ● v anchor, dock, drop anchor, land, moor, tie up. **give a wide berth to** ▷ AVOID.

beseech v ask, entreat, implore, plead. ▷ BEG.

besiege v beset, blockade, cut off, encircle, hem in, isolate, pester, plague, siege, surround.

best adj choicest, finest, first-class, foremost, incomparable, leading, matchless, optimum, outstanding, pre-eminent, superlative, supreme, top, unequalled, unrivalled, unsurpassed.

bestial adj animal, beastly, brutal, brutish, inhuman. ▷ SAVAGE.

bestow v award, confer, donate, give, grant, present.

bet n inf flutter, gamble, speculation, stake, wager. ● v bid, gamble, inf have a flutter, lay bets, speculate, stake, venture, wager.

betray v 1 be disloyal to, cheat, conspire against, deceive, double-cross, give away, inform against, inform on, let down, inf sell down the river, sell out, inf shop. 2 *betray secrets.* disclose, divulge, expose, give away, let out, let slip, reveal, show, tell.

better adj 1 preferable, recommended, superior. 2 convalescent, cured, fitter, healed, healthier, improved, inf on the mend, progressing, recovered, recovering, well. ● v ▷ IMPROVE, SURPASS.

beware v be careful, be on your guard, guard (against), heed, keep clear (of), look out, mind, steer clear (of), take care, take heed, watch out, inf watch your step.

bewilder v baffle, inf bamboozle, bemuse, confound, confuse, daze, disconcert, disorientate, inf floor, inf flummox, muddle, mystify, perplex, puzzle, inf stump.

bewitch v ▷ ENCHANT.

bias n 1 aptitude, bent, inclination, leaning, liking, partiality, penchant, predilection, predisposition, preference, proclivity, propensity, tendency. 2 [derog] bigotry, chauvinism, favouritism, injustice, nepotism, one-sidedness, partiality, partisanship, prejudice, racism, sexism, unfairness. ● v ▷ INFLUENCE.

biased *adj* bigoted, blinkered, chauvinistic, distorted, influenced, interested (*party*), loaded, one-sided, partial, partisan, prejudiced, racist, sexist, slanted, unfair, unjust. *Opp* UNBIASED.

bicycle *n* bike, cycle, *inf* push-bike, racer, tandem, *inf* two-wheeler.

bid *n* 1 offer, price, proposal, tender. 2 *winning bid*. attempt, effort, endeavour, *inf* go, try, venture. • *v* 1 make an offer, offer, propose, tender. 2 ▷ COMMAND.

big *adj* 1 above average, *inf* almighty, ample, astronomical, broad, bulky, burly, capacious, colossal, commodious, considerable, elephantine, enormous, extensive, fat, formidable, gargantuan, generous, giant, gigantic, grand, great, heavy, hefty, huge, *inf* hulking, immeasurable, immense, impressive, infinite, *inf* jumbo, *inf* king-sized, large, lofty, long, mammoth, massive, mighty, monstrous, monumental, mountainous, oversized, prodigious, roomy, sizeable, spacious, substantial, swingeing (*increase*), tall, *inf* terrific, *inf* thumping, tidy (*sum*), titanic, towering, *inf* tremendous, vast, voluminous, weighty, *inf* whacking, *inf* whopping, wide. 2 *big decision*. grave, important, major, momentous, serious, significant. 3 *big in politics*. influential, leading, prominent, powerful. 4 *big name*. ▷ FAMOUS. 5 *big noise*. ▷LOUD. *Opp* SMALL.

bigot *n* chauvinist, fanatic, prejudiced person, racist, sexist, zealot.

bigoted *adj* intolerant, one-sided, prejudiced. ▷ BIASED.

bill *n* 1 account, invoice, receipt, statement. 2 advertisement, broadsheet, circular, handbill, leaflet, notice, placard, poster. 3 *Parliamentary bill*. draft law. 4 *bird's bill*. beak.

billow *v* balloon, bulge, fill out, heave, puff out, rise, roll, surge, swell, undulate.

bind *v* 1 attach, combine, hitch, hold together, join, lash, link, rope, secure, strap, tie, unite. ▷ FASTEN. 2 *bind a wound*. bandage, cover, dress, swathe, wrap. 3 compel, constrain, force, oblige, require. **binding** ▷ COMPULSORY, FORMAL.

biography *n* autobiography, life, life-story, memoirs.

bird *n* chick, cock, *joc* feathered friend, fledgling, fowl, hen, nestling.

birth *n* 1 childbirth, confinement, delivery, labour. 2 ancestry, background, blood, breeding, derivation, descent, extraction, family, genealogy, line, lineage, parentage, pedigree, race, stock, strain. 3 ▷ BEGINNING. **give birth** bear, calve, farrow, foal. ▷ BEGIN.

bisect *v* cross, cut in half, divide, halve, intersect.

bit *n* 1 atom, chip, chunk, crumb, dollop, fraction, fragment, gobbet, grain, helping, hunk, iota, lump, morsel, mouthful, part, particle, piece, portion, sample, scrap, section, segment, share, slab, slice, snippet, speck, spot, taste, titbit, trace. 2 *Wait a bit*. instant, *inf* jiffy, minute, moment, second, *inf* tick, while.

bite *n* 1 nip, pinch, sting. 2 *bite to eat*. morsel, mouthful, nibble, snack, taste. ▷ BIT. • v 1 champ, chew, crunch, cut into, gnaw, munch, nibble, nip, sting, tear at, wound. 2 *The screw won't bite.* grip, hold.

bitter adj 1 acid, acrid, harsh, sharp, sour, unpleasant. 2 *bitter experience.* distressing, galling, heartbreaking, painful, sorrowful, unhappy, unwelcome, upsetting. 3 *bitter remarks.* acrimonious, acerbic, angry, cruel, cynical, embittered, envious, hostile, jaundiced, jealous, malicious, rancorous, resentful, savage, sharp, spiteful, stinging, vicious, waspish. 4 *bitter wind.* biting, cold, freezing, perishing, piercing, raw. Opp KIND, MILD, PLEASANT.

bizarre adj curious, eccentric, fantastic, freakish, odd, outlandish, surreal, weird. ▷ STRANGE. Opp ORDINARY.

black adj coal-black, dark, dusky, ebony, funereal, gloomy, inky, jet, jet-black, moonless, murky, pitch-black, pitch-dark, raven, sable, sooty, starless. • v 1 blacken, polish. 2 ▷ BLACKLIST.

blackleg n inf scab, strikebreaker, traitor.

blacklist v ban, boycott, exclude, ostracize, put an embargo on, repudiate, veto.

blade n dagger, edge, knife, razor, scalpel. ▷ SWORD.

blame n accusation, castigation, censure, criticism, culpability, fault, guilt, liability, inf rap, recrimination, reprimand, reproach, reproof, responsibility, inf stick, stricture. • v accuse, admonish, censure, condemn, criticize, denounce, hold responsible, incriminate, reprehend, reprimand, reproach, reprove, scold, tax, upbraid. Opp EXCUSE.

blameless adj faultless, guiltless, innocent, irreproachable, moral, unimpeachable, upright. Opp GUILTY.

bland adj banal, boring, characterless, dull, flat, gentle, insipid, mild, nondescript, smooth, soft, soothing, tasteless, trite, unappetizing, unexciting, uninspiring, uninteresting, vapid, weak, inf wishy-washy. Opp INTERESTING.

blank adj 1 bare, clean, clear, empty, plain, spotless, unadorned, unmarked, unused. 2 *blank look.* apathetic, baffled, dead, inf deadpan, emotionless, expressionless, glazed, immobile, impassive, inscrutable, lifeless, poker-faced, uncomprehending, unresponsive, vacant, vacuous. • n 1 emptiness, nothingness, vacuum, void. 2 *Fill in the blanks.* box, break, gap, line, space.

blaspheme v curse, utter profanities, swear.

blasphemous adj disrespectful, impious, irreverent, profane, sacrilegious, sinful, ungodly, wicked. Opp REVERENT.

blast n 1 gale, gust, wind. 2 blare, din, noise, racket, roar. 3 ▷ EXPLOSION. • v ▷ ATTACK, EXPLODE. **blast off** ▷ LAUNCH.

blatant adj apparent, barefaced, bold, brazen, conspicuous, evident, flagrant, glaring, obtrusive, obvious, open, overt, shameless, stark, unconcealed, undisguised, unmistakable, visible. Opp HIDDEN.

blaze n conflagration, fire, flame, flare-up, inferno, outburst.
• v burn, flame, flare.

bleach v blanch, discolour, fade, lighten, whiten.

bleak adj bare, barren, cheerless, chilly, cold, comfortless, depressing, desolate, dismal, dreary, exposed, grim, hopeless, joyless, sombre, unpromising, windswept, wintry.

bleary adj blurred, blurry, cloudy, dim, filmy, foggy, fuzzy, hazy, indistinct, misty, murky, obscured, smeary, unclear. Opp CLEAR.

blemish n blotch, blot, chip, crack, defect, deformity, disfigurement, eyesore, fault, flaw, imperfection, mark, mess, pimple, scar, smudge, speck, spot, stain. • v deface, disfigure, flaw, mar, mark, scar, spoil, stain, tarnish.

blend n alloy, amalgam, amalgamation, combination, composite, compound, concoction, fusion, mix, mixture, synthesis, union. • v 1 amalgamate, coalesce, combine, compound, fuse, harmonize, integrate, intermingle, merge, mingle, synthesize, unite. 2 blend the ingredients. beat, mix, stir together, whip, whisk.

bless v 1 anoint, consecrate, dedicate, grace, hallow, make sacred, ordain, sanctify. 2 bless the Lord. exalt, extol, glorify, praise. Opp CURSE.

blessed adj 1 divine, hallowed, holy, revered, sacred, sanctified. 2 ▷ HAPPY.

blessing n. 1 benediction, consecration, grace, prayer. 2 approbation, approval, backing, consent, leave, permission,

sanction, support. 3 The good weather was a blessing. advantage, asset, benefit, inf godsend, help. Opp CURSE, MISFORTUNE.

blight n affliction, ailment, curse, decay, disease, evil, illness, infestation, misfortune, plague, rot, scourge, sickness, trouble. • v ▷ SPOIL.

blind adj 1 blinded, eyeless, sightless, unseeing. 2 blinkered, heedless, ignorant, inattentive, indifferent, insensitive, irrational, mindless, oblivious, prejudiced, unaware, unobservant, unreasoning. • n awning, cover, screen, shade, shutters.
• v 1 dazzle, make blind. 2 ▷ DECEIVE.

blink v flash, flicker, gleam, glimmer, shimmer, sparkle, twinkle, wink.

bliss n delight, ecstasy, euphoria, felicity, glee, happiness, heaven, joy, paradise, rapture. ▷ PLEASURE. Opp MISERY.

bloated adj distended, enlarged, inflated, puffy, swollen.

block n 1 bar, brick, cake, chunk, hunk, ingot, lump, mass, piece, slab. 2 ▷ BLOCKAGE.
• v 1 block a drain. inf bung up, choke, clog, close, congest, constrict, dam, fill, jam, plug, stop up. 2 block a driveway. bar, barricade, impede, obstruct. 3 block a plan. deter, halt, hamper, hinder, hold back, prevent, prohibit, resist, inf scotch, stop, thwart.

blockage n barrier, block, bottleneck, congestion, constriction, impediment, jam, obstacle, obstruction, stoppage.

blond, blonde adjs bleached, fair, flaxen, golden, light, platinum, silvery, yellow.

bloodshed n butchery, carnage, killing, massacre, murder, slaughter, violence.

bloodthirsty adj barbaric, brutal, ferocious, fierce, homicidal, inhuman, murderous, pitiless, ruthless, sadistic, savage, vicious, violent, warlike.
▷ CRUEL. *Opp* HUMANE.

bloody adj 1 bleeding, bloodstained, raw. 2 *a bloody battle*. cruel, fierce, gory.
▷ BLOODTHIRSTY.

bloom n 1 blossom, bud, floret, flower. 2 *bloom of youth*. beauty, flush, glow, prime. ● v be healthy, blossom, bud, burgeon, *inf* come out, develop, flourish, flower, grow, open, prosper, sprout, thrive. *Opp* FADE.

blot n 1 blob, blotch, mark, smear, smudge, *inf* splodge, spot, stain. 2 *blot on the landscape*. blemish, defect, eyesore, fault, flaw. ● v bespatter, blemish, blur, disfigure, mar, mark, smudge, spoil, spot, stain. **blot out** ▷ OBLITERATE. **blot your copybook** ▷ MISBEHAVE.

blotchy adj blemished, discoloured, marked, patchy, smudged, spotty, streaked, uneven.

blow n 1 bang, bash, *sl* biff, buffet, bump, clip, clout, hit, jolt, knock, punch, rap, slap, *inf* slosh, smack, stroke, swat, swipe, thump, *sl* wallop, *inf* whack. 2 *inf* bombshell, calamity, disappointment, disaster, misfortune, shock, surprise, upset. ● v blast, breathe, exhale, fan, puff, waft, whirl, whistle. **blow up** 1 dilate, enlarge, expand, fill, inflate, pump up. 2 exaggerate, magnify, make worse, overstate. 3 blast, bomb,

burst, detonate, dynamite, erupt, explode, go off, set off, shatter. 4 [*inf*] erupt, get angry, lose your temper, rage.

blue adj 1 aquamarine, azure, cobalt, indigo, navy, sapphire, sky-blue, turquoise, ultramarine. 2 ▷ BAWDY. 3 ▷ SAD.
● v ▷ SQUANDER.

blueprint n basis, design, draft, model, outline, pattern, plan, proposal, prototype, scheme.

bluff v deceive, delude, dupe, fool, mislead.

blunder n *sl* boob, error, fault, *Fr* faux pas, gaffe, howler, indiscretion, miscalculation, misjudgement, mistake, slip, slip-up. ● v be clumsy, *inf* botch up, bumble, bungle, *inf* drop a clanger, flounder; go wrong, *inf* make a hash of something, make a mistake, mess up, miscalculate, misjudge, *inf* put your foot in it, slip up, stumble.

blunt adj 1 dull, rounded, thick, unsharpened, worn. *Opp* SHARP. 2 *blunt criticism*. abrupt, brusque, candid, curt, direct, downright, forthright, frank, honest, insensitive, outspoken, plain-spoken, rude, straightforward, tactless, undiplomatic. *Opp* TACTFUL. ● v abate, allay, anaesthetize, dampen, deaden, desensitize, dull, lessen, numb, soften, take the edge off, weaken. *Opp* SHARPEN.

blur v 1 cloud, darken, dim, fog, obscure, smear. 2 confuse, muddle.

blurred adj bleary, blurry, clouded, cloudy, confused, dim, faint, foggy, fuzzy, hazy, illdefined, indistinct, misty, nebulous, out of focus, smoky,

unclear, unfocused, vague.
Opp CLEAR.

blurt *v* blurt out *inf* blab, burst
out with, cry out, disclose,
divulge, exclaim, *inf* give the
game away, let out, let slip,
reveal, *inf* spill the beans, tell.

blush *v* be embarrassed, colour,
flush, go red, redden.

blustering *adj* angry, bullying,
defiant, domineering, hectoring,
noisy, ranting, self-assertive,
storming, swaggering,
threatening, violent.
Opp MODEST.

blustery *adj* gusty, squally,
unsettled, windy.

board *n* 1 chipboard, clapboard,
panel, plank, plywood, slat,
timber. 2 *board of directors*. cabinet, committee, council, direct-
orate, jury, panel.
• *v* 1 accommodate, billet, feed,
house, lodge, put up, quarter,
stay. 2 *board a plane*. catch,
enter, get on, go on board.

boast *v* *inf* blow your own trum-
pet, brag, crow, exaggerate,
gloat, show off, *inf* sing your
own praises, swagger, *inf* talk
big.

boaster *n* *inf* big-head, braggart,
inf loudmouth, *inf* poser, show-
off, swaggerer.

boastful *adj* *inf* big-headed, brag-
ging, *inf* cocky, conceited, egotistical, ostentatious, proud,
puffed up, swaggering, swollen-
headed, vain. *Opp* MODEST.

boat *n* craft, cruiser, motor boat,
rowing boat, ship, speedboat,
vessel, yacht.

boatman *n* ferryman, gondolier,
oarsman, rower, sailor, yachtsman. ▷ SAILOR.

bob *v* bounce, dance, hop, jerk,
jig about, jump, leap, nod, toss
about, twitch. **bob up**
▷ APPEAR.

body *n* 1 anatomy, being, build,
figure, form, frame, physique,
shape, substance, torso, trunk.
2 cadaver, carcass, corpse,
mortal remains, mummy, relics,
remains, *sl* stiff. 3 association,
band, committee, company, corporation, society. ▷ GROUP.
4 *body of material*. accumulation, collection, corpus, mass.

bodyguard *n* defender, guard,
sl minder, protector.

bog *n* fen, marsh, marshland,
mire, morass, mudflats, peat
bog, quagmire, quicksands,
swamp, wetlands. **get bogged
down** get into difficulties, get
stuck, grind to a halt, sink.

bogus *adj* counterfeit, fake, false,
fraudulent, imitation,
inf phoney, sham, spurious.
Opp GENUINE.

Bohemian *adj* *inf* arty, eccentric, nonconformist, off-beat,
unconventional, unorthodox,
inf way-out, weird.

boil *n* abscess, blister, carbuncle,
chilblain, eruption, inflammation, pimple, pustule, sore, spot,
ulcer, *sl* zit. • *v* 1 cook, heat,
simmer, stew. 2 bubble, effervesce, foam, seethe, steam.
3 ▷ RAGE.

boisterous *adj* animated, disorderly, exuberant, irrepressible,
lively, noisy, obstreperous, riotous, rough, rowdy, stormy, tempestuous, tumultuous, undisciplined, unruly, uproarious, wild.
Opp CALM.

bold *adj* 1 adventurous, brave,
confident, courageous, daredevil,
daring, dauntless, enterprising,

fearless, *derog* foolhardy, forceful, gallant, heroic, intrepid, plucky, *derog* rash, *derog* reckless, self-confident, valiant, valorous. **2** [*derog*] brash, brazen, cheeky, forward, impertinent, impudent, insolent, pert, presumptuous, rude, saucy, shameless. **3** *bold colours, writing.* big, bright, clear, conspicuous, eye-catching, large, prominent, pronounced, showy, striking, strong, vivid. *Opp* FAINT, TIMID.

bolster *n* cushion, pillow.
● *v* ▷ SUPPORT.

bolt *n* **1** arrow, dart, missile, projectile. **2** peg, pin, rivet, rod, screw. **3** *bolt on a door.* catch, fastening, latch, lock. ● *v* **1** close, fasten, latch, lock, secure. **2** dart away, dash away, escape, flee, fly, run off, rush off. **3** *bolt food.* ▷ EAT. **bolt from the blue** ▷ SURPRISE.

bomb *n* bombshell, explosive.
● *v* ▷ BOMBARD.

bombard *v* **1** attack, batter, blast, blitz, bomb, fire at, pelt, pound, shell, shoot at, strafe. **2** *bombard with questions.* assail, besiege, set upon, pester, plague.

bombardment *n* attack, barrage, blast, blitz, broadside, burst, cannonade, discharge, fusillade, salvo, volley.

bombastic *adj* extravagant, grandiloquent, grandiose, high-flown, inflated, pompous, turgid.

bond *n* **1** chain, cord, fastening, fetter, manacle, restraint, rope, shackle. **2** *bond of friendship.* affinity, attachment, connection, link, relationship, tie, unity. **3** *legal bond.* agreement, compact, covenant, guarantee, pledge, promise, word.
● *v* ▷ STICK.

bondage *n* ▷ SLAVERY.

bonus *n* **1** commission, dividend, gift, gratuity, handout, payment, *inf* perk, reward, supplement, tip. **2** addition, advantage, benefit, extra, *inf* plus.

bony *adj* angular, emaciated, gangling, gawky, lanky, lean, scraggy, scrawny, skinny, thin. *Opp* PLUMP.

book *n* album, booklet, copy, edition, guidebook, handbook, hardback, paperback, publication, textbook, tome, volume, work.
● *v* **1** *book for speeding.* take your name, write down details. **2** *book in advance.* arrange, order, organize, reserve, sign up.

booklet *n* brochure, leaflet, pamphlet.

boom *n* **1** bang, blast, crash, explosion, reverberation, roar, rumble. **2** *boom in trade.* boost, expansion, growth, improvement, increase, spurt, upsurge, upturn. ▷ PROSPERITY. **3** *boom across a river.* ▷ BARRIER.
● *v* **1** crash, explode, reverberate, roar, rumble. **2** ▷ PROSPER.

boorish *adj* ignorant, ill-mannered, loutish, oafish, philistine, uncultured, vulgar. *Opp* CULTURED.

boost *n* aid, encouragement, fillip, help, impetus, lift, push, stimulus. ● *v* advance, aid, assist, augment, bolster, build up, buoy up, encourage, enhance, expand, foster, further, give an impetus to, heighten, help, improve, increase, lift, promote, push up, raise, support. *Opp* DEPRESS.

booth *n* box, compartment, cubicle, hut, kiosk, stall, stand.

booty n contraband, gains, haul, loot, pickings, plunder, spoils, inf swag, takings, winnings.

border n 1 brim, brink, edge, edging, frame, frieze, fringe, hem, margin, perimeter, periphery, rim, surround, verge. 2 borderline, boundary, frontier, limit. 3 flower border. bed. • v be adjacent to, be alongside, join, share a border with, touch.

bore v 1 burrow, drill, mine, penetrate, sink, tunnel. ▷ PIERCE. 2 be tedious, fatigue, pall on, tire, inf turn off, weary. Opp INTEREST.

boring adj arid, commonplace, dreary, dry, dull, flat, humdrum, long-winded, monotonous, repetitive, soporific, stale, tedious, tiresome, trite, uneventful, unexciting, uninspiring, uninteresting, vapid, wearisome, wordy. Opp INTERESTING.

born adj congenital, instinctive, natural, untaught.

borrow v adopt, appropriate, inf cadge, copy, crib, make use of, imitate, pirate, plagiarize, scrounge, take, use. Opp LEND.

boss n employer, head. ▷ CHIEF.

bossy adj assertive, authoritarian, bullying, dictatorial, domineering, high-handed, imperious, officious, overbearing, peremptory, inf pushy, self-assertive, tyrannical. Opp SERVILE.

bother n 1 ado, difficulty, disorder, disturbance, fuss, inf hassle, problem, inf to-do. 2 annoyance, inconvenience, irritation, nuisance, pest, trouble, worry. • v 1 annoy, concern, dismay, disturb, exasperate, harass, inf hassle, inconvenience, irk, irritate, molest, nag, perturb, pester, plague, trouble,

upset, vex, worry. 2 be concerned, be worried, care, mind, take trouble. ▷ TROUBLE.

bottle n carafe, decanter, flagon, flask. **bottle up** ▷ SUPPRESS.

bottom adj deepest, least, lowest, minimum. • n 1 base, bed depth, floor, foot, foundation, lowest point, nadir, pedestal, substructure, underside. Opp TOP. 2 basis, essence, grounds, heart, origin, root, source. 3 sl arse, backside, behind, inf bum, buttocks, joc posterior, rear, rump, seat.

bottomless adj deep, immeasurable, unfathomable.

bounce v bob, bound, bump, jump, leap, rebound, recoil, ricochet, spring.

bound adj 1 bound to obey. compelled, committed, constrained, duty-bound, forced, obliged, required. 2 bound to help. certain, sure. 3 bound to lose her job. destined, doomed, fated. 4 bound with rope. fastened, joined, lashed together, roped, secured, tied. • v bob, bounce, caper, gambol, hop, hurdle, jump, leap, pounce, romp, skip, spring, vault. **bound for** directed towards, going to, heading for, making for, travelling towards.

boundary n border, borderline, bounds, brink, circumference, confines, demarcation, edge, end, extremity, fringe, frontier, limit, margin, perimeter, threshold, verge.

boundless adj endless, everlasting, immeasurable, incalculable, inexhaustible, infinite, limitless, unflagging, unlimited, unrestricted, untold. ▷ VAST. Opp FINITE.

bounty n alms, beneficence, charity, generosity, gift, goodness, largesse, liberality, munificence, philanthropy, unselfishness.

bouquet n 1 arrangement, bunch, buttonhole, corsage, garland, nosegay, posy, spray. 2 aroma, fragrance, scent, smell.

bout n 1 attack, fit, period, run, spell, time. 2 battle, combat, competition, contest, encounter, engagement, fight, match, round, *inf* set-to, struggle.

bow v 1 bend, bob, curtsy, genuflect, incline, kowtow, nod, stoop. 2 ▷ SUBMIT.

bowels pl n 1 entrails, guts, *inf* innards, insides, intestines, viscera, vitals. 2 core, depths, heart, inside.

bower n arbour, gazebo, hideaway, recess, retreat, shelter, summer house.

bowl n basin, casserole, container, dish, pan, tureen.
● v fling, hurl, lob, pitch, throw, toss.

box n caddy, canister, carton, case, casket, chest, coffer, container, crate, pack, trunk.
● v *inf* engage in fisticuffs, fight, punch, scrap, spar. ▷ HIT.

boy n *derog* brat, *inf* kid, lad, schoolboy, son, *derog* urchin, youngster, youth.

boycott n ban, blacklist, embargo, prohibition. ● v avoid, blacklist, exclude, *inf* give the cold-shoulder to, ignore, ostracize, outlaw, prohibit, spurn, stay away from.

bracing adj crisp, exhilarating, health-giving, invigorating, refreshing, restorative, stimulating, tonic.

brag v crow, gloat, show off.
▷ BOAST.

brain n *inf* grey matter, intellect, intelligence, mind, *inf* nous, reason, sense, understanding, wisdom, wit.

brainwash v condition, indoctrinate, re-educate.

branch n 1 arm, bough, limb, stem, twig. 2 department, division, office, offshoot, part, section, subdivision, wing.
● v diverge, divide, fork, split, subdivide. **branch out**
▷ DIVERSIFY.

brand n kind, label, line, make, sort, type, variety. ● v 1 burn, identify, label, mark, scar, stamp, tag. 2 characterize, denounce, discredit, expose, stigmatize.

brash adj brazen, insolent, rude, self-assertive. ▷ ARROGANT.

bravado n arrogance, bluster, swagger.

brave adj adventurous, audacious, bold, courageous, daring, dauntless, determined, fearless, gallant, game, *inf* gutsy, heroic, indomitable, intrepid, *derog* macho, plucky, resolute, spirited, stalwart, stoical, stouthearted, tough, unafraid, undaunted, valiant, valorous, venturesome. *Opp* COWARDLY.

bravery n audacity, boldness, *sl* bottle, courage, daring, determination, fearlessness, fibre, firmness, fortitude, gallantry, *inf* grit, guts, heroism, mettle, *inf* nerve, pluck, prowess, resolution, spirit, stoicism, tenacity, valour. *Opp* COWARDICE.

brawl n *inf* affray, altercation, *inf* bust-up, clash, *inf* dust-up, fracas, fray, *inf* free-for-all, mêlée, *inf* punch-up, quarrel, *inf* row, scrap, scuffle, *inf* set-to, tussle. • *v* ▷ FIGHT.

brazen *adj* barefaced, blatant, cheeky, defiant, flagrant, impertinent, impudent, insolent, rude, shameless, unabashed, unashamed. *Opp* SHAMEFACED.

breach *n* **1** aperture, break, chasm, crack, fissure, gap, hole, opening, rent, space, split. **2** difference, disagreement, drifting apart, estrangement, quarrel, rift, rupture, separation, split. **3** *breach of law.* contravention, infringement, offence, transgression, violation.

bread *n* **1** provisions, sustenance. ▷ FOOD. **2** [*inf*] ▷ MONEY.

break *n* **1** breach, breakage, burst, chink, cleft, crack, crevice, fissure, fracture, gap, hole, leak, opening, rift, rupture, split, tear. **2** *break from work.* *inf* breather, breathing-space, interlude, intermission, interval, *inf* let-up, lull, pause, respite, rest. **3** *break in service.* disruption, halt, interruption, lapse, suspension. • *v* **1** breach, burst, *inf* bust, chip, crack, crumble, crush, damage, demolish, fracture, fragment, knock down, ruin, shatter, smash, snap, splinter, split, wreck. ▷ DESTROY. **2** *break the law.* contravene, defy, disobey, disregard, fail to observe, flout, transgress, violate. ·**3** *break a record.* beat, better, exceed, excel, go beyond, outdo, outstrip, pass, surpass. **break down** ▷ ANALYSE, DEMOLISH. **break in** ▷ INTERRUPT, INTRUDE. **break off** ▷ FINISH. **break out** ▷ ESCAPE. **break through** ▷ PENETRATE. **break up** ▷ DISINTEGRATE.

breakdown *n* **1** collapse, disintegration, downfall, failure, malfunction, stoppage. **2** analysis, classification, dissection, itemization.

breakthrough *n* advance, development, discovery, find, improvement, innovation, invention, leap forward, progress, revolution, success.

breakwater *n* jetty, pier.

breath *n* gust, murmur, puff, sigh, waft, whiff, whisper.

breathe *v* **1** exhale, inhale, pant, respire. **2** tell, whisper.

breathless *adj* exhausted, gasping, out of breath, panting, *inf* puffed, wheezy, winded.

breed *n* clan, family, kind, line, lineage, pedigree, race, sort, species, stock, strain, type, variety. • *v* **1** bear, cultivate, increase, multiply, nourish, nurture, procreate, produce young, propagate (*plants*), raise, reproduce. **2** *breed contempt.* arouse, cause, create, develop, engender, generate, foster, induce, occasion.

breeze *n* air current, breath, draught, waft, wind.

breezy *adj* airy, blowy, draughty, fresh, gusty, windy.

brevity *n* compactness, compression, concision, curtness, economy, pithiness, succinctness, terseness.

brew *n* blend, concoction, drink, infusion, liquor, mixture, potion, punch. • *v* **1** cook, ferment, infuse, make, simmer, steep. **2** *brew mischief.* concoct, contrive, *inf* cook up, devise, foment, hatch, plan, plot, scheme, stir up.

bribe *n* *sl* backhander, *inf* carrot, enticement, *sl* graft, incentive, inducement, *inf* payola, *inf* sweetener. ● *v* buy off, corrupt, entice, *inf* grease your palm, influence, offer a bribe, pervert, suborn, tempt.

brick *n* block, breeze-block, cube, stone.

bridge *n* arch, connection, crossing, link, span, way over. ● *v* connect, cross, fill, join, link, pass over, span, straddle, tie together, traverse, unite.

bridle *v* 1 check, control, curb, restrain. 2 ▷ BRISTLE.

brief *adj* 1 cursory, ephemeral, fleeting, hasty, limited, momentary, passing, quick, sharp, short, short-lived, temporary, transient. 2 *brief comment.* abbreviated, abridged, compressed, concise, condensed, crisp, curt, curtailed, laconic, pithy, shortened, succinct, terse, thumbnail, to the point. *Opp* LONG. ● *n* 1 advice, briefing, directions, information, instructions, orders, outline, plan. 2 *barrister's brief.* argument, case, defence, dossier. ● *v* advise, direct, enlighten, *inf* fill someone in, guide, inform, instruct, prepare, prime, *inf* put someone in the picture.

brigand *n* pirate, robber, ruffian, thief. ▷ BANDIT.

bright *adj* 1 alight, beaming, blazing, burnished, colourful, dazzling, *derog* flashy, fresh, *derog* gaudy, glaring, gleaming, glistening, glittering, glossy, glowing, incandescent, lambent, light, luminous, lustrous, pellucid, polished, radiant, resplendent, scintillating, shimmering, shining, shiny, showy, sparkling, twinkling, vivid. 2 *bright sky.* clear, cloudless, fair, sunny. 3 *bright prospects.* auspicious, favourable, optimistic, rosy.

4 *bright smile.* ▷ CHEERFUL. 5 *bright ideas.* ▷ CLEVER. *Opp* DULL.

brighten *v* 1 cheer (up), gladden, illuminate, light up, liven up, *inf* perk up. 2 become sunny, clear up, lighten.

brilliant *adj* 1 dazzling, glorious, intense, shining, sparkling, vivid. ▷ BRIGHT. *Opp* DULL. 2 [*inf*] *brilliant game.* ▷ EXCELLENT.

brim *n* edge, rim, top. ▷ BRINK.

bring *v* 1 carry, convey, deliver, fetch, take, transport. 2 *bring a friend.* accompany, escort, guide, lead, usher. 3 *The book will bring her fame.* attract, cause, draw, earn, engender, give rise to, lead to, occasion, produce, prompt, provoke, result in. **bring about** ▷ CREATE. **bring in** ▷ EARN, INTRODUCE. **bring off** ▷ ACHIEVE. **bring on** ▷ ACCELERATE, CAUSE. **bring out** ▷ EMPHASIZE, PRODUCE. **bring up** ▷ EDUCATE, RAISE.

brink *n* bank, border, boundary, brim, edge, fringe, limit, lip, margin, perimeter, periphery, rim, threshold, verge.

brisk *adj* 1 active, animated, bright, businesslike, bustling, busy, crisp, decisive, energetic, lively, nimble, quick, rapid, *inf* snappy, *inf* spanking (*pace*), speedy, spirited, sprightly, vigorous. *Opp* LEISURELY. 2 *brisk wind.* bracing, fresh, invigorating, refreshing, stimulating.

bristle *n* barb, hair, prickle, quill, spine, stubble, thorn, whisker. ● *v* become angry, become indignant, bridle, flare up.

brittle *adj* breakable, crisp, crumbling, delicate, easily

broken, fragile, frail.
Opp FLEXIBLE, RESILIENT.

broad *adj* **1** ample, capacious, expansive, extensive, large, open, spacious, sweeping, vast, wide. **2** *broad daylight.* clear, full, open, plain. **3** *broad outline.* general, imprecise, non-specific, sweeping, undetailed. **4** *broad tastes.* comprehensive, encyclopaedic, universal, wide-ranging. ▷ BROAD-MINDED. **5** *broad humour.* bawdy, blue, coarse, earthy, indecent, racy, ribald, suggestive, vulgar.
Opp NARROW.

broadcast *n* programme, relay, show, transmission.
● *v* **1** advertise, announce, circulate, disseminate, make known, make public, proclaim, publish, relay, report, spread about, televise, transmit. **2** *broadcast seed.* scatter, sow at random.

broadcaster *n* anchorman, announcer, commentator, compère, disc jockey, DJ, newsreader, presenter.

broaden *v* branch out, develop, diversify, expand, extend, increase, open up, spread, widen. *Opp* LIMIT.

broad-minded *adj* all-embracing, broad, catholic, comprehensive, cosmopolitan, eclectic, enlightened, liberal, open-minded, tolerant, unbiased, unprejudiced, unshockable. *Opp* NARROW-MINDED.

brochure *n* booklet, catalogue, circular, handbill, leaflet, pamphlet, prospectus.

brooch *n* badge, clasp, clip.

brood *n* children, clutch (*of eggs*), family. ▷ YOUNG.
● *v* **1** hatch, incubate, sit on.

2 *brood over mistakes.* agonize, dwell (on), *inf* eat your heart out, fret, mope, worry. ▷ THINK.

brook *n* beck, burn, rivulet, stream, watercourse.
● *v* ▷ TOLERATE.

browbeat *v* badger, bully, coerce, cow, intimidate.
▷ FRIGHTEN.

brown *adj* beige, bronze, buff, chestnut, chocolate, fawn, khaki, russet, sepia, tan, tawny, terra-cotta, umber. ● *v* bronze, grill, tan, toast.

browse *v* **1** crop, feed, graze, pasture. **2** *browse in a book.* dip in, flick through, leaf through, look through, peruse, scan, skim.

bruise *n* bump, contusion, discoloration, *inf* shiner. ● *v* blacken, crush, damage, discolour, mark.
▷ WOUND.

brush *n* **1** besom, broom. **2** *brush with police.* ▷ CONFLICT.
● *v* **1** groom, scrub, sweep, tidy. **2** *brush the goalpost.* graze, touch. **brush aside** ▷ DISMISS. **brush-off** ▷ REBUFF. **brush up** ▷ REVISE.

brutal *adj* barbaric, bestial, bloodthirsty, brutish, callous, cold-blooded, cruel, dehumanized, ferocious, hard-hearted, heartless, inhuman, inhumane, merciless, murderous, pitiless, ruthless, sadistic, savage, vicious, violent, wild. ▷ UNKIND. *Opp* HUMANE.

brutalize *v* dehumanize, harden, inure.

brute *adj* irrational, mindless, physical, rough, unfeeling.
▷ BRUTISH. ● *n* **1** beast, creature. ▷ ANIMAL. **2** [*inf*] *cruel brute.* barbarian, bully, monster, ruffian, sadist, savage.

brutish *adj* animal, barbaric, bestial, boorish, brutal, coarse, cold-blooded, crude, cruel, *inf* gross, inhuman, insensitive, mindless, savage, senseless, stupid, unthinking. *Opp* HUMANE.

bubble *n* air pocket, blister, vesicle. • *v* boil, effervesce, fizz, foam, froth, gurgle, sparkle. **bubbles** effervescence, fizz, foam, froth, head, suds.

bubbly *adj* effervescent, fizzy, foaming, sparkling. ▷ LIVELY.

buccaneer *n* adventurer, bandit, brigand, marauder, pirate, robber.

bucket *n* can, pail, scuttle, tub.

buckle *n* catch, clasp, clip, fastener. • *v* 1 clasp, clip, do up, fasten, hook up, secure. 2 bend, bulge, cave in, collapse, crumple, distort, twist, warp.

bud *n* shoot, sprout. • *v* begin to grow, burgeon, develop, shoot, sprout. **budding** ▷ POTENTIAL, PROMISING.

budge *v* 1 give way, move, stir, yield. 2 *can't budge him.* change, dislodge, move, persuade, propel, push, shift, sway.

budget *n* accounts, allocation of funds, allowance, estimate, financial planning, means, resources. • *v* allocate money, allot resources, allow (for), estimate expenditure, ration your spending.

buff *n* ▷ ENTHUSIAST. • *v* polish, rub, shine, smooth.

buffer *n* bumper, cushion, fender, safeguard, shield, shock-absorber.

buffet *n* 1 café, counter, snack bar. 2 *stand-up buffet.* ▷ MEAL. • *v* ▷ HIT.

bug *n* 1 ▷ INSECT, MICROBE. 2 *bug in a computer program.* defect, error, failing, fault, flaw, *inf* gremlin, malfunction, mistake, virus. • *v* 1 intercept, listen in to, spy on, tap. 2 [*sl*] *Don't let it bug you.* ▷ ANNOY.

build *v* assemble, construct, develop, erect, fabricate, form, found, *inf* knock together, make, put up, raise, rear, set up. **build up** ▷ INTENSIFY.

builder *n* bricklayer, construction worker, labourer.

building *n* construction, edifice, piece of architecture, *inf* pile, premises, structure.

bulb *n* 1 corm, tuber. 2 *electric bulb.* lamp, light.

bulbous *adj* bloated, bulging, convex, distended, pot-bellied, rotund, spherical, swollen.

bulge *n* bump, distension, knob, lump, protrusion, protuberance, swelling. • *v* billow, dilate, distend, expand, project, protrude, stick out, swell.

bulk *n* 1 amplitude, body, dimensions, extent, immensity, magnitude, mass, size, substance, volume, weight. 2 *bulk of the work.* *inf* best part, greater part, majority, preponderance.

bulky *adj* awkward, chunky, cumbersome, unwieldy. ▷ BIG.

bulletin *n* announcement, communication, communiqué, dispatch, message, newsflash, notice, report, statement.

bull's-eye *n* centre, mark, target.

bully *v* browbeat, coerce, cow, harass, hector, intimidate, persecute, *inf* pick on, *inf* push around, terrorize, threaten, torment, tyrannize.

bulwark n defence, earthwork, fortification, protection, rampart, wall. ▷ BARRIER.

bump n 1 bang, blow, collision, crash, knock, thud, thump. 2 bulge, distension, hump, knob, lump, protrusion, protuberance, swelling, welt. ● v 1 bang, collide with, jar, knock, ram, smash into, thump, sl wallop. ▷ HIT. 2 bounce, jerk, jolt. **bump into** ▷ MEET. **bump off** ▷ KILL.

bumptious adj arrogant, inf big-headed, boastful, brash, inf cocky, conceited, egotistical, forward, officious, overbearing, pompous, presumptuous, inf pushy, self-assertive, self-important, smug, inf stuck-up, inf snooty, vain. Opp MODEST.

bumpy adj 1 bouncy, jarring, jerky, jolting. 2 bumpy road. broken, jagged, knobbly, pitted, rocky, rough, rutted, stony, uneven. Opp SMOOTH.

bunch n 1 batch, bundle, clump, cluster, heap, lot, quantity, set, sheaf, tuft. 2 bunch of flowers. bouquet, posy, spray. 3 [inf] bunch of friends. crowd, gang, gathering, party. ▷ GROUP. ● v cluster, congregate, crowd, flock, gather, herd, huddle, mass, pack. Opp DISPERSE.

bundle n bale, bunch, collection, package, packet, parcel, sheaf, truss. ● v bale, bind, fasten, pack, tie, truss, wrap. **bundle out** ▷ EJECT.

bung n cork, plug, stopper. ● v ▷ THROW.

bungle v blunder, botch, sl cock up, fluff, inf make a hash of, inf make a mess of, inf mess up, mismanage, inf muff, ruin, inf screw up, spoil.

buoy n beacon, float, marker, signal. ● v ▷ RAISE.

buoyant adj 1 floating, light. 2 buoyant mood. ▷ CHEERFUL.

burden n 1 cargo, encumbrance, load, weight. 2 burden of guilt. affliction, anxiety, care, cross, millstone, obligation, onus, problem, responsibility, trial, trouble, worry. ● v afflict, encumber, hamper, handicap, impose on, inf lumber (with), oppress, overload (with), inf saddle (with), tax, trouble, weigh down, worry.

burdensome adj difficult, exacting, heavy, onerous, oppressive, taxing, tiring, troublesome, wearisome, weighty, worrying. Opp EASY.

bureau n 1 desk, writing desk. 2 travel bureau. agency, department, office, service.

bureaucracy n administration, government, officialdom, paperwork, inf red tape, regulations.

burglar n housebreaker, intruder, robber. ▷ THIEF.

burglary n break-in, forcible entry, housebreaking, pilfering, robbery, stealing, theft.

burgle v break in, rob. ▷ STEAL.

burial n ▷ FUNERAL.

burlesque n caricature, imitation, mockery, parody, satire, inf send-up, inf spoof, inf take-off.

burly adj brawny, heavy, hefty, inf hulking, muscular, powerful, stocky, inf strapping, strong, sturdy, thickset, tough, well-built. Opp THIN.

burn n blister, charring. ● v 1 be alight, blaze, flame, flicker, glow, smoke, smoulder, spark. 2 consume, cremate, destroy by fire, ignite, incinerate, kindle,

reduce to ashes, set on fire.
3 *burn your skin.* blister, char,
scald, scorch, sear, shrivel,
singe, sting. ▷ FIRE, HEAT.

burning adj 1 alight, blazing,
flaming, glowing, incandescent,
on fire, raging, smouldering.
2 *burning pain.* biting, blistering, fiery, scalding, scorching,
searing, smarting, stinging.
3 *burning chemicals.* acid, caustic, corrosive. 4 *burning smell.*
acrid, pungent, reeking, smoky.
5 *burning desire.* acute, ardent,
consuming, eager, fervent,
heated, impassioned, intense,
passionate, red-hot, vehement.
6 *burning issue.* crucial, important, pressing, urgent, vital.

burrow n hole, retreat, set, shelter, tunnel, warren. • v delve,
dig, excavate, tunnel.

burst v 1 break, crack, erupt,
explode, force open, give way,
open suddenly, puncture, rupture, shatter, split. 2 ▷ RUSH.

bury v cover, embed, engulf,
entomb, immerse, implant,
inter, lay to rest, plant, secrete,
submerge. ▷ HIDE.

bus n coach, double-decker,
minibus.

bushy adj bristly, dense, fluffy,
fuzzy, luxuriant, rough, shaggy,
spreading, tangled, thick,
unruly, untidy.

business n 1 affair, concern,
duty, function, matter, problem,
question, responsibility, subject,
task. 2 calling, career, employment, job, line of work, occupation, profession, pursuit, trade,
vocation. 3 buying and selling,
commerce, dealings, industry,
merchandising, trade, trading,
transactions. 4 company, concern, corporation, enterprise,

firm, organization, *inf* outfit,
partnership, *inf* set-up, venture.

businesslike adj efficient, hard-
headed, logical, methodical,
orderly, practical, professional,
systematic, well-organized.
Opp DISORGANIZED.

businessman, businesswoman ns entrepreneur, executive, financier, industrialist,
magnate, manager, tycoon.

bustle n activity, agitation, commotion, excitement, flurry, fuss,
haste, hurly-burly, hustle, stir,
inf to-do, *inf* toing and froing.
• v dash, fuss, hasten, hurry,
hustle, rush, scamper, scramble,
scurry, scuttle, *inf* tear, whirl.

busy adj 1 active, bustling about,
diligent, employed, engaged,
engrossed, *inf* hard at it,
immersed, industrious,
involved, occupied, *inf* on the go,
slaving, *inf* tied up, *inf* up to
your eyes, working. *Opp* IDLE.
2 *busy shops.* bustling, frantic,
full, hectic, lively.

busybody n gossip, meddler,
inf Nosey Parker, *inf* snooper.
be a busybody ▷ INTERFERE.

butt n 1 handle, shaft.
2 *water-butt.* barrel, cask. 3 *cigar
butt.* remains, remnant, stub.
4 *butt of ridicule.* object, subject,
target, victim. • v buffet, bump,
jab, poke, prod, push, shove,
thump. ▷ HIT. **butt in**
▷ INTERRUPT.

buttocks n sl arse, backside,
behind, bottom, *inf* bum, *Amer*
butt, haunches, *joc* posterior,
rear, rump, seat.

buttress n prop, support.
• v brace, prop up, reinforce,
strengthen, support.

buxom adj ample, bosomy, full-figured, plump, robust, voluptuous. Opp THIN.

buy v acquire, come by, get, inf invest in, obtain, pay for, procure, purchase. Opp SELL.

buyer n client, consumer, customer, purchaser, shopper.

bypass v avoid, circumvent, dodge, evade, go round, ignore, omit, sidestep, skirt.

by-product n consequence, corollary, repercussion, side-effect.

bystander n eye-witness, observer, onlooker, passer-by, spectator, witness.

C

cabin n 1 chalet, hut, lodge, shack, shanty, shed, shelter. 2 cabin on a ship. berth, compartment, quarters.

cable n 1 chain, cord, flex, guy, hawser, lead, rope, wire. 2 news by cable. message, telegram, wire.

cacophonous adj discordant, dissonant, harsh, noisy. Opp HARMONIOUS.

cacophony n caterwauling, din, discord, dissonance, harshness, jangle, racket, inf row, inf rumpus, tumult. Opp HARMONY.

cadence n accent, beat, intonation, lilt, metre, rhythm, rise and fall, stress, tune.

cadet n learner, recruit, trainee.

cadge v ask, beg, scrounge, sponge.

café n bar, bistro, brasserie, buffet, cafeteria, canteen, coffee bar, restaurant, snack bar, take-away, teashop.

cage n coop, enclosure, hutch, pen. • v ▷ CONFINE.

cajole v inf butter up, coax, flatter, inveigle, persuade, seduce.

cake n 1 bun, gateau. 2 cake of soap. bar, block, chunk, lump, piece, slab. • v 1 coat, clog, encrust, make muddy. 2 coagulate, congeal, dry, solidify, thicken.

calamitous adj cataclysmic, catastrophic, devastating, dire, disastrous, dreadful, fatal, ruinous, serious, terrible, tragic, unlucky.

calamity n accident, cataclysm, catastrophe, disaster, misadventure, mishap, tragedy, tribulation.

calculate v add up, ascertain, assess, compute, count, determine, estimate, evaluate, figure out, gauge, judge, reckon, total, weigh, work out. **calculated** ▷ DELIBERATE. **calculating** ▷ CRAFTY.

calibre n 1 bore, diameter, gauge. 2 ability, capacity, character, distinction, excellence, genius, merit, proficiency, quality, skill, stature, talent, worth.

call n 1 bellow, cry, exclamation, shout, yell. 2 bidding, invitation, signal, summons. 3 social call. stay, visit. 4 no call for it. demand, excuse, justification, need, occasion, request.
• v 1 bellow, clamour, cry out, exclaim, hail, shout, yell. 2 call on friends. drop in, visit. 3 baptize, christen, entitle, name, title. 4 call me at 7. awaken, get someone up, rouse,

wake. 5 *call a meeting.* convene, invite, order, summon. 6 *call by phone.* contact, ring, telephone. **call for** ▷ FETCH, REQUEST. **call off** ▷ CANCEL. **call someone names** ▷ INSULT.

calligraphy *n* copperplate, handwriting, lettering, script.

calling *n* career, employment, line of work, métier, occupation, profession, pursuit, trade, vocation.

callous *adj* cold, hard-bitten, *inf* hard-boiled, hardened, hard-hearted, heartless, inhuman, insensitive, merciless, ruthless, *inf* thick-skinned, uncaring, unemotional, unfeeling, unsympathetic. ▷ CRUEL. *Opp* SENSITIVE.

callow *adj* adolescent, immature, juvenile. ▷ INEXPERIENCED. *Opp* MATURE.

calm *adj* 1 even, flat, halcyon (*days*), like a millpond, motionless, placid, quiet, slow-moving, smooth, still, unclouded, windless. 2 collected, *derog* complacent, composed, controlled, cool, dispassionate, equable, impassive, imperturbable, *inf* laid-back, level-headed, patient, peaceful, poised, quiet, relaxed, restrained, sedate, self-possessed, sensible, serene, tranquil, unemotional, *inf* unflappable, unhurried, unperturbed, unruffled, untroubled. *Opp* EXCITABLE, STORMY. ● *n* flat sea, peace, quietness, stillness, tranquillity. ▷ CALMNESS. ● *v* appease, compose, control, cool, lull, mollify, pacify, placate, quieten, settle down, soothe. *Opp* DISTURB.

calmness *n* composure, equability, equanimity, imperturbabil-ity, level-headedness, peace of mind, sang-froid, self-possession, serenity, *inf* unflappability. *Opp* ANXIETY, EXCITEMENT.

camouflage *n* cloak, cover, disguise, façade, front, guise, mask, pretence, protective colouring, screen, veil. ● *v* cloak, conceal, cover up, disguise, hide, mask, screen, veil.

camp *n* bivouac, campsite, encampment, settlement.

campaign *n* battle, crusade, drive, effort, fight, movement, offensive, operation, struggle, war.

campus *n* grounds, setting, site.

canal *n* channel, waterway.

cancel *v* abandon, abolish, abort, annul, call off, countermand, cross out, delete, drop, eliminate, erase, expunge, invalidate, overrule, postpone, quash, repeal, rescind, revoke, scrap, *inf* scrub, wipe out, write off. **cancel out** ▷ NEUTRALIZE.

cancer *n* carcinoma, growth, malignancy, tumour.

candid *adj* blunt, direct, fair, forthright, frank, honest, ingenuous, *inf* no-nonsense, objective, open, outspoken, plain, sincere, straightforward, transparent, truthful, unbiased, undisguised, unprejudiced. *Opp* INSINCERE.

candidate *n* applicant, competitor, contender, contestant, entrant, nominee, *inf* possibility, runner.

cane *n* bamboo, rod, stick. ● *v* ▷ THRASH.

canoe *n* dug-out, kayak.

canopy *n* awning, covering, shade, shelter, umbrella.

canvass *n* census, examination, investigation, market research, opinion poll, poll, scrutiny, survey. • *v* ask for, campaign, *inf* drum up support, electioneer, seek, solicit.

canyon *n* gap, gorge, pass, ravine, valley.

cap *n* covering, lid, top. ▷ HAT. • *v* ▷ COVER.

capable *adj* able, accomplished, adept, clever, competent, efficient, experienced, expert, gifted, handy, intelligent, masterly, practised, proficient, qualified, skilful, talented. *Opp* INCAPABLE. **capable of** apt to, disposed to, equal to, liable to.

capacity *n* **1** content, dimensions, magnitude, room, size, volume. **2** ability, capability, competence, intelligence, potential, power, skill, talent, wit. **3** *in an official capacity.* duty, function, job, office, place, position, post, responsibility, role.

cape *n* **1** cloak, coat, mantle, shawl, wrap. **2** head, headland, point, promontory.

caper *v* bound, cavort, dance, frisk, frolic, gambol, hop, leap, play, prance, skip, spring.

capital *adj* **1** chief, first, foremost, important, leading, main, paramount, pre-eminent, primary, principal. **2** *capital letters.* block, large, upper-case. **3** ▷ EXCELLENT. • *n* **1** chief city, centre of government. **2** assets, cash, finance, funds, investments, money, property, resources, savings, stock, wealth, *inf* the wherewithal.

capitulate *v* acquiesce, concede, give in, relent, submit, succumb, surrender, *inf* throw in the towel, yield.

capricious *adj* changeable, erratic, fanciful, fickle, flighty, impulsive, mercurial, moody, quirky, unpredictable, unreliable, unstable, variable, wayward. *Opp* STEADY.

capsize *v* flip over, keel over, overturn, tip over, *inf* turn turtle, turn upside down.

capsule *n* lozenge, medicine, pill, tablet.

captain *n* **1** boss, chief, head, leader. **2** commander, master, officer in charge, pilot, skipper.

caption *n* description, explanation, heading, title.

captivate *v* attract, beguile, bewitch, charm, delight, enchant, enslave, enthral, entrance, fascinate, hypnotize, infatuate, mesmerize, seduce, *inf* steal your heart. *Opp* DISGUST.

captive *adj* caged, captured, chained, confined, detained, enslaved, ensnared, imprisoned, incarcerated, jailed, secure, taken prisoner, *inf* under lock and key. *Opp* FREE. • *n* convict, detainee, hostage, prisoner, slave.

captivity *n* bondage, confinement, custody, detention, imprisonment, incarceration, internment, restraint, slavery. ▷ PRISON. *Opp* FREEDOM.

capture *n* apprehension, arrest, seizure. • *v* apprehend, arrest, *inf* bag, catch, *inf* collar, corner, ensnare, *inf* get, *inf* nab, net, *inf* nick, secure, seize, snare, take prisoner, trap. ▷ CONQUER. *Opp* LIBERATE.

car *n* automobile, *inf* banger, *joc* jalopy, motor, motor car, vehicle, *sl* wheels.

carcass n 1 body, corpse, meat, remains. 2 *carcass of a car*. framework, hulk, shell, skeleton.

card n 1 cardboard. 2 birthday card, business card, credit card, greetings card, playing card, postcard.

care n 1 attention, carefulness, caution, circumspection, concern, diligence, forethought, heed, meticulousness, pains, prudence, solicitude, thoroughness, thought, vigilance, watchfulness. 2 anxiety, concern, problem, responsibility, sorrow, stress, woe, worry. ▷ TROUBLE. 3 *left in my care*. charge, control, custody, guardianship, protection, safe-keeping, ward. • v bother, concern yourself, mind, worry. **care for** ▷ LOVE, TEND.

career n calling, employment, job, livelihood, living, métier, occupation, profession, trade, vocation, work. • v ▷ RUSH.

carefree adj blasé, casual, debonair, easygoing, happy-go-lucky, insouciant, inf laid-back, light-hearted, nonchalant, relaxed, unconcerned, unworried. ▷ HAPPY. 2 *carefree holiday*. leisurely, peaceful, quiet, relaxing, restful, trouble-free. Opp ANXIOUS.

careful adj 1 alert, attentive, cautious, chary, circumspect, mindful, observant, prudent, solicitous, thoughtful, vigilant, wary. 2 *careful work*. accurate, conscientious, diligent, fastidious, *derog* fussy, judicious, methodical, meticulous, neat, orderly, organized, painstaking, particular, precise, punctilious, rigorous, scrupulous, systematic, thorough, well-organized.

Opp CARELESS. **be careful** ▷ BEWARE.

careless adj 1 absent-minded, heedless, imprudent, inattentive, incautious, inconsiderate, irresponsible, negligent, rash, reckless, thoughtless, unguarded, unthinking. 2 *careless work*. casual, cursory, disorganized, hasty, inaccurate, jumbled, messy, perfunctory, scatterbrained, shoddy, slapdash, slipshod, *inf* sloppy, slovenly, untidy. Opp CAREFUL.

carelessness n inattention, irresponsibility, negligence, recklessness, *inf* sloppiness, slovenliness, thoughtlessness, untidiness. Opp CARE.

caress v cuddle, embrace, fondle, hug, kiss, make love to, nuzzle, pat, pet, rub against, stroke, touch.

caretaker n custodian, janitor, keeper, porter, warden, watchman.

careworn adj gaunt, grim, haggard. ▷ WEARY.

cargo n consignment, freight, goods, load, merchandise, payload, shipment.

caricature n burlesque, cartoon, parody, satire, *inf* send-up, *inf* spoof, *inf* take-off, travesty. • v burlesque, distort, exaggerate, make fun of, mimic, overact, parody, ridicule, satirize, *inf* send up, *inf* take off.

caring n concern, kindness, nursing, solicitude.

carnage n bloodbath, bloodshed, butchery, holocaust, killing, massacre, pogrom, slaughter.

carnal adj animal, bodily, erotic, fleshly, physical, sexual. ▷ LUSTFUL. Opp SPIRITUAL.

carnival *n* celebration, fair, festival, fête, fun and games, gala, jamboree, merrymaking, pageant, parade, revelry, show.

carp *v* cavil, find fault, *inf* go on, grumble, object, pick holes, quibble, *inf* split hairs, *inf* whinge. ▷ COMPLAIN.

carpentry *n* joinery, woodwork.

carriage *n* 1 coach. 2 bearing, demeanour, gait, manner, mien, posture, stance.

carrier *n* 1 bearer, conveyor, courier, delivery-man, delivery-woman, dispatch rider, haulier, messenger, postman, runner. 2 *carrier of a disease.* contact, host, transmitter.

carry *v* 1 bring, *inf* cart, ferry, fetch, haul, lead, lift, lug, manhandle, move, relay, ship, shoulder, take, transfer, transmit, transport. ▷ CONVEY. 2 *carry weight.* bear, maintain, support. 3 *carry a penalty.* demand, entail, involve, lead to, result in. **carry on** ▷ CONTINUE. **carry out** ▷ DO.

cart *n* truck, wagon, wheelbarrow. ● *v* ▷ CARRY.

carton *n* box, cartridge, case, container, pack, packet.

cartoon *n* animation, caricature, comic strip, drawing, sketch.

cartridge *n* 1 canister, capsule, case, cassette, container. 2 *cartridge for a gun.* magazine, round, shell.

carve *v* 1 slice. ▷ CUT. 2 *carve stone. inf* chip away at, chisel, engrave, hew, sculpture, shape.

cascade *n* cataract, flood, torrent, waterfall. ● *v* ▷ POUR.

case *n* 1 box, cabinet, carton, casket, chest, container, crate, pack, suitcase, trunk. 2 *case of*

mistaken identity. example, illustration, instance, occurrence, specimen. 3 *rules don't apply in his case.* circumstances, condition, context, plight, predicament, situation. 4 *legal case.* action, argument, cause, dispute, inquiry, investigation, lawsuit.

cash *n* change, coins, currency, *inf* dough, funds, legal tender, money, notes, *inf* (the) ready, *inf* the wherewithal. ● *v* exchange for cash, realize, sell. **cash in on** ▷ PROFIT.

cashier *n* check-out person, clerk, teller.

cask *n* barrel, butt, tub, vat.

cast *n* 1 ▷ SCULPTURE. 2 *cast of a play.* characters, company, performers, players, troupe. ● *v* 1 *inf* chuck, drop, fling, hurl, launch, lob, pelt, pitch, project, scatter, shy, sling, throw, toss. 2 form, mould, shape. ▷ SCULPTURE. **cast off** ▷ SHED, UNTIE.

castaway *adj* abandoned, deserted, exiled, marooned, rejected, shipwrecked, stranded.

caste *n* class, degree, estate, grade, level, position, rank, standing, station, status.

castigate *v* chastise, correct, discipline, punish, rebuke, scold, *inf* tell off. ▷ CRITICIZE.

castle *n* chateau, citadel, fort, mansion, palace, stately home, stronghold, tower.

castrate *v* emasculate, geld, neuter, sterilize.

casual *adj* 1 accidental, chance, fortuitous, incidental, irregular, random, unexpected, unforeseen, unintentional, unplanned, unpremeditated, unstructured, unsystematic. *Opp* DELIBERATE.

2 *casual attitude.* blasé, careless, *inf* couldn't-care-less, easygoing, *inf* free-and-easy, lackadaisical, *inf* laid-back, lax, nonchalant, offhand, relaxed, *inf* slap-happy, *inf* throwaway, unconcerned, unenthusiastic, unprofessional. *Opp* ENTHUSIASTIC. **3** *casual clothes.* comfortable, informal. *Opp* FORMAL.

casualty *n* dead person, fatality, injured person, loss, victim.

cat *n* kitten, *inf* moggy, *inf* pussy, tabby, tom, tomcat.

catacomb *n* crypt, sepulchre, tomb, vault.

catalogue *n* brochure, directory, index, inventory, list, record, register, roll. ● *v* classify, file, index, list, make an inventory of, record, register.

catapult *v* fire, fling, hurl, launch. ▷ THROW.

cataract *n* cascade, falls, rapids, torrent, waterfall.

catastrophe *n* calamity, cataclysm, crushing blow, debacle, devastation, ruin, tragedy. ▷ MISFORTUNE.

catch *n* **1** bag, booty, haul, net, prize, take. **2** difficulty, disadvantage, drawback, obstacle, problem, snag, trap, trick. **3** bolt, clasp, clip, fastener, fastening, hook, latch, lock. ● *v* **1** clutch, ensnare, grab, grasp, grip, hang on to, hold, hook, net, seize, snatch, take, tangle, trap. **2** *catch a thief.* apprehend, arrest, capture, *inf* cop, corner, discover, expose, intercept, *inf* nab, *inf* nobble, stop, take by surprise. **3** *catch unawares.* come upon, discover, surprise. **4** *catch a bus.* be in time for, get on. **5** *catch a cold.* contract, get.

catch on ▷ SUCCEED, UNDER-STAND. **catchphrase** ▷ SAYING. **catch-22** ▷ DILEMMA. **catch up** ▷ OVERTAKE.

catching *adj* ▷ CONTAGIOUS.

catchy *adj* attractive, haunting, memorable, popular, tuneful.

categorical *adj* absolute, certain, complete, decided, definite, direct, dogmatic, downright, emphatic, explicit, express, firm, forceful, out and out, positive, total, unambiguous, unconditional, unequivocal, unmitigated, unqualified, utter, vigorous. *Opp* TENTATIVE.

category *n* class, classification, division, grade, group, heading, kind, order, rank, section, set, sort, type, variety.

cater *v* cook, make arrangements, minister, provide, serve, supply.

catholic *adj* all-embracing, broad, broad-minded, comprehensive, cosmopolitan, eclectic, general, liberal, universal, varied, wide, wide-ranging.

cattle *pl n* bullocks, bulls, calves, cows, heifers, livestock.

catty *adj inf* bitchy, malicious, mean, nasty, sly, spiteful. ▷ UNKIND. *Opp* KIND.

cause *n* **1** basis, beginning, genesis, grounds, motive, occasion, origin, reason, root, source, stimulus. **2** agent, author, creator, initiator, inspiration, inventor, originator, producer. **3** excuse, explanation, pretext, reason. **4** *good cause.* aim, belief, concern, end, ideal, object, purpose, undertaking. ● *v* **1** arouse, awaken, begin, bring about, bring on, create, effect, engender, generate, give rise to, incite, kindle, lead to, occasion, precipitate, produce, provoke, result in, set off, stimulate, trigger off, *inf* whip up. 2 compel, force, induce, motivate.

caustic *adj* 1 acid, astringent, burning, corrosive. 2 *caustic criticism.* acrimonious, biting, bitter, cutting, mordant, sarcastic, scathing, severe, sharp, stinging, trenchant, waspish. Opp MILD.

caution *n* 1 alertness, care, carefulness, circumspection, discretion, forethought, heed, prudence, vigilance, wariness, watchfulness. 2 *let off with a caution.* admonition, *inf* dressing-down, reprimand, *inf* talking-to, *inf* ticking-off, warning. ● *v* 1 advise, alert, counsel, inform, tip off, warn. 2 *the police will caution him.* admonish, give a warning, reprehend, reprimand, *inf* tell off, *inf* tick off.

cautious *adj* 1 alert, attentive, careful, heedful, prudent, vigilant, watchful. 2 *cautious comments.* inf cagey, calculating, chary, circumspect, discreet, grudging, guarded, hesitant, judicious, noncommittal, suspicious, tactful, tentative, wary, watchful. Opp RECKLESS.

cavalcade *n* march-past, parade, procession, spectacle, troop.

cave *n* cavern, cavity, den, grotto, hole, pothole, underground chamber. ● *v* **cave in** ▷ COLLAPSE, SURRENDER.

cavity *n* cave, crater, hole, pit.

cease *v* break off, call a halt, conclude, desist, discontinue, finish, halt, *inf* kick (a habit), *inf* knock off, *inf* lay off, leave off, *inf* pack in, refrain, stop, terminate. Opp BEGIN.

ceaseless *adj* chronic, constant, continuous, everlasting, incessant, interminable, never-ending, non-stop, perpetual, persistent, relentless, unending, unremitting, untiring. Opp INTERMITTENT, TEMPORARY.

celebrate *v* 1 have a celebration, let yourself go, *inf* live it up, make merry, *inf* paint the town red, rejoice, revel. 2 commemorate, hold, honour, keep, observe, officiate at, remember, solemnize. **celebrated** ▷ FAMOUS.

celebration *n* banquet, binge, carnival, commemoration, feast, festivity, *inf* jamboree, *inf* jollification, merrymaking, observance, *inf* orgy, party, *inf* rave-up, revelry, *inf* shindig, solemnization.

celebrity *n* 1 ▷ FAME. 2 big name, *inf* bigwig, famous person, idol, personality, public figure, star, *inf* superstar, VIP.

celestial *adj* 1 cosmic, galactic, interplanetary, starry, stellar. 2 *celestial beings.* angelic, divine, ethereal, godlike, heavenly, seraphic, spiritual, sublime, transcendental.

celibacy *n* bachelorhood, chastity, purity, self-restraint, spinsterhood, virginity.

celibate *adj* abstinent, chaste, single, unmarried, virgin. ● *n* bachelor, spinster, virgin.

cell *n* cavity, chamber, compartment, cubicle, den, enclosure, prison, room, space, unit.

cellar *n* basement, crypt, vault, wine cellar.

cemetery *n* burial ground, churchyard, graveyard.

censor v ban, bowdlerize, *inf* clean up, cut, edit, expurgate, prohibit, remove.

censorious adj fault-finding, judgemental, moralistic, self-righteous. ▷ CRITICAL.

censure n blame, castigation, condemnation, criticism, denunciation, diatribe, disapproval, *inf* dressing-down, harangue, rebuke, reprimand, reproach, reproof, *inf* slating, stricture, *inf* talking-to, *inf* telling-off, tirade, verbal attack.
● v admonish, berate, blame, *inf* carpet, castigate, caution, *old use* chide, condemn, criticize, denounce, rebuke, reproach, scold, take to task, *inf* tear (someone) off a strip, *inf* tell off, *inf* tick off, upbraid.

census n count, survey, tally.

central adj 1 focal, inner, innermost, middle. 2 *central facts*. chief, crucial, essential, fundamental, important, key, major, pivotal, primary, principal, vital. *Opp* PERIPHERAL.

centralize v amalgamate, concentrate, rationalize, streamline, unify. *Opp* DISPERSE.

centre n bull's-eye, core, focal point, focus, heart, hub, interior, kernel, mid-point, nucleus, pivot. *Opp* PERIMETER.
● v concentrate, converge, focus.

centrifugal adj dispersing, diverging, moving outwards, scattering, spreading. *Opp* CENTRIPETAL.

centripetal adj converging. *Opp* CENTRIFUGAL.

cereal n barley, corn, grain, maize, oats, rice, rye, wheat.

ceremonial adj celebratory, liturgical, majestic, official,

ritual, stately. ▷ FORMAL. *Opp* INFORMAL.

ceremonious adj courtly, dignified, formal, grand, *derog* pompous, punctilious, *derog* starchy. ▷ POLITE. *Opp* CASUAL.

ceremony n 1 celebration, commemoration, *inf* do, function, occasion, parade, reception, rite, ritual, service, solemnity. 2 decorum, etiquette, formality, grandeur, pageantry, pomp and circumstance, protocol, ritual, spectacle.

certain adj 1 adamant, assured, confident, convinced, decided, determined, firm, invariable, positive, resolved, satisfied, settled, steady, sure, unshakable, unwavering. 2 *certain proof*. absolute, categorical, certified, clear, clear-cut, conclusive, convincing, definite, established, genuine, guaranteed, incontestable, incontrovertible, infallible, irrefutable, official, plain, reliable, settled, sure, true, trustworthy, unarguable, undeniable, undisputed, undoubted, unmistakable, unquestionable, valid, verifiable. 3 *certain disaster*. fated, guaranteed, imminent, inescapable, inevitable, inexorable, predestined, unavoidable. 4 *certain to pay up*. bound, compelled, required, sure. 5 *certain people*. individual, particular, some, specific, unnamed. *Opp* UNCERTAIN. **be certain** ▷ KNOW. **for certain** ▷ DEFINITELY. **make certain** ▷ ENSURE.

certainty n 1 actuality, certain fact, *inf* foregone conclusion, inevitability, *inf* sure thing. 2 assertiveness, assurance, authority, confidence, conviction, knowledge, proof, sureness, truth, validity. *Opp* DOUBT.

certificate *n* authorization, degree, diploma, document, guarantee, licence, pass, permit, qualification, warrant.

certify *v* 1 affirm, attest, authenticate, avow, bear witness, confirm, declare, endorse, guarantee, notify, sign, swear, testify, verify, vouch, witness. 2 *certify as competent.* authorize, charter, franchise, license, recognize, validate.

chain *n* 1 bond, coupling, fetter, link, manacle, shackle. 2 *chain of events.* combination, concatenation, line, progression, row, sequence, series, set, string, succession, train. ● *v* bind, fetter, handcuff, link, manacle, shackle, tether, tie. ▷ FASTEN.

chair *n* armchair, deckchair, easy chair, recliner, seat.
● *v* ▷ PRESIDE.

chairperson *n* chair, chairman, chairwoman, convenor, leader, moderator, president, speaker.

challenge *v* 1 accost, confront, dare, defy, *inf* have a go at, provoke, summon, take on, tax. 2 *challenge a decision.* argue against, call in doubt, contest, dispute, impugn, object to, oppose, protest against, query, question, take exception to.

challenging *adj* inspiring, stimulating, testing, thought-provoking. ▷ DIFFICULT. *Opp* EASY.

chamber *n* cavity, cell, compartment, niche, room, space.

champion *adj* great, leading, record-breaking, supreme, top, unrivalled, victorious, world-beating. ● *n* 1 conqueror, hero, medallist, prize-winner,

record-breaker, superman, superwoman, title-holder, victor; winner. 2 *champion of the poor.* backer, defender, guardian, patron, protector, supporter, upholder, vindicator.
● *v* ▷ SUPPORT.

championship *n* competition, contest, series, tournament.

chance *adj* accidental, casual, coincidental, *inf* fluky, fortuitous, fortunate, inadvertent, incidental, lucky, random, unexpected, unforeseen, unfortunate, unplanned, unpremeditated. *Opp* DELIBERATE. ● *n* 1 accident, coincidence, fate, fluke, fortune, gamble, luck, misfortune, serendipity. 2 *chance of rain.* danger, likelihood, possibility, probability, prospect, risk. 3 occasion, opportunity, time, turn.
● *v* 1 ▷ RISK. 2 ▷ HAPPEN.

chancy *adj* dangerous, *inf* dicey, *inf* dodgy, hazardous, *inf* iffy, insecure, precarious, risky, tricky, uncertain, unpredictable, unsafe. *Opp* SAFE.

change *n* 1 adaptation, adjustment, alteration, break, conversion, deterioration, development, difference, improvement, innovation, metamorphosis, modification, mutation, new look, rearrangement, reformation, reorganization, revolution, shift, substitution, swing, transfiguration, transformation, transition, translation, transposition, *inf* turnabout, U-turn, variation, variety, vicissitude. 2 *small change.* ▷ CASH.
● *v* 1 acclimatize, accommodate, adapt, adjust, affect, alter, amend, convert, diversify, influence, modify, rearrange, recon-

struct, reform, remodel, reorganize, reshape, restyle, tailor, transfigure, transform, translate, transmute. **3** *change one thing for another.* displace, exchange, replace, substitute, switch, swap, transpose. **4** *change money.* barter, convert, trade in. **change into** ▷ BECOME. **change someone's mind** ▷ CONVERT. **change your mind** ▷ RECONSIDER.

changeable *adj* capricious, chequered (*career*), erratic, fickle, fitful, fluctuating, fluid, inconsistent, irregular, mercurial, mutable, protean, shifting, temperamental, uncertain, unpredictable, unreliable, unsettled, unstable, *inf* up and down, vacillating, variable, volatile, wavering. *Opp* CONSTANT.

channel *n* **1** aqueduct, canal, conduit, ditch, duct, groove, gully, gutter, moat, overflow, pipe, sluice, sound, strait, trench, trough, waterway. ▷ STREAM. **2** avenue, means, medium, path, route, way. **3** *TV channel.* *inf* side, station, wavelength. • *v* conduct, convey, direct, guide, lead, route, transmit.

chant *n* hymn, plainsong, psalm. ▷ SONG. • *v* intone. ▷ SING.

chaos *n* anarchy, bedlam, confusion, disorder, *inf* mayhem, muddle, pandemonium, *inf* shambles, tumult, turmoil. *Opp* ORDER.

chaotic *adj* anarchic, confused, disordered, disorganized, haphazard, *inf* haywire, *inf* higgledy-piggledy, jumbled, lawless, muddled, riotous, *inf* shambolic, *inf* topsy-turvy, tumultuous, uncontrolled, unruly, untidy, *inf* upside-down. *Opp* ORDERLY.

char *v* blacken, brown, burn, scorch, sear, singe.

character *n* **1** distinctiveness, flavour, individuality, integrity, stamp, uniqueness. ▷ CHARACTERISTIC. **2** *forceful character.* constitution, disposition, *inf* make-up, manner, nature, personality, reputation, temper, temperament. **3** *famous character.* figure, individual, person, personality, *inf* type. **4** *She's a character!* *inf* case, comedian, eccentric, *inf* nut-case, *derog* weirdo. **5** *character in a play.* part, persona, role. **6** *written character.* cipher, figure, hieroglyphic, letter, mark, sign, symbol.

characteristic *adj* **1** [*of an individual*] distinctive, distinguishing, essential, idiosyncratic, individual, particular, peculiar, singular, special, specific, symptomatic, unique. **2** [*of a kind*] representative, typical. • *n* attribute, distinguishing feature, hallmark, idiosyncrasy, peculiarity, property, quality, symptom, trait.

characterize *v* brand, delineate, depict, describe, distinguish, draw, identify, mark, portray, present, typify.

charade *n* deception, fabrication, farce, make-believe, masquerade, mockery, *inf* play-acting, pose, pretence, *inf* put-up job, sham.

charge *n* **1** cost, expenditure, expense, fare, fee, payment, price, rate, terms, toll, value. **2** *in my charge.* care, control, custody, guardianship, jurisdiction, protection, responsibility, safe-keeping, supervision, trust. 3 *criminal charge.* accusation, allegation, imputation, indictment. 4 *cavalry charge.* assault, attack, drive, incursion, invasion, offensive, onslaught, raid, sally, sortie. • *v* 1 debit, exact, levy, make you pay, require. 2 accuse, blame, impeach, indict, prosecute, tax. 3 *charge with a duty.* burden, entrust, give, impose on. 4 command, direct, exhort, instruct. 5 *charge an enemy.* assault, attack, fall on, rush, set on, storm, *inf* wade into.

charitable *adj* bountiful, liberal, munificent, open-handed, philanthropic. ▷ KIND. *Opp* MEAN.

charity *n* 1 altruism, benevolence, bounty, caring, compassion, consideration, generosity, helpfulness, humanity, kindness, love, mercy, philanthropy, self-sacrifice, sympathy, unselfishness, warm-heartedness. 2 alms-giving, bounty, donation, financial support, gift, handout, largesse, offering, patronage, relief.

charm *n* 1 allure, appeal, attractiveness, charisma, fascination, magic, magnetism, power, pull, seductiveness. ▷ BEAUTY. 2 *magic charm.* curse, enchantment, incantation, magic, mumbo-jumbo, sorcery, spell, witchcraft. 3 *lucky charm.* amulet, mascot, ornament, talisman, trinket. • *v* allure, attract, beguile, bewitch, captivate, cast a spell on, delight, disarm, enchant, enthral, entrance, fascinate, hold spellbound, hypnotize, intrigue, mesmerize, please,

seduce, win over. **charming** ▷ ATTRACTIVE.

chart *n* diagram, graph, map, plan, sketch-map, table.

charter *v* 1 employ, engage, hire, lease, rent. 2 ▷ CERTIFY.

chase *v* drive, follow, hound, hunt, pursue, run after, track.

chasm *n* abyss, canyon, cleft, crater, crevasse, fissure, gap, gulf, hole, opening, pit, ravine, rift, split, void.

chaste *adj* 1 abstinent, celibate, *inf* clean, inexperienced, innocent, moral, pure, sinless, undefiled, unmarried, virgin, virginal, virtuous. *Opp* IMMORAL. 2 *chaste dress.* austere, decent, decorous, modest, plain, restrained, severe, simple, unadorned. *Opp* INDECENT.

chasten *v* 1 restrain, subdue. ▷ HUMILIATE. 2 ▷ CHASTISE.

chastise *v* castigate, correct, discipline, rebuke, scold. ▷ PUNISH, REPRIMAND.

chastity *n* abstinence, celibacy, innocence, integrity, morality, purity, restraint, virginity, virtue. *Opp* LUST.

chat *n* chatter, *inf* chin-wag, *inf* chit-chat, conversation, gossip, *inf* heart-to-heart. • *v* chatter, gossip, *inf* natter, prattle. ▷ TALK. **chat up** ▷ WOO.

chauvinist *n* bigot, *inf* MCP (= *male chauvinist pig*), patriot, sexist, xenophobe.

cheap *adj* 1 bargain, budget, cut-price, *inf* dirt-cheap, discount, economical, economy, inexpensive, *inf* knock-down, low-priced, reasonable, reduced, *inf* rock-bottom, sale. 2 *cheap quality.* base, inferior, poor, second-rate, shoddy, tawdry, *inf* tinny, worthless. **3** *cheap insult*. contemptible, despicable, facile, glib, ill-mannered, mean, silly, tasteless, unworthy, vulgar. Opp EXPENSIVE, WORTHY.

cheapen *v* belittle, debase, degrade, demean, devalue, discredit, downgrade, lower the tone (of), vulgarize.

cheat *n* **1** charlatan, *inf* con-man, counterfeiter, deceiver, double-crosser, forger, fraud, hoaxer, impersonator, impostor, *inf* phoney, quack, rogue, *inf* shark, swindler, trickster. **2** artifice, chicanery, *inf* con, confidence trick, deception, *inf* fiddle, fraud, hoax, lie, misrepresentation, pretence, *inf* put-up job, *inf* racket, *inf* rip-off, ruse, sham, swindle, *inf* swizz, trick.
● *v* **1** *inf* bamboozle, beguile, *inf* con, deceive, defraud, *inf* diddle, *inf* do, double-cross, dupe, *inf* fiddle, fleece, fool, hoax, hoodwink, outwit, *inf* rip off, *inf* short-change, swindle, take in, trick. **2** *cheat in an exam*. copy, crib.

check *adj* ▷ CHEQUERED.
● *n* **1** delay, hesitation, hindrance, interruption, pause, restraint, stoppage. **2** *medical check*. check-up, examination, *inf* going-over, inspection, investigation, *inf* once-over, scrutiny, test. ● *v* **1** arrest, bar, bridle, control, curb, delay, halt, hamper, hinder, hold back, impede, inhibit, keep in check, obstruct, regulate, rein, repress, restrain, slow down, stem, stop, stunt (*growth*), thwart. **2** *check answers*. compare, cross-check,

examine, inspect, investigate, monitor, scrutinize, test, verify.

cheek *n* audacity, boldness, effrontery, impertinence, impudence, insolence, presumptuousness, rudeness, temerity.

cheeky *adj* audacious, bold, brazen, disrespectful, flippant, forward, impertinent, impolite, impudent, insolent, irreverent, pert, presumptuous, rude, saucy, shameless, *inf* tongue-in-cheek. Opp RESPECTFUL.

cheer *n* **1** cry of approval, hurrah, shout of applause. **2** ▷ HAPPINESS. ● *v* **1** acclaim, applaud, clap, encourage, shout, yell. Opp JEER. **2** comfort, console, encourage, exhilarate, gladden, please, solace, uplift. Opp SADDEN. **cheer someone up** ▷ COMFORT, ENTERTAIN. **cheer up** ▷ BRIGHTEN. **Cheer up!** *inf* buck up, smile, *sl* snap out of it, take heart.

cheerful *adj* animated, bouncy, bright, *inf* chirpy, contented, convivial, festive, genial, good-humoured, hearty, hopeful, jaunty, jolly, jovial, joyful, light-hearted, merry, optimistic, *inf* perky, pleased, positive, sparkling, spirited, sprightly, sunny, warm-hearted. ▷ HAPPY. Opp BAD-TEMPERED, CHEERLESS.

cheerless *adj* bleak, comfortless, dark, depressing, desolate, dingy, drab, dreary, dull, forbidding, gloomy, lacklustre, melancholy, miserable, sombre, sullen, sunless, uncongenial, uninviting, unpleasant, unpromising, woeful. ▷ SAD. Opp CHEERFUL.

chemical *n* compound, element, substance.

chemist *n* *Amer* drugstore, pharmacist, pharmacy.

chequered adj 1 check, crisscross, in squares, patchwork, tartan, tessellated. 2 chequered career. ▷ CHANGEABLE.

cherish v be fond of, care for, cosset, foster, hold dear, keep safe, love, nurse, nurture, prize, protect, treasure, value.

chest n 1 box, caddy, case, casket, coffer, crate, strongbox, trunk. 2 breast, ribcage, thorax.

chew v bite, champ, crunch, gnaw, masticate, munch, nibble. **chew over** ▷ CONSIDER.

chick n fledgling, nestling.

chicken n bantam, cockerel, fowl, hen, pullet, rooster.

chief adj 1 arch, first, greatest, head, highest, leading, major, most experienced, most important, oldest, outstanding, premier, principal, senior, supreme, top, unequalled, unrivalled. 2 chief facts. basic, cardinal, central, especial, essential, foremost, fundamental, high-priority, indispensable, key, main, necessary, overriding, paramount, predominant, primary, prime, salient, significant, uppermost, vital. Opp UNIMPORTANT. ● n inf bigwig, inf boss, captain, commander, commanding officer, commissioner, controller, director, employer, executive, foreman, forewoman, inf gaffer, inf godfather, governor, head, king, leader, manager, managing director, master, inf number one, organizer, overseer, owner, president, principal, proprietor, ringleader, ruler, superintendent, supervisor, inf supremo.

chiefly adv especially, essentially, generally, mainly, mostly,

particularly, predominantly, primarily, principally.

child n 1 inf babe, baby, inf bambino, boy, derog brat, girl, infant, juvenile, inf kid, lad, lass, minor, newborn, inf nipper, inf stripling, toddler, inf tot, derog urchin, youngster, youth. 2 daughter, descendant, heir, issue, offspring, progeny, son.

childhood n babyhood, boyhood, girlhood, infancy, minority, schooldays, inf teens, youth.

childish adj babyish, credulous, immature, juvenile, puerile. ▷ SILLY. Opp MATURE.

childlike adj artless, guileless, ingenuous, innocent, naive, simple, trustful, unaffected, unsophisticated. Opp ARTFUL.

chill n ▷ COLD. ● v cool, freeze, keep cold, make cold, refrigerate. Opp WARM.

chilly adj 1 cold, cool, crisp, frosty, icy, inf nippy, inf parky, raw, sharp, wintry. 2 chilly greeting. aloof, cool, frigid, hostile, remote, reserved, standoffish, unforthcoming, unfriendly, unresponsive, unsympathetic, unwelcoming. Opp WARM.

chime n peal, striking, tintinnabulation, tolling. ● v ▷ RING.

chimney n flue, funnel, smokestack.

china n porcelain. ▷ CROCKERY.

chink n 1 cleft, crack, cranny, crevice, fissure, gap, opening, rift, slit, slot, space. 2 clink, chime, jingle, ring, tinkle.

chip n 1 bit, flake, fleck, fragment, piece, scrap, shard, shaving, sliver, splinter, wedge. 2 chip in a cup. crack, damage, flaw, nick, notch, scratch. ● v break, crack, damage, nick, notch, scratch, splinter. **chip away** ▷ CHISEL. **chip in** ▷ CONTRIBUTE, INTERRUPT.

chisel v carve, inf chip away, cut, engrave, fashion, model, sculpture, shape.

chivalrous adj bold, brave, courageous, courteous, courtly, gallant, generous, gentlemanly, heroic, honourable, noble, polite, respectable, true, trustworthy, valiant, worthy. Opp COWARDLY, RUDE.

choice adj ▷ EXCELLENT.
● n 1 alternative, dilemma, option. 2 make your choice. choosing, decision, election, nomination, pick, preference, say, vote. 3 choice of food. array, assortment, miscellany, mixture, range, selection, variety.

choke v 1 asphyxiate, garrotte, smother, stifle, strangle, suffocate, throttle. 2 choke in smoke. cough, gag, gasp, retch. 3 cars choke the roads. block, inf bung up, clog, congest, constrict, dam, fill, jam, obstruct, stop up. **choke back** ▷ SUPPRESS.

choose v adopt, agree on, appoint, decide on, determine on, distinguish, draw lots for, elect, fix on, identify, name, nominate, opt for, pick out, inf plump for, prefer, select, settle on, single out, vote for.

choosy adj dainty, discerning, discriminating, fastidious, finicky, fussy, hard to please, particular, inf pernickety, inf picky, selective. Opp INDIFFERENT.

chop v hack, lop, split. ▷ CUT. **chop and change** ▷ CHANGE.

chopper n axe, cleaver.

choppy adj rough, ruffled, turbulent, uneven. Opp SMOOTH.

chore n burden, drudgery, duty, errand, job, task, work.

chorus n 1 choir, ensemble, singers. 2 join in the chorus. refrain, response.

christen v anoint, baptize, call, dub, name.

chronic adj 1 ceaseless, constant, deep-rooted, habitual, incessant, incurable, ineradicable, ingrained, lasting, lifelong, lingering, long-standing, never-ending, non-stop, permanent, persistent, unending. Opp ACUTE, TEMPORARY. 2 [inf] chronic driving. ▷ BAD.

chronicle n account, annals, archive, description, diary, history, journal, narrative, record, register, saga, story.

chronological adj consecutive, in order, sequential.

chronology n 1 calendar, diary, journal, log, timetable. 2 establish the chronology. dating, order, sequence, timing.

chubby adj buxom, plump, stout, tubby. ▷ FAT. Opp THIN.

chunk n bar, block, brick, hunk, lump, mass, piece, portion, slab, wedge, inf wodge.

church n abbey, basilica, cathedral, chapel, convent, monastery, nunnery, priory.

churchyard n burial ground, cemetery, graveyard.

chute n channel, incline, ramp, rapid, slide, slope.

cinema n films, inf flicks, inf movies, inf pictures.

circle n 1 band, circlet, circuit, cycle, disc, hoop, loop, orbit, ring, rotation, sphere. 2 circle of friends. association, band, body, clique, club, company, fellowship, gang, party, set, society.

▷ GROUP. ● v 1 circulate, circumnavigate, coil, curve, go round, gyrate, loop, orbit, reel, revolve, rotate, spin, spiral, swirl, swivel, tour, turn, wheel, whirl, wind. 2 *trees circle the lawn.* encircle, enclose, encompass, girdle, hem in, ring, skirt, surround.

circuit n journey round, lap, orbit, revolution, tour.

circuitous adj devious, indirect, labyrinthine, meandering, rambling, roundabout, serpentine, tortuous, twisting, winding, zigzag. Opp DIRECT.

circular adj 1 ringlike, round. 2 *circular conversation.* circumlocutory, cyclic, repetitive, roundabout, tautologous.
● n advertisement, leaflet, letter, notice, pamphlet.

circulate v 1 go round, move about, move round, orbit. ▷ CIRCLE. 2 *circulate gossip.* advertise, disseminate, distribute, issue, make known, promulgate, publicize, inf put about, send round, spread about.

circulation n 1 flow, movement, pumping, recycling. 2 broadcasting, diffusion, dissemination, distribution, publication, spreading, transmission. 3 *newspaper circulation.* distribution, sales-figures.

circumference n border, boundary, circuit, edge, fringe, limit, margin, outline, perimeter, periphery, rim, verge.

circumstance n affair, event, happening, incident, occasion, occurrence. **circumstances** 1 background, conditions, considerations, context, contingencies, details, factors, facts, particulars, position, situation,

state of affairs, surroundings. 2 finances, income, resources.

circumstantial adj conjectural, deduced, inferred, unprovable. Opp PROVABLE.

cistern n bath, reservoir, tank.

citadel n acropolis, bastion, castle, fort, fortress, garrison, stronghold, tower.

cite v adduce, advance, inf bring up, mention, name, quote, inf reel off, refer to.

citizen n denizen, dweller, freeman, householder, inhabitant, national, native, passport-holder, resident, subject, taxpayer, voter.

city n capital, conurbation, metropolis, town.

civil adj 1 affable, civilized, courteous, respectful, urbane. ▷ POLITE. Opp IMPOLITE. 2 *civil administration.* civilian, domestic, internal, national. 3 *civil liberties.* communal, public, social, state. **civil rights** human rights, legal rights, liberty, political rights. **civil servant** administrator, bureaucrat, derog mandarin.

civilization n achievements, attainments, culture, customs, mores, refinement, sophistication, urbanity, urbanization.

civilize v cultivate, domesticate, educate, enlighten, humanize, improve, refine, socialize, urbanize.

civilized adj cultivated, cultured, democratic, developed, domesticated, educated, enlightened, humane, orderly, polite, refined, sociable, sophisticated, urbane, urbanized, well-behaved, well-run. Opp UNCIVILIZED.

claim v 1 ask for, collect, demand, exact, insist on, request, require, take. 2 affirm, allege, argue, assert, contend, declare, insist, maintain, pretend, profess, state.

clairvoyant adj extra-sensory, prophetic, psychic, telepathic. • n fortune-teller, oracle, prophet, seer, soothsayer.

clamber v climb, crawl, move awkwardly, scramble.

clammy adj close, damp, dank, humid, moist, muggy, slimy, sticky, sweaty, wet.

clamour n babel, commotion, din, hubbub, hullabaloo, noise, outcry, racket, inf row, shouting, storm, uproar. • v cry out, exclaim, shout, yell.

clan n family, house, tribe.

clannish adj cliquish, close-knit, insular, united.

clap n bang, crack, crash, report, smack. • v 1 applaud, sl put your hands together. 2 clap on the back. ▷ HIT.

clarify v 1 clear up, define, elucidate, explain, gloss, illuminate, make clear, simplify, spell out, throw light on. Opp CONFUSE. 2 clarify wine. cleanse, filter, purify, refine.

clash v 1 bang, clang, clank, crash, ring. 2 ▷ CONFLICT. 3 The events clash. ▷ COINCIDE.

clasp n 1 brooch, buckle, catch, clip, fastener, fastening, hasp, hook, pin. 2 cuddle, embrace, grip, hold, hug. • v 1 ▷ FASTEN. 2 cling to, clutch, embrace, grasp, grip, hold, hug, squeeze. 3 clasp your hands. hold together, wring.

class n 1 category, classification, division, genre, genus, grade, group, kind, league, order, quality, rank, set, sort, species, sphere, type. 2 social class. caste, degree, grouping, lineage, pedigree, standing, station, status. 3 class in school. band, form, Amer grade, group, set, stream, year. • v ▷ CLASSIFY.

classic adj 1 abiding, ageless, deathless, enduring, flawless, ideal, immortal, lasting, legendary, memorable, outstanding, perfect, time-honoured, undying, unforgettable, inf vintage. ▷ EXCELLENT. Opp COMMONPLACE, EPHEMERAL. 2 classic case. archetypal, characteristic, copybook, definitive, exemplary, model, standard, typical, usual. Opp UNUSUAL. • n masterpiece, masterwork, model.

classical adj 1 ancient, Attic, Greek, Hellenic, Latin, Roman. 2 classical style. austere, dignified, elegant, pure, restrained, symmetrical, well-proportioned. 3 classical music. harmonious, highbrow, serious.

classification n categorization, codification, organization, tabulation, taxonomy. ▷ CLASS.

classify v arrange, catalogue, categorize, class, grade, group, order, organize, pigeon-hole, sort, systematize, tabulate. **classified** ▷ SECRET.

clause n article, condition, item, paragraph, part, passage, proviso, section, subsection.

claw n nail, talon. • v injure, lacerate, maul, rip, scrape, scratch, slash, tear.

clean adj 1 decontaminated, disinfected, hygienic, immaculate, laundered, perfect, polished, sanitary, scrubbed, spotless, sterile, sterilized, unsoiled, unstained, unsullied, washed, wholesome. **2** *clean water.* clarified, clear, distilled, fresh, pure, purified, unpolluted. **3** *clean paper.* blank, new, plain, uncreased, unmarked, untouched, unused. **4** *clean edge.* neat, regular, smooth, straight, tidy. **5** *clean fight.* chivalrous, fair, honest, honourable, sporting, sportsmanlike. **6** *clean fun.* chaste, decent, good, innocent, moral, respectable, upright, virtuous. *Opp* DIRTY. ● *v* cleanse, clear up, purify, sterilize, tidy up, wash. *Opp* CONTAMINATE. **make a clean breast of** ▷ CONFESS.

clean-shaven *adj* beardless, shaved, shorn, smooth.

clear *adj* **1** clean, colourless, crystalline, glassy, limpid, pellucid, pure, transparent. **2** *clear sky.* cloudless, fair, fine, sunny, starlit, unclouded. *Opp* CLOUDY. **3** *clear colours.* bright, lustrous, shining, strong, vivid. **4** *clear conscience.* blameless, easy, guiltless, innocent, quiet, satisfied, undisturbed, untarnished, untroubled, unworried. **5** *clear handwriting.* bold, definite, distinct, focused, legible, recognizable, sharp, simple, visible, well-defined. **6** *clear sound.* audible, distinct, penetrating, sharp. **7** *clear instructions.* coherent, comprehensible, explicit, intelligible, lucid, precise, specific, straightforward, unambiguous, understandable, well-presented. **8** *clear case of cheating.* apparent, blatant, clear-cut, conspicuous, evident, indisputable, manifest, obvious, palpable, perceptible, plain, pronounced, straightforward, undisguised, unmistakable. *Opp* UNCERTAIN.

9 *clear space.* empty, free, open, passable, uncluttered, uncrowded, unhindered, unimpeded, unobstructed. ● *v* **1** disappear, evaporate, fade, melt away, vanish. **2** brighten, lighten. **3** clean, make clean, polish, wipe. **4** *clear weeds.* disentangle, get rid of, remove, strip. **5** *clear a drain.* clean out, free, open up, unblock, unclog. **6** *clear of blame.* absolve, acquit, exculpate, excuse, exonerate, free, let off, release, vindicate. **7** *clear a building.* empty, evacuate. **8** *clear a fence.* bound over, jump, leap over, pass over, vault. **clear away** ▷ REMOVE. **clear off** ▷ DEPART. **clear up** ▷ CLEAN, EXPLAIN.

clearing *n* gap, glade, opening, space.

cleave *v* divide, halve, rive, slit, split. ▷ CUT.

clench *v* **1** clamp, close tightly, double up, grit (*your teeth*), squeeze tightly. **2** clasp, grasp, grip, hold.

clergyman *n* archbishop, bishop, canon, cardinal, chaplain, churchman, cleric, curate, deacon, deaconess, dean, divine, ecclesiastic, friar, guru, imam, *inf* man of the cloth, minister, missionary, monk, padre, parson, pastor, preacher, prebend, prelate, priest, rabbi, rector, vicar. *Opp* LAYMAN.

clerical *adj* **1** *clerical work.* office, secretarial, *inf* white-collar. **2** *clerical collar.* canonical, ecclesiastical, episcopal, ministerial, monastic, pastoral, priestly, rabbinical, spiritual.

clerk *n* assistant, bookkeeper, computer operator, filing clerk, office worker, *inf* pen-pusher, receptionist, scribe, secretary, shorthand-typist, stenographer, typist, word-processor operator.

clever *adj* able, academic, accomplished, acute, adroit, artful, astute, *inf* brainy, bright, brilliant, canny, capable, *derog* crafty, creative, *derog* cunning, *inf* cute, *inf* deep, deft, dexterous, discerning, expert, gifted, handy, ingenious, intellectual, intelligent, inventive, judicious, keen, knowing, knowledgeable, observant, penetrating, perceptive, perspicacious, precocious, quick, quick-witted, resourceful, sagacious, sensible, sharp, shrewd, skilful, skilled, *derog* sly, smart, subtle, talented, *derog* wily, wise, witty. *Opp* STUPID, UNSKILFUL. **clever person** *inf* egghead, expert, genius, *derog* know-all, mastermind, prodigy, sage, *derog* smart-arse, virtuoso, wizard.

cleverness *n* ability, acuteness, astuteness, brilliance, *derog* cunning, expertise, ingenuity, intellect, intelligence, mastery, sagacity, sharpness, shrewdness, skill, subtlety, talent, wisdom, wit. *Opp* STUPIDITY.

cliché *n* banality, *inf* chestnut, commonplace, hackneyed phrase, platitude, stereotype, truism, well-worn phrase.

client *n pl* clientele, consumer, customer, patient, patron, shopper, user.

cliff *n* bluff, crag, escarpment, precipice, rock face, scar.

climate *n* 1 ▷ WEATHER. 2 *climate of opinion*. ambience, atmosphere, environment, feeling, mood, spirit, temper, trend.

climax *n* 1 acme, crisis, culmination, head, highlight, high point, peak, summit, zenith. *Opp* BATHOS. 2 *sexual climax*. orgasm.

climb *n* ascent, gradient, hill, incline, rise, slope. ● *v* 1 ascend, clamber up, go up, mount, move up, scale, shin up, soar, take off. 2 incline, rise, slope up. 3 *climb a mountain*. conquer, reach the top of. **climb down** ▷ DESCEND.

clinch *v* close, complete, conclude, confirm, determine, finalize, make certain of, ratify, secure, settle, shake hands on, verify.

cling *v* adhere, attach, fasten, fix, hold fast, stick. **cling to** ▷ EMBRACE.

clinic *n* health centre, infirmary, medical centre, surgery.

clip *n* 1 ▷ FASTENER. 2 *clip from a film*. cutting, excerpt, extract, fragment, part, passage, quotation, section, snippet, trailer. ● *v* 1 pin, staple. ▷ FASTEN. 2 crop, shear, snip, trim. ▷ CUT.

cloak *n* 1 cape, cope, mantle, poncho, robe, wrap. 2 ▷ COVER. ● *v* cover, mask, shroud, veil, wrap. ▷ HIDE.

clock *n* chronometer, timepiece, watch.

clog *v* block, *inf* bung up, choke, congest, dam, impede, jam, obstruct, plug, stop up.

close *adj* 1 accessible, adjacent, at hand, convenient, handy, near, neighbouring, point-blank. 2 *close friends*. affectionate, attached, dear, devoted, familiar, fond, friendly, intimate, loving, *inf* thick. 3 *close comparison*. alike, analogous, comparable, corresponding, related, similar. 4 *close crowd*. compact, congested, cramped, crowded, dense, *inf* jam-packed, packed, thick. 5 *close scrutiny*. attentive, careful, detailed, minute, painstaking, precise, rigorous, searching, thorough. 6 *close with information*. private, reserved, reticent, secretive, taciturn. 7 *close with money*. mean, *inf* mingy, miserly, niggardly, parsimonious, penurious, stingy, tight, tight-fisted. 8 *close atmosphere*. airless, fuggy, humid, muggy, oppressive, stale, stifling, stuffy, suffocating, sweltering, unventilated. *Opp* DISTANT, OPEN.

● *n* 1 completion, conclusion, culmination, end, finish, termination. 2 cadence, coda, finale. 3 *close of a play*. denouement, last act. ● *v* 1 bolt, fasten, lock, make inaccessible, padlock, seal, secure, shut. 2 *close a road*. bar, barricade, block, make impassable, obstruct, seal off, stop up. 3 *close proceedings*. complete, conclude, culminate, discontinue, end, finish, stop, terminate, *inf* wind up. 4 *close a gap*. fill, join up, reduce, shorten. *Opp* OPEN.

closed *adj* 1 fastened, locked, sealed, shut. 2 concluded, done with, ended, finished, over, resolved, settled, tied up.

clot *n* embolism, lump, mass, thrombosis. ● *v* coagulate, coalesce, congeal, curdle, set, solidify, stiffen, thicken.

cloth *n* fabric, material, stuff, textile.

clothe *v* array, attire, cover, deck, drape, dress, fit out, garb, *inf* kit out, robe, swathe. *Opp* STRIP. **clothe yourself in** ▷ WEAR.

clothes *pl n* apparel, attire, *inf* clobber, clothing, costume, dress, ensemble, finery, footwear, garb, garments, *inf* gear, *inf* get-up, headgear, outfit, *inf* rig-out, *sl* togs, trousseau, underclothes, uniform, vestments, wardrobe, wear, weeds.

cloud *n* billow, haze, mist, storm cloud. ● *v* blur, conceal, cover, darken, eclipse, enshroud, hide, mantle, mist up, obscure, screen, shroud, veil.

cloudless *adj* bright, clear, starlit, sunny. *Opp* CLOUDY.

cloudy *adj* 1 dark, dull, gloomy, grey, leaden, lowering, overcast, sunless. *Opp* CLOUDLESS. 2 *cloudy windows*. blurred, blurry, dim, misty, opaque, steamy. 3 *cloudy liquid*. hazy, milky, muddy, murky. *Opp* CLEAR.

clown *n* buffoon, comedian, fool, jester, joker. ▷ IDIOT.

club *n* 1 bat, baton, cosh, cudgel, mace, staff, stick, truncheon. 2 association, circle, company, federation, fellowship, fraternity, group, guild, league, order, organization, party, set, society, sorority, union. ● *v* ▷ HIT. **club together** ▷ COMBINE.

clue *n* hint, idea, indication, inkling, key, lead, pointer, sign, suggestion, suspicion, tip, tip-off, trace.

clump *n* bunch, bundle, cluster, mass, shock (*of hair*), thicket, tuft. ▷ GROUP.

clumsy *adj* 1 awkward, blundering, bungling, fumbling, gangling, gawky, graceless, *inf* ham-fisted, heavy-handed, *inf* hulking, lumbering, maladroit, uncoordinated, ungainly, ungraceful. *Opp* SKILFUL.

2 amateurish, badly-made, bulky, cumbersome, heavy, inelegant, large, ponderous, rough, unmanageable, unwieldy. Opp NEAT. 3 clumsy remark. gauche, ill-judged, inappropriate, indelicate, indiscreet, inept, insensitive, tactless, uncouth, undiplomatic, unsubtle.

cluster n batch, bunch, clump, collection, knot. ▷ GROUP.
• v ▷ GATHER.

clutch n clasp, control, grasp, grip, hold, possession, power.
• v catch, clasp, cling to, grab, grasp, embrace, hang on to, seize, snatch, take hold of.

clutter n chaos, confusion, disorder, jumble, junk, litter, mess, muddle, odds and ends, rubbish, tangle, untidiness. • v be scattered about, litter, make untidy, inf mess up, muddle, strew.

coach n 1 bus, carriage. 2 games coach. instructor, teacher, trainer, tutor. • v direct, drill, guide, instruct, prepare, teach, train, tutor.

coagulate v clot, congeal, curdle, inf jell, set, solidify, thicken.

coarse adj 1 bristly, gritty, hairy, harsh, prickly, rough, scratchy, sharp, stony, uneven. Opp FINE, SOFT. 2 coarse language. bawdy, blasphemous, boorish, common, crude, earthy, foul, impolite, improper, indecent, indelicate, offensive, ribald, rude, smutty, uncouth, vulgar. Opp REFINED.

coast n beach, coastline, seaboard, seashore, seaside, shore.
• v cruise, drift, freewheel, glide, sail, skim, slide, slip.

coastal adj maritime, nautical, seaside.

coat n 1 jacket, inf mac, overcoat, raincoat. 2 animal's coat. fleece, fur, hair, hide, pelt, skin. 3 coat of paint. coating, finish, glaze, layer, overlay, patina, veneer, wash. ▷ COVERING.
• v ▷ COVER. coat of arms ▷ CREST.

coax v allure, cajole, charm, entice, induce, inveigle, manipulate, persuade, tempt, wheedle.

cobble v cobble together botch, knock up, make, mend, patch up, put together.

code n 1 etiquette, laws, regulations, rule-book, rules, system. 2 message in code. cipher, secret language, signals.

coerce v bludgeon, browbeat, bully, compel, constrain, dragoon, force, intimidate, pressgang, pressurize, terrorize.

coercion n browbeating, bullying, compulsion, conscription, constraint, duress, force, intimidation, pressure, inf strong-arm tactics, threats.

coffer n box, cabinet, case, casket, chest, crate, trunk.

cog n ratchet, sprocket, tooth.

cogent adj compelling, conclusive, convincing, effective, forceful, indisputable, irresistible, persuasive, potent, powerful, strong, unanswerable, well-argued. ▷ COHERENT. Opp IRRATIONAL.

cohere v bind, cake, coalesce, combine, fuse, hold together, join, stick together, unite.

coherent adj articulate, cohesive, connected, consistent, integrated, logical, lucid, orderly, organized, rational, reasoned, sound, systematic, unified, united, well-ordered, well-structured. *Opp* INCOHERENT.

coil *n* convolution, corkscrew, curl, helix, kink, loop, roll, spiral, twist, vortex, whirl, whorl. ● *v* curl, entwine, loop, roll, snake, spiral, twine, twirl, twist, wind, writhe.

coin *n* 1 bit, piece. 2 [*pl*] coppers, silver, small change. ▷ MONEY. ● *v* 1 make, mint, mould, stamp. 2 *coin a name*. conceive, concoct, create, devise, dream up, fabricate, introduce, invent, make up, originate, think up.

coincide *v* accord, agree, be congruent, be identical, be in unison, clash, coexist, concur, correspond, happen together, harmonize, match, square, synchronize, tally.

coincidence *n* 1 accord, agreement, coexistence, concurrence, congruence, correspondence, harmony, similarity. 2 *meet by coincidence*. accident, chance, fluke, luck.

cold *adj* 1 arctic, biting, bitter, bleak, chill, chilly, cool, crisp, cutting, draughty, freezing, fresh, frosty, glacial, ice-cold, icy, inclement, keen, *inf* nippy, numbing, *inf* parky, perishing, piercing, polar, raw, shivery, Siberian, snowy, unheated, wintry. 2 *cold hands*. blue with cold, chilled, frostbitten, frozen, numbed, shivering. 3 *cold heart*. aloof, callous, cold-blooded, hard-hearted, heartless, indifferent, inhuman, insensitive, passionless, stony, uncaring, unconcerned, undemonstrative, unemotional, unfeeling, unresponsive. ▷ UNFRIENDLY. *Opp* HOT, KIND. ● *n* 1 chill, coolness, frostiness, iciness, wintriness. *Opp* HEAT. 2 *cold in the head*. catarrh, *inf* flu, *inf* the sniffles. **feel the cold** freeze, quiver, shake, shiver, shudder, tremble.

cold-blooded *adj* brutal, callous, inhuman, ruthless, savage. ▷ CRUEL. *Opp* HUMANE.

cold-hearted *adj* callous, dispassionate, heartless, impassive, insensitive, *inf* thick-skinned, uncaring, unemotional, unfeeling. ▷ UNFRIENDLY.

collaborate *v* 1 cooperate, join forces, *inf* pull together, team up, work together. 2 [*derog*] collude, connive, conspire, join the opposition, *inf* rat, turn traitor.

collaboration *n* 1 association, concerted effort, cooperation, partnership, teamwork. 2 [*derog*] collusion, connivance, conspiracy, treachery.

collaborator *n* 1 accomplice, ally, assistant, associate, co-author, colleague, confederate, fellow-worker, helper, partner, *joc* partner-in-crime, team-mate. 2 [*derog*] blackleg, *inf* Judas, quisling, *inf* scab, traitor, turncoat.

collapse *n* breakdown, break-up, cave-in, disintegration, downfall, end, fall, ruin, subsidence. ● *v* 1 break down, break up, buckle, cave in, crumble, crumple, deflate, disintegrate, double up, fall apart, fall in, fold up, give in, sink, subside, tumble down. 2 *collapse in the heat*. become ill, *inf* bite the dust, black out, *inf* crack up, faint, *inf* keel over, pass out, swoon. 3 *sales will collapse*. crash, deteriorate, diminish, drop, fall, slump, worsen.

collapsible *adj* adjustable, folding, retractable, telescopic.

colleague *n* associate, business partner, fellow-worker.
▷ COLLABORATOR.

collect *v* 1 accumulate, amass, assemble, bring together, cluster, come together, concentrate, congregate, convene, converge, crowd, garner, gather, group, harvest, heap, hoard, lay up, muster, pile up, put by, rally, save, scrape together, stack up, stockpile, store. *Opp* DISPERSE. 2 *collect money for charity*. be given, raise, secure, take. 3 *collect goods from a shop*. bring, fetch, get, load up, obtain, pick up. **collected** ▷ CALM.

collection *n* 1 accumulation, array, assortment, cluster, heap, mass, pile, set, stack, store. ▷ GROUP. 2 flag-day, voluntary contributions, *inf* whip-round.

collective *adj* combined, common, cooperative, corporate, group, joint, shared, united. *Opp* INDIVIDUAL.

college *n* academy, conservatory, institute, polytechnic, school, university.

collide *v* collide with bump into, cannon into, crash into, knock, meet, run into, smash into, strike. ▷ HIT.

collision *n* accident, bump, clash, crash, head-on collision, impact, knock, pile-up, smash.

colloquial *adj* conversational, informal, slangy, vernacular. *Opp* FORMAL.

colonist *n* colonizer, explorer, pioneer, settler. *Opp* NATIVE.

colonize *v* occupy, people, populate, settle in, subjugate.

colony *n* 1 dependency, dominion, possession, province, settlement, territory. 2 ▷ GROUP.

colossal *adj* enormous, gargantuan, giant, gigantic, herculean, huge, immense, *inf* jumbo, mammoth, massive, monstrous, prodigious, vast. ▷ BIG. *Opp* SMALL.

colour *n* 1 coloration, colouring, hue, pigment, pigmentation, shade, tincture, tinge, tint, tone. 2 *colour in your cheeks*. bloom, blush, flush, glow, rosiness, ruddiness. ● *v* 1 crayon, dye, paint, pigment, shade, stain, tinge, tint. 2 blush, bronze, brown, burn, flush, redden, tan. *Opp* FADE. 3 *It will not colour his decision*. affect, bias, distort, influence, pervert, prejudice, slant, sway. **colours** ▷ FLAG.

colourful *adj* 1 bright, brilliant, chromatic, gaudy, iridescent, multicoloured, psychedelic, showy, vibrant. 2 *colourful personality*. dashing, distinctive, dynamic, eccentric, energetic, exciting, flamboyant, glamorous, unusual, vigorous. 3 *colourful description*. graphic, lively, picturesque, rich, stimulating, striking, telling, vivid. *Opp* COLOURLESS.

colouring *n* colourant, dye, pigment, stain. ▷ COLOUR.

colourless *adj* 1 ashen, blanched, grey, monochrome, neutral, pale, pallid, sickly, wan, *inf* washed out, waxen. ▷ WHITE. 2 bland, boring, characterless, dowdy, drab, dreary, dull, insipid, lacklustre, lifeless, tame, uninspiring, uninteresting, vacuous, vapid. *Opp* COLOURFUL.

column *n* 1 pilaster, pillar, pole, post, shaft, support, upright. 2 *newspaper column*. article, feature, leader, piece. **3** *column of soldiers*. cavalcade, file, line, procession, queue, rank, row, string, train.

comb *v* **1** arrange, groom, neaten, smarten up, tidy, untangle. **2** *comb the house*. ransack, rummage through, scour, search thoroughly.

combat *n* action, battle, conflict, contest, encounter, fight, skirmish, struggle, warfare.
• *v* battle against, contest, counter, defy, face up to, oppose, resist, stand up to, struggle against, tackle, withstand.
▷ FIGHT.

combination *n* aggregate, amalgam, blend, compound, conjunction, fusion, marriage, mix, mixture, synthesis, unification. **2** alliance, amalgamation, association, coalition, confederation, consortium, conspiracy, federation, grouping, link-up, merger, partnership, syndicate, union.

combine *v* **1** add together, amalgamate, bind, blend, compound, fuse, incorporate, integrate, interweave, join, link, *inf* lump together, marry, merge, mingle, mix, pool, put together, synthesize, unify, unite. *Opp* DIVIDE. **2** *combine as a team*. ally, associate, band together, club together, coalesce, connect, cooperate, form an alliance, *inf* gang up, join forces, team up. *Opp* DISPERSE.

combustible *adj* flammable, inflammable.
Opp INCOMBUSTIBLE.

come *v* **1** advance, appear, approach, arrive, draw near, enter, get to, move (towards), near, reach, visit. **2** *whatever may come*. happen, materialize,

occur, turn up. **come about**
▷ HAPPEN. **come across**
▷ FIND. **come apart** ▷ DISINTEGRATE. **come clean** ▷ CONFESS. **come out with** ▷ SAY. **come round** ▷ RECOVER. **come up** ▷ ARISE. **come upon** ▷ FIND.

comedian *n* buffoon, clown, comic, fool, humorist, jester, joker, wag.

comedy *n* clowning, facetiousness, farce, hilarity, humour, jesting, joking, slapstick, wit.

comfort *n* **1** aid, cheer, consolation, encouragement, help, moral support, reassurance, relief, solace, succour. **2** *living in comfort*. abundance, affluence, contentment, cosiness, ease, luxury, plenty, relaxation, well-being. *Opp* DISCOMFORT, POVERTY. • *v* calm, cheer up, console, ease, encourage, gladden, hearten, help, reassure, relieve, solace, soothe, sympathize with.

comfortable *adj* **1** comfy, convenient, cosy, easy, padded, relaxing, roomy, snug, soft, upholstered. **2** *comfortable clothes*. informal, loose-fitting, well-fitting. **3** *comfortable life*. affluent, agreeable, contented, happy, homely, luxurious, pleasant, prosperous, relaxed, restful, serene, tranquil, untroubled, well-off. *Opp* UNCOMFORTABLE.

comic *adj* **1** absurd, amusing, comical, diverting, droll, facetious, farcical, funny, hilarious, humorous, hysterical, joking, laughable, ludicrous, *inf* priceless, *inf* rich, ridiculous, satirical, *inf* side-splitting, silly, uproarious, waggish, witty.

Opp SERIOUS. • *n* 1 ▷ COMEDIAN.
2 ▷ MAGAZINE.

command *n* 1 behest, bidding,
decree, directive, edict, injunction, instruction, mandate,
order, requirement, ultimatum.
2 authority, charge, control, direction, government, jurisdiction,
management, power, rule, sovereignty, supervision, sway.
3 *command of a language.* grasp,
knowledge, mastery. • *v* 1 bid,
charge, compel, decree, demand,
direct, enjoin, instruct, ordain,
order, prescribe, request,
require. 2 *command a ship.*
administer, be in charge of, control, govern, have authority
over, head, lead, manage, reign
over, rule, supervise.

commandeer *v* appropriate, confiscate, hijack, requisition, seize,
take over.

commander *n* captain, com-
mandant, general, head, leader,
officer-in-charge. ▷ CHIEF.

commemorate *v* be a memorial
to, celebrate, honour, immortalize, keep alive the memory of,
pay your respects to, pay tribute
to, remember, salute, solemnize.

commence *v* embark on, enter
on, initiate, launch, set off, set
up, start. ▷ BEGIN. *Opp* FINISH.

commend *v* acclaim, applaud,
approve of, compliment, congratulate, eulogize, extol, praise,
recommend. *Opp* CRITICIZE.

commendable *adj* admirable,
creditable, deserving, laudable,
meritorious, praiseworthy.
▷ GOOD. *Opp* DEPLORABLE.

comment *n* annotation, commentary, criticism, elucidation,
explanation, footnote, gloss,
interjection, interpolation, mention, note, observation, opinion,

reaction, reference, remark,
statement. • *v* criticize, elucidate, explain, interject, interpose,
mention, note, observe, remark,
say, state.

commentary *n* 1 account, broadcast, description, report.
2 *commentary on a poem.* analysis, criticism, critique, discourse, explanation, interpretation, notes, review.

commentator *n* broadcaster,
journalist, reporter.

commerce *n* business, buying
and selling, dealings, financial
transactions, marketing, trade,
trading, traffic.

commercial *adj* business, economic, financial, mercantile,
monetary, money-making,
profitable, profit-making, trading. • *n inf* advert, advertisement, *inf* break, *inf* plug.

commiserate *v* be sorry (for), be
sympathetic, comfort, condole,
console, feel (for), grieve,
mourn, sympathize.
Opp CONGRATULATE.

commission *n* 1 appointment,
warrant. 2 *commission to do a
job.* order, request. 3 *commission
on a sale.* allowance, *inf* cut, fee,
percentage, *inf* rake-off, reward.
4 ▷ COMMITTEE.

commit *v* 1 carry out, do, enact,
execute, perform, perpetrate.
2 *commit to safe-keeping.* consign, deliver, entrust, give, hand
over, transfer. **commit yourself**
▷ PROMISE.

commitment *n* 1 assurance,
duty, guarantee, liability,
pledge, promise, undertaking,
vow, word. 2 *commitment to a
cause.* adherence, dedication,
determination, devotion, loyalty,
zeal. 3 *social commitment.*

appointment, arrangement, engagement.

committed adj active, ardent, inf card-carrying, dedicated, devoted, earnest, enthusiastic, fervent, firm, keen, passionate, resolute, staunch, unwavering, wholehearted, zealous. Opp APATHETIC.

committee n board, body, commission, council, panel, thinktank. ▷ GROUP.

common adj 1 average, inf common or garden, conventional, customary, daily, everyday, familiar, frequent, habitual, normal, ordinary, popular, prevalent, regular, inf run-of-the-mill, standard, stock, traditional, typical, undistinguished, unexceptional, usual, well-known, widespread, workaday. ▷ COMMONPLACE. 2 common knowledge. accepted, collective, communal, general, joint, mutual, open, popular, public, shared, universal. 3 boorish, churlish, coarse, crude, disreputable, loutish, low, plebeian, proletarian, rude, uncouth, unrefined, vulgar, inf yobbish. Opp ARISTOCRATIC, DISTINCTIVE, UNUSUAL.
• n heath, park, parkland.

commonplace adj banal, boring, forgettable, hackneyed, humdrum, mediocre, obvious, ordinary, pedestrian, plain, platitudinous, predictable, prosaic, routine, standard, trite, unexciting, unremarkable. ▷ COMMON. Opp MEMORABLE.
• n ▷ PLATITUDE.

commotion n inf ado, agitation, bedlam, bother, brawl, inf brouhaha, inf bust-up, chaos, clamour, confusion, contre-

temps, din, disorder, disturbance, excitement, ferment, fracas, fray, furore, fuss, hubbub, hullabaloo, inf kerfuffle, noise, inf palaver, pandemonium, racket, riot, inf row, inf rumpus, sensation, inf shemozzle, inf stir, inf to-do, tumult, turmoil, upheaval, uproar, upset.

communal adj collective, common, general, joint, mutual, open, public, shared. Opp PRIVATE.

communicate v 1 commune, confer, converse, correspond, discuss, get in touch, speak, talk, write (to). 2 communicate information. announce, broadcast, convey, declare, disclose, divulge, express, get across, impart, indicate, inform, intimate, make known, mention, network, notify, pass on, proclaim, promulgate, publish, put over, relay, report, reveal, show, speak, spread, state, transfer, transmit, write. 3 communicate a disease. give, infect someone with, pass on, spread, transmit. 4 The rooms communicate with each other. be connected, lead (to).

communication n 1 announcement, communion, contact, conversation, correspondence, dispatch, information, intelligence, interaction, message, report, statement. 2 mass communication. advertising, radio, television, the media, the press.

communicative adj chatty, frank, informative, outgoing, responsive, sociable. ▷ TALKATIVE. Opp SECRETIVE.

community n commonwealth, commune, kibbutz, nation, society, state. ▷ GROUP.

commute v 1 adjust, decrease, mitigate, reduce, shorten. 2 ▷ TRAVEL.

compact adj 1 compressed, consolidated, dense, firm, packed, solid, tight-packed. Opp LOOSE. 2 handy, neat, portable. 3 abridged, brief, concentrated, condensed, short, small, succinct, terse. ▷ CONCISE. Opp LARGE. ● n ▷ AGREEMENT.

companion n accomplice, chaperon, colleague, confederate, confidant(e), consort, inf crony, escort, fellow, follower, inf henchman, partner. ▷ FRIEND, HELPER.

company n 1 companionship, friendship, society. 2 [inf] company for tea. callers, guests, visitors. 3 mixed company. assemblage, band, body, circle, club, community, coterie, crew, crowd, entourage, gang, gathering, society, throng, troop, troupe (of actors). 4 trading company. business, cartel, concern, consortium, corporation, establishment, firm, house, organization, partnership, inf set-up, syndicate. ▷ GROUP.

comparable adj analogous, cognate, commensurate, compatible, corresponding, equal, equivalent, matching, parallel, proportionate, related, similar, twin. Opp DISSIMILAR.

compare v check, contrast, correlate, draw parallels (between), equate, juxtapose, liken, make comparisons, measure (against), relate (to), set side by side, weigh (against). **compare with** ▷ EQUAL.

comparison n analogy, contrast, correlation, difference, distinction, juxtaposition, likeness, parallel, relationship, resemblance, similarity.

compartment n alcove, bay, berth, booth, cell, chamber, inf cubbyhole, cubicle, division, kiosk, locker, niche, nook, pigeon-hole, section, slot, space.

compatible adj 1 harmonious, like-minded, similar, well-matched. ▷ FRIENDLY. 2 compatible claims. congruent, consistent, matching, reconcilable. Opp INCOMPATIBLE.

compel v coerce, constrain, dragoon, drive, force, impel, necessitate, oblige, order, press, press-gang, pressurize, require, inf shanghai, urge.

compendium n anthology, collection, digest, handbook, summary.

compensate v 1 atone, expiate, indemnify, make amends, make good, make restitution, make up for, pay back, recompense, redress, reimburse, remunerate, repay, requite. 2 counterbalance, even up, neutralize, offset.

compensation n amends, damages, indemnity, recompense, reimbursement, reparation, repayment, restitution.

compère n announcer, disc jockey, host, hostess, Master of Ceremonies, MC, presenter.

compete v 1 enter, participate, perform, take part. 2 be in competition, contend, emulate, oppose, rival, strive, undercut, vie. ▷ FIGHT. Opp COOPERATE. **compete with** ▷ RIVAL.

competent adj able, accomplished, adept, adequate, capable, clever, effective, efficient, experi-

enced, expert, fit, handy, practical, proficient, qualified, satisfactory, skilful, skilled, trained, workmanlike.
Opp INCOMPETENT.

competition n 1 competitiveness, conflict, contention, emulation, rivalry, struggle. 2 challenge, championship, contest, event, game, heat, match, quiz, race, rally, tournament, trial.

competitive adj 1 aggressive, antagonistic, combative, contentious, hard-fought, keen, lively, sporting. 2 competitive prices. fair, moderate, reasonable, similar to others.

competitor n adversary, antagonist, candidate, contender, contestant, entrant, finalist, opponent, participant, rival.

compile v accumulate, amass, arrange, assemble, collate, collect, compose, edit, gather, marshal, organize, put together.

complain v inf beef, inf bellyache, carp, cavil, find fault, fuss, inf gripe, inf grouch, inf grouse, grumble, lament, inf moan, object, protest, wail, whine, inf whinge. Opp PRAISE. **complain about** ▷ CRITICIZE.

complaint n 1 accusation, inf beef, charge, criticism, grievance, inf gripe, inf grouse, grumble, inf moan, objection, protest, whine, inf whinge. 2 medical complaint. disease, infection, sickness. ▷ ILLNESS.

complaisant adj accommodating, acquiescent, amenable, biddable, compliant, cooperative, docile, obedient, obliging, pliant, polite, tractable, willing.
Opp OBSTINATE.

complement n 1 completion, inf finishing touch. 2 full complement. aggregate, capacity, quota, sum, total. • v complete, make whole, perfect, round off.

complementary adj interdependent, matching, reciprocal, toning, twin.

complete adj 1 comprehensive, entire, exhaustive, full, intact, total, unabridged, uncut, unedited, unexpurgated, whole. 2 accomplished, achieved, concluded, done, finished, over. ▷ PERFECT. 3 complete disaster. absolute, downright, extreme, out and out, outright, pure, rank, sheer, thorough, total, unmitigated, unmixed, unqualified, utter, inf wholesale. Opp INCOMPLETE. • v 1 accomplish, achieve, carry out, clinch, close, conclude, crown, do, end, finalize, finish, fulfil, perfect, perform, round off, terminate, inf wind up. 2 complete forms. answer, fill in.

complex adj complicated, composite, compound, convoluted, elaborate, inf fiddly, intricate, involved, inf knotty, labyrinthine, mixed, multifarious, multiple, ornate, problematic, sophisticated, tortuous, tricky. Opp SIMPLE.

complexion n appearance, colour, colouring, look, pigmentation, skin, texture.

complicate v compound, confound, confuse, elaborate, entangle, make complicated, mix up, muddle, inf snarl up, tangle, twist. Opp SIMPLIFY. **complicated** ▷ COMPLEX.

complication n complexity, confusion, convolution, difficulty, intricacy, inf mix-up, obstacle, compliment 79 compromise

problem, ramification, set-back, snag, tangle.

compliment n [often pl] accolade, admiration, appreciation, commendation, congratulations, eulogy, felicitations, flattery, honour, plaudits, praise, tribute. ● v applaud, commend, congratulate, eulogize, felicitate, flatter, give credit, laud, praise, salute, speak highly of. Opp INSULT.

complimentary adj admiring, appreciative, approving, commendatory, congratulatory, eulogistic, favourable, flattering, derog fulsome, generous, laudatory, rapturous, supportive. Opp ABUSIVE, CRITICAL.

comply v abide (by), accede, accord, acquiesce, adhere (to), agree, assent, be in accordance, concur, consent, defer, fall in (with), fit in, follow, fulfil, harmonize, keep (to), match, meet, obey, observe, perform, respect, satisfy, square (with), submit, yield. ▷ CONFORM. Opp DEFY.

component n bit, constituent, element, essential part, ingredient, item, part, piece, inf spare, spare part, unit.

compose v 1 build, constitute, construct, fashion, form, frame, make, put together. 2 compose music. arrange, create, devise, imagine, produce, write. 3 compose yourself. calm, control, pacify, quieten, soothe. **be composed of** ▷ COMPRISE. **composed** ▷ CALM.

composition n 1 assembly, constitution, creation, establishment, formation, inf make-up, setting up. 2 configuration, layout, organization, structure. 3 literary composition. article,

essay, story. 4 musical composition. opus, piece, work.

compound adj complex, complicated, composite, intricate, involved, multiple. Opp SIMPLE. ● n 1 alloy, amalgam, blend, combination, composite, composition, fusion, mixture, synthesis. 2 compound for cattle. corral, enclosure, pen, run. ● v ▷ COMBINE, COMPLICATE.

comprehend v appreciate, conceive, fathom, grasp, realize. ▷ UNDERSTAND.

comprehensible adj clear, easy, intelligible, lucid, meaningful, plain, self-explanatory, simple, straightforward, understandable. Opp INCOMPREHENSIBLE.

comprehensive adj all-embracing, broad, catholic, compendious, complete, detailed, encyclopaedic, exhaustive, extensive, far-reaching, full, sweeping, thorough, total, universal, wholesale, wide-ranging. Opp SELECTIVE.

compress v abbreviate, abridge, concentrate, condense, constrict, contract, cram, crush, flatten, inf jam, précis, press, shorten, squash, squeeze, stuff, summarize, truncate. Opp EXPAND. **compressed** ▷ COMPACT, CONCISE.

comprise v be composed of, comprehend, consist of, contain, cover, embody, include, incorporate, involve.

compromise n bargain, concession, inf give-and-take, inf halfway house, middle way, settlement. ● v 1 concede a point, make concessions, meet halfway, negotiate a settlement, reach a formula, settle, inf split the difference, strike a balance. 2 compromise your reputation.

damage, discredit, disgrace, dishonour, jeopardize, prejudice, risk, undermine, weaken. **compromising** ▷ SHAMEFUL.

compulsion n 1 coercion, duress, force, necessity. 2 *compulsion to smoke*. addiction, drive, habit, pressure, urge.

compulsive adj 1 besetting, compelling, driving, involuntary, irresistible, overpowering, overwhelming, uncontrollable, urgent. 2 *compulsive drinker*. addicted, habitual, incorrigible, obsessive, persistent.

compulsory adj binding, contractual, enforceable, essential, imperative, incumbent, indispensable, mandatory, necessary, obligatory, official, prescribed, required, requisite, set, statutory, stipulated, unavoidable. *Opp* OPTIONAL.

compunction n contrition, hesitation, pang of conscience, qualm, regret, remorse, scruple.

compute v add up, ascertain, assess, calculate, count, determine, estimate, evaluate, measure, reckon, total, work out.

computer n mainframe, micro, microcomputer, PC, personal computer, word-processor.

comrade n associate, colleague, companion. ▷ FRIEND.

conceal v blot out, bury, camouflage, cloak, cover up, disguise, gloss over, hide, hush up, keep secret, mask, obscure, screen, secrete, suppress, veil. *Opp* REVEAL. **concealed** ▷ HIDDEN.

concede v accept, acknowledge, admit, agree, allow, confess, grant, own, profess, recognize. **concede defeat** capitulate,

inf cave in, cede, give in, resign, submit, surrender, yield.

conceit n self-love, vanity. ▷ PRIDE.

conceited adj arrogant, *inf* big-headed, boastful, bumptious, *inf* cocky, egocentric, egotistical, haughty, *inf* high and mighty, immodest, narcissistic, overweening, pleased with yourself, proud, self-centred, self-important, self-satisfied, smug, snobbish, *inf* snooty, *inf* stuck-up, supercilious, *inf* swollen-headed, *inf* toffee-nosed, vain. *Opp* MODEST.

conceive v 1 become pregnant. 2 *conceive a plan*. conjure up, contrive, create, design, devise, *inf* dream up, envisage, form, formulate, frame, hatch, imagine, invent, make up, originate, plan, plot, produce, realize, suggest, think up, visualize, work out. ▷ THINK.

concentrate n distillation, essence, extract. ● v 1 apply yourself, attend, be attentive, engross yourself, think, work hard. 2 centre, cluster, collect, congregate, converge, crowd, focus, gather, mass. *Opp* DISPERSE. 3 *concentrate a liquid*. condense, reduce, thicken. *Opp* DILUTE. **concentrated** 1 ▷ INTENSIVE. 2 condensed, evaporated, reduced, strong, thick, undiluted.

conception n 1 begetting, conceiving, fathering, fertilization, genesis, impregnation, origin. ▷ BEGINNING. 2 ▷ IDEA.

concern n 1 attention, care, consideration, heed, interest, regard. 2 *no concern of yours*. affair, business, involvement, matter, problem, responsibility, task. **3** *matter for concern.* anxiety, disquiet, distress, fear, solicitude, worry. **4** *business concern.* company, corporation, enterprise, establishment, firm, organization. • *v* affect, be important to, interest, involve, matter to, pertain to, refer to, relate to.

concerned *adj* **1** *concerned parents.* bothered, caring, distressed, solicitous, troubled, unhappy, worried. ▷ ANXIOUS. **2** *the people concerned.* connected, implicated, interested, involved, referred to, relevant. ▷ RESPONSIBLE.

concerning *prep* about, apropos of, involving, re, regarding, relating to, relevant to, with reference to, with regard to.

concert *n* performance, programme, show.

concerted *adj* collaborative, collective, combined, cooperative, joint, mutual, united.

concession *n* adjustment, allowance, reduction.

concise *adj* brief, compact, compressed, concentrated, condensed, laconic, pithy, short, small, succinct, terse.
▷ ABRIDGED. *Opp* DIFFUSE.

conclude *v* **1** cease, close, complete, culminate, end, finish, round off, stop, terminate. **2** assume, decide, deduce, gather, infer, judge. ▷ THINK.

conclusion *n* **1** close, completion, culmination, end, epilogue, finale, finish, termination. **2** answer, belief, decision, deduction, inference, judgement, opinion, outcome, resolution, result, solution, upshot, verdict.

conclusive *adj* certain, convincing, decisive, definite, persuasive, unanswerable, unequivocal. *Opp* INCONCLUSIVE.

concoct *v* contrive, devise, fabricate, feign, formulate, hatch, invent, make up, plan, prepare, put together, think up.

concord *n* agreement, euphony, harmony, peace.

concrete *adj* actual, definite, existing, factual, firm, material, objective, palpable, physical, real, solid, substantial, tangible, visible. *Opp* ABSTRACT.

concur *v* accord, agree.
▷ COMPLY.

concurrent *adj* coexisting, coinciding, concomitant, contemporary, overlapping, parallel, simultaneous, synchronous.

condemn *v* **1** blame, castigate, censure, criticize, damn, decry, denounce, deplore, deprecate, disapprove of, disparage, execrate, rebuke, reprove, revile, *inf* slam, *inf* slate, upbraid. *Opp* COMMEND. **2** convict, find guilty, judge, punish, sentence. *Opp* ACQUIT.

condense *v* **1** abbreviate, abridge, compress, curtail, précis, reduce, shorten, summarize. *Opp* EXPAND. **2** *condense a liquid.* concentrate, distil, reduce, solidify, thicken. *Opp* DILUTE.

condensation *n* haze, mist, precipitation, steam.

condescend *v* deign, demean yourself, lower yourself, stoop. **condescending** ▷ HAUGHTY.

condition *n* **1** case, circumstance, fitness, form, health, *inf* nick, order, shape, situation, state, *inf* trim,

working order. **2** limitation, prerequisite, proviso, qualification, requirement, requisite, restriction, stipulation, terms. **3** *medical condition.* ▷ ILLNESS.
● *v* acclimatize, accustom, brainwash, educate, mould, prepare, *inf* soften up, train.

conditional *adj* dependent, limited, provisional, qualified, restricted, *inf* with strings attached. *Opp* UNCONDITIONAL.

condone *v* connive at, disregard, endorse, excuse, forgive, overlook, pardon, tolerate.

conducive *adj* advantageous, beneficial, encouraging, favourable, helpful, supportive. **be conducive to** ▷ ENCOURAGE.

conduct *n* **1** actions, attitude, bearing, behaviour, demeanour, deportment, manners, ways. **2** *conduct of affairs.* administration, control, direction, discharge, government, guidance, handling, management, organization, regulation, running, supervision. ● *v* **1** administer, be in charge of, chair, command, control, direct, govern, handle, head, manage, organize, oversee, preside over, regulate, rule, run, steer, supervise. **2** accompany, escort, guide, lead, take, usher. **3** *conduct electricity.* carry, channel, convey, transmit. **conduct yourself** ▷ BEHAVE.

confer *v* **1** accord, award, bestow, give, grant, honour with, impart, invest, present. **2** compare notes, consult, debate, deliberate, discuss, exchange ideas, *inf* put your heads together. ▷ TALK.

conference *n* congress, consultation, convention, council, discus-

sion, forum, meeting, seminar, symposium.

confess *v* acknowledge, admit, *inf* come clean, concede, disclose, divulge, *inf* make a clean breast (of), own up, unburden yourself.

confession *n* acknowledgement, admission, declaration, disclosure, expression, revelation.

confide *v* consult, speak confidentially, *inf* spill the beans, open your heart, *inf* tell all, tell your secrets, trust.

confidence *n* **1** belief, certainty, faith, hope, optimism, reliance, trust. **2** aplomb, assurance, boldness, composure, conviction, firmness, *inf* nerve, panache, self-assurance, self-possession, spirit, verve. *Opp* DOUBT, HESITATION. **have confidence in** ▷ TRUST.

confident *adj* **1** certain, convinced, hopeful, optimistic, positive, sanguine, sure. **2** *confident person.* assertive, assured, bold, *derog* cocksure, composed, cool, definite, fearless, secure, self-assured, self-possessed, unafraid. *Opp* DOUBTFUL.

confidential *adj* **1** classified, *inf* hush-hush, *inf* off the record, restricted, secret, top secret. **2** *confidential secretary.* personal, private, trusted.

confine *v* box in, cage, circumscribe, constrain, *inf* coop up, cramp, enclose, hedge in, hem in, *inf* hold down, isolate, keep in, limit, localize, restrain, restrict, rope off, shut in, shut up, surround, wall up.
▷ IMPRISON. *Opp* FREE.

confirm *v* **1** authenticate, back up, bear out, corroborate, demonstrate, endorse, establish, give credence to, justify, lend force to, prove, reinforce, settle, strengthen, substantiate, support, underline, vindicate. 2 *confirm a deal.* clinch, formalize, guarantee, make official, ratify, sanction, validate, verify.

confiscate *v* appropriate, commandeer, expropriate, impound, remove, seize, sequestrate, take away, take possession of.

conflict *n* 1 antagonism, antipathy, contradiction, disagreement, dissension, friction, hostility, incompatibility, inconsistency, opposition, strife. 2 battle, *inf* brush, clash, combat, confrontation, dispute, encounter, engagement, feud, *inf* row, *inf* set-to, skirmish, struggle, war, wrangle. ● *v* 1 be at variance, be incompatible, clash, compete, contradict, contrast, *inf* cross swords, disagree. ▷ FIGHT, QUARREL.

conform *v* agree, behave conventionally, blend in, *inf* do what you are told, *inf* keep in step, obey, *inf* toe the line. ▷ COMPLY.

conformist *n* traditionalist, yesman. *Opp* REBEL.

conformity *n* compliance, conventionality, orthodoxy, submission, uniformity.

confront *v* accost, challenge, defy, encounter, face up to, oppose, resist, stand up to, take on, withstand. *Opp* AVOID.

confuse *v* 1 disarrange, disorder, garble, jumble, *inf* mess up, mix up, muddle, tangle, *inf* throw into disarray, upset. 2 *rules confuse me.* baffle, befuddle, bemuse, bewilder, confound, disconcert, disorientate, distract, *inf* flummox, fluster, mislead, mystify, perplex, puzzle,

inf rattle, *inf* throw. **confusing** ▷ PUZZLING.

confused *adj* 1 chaotic, disordered, disorganized, *inf* higgledy-piggledy, jumbled, messy, mixed up, muddled, *inf* shambolic, *inf* topsy-turvy, twisted. 2 *confused ideas.* aimless, contradictory, disjointed, garbled, incoherent, inconsistent, irrational, misleading, obscure, rambling, unclear, unstructured, woolly. 3 *confused mind.* addled, baffled, bewildered, dazed, disorientated, distracted, flustered, fuddled, *inf* in a tizzy, muddle-headed, mystified, nonplussed, perplexed, puzzled. ▷ MAD. *Opp* ORDERLY.

confusion *n* 1 *inf* ado, anarchy, bedlam, bother, chaos, clutter, commotion, disorder, disorganization, fuss, hubbub, hullabaloo, jumble, *inf* mayhem, mêlée, mess, *inf* mix-up, muddle, pandemonium, riot, *inf* rumpus, *inf* shambles, tumult, turmoil, upheaval, uproar, whirl. 2 *mental confusion.* bemusement, bewilderment, disorientation, distraction, mystification, perplexity, puzzlement. *Opp* ORDER.

congeal *v* clot, coagulate, curdle, harden, *inf* jell, set, solidify, stiffen, thicken.

congenial *adj* acceptable, agreeable, pleasant, suitable, understanding. ▷ FRIENDLY. *Opp* UNCONGENIAL.

congenital *adj* hereditary, inborn, inherent, inherited, innate, natural.

congested *adj* blocked, choked, clogged, crammed, crowded, full, jammed, obstructed, overcrowded, stuffed. *Opp* CLEAR.

congratulate *v* applaud, compliment, felicitate, praise.

congregate *v* assemble, collect, convene, converge, gather, mass, meet, muster, rally, rendezvous. ▷ GROUP.

conjure *v* invoke, raise, summon. **conjure up** ▷ PRODUCE.

conjuring *n* illusions, magic, sleight of hand, tricks.

connect *v* 1 attach, combine, couple, fix, interlock, join, link, switch on, tie, unite. ▷ FASTEN. 2 associate, bracket together, compare, put together, relate, tie up. *Opp* SEPARATE.

connection *n* affinity, association, bond, contact, correlation, correspondence, link, relationship, relevance, tie, *inf* tie-up, unity. *Opp* SEPARATION.

conquer *v* 1 annex, best, capture, crush, defeat, get the better of, humble, *inf* lick, master, occupy, outdo, overpower, overrun, overthrow, overwhelm, quell, rout, seize, subdue, subjugate, surmount, take, *inf* thrash, triumph over, vanquish, worst. ▷ WIN. 2 *conquer a mountain*. climb, reach the top of.

conquest *n* annexation, appropriation, capture, defeat, domination, invasion, occupation, overthrow, subjection, subjugation, *inf* takeover. ▷ VICTORY.

conscience *n* compunction, ethics, honour, morality, principles, qualms, reservations, scruples, standards.

conscientious *adj* attentive, careful, diligent, dutiful, hardworking, honest, meticulous, painstaking, particular, punctilious, responsible, rigorous, scrupulous, serious, thorough. *Opp* CARELESS.

conscious *adj* 1 alert, awake, aware, compos mentis, sensible. 2 *conscious act*. calculated, deliberate, intended, intentional, knowing, planned, premeditated, studied, voluntary, wilful. *Opp* UNCONSCIOUS.

consecrate *v* bless, dedicate, devote, hallow, make sacred, sanctify. *Opp* DESECRATE.

consecutive *adj* continuous, following, one after the other, running (*3 days running*), sequential, successive.

consent *n* acquiescence, agreement, assent, concurrence, permission, seal of approval. ● *v* accede, acquiesce, agree, approve, comply, concede, concur, undertake, yield. *Opp* REFUSE. **consent to** ▷ ALLOW.

consequence *n* 1 aftermath, by-product, corollary, effect, end, *inf* follow-up, outcome, repercussion, result, side-effect, upshot. 2 *of no consequence*. concern, importance, moment, note, significance, value.

consequent *adj* consequential, ensuing, following, resultant, resulting, subsequent.

conservation *n* economy, maintenance, preservation, protection, safeguarding, saving, upkeep. *Opp* DESTRUCTION.

conservationist *n* ecologist, environmentalist, *inf* green.

conservative *adj* 1 conventional, die-hard, hidebound, moderate, narrow-minded, old-fashioned, reactionary, sober, traditional, unadventurous. 2 *conservative estimate*. cautious, reasonable, under-

stated. 3 *conservative politics.*
right-of-centre, right-wing, Tory.
Opp PROGRESSIVE.
● *n* conformist, die-hard, right-
winger, Tory, traditionalist.

conserve *v* hold in reserve,
keep, look after, maintain, preserve, protect, safeguard, save,
store up, use sparingly.
Opp DESTROY, WASTE.

consider *v* 1 chew over, contemplate, discuss, examine,
muse, puzzle over, reflect, study,
inf turn over, weigh up.
▷ THINK. 2 believe, deem, judge,
reckon.

considerable *adj* appreciable,
big, comfortable, noteworthy,
noticeable, perceptible, reasonable, respectable, significant,
sizeable, substantial, *inf* tidy
(amount), tolerable, worthwhile.
Opp NEGLIGIBLE.

considerate *adj* accommodating,
altruistic, caring, cooperative,
friendly, generous, gracious,
helpful, kind, kind-hearted,
neighbourly, obliging, polite,
sensitive, solicitous, sympathetic, tactful, thoughtful,
unselfish. *Opp* SELFISH.

consign *v* commit, convey,
deliver, devote, entrust, give,
hand over, pass on, relegate,
send, ship, transfer.

consignment *n* batch, cargo,
delivery, goods, load, shipment.

consist *v* consist of add up to,
amount to, be composed of, comprise, contain, embody, include,
incorporate, involve.

consistent *adj* 1 constant,
dependable, faithful, predictable,
regular, reliable, stable, steady,
unchanging, undeviating, unfailing, uniform. 2 *The stories are
consistent.* compatible, conson-

ant, in accordance, in agreement, of a piece.
Opp INCONSISTENT.

console *v* calm, cheer, comfort,
ease, hearten, relieve, solace,
soothe, sympathize with.

consolidate *v* make secure,
make strong, reinforce, stabilize,
strengthen. *Opp* WEAKEN.

consort *v* consort with associate with, be seen with, fraternize
with, *inf* gang up with, keep company with, mix with.

conspicuous *adj* apparent, blatant, clear, discernible, dominant, eminent, evident, flagrant,
glaring, impressive, manifest,
marked, notable, noticeable,
obtrusive, obvious, ostentatious,
outstanding, patent, perceptible,
plain, prominent, pronounced,
self-evident, shining (*example*),
showy, striking, unmistakable,
visible. *Opp* INCONSPICUOUS.

conspiracy *n* collusion,
inf frame-up, insider dealing,
intrigue, machinations, plot,
inf racket, scheme, treason.

conspirator *n* plotter, schemer.

conspire *v* be in league, collude,
combine, connive, cooperate,
hatch a plot, have designs,
intrigue, plot, scheme.

constant *adj* 1 ceaseless,
chronic, consistent, continuous,
endless, everlasting, fixed,
immutable, incessant, invariable, non-stop, permanent, perpetual, persistent, regular,
relentless, repeated, stable,
steady, sustained, unbroken,
unchanging, unending, unflagging, uniform, uninterrupted,
unremitting. 2 *constant friend.*
dedicated, dependable, devoted,
faithful, firm, indefatigable,
loyal, reliable, resolute, staunch,

steadfast, tireless, true, trustworthy, trusty, unswerving. *Opp* CHANGEABLE.

constitute *v* appoint, bring together, compose, comprise, create, establish, form, found, inaugurate, make (up), set up.

construct *v* assemble, build, create, engineer, erect, fabricate, fashion, form, *inf* knock together, make, manufacture, produce, put together, put up, set up. *Opp* DEMOLISH.

construction *n* 1 assembly, building, creation, manufacture, production, putting-up, setting-up. 2 building, edifice, structure.

constructive *adj* advantageous, beneficial, cooperative, creative, helpful, positive, practical, productive, useful, valuable, worthwhile. *Opp* DESTRUCTIVE.

consult *v* confer, debate, discuss, exchange views, *inf* put your heads together, refer (to), seek advice, speak (to), *inf* talk things over. ▷ QUESTION.

consume *v* 1 devour, drink, *inf* gobble up, guzzle, *inf* put away. ▷ EAT. 2 *consume energy.* absorb, deplete, drain, exhaust, expend, swallow up, use up, utilize.

contact *n* connection, junction, touch, union.
▷ COMMUNICATION. ● *v* apply to, approach, call on, communicate with, *inf* drop a line to, *inf* get hold of, get in touch with, make overtures to, notify, ring, speak to, telephone.

contagious *adj* catching, communicable, infectious, spreading, transmissible, transmittable.

contain *v* 1 accommodate, enclose, hold. 2 comprise, consist of, embody, embrace, include, incorporate, involve. 3 *contain your anger.* check, control, curb, hold back, limit, repress, restrain, stifle.

container *n* holder, receptacle, vessel.

contaminate *v* adulterate, corrupt, debase, defile, foul, infect, poison, pollute, soil, spoil, stain, taint. *Opp* PURIFY.

contemplate *v* 1 eye, gaze at, observe, stare at, survey, watch. ▷ SEE. 2 consider, examine, mull over, muse, plan, reflect, ruminate, study. ▷ THINK. 3 envisage, expect, intend, propose.

contemporary *adj* 1 *contemporary events.* coexistent, concurrent, contemporaneous, simultaneous, synchronous. 2 *contemporary music.* current, fashionable, the latest, modern, novel, present-day, *inf* trendy, topical, up-to-date.

contempt *n* derision, disdain, disgust, disrespect, ridicule, scorn. ▷ HATRED.
Opp ADMIRATION. **feel contempt for** ▷ DESPISE.

contemptible *adj* base, beneath contempt, discreditable, disgraceful, disreputable, ignominious, mean, pitiful, shabby, shameful, worthless, wretched. ▷ HATEFUL. *Opp* ADMIRABLE.

contemptuous *adj* arrogant, belittling, condescending, derisive, disdainful, dismissive, haughty, insolent, insulting, jeering, patronizing, sarcastic, scornful, sneering, *inf* snide, *inf* snooty, *sl* snotty, supercilious, superior, withering.

contend *v* 1 compete, contest, cope, grapple, strive, struggle, vie. ▷ FIGHT, QUARREL. 2 *contend that you're innocent.* affirm, allege, argue, assert, claim, declare, maintain, plead.

content *adj* ▷ CONTENTED. ● *n* 1 constituent, element, ingredient, part. 2 ▷ CONTENTMENT. ● *v* ▷ SATISFY.

contented *adj* comfortable, fulfilled, peaceful, relaxed, satisfied, serene, smug, uncomplaining, untroubled, well-fed. ▷ HAPPY. *Opp* DISSATISFIED.

contentment *n* comfort, content, ease, fulfilment, relaxation, satisfaction, serenity, smugness, tranquillity, well-being. ▷ HAPPINESS. *Opp* DISSATISFACTION.

contest *n* ▷ COMPETITION, FIGHT. ● *v* 1 compete for, contend for, fight for, *inf* make a bid for, strive for, struggle for, vie for. 2 *contest a decision.* argue against, challenge, debate, dispute, doubt, oppose, query, question, refute, resist.

contestant *n* candidate, opponent, participant. ▷ ENTRANT.

context *n* background, environment, frame of reference, framework, milieu, setting, situation, surroundings.

continual *adj* eternal, everlasting, frequent, limitless, ongoing, perennial, perpetual, recurrent, regular, repeated. ▷ CONTINUOUS. *Opp* OCCASIONAL.

continuation *n* 1 extension, prolongation, protraction, resumption. 2 addition, appendix, postscript, sequel, supplement.

continue *v* 1 carry on, endure, go on, last, linger, persevere, persist, proceed, pursue, remain, stay, survive, sustain. 2 *continue after lunch.* *inf* pick up the threads, restart, resume. 3 *continue a series.* extend, keep going, lengthen, maintain, prolong.

continuous *adj* constant, continuing, endless, incessant, interminable, never-ending, non-stop, relentless, *inf* round-the-clock, solid, sustained, unbroken, unceasing, uninterrupted, unremitting. ▷ CHRONIC, CONTINUAL. *Opp* INTERMITTENT.

contour *n* form, outline, shape.

contract *n* agreement, bargain, bond, commitment, concordat, covenant, deal, lease, pact, settlement, treaty, understanding, undertaking. ● *v* 1 become smaller, close up, condense, decrease, diminish, draw together, dwindle, lessen, narrow, reduce, shrink, shrivel, slim down, wither. *Opp* EXPAND. 2 agree, arrange, close a deal, covenant, negotiate a deal, promise, sign an agreement, undertake. 3 *contract a disease.* become infected with, catch, develop, get.

contraction *n* 1 diminution, narrowing, shortening, shrinkage, shrivelling. 2 abbreviation, diminutive, shortened form.

contradict *v* argue with, challenge, confute, deny, disagree with, dispute, gainsay, impugn, oppose, speak against.

contradictory *adj* antithetical, conflicting, contrary, different, incompatible, inconsistent, irreconcilable, opposed, opposite. *Opp* COMPATIBLE.

contraption n apparatus, contrivance, device, gadget, invention, machine, mechanism.

contrary adj 1 conflicting, contradictory, different, opposed, opposite, reverse. 2 contrary winds. adverse, hostile, opposing, unfavourable. 3 contrary child. awkward, cantankerous, defiant, difficult, disobedient, disruptive, intractable, obstinate, perverse, rebellious, inf stroppy, stubborn, uncooperative, unhelpful, wayward, wilful. Opp HELPFUL.

contrast n antithesis, comparison, difference, disparity, dissimilarity, distinction, divergence, foil, opposition. Opp SIMILARITY. • v 1 compare, differentiate, discriminate, distinguish, make a distinction, set one against the other. 2 be set off (by), clash, conflict, differ (from). contrasting ▷ DISSIMILAR.

contribute v add, bestow, inf chip in, donate, inf fork out, furnish, give, present, provide, put up, subscribe, supply. contribute to ▷ SUPPORT.

contribution n 1 donation, fee, gift, grant, handout, offering, payment, sponsorship, subscription. 2 addition, input, support. ▷ HELP.

contributor n 1 backer, benefactor, donor, giver, helper, patron, sponsor, subscriber, supporter. 2 ▷ WRITER.

control n 1 administration, authority, charge, command, direction, discipline, government, grip, guidance, influence, jurisdiction, leadership, management, mastery, organization, oversight, power, regulation, restraint, rule, supervision, supremacy, sway. 2 dial, key, lever, switch. • v 1 administer, inf be at the helm, be in charge, command, conduct, cope with, deal with, direct, dominate, engineer, govern, guide, handle, lead, look after, manage, manipulate, order about, oversee, regulate, rule, run, superintend, supervise. 2 control animals. check, confine, contain, curb, hold back, keep in check, master, repress, restrain, subdue.

controversial adj 1 arguable, debatable, disputable, doubtful, problematic, questionable. Opp ACCEPTED. 2 argumentative, contentious, litigious, polemical, provocative.

controversy n argument, contention, debate, disagreement, dispute, dissension, polemic, quarrel, war of words, wrangle.

convalesce v get better, make progress, mend, recover, recuperate, regain strength.

convalescent adj getting better, healing, improving, making progress, inf on the mend, recovering, recuperating.

convene v bring together, call, convoke, summon. ▷ GATHER.

convenient adj accessible, appropriate, at hand, available, expedient, handy, helpful, labour-saving, nearby, opportune, suitable, timely, useful. Opp INCONVENIENT.

convention n 1 custom, etiquette, formality, practice, rule, tradition. 2 ▷ ASSEMBLY.

conventional adj 1 accepted, correct, customary, decorous, expected, formal, mainstream, orthodox, prevalent, received, standard, *inf* straight, traditional, unadventurous, unimaginative, unoriginal. ▷ ORDINARY. **2** [*derog*] bourgeois, conservative, hidebound, pedestrian, reactionary, rigid, stereotyped, *inf* stuffy. *Opp* UNCONVENTIONAL.

converge *v* coincide, combine, come together, join, link up, meet, merge, unite. *Opp* DIVERGE.

conversation *n inf* chat, communication, discourse, discussion, gossip, *inf* heart-to-heart, intercourse, *inf* natter, tête-à-tête. ▷ TALK.

convert *v* change someone's mind, convince, persuade, re-educate, reform, rehabilitate, save, win over. ▷ CHANGE.

convey *v* **1** bear, bring, carry, conduct, deliver, ferry, fetch, forward, move, send, shift, ship, take, transfer, transport. **2** *convey a message*. communicate, disclose, impart, imply, indicate, mean, relay, reveal, signify, tell, transmit.

convict *n* criminal, culprit, felon, malefactor, prisoner, wrongdoer. ● *v* condemn, declare guilty, prove guilty, sentence. *Opp* ACQUIT.

conviction *n* **1** assurance, certainty, confidence. **2** *religious conviction*. belief, creed, faith, opinion, persuasion, position, principle, tenet, view.

convince *v* assure, *inf* bring round, convert, persuade, reassure, satisfy, sway, win over. **convincing** ▷ PERSUASIVE.

convulsion *n* **1** eruption, tremor, turbulence, upheaval.

2 [*medical*] attack, fit, paroxysm, seizure, spasm.

convulsive *adj* jerky, shaking, spasmodic, *inf* twitchy, uncontrolled, violent, wrenching.

cook *v* bake, cater, concoct, make, prepare. **cook up** ▷ PLOT.

cooking *n* baking, catering, cookery, cuisine.

cool *adj* **1** chilled, chilly, iced, refreshing. ▷ COLD. *Opp* HOT. **2** calm, collected, composed, dignified, *inf* laid-back, level-headed, phlegmatic, quiet, relaxed, self-possessed, sensible, serene, unexcited, unflustered, unruffled, urbane. **3** [*derog*] aloof, apathetic, cold-blooded, dispassionate, distant, frigid, half-hearted, indifferent, lukewarm, offhand, reserved, standoffish, unemotional, unenthusiastic, unfriendly, unresponsive, unsociable, unwelcoming. *Opp* PASSIONATE. **4** [*inf*] *cool customer*. ▷ INSOLENT. ● *v* **1** chill, freeze, refrigerate. *Opp* HEAT. **2** *cool your enthusiasm*. abate, allay, assuage, calm, dampen, diminish, lessen, moderate, *inf* pour cold water on, quiet, temper. *Opp* INFLAME.

cooperate *v* collaborate, combine, conspire, help, *inf* join forces, *inf* pitch in, *inf* play along, *inf* play ball, *inf* pull together, unite, work as a team, work together. *Opp* COMPETE.

cooperation *n* assistance, collaboration, help, joint action, mutual support, teamwork. *Opp* COMPETITION.

cooperative *adj* **1** accommodating, hard-working, helpful, obliging, supportive, united, willing, working as a team. **2** *cooperative effort*.

collective, combined, communal, concerted, coordinated, corporate, joint, shared.

cope *v* get by, make do, manage, survive, win through. **cope with** ▷ ENDURE, MANAGE.

copious *adj* abundant, ample, bountiful, extravagant, generous, great, inexhaustible, large, lavish, liberal, luxuriant, overflowing, plentiful, profuse, unstinting. *Opp* SCARCE.

copy *n* 1 carbon copy, clone, counterfeit, double, duplicate, facsimile, fake, forgery, imitation, likeness, model, pattern, photocopy, print, replica, representation, reproduction, tracing, transcript, twin, Xerox. 2 *copy of a book.* edition, volume. ● *v* 1 counterfeit, crib, duplicate, emulate, follow, forge, imitate, photocopy, plagiarize, reproduce, simulate, transcribe. 2 ape, imitate, impersonate, mimic.

cord *n* cable, lace, line, rope, strand, string, twine, wire.

cordon *n* barrier, chain, line. **cordon off** ▷ ISOLATE.

core *n* 1 centre, heart, nucleus. 2 *core of a problem.* central issue, crux, essence, gist, kernel, *sl* nitty-gritty, nub.

cork *n* bung, plug, stopper.

corner *n* 1 angle, crook, joint. 2 bend, crossroads, intersection, junction, turning. 3 *quiet corner.* hideaway, hiding-place, niche, nook, recess, retreat. ● *v* capture, catch, trap.

corporation *n* company, concern, council, enterprise, firm, organization.

corpse *n* body, cadaver, carcass, mortal remains, *sl* stiff.

correct *adj* 1 accurate, confirmed, exact, factual, faithful, faultless, flawless, genuine, literal, precise, reliable, right, strict, true, truthful, verified. 2 acceptable, appropriate, fitting, just, proper, regular, standard, suitable, tactful, well-mannered. *Opp* WRONG. ● *v* 1 adjust, alter, cure, put right, rectify, redress, remedy, repair. 2 *correct pupils' work.* assess, mark. 3 ▷ REPRIMAND.

correspond *v* accord, agree, be consistent, coincide, concur, conform, correlate, fit, harmonize, match, parallel, square, tally. **corresponding** ▷ EQUIVALENT. **correspond with** communicate with, write to.

correspondence *n* letters, memoranda, *inf* memos, messages, notes, writings.

correspondent *n* contributor, journalist, reporter, writer.

corridor *n* aisle, hallway, passage, passageway.

corrode *v* 1 consume, eat into, erode, oxidize, rot, rust, tarnish. 2 crumble, deteriorate.

corrugated *adj* creased, *inf* crinkly, furrowed, lined, puckered, ridged, wrinkled.

corrupt *adj inf* bent, criminal, *inf* crooked, debauched, decadent, degenerate, depraved, *inf* dirty, dishonest, dishonourable, dissolute, evil, false, fraudulent, illegal, immoral, iniquitous, low, perverted, rotten, sinful, unethical, unprincipled, unscrupulous, untrustworthy, venal, vicious, wicked. *Opp* HONEST. ● *v* 1 bribe, divert, *inf* fix, influence, pervert, suborn, subvert. 2 *corrupt the* *innocent.* debauch, deprave, lead astray, tempt, seduce.

cosmetics n make-up, toiletries.

cosmic adj boundless, endless, infinite, limitless, universal.

cosmopolitan adj international, multicultural, sophisticated, urbane. *Opp* PROVINCIAL.

cost n amount, charge, expenditure, expense, fare, figure, outlay, payment, price, rate, tariff, value. ● v be worth, fetch, go for, realize, sell for, *inf* set you back.

costume n clothing, dress, fancy-dress, livery, period dress, *old use* raiment, robes.
▷ CLOTHES.

cosy adj comfortable, *inf* comfy, homely, intimate, reassuring, restful, secure, snug, warm.
Opp UNCOMFORTABLE.

council n committee, corporation, meeting. ▷ ASSEMBLY.

counsel n ▷ LAWYER. ● v advise, discuss (with), give help, guide, warn.

count v 1 add up, calculate, check, compute, enumerate, estimate, figure out, *inf* notch up, number, reckon, score, take stock of, tell, total, *inf* tot up, work out. 2 be important, matter, signify. **count on**
▷ EXPECT.

countenance n aspect, demeanour, expression, face, features, look. ● v ▷ APPROVE.

counter n 1 bar, service-point, table. 2 chip, disc, piece, token. ● v answer, *inf* come back at, contradict, defend yourself against, hit back at, parry, react to, refute, reply to, ward off.

counteract v act against, annul, be an antidote to, cancel out, counterbalance, foil, invalidate,

negate, neutralize, offset, oppose, resist, thwart, withstand, work against.

counterbalance v balance, compensate for, counteract, counterpoise, equalize.

counterfeit adj artificial, bogus, copied, ersatz, fake, false, feigned, forged, fraudulent, imitation, *inf* phoney, *inf* pseudo, sham, simulated, spurious, synthetic.
Opp GENUINE. ● v copy, fake, falsify, feign, forge, imitate, pretend, *inf* put on, simulate.

countless adj endless, immeasurable, incalculable, infinite, innumerable, limitless, many, myriad, numerous, unnumbered, untold.
Opp FINITE.

country n 1 commonwealth, domain, empire, kingdom, land, nation, people, power, realm, state, territory. 2 *open country.* countryside, green belt, landscape, scenery.

couple n brace, duo, pair, twosome. ● v 1 connect, fasten, hitch, join, link, match, pair, unite, yoke. 2 ▷ MATE.

coupon n tear-off slip, ticket, token, voucher.

courage n audacity, boldness, *sl* bottle, bravery, daring, determination, fearlessness, firmness, fortitude, gallantry, *inf* grit, *inf* guts, heroism, indomitability, mettle, *inf* nerve, patience, pluck, resolution, spirit, stoicism, tenacity, valour.
Opp COWARDICE.

courageous adj audacious, bold, brave, daring, dauntless, determined, fearless, gallant, game, *inf* gutsy, heroic, indomitable, intrepid, noble, plucky, resolute, spirited, stalwart, stout-hearted, tough, unafraid, uncomplaining, undaunted, unshrinking, valiant, valorous. *Opp* COWARDLY.

course *n* 1 bearings, direction, orbit, path, route, track, way. 2 *course of events.* development, movement, passage, progress, progression, succession. 3 *course of lectures.* curriculum, programme, schedule, series, syllabus.

court *n* 1 assizes, bench, law court, tribunal. 2 entourage, followers, retinue. 3 ▷ COURTYARD. ● *v* 1 *inf* ask for, invite, provoke, seek, solicit. 2 date, *inf* go out with, pursue, try to win, woo.

courteous *adj* civil, considerate, gentlemanly, ladylike, urbane, well-mannered. ▷ POLITE.

courtier *n* attendant, follower, lady, lord, noble, page, steward.

courtyard *n* court, enclosure, patio, *inf* quad, quadrangle.

cover *n* 1 ▷ COVERING. 2 binding, case, dust jacket, envelope, folder, wrapper. 3 camouflage, cloak, concealment, cover-up, deception, disguise, façade, front, hiding-place, mask, pretence, refuge, shelter, smokescreen. 3 *air cover.* defence, guard, protection. ● *v* 1 blot out, bury, camouflage, cap, cloak, clothe, coat, conceal, curtain, disguise, drape, dress, encase, enclose, envelop, hide, hood, mantle, mask, obscure, overlay, plaster, protect, screen, shade, sheathe, shield, shroud, spread over, surface, veil, veneer, wrap up. 2 *cover expenses.* be enough for, match, meet, pay for, suffice for. 3 *The talk will cover many subjects.* comprise, deal with, embrace,

encompass, include, involve, treat.

covering *n* blanket, canopy, cap, carpet, casing, cloak, coat, cocoon, crust, facing, film, incrustation, layer, mantle, rind, roof, screen, sheath, sheet, shell, shield, shroud, skin, tarpaulin, veil, veneer, wrapping. ▷ BEDCLOTHES.

coward *n inf* chicken, deserter, *inf* wimp.

cowardice *n* cowardliness, desertion, faint-heartedness, *inf* funk, spinelessness, timidity. ▷ FEAR. *Opp* COURAGE.

cowardly *adj* abject, afraid, cowering, craven, faint-hearted, fearful, *inf* gutless, *inf* lily-livered, pusillanimous, spineless, submissive, timid, unchivalrous, unheroic, *inf* wimpish, *sl* yellow. ▷ FRIGHTENED. *Opp* COURAGEOUS.

cower *v* cringe, crouch, flinch, quail, shiver, shrink, tremble.

coy *adj* bashful, coquettish, demure, diffident, embarrassed, evasive, hesitant, modest, timid, unforthcoming. ▷ SHY. *Opp* BOLD.

crack *n* 1 break, chink, cranny, crevice, fissure, flaw, fracture, gap, opening, rift, rupture, slit, split. 2 bang, clap, explosion, shot, snap. 3 ▷ JOKE. ● *v* break, fracture, snap, splinter, split. **crack up** ▷ DISINTEGRATE.

craft *n* 1 handicraft, job, trade. ▷ CRAFTSMANSHIP, CUNNING. 2 *sea-going craft.* boat, ship, vessel. ● *v* ▷ MAKE.

craftsmanship *n* art, artistry, expertise, handiwork, *inf* know-how, workmanship. ▷ SKILL.

crafty adj artful, astute, calculating, canny, clever, conniving, cunning, deceitful, devious, inf dodgy, furtive, ingenious, knowing, machiavellian, manipulative, scheming, shrewd, sly, sneaky, wily. Opp HONEST, NAIVE.

craggy adj jagged, rocky, rough, rugged.

cram v 1 compress, crowd, crush, force, jam, overfill, pack, press, squeeze, stuff. 2 ▷ STUDY.

cramped adj crowded, restricted, tight, uncomfortable. Opp ROOMY.

crash n 1 bang, blast, boom, explosion, smash. 2 accident, collision, disaster, impact, pile-up, smash, wreck. 3 crash on the stock market. collapse, depression, fall. ● v 1 bump, collide, knock, smash. ▷ HIT. 2 collapse, crash-dive, dive, fall, plummet, plunge, topple.

crate n box, case, packing case.

crater n abyss, chasm, hole, hollow, pit.

crawl v 1 clamber, creep, edge, slither, wriggle. 2 [inf] be obsequious, fawn, flatter, grovel, inf suck up, toady. 3 ▷ TEEM.

craze n enthusiasm, fad, fashion, infatuation, mania, novelty, obsession, passion, rage, trend.

crazy adj 1 berserk, demented, deranged, frantic, hysterical, insane, inf potty, unbalanced, unhinged, wild. ▷ MAD. 2 crazy ideas. absurd, confused, foolish, idiotic, illogical, impractical, ridiculous, senseless, silly, unrealistic, unreasonable, unwise. ▷ STUPID. 3 ▷ ENTHUSIASTIC. Opp SENSIBLE.

creamy adj milky, oily, smooth, thick, velvety.

crease n corrugation, fold, furrow, groove, pleat, pucker, ridge, tuck, wrinkle. ● v crimp, crinkle, crumple, crush, fold, pleat, pucker, rumple, wrinkle.

create v old use beget, breed, bring into existence, build, cause, compose, conceive, constitute, construct, design, inf dream up, engender, engineer, establish, father, forge, found, generate, give rise to, imagine, institute, invent, make up, manufacture, originate, produce, shape, sire, think up. ▷ MAKE. Opp DESTROY.

creation n 1 beginning, birth, conception, constitution, construction, formation, foundation, genesis, inception, institution, making, origin, procreation, production. 2 achievement, brainchild, concept, handiwork, invention, product. Opp DESTRUCTION.

creative adj artistic, clever, fertile, imaginative, ingenious, inspired, inventive, original, productive, resourceful, talented. Opp DESTRUCTIVE.

creator n architect, author, begetter, composer, craftsman, designer, deviser, initiator, inventor, manufacturer, originator. ▷ ARTIST.

creature n beast, being, brute, organism. ▷ ANIMAL.

credentials n authorization, documents, licence, passport, proof of identity, warrant.

credible adj believable, conceivable, convincing, likely, persuasive, plausible, possible, tenable, trustworthy. Opp INCREDIBLE.

credit n approval, commendation, distinction, esteem, fame, honour, *inf* kudos, merit, praise, prestige, recognition, reputation. ● *v* 1 accept, believe, count on, depend on, have faith in, rely on, subscribe to, *inf* swallow, swear by, trust. *Opp* DOUBT. 2 *credit you with sense*. assign to, attribute to. 3 *credit £10 to my account*. add, enter. *Opp* DEBIT.

creditable *adj* admirable, commendable, estimable, honourable, laudable, meritorious, praiseworthy, worthy. *Opp* UNWORTHY.

credulous *adj* easily taken in, *inf* green, gullible, trusting, unsuspecting. ▷ NAIVE. *Opp* SCEPTICAL.

creed *n* belief, conviction, doctrine, dogma, faith, principle, tenet.

creek *n* bay, cove, estuary, harbour, inlet.

creep *v* crawl, edge, move quietly, move slowly, slip, slither, sneak, steal, tiptoe, worm.

creepy *adj* disturbing, eerie, frightening, hair-raising, macabre, ominous, *inf* scary, sinister, spine-chilling, *inf* spooky, supernatural, threatening, weird.

crest *n* 1 comb, plume. 2 *crest of a hill*. apex, brow, crown, peak, pinnacle, summit. 3 badge, coat of arms, device, emblem, heraldic device, insignia, seal, shield, symbol.

crevice *n* break, chink, cleft, crack, cranny, fissure, groove, rift, slit.

crew *n* band, company, gang, team. ▷ GROUP.

crime *n* delinquency, dishonesty, felony, law-breaking, law-

lessness, misconduct, misdemeanour, offence, *inf* racket, sin, wrongdoing.

criminal *adj inf* bent, corrupt, *inf* crooked, culpable, dishonest, felonious, illegal, indictable, nefarious, *inf* shady, unlawful. ▷ WICKED, WRONG. *Opp* LAWFUL. ● *n* convict, *inf* crook, culprit, delinquent, desperado, felon, lawbreaker, malefactor, miscreant, offender, outlaw, recidivist, transgressor, villain. ▷ GANGSTER.

cringe *v* cower, crouch, flinch, grovel, quail, quiver, shy away, wince.

cripple *v* 1 disable, hamper, hamstring, incapacitate, lame, maim, mutilate, paralyse, weaken. 2 damage, make useless, sabotage. **crippled** ▷ HANDICAPPED.

crisis *n* calamity, catastrophe, critical moment, danger, difficulty, disaster, emergency, turning point.

crisp *adj* 1 brittle, crackly, crunchy, friable, hard and dry. 2 ▷ BRACING, BRISK.

criterion *n* measure, principle, standard, yardstick.

critic *n* 1 authority, judge, pundit, reviewer. 2 attacker, detractor.

critical *adj* 1 carping, censorious, criticizing, deprecatory, derogatory, disapproving, disparaging, hypercritical, judgemental, *inf* nit-picking, scathing, uncomplimentary. *Opp* COMPLIMENTARY. 2 analytical, discerning, discriminating, intelligent, perceptive, probing, sharp. 3 *critical moment*. crucial, dangerous, decisive, important, key,

momentous, pivotal, vital.
Opp UNIMPORTANT.

criticism n 1 censure, condemnation, disapproval, disparagement, reprimand, verbal attack. 2 literary criticism. analysis, appraisal, appreciation, commentary, critique, evaluation, judgement.

criticize v 1 belittle, berate, blame, inf cast aspersions on, castigate, censure, old use chide, condemn, complain about, disapprove of, disparage, find fault with, inf get at, impugn, inf knock, inf pan, inf pick holes in, inf rap, rate, rebuke, reprimand, satirize, scold, inf slam, inf slate. Opp PRAISE. 2 analyse, appraise, assess, evaluate, judge, review.

crockery n china, crocks, dishes, earthenware, porcelain, pottery, tableware.

crook n 1 angle, corner, hook. 2 ▷ CRIMINAL.

crooked adj 1 angled, askew, bent, contorted, curved, deformed, gnarled, lopsided, misshapen, off-centre, tortuous, twisted, warped, winding. ▷ INDIRECT. 2 ▷ CRIMINAL.

crop n harvest, produce, yield. ● v browse, graze, nibble, shear, trim. ▷ CUT, HARVEST. **crop up** ▷ ARISE.

cross adj bad-tempered, cantankerous, grumpy, irascible, irate, irritable, peevish, short-tempered, testy, upset. ▷ ANGRY, ANNOYED. Opp GOOD-TEMPERED. ● n 1 intersection, X. 2 cross to bear. burden, grief, misfortune, problem, trial, tribulation, trouble. 3 cross of breeds. amalgam, combination, crossbreed, hybrid, mixture, mongrel.

● v 1 criss-cross, intersect, meet. 2 cross a river. bridge, ford, go across, traverse. 3 cross someone. annoy, block, frustrate, impede, oppose, thwart. **cross out** ▷ CANCEL. **cross swords** ▷ CONFLICT.

crossing v 1 bridge, causeway, flyover, ford, overpass, pedestrian crossing, underpass. 2 sea crossing. ▷ JOURNEY.

crossroads n interchange, intersection, junction.

crouch v bend, cower, cringe, duck, squat, stoop.

crowd n 1 assembly, bunch, cluster, collection, company, crush, flock, gathering, horde, mob, multitude, pack, swarm, throng. ▷ GROUP. 2 football crowd. audience, spectators. ● v assemble, cluster, collect, compress, congregate, cram, flock, gather, jostle, mass, muster, overcrowd, pack, inf pile, press, push, squeeze, swarm, throng.

crowded adj congested, cramped, full, jammed, jostling, overcrowded, overflowing, packed, teeming. Opp EMPTY.

crown n 1 circlet, coronet, tiara. 2 crown of a hill. apex, brow, peak, summit, top. ● v 1 anoint, appoint, enthrone, install. 2 complete, conclude, culminate, finish off, perfect, round off.

crucial adj central, critical, essential, important, momentous, pivotal. Opp UNIMPORTANT.

crude adj 1 natural, raw, unprocessed, unrefined. 2 crude work. amateurish, awkward, clumsy, inelegant, inept, makeshift, primitive, rough, rudimentary, unpolished, unskilful. Opp REFINED. 3 ▷ VULGAR.

cruel adj atrocious, barbaric, beastly, bestial, bloodthirsty, brutal, callous, cold-blooded, diabolical, ferocious, fiendish, fierce, grim, hard, hard-hearted, harsh, heartless, hellish, implacable, inhuman, malevolent, merciless, murderous, pitiless, relentless, ruthless, sadistic, savage, spiteful, tyrannical, unfeeling, unjust, unkind, unmerciful, unrelenting, vengeful, venomous, vicious, violent. Opp KIND.

cruelty n barbarity, brutality, callousness, cold-bloodedness, ferocity, heartlessness, inhumanity, malevolence, ruthlessness, sadism, savagery, unkindness, viciousness, violence.

cruise v coast, sail, travel, voyage. • n boat-trip, journey, passage, voyage.

crumb n bit, fragment, grain, morsel, particle, scrap, speck.

crumble v break into pieces, crush, decompose, deteriorate, disintegrate, fall apart, fragment, perish, powder, pulverize.

crumbly adj friable, granular, powdery. Opp SOLID.

crumple v crease, crush, dent, mangle, rumple, wrinkle.

crunch v chew, crush, grind, masticate, munch, scrunch, smash.

crusade n campaign, holy war, jihad, struggle, war.

crush n congestion, jam. ▷ CROWD. • v 1 break, bruise, compress, crunch, mangle, mash, pound, press, pulp, pulverize, smash, squeeze. 2 *crush opponents*. humiliate, mortify, overwhelm, rout, thrash, vanquish. ▷ CONQUER.

crust n incrustation, outer layer, rind, scab, shell, skin, surface. ▷ COVERING.

crux n centre, core, crucial issue, essence, nub.

cry n bellow, call, caterwaul, exclamation, howl, roar, scream, shout, shriek, whoop, yell. • v bawl, blubber, shed tears, snivel, sob, weep, inf whinge. **cry off** ▷ WITHDRAW. **cry out** ▷ SHOUT.

crypt n catacomb, cellar, grave, sepulchre, tomb, vault.

cryptic adj arcane, coded, enigmatic, hidden, mysterious, mystical, obscure, perplexing, recondite, secret, unintelligible, veiled. Opp INTELLIGIBLE.

cuddle v caress, clasp lovingly, embrace, fondle, hold closely, hug, make love, nestle against, nurse, pet, snuggle up to.

cudgel n baton, bludgeon, club, cosh, truncheon. • v batter, beat, bludgeon, inf clobber, cosh, pummel, thrash, thump. ▷ HIT.

cue n hint, prompt, sign, signal.

culminate v climax, conclude, reach a finale. ▷ END.

culpable adj criminal, guilty, liable, punishable, reprehensible, wrong. ▷ DELIBERATE. Opp INNOCENT.

culprit n miscreant, offender, troublemaker, wrongdoer. ▷ CRIMINAL.

cult n 1 craze, fan-club, fashion, party, trend, vogue. 2 *religious cult.* ▷ DENOMINATION.

cultivate v 1 dig, farm, manure, plough, prepare, till, turn, work. 2 grow, plant, produce, raise, take cuttings, tend. 3 *cultivate a friendship.* court, develop, encourage, foster, further, improve, promote, pursue.

cultivated adj 1 farmed, planted, prepared, tilled. 2 ▷ CULTURED.

cultivation n agriculture, agronomy, breeding, farming, gardening, horticulture, husbandry, nurturing.

cultural adj aesthetic, artistic, educational, enlightening, highbrow, intellectual.

culture n 1 art, civilization, customs, education, learning, traditions, way of life. 2 ▷ CULTIVATION.

cultured adj 1 civilized, discriminating, educated, elegant, erudite, refined, scholarly, sophisticated, well-bred, well-educated. Opp IGNORANT. 2 ▷ CULTIVATED.

cunning adj 1 devious, guileful, knowing, machiavellian, sly, subtle, tricky, wily. ▷ CRAFTY. 2 adroit, astute, ingenious, skilful. ▷ CLEVER. • n 1 artlessness, chicanery, craft, deceit, deviousness, duplicity, guile, trickery. 2 cleverness, expertise, ingenuity, skill.

cup n 1 mug, tankard, teacup. 2 award, prize, trophy.

cupboard n cabinet, chiffonier, closet, larder, locker, wardrobe.

curable adj remediable, treatable. Opp INCURABLE.

curb v check, control, deter, hinder, hold back, impede, inhibit, moderate, restrain, restrict, suppress. Opp ENCOURAGE.

curdle v clot, coagulate, congeal, go sour.

cure n 1 antidote, medication, medicine, palliative, panacea, prescription, remedy, therapy.

2 healing, recovery, restoration, revival. • v alleviate, correct, counteract, ease, inf fix, heal, mend, rectify, relieve, remedy, repair, treat. Opp AGGRAVATE.

curiosity n inquisitiveness, interest, interference, nosiness, inf snooping.

curious adj 1 inquiring, inquisitive, interested, puzzled, questioning, searching. 2 meddlesome, inf nosy, prying. 3 ▷ STRANGE. **be curious** ▷ PRY.

curl n coil, curve, kink, loop, ringlet, scroll, spiral, swirl, twist, whorl. • v 1 coil, corkscrew, entwine, loop, spiral, twist, wreathe, writhe. 2 curl your hair. crimp, frizz, perm.

curly adj crimped, curled, frizzy, permed, wavy. Opp STRAIGHT.

current adj 1 contemporary, existing, fashionable, living, modern, ongoing, present-day, prevailing, reigning, remaining, inf trendy, up-to-date. 2 current passport. valid. Opp OLD. • n course, drift, flow, river, tide, trend, undertow.

curriculum n course, programme of study, syllabus.

curse n blasphemy, expletive, imprecation, malediction, oath, profanity, swear word. Opp BLESSING. • v blaspheme, damn, swear. Opp BLESS. **cursed** ▷ HATEFUL.

cursory adj brief, careless, casual, desultory, hasty, perfunctory, slapdash, superficial. Opp THOROUGH.

curt adj abrupt, blunt, brief, brusque, crusty, gruff, monosyllabic, offhand, rude, short, succinct, tart, terse, uncommunicat-

ive, ungracious. ▷ RUDE.
Opp EXPANSIVE.

curtail *v* abbreviate, break off,
cut short, decrease, *inf* dock,
halt, lessen, restrict, shorten,
truncate. ▷ SHORTEN.
Opp EXTEND.

curtain *n* blind, drape, screen.
● *v* drape, mask, screen, veil.
▷ HIDE.

curtsy *v* bend the knee, bow,
genuflect.

curve *n* arc, arch, bend, bow,
bulge, circle, corkscrew, crescent, curl, loop, spiral, swirl, trajectory, turn, twist, undulation,
whorl. ● *v* arc, arch, bend, bow,
bulge, corkscrew, curl, loop,
snake, spiral, swerve, twist.
▷ CIRCLE.

curved *adj* concave, convex, crescent, crooked, curvy, rounded,
serpentine, sinuous, swelling,
tortuous, turned, undulating.

cushion *n* bolster, hassock, pad,
pillow. ● *v* absorb, deaden, insulate, mitigate, protect from,
reduce the effect of, support.

custodian *n* caretaker, curator,
guardian, keeper, warder,
inf watchdog, watchman.

custody *n* 1 care, guardianship,
observation, possession, preservation, protection, safe-keeping.
2 *in police custody*. confinement,
detention, imprisonment, incarceration, remand.

custom *n* 1 convention, etiquette, fashion, formality, habit,
institution, observance, policy,
practice, procedure, routine, tradition, way. 2 business, cus-
tomers, patronage, support,
trade.

customary *adj* accepted, accustomed, common, commonplace,

conventional, established, everyday, expected, fashionable, general, habitual, normal, ordinary,
popular, prevailing, regular, routine, traditional, typical, usual,
wonted *Opp* UNUSUAL.

customer *n* buyer, client, consumer, patron, purchaser, shopper. *Opp* SELLER.

cut *n* 1 gash, graze, incision,
laceration, nick, rent, rip, slash,
slit, snick, snip, stab, tear.
▷ INJURY. 2 *cut in prices.* cutback, decrease, fall, lowering,
reduction, saving.
● *v* 1 amputate, axe, carve,
chisel, chop, cleave, crop, dice,
dissect, divide, dock, engrave,
gash, gouge, grate, graze, guillotine, hack, halve, hew, incise,
knife, lacerate, lance, lop, mince,
mow, nick, notch, pierce, prune,
reap, saw, scalp, score, sever,
shave, shear, shred, slash, slice,
slit, snick, snip, split, stab, trim,
wound. 2 abbreviate, abridge,
censor, condense, edit, précis,
shorten, summarize, truncate.
▷ REDUCE. **cut and dried**
▷ DEFINITE. **cut in** ▷ INTER-
RUPT. **cut off** ▷ REMOVE,
STOP. **cut short** ▷ CURTAIL.

cutlery *n* knives, forks, and
spoons, silver, tableware.

cutting *adj* acute, biting, caustic,
incisive, keen, sarcastic, satirical, sharp. ▷ HURTFUL.

cycle *n* 1 circle, repetition,
revolution, rotation, sequence,
series. 2 bicycle, *inf* bike, moped,
inf motor bike, scooter. ● *v* travel
by cycle.

cyclic *adj* circular, recurring,
repeating, repetitive, rotating.

cynical *adj* doubting, *inf* hard,
incredulous, mocking, negative,

pessimistic, questioning, sceptical. *Opp* OPTIMISTIC.

D

dabble *v* 1 dip, paddle, splash. 2 *dabble in a hobby.* potter about, tinker, work casually.

dabbler *n* ▷ AMATEUR.

dagger *n* bayonet, blade, knife, stiletto.

daily *adj* diurnal, everyday, regular.

dainty *adj* 1 charming, delicate, exquisite, fine, meticulous, neat, pretty, skilful. 2 discriminating, fastidious, finicky, fussy, genteel, sensitive, squeamish, well-mannered. 3 *dainty morsel.* appealing, appetizing, choice, delectable, delicious. *Opp* CLUMSY, GROSS.

dally *v* dawdle, delay, *inf* dilly-dally, hang about, idle, linger, loaf, loiter, play about, procrastinate, *old use* tarry.

dam *n* bank, barrage, barrier, dyke, embankment, wall, weir. ● *v* block, check, hold back, obstruct, stanch, stem, stop.

damage *n* destruction, devastation, harm, havoc, injury, mutilation, sabotage. ● *v* 1 break, buckle, burst, *inf* bust, chip, crack, cripple, deface, destroy, disable, disfigure, harm, hurt, immobilize, impair, incapacitate, injure, make inoperative, make useless, mar, mark, mutilate, ruin, rupture, sabotage, scar, scratch, spoil, vandalize, warp, weaken, wound, wreck.

damaged ▷ FAULTY. **damages**

▷ COMPENSATION. **damaging** ▷ HARMFUL.

damn *v* attack, berate, castigate, condemn, criticize, curse, denounce, doom, execrate, swear at.

damnation *n* doom, everlasting fire, hell, perdition, ruin. *Opp* SALVATION.

damp *adj* clammy, dank, dripping, drizzly, foggy, humid, misty, moist, muggy, perspiring, rainy, soggy, steamy, sticky, sweaty, unaired, unventilated, wet. *Opp* DRY. ● *v* 1 dampen, moisten, sprinkle. 2 ▷ DISCOURAGE.

dance *n* disco, ball, party. ● *v* caper, cavort, frisk, frolic, gambol, hop about, jig, leap, prance, sway, whirl.

danger *n* 1 hazard, insecurity, jeopardy, menace, peril, pitfall, trouble. 2 chance, possibility, risk, threat.

dangerous *adj* 1 critical, destructive, explosive, grave, harmful, hazardous, insecure, menacing, *inf* nasty, noxious, perilous, precarious, reckless, risky, threatening, toxic, unsafe. 2 *dangerous men.* desperate, ruthless, treacherous, unmanageable, unpredictable, violent, volatile, wild. *Opp* HARMLESS.

dangle *v* be suspended, flap, hang, sway, swing, trail, wave about.

dank *adj* chilly, clammy, damp, moist, unaired.

dappled *adj* blotchy, brindled, dotted, flecked, freckled, marbled, mottled, patchy, pied, speckled, spotted, stippled, streaked, variegated.

dare v 1 gamble, have the courage, risk, take a chance, venture. 2 challenge, defy, provoke, taunt. **daring** ▷ BOLD.

dark adj 1 black, cheerless, cloudy, dim, dingy, dismal, drab, dreary, dull, dusky, funereal, gloomy, glowering, glum, grim, inky, moonless, murky, overcast, pitch-black, pitch-dark, shadowy, shady, sombre, starless, sullen, sunless, unlit. 2 dark colours. dense, heavy, strong. 3 dark complexion. black, brown, dark-skinned, dusky, swarthy, tanned. 4 ▷ HIDDEN, MYSTERIOUS. Opp LIGHT, PALE.

darken v 1 become overcast, cloud over. 2 blacken, dim, eclipse, obscure, overshadow, shade. Opp LIGHTEN.

darling n beloved, inf blue-eyed boy, dear, dearest, favourite, honey, love, loved one, pet, sweetheart, true love.

dart n arrow, bolt, missile, shaft. • v bound, flit, fly, hurtle, leap, move suddenly, shoot, spring, streak, inf whiz, inf zip. ▷ DASH.

dash n race, run, rush, sprint, spurt. • v 1 bolt, chase, dart, fly, hasten, hurry, move quickly, rush, speed, tear, zoom. 2 ▷ HIT.

dashing adj dapper, dynamic, elegant, lively, smart, spirited, stylish, vigorous.

data pl n details, facts, figures, information, statistics.

date n 1 day. ▷ TIME. 2 date with a friend. appointment, assignation, engagement, meeting, rendezvous. **out-of-date** ▷ OBSOLETE. **up-to-date** ▷ MODERN.

daunt v deter, discourage, dishearten, dismay, intimidate, overawe, put off, unnerve. ▷ FRIGHTEN. Opp ENCOURAGE.

dawdle v be slow, dally, delay, inf dilly-dally, hang about, idle, lag behind, linger, loaf about, loiter, inf take your time, trail behind. ▷ HURRY.

dawn n daybreak, first light, sunrise. ▷ BEGINNING.

day n 1 daylight, daytime. 2 age, epoch, era, period, time.

daydream n fantasy, hope, illusion, meditation, reverie, vision, woolgathering. • v dream, fantasize, imagine, meditate.

daze v paralyse, shock, stun, stupefy. ▷ AMAZE.

dazzle v blind, confuse, disorientate. **dazzling** ▷ BRILLIANT.

dead adj 1 deceased, inf done for, inanimate, inert, killed, late, lifeless, perished, rigid, stiff. Opp ALIVE. 2 dead language. died out, extinct, obsolete. 3 dead with cold. insensitive, numb, paralysed, without feeling. 4 dead battery, engine. burnt out, defunct, flat, inoperative, not working, out of order, unresponsive, used up, useless, worn out. 5 dead party. boring, dull, slow, uninteresting. Opp LIVELY. 6 dead centre. ▷ EXACT. **dead person** ▷ CORPSE. **dead to the world** ▷ ASLEEP.

deaden v 1 anaesthetize, desensitize, numb, paralyse. 2 blunt, cushion, damp, dampen, diminish, lessen, muffle, mute, quieten, reduce, smother, soften, stifle, suppress, weaken.

deadlock n impasse, stalemate, standstill, stop, stoppage, tie.

deadly adj dangerous, fatal, lethal, mortal, noxious, terminal. ▷ HARMFUL.

deafen v drown out, make deaf, overwhelm. **deafening** ▷ LOUD.

deal n 1 agreement, arrangement, bargain, contract, pact, understanding. 2 amount, quantity, volume. ● v 1 allot, dispense, distribute, divide, inf dole out, give out, share out. 2 deal someone a blow. administer, deliver, inflict, mete out. 3 deal in stocks and shares. buy and sell, do business, trade, traffic. deal with ▷ MANAGE, TREAT.

dealer n agent, broker, distributor, merchant, retailer, shopkeeper, trader, tradesman, vendor, wholesaler.

dear adj 1 adored, beloved, darling, intimate, loved, precious, treasured, valued. ▷ LOVABLE. Opp HATEFUL. 2 costly, exorbitant, expensive, high-priced, over-priced. Opp CHEAP. ● n ▷ DARLING.

death n 1 demise, dying, loss. ▷ END. 2 casualty, fatality. put to death ▷ EXECUTE.

debase v belittle, commercialize, degrade, demean, depreciate, devalue, diminish, reduce the value of, ruin, spoil, vulgarize.

debatable adj arguable, contentious, controversial, disputable, doubtful, dubious, open to question, problematic, questionable, uncertain, unsettled. Opp CERTAIN.

debate n argument, conference, consultation, controversy, deliberation, dialectic, discussion, disputation. ● v argue, consider, deliberate, discuss, dispute, mull over, question, reflect on, wrangle.

debit v subtract, take away. Opp CREDIT.

debris n bits, detritus, flotsam, fragments, litter, pieces, remains, rubbish, ruins, wreckage.

debt n account, arrears, bill, debit, dues, liability, obligation. in debt bankrupt, defaulting, insolvent. ▷ POOR.

decadent adj corrupt, debauched, declining, degenerate, immoral, self-indulgent. Opp MORAL.

decay v atrophy, break down, corrode, decompose, degenerate, deteriorate, disintegrate, dissolve, fester, go bad, mortify, moulder, oxidize, putrefy, rot, spoil, waste away, weaken, wither.

deceit n artifice, chicanery, craftiness, cunning, deceitfulness, dishonesty, dissimulation, duplicity, guile, hypocrisy, insincerity, lying, pretence, slyness, treachery, trickery, underhandedness, untruthfulness. ▷ DECEPTION. Opp HONESTY.

deceitful adj crafty, cunning, deceiving, deceptive, dishonest, double-dealing, duplicitous, false, fraudulent, furtive, insincere, lying, secretive, sneaky, treacherous, tricky, underhand, untrustworthy, wily. Opp HONEST.

deceive v inf bamboozle, beguile, betray, bluff, cheat, inf con, defraud, delude, inf double-cross, dupe, fool, inf fox, hoax, hoodwink, inf kid, inf lead on, lie, mislead, mystify, inf outsmart, outwit, swindle, inf take for a ride, take in, trick.

decelerate v brake, decrease speed, go slower, slow down. *Opp* ACCELERATE.

decent adj 1 appropriate, chaste, courteous, decorous, delicate, fitting, honourable, modest, polite, presentable, proper, respectable, seemly, sensitive, tasteful. *Opp* INDECENT. 2 agreeable, pleasant, satisfactory. ▷ GOOD. *Opp* BAD.

deception n charade, cheat, *inf* con, confidence trick, cover-up, *inf* fiddle, fraud, hoax, lie, pretence, ruse, sham, subterfuge, swindle, trick, wile. ▷ DECEIT.

deceptive adj ambiguous, deceiving, dishonest, equivocal, fallacious, false, fraudulent, illusory, insincere, lying, mendacious, misleading, specious, spurious, unreliable, wrong. *Opp* GENUINE.

decide v adjudicate, arbitrate, choose, conclude, determine, elect, judge, make up your mind, opt for, reach a decision, resolve, select, settle. **decided** ▷ DEFINITE.

decipher v disentangle, *inf* figure out, work out. ▷ DECODE.

decision n conclusion, decree, finding, judgement, outcome, ruling, verdict.

decisive adj 1 conclusive, convincing, crucial, final, positive, significant. 2 *decisive action*. certain, confident, definite, determined, firm, forceful, forthright, incisive, resolute, unhesitating. *Opp* TENTATIVE.

declaration n affirmation, announcement, assertion, avowal, confirmation, deposition, disclosure, edict, manifesto, proclamation, profession, pronouncement, protestation, statement, testimony.

declare v affirm, announce, assert, attest, avow, broadcast, certify, claim, confirm, contend, disclose, insist, maintain, make known, proclaim, profess, pronounce, protest, report, reveal, state, swear, testify.

decline n decrease, degeneration, deterioration, downturn, drop, fall, recession, reduction, slump. ● v 1 decrease, degenerate, deteriorate, die away, diminish, dwindle, ebb, fail, fall off, flag, lessen, peter out, reduce, slacken, subside, tail off, taper off, wane, weaken, wilt, worsen. *Opp* IMPROVE. 2 *decline an invitation*. abstain from, forgo, refuse, reject, *inf* turn down, veto. *Opp* ACCEPT.

decode v *inf* crack, decipher, explain, *inf* figure out, interpret, make out, read, solve, understand, unscramble.

decompose v break down, decay, disintegrate, *inf* go off, moulder, putrefy, rot.

decorate v 1 adorn, beautify, *old use* bedeck, colour, *inf* do up, embellish, embroider, festoon, garnish, ornament, paint, *derog* prettify, refurbish, renovate, smarten up, spruce up, trim, wallpaper. 2 give a medal to, honour, reward.

decoration n 1 adornment, elaboration, embellishment, finery, flourish, ornament, ornamentation, trimming. 2 award, badge, colours, medal, order, ribbon, star.

decorative adj elaborate, fancy, non-functional, ornamental, ornate. *Opp* FUNCTIONAL.

decorous *adj* appropriate, becoming, befitting, correct, dignified, genteel, polite, presentable, proper, refined, respectable, sedate, seemly, suitable, well-behaved. ▷ DECENT. *Opp* INDECOROUS.

decorum *n* decency, dignity, etiquette, good manners, gravity, modesty, politeness, propriety, protocol, respectability, seemliness.

decoy *n* bait, distraction, diversion, enticement, inducement, lure, red herring, trap. • *v* bait, draw, entice, inveigle, lead, lure, seduce, tempt, trick.

decrease *n* abatement, contraction, curtailment, cut, decline, diminution, downturn, drop, dwindling, easing-off, ebb, fall, falling off, lessening, lowering, reduction, shrinkage, wane. *Opp* INCREASE. • *v* 1 abate, cut, ease off, lower, reduce, turn down. 2 condense, contract, decline, die away, diminish, dwindle, lessen, peter out, shrink, slacken, subside, tail off, taper off, wane. *Opp* INCREASE.

decree *n* act, command, declaration, dictate, dictum, directive, edict, enactment, fiat, injunction, judgement, law, mandate, order, ordinance, proclamation, regulation, ruling, statute. • *v* command, decide, declare, determine, dictate, direct, order, prescribe, proclaim, promulgate, pronounce, rule.

decrepit *adj* battered, broken down, derelict, dilapidated, feeble, frail, ramshackle, tumbledown, weak, worn out. ▷ OLD.

dedicate *v* 1 commit, consecrate, devote, give, pledge, sanctify. 2 *dedicate a book.* address, inscribe. **dedicated** ▷ KEEN, LOYAL.

dedication *n* 1 allegiance, commitment, devotion, enthusiasm, faithfulness, fidelity, loyalty, single-mindedness, zeal. 2 inscription, legend.

deduce *v* conclude, divine, draw the conclusion, extrapolate, glean, infer, *inf* reason, surmise, *sl* suss out, understand, work out.

deduct *v* subtract, take away. *Opp* ADD.

deduction *n* 1 allowance, decrease, diminution, discount, reduction, subtraction, withdrawal. 2 conclusion, finding, inference, reasoning.

deed *n* 1 accomplishment, achievement, act, adventure, effort, endeavour, enterprise, exploit, feat, stunt, undertaking. 2 ▷ DOCUMENT.

deep *adj* 1 profound, unfathomable, unplumbed, yawning. 2 *deep feelings.* earnest, extreme, genuine, heartfelt, intense, serious, sincere. 3 *deep in thought.* absorbed, concentrating, engrossed, immersed, preoccupied, rapt, thoughtful. 4 *deep matters.* esoteric, intellectual, learned, obscure, recondite. ▷ DIFFICULT. 5 *deep sleep.* heavy, sound. 6 *deep colour.* dark, rich, strong, vivid. 7 *deep sound.* bass, booming, growling, low-pitched, resonant, reverberating, sonorous. *Opp* SHALLOW, SUPERFICIAL.

deface *v* blemish, damage, disfigure, harm, impair, injure, mar, mutilate, ruin, spoil, vandalize.

defeat *n* beating, downfall, *inf* drubbing, failure, humiliation, *inf* licking, overthrow, rebuff, repulse, rout, set-back, subjugation, thrashing, trouncing. *Opp* VICTORY. ● *v* beat, be victorious over, check, *inf* clobber, confound, conquer, crush, destroy, *inf* flatten, foil, frustrate, get the better of, *sl* hammer, *inf* lick, master, outdo, outwit, overcome, overpower, overthrow, overwhelm, prevail over, put down, quell, repulse, rout, ruin, *inf* smash, stop, subdue, subjugate, suppress, *inf* thrash, thwart, triumph over, vanquish, whip. *Opp* LOSE. **be defeated** ▷ LOSE. **defeated** ▷ UNSUCCESSFUL.

defect *n* blemish, (*computing*) bug, deficiency, error, failing, fault, flaw, imperfection, irregularity, mark, mistake, shortcoming, shortfall, spot, stain, weakness, weak point. ● *v* change sides, desert, go over.

defective *adj* broken, deficient, faulty, flawed, imperfect, incomplete, *inf* on the blink, unsatisfactory. *Opp* PERFECT.

defence *n* 1 deterrence, guard, protection, guard, security, shelter, shield. ▷ BARRIER. 2 alibi, apology, case, excuse, explanation, justification, plea, testimony, vindication.

defenceless *adj* exposed, helpless, insecure, powerless, unguarded, unprotected, vulnerable, weak.

defend *v* 1 fight for, fortify, guard, keep safe, preserve, protect, safeguard, screen, shelter, shield, *inf* stick up for, watch over. 2 champion, justify, plead for, speak up for, stand up for, support, uphold, vindicate. *Opp* ATTACK.

defendant *n* accused, appellant, offender, prisoner.

defensive *adj* 1 protective, wary, watchful. 2 apologetic, faint-hearted. *Opp* AGGRESSIVE.

defer *v* 1 adjourn, delay, hold over, postpone, prorogue (*parliament*), put off, *inf* shelve, suspend. 2 ▷ YIELD.

deference *n* acquiescence, compliance, obedience, submission. ▷ RESPECT.

defiant *adj* antagonistic, belligerent, bold, brazen, challenging, daring, disobedient, headstrong, insolent, insubordinate, mutinous, obstinate, rebellious, recalcitrant, self-willed, stubborn, truculent, uncooperative, unruly, unyielding. *Opp* COOPERATIVE.

deficient *adj* defective, inadequate, insufficient, lacking, scanty, scarce, short, unsatisfactory, wanting, weak. *Opp* ADEQUATE, EXCESSIVE.

defile *v* contaminate, corrupt, degrade, desecrate, dirty, dishonour, foul, poison, pollute, soil, stain, sully, taint, tarnish.

define *v* 1 be the boundary of, bound, circumscribe, delineate, demarcate, describe, fix, limit, mark off, mark out, outline, specify. 2 *define a word*. explain, formulate, give the meaning of, interpret, spell out.

definite *adj* assured, categorical, certain, clear, clear-cut, confident, confirmed, cut and dried, decided, determined, distinct, emphatic, exact, explicit, fixed, incisive, marked, noticeable, obvious, particular, perceptible, positive, precise, pronounced, settled, specific, sure, unambiguous, unequivocal, unmistakable, well-defined. Opp VAGUE.

definitely adv beyond doubt, certainly, doubtless, for certain, indubitably, positively, surely, unquestionably, without doubt, without fail.

definition n 1 elucidation, explanation, interpretation. 2 clarity, clearness, focus, precision, sharpness.

definitive adj agreed, authoritative, complete, conclusive, correct, decisive, final, last (word), official, reliable, settled, standard, ultimate. Opp PROVISIONAL.

deflect v avert, deviate, divert, fend off, head off, intercept, parry, sidetrack, swerve, turn aside, veer, ward off.

deformed adj bent, buckled, contorted, crippled, crooked, disfigured, distorted, gnarled, grotesque, malformed, mangled, misshapen, mutilated, twisted, ugly, warped.

defraud v inf con, inf diddle, embezzle, fleece, rob, swindle. ▷ CHEAT.

deft adj adept, adroit, agile, clever, dexterous, expert, neat, inf nifty, nimble, proficient, quick, skilful. Opp CLUMSY.

defy v 1 challenge, confront, dare, disobey, rebel against, refuse to obey, resist, stand up to, withstand. 2 baffle, beat, elude, foil, frustrate, repel, repulse, resist, thwart, withstand.

degenerate adj ▷ CORRUPT. ● v become worse, decline, deteriorate, retrogress, sink, weaken, worsen. Opp IMPROVE.

degrade v 1 demote, depose, downgrade. 2 abase, brutalize,

cheapen, corrupt, debase, dehumanize, deprave, desensitize, dishonour, humiliate. **degrading** ▷ SHAMEFUL.

degree n 1 calibre, class, grade, order, position, rank, standard, standing, station, status. 2 extent, intensity, level, measure.

deify v idolize, treat as a god, venerate, worship.

deign v concede, condescend, demean yourself, lower yourself, stoop.

deity n divinity, god, goddess, godhead, idol, immortal, spirit, supreme being.

dejected adj depressed, disconsolate, dispirited, downhearted, heavy-hearted, in low spirits. ▷ SAD.

delay n check, deferment, hiatus, hitch, hold-up, interruption, pause, postponement, set-back, stay (of execution), stoppage, wait. ● v 1 defer, detain, halt, hinder, hold up, impede, keep back, keep waiting, obstruct, postpone, put off, retard, set back, slow down, stay, stop, suspend. 2 be late, be slow, dally, dawdle, inf drag your feet, inf get bogged down, hang about, hang back, hang fire, hesitate, loiter, mark time, pause, inf play for time, procrastinate, stall, old use tarry, temporize, vacillate. Opp HURRY.

delegate n agent, ambassador, emissary, envoy, go-between, legate, messenger, representative, spokesperson. ● v appoint, assign, authorize, charge, commission, depute, entrust, mandate, nominate.

delegation n commission, deputation, mission.

delete v blot out, cancel, cross out, cut out, efface, eliminate, eradicate, erase, expunge, obliterate, remove, rub out, wipe out.

deliberate adj 1 arranged, calculated, cold-blooded, conscious, contrived, intentional, malicious, organized, planned, prearranged, preconceived, premeditated, prepared, purposeful, studied, thought out, wilful, worked out. 2 careful, cautious, circumspect, considered, diligent, measured, methodical, orderly, painstaking, regular, slow, thoughtful, unhurried. *Opp* HASTY, INSTINCTIVE. • v ▷ THINK.

delicacy n accuracy, care, cleverness, daintiness, discrimination, exquisiteness, fineness, finesse, fragility, intricacy, precision, sensitivity, subtlety, tact.

delicate adj 1 dainty, easily broken, easily damaged, elegant, exquisite, fine, flimsy, fragile, frail, gauzy, gentle, feathery, intricate, light, sensitive, soft, tender. *Opp* TOUGH. 2 *delicate work*. accurate, careful, clever, deft, precise, skilled. *Opp* CLUMSY. 3 *delicate flavour, colour*. faint, muted, pale, slight, subtle. 4 *delicate health*. feeble, puny, sickly, squeamish, unhealthy, weak. 5 *delicate situation*. awkward, confidential, embarrassing, private, problematic, ticklish, touchy. 6 *delicate handling*. considerate, diplomatic, discreet, judicious, prudent, sensitive, tactful. *Opp* CRUDE.

delicious adj appetizing, choice, delectable, enjoyable, luscious, *inf* mouth-watering, savoury, *inf* scrumptious, succulent, tasty, tempting, *sl* yummy.

delight n bliss, delectation, ecstasy, enchantment, enjoyment, felicity, gratification, happiness, joy, pleasure, rapture, satisfaction. • v amuse, bewitch, captivate, charm, cheer, enchant, entertain, enthral, entrance, fascinate, gladden, gratify, please, thrill, transport. *Opp* DISMAY. **delighted** ▷ HAPPY, PLEASED.

delightful adj agreeable, attractive, captivating, charming, congenial, delectable, enjoyable, *inf* nice, pleasant, pleasing, pleasurable, rewarding, satisfying. ▷ BEAUTIFUL.

delinquent n culprit, hooligan, lawbreaker, malefactor, miscreant, offender, roughneck, ruffian, *inf* tearaway, vandal, wrongdoer.

delirious adj *inf* beside yourself, crazy, demented, distracted, ecstatic, excited, feverish, frantic, frenzied, hysterical, incoherent, light-headed, rambling, wild. ▷ DRUNK, MAD. *Opp* SANE, SOBER.

deliver v 1 bear, bring, carry, convey, distribute, give out, hand over, present, purvey, supply, surrender, take round, transfer, transport, turn over. 2 *deliver a lecture*. broadcast, express, give, make, read. ▷ SPEAK. 3 *deliver a blow*. administer, aim, deal, direct, fire, inflict, launch, strike, throw. ▷ HIT. 4 ▷ RESCUE.

delivery n 1 dispatch, distribution, shipment, transmission, transportation. 2 *delivery of goods*. batch, consignment. 3 *delivery of a speech*. execution,

performance, presentation.
4 childbirth, confinement,
parturition.

deluge n downpour, flood,
inundation, rainfall, rainstorm,
spate. • v drown, engulf, flood,
inundate, overwhelm, submerge,
swamp.

delusion n dream, fantasy, hallucination, illusion, mirage, misconception, self-deception.

delve v burrow, dig, explore,
investigate, probe, search.

demand n old use behest, claim,
command, desire, expectation,
importunity, need, order,
request, requirement, requisition, want. • v call for, claim, cry
out for, exact, insist on, order,
request, require, requisition.
▷ ASK. **demanding**
▷ DIFFICULT, IMPORTANATE. **in
demand** ▷ POPULAR.

demean v cheapen, debase,
degrade, disgrace, humble, humiliate, lower, make (yourself)
cheap, sacrifice (your) pride,
undervalue. **demeaning**
▷ SHAMEFUL.

democratic adj 1 classless,
egalitarian. 2 chosen, elected,
popular, representative.
Opp TOTALITARIAN.

demolish v bulldoze, dismantle,
flatten, knock down, level, raze,
tear down, wreck. ▷ DESTROY.
Opp BUILD.

demon n devil, evil spirit, fiend,
goblin, imp, spirit.

demonstrable adj conclusive,
confirmable, evident, incontro-,
vertible, indisputable, irrefutable, palpable, provable, undeniable, unquestionable, verifiable.

demonstrate v 1 display,
embody, establish, evince, exem-

plify, exhibit, explain, express,
illustrate, indicate, manifest,
prove, represent, show, substantiate, teach, typify, verify.
2 lobby, march, parade, picket,
protest, rally.

demonstration n 1 confirmation, display, exhibition, experiment, expression, illustration,
indication, manifestation,
presentation, proof, representation, substantiation, test, verification. 2 inf demo, march,
parade, picket, protest, rally,
sit-in, vigil.

demonstrative adj affectionate,
effusive, emotional, fulsome,
loving, open, uninhibited, unreserved. Opp RETICENT.

demote v downgrade, reduce,
relegate. Opp PROMOTE.

demure adj bashful, coy, diffident, modest, prim, reserved, reticent, sedate, shy, sober, staid.
Opp CONCEITED.

den n hideaway, inf hideout,
hiding-place, lair, retreat, sanctuary, secret place, shelter.

denial n abnegation, disavowal,
disclaimer, negation, refutation,
rejection, renunciation, repudi-
ation, veto. Opp ADMISSION.

denigrate v belittle, blacken the
reputation of, criticize, decry,
disparage, impugn, malign,
inf put down, inf run down,
sneer at, inf turn your nose up,
vilify. ▷ DESPISE. Opp PRAISE.

denomination n 1 category,
classification, designation, kind,
size, sort, species, type, value.
2 church, communion, creed,
cult, persuasion, schism, sect.

denote v be the sign for, designate, express, indicate, represent, signify, stand for,
symbolize.

denouement n climax, inf pay-off, resolution, solution, inf sorting out, inf tidying up. ▷ END.

denounce v accuse, attack verbally, betray, blame, censure, complain about, condemn, criticize, declaim against, inf hold forth against, impugn, incriminate, inform against, pillory, report, reveal, stigmatize, vilify, vituperate. Opp PRAISE.

dense adj 1 close, compact, concentrated, heavy, impassable, impenetrable, inf jam-packed, packed, solid, thick, tight. Opp THIN. 2 ▷ STUPID.

dent n concavity, depression, dimple, dint, hollow, indentation. ● v bend, crumple, knock in.

denude v defoliate, deforest, expose, remove, strip, unclothe, uncover. Opp CLOTHE.

deny v 1 contradict, disagree with, disclaim, disown, dispute, gainsay, negate, refute, reject, repudiate. Opp AGREE. 2 begrudge, deprive of, disallow, refuse, withhold. Opp GRANT.

deny yourself ▷ ABSTAIN.

depart v 1 abscond, inf clear off, decamp, disappear, embark, exit, go away, sl hit the road, leave, make off, inf make tracks, inf make yourself scarce, migrate, move away, move off, inf push off, quit, retreat, run away, run off, sl scarper, sl scram, set off, set out, start, take your leave, vanish, withdraw. 2 ▷ DEVIATE. **departed** ▷ DEAD.

department n 1 branch, division, office, section, sector, subdivision, unit. 2 [inf] not my department. area, concern, field, function, job, line, province,

responsibility, specialism, sphere.

departure n disappearance, embarkation, exit, exodus, going, retirement, withdrawal. Opp ARRIVAL.

depend v 1 depend on inf bank on, count on, hinge on, need, put your faith in, inf reckon on, rely on, trust. 2 hang, dangle.

dependable adj conscientious, consistent, faithful, honest, regular, reliable, safe, steady, true, trustworthy, unfailing. Opp UNRELIABLE.

dependence n 1 need, reliance, trust. 2 ▷ ADDICTION.

dependent adj dependent on 1 conditional on, determined by, subject to, vulnerable to. Opp INDEPENDENT. 2 dependent on drugs. addicted to, inf hooked on, reliant on.

depict v describe, draw, illustrate, narrate, outline, paint, picture, portray, represent, reproduce, show.

deplete v consume, cut, decrease, drain, reduce, use up. Opp INCREASE.

deplorable adj awful, discreditable, disgraceful, disreputable, dreadful, execrable, lamentable, regrettable, reprehensible, scandalous, shameful, shocking, unfortunate. ▷ BAD. Opp COMMENDABLE.

deplore v 1 lament, mourn, regret. 2 ▷ CONDEMN.

deploy v arrange, distribute, manage, position, use systematically, utilize.

deport v banish, exile, expatriate, expel, send abroad, transport.

depose v demote, dethrone, displace, get rid of, oust, remove, inf topple.

deposit n 1 advance payment, down-payment, initial payment, part-payment, retainer, security. 2 accumulation, dregs, layer, precipitate, sediment, silt, sludge. • v 1 drop, dump, leave, inf place, put down, set down. 2 deposit money. bank, pay in, save.

depot n 1 arsenal, cache, depository, dump, store, storehouse. 2 bus depot. garage, headquarters, station, terminus.

deprave v brutalize, corrupt, debase, degrade. **depraved** ▷ CORRUPT.

depreciate v become less, decrease, deflate, drop, fall, lessen, reduce, slump, weaken. Opp APPRECIATE.

depress v 1 burden, discourage, dishearten, dismay, dispirit, enervate, lower the spirits of, oppress, sadden, tire, upset, weary. Opp CHEER. 2 depress the market. bring down, deflate, make less active, push down, weaken. Opp BOOST. **depressed**, **depressing** ▷ SAD.

depression n 1 inf blues, dejection, desolation, despair, despondency, gloom, glumness, hopelessness, low spirits, melancholy, misery, pessimism, sadness, weariness. Opp HAPPINESS. 2 cavity, concavity, dent, dimple, dip, excavation, hole, hollow, indentation, recess, sunken area. Opp BUMP. 3 economic depression. decline, hard times, recession, slump. Opp BOOM, HIGH.

deprive v deprive of deny, prevent from using, refuse, starve

of, strip of, take away, withdraw, withhold. **deprived** ▷ POOR.

deputize v deputize for act as stand-in for, cover for, do the job of, replace, represent, stand in for, substitute for, take over from, understudy.

deputy n agent, assistant, delegate, emissary, inf locum, proxy, relief, replacement, representative, reserve, second-in-command, stand-in, substitute, supply, surrogate, understudy, vice-president.

derelict adj abandoned, broken down, decrepit, deserted, desolate, dilapidated, forsaken, neglected, overgrown, ruined, run-down, tumbledown, uncared-for, untended.

derivation n ancestry, descent, etymology, extraction, origin. ▷ BEGINNING.

derive v draw, extract, gain, gather, get, glean, inf lift, obtain, pick up, procure, receive, secure, take. **be derived** ▷ ORIGINATE.

descend v 1 climb down, come down, drop, fall, move down, plummet, plunge, sink. 2 dip, incline, slant, slope. 3 alight, dismount, get down, get off. Opp ASCEND. **be descended** ▷ ORIGINATE. **descend on** ▷ ATTACK.

descendant n child, heir, scion, successor. Opp ANCESTOR. **descendants** family, issue, line, lineage, offspring, progeny.

descent n 1 declivity, dip, drop, fall, incline, slant, slope, way down. Opp ASCENT. 2 aristocratic descent. ancestry, extraction, family, genealogy, heredity, lin-

eage, parentage, pedigree, stock.
▷ ORIGIN.

describe v 1 characterize, define, delineate, depict, detail, explain, give an account of, narrate, outline, portray, present, recount, relate, report, represent, sketch, speak of. 2 *describe a circle.* draw, mark out, trace.

description n account, characterization, commentary, definition, delineation, depiction, explanation, narration, outline, portrait, report, representation, sketch, story.

descriptive adj detailed, explanatory, expressive, graphic, illustrative, vivid.

desecrate v contaminate, corrupt, debase, defile, degrade, dishonour, pervert, pollute, profane, treat disrespectfully, treat irreverently, vandalize, violate. Opp REVERE.

desert adj arid, barren, desolate, infertile, isolated, lonely, sterile, uncultivated, uninhabited, waterless. Opp FERTILE. ● n dust bowl, wasteland, wilderness. ● v 1 abandon, betray, forsake, jilt, *inf* leave in the lurch, maroon, renounce, strand, vacate, *inf* wash your hands of. 2 abscond, defect, go absent, run away. **deserted** ▷ EMPTY, LONELY.

deserter n absconder, betrayer, defector, escapee, fugitive, outlaw, renegade, runaway, traitor, truant, turncoat.

deserve v be worthy of, earn, justify, merit, rate, warrant. **deserving** ▷ WORTHY.

design n 1 blueprint, conception, drawing, model, pattern, plan, proposal, prototype, sketch. 2 style, type, version.

3 arrangement, composition, configuration, form, pattern, shape. 4 aim, goal, intention, objective, purpose. ● v conceive, construct, create, devise, draft, draw, draw up, fashion, form, intend, invent, lay out, make, originate, plan, plot, project, propose, shape. **designing** ▷ CRAFTY. **have designs** ▷ PLOT.

designer n architect, artist, creator, inventor, originator.

desire n 1 ambition, appetite, craving, fancy, hankering, hunger, longing, urge, want, wish, yearning, *inf* yen. 2 covetousness, cupidity, greed. 3 *sexual desire.* ardour, libido, love, lust, passion. ● v ache for, ask for, covet, crave, dream of, fancy, *inf* have a yen for, hope for, hunger for, itch for, long for, lust after, need, pursue, *inf* set your heart on, want, wish for, yearn for.

desolate adj 1 abandoned, bare, barren, bleak, cheerless, deserted, dismal, dreary, empty, forsaken, gloomy, godforsaken, inhospitable, isolated, lonely, remote, uninhabited, wild. 2 dejected, depressed, despairing, disconsolate, forlorn, forsaken, inconsolable, lonely, melancholy, miserable, neglected, solitary, wretched. ▷ SAD. Opp CHEERFUL.

despair n anguish, depression, desperation, despondency, hopelessness, pessimism, resignation, wretchedness. ▷ MISERY. ● v give in, give up, lose heart, lose hope. Opp HOPE.

desperate adj 1 *inf* at your wits' end, beyond hope, despairing, wretched. 2 *desperate situation.*

acute, critical, dangerous, grave, hopeless, irretrievable, pressing, serious, severe, urgent.
3 *desperate criminals.* dangerous, impetuous, rash, reckless, violent, wild. **4** ▷ ANXIOUS.

despise *v* be contemptuous of, condemn, deride, disapprove of, disdain, feel contempt for, hate, look down on, scorn, spurn, undervalue. ▷ DENIGRATE.
Opp ADMIRE.

despondent *adj* dejected, depressed, disheartened, downcast, *inf* down in the mouth, melancholy, morose, pessimistic, sorrowful. ▷ MISERABLE.

despotic *adj* ▷ DICTATORIAL.
Opp DEMOCRATIC.

destination *n* goal, objective, purpose, target.

destined *adj* **1** inescapable, inevitable, intended, ordained, predetermined, unavoidable.
2 *destined to fail.* bound, certain, doomed.

destiny *n* doom, fate, fortune, karma, kismet, luck, providence.

destitute *adj* deprived, down-and-out, homeless, impecunious, impoverished, penniless, poverty-stricken. ▷ POOR.
Opp WEALTHY.

destroy *v* annihilate, blast, break down, burst, *inf* bust, crush, decimate, demolish, devastate, devour, dismantle, eliminate, eradicate, erase, exterminate, extinguish, flatten, get rid of, knock down, lay waste, level, liquidate, nullify, pull down, pulverize, raze, ruin, sabotage, scuttle, shatter, smash, stamp out, uproot, vaporize, wipe out, wreck, write off. ▷ DEFEAT, END, KILL. *Opp* CONSERVE, CREATE.

destruction *n* annihilation, decimation, demolition, depredation, devastation, elimination, eradication, extermination, extinction, liquidation, overthrow, ruin, ruination, shattering, smashing, undoing, uprooting, wiping out, wrecking. ▷ KILLING. *Opp* CONSERVATION, CREATION.

destructive *adj* adverse, antagonistic, baleful, catastrophic, damaging, dangerous, deadly, deleterious, detrimental, devastating, disastrous, fatal, harmful, injurious, lethal, malignant, negative, pernicious, pestilential, ruinous, violent.
Opp CONSTRUCTIVE.

detach *v* cut loose, cut off, disconnect, disengage, disentangle, free, isolate, pull off, release, remove, separate, sever, take off, tear off, uncouple, undo, unfasten, unfix, unhitch.
Opp ATTACH. **detached**
▷ ALOOF, IMPARTIAL, SEPARATE.

detail *n* aspect, complexity, complication, component, element, fact, factor, feature, intricacy, item, *pl* minutiae, nicety, particular, point, refinement, specific, technicality.

detailed *adj* *inf* blow-by-blow, complete, complex, comprehensive, descriptive, exact, exhaustive, full, *derog* fussy, *derog* hair-splitting, intricate, itemized, minute, specific. *Opp* GENERAL.

detain *v* **1** arrest, capture, confine, hold, imprison, intern.
2 delay, hinder, hold up, impede, keep, keep waiting, restrain, slow, waylay.

detect *v* ascertain, become aware of, diagnose, discern, discover, expose, feel, *inf* ferret out, find, identify, locate, note, observe, perceive, recognize, reveal, scent, see, sense, sniff out, spy, taste, track down, uncover, unearth.

detective n investigator, police officer, inf private eye, sleuth.

detention n captivity, confinement, custody, imprisonment, incarceration, internment.

deter v check, daunt, discourage, dismay, dissuade, hinder, impede, intimidate, obstruct, prevent, put off, repel, inf turn off, warn off. Opp ENCOURAGE.

deteriorate v decay, decline, degenerate, depreciate, disintegrate, fall off, get worse, inf go downhill, slip, weaken, worsen. Opp IMPROVE.

determination n backbone, commitment, courage, dedication, doggedness, firmness, fortitude, inf grit, inf guts, perseverance, persistence, resoluteness, resolve, single-mindedness, spirit, steadfastness, derog stubbornness, tenacity, will-power.

determine v 1 conclude, decide, establish, find out, identify, judge, settle. 2 choose, decide on, resolve, select. 3 What determined your choice? affect, dictate, govern, influence, regulate.

determined adj adamant, assertive, certain, convinced, decided, decisive, definite, dogged, firm, insistent, intent, derog obstinate, persistent, purposeful, resolute, single-minded, steadfast, strong-minded, strong-willed, derog stubborn, sure, tenacious, tough, unwavering. Opp IRRESOLUTE.

deterrent n barrier, check, curb, discouragement, disincentive, hindrance, impediment, obs-tacle, restraint, threat, warning. Opp ENCOURAGEMENT.

detest v abhor, abominate, despise, execrate, loathe. ▷ HATE.

detour n deviation, diversion, indirect route. **make a detour** ▷ DEVIATE.

detract v **detract from** diminish, lessen, lower, reduce, take away from.

detrimental adj damaging, deleterious, disadvantageous, harmful, hurtful, injurious, prejudicial, unfavourable. Opp ADVANTAGEOUS.

devastate v 1 damage severely, demolish, destroy, flatten, lay waste, level, obliterate, ravage, raze, ruin, waste, wreck. 2 ▷ DISMAY.

develop v 1 advance, age, inf blow up, come into existence, evolve, grow, flourish, improve, mature, move on, progress, ripen. Opp REGRESS. 2 develop habits. acquire, contract, cultivate, evolve, foster, pick up. 3 develop ideas. amplify, augment, elaborate, enlarge on. 4 develop a business. branch out, build up, diversify, enlarge, expand, extend, increase.

development n 1 advancement, enlargement, evolution, expansion, extension, furtherance, growth, improvement, increase, progress, promotion, regeneration, reinforcement, spread. 2 incident, occurrence, outcome, result, upshot.

deviate v branch off, digress, diverge, divert, drift, go astray, go round, make a detour; stray, swerve, turn aside, turn off, veer, wander.

device n 1 apparatus, appliance, contraption, contrivance, gadget, implement, invention, machine, tool, utensil. **2** expedient, gambit, manoeuvre, plan, ploy, ruse, scheme, stratagem, tactic, trick. **3** *heraldic device*. badge, crest, design, logo, motif, symbol.

devil *n* demon, fiend, imp, spirit. **The Devil** Beelzebub, Lucifer, *inf* Old Nick, the Prince of Darkness, Satan.

devilish *adj* demoniac(al), demonic, diabolic(al), fiendish, impish, inhuman, satanic. ▷ EVIL. *Opp* SAINTLY.

devious *adj* **1** circuitous, crooked, indirect, periphrastic, round-about, sinuous, tortuous, winding. **2** [*derog*] calculating, cunning, deceitful, evasive, insincere, misleading, scheming, slippery, sly, sneaky, treacherous, underhand, wily. ▷ DISHONEST. *Opp* DIRECT.

devise *v* arrange, conceive, concoct, contrive, *inf* cook up, create, design, formulate, invent, make up, plan, plot, prepare, project, scheme, think up, work out.

devoted *adj* committed, dedicated, enthusiastic, faithful, loving, staunch, true, zealous. ▷ LOYAL. *Opp* DISLOYAL, HALF-HEARTED.

devotee *n inf* addict, aficionado, *inf* buff, enthusiast, fan, follower, supporter.

devotion *n* allegiance, attachment, commitment, dedication, *derog* fanaticism, fervour, loyalty, zeal. ▷ LOVE, PIETY.

devour *v* consume, demolish, eat up, engulf, swallow up, take in. ▷ DESTROY, EAT.

devout *adj* God-fearing, godly, holy, religious, sincere, spiritual. ▷ PIOUS. *Opp* IRRELIGIOUS.

dexterous *adj* adroit, agile, clever, deft, nimble, quick, skilful. *Opp* CLUMSY.

diabolical *adj* evil, fiendish, inhuman, satanic, wicked. ▷ DEVILISH. *Opp* SAINTLY.

diagnose *v* detect, determine, identify, isolate, name, recognize.

diagnosis *n* analysis, conclusion, explanation, identification, interpretation, verdict.

diagram *n* chart, drawing, figure, graph, illustration, outline, plan, representation, sketch, table.

dial *n* clock, digital display, face, instrument, speedometer.

dialect *n* accent, brogue, creole, idiom, language, patois, pronunciation, register, slang, tongue, vernacular.

dialogue *n inf* chat, *inf* chin-wag, communication, conversation, debate, discourse, discussion, exchange, interchange, intercourse, talk, *inf* tête-à-tête.

diary *n* appointment book, calendar, chronicle, engagement book, journal, log, record.

dictate *v* **1** read aloud, recite. **2** command, decree, enforce, give orders, impose, *inf* lay down the law, make the rules, order, prescribe.

dictator *n* autocrat, despot, tyrant. ▷ RULER.

dictatorial *adj* absolute, authoritarian, autocratic, *inf* bossy, despotic, dogmatic, dominant, domineering, imperious, intolerant, omnipotent, oppressive, overbearing, repressive, totalitarian, tyrannical, undemocratic. *Opp* DEMOCRATIC.

dictionary n glossary, lexicon, thesaurus, vocabulary.

didactic adj instructive, lecturing, pedagogic, pedantic.

die v 1 inf bite the dust, cease to exist, decease, depart, expire, inf give up the ghost, sl kick the bucket, pass away, sl peg out, perish, sl snuff it. 2 decline, decrease, die away, disappear, droop, dwindle, end, fade, fail, fizzle out, go out, languish, lessen, stop, subside, vanish, wane, weaken, wilt, wither.

diet n fare, food, intake, nourishment, nutriment, nutrition, sustenance. ● v inf cut down, fast, lose weight, ration yourself, reduce, slim.

differ v 1 be different, be distinct, contrast, deviate, diverge, vary. 2 argue, be at odds, be at variance, clash, conflict, contradict, disagree, dispute, dissent, fall out, quarrel. Opp AGREE.

difference n 1 alteration, change, comparison, contrast, deviation, dissimilarity, distinction, diversity, incompatibility, inconsistency, modification, variation, variety. Opp SIMILARITY. 2 argument, clash, conflict, controversy, debate, disagreement, dispute, dissent, quarrel, strife, tiff, wrangle. Opp AGREEMENT.

different adj 1 assorted, conflicting, contradictory, contrasting, discordant, disparate, dissimilar, divergent, diverse, heterogeneous, inconsistent, miscellaneous, mixed, multifarious, opposed, opposite, varied, various. Opp SIMILAR. 2 abnormal, anomalous, atypical, bizarre, distinct, distinctive, eccentric, extraordinary, fresh, individual, new, original, particular, peculiar, separate, singular, special, specific, strange, uncommon, unconventional, unique, unorthodox, unusual. Opp CONVENTIONAL.

differentiate v discriminate, distinguish.

difficult adj 1 baffling, complex, complicated, deep, enigmatic, hard, intractable, intricate, involved, inf knotty, obscure, perplexing, problematic, inf thorny, ticklish, tricky. 2 arduous, back-breaking, burdensome, challenging, daunting, demanding, exacting, formidable, gruelling, heavy, herculean, laborious, onerous, punishing, rigorous, severe, strenuous, taxing, tough. 3 difficult children. annoying, disruptive, fussy, headstrong, intractable, obstinate, obstreperous, tiresome, troublesome, trying, uncooperative, unfriendly, unhelpful, unresponsive, unruly. Opp COOPERATIVE, EASY.

difficulty n adversity, complication, dilemma, embarrassment, inf fix, hardship, hindrance, hurdle, impediment, inf jam, inf mess, obstacle, perplexity, inf pickle, plight, predicament, problem, puzzle, quandary, snag, inf spot, stumbling block, tribulation, trouble.

diffident adj backward, bashful, coy, distrustful, doubtful, fearful, hesitant, inhibited, insecure, introvert, meek, modest, nervous, private, reluctant, reserved, retiring, self-effacing, sheepish, shrinking, shy, tentative, timid, timorous, unadventurous, unas-

suming, unsure, withdrawn.
Opp CONFIDENT.

diffuse adj discursive, long-
winded, meandering, rambling,
spread out, unstructured, vague,
inf waffly, wandering. ▷ WORDY.
Opp CONCISE. • v ▷ SPREAD.

dig v 1 burrow, delve, excavate,
gouge, hollow, mine, quarry,
tunnel. 2 cultivate, fork over,
till, trench, turn over. 3 jab,
nudge, poke, prod, punch, shove.
dig out ▷ FIND. **dig up** disinter,
exhume.

digest n ▷ SUMMARY.
• v 1 absorb, assimilate, dissolve,
process, utilize. ▷ EAT.
2 consider, ponder, study, take
in, understand.

digit n 1 figure, integer, number,
numeral. 2 finger, toe.

dignified adj august, calm,
courtly, decorous, distinguished,
elegant, exalted, formal, grave,
imposing, impressive, lofty,
lordly, majestic, noble, proper,
refined, regal, sedate, serious,
sober, solemn, stately. ▷ PROUD.
Opp UNBECOMING.

dignitary n important person,
luminary, official, inf VIP,
worthy.

dignity n calmness, decorum,
formality, grandeur, gravity,
majesty, nobility, propriety,
respectability, seriousness, sobriety, solemnity, stateliness.

digress v depart, deviate,
diverge, drift, get off the subject,
inf lose the thread, ramble,
stray, veer, wander.

dilapidated adj broken down,
crumbling, decayed, decrepit,
derelict, falling down, in disrepair, in ruins, neglected, ramshackle, rickety, ruined, run-

down, shaky, tumbledown,
uncared-for.

dilemma n inf catch-22, deadlock, difficulty, inf fix, impasse,
inf jam, inf pickle, plight, predicament, problem, quandary,
stalemate.

diligent adj assiduous, busy,
careful, conscientious, devoted,
earnest, hardworking, indefatigable, industrious, meticulous,
painstaking, persevering, persistent, punctilious, scrupulous,
sedulous, studious, thorough,
tireless. Opp LAZY.

dilute v adulterate, reduce the
strength of, thin, water down,
weaken. Opp CONCENTRATE.

dim adj 1 bleary, blurred,
clouded, cloudy, dark, dull,
faint, foggy, fuzzy, gloomy, grey,
hazy, ill-defined, indistinct,
misty, murky, nebulous,
obscure, pale, shadowy, sombre,
unclear, vague. 2 ▷ STUPID.
Opp BRIGHT. • v 1 blacken, cloud,
darken, dull, obscure, shade,
shroud. 2 become dim, fade, go
out. Opp BRIGHTEN. **take a dim
view** ▷ DISAPPROVE.

dimensions pl n capacity,
extent, magnitude, measurements, proportions, scale, scope,
size.

diminish v 1 abate, contract,
decline, decrease, depreciate, die
down, dwindle, ease off, ebb,
fade, lessen, inf let up, peter out,
recede, reduce, shrink, subside,
wane, inf wind down.
Opp INCREASE. 2 belittle,
demean, deprecate, devalue, disparage, minimize, undervalue.
Opp EXAGGERATE.

diminutive adj microscopic,
miniature, minuscule, minute,
tiny. ▷ SMALL.

din n clamour, clatter, commotion, crash, hubbub, hullabaloo, noise, outcry, pandemonium, racket, roar, inf row, inf rumpus, shouting, tumult, uproar.

dingy adj colourless, dark, depressing, dim, dirty, dismal, drab, dreary, dull, faded, gloomy, grimy, murky, old, seedy, shabby, soiled, worn. Opp BRIGHT.

dinner n banquet, feast.
▷ MEAL.

dip n 1 concavity, declivity, dent, depression, fall, hollow, incline, slope. 2 dip in the sea. bathe, dive, immersion, plunge, swim. • v 1 decline, descend, dive, fall, go down, sag, sink, slope down, slump, subside. 2 douse, drop, duck, dunk, immerse, lower, plunge, submerge. take a dip ▷ BATHE.

diplomacy n delicacy, discretion, finesse, negotiation, skill, tact.

diplomat n ambassador, consul, negotiator, official, peacemaker, politician, statesman.

diplomatic adj careful, delicate, discreet, judicious, polite, politic, prudent, sensitive, subtle, tactful, understanding. Opp TACTLESS.

direct adj 1 non-stop, shortest, straight, undeviating, unswerving. 2 blunt, candid, clear, decided, explicit, forthright, frank, honest, open, outspoken, plain, sincere, straightforward, derog tactless, to the point, unambiguous, uncomplicated, derog undiplomatic, unequivocal, unreserved. 3 direct experience. empirical, first-hand, personal. 4 direct opposites. absolute, complete, diametrical,

exact, out and out, utter. Opp INDIRECT. • v 1 escort, guide, indicate the way, point, send, show the way, usher. 2 aim, focus, target. 3 administer, be in charge of, conduct, control, govern, handle, lead, manage, mastermind, oversee, regulate, rule, run, stage-manage, supervise, take charge of. 4 advise, bid, command, counsel, instruct, order, require, tell.

direction n aim, approach, (compass) bearing, course, orientation, path, road, route, tack, track, way. **directions** guidelines, instructions, orders, plans.

director n administrator, inf boss, governor, manager, organizer, president, principal. ▷ CHIEF.

directory n catalogue, index, list, register.

dirt n 1 dust, filth, grime, impurity, mess, mire, muck, ooze, pollution, smut, soot, stain. ▷ OBSCENITY, RUBBISH. 2 clay, earth, loam, mud, soil.

dirty adj 1 dingy, dusty, filthy, foul, grimy, grubby, marked, messy, mucky, muddy, smeary, smudged, soiled, sooty, sordid, squalid, stained, sullied, tarnished, travel-stained, unclean, unwashed. 2 dirty water. cloudy, contaminated, impure, muddy, murky, polluted, tainted, untreated. 3 dirty tactics. dishonest, dishonourable, illegal, inf low-down, mean, rough, treacherous, unfair, unscrupulous, unsporting. ▷ CORRUPT. 4 dirty talk. coarse, crude, improper, indecent, offensive, rude, smutty, vulgar. ▷ OBSCENE. Opp CLEAN. • v foul, mark, inf mess up, smear, smudge, soil, spatter, spot, stain, streak, tarnish. ▷ DEFILE. *Opp* CLEAN.

disability *n* affliction, defect, disablement, handicap, impairment, incapacity, infirmity, weakness.

disable *v* cripple, damage, debilitate, enfeeble, *inf* hamstring, handicap, immobilize, impair, incapacitate, injure, lame, maim, paralyse, put out of action, weaken. **disabled** ▷ HANDICAPPED.

disadvantage *n* drawback, handicap, hardship, hindrance, impediment, inconvenience, liability, *inf* minus, nuisance, snag, trouble, weakness.

disagree *v* argue, bicker, conflict, contend, differ, dispute, dissent, fall out, fight, quarrel, squabble, wrangle. **disagree with** ▷ OPPOSE.

disagreeable *adj* distasteful, nasty, objectionable, offensive, sickening, unsavoury. ▷ UNPLEASANT. *Opp* PLEASANT.

disagreement *n* altercation, argument, clash, conflict, controversy, debate, difference, disharmony, dispute, dissension, dissent, divergence, incompatibility, inconsistency, misunderstanding, opposition, quarrel, squabble, strife, *inf* tiff, variance, wrangle. *Opp* AGREEMENT.

disappear *v* 1 become invisible, clear, disperse, dissolve, dwindle, ebb, evaporate, fade, melt away, recede, vanish, vaporize, wane. ▷ DIE. 2 escape, flee, fly, run away, walk away, withdraw. *Opp* APPEAR.

disappoint *v* disenchant, disillusion, dismay, displease, dissat-

isfy, fail to satisfy, *inf* let down, sadden, upset. ▷ FRUSTRATE. *Opp* SATISFY. **disappointed** disillusioned, frustrated, *inf* let down. ▷ SAD.

disapproval *n* censure, condemnation, criticism, disfavour, dislike, displeasure, dissatisfaction, hostility. *Opp* APPROVAL.

disapprove *v* **disapprove of** be displeased by, censure, condemn, criticize, denounce, deplore, deprecate, dislike, disparage, frown on, look askance at, make unwelcome, object to, reject, *inf* take a dim view of, take exception to. *Opp* APPROVE. **disapproving** ▷ CRITICAL.

disarm *v* 1 demilitarize, demobilize, make powerless, take weapons from. 2 charm, mollify, pacify, placate.

disaster *n* accident, blow, calamity, cataclysm, catastrophe, crash, debacle, failure, fiasco, *inf* flop, misadventure, mischance, misfortune, mishap, reverse, tragedy, *inf* wash-out. *Opp* SUCCESS.

disastrous *adj* appalling, awful, calamitous, cataclysmic, catastrophic, devastating, dire, dreadful, fatal, ruinous, terrible, tragic. *Opp* SUCCESSFUL.

disbelieve *v* be sceptical of, discount, discredit, doubt, have no faith in, mistrust, reject, suspect. *Opp* BELIEVE. **disbelieving** ▷ INCREDULOUS.

disc *n* 1 circle, counter, token. 2 album, CD, LP, record, single. 3 [*computing*] CD-ROM, disk, diskette, floppy disk, hard disk.

discard *v* abandon, cast off, dispense with, dispose of, *inf* ditch, dump, get rid of, jettison, junk, reject, scrap, shed, throw away, toss out.

discern v be aware of, detect, discover, distinguish, make out, mark, notice, observe, perceive, recognize, spy. ▷ SEE. **discerning** ▷ PERCEPTIVE.

discernible adj detectable, distinguishable, measurable, perceptible. ▷ NOTICEABLE.

discharge n 1 release, dismissal. 2 emission, ooze, pus, secretion, suppuration. ● v 1 belch, eject, emit, expel, exude, give off, pour out, produce, release, secrete, send out, spew, spit out. 2 discharge guns. detonate, explode, fire, let off, shoot. 3 discharge employees. dismiss, fire, make redundant, sack, throw out. 4 discharge a prisoner. absolve, acquit, clear, dismiss, excuse, exonerate, free, liberate, pardon, release. 5 discharge duties. accomplish, carry out, execute, fulfil, perform.

disciple n adherent, admirer, apostle, apprentice, devotee, follower, learner, pupil, scholar, student, supporter.

disciplinarian n authoritarian, autocrat, despot, dictator, inf hard taskmaster, inf slave-driver, tyrant.

discipline n 1 control, drill, indoctrination, instruction, management, training. 2 obedience, order, orderliness, routine, self-control, self-restraint. ● v 1 coach, control, drill, educate, govern, indoctrinate, instruct, keep in check, manage, restrain, school, train. 2 castigate, chastise, correct, penalize, punish, rebuke, reprim-

and, reprove, scold. **disciplined** ▷ OBEDIENT.

disclaim v deny, disown, reject, renounce, repudiate. Opp ACKNOWLEDGE.

disclose v divulge, expose, let out, make known. ▷ REVEAL.

discolour v bleach, dirty, fade, mark, stain, tarnish, tinge.

discomfort n distress, inconvenience, irritation, soreness, uneasiness. ▷ PAIN. Opp COMFORT.

disconcert v agitate, bewilder, confuse, discomfit, distract, disturb, fluster, nonplus, perplex, puzzle, inf rattle, ruffle, throw off balance, trouble, unsettle, upset, worry. Opp REASSURE.

disconnect v break off, cut off, detach, disengage, divide, part, sever, switch off, turn off, undo, unhook, unplug. **disconnected** ▷ INCOHERENT.

discontented adj annoyed, disgruntled, displeased, dissatisfied, fed up, restless, sulky, unhappy, unsettled.

discord n 1 argument, conflict, difference of opinion, disagreement, disharmony, dispute, friction, strife. ▷ QUARREL. 2 [music] cacophony, jangle. ▷ NOISE. Opp HARMONY.

discordant adj 1 conflicting, contrary, differing, dissimilar, divergent, incompatible, inconsistent, opposed, opposite. 2 cacophonous, clashing, dissonant, grating, harsh, jangling, jarring, shrill, strident, tuneless, unmusical. Opp HARMONIOUS.

discount n concession, cut, deduction, inf mark-down, rebate, reduction. ● v disbelieve, dismiss, disregard, ignore, overlook, reject.

discourage v 1 cow, damp, dampen, daunt, demoralize, depress, disenchant, dishearten, dismay, dispirit, frighten, inhibit, intimidate, overawe, *inf* put off, scare, *inf* throw cold water on, unnerve. 2 *discourage vandalism.* check, deter, dissuade, hinder, prevent, put an end to, repress, restrain, stop, suppress. *Opp* ENCOURAGE.

discouragement n constraint, *inf* damper, deterrent, disincentive, hindrance, impediment, obstacle, restraint.
Opp ENCOURAGEMENT.

discourse n 1 ▷ CONVERSATION. 2 dissertation, essay, paper, thesis, treatise. • v ▷ SPEAK.

discover v ascertain, bring to light, come across, detect, dig up, disclose, expose, *inf* ferret out, find, hit on, identify, learn, locate, notice, observe, perceive, recognize, reveal, search out, spot, track down, turn up, uncover, unearth. ▷ INVENT. *Opp* HIDE.

discoverer n explorer, finder, initiator, inventor, originator, pioneer, traveller.

discovery n breakthrough, detection, disclosure, exploration, *inf* find, innovation, invention, revelation.

discredit v 1 defame, disgrace, dishonour, slander, slur, smear, vilify. 2 challenge, disbelieve, disprove, refuse to believe.

discreet adj careful, cautious, circumspect, considerate, delicate, diplomatic, guarded, judicious, low-key, muted, politic, prudent, restrained, sensitive,

subdued, tactful, thoughtful, wary. *Opp* INDISCREET.

discrepancy n conflict, difference, disparity, dissimilarity, divergence, incompatibility, incongruity, inconsistency, variance. *Opp* SIMILARITY.

discretion n circumspection, diplomacy, good sense, judgement, maturity, prudence, responsibility, sensitivity, tact, wisdom. *Opp* TACTLESSNESS.

discriminate v 1 differentiate, distinguish, draw a distinction, separate, tell apart. 2 be biased, be prejudiced. **discriminating** ▷ PERCEPTIVE.

discrimination n 1 discernment, good taste, insight, judgement, perceptiveness, refinement, subtlety, taste. 2 [*derog*] bias, bigotry, chauvinism, favouritism, prejudice, racism, sexism, unfairness. *Opp* IMPARTIALITY.

discuss v confer about, consider, consult, debate, deliberate, examine, talk about, *inf* weigh up the pros and cons of.

discussion n argument, colloquy, conference, consideration, consultation, debate, deliberation, dialogue, discourse, examination, exchange of views, symposium. ▷ TALK.

disdainful adj contemptuous, mocking, scornful, supercilious, superior. ▷ PROUD.

disease n affliction, ailment, *inf* bug, complaint, contagion, disorder, infection, infirmity, malady, sickness. ▷ ILLNESS.

diseased adj ailing, infirm, sick, unwell. ▷ ILL.

disembark v alight, get off, go ashore, land. *Opp* EMBARK.

disfigure v blemish, damage, deface, deform, distort, impair, injure, make ugly, mar, mutilate, ruin, scar, spoil. *Opp* BEAUTIFY.

disgrace n 1 degradation, discredit, dishonour, disrepute, embarrassment, humiliation, ignominy, opprobrium, scandal, shame, slur, stain, stigma. 2 ▷ OUTRAGE.

disgraceful adj contemptible, degrading, dishonourable, embarrassing, humiliating, ignominious, shameful, shaming, wicked. ▷ BAD.

disgruntled adj annoyed, cross, disaffected, disappointed, discontented, dissatisfied, fed up, grumpy, moody, sulky, sullen. ▷ BAD-TEMPERED.

disguise n camouflage, costume, cover, front, *inf* get-up, impersonation, mask, pretence, smokescreen. ● v camouflage, conceal, cover up, dress up, falsify, gloss over, hide, make inconspicuous, mask, misrepresent, screen, shroud, veil. **disguise yourself as** ▷ IMPERSONATE.

disgust n abhorrence, aversion, contempt, detestation, dislike, distaste, hatred, loathing, nausea, outrage, repugnance, revulsion, sickness. ● v appal, be distasteful to, horrify, nauseate, offend, outrage, repel, revolt, sicken, shock, *inf* turn your stomach. *Opp* PLEASE. **disgusting** ▷ HATEFUL.

dish n 1 basin, bowl, casserole, container, plate, platter, tureen. 2 entrée, food, item on the menu, recipe. **dish out** ▷ DISTRIBUTE. **dish up** ▷ SERVE.

dishearten v depress, deter, discourage, dismay, put off, sadden.

Opp ENCOURAGE. **disheartened** ▷ SAD.

dishevelled adj bedraggled, disordered, messy, ruffled, rumpled, *inf* scruffy, slovenly, tangled, tousled, uncombed, unkempt, untidy. *Opp* NEAT.

dishonest adj *inf* bent, cheating, corrupt, criminal, *inf* crooked, deceitful, deceptive, devious, dishonourable, disreputable, false, fraudulent, hypocritical, immoral, insincere, lying, mendacious, misleading, perfidious, *inf* shady, slippery, swindling, thieving, treacherous, *inf* two-faced, *inf* underhand, unprincipled, unscrupulous, untrustworthy, untruthful. *Opp* HONEST.

dishonour n blot, degradation, discredit, disgrace, humiliation, ignominy, indignity, loss of face, opprobrium, reproach, scandal, shame, slander, slur, stain, stigma. *Opp* HONOUR. ● v abuse, debase, defile, degrade, disgrace, profane, shame, slight.

dishonourable adj base, despicable, discreditable, disgraceful, dishonest, disloyal, disreputable, ignoble, ignominious, improper, infamous, mean, outrageous, perfidious, reprehensible, scandalous, shabby, shameful, shameless, treacherous, unchivalrous, unscrupulous, unworthy. ▷ CORRUPT. *Opp* HONOURABLE.

disillusion v disabuse, disappoint, disenchant, enlighten.

disinfect v chlorinate, clean, cleanse, decontaminate, fumigate, purify, sanitize, sterilize.

disinfectant n antiseptic, decontaminant, germicide.

disinherit v cut off, cut out of a will, deprive someone of their inheritance.

disintegrate v break up, come apart, crack up, crumble, decay, decompose, deteriorate, fall apart, rot, shatter, smash, splinter.

disinterested adj detached, dispassionate, impartial, impersonal, neutral, objective, unbiased, uninvolved, unprejudiced. Opp BIASED.

disjointed adj confused, disconnected, dislocated, disordered, incoherent, jumbled, mixed up, muddled, rambling, uncoordinated, wandering. Opp COHERENT.

dislike n antagonism, antipathy, aversion, detestation, disapproval, disgust, distaste, hatred, hostility, ill will, loathing, repugnance, revulsion. ● v despise, detest, disapprove of, scorn, inf take against. ▷ HATE. Opp LOVE.

dislocate v disengage, disjoint, displace, put out of joint.

disloyal adj faithless, false, insincere, perfidious, renegade, seditious, subversive, treacherous, inf two-faced, unfaithful, unreliable, untrustworthy. Opp LOYAL.

disloyalty n betrayal, double-dealing, duplicity, inconstancy, infidelity, perfidy, treachery, treason, unfaithfulness. Opp LOYALTY.

dismal adj bleak, cheerless, depressing, dreary, dull, funereal, gloomy, grey, grim, miserable, sombre, wretched. ▷ SAD.

dismantle v demolish, strip down, take apart, take down. Opp ASSEMBLE.

dismay n agitation, alarm, anxiety, apprehension, consternation, disappointment, distress, dread, gloom, horror, surprise. ▷ FEAR. ● v alarm, appal, daunt, depress, devastate, disappoint, discourage, dishearten, dispirit, distress, shock, take aback, unnerve. ▷ FRIGHTEN. Opp PLEASE.

dismiss v 1 disband, free, let go, inf pack off, release, send away. 2 belittle, brush aside, discount, disregard, drop, give up, reject, repudiate, set aside, shrug off, wave aside. 3 dismiss a worker. discharge, inf fire, get rid of, give notice to, inf someone their cards, give the push to, lay off, make redundant, sack.

disobedient adj anarchic, contrary, defiant, disorderly, disruptive, headstrong, insubordinate, intractable, mutinous, obstinate, obstreperous, perverse, rebellious, recalcitrant, refractory, riotous, self-willed, uncontrollable, undisciplined, unmanageable, unruly, wayward, wild, wilful. ▷ NAUGHTY. Opp OBEDIENT.

disobey v 1 be disobedient, mutiny, protest, rebel, revolt, rise up. 2 break, contravene, defy, disregard, flout, ignore, infringe, oppose, transgress, violate. Opp OBEY.

disorder n 1 anarchy, chaos, confusion, disarray, disorganization, disturbance, fighting, fracas, fuss, jumble, lawlessness, mess, muddle, inf shambles, tangle, untidiness, uproar. ▷ COMMOTION. Opp ORDER. 2 ▷ ILLNESS.

disorderly adj ▷ DISOBEDIENT, DISORGANIZED.

disorganized adj aimless, careless, chaotic, confused, disorderly, haphazard, jumbled, messy, muddled, rambling, scatterbrained, slapdash, slipshod, inf sloppy, slovenly, unplanned, unstructured, unsystematic, untidy. Opp SYSTEMATIC.

disown v disclaim knowledge of, renounce, repudiate.

disparage v belittle, demean, discredit, insult, inf put down, slight, undervalue. ▷ CRITICIZE. **disparaging**
▷ UNCOMPLIMENTARY.

dispassionate adj calm, composed, cool, equable, even-tempered, level-headed, sober.
▷ IMPARTIAL, UNEMOTIONAL.
Opp EMOTIONAL.

dispatch n bulletin, communiqué, letter, message, report.
● v 1 consign, convey, forward, mail, post, send, ship. 2 ▷ KILL.

dispense v 1 allocate, allot, apportion, assign, distribute, inf dole out, give out, issue, measure out, provide, ration out, share. 2 dispense medicine. make up, prepare, supply. **dispense with** ▷ OMIT, REMOVE.

disperse v 1 break up, disband, dismiss, dispel, dissipate, drive away, send in different directions, separate, spread.
Opp GATHER. 2 disappear, dissolve, melt away, scatter, spread out, vanish.

displace v 1 disarrange, dislocate, dislodge, disturb, move, put out of place, shift. 2 crowd out, depose, oust, replace, succeed, supersede, supplant, take the place of, unseat, usurp.

display n 1 array, demonstration, exhibition, manifestation, pageant, parade, presentation,

show, spectacle. 2 ceremony, ostentation, pageantry, pomp.
● v advertise, air, demonstrate, disclose, exhibit, expose, flaunt, flourish, give evidence of, parade, present, produce, put on show, reveal, show, show off, unfold, unfurl, unveil, vaunt.
Opp HIDE.

displease v anger, offend, put out, upset. ▷ ANNOY.

disposable adj 1 available, usable. 2 expendable, non-returnable, replaceable, inf throwaway.

dispose v distribute, place, position. ▷ ARRANGE. **disposed**
▷ LIABLE. **dispose of**
▷ DESTROY, DISCARD.

disproportionate adj excessive, incongruous, inordinate, out of proportion, unbalanced, uneven, unreasonable.
Opp PROPORTIONAL.

disprove v confute, contradict, discredit, inf explode, invalidate, negate, rebut, refute, show to be wrong. Opp PROVE.

dispute n ▷ QUARREL. ● v argue against, challenge, contest, contradict, deny, disagree with, doubt, gainsay, impugn, object to, oppose, inf pick holes in, quarrel with, query, question, raise doubts about. ▷ DEBATE.
Opp ACCEPT.

disqualify v debar, declare ineligible, exclude, preclude, prohibit, reject.

disregard v brush aside, discount, dismiss, disobey, inf fly in the face of, forget, ignore, leave out, inf make light of, miss out, neglect, omit, overlook, pass over, pay no attention to, reject, shrug off, skip, inf turn a blind eye to. Opp HEED.

disreputable adj dishonest, dishonourable, inf dodgy, dubious, infamous, questionable, inf shady, suspect, suspicious, untrustworthy. Opp REPUTABLE.

disrespectful adj bad-mannered, discourteous, disparaging, impolite, impudent, inconsiderate, insolent, insulting, irreverent, mocking, scornful, uncivil. ▷ RUDE. Opp RESPECTFUL.

disrupt v break up, dislocate, disorder, disturb, interfere with, interrupt, intrude on, spoil, throw into disorder, unsettle, upset.

dissatisfaction n annoyance, chagrin, disappointment, discontentment, dismay, displeasure, disquiet, exasperation, frustration, irritation, malaise, regret, unhappiness. Opp SATISFACTION.

dissatisfied adj disaffected, disappointed, discontented, disgruntled, displeased, fed up, frustrated, unfulfilled. ▷ UNHAPPY. Opp CONTENTED.

dissident n derog agitator, dissenter, independent thinker, protester, rebel, revolutionary. Opp CONFORMIST.

dissimilar adj antithetical, conflicting, contrasting, different, disparate, distinct, distinguishable, divergent, diverse, heterogeneous, incompatible, opposite, unrelated, various. Opp SIMILAR.

dissipate v 1 break up, diffuse, disappear, disperse, scatter. 2 ▷ SQUANDER. **dissipated** ▷ IMMORAL.

dissociate v cut off, detach, distance, divorce, isolate. ▷ SEPARATE. Opp ASSOCIATE.

dissolve v 1 become liquid, decompose, dematerialize, diffuse, disappear, disintegrate, disperse, liquefy, melt away, vanish. 2 dissolve a meeting, partnership. break up, cancel, dismiss, divorce, end, sever, split up, terminate, inf wind up.

dissuade v dissuade from advise against, argue out of, deter from, discourage from, persuade not to, put off, warn against. Opp PERSUADE.

distance n 1 breadth, extent, gap, interval, journey, length, measurement, mileage, range, reach, space, span, stretch, width. 2 aloofness, coolness, unfriendliness. • v distance yourself be unfriendly, dissociate yourself, keep away, separate yourself, set yourself apart, stay away. Opp INVOLVE.

distant adj 1 far, far-away, far-flung, outlying, out-of-the-way, remote. Opp CLOSE. 2 aloof, cool, formal, haughty, reserved, reticent, stiff, unapproachable, unfriendly, withdrawn. Opp FRIENDLY.

distasteful adj disgusting, displeasing, nasty, objectionable, offensive, inf off-putting, revolting, unpalatable. ▷ UNPLEASANT. Opp PLEASANT.

distinct adj 1 apparent, clear, clear-cut, definite, evident, noticeable, obvious, patent, perceptible, plain, precise, recognizable, sharp, unambiguous, unequivocal, unmistakable, visible, well-defined. Opp INDISTINCT. 2 contrasting, detached, different, dissimilar, distinguishable, individual, separate, unconnected, unique.

distinction n 1 contrast, difference, differentiation, dissimilarity, distinctiveness, dividing

line, division, individuality, particularity, peculiarity, separation. Opp SIMILARITY.
2 celebrity, credit, eminence, excellence, fame, glory, greatness, honour, importance, merit, prestige, renown, reputation, superiority.

distinctive adj characteristic, different, distinguishing, idiosyncratic, individual, original, peculiar, personal, singular, special, striking, typical, uncommon, unique. Opp COMMON.

distinguish v 1 choose, decide, differentiate, discriminate, judge, make a distinction, separate, tell apart. 2 ascertain, determine, discern, know, make out, perceive, pick out, recognize, see, single out, tell.
distinguished ▷ FAMOUS.

distort v 1 bend, buckle, contort, deform, twist, warp, wrench. 2 exaggerate, falsify, garble, misrepresent, pervert, slant, twist.
distorted ▷ GNARLED, FALSE.

distract v bewilder, bother, confuse, deflect, disconcert, divert, harass, mystify, perplex, puzzle, sidetrack, trouble, worry. **distracted** ▷ DISTRAUGHT, MAD.

distraction n 1 disturbance, interference, interruption. 2 agitation, bewilderment, confusion, delirium, frenzy, insanity, madness. 3 ▷ DIVERSION.

distraught adj agitated, inf beside yourself, distracted, distressed, disturbed, emotional, excited, frantic, hysterical, overwrought, troubled, upset, worked up. ▷ ANXIOUS. Opp CALM.

distress n adversity, affliction, angst, anguish, anxiety, danger, desolation, difficulty, dismay,

fright, grief, heartache, misery, privation, sadness, sorrow, stress, suffering, torment, tribulation, trouble, unhappiness, woe, worry, wretchedness.
▷ PAIN. • v afflict, alarm, bother, dismay, disturb, frighten, grieve, harass, hurt, make miserable, pain, perplex, perturb, plague, sadden, shake, shock, terrify, torment, torture, trouble, upset, worry, wound. Opp COMFORT.

distribute v allocate, allot, apportion, arrange, assign, circulate, deliver, inf dish out, dispense, disperse, disseminate, inf dole out, give out, hand round, issue, partition, scatter, share out, spread, strew, take round. Opp COLLECT.

district n area, community, division, locality, neighbourhood, parish, part, province, quarter, region, sector, territory, vicinity, ward, zone.

distrust v disbelieve, doubt, have misgivings about, have qualms about, mistrust, question, suspect. Opp TRUST.

distrustful adj cautious, dubious, uncertain. ▷ SUSPICIOUS. Opp TRUSTFUL.

disturb v 1 agitate, alarm, annoy, bother, disrupt, distract, distress, excite, fluster, frighten, interrupt, intrude on, perturb, pester, ruffle, scare, shake, startle, stir up, trouble, unsettle, upset, worry. 2 disorder, interfere with, jumble up, move, muddle, rearrange. **disturbed** ▷ DISTRAUGHT.

disturbance n disruption, interference, upheaval, upset. ▷ COMMOTION.

disunited adj divided, opposed, polarized, split. Opp UNITED.

disunity n difference, disagreement, discord, disharmony, disintegration, division, fragmentation, incoherence, opposition, polarization. *Opp* UNITY.

disused adj abandoned, closed, dead, discarded, discontinued, idle, neglected, obsolete, superannuated, withdrawn. ▷ OLD. *Opp* CURRENT.

ditch n channel, drain, dyke, gully, gutter, moat, trench. ● v ▷ ABANDON.

dive v crash-dive, dip, drop, fall, go under, jump, leap, nosedive, pitch, plummet, plunge, sink, submerge, subside, swoop.

diverge v branch, deviate, divide, fork, part, radiate, separate, split, spread, subdivide. ▷ DIFFER. *Opp* CONVERGE.

diverse adj ▷ VARIOUS.

diversify v branch out, develop, divide, enlarge, expand, extend, spread out, vary.

diversion n 1 detour, deviation. 2 amusement, distraction, entertainment, fun, game, hobby, interest, pastime, play, recreation, relaxation, sport.

divert v 1 avert, change direction, deflect, deviate, redirect, reroute, shunt, sidetrack, switch, turn aside. 2 amuse, beguile, cheer up, delight, distract, engage, entertain, keep happy, occupy, regale.

diverting ▷ FUNNY.

divide v 1 branch, diverge, fork, move apart, part, separate, sunder. 2 allocate, allot, apportion, deal out, dispense, distribute, *inf* dole out, give out, halve, measure out, parcel out, pass round, share out. 3 disunite, polarize, split. 4 *divide into sets*. arrange, categorize, classify,

grade, group, sort out, subdivide. *Opp* GATHER, UNITE.

divine adj angelic, celestial, godlike, hallowed, heavenly, holy, immortal, mystical, religious, sacred, saintly, seraphic, spiritual, transcendental. *Opp* MORTAL. ● n ▷ CLERGYMAN. ● v ▷ PROPHESY.

divinity n 1 ▷ GOD. 2 religion, religious studies, theology.

division n 1 allocation, allotment, cutting up, dividing, partition, segmentation, separation. 2 disagreement, discord, disunity, feud, quarrel, rupture, schism, split. 3 alcove, compartment, part, recess, section, segment. 4 border, borderline, boundary line, demarcation, dividing wall, fence, frontier, margin, partition, screen. 5 *division of a business*. branch, department, section, subdivision, unit.

divorce n annulment, *inf* breakup, dissolution, separation, *inf* split-up. ● v annul marriage, dissolve marriage, part, separate, *inf* split up.

dizziness n faintness, giddiness, light-headedness, vertigo.

dizzy adj confused, dazed, faint, giddy, light-headed, muddled, reeling, shaky, unsteady, *inf* woozy.

do v 1 accomplish, achieve, carry out, commit, complete, effect, execute, finish, fulfil, implement, initiate, instigate, organize, perform, produce, undertake. 2 *do the garden*. arrange, attend to, cope with, deal with, handle, look after, manage, work at. 3 *do sums*. give your mind to, solve, work out. 4 *Will this do?* be acceptable, be enough, be suitable, satisfy, serve, suffice. 5 *Do as you like.* act, behave, conduct yourself. **do away with** ▷ ABOLISH. **do up** ▷ DECORATE, FASTEN.

docile *adj* cooperative, domesticated, obedient. ▷ TAME.

dock *n* berth, dockyard, dry dock, harbour, jetty, landing stage, pier, quay, wharf.
• *v* 1 anchor, berth, drop anchor, land, moor, put in, tie up.
2 ▷ CUT.

doctor *n* general practitioner, *inf* GP, medical officer, medical practitioner, *inf* MO, physician, *derog* quack, surgeon.

doctrine *n* axiom, belief, conviction, creed, dogma, precept, principle, teaching, tenet.

document *n* certificate, charter, chronicle, deed, diploma, form, instrument, licence, manuscript, *inf* MS, paper, passport, policy, record, typescript, visa, warrant, will. • *v* ▷ RECORD.

documentary *adj* 1 authenticated, recorded, substantiated, written. 2 factual, historical, non-fiction, real life.

dodge *n* contrivance, device, manoeuvre, ploy, ruse, scheme, stratagem, subterfuge, trick, *inf* wheeze. • *v* 1 avoid, duck, elude, escape, evade, fend off, move out of the way, sidestep, swerve, turn away, veer. 2 *dodge work.* shirk, *sl* skive, *inf* wriggle out of. 3 *dodge a question.* equivocate, fudge, hedge, *inf* waffle.

dog *n* bitch, hound, mongrel, pedigree, pup, puppy.
• *v* ▷ FOLLOW.

dogma *n* article of faith, belief, conviction, creed, doctrine, precept, principle, teaching, tenet.

dogmatic *adj* assertive, arbitrary, authoritarian, categorical, certain, dictatorial, doctrinaire, *inf* hard-line, imperious, inflexible, intolerant, narrow-minded, obdurate, opinionated.
▷ STUBBORN. *Opp* AMENABLE.

dole *n* [*inf*] benefit, income support, social security, unemployment benefit. **dole out**
▷ DISTRIBUTE. **on the dole**
▷ UNEMPLOYED.

doll *n* marionette, puppet, rag doll.

domestic *adj* 1 family, household, private. 2 internal, national.

domesticated *adj* house-trained, tame, trained. *Opp* WILD.

dominant *adj* 1 biggest, chief, commanding, conspicuous, eye-catching, highest, largest, main, major, obvious, outstanding, pre-eminent, prevailing, primary, principal, uppermost. 2 ascendant, controlling, domineering, governing, influential, leading, powerful, predominant, presiding, reigning, ruling, supreme.

dominate *v* 1 be in the majority, control, direct, govern, influence, lead, manage, master, monopolize, outnumber, prevail, rule, subjugate, take control, tyrannize. 2 look down on, overshadow, tower over.

domineering *adj* authoritarian, autocratic, *inf* bossy, despotic, dictatorial, high-handed, oppressive, overbearing, *inf* pushy, strict, tyrannical. *Opp* SUBMISSIVE.

donate *v* contribute, give, grant, hand over, make a donation, present, supply.

donation *n* alms, contribution, offering. ▷ GIFT.

donor *n* backer, benefactor, contributor, giver, philanthropist, sponsor, supporter.

doom *n* destiny, end, fate, fortune, karma, kismet, lot.

doomed *adj* 1 condemned, destined, fated, ordained, predestined. 2 *doomed enterprise*. cursed, damned, hopeless, ill-fated, ill-starred, luckless, star-crossed, unlucky.

door *n* barrier, doorway, entrance, exit, gate, gateway, opening, portal, swing door, way out.

dormant *adj* 1 asleep, hibernating, inactive, inert, passive, quiescent, quiet, resting, sleeping. 2 *dormant talent*. hidden, latent, potential, untapped, unused. *Opp* ACTIVE.

dose *n* amount, dosage, measure, prescribed amount, quantity. ● *v* administer, dispense, prescribe.

dossier *n* file, folder, records, set of documents.

dot *n* decimal point, fleck, full stop, iota, jot, mark, point, speck, spot. ● *v* fleck, speckle, spot, stipple.

dote *v* dote on adore, idolize, worship. ▷ LOVE.

double *adj* doubled, dual, duplicated, paired, twin, twofold. ● *n* clone, copy, counterpart, duplicate, *inf* look-alike, *inf* spitting image, twin. ● *v* duplicate, multiply by two, repeat. double back ▷ RETURN. double up ▷ COLLAPSE.

double-cross *v* cheat, deceive, let down, trick. ▷ BETRAY.

doubt *n* 1 anxiety, apprehension, cynicism, diffidence, disbelief, disquiet, distrust, fear, hesitation, incredulity, indecision, misgiving, mistrust, perplexity, qualm, reservation, scepticism, suspicion, worry. 2 ambiguity, difficulty, dilemma, problem, query, question, uncertainty. *Opp* CERTAINTY. ● *v* be dubious, be sceptical about, disbelieve, distrust, fear, feel uncertain about, have misgivings about, hesitate, lack confidence, mistrust, query, question, suspect. *Opp* TRUST.

doubtful *adj* 1 cynical, diffident, distrustful, dubious, hesitant, incredulous, sceptical, suspicious, tentative, uncertain, unconvinced, undecided, unsure. 2 *doubtful decision*. ambiguous, debatable, dubious, equivocal, inconclusive, problematic, questionable, suspect, worrying. 3 *doubtful ally*. irresolute, uncommitted, unreliable, untrustworthy, vacillating, wavering. *Opp* CERTAIN, DEPENDABLE.

dowdy *adj* colourless, dingy, drab, dull, *inf* frumpish, shabby, unattractive, unstylish. *Opp* SMART.

downfall *n* collapse, defeat, overthrow, ruin, undoing.

downhearted *adj* dejected, depressed, discouraged, downcast, miserable. ▷ SAD.

downward *adj* declining, descending, downhill, falling, going down. *Opp* UPWARD.

downy *adj* feathery, fleecy, fluffy, furry, fuzzy, soft, woolly.

drab *adj* cheerless, colourless, dingy, dismal, dowdy, dreary, dull, flat, gloomy, grey, lacklustre, shabby, sombre, uninteresting. *Opp* BRIGHT.

draft *n* 1 notes, outline, plan, rough version, sketch. 2 *bank draft*. cheque, order. ● *v* compose, draw up, outline, plan, prepare, put together, sketch out, work out.

drag *v* 1 draw, haul, lug, pull, tow, trail, tug. 2 crawl, creep, go slowly, lose momentum, pass slowly.

drain *n* channel, conduit, ditch, dyke, drainpipe, duct, gutter, outlet, pipe, sewer, trench, watercourse. ● *v* 1 bleed, draw off, dry out, empty, extract, pump out, remove, tap. 2 drip, ebb, leak out, ooze, seep, strain, trickle. 3 *drain resources*. consume, deplete, exhaust, sap, spend, use up.

drama *n* 1 acting, dramatics, improvisation, stagecraft, theatre, theatricals. 2 comedy, dramatization, farce, melodrama, musical, opera, operetta, pantomime, performance, play, production, screenplay, script, show, tragedy. 3 *real-life drama*. action, crisis, excitement, suspense.

dramatic *adj* 1 ▷ THEATRICAL. 2 *dramatic gestures*. exaggerated, flamboyant, showy. 3 ▷ EXCITING.

dramatist *n* playwright, scriptwriter.

dramatize *v* 1 adapt, make into a play. 2 exaggerate, make too much of, overdo, overstate.

drape *n* curtain, hanging, screen. ● *v* cover, decorate, festoon, hang, swathe.

drastic *adj* desperate, dire, draconian, extreme, far-reaching,

harsh, radical, rigorous, severe, strong.

draught *n* 1 breeze, current, movement, puff, wind. 2 dose, drink, gulp, measure, pull, swallow, *inf* swig.

draw *n* 1 attraction, enticement, lure, *inf* pull. 2 dead-heat, stalemate, tie. 3 competition, lottery, raffle. ● *v* 1 drag, haul, lug, pull, tow, tug. 2 *draw a crowd*. attract, bring in, entice, lure, persuade, pull in, win over. 3 *draw a sword*. extract, remove, take out, unsheathe. 4 *draw lots*. choose, pick, select. 5 *draw a conclusion*. arrive at, come to, deduce, infer, work out. 6 *draw 1-1*. be equal, finish equal, tie. 7 *draw pictures*. depict, map out, outline, paint, pen, portray, represent, sketch, trace. **draw off** ▷ DRAIN. **draw out** ▷ EXTEND. **draw up** ▷ DRAFT, HALT.

drawback *n* difficulty, disadvantage, hindrance, obstacle, problem, snag, stumbling block.

drawing *n* cartoon, design, illustration, outline, picture, sketch.

dread *n* anxiety, apprehension, awe, dismay, fear, nervousness, qualm, trepidation, uneasiness, worry. ● *v* be afraid of, shrink from, view with horror. ▷ FEAR.

dreadful *adj* alarming, appalling, awful, dire, distressing, frightful, ghastly, grisly, gruesome, harrowing, hideous, horrible, indescribable, monstrous, shocking, terrible, tragic, unspeakable, upsetting. ▷ BAD, FRIGHTENING.

dream *n* 1 daydream, delusion, fantasy, hallucination, illusion, mirage, nightmare, reverie, trance, vision. 2 ambition, aspiration, ideal, pipedream, wish. • *v* conjure up, daydream, fancy, fantasize, hallucinate, imagine, think. **dream up** ▷ INVENT.

dreary *adj* bleak, boring, depressing, dismal, dull, gloomy, sombre, uninteresting. ▷ MISERABLE.

dregs *n* deposit, grounds (*of coffee*), lees, precipitate, remains, residue, sediment.

drench *v* douse, drown, flood, inundate, saturate, soak, souse, steep, wet thoroughly.

dress *n* 1 apparel, attire, clothing, costume, garb, garments, *inf* gear, *inf* get-up, outfit, *old use* raiment. ▷ CLOTHES. 2 frock, gown, robe, shift. • *v* 1 array, attire, clothe, cover, fit out, provide clothes for, robe. 2 *dress a wound*. bandage, bind up, put a dressing on, tend, treat.

dressing *n* bandage, compress, plaster, poultice.

dribble *v* 1 drool, slaver, slobber. 2 drip, flow, leak, ooze, run, seep, trickle.

drift *n* 1 bank, dune, heap, mound, pile, ridge. 2 *drift of a speech*. ▷ GIST. • *v* 1 be carried, coast, float, meander, move casually, ramble, roam, stray, waft, walk aimlessly, wander. 2 accumulate, gather, make drifts, pile up.

drill *n* discipline, exercises, instruction, practice, training. • *v* 1 coach, discipline, exercise, indoctrinate, instruct, practise, rehearse, school, teach, train. 2 bore, penetrate, perforate, pierce.

drink *n* 1 beverage, *inf* dram, draught, glass, *inf* nightcap, *inf* nip, pint, sip, swallow, swig, *inf* tipple, tot. 2 alcohol,

inf booze, *joc* liquid refreshment, liquor. • *v* 1 gulp, guzzle, imbibe, *inf* knock back, lap, partake of, quaff, sip, swallow, swig, *inf* swill. 2 *inf* booze, carouse, *inf* indulge, tipple.

drip *n* bead, drop, splash, spot, tear, trickle. • *v* dribble, drizzle, drop, leak, plop, splash, sprinkle, trickle, weep.

drive *n* 1 excursion, jaunt, journey, outing, ride, run, *inf* spin, trip. 2 ambition, determination, energy, enterprise, enthusiasm, *inf* get-up-and-go, impetus, initiative, keenness, motivation, persistence, *inf* push, vigour, zeal. 3 campaign, crusade, effort. • *v* 1 bang, dig, hammer, hit, knock, push, ram, sink, stab, strike, thrust. 2 coerce, compel, constrain, force, oblige, press, urge. 3 control, direct, guide, handle, manage, pilot, propel, send, steer. ▷ TRAVEL. **drive out** ▷ EXPEL.

droop *v* be limp, fall, flop, hang, sag, slump, wilt, wither.

drop *n* 1 bead, blob, bubble, dab, drip, droplet, globule, pearl, spot, tear. 2 *drop of whisky*. dash, *inf* nip, *inf* tot. 3 *steep drop*. declivity, descent, dive, fall, incline, plunge, precipice. 4 *drop in price*. cut, decrease, reduction, slump. *Opp* RISE. • *v* 1 collapse, descend, dive, fall, jump down, lower, nosedive, plummet, plunge, sink, slump, subside, swoop, tumble. 2 *drop from a team*. eliminate, exclude, leave out, omit. 3 *drop a friend, a plan*. abandon, discard, *inf* dump, forsake, give up, jilt, leave, reject, scrap. **drop behind** ▷ LAG. **drop in on** ▷ VISIT. **drop off** ▷ SLEEP.

drown v 1 engulf, flood, immerse, submerge, swamp. 2 be louder than, overpower, overwhelm, silence.

drowsy adj dozing, heavy-eyed, inf nodding off, sleepy, sluggish, somnolent, tired. Opp LIVELY.

drudgery n chore, inf donkey work, inf grind, labour, slavery, inf slog, toil. ▷ WORK.

drug n 1 cure, medicament, medication, medicine, remedy, treatment. 2 inf dope, narcotic, opiate. • v anaesthetize, inf dope, dose, inf knock out, medicate, poison, sedate, stupefy, tranquillize.

drum n ▷ BARREL.

drunk adj delirious, fuddled, incapable, inebriate, inebriated, intoxicated, maudlin, [sl] blotto, legless, merry, paralytic, pie-eyed, pissed, plastered, sloshed, sozzled, tiddly, tight, tipsy. Opp SOBER.

drunkard n alcoholic, dipsomaniac, drunk, inf sot, tippler, sl wino. Opp TEETOTALLER.

dry adj 1 arid, baked, barren, dead, dehydrated, desiccated, parched, scorched, shrivelled, thirsty, waterless. Opp WET. 2 boring, dreary, dull, flat, prosaic, tedious, tiresome, uninspired, uninteresting. Opp LIVELY. 3 dry humour. inf dead-pan, droll, laconic. • v become dry, dehumidify, dehydrate, desiccate, parch, shrivel, wilt, wither.

dual adj double, duplicate, linked, paired, twin.

dubious adj 1 ▷ DOUBTFUL. 2 a dubious character. inf fishy, inf shady, suspect, suspicious, unreliable, untrustworthy.

duck v 1 avoid, bob down, crouch, dodge, evade, sidestep, stoop, swerve. 2 immerse, plunge, push under, submerge.

due adj 1 outstanding, owed, owing, payable, unpaid. 2 due consideration. adequate, appropriate, deserved, fitting, just, merited, proper, requisite, right, rightful, sufficient, suitable, well-earned. • n deserts, entitlement, merits, reward, rights.

dues n ▷ DUTY.

dull adj 1 dim, dingy, dowdy, drab, dreary, faded, flat, gloomy, lacklustre, lifeless, sombre, subdued. 2 dull sky. cloudy, dismal, grey, heavy, leaden, murky, overcast, sunless. 3 dull sound. deadened, indistinct, muffled, muted. 4 dull student. dense, dim, obtuse, inf thick, unimaginative, unintelligent, unresponsive. ▷ STUPID. 5 dull edge. blunt, blunted. 6 dull book. tedious, uninteresting. ▷ BORING. Opp BRIGHT, SHARP.

dumb adj mute, silent, speechless, tongue-tied, unable to speak.

dummy n 1 copy, counterfeit, duplicate, imitation, model, reproduction, sample, simulation, substitute, toy. 2 doll, figure, puppet.

dump n 1 rubbish-heap, tip. 2 arms dump. arsenal, cache, depot, hoard, store. • v deposit, discard, dispose of, inf ditch, drop, get rid of, jettison, offload, put down, reject, scrap, throw away, tip, unload.

dune n drift, hillock, hummock, mound, sand dune.

dungeon n gaol, keep, lock-up, prison, vault.

duplicate adj copied, corresponding, identical, matching, second, twin. • n carbon copy, clone, copy, double, facsimile, imitation, likeness, inf look-alike, match, photocopy, replica, reproduction, twin, Xerox. • v copy, photocopy, print, repeat, reproduce, Xerox.

durable adj enduring, hard-wearing, indestructible, long-lasting, permanent, resilient, stout, strong, substantial, thick, tough. Opp IMPERMANENT, WEAK.

dusk n evening, sundown, sunset, twilight.

dust n dirt, grime, grit, particles, powder.

dusty adj 1 chalky, crumbly, dry, fine, friable, powdery, sandy, sooty. 2 dirty, grubby, un-cleaned, unswept.

dutiful adj careful, compliant, conscientious, devoted, diligent, faithful, hard-working, loyal, obedient, obliging, reliable, responsible, scrupulous, thorough, trustworthy. Opp IRRESPONSIBLE.

duty n 1 allegiance, loyalty, obedience, obligation, onus, responsibility, service. 2 assignment, business, chore, function, job, office, role, stint, task, work. 3 charge, dues, fee, levy, tariff, tax, toll.

dwarf adj ▷ SMALL. • n midget, pigmy. • v dominate, over-shadow, tower over.

dwell v dwell in ▷ INHABIT.

dwelling n abode, domicile, habitation, home, house, lodging, quarters, residence.

dying adj declining, expiring, fading, failing, moribund, obsolescent. Opp ALIVE.

dynamic adj active, driving, energetic, enterprising, enthusiastic, forceful, inf go-ahead, inf go-getting, high-powered, lively, motivated, powerful, inf pushy, spirited, vigorous, zealous. Opp APATHETIC.

E

eager adj agog, animated, anxious (to please), ardent, avid, desirous, earnest, enthusiastic, excited, fervent, hungry, impatient, intent, itching, keen, keyed up, motivated, passionate, inf raring (to go), voracious, yearning, zealous. Opp APATHETIC.

eagerness n alacrity, anxiety, appetite, ardour, desire, enthusiasm, excitement, fervour, hunger, impatience, interest, keenness, longing, motivation, passion, thirst, zeal. Opp APATHY.

early adj 1 advance, before time, first, forward, premature. Opp LATE. 2 ancient, initial, original. ▷ OLD. Opp RECENT.

earn v 1 be paid, inf bring in, inf clear, draw, gain, get, inf gross, make, net, obtain, pocket, realize, receive, inf take home, yield. 2 attain, be worthy of, deserve, merit, warrant, win.

earnest adj 1 assiduous, committed, conscientious, dedicated, determined, devoted, diligent, eager, hard-working, industrious, purposeful, resolved, zealous. *Opp* CASUAL. **2** grave, heartfelt, impassioned, serious, sincere, sober, solemn, thoughtful, well-meant.

earnings *pl n* income, salary, stipend, wages. ▷ PAY.

earth *n* clay, dirt, ground, land, loam, soil, topsoil.

earthenware *n* ceramics, china, crockery, porcelain, pottery.

earthly *adj* human, material, mortal, mundane, physical, secular, temporal, terrestrial, worldly. *Opp* SPIRITUAL.

earthquake *n* quake, shock, tremor, upheaval.

earthy *adj* bawdy, coarse, crude, down to earth, frank, lusty, ribald, uninhibited.

ease *n* **1** aplomb, calmness, comfort, composure, contentment, enjoyment, happiness, leisure, luxury, peace, quiet, relaxation, repose, rest, serenity, tranquillity. **2** dexterity, effortlessness, facility, skill, speed, straightforwardness. *Opp* DIFFICULTY.
● *v* **1** allay, alleviate, assuage, calm, comfort, decrease, lessen, lighten, mitigate, moderate, pacify, quell, quieten, reduce, relax, relieve, slacken, soothe. **2** edge, guide, inch, manoeuvre, move gradually, slide.

easy *adj* **1** carefree, comfortable, contented, cosy, *inf* cushy, effortless, leisurely, light, painless, peaceful, pleasant, relaxed, relaxing, restful, serene, soft, tranquil, undemanding, unhurried, untroubled. **2** clear, elementary, foolproof, manageable, plain, simple, straightforward, uncomplicated, understandable, user-friendly. **3** ▷ EASYGOING. *Opp* DIFFICULT.

easygoing *adj* accommodating, affable, amenable, calm, carefree, casual, cheerful, eventempered, flexible, *inf* free and easy, friendly, genial, *inf* happy-go-lucky, indulgent, informal, *inf* laid-back, *derog* lax, lenient, liberal, mellow, nonchalant, open, patient, permissive, placid, relaxed, tolerant, unruffled. *Opp* STRICT.

eat *v* **1** bolt, chew, consume, devour, digest, feed on, gnaw, gobble, gorge, graze, gulp, guzzle, live on, munch, nibble, *inf* scoff, swallow, *inf* tuck in. **2** breakfast, dine, feast, lunch. **eat away, eat into** ▷ ERODE.

eatable *adj* digestible, edible, fit to eat, palatable, wholesome. ▷ TASTY. *Opp* INEDIBLE.

ebb *v* fall, flow back, go down, recede, retreat, subside. ▷ DECLINE.

eccentric *adj* **1** aberrant, abnormal, anomalous, atypical, bizarre, curious, freakish, idiosyncratic, odd, outlandish, out of the ordinary, peculiar, quaint, queer, quirky, singular, strange, unconventional, unusual, *inf* way-out, *inf* weird, zany. ▷ ABSURD, MAD. **2** *eccentric circles.* irregular, off-centre. ● *n* ▷ CHARACTER.

echo *v* **1** resound, reverberate, ring, sound again. **2** copy, emulate, imitate, mimic, mirror, reiterate, repeat.

eclipse *v* **1** blot out, cloud, darken, dim, obscure, veil. ▷ COVER. **2** excel, outdo, outshine, overshadow, *inf* put in the shade, surpass, top.

economic *adj* business, commercial, financial, fiscal, monetary, trading.

economical adj 1 careful, frugal, provident, prudent, sparing, thrifty. ▷ MISERLY. Opp WASTEFUL. 2 cheap, cost-effective, inexpensive, low-priced, reasonable, inf value-for-money. Opp EXPENSIVE.

economize v cut back, save, inf scrimp, skimp, spend less, inf tighten your belt. Opp SQUANDER.

economy n 1 frugality, derog miserliness, parsimony, providence, prudence, saving, thrift. Opp WASTE. 2 national economy: budget, economic affairs, wealth. 3 ▷ BREVITY.

ecstasy n bliss, delight, elation, euphoria, exaltation, fervour, frenzy, happiness, joy, rapture, thrill, trance, transport.

ecstatic adj blissful, delighted, delirious, elated, enraptured, euphoric, exhilarated, exultant, frenzied, joyful, orgasmic, overjoyed, inf over the moon, rapturous, transported. ▷ HAPPY.

eddy n maelstrom, swirl, vortex, whirl, whirlpool, whirlwind. ● v move in circles, spin, swirl, turn, whirl.

edge n 1 border, boundary, brim, brink, circumference, frame, kerb, limit, lip, margin, outline, perimeter, periphery, rim, side, verge. 2 outskirts, suburbs. 3 incisiveness, keenness, sharpness. 4 edge of a curtain: edging, fringe, hem. ● v 1 bind, border, fringe, hem, trim. 2 edge away: crawl, creep, inch, move stealthily, sidle, slink, steal, worm.

edible adj digestible, eatable, fit to eat, palatable, wholesome. ▷ TASTY. Opp INEDIBLE.

edit v abridge, adapt, alter, amend, arrange, assemble, censor, compile, condense, correct, cut, emend, organize, polish, prepare, put together, rephrase, revise, rewrite, select.

edition n 1 copy, issue, number. 2 impression, printing, print-run, publication, version.

educate v bring up, civilize, coach, cultivate, discipline, drill, edify, enlighten, guide, improve, indoctrinate, inform, instruct, lecture, rear, school, teach, train, tutor.

educated adj cultured, enlightened, erudite, knowledgeable, learned, literate, numerate, trained, well-bred, well-read.

education n coaching, enlightenment, guidance, indoctrination, instruction, schooling, teaching, training, tuition.

eerie adj inf creepy, frightening, ghostly, mysterious, inf scary, inf spooky, strange, uncanny, unearthly, unnatural, weird.

effect n 1 aftermath, conclusion, consequence, impact, issue, outcome, repercussion, result, sequel, upshot. 2 feeling, illusion, impression, sensation, sense. ● v accomplish, achieve, bring about, carry out, cause, create, enforce, execute, implement, initiate, make, produce, put into effect, secure.

effective adj 1 capable, competent, functional, impressive, potent, powerful, productive, proficient, serviceable, strong, successful, useful, worthwhile. ▷ EFFICIENT. 2 effective argument: cogent, compelling, convincing, meaningful, persuasive, striking, telling. Opp INEFFECTIVE.

effeminate *adj* camp, effete, girlish, *inf* sissy, unmanly, weak. Opp MANLY.

effervesce *v* bubble, ferment, fizz, foam, froth, sparkle.

effervescent *adj* bubbling, bubbly, carbonated, fizzy, foaming, frothy, gassy, sparkling.

efficient *adj* businesslike, cost-effective, economic, streamlined. ▷ EFFECTIVE. Opp INEFFICIENT.

effort *n* 1 application, *inf* elbow grease, endeavour, exertion, industry, labour, pains, strain, stress, striving, struggle, toil, trouble, work. 2 *brave effort.* attempt, endeavour, go, try, venture. 3 *successful effort.* achievement, exploit, feat, outcome, product, production, result.

effusive *adj* demonstrative, ebullient, enthusiastic, exuberant, fulsome, gushing, lavish, *inf* over the top, profuse, voluble. Opp RETICENT.

egotism *n* egocentricity, egoism, narcissism, pride, self-importance, self-interest, selfishness, self-love, vanity.

egotistical *adj* self-centred, selfish. ▷ CONCEITED.

eject *v* 1 banish, *inf* bundle out, deport, discharge, dismiss, drive out, evict, exile, expel, *inf* kick out, oust, push out, put out, remove, sack, shoot out, throw out, turn out. 2 ▷ EMIT.

elaborate *adj* complex, complicated, detailed, exhaustive, intricate, involved, painstaking, thorough. 2 *elaborate decor.* baroque, decorative, fancy, fantastic, fussy, intricate, ornamental, ornate, rococo, showy. Opp SIMPLE. ● *v* add to, adorn, amplify, complicate, decorate, develop, embellish, enlarge on,

expand, fill out, give details of, improve on, ornament. Opp SIMPLIFY.

elapse *v* go by, pass, slip by.

elastic *adj inf* bendy, bouncy, flexible, plastic, pliable, pliant, resilient, rubbery, *inf* springy, *inf* stretchy, yielding. Opp RIGID.

elderly *adj* ageing, *inf* getting on. ▷ OLD.

elect *adj* chosen, elected, prospective, selected. ● *v* adopt, appoint, choose, name, nominate, opt for, pick, select, vote for.

election *n* ballot, choice, poll, referendum, selection, vote, voting.

electioneer *v* campaign, canvass.

electorate *n* constituents, electors, voters.

electric *adj* 1 battery-operated, electrical. 2 electrifying. ▷ EXCITING.

electricity *n* current, energy, power, power supply.

elegant *adj* beautiful, chic, courtly, cultivated, debonair, dignified, exquisite, fashionable, fine, genteel, graceful, gracious, handsome, luxurious, pleasing, *inf* plush, *inf* posh, refined, smart, sophisticated, splendid, stately, stylish, suave, tasteful, urbane, well-bred. Opp INELEGANT.

elegy *n* dirge, lament, requiem.

element *n* 1 component, constituent, detail, factor, feature, fragment, ingredient, part, piece, trace, unit. 2 *in your element.* domain, environment, habitat, medium, sphere, territory. **elements** ▷ RUDIMENTS, WEATHER.

elementary *adj* basic, early, first, fundamental, initial, introductory, primary, rudimentary,

simple, straightforward. ▷ EASY.
Opp ADVANCED.

elevate *v* exalt, lift, make higher,
promote. ▷ RAISE. **elevated**
▷ HIGH, NOBLE.

elicit *v* bring out, derive, draw
out, evoke, extract, get, obtain,
wrest, wring.

eligible *adj* acceptable, allowed,
appropriate, authorized, competent, equipped, fit, proper, qualified, suitable, worthy.
Opp INELIGIBLE.

eliminate *v* 1 abolish, annihilate, delete, destroy, dispense
with, do away with, eject, end,
eradicate, exterminate, extinguish, get rid of, remove, stamp
out. ▷ KILL. 2 drop, exclude,
knock out, leave out, omit,
reject.

elite *n* aristocracy, best,
inf cream, flower, nobility, pick,
inf upper crust.

eloquent *adj* articulate, expressive, fluent, *derog* glib, persuasive, plausible, powerful.
Opp INARTICULATE.

elude *v* avoid, circumvent,
dodge, *inf* duck, escape, evade,
foil, *inf* give (someone) the slip,
shake off.

elusive *adj* 1 evasive, hard to
find, slippery. 2 *elusive meaning.*
ambiguous, baffling, deceptive,
hard to pin down, indefinable,
intangible, puzzling.

emaciated *adj* bony, cadaverous, gaunt, haggard, skeletal,
skinny, starved, underfed, undernourished, wizened. ▷ THIN.

emancipate *v* deliver, discharge,
enfranchise, free, let go, liberate,
loose, release, set free.
Opp ENSLAVE.

embankment *n* bank, dam,
earthwork, mound.

embark *v* board, depart, go
aboard, leave, set out.
Opp DISEMBARK. **embark on**
▷ BEGIN.

embarrass *v* abash, confuse, discomfit, disconcert, disgrace, distress, fluster, humiliate, mortify,
shame, *inf* show up, upset.
embarrassed ▷ ASHAMED.
embarrassing ▷ AWKWARD,
SHAMEFUL.

embellish *v* adorn, beautify,
deck, decorate, embroider, garnish, ornament. ▷ ELABORATE.

embezzle *v* appropriate, misappropriate, *inf* put your hand in
the till. ▷ STEAL.

embezzlement *n* fraud, misappropriation, misuse of funds,
stealing, theft.

embittered *adj* bitter, disillusioned, envious, rancorous,
resentful, sour. ▷ ANGRY.

emblem *n* badge, crest, device,
image, insignia, mark, regalia,
seal, sign, symbol, token.

embody *v* 1 exemplify, express,
incarnate, manifest, personify,
represent, stand for, symbolize.
2 combine, comprise, embrace,
enclose, include, incorporate,
integrate, involve, unite.

embrace *v* 1 clasp, cling to,
cuddle, enfold, grasp, hold, hug,
kiss, snuggle up to. 2 *embrace
new ideas.* accept, espouse,
receive, take on, welcome.
3 ▷ EMBODY.

embryonic *adj* early, immature,
just beginning, rudimentary,
undeveloped, unformed.
Opp MATURE.

emerge *v* appear, arise, be
revealed, come out, come to

light, emanate, leak out, *inf* pop up, proceed, surface, transpire, *inf* turn out.

emergency *n* crisis, danger, difficulty, predicament, serious situation.

emigrate *v* depart, go abroad, leave, relocate, resettle.

eminent *adj* august, celebrated, conspicuous, distinguished, elevated, esteemed, exalted, famous, great, honoured, illustrious, important, notable, noteworthy, outstanding, pre-eminent, prominent, renowned, well-known. *Opp* LOWLY.

emit *v* belch, discharge, eject, exhale, expel, exude, give off, give out, issue, radiate, send out, spew out, spout, transmit.

emotion *n* excitement, feeling, fervour, passion, sentiment, warmth.

emotional *adj* 1 ardent, demonstrative, enthusiastic, excited, fervent, fiery, heated, hot-headed, impassioned, intense, irrational, passionate, romantic, touched, warm-hearted, worked up. 2 *emotional language.* affecting, emotive, heart-rending, inflammatory, loaded, moving, pathetic, poignant, provocative, sentimental, stirring, subjective, *inf* tear-jerking, tender, touching. *Opp* UNEMOTIONAL.

emphasis *n* accent, attention, force, importance, intensity, priority, prominence, stress, urgency, weight.

emphasize *v* accent, accentuate, bring out, dwell on, focus on, highlight, impress, insist on, make obvious, *inf* play up, point up, *inf* press home, *inf* rub it in,

spotlight, stress, underline, underscore.

emphatic *adj* assertive, categorical, dogmatic, definite, firm, forceful, insistent, positive, pronounced, resolute, strong, uncompromising, unequivocal. *Opp* TENTATIVE.

empirical *adj* experimental, observed, practical, pragmatic. *Opp* THEORETICAL.

employ *v* 1 commission, engage, enlist, hire, pay, sign up, take on, use the services of. 2 apply, use, utilize.

employed *adj* active, earning, hired, involved, in work, occupied, practising, working. ▷ BUSY. *Opp* UNEMPLOYED.

employee *n* worker. **employees** staff, workforce.

employer *n* boss, chief, *inf* gaffer, *inf* governor, head, manager, owner, proprietor.

employment *n* business, calling, craft, job, line, livelihood, living, métier, occupation, profession, pursuit, trade, vocation, work.

empty *adj* 1 bare, blank, clean, clear, deserted, desolate, forsaken, hollow, unfilled, unfurnished, uninhabited, unoccupied, unused, vacant, void. *Opp* FULL. 2 *empty threats.* futile, idle, impotent, ineffective, meaningless, pointless, purposeless, senseless, silly, worthless. ● *v* clear, discharge, drain, evacuate, exhaust, pour out, unload, vacate, void. *Opp* FILL.

enable *v* allow, assist, authorize, empower, entitle, equip, facilitate, help, license, make it possible, permit, provide the means, qualify. *Opp* PREVENT.

enchant *v* allure, beguile, bewitch, captivate, cast a spell on, charm, delight, enthral, entrance, fascinate, hypnotize, mesmerize. **enchanting** ▷ ATTRACTIVE.

enchantment *n* charm, magic, sorcery, spell, witchcraft, wizardry. ▷ DELIGHT.

enclose *v* box, cage, conceal, confine, contain, cover, encircle, encompass, enfold, envelop, fence in, hedge in, hem in, insert, limit, package, pen, restrict, ring, secure, sheathe, shut in, surround, wall in, wall up, wrap. ▷ IMPRISON.

enclosure *n* 1 cage, compound, coop, corral, courtyard, farmyard, field, fold, paddock, pen, pound, ring, run, stockade, sty, yard. 2 *enclosure in an envelope.* contents, insertion.

encounter *n* 1 confrontation, meeting. 2 [*military*] battle, clash, dispute, skirmish, struggle. ▷ FIGHT. ● *v inf* bump into, chance upon, clash with, come upon, confront, contend with, *inf* cross swords with, face, happen upon, meet, run into.

encourage *v* 1 applaud, cheer, egg on, give hope to, hearten, incite, inspire, persuade, prompt, rally, reassure, rouse, spur on, support, urge. 2 *encourage sales.* aid, be an incentive to, be conducive to, boost, foster, further, generate, help, increase, induce, promote, stimulate. *Opp* DISCOURAGE.

encouragement *n* approval, boost, cheer, exhortation, incentive, inspiration, reassurance, *inf* shot in the arm, stimulus, support. *Opp* DISCOURAGEMENT.

encouraging *adj* comforting, heartening, hopeful, inspiring, optimistic, positive, promising, reassuring. ▷ FAVOURABLE.

encroach *v* enter, impinge, infringe, intrude, invade, make inroads, trespass, violate.

end *n* 1 boundary, edge, extremity, limit, tip. 2 cessation, close, coda, completion, conclusion, culmination, curtain (*of play*), denouement (*of plot*), ending, expiry, finale, finish, *inf* pay-off, resolution. 3 *journey's end.* destination, home, termination. 4 *end of a queue.* back, rear, tail. 5 *end of your life.* death, destruction, destiny, doom, extinction, fate, passing. 6 *end in view.* aim, aspiration, design, intention, objective, outcome, plan, purpose, result, upshot. *Opp* BEGINNING. ● *v* 1 abolish, break off, complete, conclude, cut off, destroy, discontinue, *inf* drop, eliminate, exterminate, finalize, *inf* get rid of, halt, phase out, *inf* round off, ruin, terminate, *inf* wind up. 2 break up, cease, close, culminate, die, disappear, expire, fade away, finish, *inf* pack up, stop. *Opp* BEGIN.

endanger *v* jeopardize, put at risk, threaten. ▷ PROTECT.

endearing *adj* appealing, attractive, captivating, charming, disarming, enchanting, engaging, likable, lovable, sweet, winning. *Opp* REPULSIVE.

endeavour *v* ▷ TRY.

endless *adj* 1 boundless, immeasurable, inexhaustible, infinite, limitless, unbounded, unlimited. 2 abiding, ceaseless, constant, continual, continuous, enduring, eternal, everlasting, immortal, incessant, interminable, never-ending, nonstop, perpetual, persistent, unbroken, undying.

endorse v 1 advocate, agree with, approve, authorize, *inf* back, condone, confirm, *inf* OK, sanction, subscribe to, support. 2 *endorse a cheque*. countersign, sign.

endurance n determination, fortitude, patience, perseverance, persistence, resolution, stamina, staying-power, strength, tenacity.

endure v 1 carry on, continue, exist, last, live on, persevere, persist, prevail, remain, stay, survive. 2 bear, cope with, experience, go through, put up with, stand, stomach, submit to, suffer, tolerate, undergo, weather, withstand. **enduring** ▷ PERMANENT.

enemy n adversary, antagonist, competitor, foe, opponent, opposition, the other side, rival. *Opp* FRIEND.

energetic adj active, animated, brisk, dynamic, enthusiastic, forceful, indefatigable, lively, powerful, quick-moving, spirited, strenuous, tireless, unflagging, vigorous, zestful. *Opp* LETHARGIC.

energy n 1 animation, ardour, drive, dynamism, élan, enthusiasm, exertion, fire, force, *inf* get-up-and-go, *inf* go, life, liveliness, spirit, stamina, strength, verve, vigour, vitality, vivacity, zeal, zest. *Opp* LETHARGY. 2 fuel, power.

enforce v apply, carry out, compel, execute, implement, impose, inflict, insist on, prosecute, put into effect, require. *Opp* WAIVE.

engage v 1 employ, enlist, hire, recruit, sign up, take on. 2 *cogs engage*. bite, fit together, interlock. 3 *engage to do something.* ▷ PROMISE. 4 *engage in gossip.* ▷ OCCUPY. 5 *engage in sport.* ▷ PARTICIPATE.

engaged adj 1 affianced, betrothed, *old use* spoken for. 2 ▷ BUSY.

engagement n 1 betrothal, promise to marry. 2 *social engagement.* appointment, arrangement, commitment, date, fixture, meeting, obligation, rendezvous. 3 ▷ BATTLE.

engine n 1 machine, motor. 2 locomotive.

engineer n mechanic, technician. ● v ▷ CONSTRUCT, DEVISE.

engrave v carve, chisel, etch, inscribe. ▷ CUT.

enigma n conundrum, mystery, problem, puzzle, riddle.

enjoy v 1 appreciate, bask in, delight in, *inf* go in for, indulge in, *inf* lap up, luxuriate in, relish, revel in, savour, take pleasure in. ▷ LIKE. 2 benefit from, experience, take advantage of, use. **enjoy yourself** celebrate, have a good time, make merry.

enjoyable adj agreeable, amusing, delicious, delightful, entertaining, *inf* nice, pleasurable, rewarding, satisfying. ▷ PLEASANT. *Opp* UNPLEASANT.

enlarge v amplify, augment, blow up, broaden, build up, develop, dilate, distend, elongate, expand, extend, fill out, grow, increase, inflate, lengthen, magnify, multiply, spread, stretch, swell, widen. *Opp* DECREASE. **enlarge on** ▷ ELABORATE.

enlighten v edify, illuminate, inform, make aware. ▷ TEACH.

enlist v 1 conscript, muster, recruit, sign up. 2 *enlist in the army*. enrol, enter, join up, register, sign on, volunteer. 3 *enlist help*. ▷ OBTAIN.

enliven v animate, arouse, brighten, cheer up, energize, inspire, *inf* pep up, rouse, stimulate, wake up.

enormous adj colossal, elephantine, gargantuan, giant, gigantic, gross, huge, immense, *inf* jumbo, mammoth, massive, mighty, monstrous, mountainous, prodigious, stupendous, titanic, towering, vast. ▷ BIG. *Opp* SMALL.

enough adj adequate, ample, as much as necessary, sufficient.

enquire v ask, inquire, query, question. **enquire about** ▷ INVESTIGATE.

enrage v incense, infuriate, madden. ▷ ANGER.

enslave v dominate, subjugate, take away the rights of. *Opp* EMANCIPATE.

ensure v confirm, guarantee, make certain, secure.

entail v call for, demand, give rise to, involve, lead to, necessitate, require.

enter v 1 arrive, come in, get in, go in, infiltrate, invade, step in. *Opp* DEPART. 2 penetrate, pierce, puncture, push into. 3 *enter a contest*. engage in, enlist in, enrol in, *inf* go in for, join, participate in, sign up for, take part in, volunteer for. 4 *enter names on a list*. add, insert, note down, put down, record, register, sign, write. *Opp* REMOVE. **enter into** ▷ BEGIN.

enterprise n 1 adventure, effort, endeavour, operation, programme, project, undertaking, venture. 2 ambition, courage, daring, determination, drive, energy, *inf* get-up-and-go, initiative. 3 business, company, concern, firm, organization.

enterprising adj adventurous, ambitious, bold, courageous, daring, determined, eager, energetic, enthusiastic, *inf* go-ahead, *inf* go-getting, imaginative, indefatigable, industrious, intrepid, keen, purposeful, *inf* pushy, resourceful, spirited, vigorous, zealous. *Opp* UNADVENTUROUS.

entertain v 1 amuse, cheer up, delight, divert, occupy, please, regale, *inf* tickle. *Opp* BORE. 2 *entertain friends*. accommodate, be host to, cater for, *inf* put up, receive, treat, welcome. 3 *entertain an idea*. accept, agree to, approve, consent to, consider, contemplate, support, take seriously. *Opp* IGNORE. **entertaining** ▷ INTERESTING.

entertainer n actor, actress, artist, artiste, musician, performer, player, singer.

entertainment n 1 amusement, distraction, diversion, enjoyment, fun, nightlife, pastime, play, pleasure, recreation, sport. 2 drama, exhibition, extravaganza, performance, presentation, production, show, spectacle.

enthusiasm n 1 ambition, ardour, drive, eagerness, excitement, exuberance, *derog* fanaticism, fervour, gusto, keenness, passion, relish, spirit, verve, zeal, zest. *Opp* APATHY. 2 craze, fad, hobby, interest, passion, pastime.

enthusiast n addict, admirer, aficionado, *inf* buff, champion, devotee, fan, fanatic, *inf* fiend, lover, supporter.

enthusiastic adj ambitious, ardent, avid, committed, *inf* crazy, devoted, eager, earnest, ebullient, energetic, excited, exuberant, fervent, hearty, impassioned, interested, involved, irrepressible, keen, lively, *inf* mad (about), passionate, positive, rapturous, raring (to go), spirited, unstinting, vigorous, wholehearted, zealous. *Opp* APATHETIC. **be enthusiastic** enthuse, get excited, *inf* go into raptures, *inf* go overboard, rave.

entice v allure, attract, coax, decoy, inveigle, lead on, lure, persuade, seduce, tempt, trap.

entire adj complete, full, intact, sound, total, unbroken, undivided, uninterrupted, whole.

entitle v 1 call, christen, designate, dub, name, style, term, title. 2 allow, authorize, empower, enable, license, permit, qualify, warrant.

entitlement n claim, ownership, prerogative, right, title.

entity n article, being, object, organism, thing, whole.

entrails pl n bowels, guts, *inf* innards, inner organs, *inf* insides, intestines, viscera.

entrance n 1 access, admission, admittance. 2 appearance, arrival, entry. 3 door, doorway, gate, ingress, opening, turnstile, way in. 4 ante-room, foyer, lobby, passage, passageway, porch, vestibule. *Opp* EXIT.

entrant n applicant, candidate, competitor, contender, contestant, participant, player, rival.

entreat v beg, beseech, implore, sue. ▷ REQUEST.

entry n 1 insertion, item, listing, note, record. 2 ▷ ENTRANCE. 3 ▷ ENTRANT.

envelop v cloak, enfold, enshroud, swathe, wrap. ▷ HIDE.

envelope n cover, sheath, wrapper, wrapping.

enviable adj attractive, covetable, desirable, sought-after.

envious adj bitter, covetous, *inf* green with envy, grudging, jaundiced, jealous, resentful.

environment n conditions, context, ecosystem, environs, habitat, location, milieu, setting, situation, surroundings.

envisage v anticipate, contemplate, dream of, envision, fancy, forecast, foresee, imagine, picture, predict, visualize.

envy n bitterness, covetousness, cupidity, desire, discontent, ill will, jealousy, longing, resentment. • v begrudge, grudge, resent.

ephemeral adj brief, evanescent, fleeting, fugitive, impermanent, momentary, passing, short-lived, transient, transitory. *Opp* PERMANENT.

epidemic adj general, prevalent, rife, spreading, universal, widespread. • n outbreak, pestilence, plague, rash, upsurge.

episode n 1 affair, event, happening, incident, matter, occurrence. 2 chapter, instalment, part, passage, scene.

epitome n 1 archetype, embodiment, essence, exemplar, incarnation, personification, quintessence, type. 2 ▷ SUMMARY.

equal *adj* balanced, commensurate, congruent, egalitarian, even, fair, identical, indistinguishable, interchangeable, level, like, matching, proportionate, regular, the same, symmetrical, uniform. ▷ EQUIVALENT.
Opp UNEQUAL. ● *n* counterpart, equivalent, fellow, peer, twin.
● *v* 1 balance, correspond to, draw with, tie with. 2 *No one equals her.* be in the same class as, compare with, match, resemble, rival.

equality *n* 1 balance, correspondence, equivalence, identity, similarity, uniformity. 2 *social equality.* egalitarianism, even-handedness, fairness, parity.
Opp BIAS, INEQUALITY.

equalize *v* balance, compensate, even up, level, match, regularize, square, standardize.

equate *v* assume to be equal, compare, juxtapose, liken, match, set side by side.

equilibrium *n* balance, equanimity, evenness, poise, stability, steadiness, symmetry.

equip *v* arm, array, attire, clothe, dress, fit out, fit up, furnish, *inf* kit out, provide, stock, supply.

equipment *n* accoutrements, apparatus, *inf* clobber, furnishings, *inf* gear, hardware, implements, instruments, kit, machinery, materials, outfit, paraphernalia, rig, stuff, supplies, tackle, things, tools, trappings.

equivalent *adj* alike, analogous, comparable, corresponding, parallel, similar, synonymous.
▷ EQUAL.

equivocal *adj* ambiguous, circumlocutory, doubtful, equivoc-

ating, evasive, noncommittal, questionable, roundabout.

equivocate *v inf* beat about the bush, dodge the issue, fence, *inf* have it both ways, hedge, prevaricate, quibble.

era *n* age, date, day, epoch, period, time.

eradicate *v* eliminate, get rid of, uproot. ▷ DESTROY.

erase *v* cancel, cross out, delete, eradicate, obliterate, rub out, wipe away. ▷ REMOVE.

erect *adj* perpendicular, rigid, standing, straight, upright, vertical. ● *v* build, construct, elevate, establish, lift up, pitch (*a tent*), put up, raise.

erode *v* corrode, eat away, eat into, gnaw away, grind down, wash away, wear away.

erotic *adj* aphrodisiac, arousing, seductive, sensual, voluptuous.
▷ SEXY.

err *v* be mistaken, *sl* boob, *inf* get it wrong, go astray, go wrong, misbehave, miscalculate, sin, *inf* slip up, transgress.

errand *n* assignment, commission, duty, job, journey, mission, task, trip.

erratic *adj* capricious, changeable, fickle, fitful, fluctuating, inconsistent, irregular, shifting, spasmodic, sporadic, uneven, unpredictable, unsteady, variable, wayward. *Opp* REGULAR. 2 aimless, haphazard, meandering, wandering.

error *n inf* bloomer, blunder, *sl* boob, fallacy, fault, flaw, gaffe, *inf* howler, inaccuracy, inconsistency, lapse, misapprehension, miscalculation, misconception, misprint, mistake, misunderstanding, omission, oversight, sin, *inf* slip-up, solecism, transgression, wrongdoing.

erupt *v* be discharged, belch, break out, burst out, explode, gush, issue, pour out, shoot out, spew, spout, spurt.

eruption *n* emission, explosion, outbreak, outburst, rash.

escapade *n* adventure, exploit, *inf* lark, mischief, practical joke, prank, scrape, stunt.

escape *n* 1 break-out, departure, flight, flit, getaway, retreat. 2 discharge, emission, leak, leakage, seepage. 3 avoidance, distraction, diversion, escapism, evasion, relaxation, relief. ● *v* 1 abscond, *sl* beat it, bolt, break free, break out, *inf* cut and run, decamp, disappear, *sl* do a bunk, elope, flee, fly, get away, *inf* give someone the slip, run away, *sl* scarper, *inf* slip the net, *inf* take to your heels, *inf* turn tail. 2 discharge, drain, leak, ooze, pour out, seep. 3 *escape the nasty jobs.* avoid, dodge, duck, elude, evade, shirk, *sl* skive off.

escapism *n* daydreaming, fantasy, wishful thinking.

escort *n* 1 bodyguard, convoy, guard, guide, protection, protector, safe-conduct. 2 *royal escort.* attendant, entourage, retinue, train. 3 *escort at a dance.* chaperon, companion, *inf* date, partner. ● *v* accompany, attend, chaperon, conduct, guard, look after, protect, shepherd, stay with, usher, watch.

essence *n* 1 centre, character, core, crux, essential quality, heart, kernel, life, meaning, nature, pith, quintessence, soul, spirit, substance. 2 concentrate, elixir, extract, flavouring, fragrance, perfume, scent, tincture.

essential *adj* basic, characteristic, chief, crucial, fundamental, important, indispensable, inherent, innate, intrinsic, irreplaceable, key, leading, main, necessary, primary, principal, quintessential, requisite, vital. *Opp* INESSENTIAL.

establish *v* 1 base, constitute, construct, create, decree, found, form, inaugurate, institute, introduce, organize, originate, set up, start. 2 *establish yourself in a job.* confirm, ensconce, entrench, install, lodge, secure, settle. 3 *establish facts.* accept, agree, authenticate, confirm, corroborate, decide, demonstrate, fix, prove, ratify, recognize, substantiate, verify.

established *adj* deep-rooted, deep-seated, ineradicable, ingrained, long-standing, permanent, proven, reliable, respected, secure, traditional, well-known, well-tried. *Opp* NEW.

establishment *n* 1 constitution, creation, formation, foundation, inauguration, institution, introduction, setting up. 2 *well-run establishment.* business, company, concern, enterprise, factory, household, institution, office, organization, shop.

estate *n* 1 area, development, domain, land. 2 assets, capital, chattels, effects, fortune, goods, inheritance, lands, possessions, property, wealth.

esteem *n* admiration, credit, estimation, favour, honour, regard, respect, reverence, veneration. ● *v* ▷ RESPECT.

estimate *n* appraisal, approximation, assessment, calculation, conjecture, estimation, evaluation, guess, judgement, opinion, price, quotation, reckoning, valuation. ● *v* appraise, assess, calculate, compute, conjecture, consider, count up, evaluate, gauge, guess, judge, project, reckon, surmise, weigh up, work out.

estimation *n* appraisal, appreciation, assessment, calculation, consideration, estimate, evaluation, judgement, opinion, rating, view.

estuary *n* creek, firth, fjord, inlet, loch, river mouth.

eternal *adj* ceaseless, endless, everlasting, heavenly, immeasurable, immortal, infinite, lasting, measureless, never-ending, permanent, perpetual, timeless, unchanging, undying, unending, unlimited. ▷ CONTINUAL. *Opp* OCCASIONAL, TRANSIENT.

eternity *n* afterlife, immortality, infinity, perpetuity.

ethical *adj* decent, fair, good, honest, just, moral, noble, principled, righteous, upright, virtuous. *Opp* IMMORAL.

ethnic *adj* cultural, folk, national, racial, traditional.

etiquette *n* ceremony, civility, code, conventions, courtesy, decency, decorum, form, formalities, manners, politeness, propriety, protocol, rules, standards.

evacuate *v* 1 clear, move out, remove, send away. 2 abandon, desert, empty, leave, pull out of, quit, relinquish, vacate, withdraw from.

evade *v* 1 avoid, circumvent, dodge, duck, elude, escape from, fend off, get away from, shirk, shrink from, shun, sidestep, *sl* skive, steer clear of. 2 *evade a question.* fudge, hedge, parry. ▷ EQUIVOCATE. *Opp* CONFRONT.

evaluate *v* assess, estimate, judge, value, weigh up.

evaporate *v* disappear, disperse, dissipate, dissolve, dry up, melt away, vanish, vaporize.

evasive *adj* ambiguous, *inf* cagey, circumlocutory, deceptive, devious, equivocal, indirect, misleading, noncommittal, oblique, prevaricating, roundabout, *inf* shifty, uninformative. *Opp* DIRECT.

even *adj* 1 flat, flush, horizontal, level, plane, smooth, straight, true. 2 *even pulse.* consistent, constant, measured, regular, rhythmical, unbroken, uniform, unvarying. 3 *even scores.* balanced, equal, identical, level, matching, the same. 4 ▷ EVEN-TEMPERED. *Opp* IRREGULAR. **even out** ▷ FLATTEN. **even up** ▷ EQUALIZE. **get even** ▷ RETALIATE.

evening *n* dusk, nightfall, sundown, sunset, twilight.

event *n* 1 affair, business, chance, circumstance, contingency, episode, eventuality, experience, happening, incident, occurrence. 2 ceremony, entertainment, function, occasion. 3 *sporting event.* championship, competition, contest, engagement, fixture, game, match, meeting, tournament.

even-tempered *adj* balanced, calm, composed, cool, equable, impassive, imperturbable, peaceable, peaceful, placid, poised, reliable, self-possessed, serene, stable, steady, tranquil, unemotional, unexcitable, unruffled. *Opp* EXCITABLE.

eventual *adj* concluding, destined, ensuing, final, last, resultant, resulting, ultimate.

everlasting adj ceaseless, deathless, endless, eternal, immortal, incorruptible, infinite, limitless, measureless, never-ending, permanent, perpetual, timeless, unchanging, undying, unending. Opp TRANSIENT.

evermore adv always, eternally, for ever, unceasingly.

evict v dislodge, dispossess, eject, expel, sl give (someone) the boot, inf kick out, oust, remove, throw out, inf turf out.

evidence n attestation, confirmation, corroboration, data, demonstration, documentation, facts, grounds, information, proof, sign, statistics. **give evidence** ▷ TESTIFY.

evident adj apparent, clear, discernible, manifest, obvious, palpable, patent, perceptible, plain, self-explanatory, undeniable, unmistakable, visible. Opp UNCERTAIN.

evil adj 1 amoral, atrocious, base, black-hearted, blasphemous, corrupt, devilish, diabolical, dishonest, fiendish, foul, harmful, hateful, heinous, hellish, impious, iniquitous, irreligious, machiavellian, malevolent, nefarious, pernicious, perverted, reprobate, satanic, sinful, sinister, treacherous, ungodly, unprincipled, vicious, vile, wicked, wrong. ▷ BAD. Opp GOOD. 2 evil smell. foul, nasty, pestilential, poisonous, unpleasant, unspeakable, vile. Opp PLEASANT. ● n 1 amorality, blasphemy, corruption, criminality, cruelty, depravity, dishonesty, fiendishness, immorality, impiety, iniquity, malevolence, malice, mischief, sin, sinfulness, treachery, turpitude, ungodli-ness, unrighteousness, vice, viciousness, villainy, wickedness. 2 affliction, bane, calamity, catastrophe, curse, disaster, enormity, hardship, harm, ill, misfortune, wrong.

evocative adj atmospheric, emotive, graphic, imaginative, realistic, stimulating, suggestive, vivid.

evoke v arouse, awaken, call up, conjure up, elicit, excite, kindle, produce, provoke, raise, rouse, stimulate, stir up, suggest, summon up.

evolution n advance, development, emergence, formation, growth, improvement, maturation, progress, unfolding.

evolve v develop, emerge, grow, improve, mature, progress, unfold.

exact adj 1 accurate, correct, dead (centre), faithful, faultless, meticulous, painstaking, precise, punctilious, right, rigorous, scrupulous, specific, inf spot-on, strict, true, truthful. Opp IMPRECISE. 2 exact copy. identical, indistinguishable, literal, perfect. ● v claim, compel, demand, enforce, extort, extract, get, insist on, obtain, require. **exacting** ▷ DIFFICULT.

exaggerate v 1 amplify, embellish, embroider, enlarge, inflate, magnify, make too much of, maximize, overdo, overemphasize, overestimate, overstate, inf pile it on. Opp MINIMIZE. 2 ▷ CARICATURE. **exaggerated** ▷ EXCESSIVE.

exalt v boost, elevate, lift, promote, raise, uplift. ▷ PRAISE. **exalted** ▷ HIGH.

examination n 1 analysis, appraisal, assessment, audit,

inf exam, inspection, investigation, paper, post-mortem, review, scrutiny, study, survey, test. 2 [*medical*] *inf* check-up, scan. 3 *police examination.* cross-examination, enquiry, inquiry, inquisition, interrogation, probe, questioning, trial.

examine *v* 1 analyse, appraise, audit (*accounts*), check, *inf* check out, explore, inquire into, inspect, investigate, peruse, probe, research, scan, scrutinize, sift, sort out, study, test, vet, weigh up. 2 *examine a witness.* catechize, cross-examine, cross-question, *inf* grill, interrogate, *inf* pump, question, sound out, try.

example *n* 1 case, illustration, instance, occurrence, sample, specimen. 2 *example to follow.* ideal, lesson, model, paragon, pattern, prototype. **make an example of** ▷ PUNISH.

exasperate *v inf* aggravate, gall, infuriate, irk, irritate, pique, vex. ▷ ANNOY.

excavate *v* burrow, dig, hollow out, mine, unearth.

exceed *v* do more than, go beyond, outnumber, outstrip, overstep, overtake, pass, transcend. ▷ EXCEL.

exceedingly *adv* amazingly, especially, exceptionally, excessively, extremely, outstandingly, unusually, very.

excel *v* beat, better, eclipse, exceed, outdo, outshine, shine, stand out, surpass, top.

excellent *adj inf* ace, admirable, *inf* brilliant, capital, champion, choice, consummate, distinguished, exceptional, exemplary, extraordinary, *inf* fabulous, *inf* fantastic, fine, first-class,

first-rate, gorgeous, great, ideal, impressive, magnificent, marvellous, model, outstanding, perfect, *inf* phenomenal, remarkable, *inf* smashing, splendid, sterling, *inf* stunning, *inf* super, superb, superlative, supreme, surpassing, *inf* terrific, *inf* tip-top, *inf* top-notch, *inf* tremendous, unequalled, wonderful. *Opp* BAD.

except *v* exclude, leave out, omit.

exception *n* 1 exclusion, omission, rejection. 2 anomaly, departure, deviation, eccentricity, freak, irregularity, oddity, peculiarity, quirk, rarity. **take exception** ▷ OBJECT.

exceptional *adj* 1 abnormal, anomalous, atypical, curious, eccentric, extraordinary, isolated, memorable, notable, odd, out of the ordinary, peculiar, phenomenal, quirky, rare, remarkable, singular, special, strange, surprising, uncommon, unconventional, unexpected, unheard-of, unique, unparalleled, unprecedented, untypical, unusual. 2 ▷ EXCELLENT. *Opp* ORDINARY.

excerpt *n* citation, clip, extract, fragment, part, passage, quotation, section, selection.

excess *n* 1 abundance, glut, overabundance, overflow, profit, superfluity, surfeit, surplus. *Opp* SCARCITY. 2 debauchery, dissipation, extravagance, intemperance, overindulgence, profligacy, wastefulness. *Opp* MODERATION.

excessive *adj* 1 disproportionate, exaggerated, extravagant, extreme, immoderate, inordinate, intemperate, needless, overdone, prodigal, profligate, profuse, superfluous, undue, unnecessary, wasteful. ▷ HUGE. *Opp* INADEQUATE. **2** *excessive prices.* exorbitant, extortionate, unjustifiable, unrealistic, unreasonable. *Opp* MODERATE.

exchange *n* deal, interchange, replacement, substitution, swap, switch. ● *v* bargain, barter, change, convert (*currency*), interchange, reciprocate, replace, substitute, swap, switch, trade, trade in. **exchange words** ▷ TALK.

excitable *adj* edgy, emotional, explosive, fidgety, fiery, highly-strung, hot-tempered, irrepressible, jumpy, lively, mercurial, nervous, passionate, quick-tempered, restive, temperamental, unstable, volatile. *Opp* CALM.

excite *v* **1** agitate, amaze, animate, arouse, awaken, disturb, elate, electrify, enthral, exhilarate, fluster, *inf* get going, incite, inflame, interest, intoxicate, move, perturb, provoke, rouse, stimulate, stir up, thrill, *inf* turn on, upset, urge, work up. **2** *excite interest.* activate, cause, elicit, encourage, engender, evoke, fire, generate, kindle, produce, whet. *Opp* CALM.

excited *adj* agitated, eager, enthusiastic, exuberant, feverish, frantic, frenzied, heated, *inf* het up, hysterical, impassioned, intoxicated, lively, nervous, overwrought, restless, spirited, vivacious, wild. *Opp* APATHETIC.

exciting *adj* dramatic, electrifying, eventful, fast-moving, galvanizing, gripping, heady, hair-raising, intoxicating,

inf nail-biting, provocative, riveting, rousing, sensational, spectacular, spine-tingling, stimulating, stirring, tense, thrilling. ▷ AMAZING. *Opp* BORING.

excitement *n* action, activity, adventure, agitation, animation, commotion, drama, eagerness, enthusiasm, furore, fuss, heat, intensity, *inf* kicks, passion, stimulation, suspense, tension, thrill, unrest.

exclaim *v* bawl, bellow, blurt out, call, cry out, declare, proclaim, shout, utter, yell.

exclamation *n* bellow, call, cry, expletive, interjection, oath, shout, utterance, yell.

exclude *v* ban, bar, blacklist, debar, disallow, except, expel, forbid, keep out, leave out, omit, ostracize, outlaw, prohibit, proscribe, put an embargo on, refuse, reject, repudiate, rule out, shut out, veto. ▷ REMOVE. *Opp* INCLUDE.

exclusive *adj* **1** limiting, restricted, sole, unique, unshared. **2** *exclusive club.* *inf* classy, fashionable, *inf* posh, private, select, selective, snobbish, up-market.

excreta *pl n* droppings, dung, excrement, faeces, manure, sewage, waste matter.

excursion *n* expedition, jaunt, journey, outing, trip.

excuse *n* alibi, apology, defence, explanation, extenuation, justification, mitigation, plea, pretext, reason, vindication.

● *v* **1** apologize for, condone, disregard, explain away, forgive, ignore, justify, mitigate, overlook, pardon, pass over, sanction, tolerate, vindicate, warrant. **2** absolve, acquit, clear, discharge, exculpate, exempt, exonerate, free, let off, *inf* let off the hook, liberate, release. *Opp* BLAME.

execute v 1 accomplish, achieve, bring off, carry out, complete, discharge, do, effect, implement, perform, *inf* pull off. 2 kill, put to death.

executive n administrator, manager, officer. ▷ CHIEF.

exemplary adj admirable, commendable, faultless, flawless, ideal, model, perfect, praiseworthy.

exemplify v demonstrate, depict, embody, illustrate, personify, represent, show, symbolize, typify.

exempt v except, exclude, excuse, free, let off, liberate, release, spare.

exercise n 1 action, activity, aerobics, callisthenics, exertion, games, gymnastics, sport, *inf* work-out. 2 *military exercise.* discipline, drill, manoeuvre, operation, practice, training. ● v 1 apply, bring to bear, display, effect, employ, exert, expend, implement, put to use, show, use, utilize, wield. 2 *exercise your body.* discipline, drill, keep fit, practise, train, *inf* work out. 3 ▷ WORRY.

exertion n action, effort, endeavour, strain. ▷ WORK.

exhaust n emission, fumes, gases, smoke. ● v 1 consume, deplete, drain, dry up, empty, expend, finish off, *inf* run through, sap, use up. 2 debilitate, enervate, fatigue, prostrate, tax, tire, wear out, weary. **exhausted** ▷ BREATHLESS, WEARY.

exhausting adj arduous, back-breaking, crippling, debilitating, demanding, enervating, gruelling, hard, laborious, punishing, severe, strenuous, taxing, tiring, wearying.

exhaustion n tiredness, weariness. ▷ FATIGUE.

exhaustive adj careful, comprehensive, full-scale, intensive, meticulous, thorough. *Opp* INCOMPLETE.

exhibit v 1 arrange, display, offer, present, put up, set up, show. 2 air, betray, demonstrate, disclose, express, *derog* flaunt, indicate, manifest, *derog* parade, reveal, *derog* show off. *Opp* HIDE.

exhibition n demonstration, display, *inf* expo, exposition, presentation, show.

exhilarating adj bracing, cheering, exciting, invigorating, refreshing, stimulating, tonic, uplifting. ▷ HAPPY.

exhort v advise, encourage, harangue, recommend, urge.

exile n 1 banishment, deportation, expatriation, expulsion. 2 displaced person, émigré, expatriate, outcast, refugee, wanderer. ● v ban, banish, bar, deport, drive out, eject, evict, expatriate, expel, oust, send away.

exist v 1 be, be found, be real, happen, occur. 2 continue, endure, hold out, keep going, last, live, remain alive, subsist, survive. **existing** ▷ ACTUAL, CURRENT, LIVING.

existence n actuality, being, continuance, life, living, persistence, reality, survival.

exit n 1 barrier, door, doorway, gate, gateway, opening, portal, way out. **2** *hurried exit.* departure, escape, exodus, flight, leave-taking, retreat, withdrawal. ● *v* ▷ DEPART.

exorbitant *adj* disproportionate, excessive, extortionate, extravagant, high, inordinate, outrageous, prohibitive, *inf* sky-high, *inf* steep, swingeing, unjustifiable, unrealistic, unreasonable, unwarranted. ▷ EXPENSIVE. *Opp* REASONABLE.

exotic *adj* **1** far-away, foreign, remote. **2** colourful, different, exciting, extraordinary, glamorous, novel, odd, outlandish, peculiar, rare, romantic, singular, strange, striking, unfamiliar, unusual, wonderful. *Opp* ORDINARY.

expand *v* **1** amplify, augment, broaden, build up, develop, diversify, elaborate, enlarge, extend, fill out, heighten, increase, prolong. **2** dilate, distend, grow, increase, lengthen, open out, stretch, swell, thicken, widen. *Opp* CONTRACT.

expanse *n* area, breadth, extent, range, space, spread, stretch, sweep, surface, tract.

expansive *adj* **1** affable, amiable, communicative, effusive, extrovert, friendly, genial, open, outgoing, sociable, well-disposed. ▷ TALKATIVE. *Opp* TACITURN. **2** ▷ BROAD.

expect *v* **1** anticipate, await, *inf* bank on, bargain for, be prepared for, contemplate, count on, envisage, forecast, foresee, hope for, imagine, look forward to, plan for, predict, prophesy, reckon on, wait for. **2** *expect obedience.* demand, insist on, look for, rely on, require, want. **3** *I expect he'll come.* assume,

believe, conjecture, imagine, judge, presume, suppose, surmise, think. **expected** ▷ PREDICTABLE.

expectant *adj* **1** eager, hopeful, keyed up, *inf* on tenterhooks, optimistic, ready. **2** *expectant mother.* *inf* expecting, pregnant.

expedient *adj* advantageous, advisable, appropriate, beneficial, convenient, desirable, helpful, judicious, opportune, politic, practical, pragmatic, profitable, prudent, right, sensible, suitable, to your advantage, useful, worthwhile. ● *n* contrivance, device, means, measure, method, ploy, recourse, resort, ruse, scheme, stratagem, tactics.

expedition *n* crusade, excursion, exploration, journey, mission, pilgrimage, quest, raid, safari, tour, trek, trip, undertaking, voyage.

expel *v* **1** ban, banish, cast out, dismiss, drive out, eject, evict, exile, exorcise, *inf* kick out, oust, remove, send away, throw out, *inf* turf out, turn out. **2** *expel fumes.* belch, discharge, emit, exhale, give out, push out, send out, spew out.

expend *v* consume, employ, pay out, spend, use.

expendable *adj* disposable, inessential, replaceable, *inf* throw-away, unimportant.

expense *n* charge, cost, expenditure, fee, outgoings, outlay, overheads, payment, price, rate, spending.

expensive *adj* costly, dear, generous, high-priced, over-priced, *inf* pricey, *inf* steep, up-market, valuable. ▷ EXORBITANT. *Opp* CHEAP.

experience n 1 familiarity, involvement, observation, participation, practice, taking part. 2 background, expertise, *inf* know-how, knowledge, *Fr* savoir faire, skill, understanding, wisdom. 3 *nasty experience.* adventure, episode, event, happening, incident, occurrence, ordeal, trial. ● v encounter, endure, face, go through, have a taste of, know, meet, sample, suffer, test out, try, undergo.
experienced ▷ EXPERT.

experiment n demonstration, investigation, *inf* practical, research, test, trial, try-out. ● v examine, investigate, probe, research, test, try out.

experimental adj 1 exploratory, pilot, provisional, tentative, trial. 2 *experimental evidence.* empirical, proved, tested.

expert adj able, *inf* ace, *inf* brilliant, capable, competent, *inf* crack, experienced, knowing, knowledgeable, master, masterly, practised, professional, proficient, qualified, skilful, skilled, specialized, trained, well-versed. ▷ CLEVER. *Opp* UNSKILFUL. ● n *inf* ace, authority, connoisseur, *inf* dab hand, genius, *derog* know-all, master, *inf* old hand, professional, pundit, specialist, virtuoso, *inf* wizard. *Opp* AMATEUR.

expertise n dexterity, judgement, *inf* know-how, knowledge, *Fr* savoir faire, skill.

expire v cease, come to an end, finish, lapse, *inf* run out, terminate. ▷ DIE.

explain v 1 clarify, clear up, decipher, define, demonstrate, describe, disentangle, elucidate, expound, *inf* get across, *inf* get over, gloss, illustrate, interpret, make clear, make plain, resolve, shed light on, simplify, solve, *inf* sort out, spell out, teach, translate, unravel. 2 *explain a mistake.* account for, excuse, give reasons for, justify, legitimize, make excuses for, rationalize, vindicate.

explanation n 1 account, analysis, clarification, definition, demonstration, description, elucidation, exegesis, exposition, gloss, illustration, interpretation, key, meaning, rubric, significance, solution. 2 cause, excuse, justification, motive, reason, vindication.

explanatory adj descriptive, expository, helpful, illuminating, illustrative.

explicit adj categorical, clear, definite, detailed, direct, exact, express, frank, manifest, open, outspoken, patent, plain, positive, precise, specific, *inf* spelt out, spoken, stated, straightforward, unambiguous, unconcealed, unequivocal, unreserved, well-defined. *Opp* IMPLICIT.

explode v 1 backfire, blast, blow up, burst, detonate, erupt, go off, set off, shatter. 2 *explode a theory.* debunk, destroy, discredit, disprove, put an end to, rebut, refute, reject.

exploit n achievement, adventure, attainment, deed, feat. ● v 1 build on, capitalize on, *inf* cash in on, develop, make use of, profit by, profit from, trade on, work on, use, utilize. 2 *exploit people. inf* bleed, ill-treat, impose on, keep down, manipulate, *inf* milk, misuse, oppress, *inf* rip off, *inf* squeeze

explore v 1 break new ground, prospect, reconnoitre, scout, search, survey, tour, travel through. 2 *explore a problem.* analyse, examine, inspect, investigate, look into, probe, research, scrutinize, study.

explosion n 1 bang, blast, burst, clap, crack, detonation, eruption, firing, report. 2 *explosion of anger.* fit, outbreak, outburst, paroxysm, spasm.

explosive adj dangerous, highly-charged, sensitive, unstable, volatile. *Opp* STABLE. ● n cordite, dynamite, gelignite, gunpowder, TNT.

exponent n 1 interpreter, performer, player. 2 advocate, champion, defender, expounder, presenter, proponent, supporter, upholder.

expose v bare, betray, dig up, disclose, display, show (up), uncover, unmask. ▷ REVEAL. *Opp* HIDE.

express v air, articulate, give vent to, phrase, put into words, release, vent, voice, word. ▷ COMMUNICATE.

expression n 1 cliché, formula, phrase, phraseology, remark, statement, term, turn of phrase, usage, utterance, wording. ▷ SAYING. 2 articulation, confession, declaration, disclosure, revelation, statement. 3 *expression in your voice.* depth, emotion, expressiveness, feeling, nuance, sensitivity, sympathy, tone. 4 *facial expression.* air, appearance, aspect, countenance, face, look, mien.

expressionless adj 1 blank, *inf* dead-pan, emotionless, empty, glassy, impassive, inscrutable, poker-faced, uncommunicative, wooden. 2 boring, dull, flat, monotonous, uninspiring, unmodulated, unvarying. *Opp* EXPRESSIVE.

expressive adj 1 meaningful, revealing, significant, striking, suggestive, telling. 2 articulate, eloquent, lively, modulated, varied. *Opp* EXPRESSIONLESS.

exquisite adj delicate, elegant, fine, intricate, well-crafted. ▷ BEAUTIFUL. *Opp* CRUDE.

extend v 1 add to, broaden, build up, develop, draw out, enlarge, expand, increase, keep going, lengthen, open up, pad out, perpetuate, prolong, protract, *inf* spin out, spread, stretch, widen. 2 *extend a deadline.* defer, delay, postpone, put back, put off. 3 *extend your hand.* give, hold out, offer, outstretch, present, proffer, put out, raise, reach out, stretch out. 4 *The grounds extend to the lake.* continue, range, reach.

extensive adj broad, comprehensive, expansive, far-ranging, far-reaching, sweeping, vast, wide, widespread. ▷ LARGE.

extent n amount, area, bounds, breadth, compass, degree, dimensions, distance, expanse, length, limit, magnitude, measure, proportions, quantity, range, reach, scale, scope, size, spread, sweep, width.

exterior adj external, outer, outside, outward, superficial. ● n coating, covering, façade, front, outside, shell, skin, surface. *Opp* INTERIOR.

exterminate v annihilate, destroy, eliminate, eradicate, extirpate, get rid of, obliterate, root out, terminate. ▷ KILL.

external adj exterior, outer, outside, outward, superficial. Opp INTERNAL.

extinct adj dead, defunct, died out, extinguished, gone, inactive, vanished. ▷ OLD. Opp LIVING.

extinguish v blow out, damp down, douse, put out, quench, slake, smother, snuff out, switch off. ▷ DESTROY. Opp KINDLE.

extort v blackmail, bully, coerce, exact, extract, force, obtain by force.

extra adj accessory, added, additional, auxiliary, excess, further, left over, more, other, reserve, spare, superfluous, supplementary, surplus, temporary, unneeded, unused, unwanted.

extract n 1 concentrate, distillation, essence, quintessence. 2 abstract, citation, inf clip, clipping, cutting, excerpt, passage, quotation, selection. • v 1 draw out, extricate, pull out, remove, take out, withdraw. 2 extract a confession. extort, force out, inf worm out, wrench, wrest, wring. 3 extract what you need. choose, derive, gather, glean, quote, select. ▷ OBTAIN.

extraordinary adj abnormal, amazing, astonishing, astounding, bizarre, breathtaking, curious, exceptional, extreme, fantastic, inf funny, incredible, marvellous, miraculous, mysterious, notable, noteworthy, odd, outstanding, peculiar, inf phenomenal, prodigious, queer, rare, remarkable, inf sensational, singular, special, staggering, strange, striking, stunning, stupendous, surpris-

ing, inf unbelievable, uncommon, unheard-of, unimaginable, unique, unprecedented, unusual, inf weird, wonderful. Opp ORDINARY.

extravagance n excess, improvidence, lavishness, overindulgence, prodigality, profligacy, self-indulgence, wastefulness. Opp ECONOMY.

extravagant adj exaggerated, excessive, flamboyant, grandiose, immoderate, improvident, lavish, outrageous, overdone, pretentious, prodigal, profligate, profuse, self-indulgent, inf showy, spendthrift, uneconomical, unreasonable, wasteful. ▷ EXPENSIVE. Opp ECONOMICAL.

extreme adj 1 acute, drastic, excessive, greatest, maximum, utmost. ▷ EXTRAORDINARY. 2 distant, furthermost, furthest, last, outermost, ultimate, uttermost. 3 extreme opinions. absolute, avant-garde, exaggerated, extravagant, extremist, fanatical, inf hard-line, immoderate, intemperate, intransigent, left-wing, militant, outrageous, radical, right-wing, uncompromising, inf way-out. • n bounds, edge, end, extremity, left wing, limit, maximum, minimum, pole, right wing, top, ultimate.

extroverted adj active, confident, exhibitionist, outgoing, positive. ▷ SOCIABLE. Opp INTROVERTED.

exuberant adj 1 animated, boisterous, inf bubbly, buoyant, eager, ebullient, effervescent, energetic, enthusiastic, excited, exhilarated, exultant, high-spirited, irrepressible, lively, spirited, sprightly, vivacious.

▷ CHEERFUL. **2** *exuberant decoration.* baroque, exaggerated, ornate, overdone, rich, rococo. **3** *exuberant growth.* abundant, copious, lush, luxuriant, overflowing, profuse, rank, teeming. *Opp* AUSTERE.

exultant *adj* delighted, ecstatic, elated, joyful, jubilant, *inf* on top of the world, overjoyed, rejoicing. ▷ EXUBERANT.

eye *n* **1** eyeball, *inf* peeper. **2** discernment, perception, sight, vision. ● *v* contemplate, examine, inspect, scrutinize, study, watch. ▷ SEE.

eye-witness *n* bystander, observer, onlooker, passer-by, spectator, watcher, witness.

F

fabric *n* **1** cloth, material, stuff, textile. **2** *fabric of a building.* construction, framework, make-up, structure, substance.

fabulous *adj* **1** fabled, fairy-tale, fanciful, fictitious, imaginary, legendary, mythical, story-book. **2** ▷ EXCELLENT.

face *n* **1** appearance, countenance, expression, features, lineaments, look, *sl* mug, visage. **2** *face of building.* aspect, exterior, façade, front, outside, side, surface. ● *v* **1** be opposite, front onto, look towards, overlook. **2** *face danger.* brave, come to terms with, confront, cope with, defy, encounter, experience, face up to, meet, oppose, stand up to, tackle. **3** *face a wall with plaster.* ▷ COVER.

facetious *adj* cheeky, flippant, impudent, irreverent. ▷ FUNNY.

facile *adj* **1** cheap, easy, effortless, hasty, obvious, easy, simple, superficial, unconsidered. **2** *facile talker.* fluent, glib, insincere, plausible, ready, shallow, slick, *inf* smooth.

facility *n* **1** adroitness, ease, expertise, fluency, skill, smoothness. **2** *useful facility.* amenity, convenience, help, provision, resource, service.

fact *n* actuality, certainty, *Fr* fait accompli, reality, truth. *Opp* FICTION. **the facts** circumstances, data, details, evidence, information, *sl* the lowdown, particulars, statistics.

factor *n* aspect, cause, circumstance, component, consideration, constituent, contingency, detail, element, fact, influence, ingredient, item, part, particular.

factory *n* forge, foundry, manufacturing plant, mill, plant, refinery, works, workshop.

factual *adj* **1** accurate, bona fide, circumstantial, correct, demonstrable, empirical, faithful, genuine, matter-of-fact, objective, plain, prosaic, realistic, straightforward, true, unadorned, unbiased, unimaginative, unvarnished, valid, verifiable, well-documented. *Opp* FALSE. **2** *factual film.* biographical, documentary, historical, real-life. *Opp* FICTIONAL.

faculty *n* ability, aptitude, capability, capacity, flair, genius, gift, knack, power, talent.

fade *v* **1** blanch, bleach, dim, discolour, dull, grow pale, whiten. *Opp* BRIGHTEN. **2** become less, decline, diminish, disappear, dwindle, evanesce, fail, melt away, vanish, wane, weaken. **3** *flowers fade.* droop, flag, wilt, wither.

fail *v* **1** be unsuccessful, break down, close down, come to an end, *inf* come to grief, come to nothing, *sl* conk out, *inf* crash, cut out, fall through, *inf* fizzle out, *inf* flop, *inf* fold, founder, give up, go bankrupt, *inf* go bust, go out of business, miscarry, misfire, *inf* miss out, peter out, stop working. **2** *the light will fail soon.* decline, deteriorate, diminish, disappear, dwindle, ebb, fade, give out, melt away, vanish, wane, weaken. **3** *fail to do something.* forget, neglect, omit. **4** *fail someone.* disappoint, *inf* let down. *Opp* IMPROVE, SUCCEED.

failing *n* blemish, defect, fault, flaw, foible, imperfection, shortcoming, weakness, weak spot.

failure *n* **1** defeat, disappointment, disaster, downfall, fiasco, *inf* flop, loss, miscarriage, *inf* wash-out, wreck. **2** breakdown, collapse, crash, stoppage. **3** *failure to do your duty.* dereliction, neglect, omission. *Opp* SUCCESS.

faint *adj* **1** blurred, blurry, dim, faded, feeble, hazy, ill-defined, indistinct, misty, muzzy, pale, pastel (*colours*), shadowy, unclear, vague. **2** *faint smell.* delicate, slight. **3** *faint sounds.* distant, hushed, low, muffled, muted, soft, stifled, subdued, thin, weak. **4** *feel faint.* dizzy, exhausted, feeble, giddy, lightheaded, unsteady, weak, *inf* woozy. *Opp* CLEAR, STRONG.
● *v* black out, collapse, *inf* flake

out, *inf* keel over, pass out, swoon.

fair *adj* **1** blond, blonde, flaxen, golden, light, yellow. **2** *fair weather.* bright, clear, clement, cloudless, dry, favourable, fine, pleasant, sunny. *Opp* DARK. **3** *fair decision.* disinterested, even-handed, honest, honourable, impartial, just, lawful, legitimate, non-partisan, open-minded, proper, right, unbiased, unprejudiced, upright. *Opp* UNJUST. **4** *fair standard.* acceptable, adequate, average, mediocre, middling, moderate, passable, reasonable, respectable, satisfactory, *inf* so-so, tolerable. *Opp* UNACCEPTABLE. **5** ▷ BEAUTIFUL.
● *n* **1** amusement park, funfair. **2** bazaar, carnival, exhibition, festival, fête, gala, market, sale, show.

fairly *adv* moderately, pretty, quite, rather, reasonably, somewhat, tolerably, up to a point.

faith *n* **1** assurance, belief, confidence, credence, reliance, trust. *Opp* DOUBT. **2** conviction, creed, doctrine, dogma, persuasion, religion.

faithful *adj* **1** constant, dependable, devoted, dutiful, loyal, reliable, staunch, steadfast, trusted, trustworthy, unswerving. **2** *faithful account.* accurate, exact, factual, literal, precise. ▷ TRUE. *Opp* FALSE.

fake *adj* artificial, bogus, counterfeit, ersatz, false, fictitious, forged, fraudulent, imitation, invented, made-up, mock, *inf* phoney, pretended, sham, simulated, spurious, synthetic, trumped-up, unreal. *Opp* GENUINE. ● *n* **1** copy, counterfeit, duplicate, forgery, hoax, imitation, replica, reproduction, sham, simulation. **2** charlatan, cheat, fraud, hoaxer, impostor, *inf* phoney, quack. ● *v* affect, copy, counterfeit, dissemble, falsify, feign, forge, fudge, imitate, pretend, put on, reproduce, sham, simulate.

fall *n* **1** collapse, crash, decline, decrease, depreciation, descent, dip, dive, downswing, downturn, drop, lowering, nosedive, plunge, reduction, slump, tumble. **2** *fall of a town.* capitulation, capture, defeat, overthrow, seizure, submission, surrender. ● *v* **1** come a cropper, crash down, dive, drop down, founder, keel over, overbalance, pitch, plummet, plunge, sink, slump, spiral, stumble, topple, trip over, tumble. **2** decline, decrease, diminish, dwindle, ebb, lessen, subside. **3** descend, drop, fall away, slope down. **4** *curtains fell in folds.* be suspended, cascade, dangle, hang. **5** *Christmas falls on a Friday this year.* come, happen, occur. **6** ▷ DIE. **7** ▷ SURRENDER. **fall apart** ▷ DISINTEGRATE. **fall back** ▷ RETREAT. **fall behind** ▷ LAG. **fall down, fall in** ▷ COLLAPSE. **fall off** ▷ DECLINE. **fall out** ▷ QUARREL. **fall through** ▷ FAIL.

fallacy *n* delusion, misconception. ▷ ERROR.

fallible *adj* erring, frail, human, imperfect, liable to make mistakes, uncertain, unpredictable, unreliable, weak. *Opp* INFALLIBLE.

fallow *adj* resting, uncultivated, unplanted, unused.

false *adj* **1** deceptive, distorted, erroneous, fabricated, fallacious, fictitious, flawed, imprecise, inaccurate, incorrect, invalid, misleading, mistaken, spurious, untrue, wrong. ▷ FAKE. **2** *false friends.* deceitful, dishonest, disloyal, double-dealing, faithless, lying, treacherous, *inf* two-faced, unfaithful, unreliable, untrustworthy. *Opp* TRUE. **false name** ▷ PSEUDONYM.

falsehood *n* fabrication, *inf* fib, *inf* story. ▷ LIE.

falsify *v* alter, *inf* cook (*the books*), counterfeit, distort, exaggerate, fake, forge, fudge, misrepresent, mock up, pervert, slant, tamper with, twist.

falter *v* **1** flag, flinch, hesitate, hold back, lose confidence, pause, quail, stagger, stumble, totter, waver. *Opp* PERSIST. **2** stammer, stutter. **faltering** ▷ HESITANT.

fame *n* acclaim, celebrity, distinction, eminence, glory, honour, importance, name, *derog* notoriety, pre-eminence, prestige, prominence, renown, reputation, repute, *inf* stardom.

familiar *adj* **1** accustomed, common, conventional, customary, everyday, frequent, habitual, mundane, normal, ordinary, predictable, regular, routine, stock, traditional, usual, well-known. *Opp* STRANGE. **2** chatty, close, confidential, *derog* forward, *inf* free-and-easy, *derog* impudent, informal, intimate, *derog* presumptuous, relaxed, sociable, unceremonious. ▷ FRIENDLY. *Opp* FORMAL. **familiar with** acquainted with, *inf* at home with, aware of, conscious of, knowledgeable about, trained in, versed in.

family n 1 brood, children, *inf* flesh and blood, issue, kindred, kith and kin, litter, *inf* nearest and dearest, offspring, progeny, relations, relatives, *inf* tribe. 2 ancestry, blood, clan, dynasty, extraction, forebears, genealogy, house, line, lineage, pedigree, race, strain, tribe.

famine n dearth, hunger, lack, malnutrition, scarcity, shortage, starvation, want. *Opp* PLENTY.

famished adj hungry, ravenous, starved, starving.

famous adj acclaimed, big, celebrated, distinguished, eminent, exalted, glorious, great, historic, illustrious, important, legendary, notable, noted, *derog* notorious, outstanding, popular, prominent, proverbial, renowned, revered, time-honoured, venerable, well-known, world-famous. *Opp* UNKNOWN.

fan n 1 extractor, ventilator. 2 *soccer fan*. addict, admirer, aficionado, *inf* buff, devotee, enthusiast, *inf* fiend, follower, lover, supporter. ▷ FANATIC.

fanatic n activist, adherent, bigot, extremist, fiend, freak, maniac, militant, zealot.

fanatical adj bigoted, extreme, fervent, immoderate, irrational, maniacal, militant, obsessive, over-enthusiastic, passionate, rabid, single-minded, zealous. *Opp* MODERATE.

fanciful adj capricious, fantastic, illusory, imaginary, make-believe, unrealistic, whimsical.

fancy adj decorative, elaborate, embellished, embroidered, intricate, ornate. ● n ▷ IMAGINATION,

WHIM. ● v 1 envisage, imagine, picture, visualize. ▷ THINK. 2 be attracted to, crave, like, long for, prefer, want, wish for. ▷ DESIRE.

fantastic adj 1 absurd, amazing, elaborate, exaggerated, extraordinary, extravagant, fabulous, fanciful, far-fetched, grotesque, imaginative, implausible, incredible, odd, quaint, remarkable, strange, surreal, unbelievable, unlikely, weird. 2 ▷ EXCELLENT. *Opp* ORDINARY.

fantasy n chimera, daydream, delusion, dream, fancy, hallucination, illusion, make-believe, mirage, pipedream, reverie, vision. *Opp* REALITY.

far adj distant, far-away, far-off, outlying, remote. *Opp* NEAR.

farcical adj absurd, foolish, ludicrous, preposterous. ▷ FUNNY.

fare n 1 charge, cost, fee, payment, price. 2 ▷ FOOD.

farewell adj leaving, parting, valedictory. ● n departure, leave-taking, send-off, valediction. ▷ GOODBYE.

farm n farmhouse, farmstead, grange, smallholding.

farming n agriculture, crofting, cultivation, husbandry.

fascinate v allure, attract, beguile, bewitch, captivate, charm, delight, enchant, engross, enthral, entrance, interest, mesmerize, rivet. **fascinating** ▷ ATTRACTIVE.

fashion n 1 manner, method, mode, way. 2 convention, craze, fad, look, rage, style, taste, trend, vogue.

fashionable adj chic, contemporary, current, elegant, *inf* in, in vogue, the latest, modern, popular, smart, *inf* snazzy, sophisticated, stylish, tasteful, *inf* trendy, up-to-date. *Opp* UNFASHIONABLE.

fast *adv* at full tilt, briskly, posthaste, quickly, rapidly, swiftly. ● *adj* 1 breakneck, brisk, express, hasty, headlong, high-speed, hurried, lively, *inf* nippy, precipitate, quick, rapid, smart, *inf* spanking, speedy, swift. *Opp* SLOW. 2 attached, bound, fastened, firm, fixed, immobile, immovable, secure, tight. 3 *fast colours*. indelible, lasting, permanent, stable. 4 *fast living*. ▷ IMMORAL. ● *v* abstain, deny yourself, diet, go hungry, go without food, starve. *Opp* INDULGE.

fasten *v* affix, anchor, attach, bind, bolt, buckle, button, chain, clasp, cling, close, connect, couple, do up, fix, grip, hitch, hook, knot, join, lace, latch on, link, lock, make fast, moor, nail, padlock, paste, peg, pin, rope, screw down, seal, secure, staple, strap, tack, tape, tether, tie, unite, weld. ▷ STICK. *Opp* UNDO.

fastener *n* bond, connection, connector, coupling, fastening, link, linkage. 2 buckle, button, catch, clasp, clip, hook, lace, latch, lock, peg, pin, zip.

fastidious *adj inf* choosy, dainty, discriminating, finicky, fussy, hard to please, nice, particular, *inf* pernickety, *inf* picky, selective, squeamish.

fat *adj* 1 bloated, *inf* broad in the beam, bulky, chubby, corpulent, dumpy, flabby, fleshy, gross, heavy, obese, overweight, paunchy, plump, podgy, portly, pot-bellied, pudgy, rotund, round, solid, squat, stocky, stout, thick, tubby, well-fed.

▷ BIG. 2 *fat meat*. fatty, greasy, oily. *Opp* LEAN. ● *n* blubber, grease, oil.

fatal *adj* 1 deadly, final, incurable, lethal, malignant, mortal, terminal. 2 ▷ DISASTROUS.

fatality *n* casualty, death, loss.

fate *n* 1 chance, destiny, doom, fortune, karma, kismet, lot, luck, nemesis, predestination, providence, the stars. 2 death, demise, destruction, downfall, end, ruin.

fated *adj* certain, cursed, damned, decreed, destined, doomed, inescapable, inevitable, intended, predestined, predetermined, preordained, sure.

father *n* begetter, *inf* dad, *inf* daddy, *inf* pa, *inf* papa, parent, *inf* pop, sire.

fatigue *n* debility, exhaustion, languor, lassitude, lethargy, tiredness, weakness, weariness. ● *v* debilitate, drain, enervate, exhaust, tire, weaken, weary. **fatigued** ▷ WEARY.

fault *n* 1 blemish, defect, deficiency, failure, fallacy, flaw, foible, frailty, imperfection, inaccuracy, malfunction, snag, weakness. 2 blunder, *sl* boob, error, failing, *Fr* faux pas, gaffe, *inf* howler, indiscretion, lapse, miscalculation, misconduct, misdeed, mistake, negligence, offence, omission, oversight, peccadillo, shortcoming, sin, slip, transgression, vice, wrongdoing. 3 *It was my fault*. blame, culpability, guilt, liability, responsibility. ● *v* ▷ CRITICIZE.

faultless *adj* accurate, correct, exemplary, flawless, ideal, in mint condition, unimpeachable. ▷ PERFECT. *Opp* FAULTY.

faulty adj broken, damaged, defective, flawed, illogical, imperfect, inaccurate, incorrect, inoperative, invalid, not working, out of order, shopsoiled, unusable, useless. Opp FAULTLESS.

favour n 1 acceptance, approval, bias, favouritism, friendliness, goodwill, grace, liking, partiality, preference, support. 2 Do me a favour. courtesy, gift, good turn, indulgence, kindness, service. • v 1 approve of, be in sympathy with, champion, choose, commend, esteem, inf fancy, inf go for, like, opt for, prefer, think well of, value. Opp DISLIKE. 2 abet, advance, back, be advantageous to, befriend, promote, support. ▷ HELP. Opp HINDER.

favourable adj 1 advantageous, appropriate, auspicious, beneficial, benign, convenient, following (wind), friendly, generous, helpful, kind, opportune, promising, propitious, reassuring, suitable, supportive, sympathetic, understanding, well-disposed. 2 favourable review. approving, commendatory, complimentary, encouraging, enthusiastic. 3 favourable reputation. desirable, enviable, good, pleasing, satisfactory. Opp UNFAVOURABLE.

favourite adj beloved, best, chosen, dearest, ideal, liked, loved, popular, preferred, well-liked. • n 1 choice, pick, preference. 2 inf apple of your eye, darling, idol, pet.

fear n alarm, anxiety, apprehension, awe, concern, cowardice, dismay, doubt, dread, faintheartedness, foreboding, fright,

inf funk, horror, misgiving, nervousness, panic, qualm, suspicion, terror, timidity, trepidation, uneasiness, worry. ▷ PHOBIA. Opp COURAGE. • v be afraid of, dread, quail at, shrink from, suspect, tremble at, worry about.

fearful adj 1 alarmed, apprehensive, frightened, nervous, scared, terrified, timid. ▷ AFRAID. Opp FEARLESS. 2 ▷ FEARSOME.

fearless adj bold, brave, dauntless, intrepid, resolute, stoical, unafraid, unconcerned, undaunted, valiant, valorous. ▷ COURAGEOUS. Opp FEARFUL.

fearsome adj appalling, aweinspiring, awesome, dreadful, fearful, frightful, terrible, terrifying. ▷ FRIGHTENING.

feasible adj 1 attainable, easy, possible, practicable, practical, viable, workable. Opp IMPRACTICAL. 2 feasible excuse. credible, likely, plausible, reasonable. Opp IMPLAUSIBLE.

feast n banquet, sl blow-out, dinner, inf spread. • v dine, gorge, inf wine and dine.

feat n accomplishment, achievement, act, action, attainment, deed, exploit, performance.

feather n plume, quill. **feathers** down, plumage.

feathery adj downy, fluffy, wispy.

feature n 1 aspect, attribute, characteristic, detail, facet, hallmark, idiosyncrasy, mark, peculiarity, point, property, quality, trait. 2 newspaper feature. article, column, item, piece, report, story. • v 1 emphasize, focus on, highlight, inf play up, present, promote, show up, *inf* spotlight, stress. **2** *feature in a film.* act, appear, figure, participate, perform, play a role, star, take a part. **features** ▷ FACE.

fee *n* bill, charge, cost, dues, fare, payment, price, remuneration, subscription, sum, tariff, terms, toll, wage.

feeble *adj* **1** ailing, debilitated, decrepit, delicate, exhausted, faint, fragile, frail, helpless, ill, impotent, inadequate, ineffective, infirm, languid, listless, powerless, puny, sickly, slight, useless, weak. *Opp* STRONG. **2** hesitant, incompetent, indecisive, ineffectual, namby-pamby, *inf* namby-pamby, spineless, vacillating, weedy, *inf* wimpish, *inf* wishy-washy. **3** *feeble excuses.* flimsy, insubstantial, lame, poor, tame, thin, unconvincing.

feed *v* **1** cater for, nourish, nurture, provide for, provision, strengthen, suckle, support, sustain, *inf* wine and dine. **2** dine, eat, graze, pasture. **feed on** ▷ EAT.

feel *v* **1** caress, finger, handle, hold, manipulate, maul, *inf* paw, pet, stroke, touch. **2** *feel your way.* explore, fumble, grope. **3** *feel the cold.* be aware of, be conscious of, detect, experience, know, notice, perceive, sense, suffer, undergo. **4** *feel empty.* appear, seem. **5** *feel something's true.* believe, consider, deem, guess, *inf* have a feeling, *inf* have a hunch, judge, think.

feeling *n* **1** perception, sensation, sense of touch, sensitivity. **2** emotion, passion, sentiment. **3** *religious feelings.* attitude, belief, consciousness, guess, hunch, idea, impression, instinct, intuition, notion, opinion, thought, view. **4** *feeling for music.* sympathy, understanding. **5** [*inf*] *autumnal feeling.* atmosphere, mood, tone.

fell *v* cut down, flatten, floor, knock down, mow down, prostrate. ▷ KILL.

female *adj* ▷ FEMININE. *Opp* MALE. ● *n* girl, woman.

feminine *adj derog of men* effeminate, female, *derog* girlish, ladylike, womanly. *Opp* MASCULINE.

fen *n* bog, lowland, marsh, morass, quagmire, swamp.

fence *n* barricade, barrier, hedge, hurdle, paling, palisade, railing, rampart, stockade, wall, wire. ● *v* **1** bound, circumscribe, confine, coop up, encircle, enclose, hedge in, pen, surround, wall in. **2** ▷ FIGHT.

fend *v* **fend for yourself** *inf* get along, *inf* get by, look after yourself, manage, *inf* scrape along, support yourself, survive. **fend off** ▷ REPEL.

ferment *n* ▷ COMMOTION. ● *v* **1** boil, bubble, effervesce, *inf* fizz, foam, froth, seethe. **2** agitate, excite, foment, incite, instigate, provoke, rouse, stir up.

ferocious *adj* bestial, bloodthirsty, brutal, cruel, fiendish, fierce, harsh, inhuman, merciless, murderous, pitiless, sadistic, savage, vicious, wild. *Opp* GENTLE.

ferry *n* boat, craft, ship, vessel. ● *v* carry, export, import, ship, take across, transport. ▷ CONVEY.

fertile *adj* abundant, fecund, flourishing, fruitful, lush, luxuriant, productive, prolific, rich, teeming. Opp STERILE.

fertilize v 1 impregnate, inseminate, pollinate. 2 cultivate, enrich, feed, make fertile, manure, mulch, nourish.

fertilizer n compost, dressing, manure, mulch, nutrient.

fervent adj ardent, avid, burning, committed, devout, eager, emotional, enthusiastic, excited, fanatical, fervid, fiery, frenzied, heated, impassioned, intense, keen, passionate, spirited, vehement, vigorous, warm, wholehearted, zealous. Opp COOL.

fervour n ardour, eagerness, energy, enthusiasm, excitement, fire, heat, intensity, keenness, passion, sparkle, spirit, vehemence, vigour, warmth, zeal.

fester v become infected, decay, discharge, go bad, go septic, ooze, putrefy, rot, run, suppurate, ulcerate.

festival n anniversary, carnival, commemoration, fair, feast, fête, fiesta, gala, jamboree, jubilee. ▷ FESTIVITY.

festive adj celebratory, cheerful, cheery, convivial, gay, gleeful, jolly, jovial, joyful, joyous, lighthearted, merry. ▷ HAPPY.

festivity n celebration, conviviality, entertainment, feasting, inf jollification, jollity, jubilation, merrymaking, merriment, mirth, rejoicing, revelry, revels. ▷ PARTY.

fetch v 1 bear, bring, carry, collect, convey, get, obtain, pick up, retrieve, transfer, transport. 2 fetch a good price. bring in, earn, go for, make, produce, raise, realize, sell for. **fetching** ▷ ATTRACTIVE.

feud n animosity, antagonism, inf bad blood, dispute, enmity, grudge, hostility, rivalry, vendetta. ▷ QUARREL.

fever n delirium, feverishness, high temperature.

feverish adj 1 burning, febrile, fevered, flushed, hot, inflamed, trembling. Opp COOL. 2 feverish activity. agitated, excited, frantic, frenetic, frenzied, hectic, hurried, impatient, restless.

few adj inf few and far between, hardly any, inadequate, infrequent, rare, scarce, sparse, sporadic, inf thin on the ground, uncommon. Opp MANY.

fibre n 1 filament, hair, strand, thread. 2 moral fibre. backbone, character, determination, spirit, tenacity. ▷ COURAGE.

fickle adj capricious, changeable, changing, disloyal, erratic, faithless, flighty, inconsistent, inconstant, mercurial, mutable, treacherous, unfaithful, unpredictable, unreliable, unstable, unsteady, inf up and down, vacillating, volatile. Opp CONSTANT.

fiction n 1 concoction, fabrication, fantasy, figment of the imagination, flight of fancy, invention, lies, story-telling, inf tall story. 2 novel, romance, story, tale. Opp FACT.

fictional adj fabulous, fanciful, imaginary, invented, legendary, made-up, make-believe, mythical, story-book. Opp FACTUAL.

fictitious adj apocryphal, assumed, fabricated, fraudulent, imagined, invented, made-up, spurious, unreal, untrue. ▷ FALSE. Opp GENUINE.

fiddle v interfere, meddle, play about, tamper. ▷ FIDGET.

fiddling ▷ TRIVIAL.

fidget *v* be restless, fiddle, fret, fuss, jiggle, *inf* mess about, *inf* play about, shuffle, squirm, twitch, worry, wriggle about.

fidgety *adj* agitated, impatient, *inf* jittery, jumpy, nervous, on edge, restless, *inf* twitchy, uneasy. *Opp* CALM.

field *n* 1 arable land, clearing, enclosure, grassland, green, meadow, paddock, pasture. 2 *games field.* arena, ground, pitch, playing field, stadium. 3 *field of activity.* area, *inf* department, domain, province, sphere, subject, territory.

fiend *n* 1 demon, devil, evil spirit, goblin, hobgoblin, imp, Satan, spirit. 2 ▷ FANATIC.

fierce *adj* 1 angry, barbaric, barbarous, bloodthirsty, bloody, brutal, cold-blooded, cruel, dangerous, fearsome, ferocious, fiendish, fiery, homicidal, inhuman, merciless, murderous, pitiless, ruthless, sadistic, savage, untamed, vicious, violent, wild. 2 *fierce opposition.* active, aggressive, competitive, eager, furious, heated, intense, keen, passionate, relentless, strong. *Opp* GENTLE.

fiery *adj* 1 aflame, blazing, burning, fierce, flaming, glowing, hot, incandescent, raging, red, redhot. 2 *fiery temper.* angry, choleric, excitable, fervent, furious, hot-headed, intense, irascible, livid, mad, passionate, touchy, violent. *Opp* COOL.

fight *n* action, affray, attack, battle, bout, brawl, *inf* brush, *inf* bust-up, clash, combat, competition, conflict, confrontation, contest, dispute, dogfight, duel, *inf* dust-up, encounter, engagement, feud, fisticuffs, fracas, fray, *inf* free-for-all, hostilities, match, mêlée, *inf* punch-up, riot, rivalry, *inf* row, scramble, scrap, scrimmage, scuffle, *inf* set-to, skirmish, squabble, strife, struggle, tussle, war, wrangle. ▷ QUARREL. ● *v* 1 attack, battle, box, brawl, *inf* brush, clash, compete, conflict, contend, duel, engage, fence, feud, grapple, quarrel, *inf* row, scrap, scuffle, skirmish, spar, squabble, stand up (to), strive, struggle, tussle, wage war, wrestle. 2 *fight a decision.* campaign against, contest, defy, oppose, resist, take a stand against.

fighter *n* aggressor, antagonist, attacker, campaigner, combatant, contender, defender. ▷ SOLDIER.

figure *n* 1 amount, cipher, digit, integer, number, numeral, sum, symbol, value. 2 diagram, drawing, graph, illustration, outline, picture, plate, representation. 3 *plump figure.* body, build, form, outline, physique, shape, silhouette. 4 *bronze figure.* ▷ SCULPTURE. 5 *well-known figure.* ▷ PERSON. ● *v* ▷ FEATURE. **figure out** ▷ CALCULATE, UNDERSTAND.

figures ▷ STATISTICS.

file *n* 1 binder, box-file, case, cover, dossier, folder, portfolio, ring-binder. 2 *single file.* column, line, procession, queue, rank, row, stream, string, train. ● *v* 1 arrange, categorize, classify, enter, organize, pigeonhole, put away, record, register, store, systematize. 2 *file through a door.* march, parade, proceed in a line, stream, troop.

fill *v* 1 be full of, block, *inf* bung up, clog, close up, cram, crowd, flood, jam, load, pack, plug, refill, replenish, seal, stock up, stop up, stuff, *inf* top up. *Opp* EMPTY. 2 *fill a need.* answer, fulfil, meet, provide, satisfy, supply. 3 *fill a post.* hold, occupy, take over, take up. **fill out** ▷ SWELL.

filling *n* contents, insides, padding, stuffing, wadding.

film *n* 1 coat, coating, covering, haze, layer, membrane, mist, sheet, skin, slick, tissue, veil. 2 *inf* flick, *inf* movie, *inf* picture, video.

filter *n* colander, gauze, mesh, riddle, screen, sieve, strainer. • *v* clarify, percolate, purify, refine, screen, sieve, sift, strain.

filth *n* decay, dirt, effluent, garbage, grime, *inf* gunge, muck, mud, ordure, pollution, refuse, rubbish, scum, sewage, slime, sludge. ▷ EXCRETA.

filthy *adj* 1 caked, defiled, dirty, disgusting, dusty, foul, grimy, grubby, messy, mucky, muddy, nasty, polluted, scummy, slimy, smelly, soiled, sooty, sordid, squalid, stinking, tainted, unkempt, unwashed, vile. 2 ▷ OBSCENE. *Opp* CLEAN.

final *adj* closing, concluding, conclusive, decisive, dying, end, eventual, finishing, last, settled, terminal, ultimate. *Opp* INITIAL.

finalize *v* clinch, complete, conclude, settle, *inf* sew up, *inf* wrap up.

finance *n* accounting, banking, business, commerce, economics, investment, stocks and shares. • *v* back, fund, guarantee, invest in, pay for, provide money for, subsidize, support, underwrite. **finances** assets, capital, cash, funds, holdings, income, money,

resources, wealth, *inf* the wherewithal.

financial *adj* economic, fiscal, monetary, pecuniary.

find *v* 1 acquire, become aware of, *inf* bump into, chance upon, come across, come upon, detect, diagnose, dig out, dig up, discover, encounter, expose, *inf* ferret out, happen on, hit on, identify, learn, light on, locate, meet, note, notice, observe, *inf* put your finger on, recognize, reveal, spot, stumble on, uncover, unearth. 2 get back, recover, rediscover, regain, repossess, retrieve, trace, track down. 3 *found me a job.* give, pass on, procure, provide, supply. *Opp* LOSE.

finding *n* conclusion, decision, decree, judgement, verdict.

fine *adj* 1 admirable, beautiful, choice, classic, excellent, first-class, handsome, noble, select, superior, worthy. ▷ GOOD. 2 *fine workmanship.* consummate, craftsmanlike, meticulous, skilful, skilled. 3 *fine sand.* minute, powdery, soft. 4 *fine fabric.* dainty, delicate, exquisite, flimsy, fragile, silky. 5 *fine distinction.* acute, discriminating, hair-splitting, nice, precise, subtle. 6 *fine weather.* bright, clear, cloudless, dry, fair, nice, pleasant, sunny. 7 *fine point.* ▷ SHARP. • *n* charge, forfeit, penalty.

finish *n* 1 cessation, close, completion, conclusion, culmination, end, ending, finale, resolution, result, termination. 2 *finish on furniture.* appearance, gloss, lustre, patina, polish, shine, smoothness, surface, texture. • *v* 1 accomplish, achieve, break off, bring to an end, cease, clinch, complete, conclude, discontinue, end, finalize, fulfil, halt, pack up, perfect, phase out, reach the end, round off, sign off, stop, terminate, *inf* wind up, *inf* wrap up. **2** consume, drink up, eat up, empty, exhaust, expend, get through, *inf* polish off, use up. **finish off** ▷ KILL.

finite *adj* bounded, definable, defined, fixed, known, limited, measurable, numbered, rationed, restricted.
Opp INFINITE.

fire *n* **1** blaze, combustion, conflagration, flames, holocaust, inferno, pyre. **2** fireplace, furnace, grate, hearth. **3** *fire in your veins.* ▷ PASSION. ● *v* **1** bake, burn, heat, ignite, kindle, light, set alight, set fire to, spark off. **2** animate, awaken, enliven, excite, incite, inflame, inspire, motivate, rouse, stimulate, stir. **3** *fire a gun or missile.* catapult, detonate, discharge, explode, launch, let off, set off, shoot, trigger off. **4** *fire a worker.* dismiss, make redundant, sack, throw out. **fire at** ▷ BOMBARD.
hang fire ▷ DELAY.

fireproof *adj* flameproof, incombustible, non-flammable.
Opp INFLAMMABLE.

firm *adj* **1** compact, compressed, dense, hard, rigid, set, solid, stable, stiff, unyielding. **2** anchored, embedded, fast, fastened, fixed, immovable, secure, steady, tight. **3** *firm convictions.* adamant, decided, determined, dogged, inflexible, obstinate, persistent, resolute, unshakeable, unwavering. **4** *firm price.* agreed, settled, unchangeable. **5** *firm friends.* constant,

dependable, devoted, faithful, loyal, reliable. ● *n* business, company, concern, corporation, establishment, organization, partnership.

first *adj* **1** cardinal, chief, dominant, foremost, head, key, leading, main, outstanding, paramount, predominant, primary, prime, principal, top, uppermost. **2** *first steps.* basic, elementary, initial, introductory, preliminary, rudimentary. **3** *first version.* archetypal, earliest, eldest, embryonic, oldest, original, primeval. **first-class**, **first-rate** ▷ EXCELLENT.

fish *v* angle, go fishing, trawl.

fisher *n* angler, fisherman, trawlerman.

fit *adj* **1** adapted, adequate, applicable, apposite, appropriate, apt, becoming, befitting, correct, decent, equipped, fitting, good enough, proper, right, satisfactory, seemly, sound, suitable, suited, timely. **2** able, capable, competent, in good form, on form, prepared, ready, strong, well enough. ▷ HEALTHY.
Opp UNFIT. ● *n* attack, bout, convulsion, eruption, explosion, outburst, paroxysm, seizure, spasm, spell. ● *v* **1** accord with, become, be fitting for, conform with, correspond to, go with, suit. **2** *fit things into place.* arrange, assemble, build, construct, dovetail, install, interlock, join, match, position, put in place, put together. **fit out, fit up** ▷ EQUIP.

fix *n inf* catch-22, corner, difficulty, dilemma, *inf* hole, *inf* jam, mess, *inf* pickle, plight, predicament, problem, quandary.
● *v* **1** attach, connect, implant,

install, join, link, make firm, plant, position, secure, stabilize, stick. ▷ FASTEN. **2** *fix a price.* agree, appoint, arrange, arrive at, conclude, confirm, decide, define, establish, finalize, name, set, settle, sort out, specify. **3** *fix a broken window.* correct, make good, mend, put right, rectify, remedy, repair.

fixture *n* date, engagement, event, game, match, meeting.

fizz *v* bubble, effervesce, fizzle, foam, froth, hiss, sizzle, sparkle, sputter.

fizzy *adj* bubbly, effervescent, foaming, sparkling.

flag *n* banner, bunting, colours, ensign, pennant, pennon, standard, streamer. ● *v* **1** ▷ SIGNAL. **2** *enthusiasm began to flag.* ▷ DECLINE.

flake *n* chip, leaf, scale, shaving, sliver, splinter, wafer.

flame *n* blaze, light, tongue. ▷ FIRE. ● *v* ▷ FLARE.

flap *v* beat, flutter, sway, swing, thrash about, *inf* waggle, wave about.

flare *v* **1** blaze, brighten, burst out, erupt, flame, shine. ▷ BURN. **2** ▷ WIDEN.

flash *v* dazzle, flicker, glare, glint, glitter, light up, reflect, scintillate, shine, spark, sparkle, twinkle. ▷ BURN.

flat *adj* **1** calm, even, horizontal, level, smooth, unbroken, unruffled. **2** outstretched, prone, prostrate, recumbent, spread-eagled, spread out, supine. **3** *flat voice.* bland, boring, dead, dull, featureless, insipid, lacklustre, lifeless, monotonous, stale, tedious, tired, unexciting, uninteresting, unvarying. **4** *flat tyre.*

blown out, burst, deflated, punctured. ● *n* apartment, bedsitter, penthouse, rooms.

flatten *v* **1** compress, even out, iron out, level out, press, roll, smooth. **2** crush, demolish, level, raze, run over, squash, trample. ▷ DESTROY. **3** *flatten an opponent.* fell, floor, knock down, prostrate. ▷ DEFEAT.

flatter *v* *inf* butter up, compliment, court, curry favour with, fawn on, humour, *inf* play up to, praise, *inf* suck up to.
Opp INSULT. **flattering** ▷ COMPLIMENTARY, OBSEQUIOUS.

flatterer *n* *inf* crawler, *inf* creep, groveller, sycophant, toady, *inf* yes-man.

flattery *n* adulation, blandishments, *inf* blarney, cajolery, fawning, *inf* flannel, insincerity, obsequiousness, servility, *inf* soft soap, sycophancy.

flavour *n* **1** savour, taste. ▷ FLAVOURING. **2** air, ambience, atmosphere, aura, character, characteristic, feel, feeling, property, quality, style. ● *v* add flavour to, season, spice.

flavouring *n* additive, essence, extract, seasoning.

flaw *n* break, defect, error, fallacy, fault, imperfection, inaccuracy, loophole, mistake, slip, weakness. ▷ BLEMISH. **flawed** ▷ IMPERFECT.

flawless *adj* accurate, clean, faultless, immaculate, mint, pristine, sound, spotless, undamaged, unmarked. ▷ PERFECT.
Opp IMPERFECT.

flee *v* abscond, *inf* beat a retreat, *sl* beat it, bolt, clear off, *inf* cut and run, decamp, disappear, escape, fly, get away, *inf* make a run for it, make off, retreat, run away, *sl* scarper, take flight, *inf* take to your heels, vanish, withdraw.

fleet *n* armada, convoy, flotilla, navy, squadron, task force.

fleeting *adj* brief, ephemeral, evanescent, fugitive, impermanent, momentary, passing, short, short-lived, temporary, transient, transitory. *Opp* PERMANENT.

flesh *n* carrion, fat, meat, muscle, tissue.

flex *n* cable, cord, extension, lead, wire. ● *v* ▷ BEND.

flexible *adj* 1 bendable, *inf* bendy, elastic, floppy, lithe, plastic, pliable, pliant, rubbery, soft, springy, stretchy, supple, whippy, yielding. 2 adjustable, fluid, open, provisional, variable. 3 *flexible person.* accommodating, adaptable, amenable, compliant, cooperative, docile, easygoing, malleable, open-minded, responsive, tractable, willing. *Opp* RIGID.

flicker *v* blink, flutter, glimmer, quiver, shimmer, sparkle, tremble, twinkle, waver.

flight *n* 1 journey, trajectory. 2 ▷ ESCAPE.

flimsy *adj* 1 breakable, brittle, delicate, fine, fragile, frail, insubstantial, light, slight, thin, weak. 2 *flimsy building.* decrepit, dilapidated, gimcrack, makeshift, rickety, shaky, tottering, wobbly. 3 *flimsy argument.* feeble, implausible, inadequate, superficial, trivial, unbelievable, unconvincing, unsatisfactory. *Opp* STRONG.

flinch *v* blench, cower, cringe, dodge, draw back, duck, falter, jump, quail, recoil, shrink back,

shy away, start, swerve, wince. flinch from ▷ EVADE.

fling *v inf* bung, cast, *inf* chuck, heave, hurl, launch, lob, pitch, sling, throw, toss.

flippant *adj* cheeky, facetious, *inf* frivolous, light-hearted, shallow, superficial, thoughtless. *Opp* SERIOUS.

flirt *n female* coquette, *male* philanderer, *inf* tease. ● *v sl* chat someone up, lead someone on, make love, philander.

flirtatious *adj* amorous, coquettish, flirty, playful, teasing.

float *v* 1 bob, drift, glide, hang, hover, sail, swim, waft. 2 *float a ship.* launch. *Opp* SINK.

flock *n* congregation, crowd, drove, gathering, herd, horde. ▷ GROUP. ● *v* ▷ GATHER.

flog *v* beat, birch, cane, flagellate, flay, lash, scourge, thrash, whip. ▷ HIT.

flood *n* 1 cataract, deluge, downpour, flash-flood, inundation, overflow, rush, spate, stream, tide, torrent. 2 abundance, excess, glut, plethora, superfluity, surfeit, surge. ● *v* cover, deluge, drown, engulf, fill up, immerse, inundate, overflow, overwhelm, saturate, sink, submerge, swamp.

floor *n* 1 floorboards, flooring. 2 deck, level, storey, tier.

flop *v* 1 collapse, dangle, droop, drop, fall, flag, sag, slump, topple, tumble, wilt. 2 ▷ FAIL.

floppy *adj* dangling, droopy, loose, limp, pliable, soft. ▷ FLEXIBLE. *Opp* RIGID.

flounder *v* 1 blunder, flail, fumble, grope, move clumsily, plunge about, stagger, struggle, tumble, wallow. **2** falter, get confused, make mistakes.

flourish *n* ▷ GESTURE. ● *v* **1** be successful, bloom, blossom, boom, burgeon, develop, do well, flower, grow, increase, prosper, strengthen, succeed, thrive. **2** *flourish an umbrella.* brandish, flaunt, gesture with, shake, swing, twirl, wag, wave, wield.

flow *n* cascade, course, current, drift, ebb, effusion, flood, gush, outpouring, spate, spurt, stream, tide, trickle. ● *v* cascade, course, dribble, drift, drip, flood, flush, glide, gush, issue, leak, ooze, overflow, pour, ripple, roll, run, seep, spill, spring, spurt, squirt, stream, swirl, trickle, well, well up.

flower *n* **1** bloom, blossom, bud, floret, petal. ● *v* bloom, blossom, bud, burgeon, come out, open out, unfold. ▷ FLOURISH. **bunch of flowers** arrangement, bouquet, corsage, garland, posy, spray, wreath.

fluctuate *v* alternate, be unsteady, change, go up and down, oscillate, seesaw, shift, swing, vacillate, vary, waver.

fluent *adj* articulate, effortless, eloquent, *derog* facile, flowing, *derog* glib, natural, polished, ready, smooth, voluble, unhesitating. *Opp* HESITANT.

fluff *n* down, dust, feathers, fuzz, thistledown.

fluffy *adj* downy, feathery, fleecy, furry, fuzzy, light, silky, soft, velvety, wispy, woolly.

fluid *adj* **1** aqueous, flowing, liquefied, liquid, melted, molten, running, *inf* runny, sloppy, watery. *Opp* SOLID. **2** *fluid situation.* changing, flexible, open,

variable, undefined. ● *n* juice, liquid, plasma, sap.

fluke *n* accident, chance, stroke of good luck.

flush *v* **1** blush, colour, glow, go red, redden. **2** *flush a lavatory.* cleanse, rinse out. **3** *flush from a hiding-place.* chase out, drive out, expel.

fluster *v* agitate, bewilder, bother, distract, flurry, perplex, put off, put out, *inf* rattle, *inf* throw, upset. ▷ CONFUSE.

flutter *v* bat (*eyelid*), flap, flicker, flit, oscillate, palpitate, quiver, shake, tremble, twitch, vibrate, wave.

fly *v* **1** ascend, flit, glide, hover, rise, sail, soar, swoop, take flight, take wing. **2** *fly a plane.* control, pilot. **3** *fly a flag.* display, flutter, hang up, hoist, raise, show, wave. **4** *fly from danger.* flee, hurry, run. ▷ ESCAPE. **fly at** ▷ ATTACK. **fly in the face of** ▷ DISREGARD.

flying *n* aeronautics, air-travel, aviation, flight.

foam *n* **1** bubbles, effervescence, froth, head (*on beer*), lather, scum, spume, suds. **2** sponge. ● *v* boil, bubble, effervesce, fizz, froth, lather.

focus *n* centre, core, focal point, heart, hub, pivot, target. ● *v* aim, centre, concentrate, direct attention, home in, spotlight.

fog *n* cloud, haze, miasma, mist, smog, smoke, vapour.

foggy *adj* blurred, cloudy, dim, hazy, indistinct, misty, murky, obscure. *Opp* CLEAR.

foil *v* baffle, block, check, frustrate, halt, hamper, hinder, obstruct, outwit, prevent, stop, thwart. ▷ DEFEAT.

foist v inf fob off, get rid of, impose, offload, palm off.

fold n 1 bend, corrugation, crease, crinkle, furrow, pleat, pucker, wrinkle. 2 *fold for sheep*. ▷ ENCLOSURE. ● v 1 bend, crease, crinkle, double over, jack-knife, overlap, pleat, pucker, tuck in, turn over. 2 close, collapse, let down, put down, shut. 3 *fold in your arms*. clasp, embrace, enclose, enfold, envelop, hold, hug, wrap. 4 *business folded*. ▷ FAIL.

folk n clan, nation, people, the public, race, society, tribe.

follow v 1 accompany, chase, come after, dog, escort, go after, hound, hunt, keep pace with, pursue, replace, shadow, stalk, succeed, supersede, supplant, *inf* tag along with, *inf* tail, take the place of, track, trail. 2 *follow a path*. keep to, trace. 3 *follow rules*. abide by, adhere to, comply with, conform to, heed, honour, obey, observe, pay attention to, stick to, take notice of. 4 *follow my example*. adopt, copy, imitate, mirror. 5 *follow an argument*. appreciate, comprehend, grasp, keep up with, take in, understand. 6 *follow football*. be a fan of, keep abreast of, know about, take an interest in, support. 7 *It doesn't follow*. be inevitable, be logical, ensue, happen, mean, result. **following** ▷ SUBSEQUENT.

folly n foolishness, insanity, lunacy, madness. ▷ STUPIDITY.

foment v arouse, incite, instigate, kindle, provoke, rouse, stir up. ▷ STIMULATE.

fond adj 1 adoring, affectionate, caring, loving, tender, warm.

2 *a fond hope*. ▷ FOOLISH. **be fond of** ▷ LOVE.

fondle v caress, cuddle, handle, pat, pet, squeeze, touch.

food n comestibles, cooking, cuisine, delicacies, diet, eatables, *inf* eats, fare, feed, fodder, foodstuff, *inf* grub, meat, *sl* nosh, nourishment, nutriments, provisions, rations, recipe, refreshments, sustenance, *old use* victuals.

fool n 1 [*most synonyms inf*] ass, blockhead, buffoon, dimwit, dope, dunce, dunderhead, dupe, half-wit, ignoramus, mug, muggins, ninny, nit, nitwit, simpleton, sucker, twerp, wally. ▷ IDIOT. 2 clown, comic, entertainer, jester. ● v inf bamboozle, bluff, cheat, *inf* con, deceive, defraud, delude, dupe, fleece, gull, hoax, hoodwink, *inf* kid, mislead, swindle, take in, tease, trick. **fool about** ▷ MISBEHAVE.

foolish adj absurd, asinine, brainless, childish, crazy, *inf* daft, *inf* dopey, *inf* dotty, fatuous, feather-brained, frivolous, *inf* half-baked, hare-brained, idiotic, immature, inane, infantile, irrational, laughable, ludicrous, mad, meaningless, mindless, misguided, naive, nonsensical, pointless, preposterous, ridiculous, *inf* scatty, senseless, shallow, silly, simple, simple-minded, simplistic, *inf* soppy, stupid, thoughtless, unintelligent, unreasonable, unwise, witless. *Opp* WISE.

foot n 1 claw, hoof, paw, trotter. 2 ▷ BASE.

footprint n footmark, spoor, track.

forbid v ban, bar, debar, deny, disallow, exclude, outlaw, preclude, prevent, prohibit, proscribe, refuse, rule out, stop, veto. *Opp* ALLOW.

forbidden adj 1 against the law, taboo, unlawful, wrong. 2 *forbidden area*. closed, out of bounds, restricted, secret.

forbidding adj gloomy, grim, menacing, ominous, stern, threatening, uninviting. ▷ UNFRIENDLY. *Opp* FRIENDLY.

force n 1 aggression, *inf* arm-twisting, coercion, compulsion, constraint, duress, effort, might, power, pressure, strength, vehemence, vigour, violence. 2 energy, impact, intensity, momentum, shock. 3 *military force*. army, body, group, troops. 4 *force of an argument*. cogency, effectiveness, persuasiveness, thrust, validity, weight. ● v 1 *inf* bulldoze, coerce, compel, constrain, drive, impel, make, oblige, order, press-gang, pressurize. 2 *force a door*. break open, burst open, prise open, smash, wrench. 3 *force something on someone*. impose, inflict.

foreboding n anxiety, apprehension, dread, fear, intimation, intuition, misgiving, omen, portent, premonition, presentiment, suspicion, warning, worry.

forecast n augury, outlook, prediction, prognosis, projection, prophecy. ● v ▷ FORESEE.

forefront n avant-garde, front, lead, vanguard.

foreign adj 1 distant, exotic, far-away, outlandish, remote, strange, unfamiliar, unknown. 2 alien, external, imported, incoming, international, outside,

overseas, visiting. 3 extraneous, odd, uncharacteristic, unnatural, untypical, unusual, unwanted. *Opp* NATIVE.

foreigner n alien, immigrant, newcomer, outsider, overseas visitor, stranger. *Opp* NATIVE.

foremost adj first, leading, main, primary. ▷ CHIEF.

forerunner n advance messenger, harbinger, herald, precursor, predecessor. ▷ ANCESTOR.

foresee v anticipate, envisage, expect, forecast, picture. ▷ FORETELL.

foresight n ▷ FORETHOUGHT.

forest n jungle, plantation, trees, woodland, woods.

foretaste n advance warning, augury, example, forewarning, indication, omen, premonition, preview, sample, specimen, tip-off, trailer.

foretell v augur, bode, forebode, foreshadow, forewarn, herald, portend, predict, presage, prophesy, signify. ▷ FORESEE.

forethought n anticipation, caution, far-sightedness, foresight, looking ahead, perspicacity, planning, preparation, prudence, readiness, vision.

forewarning n advance warning, augury, omen, premonition, tip-off. ▷ FORETASTE.

forfeit n damages, fee, fine, penalty. ● v abandon, give up, let go, lose, pay up, relinquish, renounce, surrender.

forge n furnace, smithy, workshop. ● v 1 beat into shape, cast, construct, hammer out, manufacture, mould, shape, work. 2 coin, copy, counterfeit, fake, falsify,

imitate, reproduce. **forge ahead**
▷ ADVANCE.

forgery n copy, counterfeit,
inf dud, fake, fraud, imitation,
inf phoney, reproduction.

forget v 1 dismiss from your
mind, disregard, fail to remember, ignore, leave out, lose track
(of), miss out, neglect, omit, overlook, skip. 2 be without, leave
behind. Opp REMEMBER.

forgetful adj absent-minded,
careless, distracted, neglectful,
negligent, oblivious, preoccupied, unmindful, unreliable,
vague, inf woolly-minded.

forgivable adj allowable, excusable, justifiable, pardonable,
petty, understandable, venial
(sin). Opp UNFORGIVABLE.

forgive v 1 absolve, acquit, clear,
excuse, exonerate, let off,
pardon, spare. 2 forgive a crime.
condone, ignore, make allowances for, overlook, pass over.

forgiveness n absolution,
amnesty, clemency, compassion,
exoneration, indulgence, leniency, mercy, pardon, reprieve.
Opp RETRIBUTION.

forgiving adj compassionate,
forbearing, generous, merciful,
tolerant, understanding. ▷ KIND.
Opp VENGEFUL.

forgo v abandon, abstain from,
do without, forswear, give up, go
without, pass up, relinquish,
renounce, sacrifice, waive.

forked adj branched, cleft,
divided, pronged, V-shaped.

forlorn adj abandoned, alone,
bereft, deserted, forsaken, friendless, lonely, outcast, solitary,
unloved. ▷ SAD.

form n 1 appearance, arrangement, cast, character, configura-

tion, design, format, framework,
genre, guise, kind, manifestation, model, mould, nature, pattern, semblance, sort, species,
structure, style, system, type,
variety. 2 human form. anatomy,
body, build, figure, frame, outline, physique, shape, silhouette.
3 school form. class, grade,
group, level, set, stream. 4 good
form. behaviour, convention,
custom, etiquette, fashion, manners, practice. 5 application
form. document, paper. 6 in good
form. condition, inf fettle, fitness, health, performance,
spirits. 7 ▷ SEAT. ● v 1 cast, constitute, construct, create, design,
establish, forge, found, give form
to, make, model, mould, organize, produce, shape. 2 appear,
arise, develop, grow, materialize, take shape. 3 form a team.
act as, compose, comprise, make
up. 4 form a habit. acquire,
develop, get.

formal adj 1 aloof, ceremonial,
conventional, cool, correct, customary, dignified, orthodox,
inf posh, proper, punctilious,
ritualistic, solemn, sophisticated, inf starchy, stately, stiff,
unbending, unfriendly. 2 formal
language. academic, impersonal,
official, precise, specialist, stilted, technical. 3 formal agreement. binding, contractual,
enforceable, legal, inf signed and
sealed. 4 formal design. geometrical, orderly, organized, regular, rigid, symmetrical.
Opp INFORMAL.

format n appearance, design,
layout, plan, shape, size, style.

former adj bygone, departed, ex-,
last, late, old, one-time, past, previous, prior, recent. **the former**

earlier, first, first-mentioned.
Opp LATTER.

formidable adj awesome, challenging, daunting, difficult, dreadful, frightening, intimidating, inf mind-boggling, onerous, overwhelming, prodigious, taxing. Opp EASY.

formula n 1 ritual, rubric, spell, wording. 2 formula for success. blueprint, method, prescription, procedure, recipe, rule, technique, way.

formulate v 1 codify, define, express clearly, set out in detail, specify, systematize. 2 concoct, create, devise, evolve, form, invent, map out, originate, plan, work out.

forsake v abandon, desert, forgo, forswear, give up, jilt, leave, quit, renounce, repudiate, surrender, throw over, inf turn your back on.

fort n castle, citadel, fortress, garrison, stronghold, tower.

forthright adj blunt, candid, decisive, direct, outspoken, straightforward, unequivocal, unhesitating, uninhibited.
▷ FRANK. Opp EVASIVE.

fortify v 1 defend, garrison, protect, reinforce, secure against attack, shore up. 2 bolster, boost, brace, buoy up, cheer, encourage, hearten, invigorate, reassure, strengthen, support, sustain. Opp WEAKEN.

fortitude n backbone, bravery, determination, endurance, firmness, patience, resolution, stoicism, valour, will-power.
▷ COURAGE. Opp COWARDICE.

fortunate adj auspicious, blessed, favourable, lucky, opportune, propitious, prosperous, providential, timely. ▷ HAPPY.

fortune n 1 accident, chance, destiny, fate, karma, kismet, luck, providence. 2 affluence, assets, estate, holdings, inheritance, inf millions, money, inf pile, possessions, property, prosperity, riches, treasure, wealth.

fortune-teller n clairvoyant, crystal-gazer, oracle, palmist, prophet, seer, soothsayer.

forward adj 1 advancing, frontal, head-first, leading, onward, progressive. 2 forward planning. advance, early, future. 3 forward child. assertive, bold, brazen, cheeky, familiar, inf fresh, impertinent, impudent, insolent, over-confident, precocious, presumptuous, inf pushy, shameless, uninhibited.
Opp BACKWARD. ● v 1 dispatch, freight, post on, re-address, send, send on, ship, transmit, transport. 2 forward your career. accelerate, advance, encourage, facilitate, foster, further, hasten, help along, promote, speed up, support. ▷ HELP. Opp HINDER.

foster v 1 advance, cultivate, encourage, further, promote, stimulate. ▷ HELP. 2 foster a child. adopt, bring up, care for, look after, raise, rear, take care of.

foul adj 1 bad, contaminated, disgusting, fetid, filthy, hateful, impure, loathsome, nasty, nauseating, noisome, obnoxious, offensive, polluted, putrid, repugnant, repulsive, revolting, rotten, sickening, squalid, stinking, vile. ▷ DIRTY, SMELLING. 2 foul crimes. abhorrent, abominable, atrocious, beastly, cruel, evil, monstrous, scandalous, shameful, vicious, villainous, violent, wicked.

3 *foul language*. abusive, blasphemous, coarse, common, crude, improper, indecent, insulting, offensive, rude, uncouth, vulgar. ▷ OBSCENE.
4 *foul weather*. foggy, rainy, rough, stormy, violent, windy. ▷ UNPLEASANT. **5** *foul play*. dishonest, illegal, invalid, unfair, unsportsmanlike. Opp CLEAN, FAIR. ● *n* infringement, violation. ● *v* ▷ DIRTY. **foul up** ▷ MUDDLE.

found *v* **1** begin, create, endow, establish, fund, *inf* get going, inaugurate, initiate, institute, organize, originate, raise, set up, start. **2** base, build, construct, erect, ground.

foundation *n* **1** beginning, endowment, establishment, inauguration, initiation, institution, setting up. **2** base, basis, bottom, cornerstone, foot, footing, substructure, underpinning. **3** *foundations of science*. basic principle, element, essential, fundamental, origin, *pl* rudiments.

founder *v* be wrecked, *inf* come to grief, fail, fall through, go down, miscarry, sink.

fountain *n* fount, jet, source, spout, spring, well.

foyer *n* ante-room, entrance, entrance hall, hall, lobby.

fraction *n* division, part, portion, section, subdivision.

fracture *n* break, breakage, chip, cleft, crack, fissure, gap, opening, rent, rift, rupture, split. ● *v* breach, break, crack, rupture, separate, snap, split.

fragile *adj* ▷ FRAIL.

fragment *n* atom, bit, chip, crumb, *pl* debris, morsel, part, particle, piece, portion, remnant, scrap, shard, shred, sliver,

pl smithereens, snippet, speck. ● *v* ▷ BREAK.

fragmentary *adj inf* bitty, broken, disconnected, disjointed, fragmented, imperfect, in bits, incoherent, incomplete, partial, scattered, scrappy, sketchy, uncoordinated. Opp COMPLETE.

fragrance *n* aroma, bouquet, nose (*of wine*), odour, perfume, redolence, scent, smell.

fragrant *adj* aromatic, odorous, perfumed, redolent, scented, sweet-smelling.

frail *adj* breakable, brittle, delicate, easily damaged, flimsy, fragile, insubstantial, light, *derog* puny, rickety, slight, thin, unsound, unsteady, vulnerable, *derog* weedy. ▷ ILL. Opp STRONG.

frame *n* **1** bodywork, chassis, construction, scaffolding, structure. ▷ FRAMEWORK. **2** *photo frame*. border, case, casing, edge, edging, mount, mounting. ● *v* **1** box in, enclose, mount, set off, surround. **2** ▷ COMPOSE. **frame of mind** ▷ ATTITUDE.

framework *n* bare bones, frame, outline, plan, shell, skeleton, support, trellis.

frank *adj* blunt, candid, direct, downright, explicit, forthright, genuine, *inf* heart-to-heart, honest, *inf* no-nonsense, open, outright, outspoken, plain, plain-spoken, revealing, sincere, straightforward, straight from the heart, to the point, trustworthy, truthful, unconcealed, undisguised, unreserved. Opp INSINCERE.

frantic *adj* agitated, anxious, berserk, *inf* beside yourself, crazy, delirious, demented, desperate, distraught, excitable, feverish, *inf* fraught, frenetic, frenzied, furious, hectic, hysterical, mad, overwrought, panicky, violent, wild, worked up. *Opp* CALM.

fraud n 1 cheating, chicanery, *inf* con-trick, counterfeit, deceit, deception, dishonesty, double-dealing, duplicity, fake, forgery, hoax, pretence, *inf* put-up job, ruse, sham, *inf* sharp practice, swindle, trick, trickery. 2 charlatan, cheat, *inf* con-man, hoaxer, impostor, *inf* phoney, quack, rogue, scoundrel, swindler.

fraudulent adj *inf* bent, bogus, cheating, corrupt, counterfeit, criminal, *inf* crooked, deceitful, devious, *inf* dirty, dishonest, duplicitous, fake, false, forged, illegal, lying, *inf* phoney, sham, specious, swindling, underhand. *Opp* HONEST.

fray n brawl, commotion, conflict, fracas, mêlée, quarrel, *inf* rumpus. ▷ FIGHT.

frayed adj tattered, threadbare, worn. ▷ RAGGED.

freak adj aberrant, abnormal, anomalous, atypical, bizarre, exceptional, extraordinary, odd, peculiar, queer, rare, unaccountable, unforeseeable, unpredictable, unusual, weird. *Opp* NORMAL. ● n 1 aberration, abnormality, anomaly, curiosity, irregularity, monster, monstrosity, mutant, oddity, *inf* one-off, quirk, rarity, variant. 2 ▷ FANATIC.

free adj 1 able, allowed, at leisure, at liberty, idle, independent, loose, not working, uncommitted, unconfined, unconstrained, unrestrained, untrammelled. 2 emancipated, liberated, released, unchained, unfettered,

unshackled. 3 *free country*. autonomous, democratic, independent, self-governing, sovereign. 4 *free access*. clear, open, permitted, unhindered, unimpeded, unrestricted. 5 *free gifts*. complimentary, gratis, *sl* on the house, unasked-for, unsolicited. 6 *free space*. available, empty, uninhabited, unoccupied, vacant. 7 *free with money*. casual, generous, lavish, liberal, ready, unstinting, willing. ● v 1 absolve, acquit, clear, deliver, discharge, emancipate, exculpate, exonerate, let go, let off, let out, liberate, loose, pardon, parole, ransom, release, reprieve, rescue, save, set free, spare, turn loose, unchain, unfetter, unleash, unlock, unloose. *Opp* CONFINE. 2 *free tangled ropes*. clear, disengage, disentangle, extricate, loose, undo, untie. *Opp* TANGLE. **free and easy** ▷ INFORMAL.

freedom n 1 autonomy, independence, liberty, self-determination, self-government, sovereignty. *Opp* CAPTIVITY. 2 deliverance, emancipation, exemption, immunity, liberation, release. 3 *freedom to choose*. ability, discretion, free hand, latitude, leeway, leisure, licence, opportunity, permission, power, privilege, right, scope.

freeze v 1 congeal, harden, ice over, ice up, solidify, stiffen. 2 chill, cool, make cold, numb. 3 chill, deep-freeze, ice, preserve, refrigerate. 4 fix, hold, immobilize, peg, stand still, stick, stop. **freezing** ▷ COLD.

freight n ▷ CARGO.

frenzy n agitation, delirium, excitement, fever, fit, fury, hysteria, insanity, lunacy, madness, mania, outburst, paroxysm, passion, turmoil.

frequent adj common, constant, continual, customary, everyday, familiar, habitual, incessant, innumerable, many, normal, numerous, persistent, recurrent, regular, repeated, usual. Opp INFREQUENT. ● v ▷ HAUNT.

fresh adj 1 additional, alternative, different, extra, new, recent, supplementary, unfamiliar, up-to-date. 2 alert, energetic, healthy, invigorated, lively, inf perky, rested, revived, sprightly, tingling, vigorous, vital. 3 fresh recruit. ▷ INEXPERIENCED. 4 fresh water. clear, drinkable, pure, refreshing, sweet, uncontaminated. 5 fresh air. airy, breezy, circulating, clean, cool, unpolluted 6 fresh wind. bracing, invigorating, sharp, stiff. 7 fresh food. healthy, natural, unprocessed, untreated, wholesome. 8 fresh sheets. clean, crisp, laundered, unused, washed-and-ironed. 9 fresh colours. bright, clean, glowing, renewed, restored, sparkling, vivid. Opp OLD, STALE.

fret v 1 agonize, be anxious, brood, worry. 2 ▷ ANNOY.

fretful adj anxious, distressed, disturbed, edgy, irritable, inf jittery, peevish, petulant, restless, touchy, worried. Opp CALM.

friction n 1 abrasion, chafing, grating, resistance, rubbing, scraping. 2 ▷ CONFLICT.

friend n acquaintance, associate, inf buddy, inf chum, companion, comrade, confidant(e), inf crony, intimate, inf mate, inf pal, partner, playmate, supporter, well-wisher. ▷ ALLY, LOVER.

Opp ENEMY. **be friends** ▷ ASSOCIATE. **make friends with** ▷ BEFRIEND.

friendless adj alienated, alone, deserted, estranged, forlorn, isolated, lonely, ostracized, shunned, solitary, unattached, unloved, unpopular.

friendliness n benevolence, camaraderie, conviviality, devotion, esteem, familiarity, goodwill, helpfulness, hospitality, kindness, regard, sociability, warmth. Opp HOSTILITY.

friendly adj accessible, affable, affectionate, agreeable, amiable, amicable, approachable, benevolent, benign, inf chummy, civil, close, companionable, compatible, conciliatory, congenial, convivial, cordial, demonstrative, expansive, favourable, genial, good-natured, gracious, helpful, hospitable, intimate, kind, kind-hearted, kindly, likeable, inf matey, neighbourly, outgoing, inf pally, sympathetic, tender, inf thick, warm, welcoming, well-disposed. ▷ FAMILIAR, LOVING, SOCIABLE. Opp UNFRIENDLY.

friendship n affection, alliance, association, attachment, closeness, fellowship, fondness, harmony, intimacy, rapport, relationship. ▷ FRIENDLINESS, LOVE. Opp HOSTILITY.

fright n 1 jolt, scare, shock, surprise. 2 alarm, apprehension, consternation, dismay, dread, fear, horror, panic, terror, trepidation.

frighten v agitate, alarm, appal, browbeat, bully, cow, daunt, dismay, distress, horrify, intimidate, inf make your blood run cold, make your hair stand on

end, menace, panic, petrify, *inf* put the wind up, scare, shake, shock, startle, terrify, terrorize, threaten, traumatize, tyrannize, unnerve, upset.
▷ DISCOURAGE. *Opp* REASSURE.

frightened *adj* afraid, aghast, alarmed, anxious, appalled, apprehensive, *inf* chicken, cowardly, daunted, fearful, horrified, horror-struck, panicky, panic-stricken, petrified, scared, shocked, terrified, trembling, unnerved, upset.

frightening *adj* alarming, appalling, blood-curdling, *inf* creepy, daunting, dire, dreadful, eerie, fearsome, formidable, ghostly, grim, hair-raising, horrifying, intimidating, *inf* scary, sinister, spine-chilling, *inf* spooky, terrifying, traumatic, uncanny, unnerving, upsetting, weird, worrying. ▷ FRIGHTFUL.

frightful *adj* 1 awful, ghastly, grisly, gruesome, harrowing, hideous, horrid, horrific, macabre, shocking, terrible.
▷ FRIGHTENING. 2 ▷ BAD.

fringe *n* 1 borders, boundary, edge, limits, marches, margin, outskirts, perimeter, periphery. 2 border, edging, flounce, frill, gathering, ruffle, trimming.

frisky *adj* active, animated, frolicsome, high-spirited, jaunty, lively, perky, playful, skittish, spirited, sportive, sprightly.

frivolity *n* facetiousness, flippancy, levity, light-heartedness, nonsense, silliness, triviality.
▷ FUN.

frivolous *adj* casual, facetious, flighty, *inf* flip, flippant, foolish, inconsequential, insignificant, jocular, joking, minor, paltry, petty, pointless, shallow, silly,

superficial, trifling, trivial, unimportant, vacuous, worthless. *Opp* SERIOUS.

frock *n* dress, gown, robe.

frolic *v* caper, cavort, dance, frisk about, gambol, have fun, jump about, lark around, leap about, play about, prance, revel, romp, skip, skylark, sport.

front *adj* facing, first, foremost, leading, most advanced.
● *n* 1 bow (*of ship*), façade, face, facing, forefront, foreground, frontage, head, nose, van, vanguard. 2 battle area, danger zone, front line. 3 *brave front.* appearance, aspect, bearing, blind, *inf* cover-up, demeanour, disguise, expression, look, mask, pretence, show. *Opp* BACK.

frontal *adj* direct, facing, head-on, oncoming, straight.

frontier *n* border, borderline, boundary, bounds, limit.

froth *n* bubbles, effervescence, foam, head (*on beer*), lather, scum, spume, suds.

frown *v* glare, glower, grimace, knit your brows, look sullen, lour, scowl. **frown on**
▷ DISAPPROVE.

fruit *n* outcome, product, profit, result.

fruitful *adj* 1 abundant, bountiful, copious, fecund, fertile, flourishing, lush, luxurious, plenteous, productive, profuse, prolific, rich. 2 advantageous, beneficial, effective, gainful, profitable, rewarding, successful, useful, worthwhile.
Opp FRUITLESS.

fruitless *adj* 1 barren, sterile, unfruitful, unproductive. 2 abortive, disappointing, futile, ineffective, pointless, profitless,

frustrate unavailing, unprofitable, unrewarding, unsuccessful, useless, vain. Opp FRUITFUL.

frustrate v baffle, block, check, disappoint, foil, halt, hinder, impede, inhibit, nullify, prevent, inf scotch, stop, inf stymie, thwart. ▷ DEFEAT.
Opp ENCOURAGE.

frustrated adj disappointed, loveless, lovesick, resentful, thwarted, unfulfilled, unsatisfied.

fuel n ammunition, energy, food, nourishment. • v encourage, feed, inflame, keep going, nourish, stoke up, supply with fuel.

fugitive adj ▷ TRANSIENT. • n deserter, escapee, escaper, refugee, renegade, runaway.

fulfil v 1 accomplish, achieve, bring about, bring off, carry out, complete, consummate, discharge, do, effect, execute, implement, perform, realize. 2 fulfil a need answer, comply with, conform to, meet, obey, respond to, satisfy.

full adj 1 brimming, bursting, inf chock-a-block, inf chock-full, congested, crammed, crowded, filled, jammed, inf jam-packed, loaded, overflowing, packed, stuffed, topped-up, well-stocked. 2 full stomach. gorged, replete, sated, satiated, satisfied, well-fed. 3 the full story. complete, comprehensive, detailed, entire, exhaustive, thorough, total, unabridged, uncensored, uncut, unedited, unexpurgated, whole. 4 full speed. greatest, highest, maximum, top, utmost. 5 full figure. ample, broad, buxom, fat, large, plump, rounded, voluptuous, well-built. 6 full skirt. baggy, voluminous, wide.

Opp EMPTY, INCOMPLETE, SMALL.

full-grown adj adult, grown-up, mature, ready, ripe.

fumble v grope at, feel your way, mishandle, stumble.

fume v emit fumes, smoke, smoulder. **fuming** ▷ ANGRY.

fumes pl n exhaust, fog, gases, pollution, smog, smoke, vapour.

fun n amusement, clowning, diversion, enjoyment, entertainment, festivity, fun and games, gaiety, games, inf high jinks, horseplay, jocularity, joking, inf jollification, jollity, laughter, merriment, merrymaking, mirth, pastimes, play, playfulness, pleasure, pranks, recreation, romp, inf skylarking, sport, teasing, tomfoolery. ▷ FRIVOLITY. **make fun of** ▷ MOCK.

function n 1 aim, purpose, use. ▷ JOB. 2 official function. affair, ceremony, inf do, event, occasion, party, reception. • v act, behave, go, operate, perform, run, work.

functional adj functioning, practical, serviceable, useful, utilitarian, working.
Opp DECORATIVE.

fund n cache, hoard, inf kitty, mine, pool, reserve, reservoir, stock, store, supply, treasurehouse. **funds** capital, investments, resources, riches, savings, wealth. ▷ MONEY.

fundamental adj axiomatic, basic, cardinal, central, crucial, elementary, essential, important, key, main, necessary, primary, prime, principal, underlying. Opp INESSENTIAL.

funeral n burial, cremation, entombment, exequies, interment, obsequies, wake.

funereal adj dark, depressing, dismal, gloomy, grave, mournful, sepulchral, solemn, sombre. ▷ SAD. Opp CHEERFUL.

funnel n chimney, flue.
• v channel, direct, filter, pour.

funny adj 1 absurd, amusing, comic, comical, crazy, inf daft, diverting, droll, eccentric, entertaining, facetious, farcical, hilarious, humorous, inf hysterical, ironic, jocular, laughable, ludicrous, mad, merry, nonsensical, inf priceless, inf rich, ridiculous, satirical, inf side-splitting, silly, slapstick, uproarious, waggish, witty, inf zany. Opp SERIOUS.
2 ▷ PECULIAR.

fur n bristles, coat, down, fleece, hair, hide, pelt, skin, wool.

furious adj 1 enraged, fuming, incensed, infuriated, irate, livid, mad, raging, savage, wrathful. ▷ ANGRY. 2 furious activity. agitated, frantic, frenzied, intense, tempestuous, tumultuous, turbulent, violent, wild. Opp CALM.

furnish v 1 equip, fit out, fit up, inf kit out. 2 furnish information. give, grant, provide, supply.

furniture n antiques, effects, equipment, fittings, fixtures, furnishings, household goods, inf movables, possessions.

furrow n channel, corrugation, crease, cut, ditch, fissure, flute, groove, gash, hollow, line, rut, track, trench, wrinkle.

furrowed adj 1 creased, crinkled, corrugated, fluted, grooved, ploughed, ribbed, ridged, rutted, scored.
2 furrowed brow. frowning,

lined, worried, wrinkled. Opp SMOOTH.

furry adj bristly, downy, feathery, fleecy, fuzzy, hairy, woolly.

further adj additional, another, auxiliary, extra, fresh, more, new, supplementary.

furthermore adv additionally, also, besides, moreover, too.

furtive adj clandestine, concealed, conspiratorial, covert, deceitful, disguised, hidden, mysterious, private, secret, secretive, inf shifty, sly, sneaky, stealthy, surreptitious, underhand. ▷ CRAFTY. Opp BLATANT.

fury n ferocity, fierceness, force, intensity, madness, power, rage, savagery, tempestuousness, turbulence, vehemence, violence, wrath. ▷ ANGER.

fuse v amalgamate, blend, coalesce, combine, compound, consolidate, join, melt, merge, mix, solder, unite, weld.

fusillade n barrage, burst, firing, outburst, salvo, volley.

fuss n ▷ COMMOTION. • v agitate, bother, complain, inf create, fidget, complain, inf flap, get worked up, grumble, worry.

fussy adj 1 inf choosy, difficult, discriminating, inf faddy, fastidious, finicky, hard to please, niggling, inf nit-picking, particular, inf pernickety, scrupulous, squeamish. 2 fussy decorations. complicated, detailed, elaborate, fancy, ornate, overdone.

futile adj abortive, barren, empty, foolish, forlorn, fruitless, hollow, ineffective, ineffectual, pointless, profitless, silly, sterile, unavailing, unproductive, unprofitable, unsuccessful, use-

less, vain, wasted, worthless.
Opp FRUITFUL.

future adj approaching, awaited,
coming, destined, expected,
forthcoming, impending, intended, planned, prospective, subsequent, unborn. ● n expecta-
tions, outlook, prospects,
time to come, tomorrow.
Opp PAST.

fuzz n down, floss, fluff, hair.

fuzzy adj 1 downy, feathery,
fleecy, fluffy, furry, woolly.
2 bleary, blurred, cloudy, dim,
faint, hazy, ill-defined, indistinct, misty, obscure, out of
focus, shadowy, unclear,
unfocused, vague. Opp CLEAR.

G

gadget n apparatus, appliance,
contraption, device, implement,
instrument, invention, machine,
tool, utensil.

gag n ▷ JOKE. ● v check, curb,
keep quiet, muffle, muzzle,
silence, stifle, still, suppress.

gaiety n brightness, cheerfulness, delight, exhilaration,
felicity, glee, happiness, high
spirits, hilarity, jollity, joyfulness, light-heartedness, liveliness, merriment, merrymaking,
mirth.

gain n achievement, acquisition,
advantage, asset, attainment,
benefit, dividend, earnings,
income, increase, proceeds,
profit, return, revenue, winnings, yield. Opp LOSS.

● v 1 acquire, bring in, capture,
earn, gather in, get, harvest,

make, net, obtain, pick up, procure, profit, realize, reap,
receive, win. Opp LOSE. 2 gain
your objective. achieve, arrive at,
attain, get to, reach, secure.
Opp MISS. **gain on** approach,
catch up with, close the gap, go
faster than, overtake.

gainful adj ▷ PROFITABLE.

gala n carnival, celebration, fair,
festival, festivity, fête,
inf jamboree, party.

gale n ▷ WIND.

gallant adj attentive, chivalrous,
courteous, courtly, dashing, gentlemanly, gracious, heroic, honourable, magnanimous, noble,
polite, valiant, well-bred.
▷ BRAVE. Opp VILLAINOUS.

gallows pl n gibbet, scaffold.

gamble v back, bet, chance,
draw lots, inf have a flutter,
hazard, lay bets, risk money,
speculate, inf take a chance, take
risks, inf try your luck, venture,
wager.

game adj ▷ BRAVE, WILLING.
● n 1 amusement, diversion,
entertainment, frolic, fun, jest,
joke, inf lark, pastime, play, playing, recreation, romp, sport.
2 competition, contest, match,
round, pl sport, tournament.
3 animals, game birds, prey,
quarry. **give the game away**
▷ REVEAL.

gang n band, crowd, pack, team.
▷ GROUP. **gang together, gang
up** ▷ COMBINE.

gangster n bandit, brigand,
criminal, inf crook, desperado,
gunman, hoodlum, mafioso,
racketeer, robber, thug.

gaol n cell, custody, dungeon,
jail, Amer penitentiary.
▷ PRISON. ● v confine, detain,

imprison, incarcerate, intern, *inf* send down, send to prison, *inf* shut away.

gaoler *n* guard, jailer, prison officer, *sl* screw, warder.

gap *n* 1 aperture, breach, break, cavity, chink, cleft, crack, cranny, crevice, gulf, hole, opening, rent, rift, rip, space, void. 2 breathing-space, discontinuity, hiatus, interlude, intermission, interruption, interval, lacuna, lapse, lull, pause, recess, respite, rest, suspension, wait. 3 *gap between political parties.* difference, disagreement, discrepancy, disparity, distance, divergence, division, incompatibility.

gape *v* 1 open, part, yawn. 2 *inf* gawp, gaze, goggle, stare.

garbage *n* debris, junk, litter, refuse, trash. ▷ RUBBISH.

garble *v* distort, falsify, misquote, misrepresent, mutilate, slant, twist, warp. ▷ CONFUSE.

garden *n* allotment, patch, plot, yard. **gardens** grounds, park.

garish *adj* ▷ GAUDY.

garment *n* ▷ CLOTHES.

garrison *n* 1 contingent, detachment, force, unit. 2 barracks, camp, citadel, fort, fortification, fortress, station, stronghold.

gas *n* exhalation, exhaust, fumes, miasma, vapour.

gash *v* chop, cleave, cut, lacerate, score, slash, slit, split, wound.

gasp *v* breathe with difficulty, choke, fight for breath, gulp, pant, puff, wheeze. **gasping** ▷ BREATHLESS, THIRSTY.

gate *n* access, barrier, door, entrance, entry, exit, gateway, opening, portal, portcullis, turnstile, way in, way out, wicket.

gather *v* 1 accumulate, amass, assemble, bring together, build up, cluster, collect, come together, concentrate, congregate, convene, crowd, flock, get together, group, grow, heap up, herd, hoard, huddle together, marshal, mass, meet, mobilize, muster, rally, round up, pick up, stockpile, store up, swarm, throng. *Opp* DISPERSE. 2 *gather flowers.* garner, glean, harvest, pick, pluck, reap. 3 *I gather he's ill.* assume, be led to believe, conclude, deduce, guess, infer, learn, surmise, understand.

gathering *n* assembly, congress, convention, convocation, function, *inf* get-together, meeting, party, rally, social. ▷ GROUP.

gaudy *adj* bright, cheap, crude, flamboyant, *inf* flashy, garish, harsh, loud, lurid, ostentatious, raffish, showy, startling, tasteless, tawdry, vivid, vulgar. *Opp* DRAB, TASTEFUL.

gauge *n* 1 benchmark, criterion, guideline, measurement, norm, standard, test, yardstick. 2 capacity, dimensions, extent, measure, size, span, thickness, width. ● *v* ▷ ESTIMATE, MEASURE.

gaunt *adj* 1 bony, cadaverous, emaciated, haggard, hollow-eyed, lean, pinched, scraggy, scrawny, skeletal, starving, underweight, wasted away. ▷ THIN. *Opp* PLUMP. 2 *gaunt ruin.* bare, bleak, desolate, dreary, forbidding, grim, stark, stern. *Opp* ATTRACTIVE.

gawky *adj* awkward, blundering, clumsy, gangling, gauche, gawky, inept, lumbering, maladroit, uncoordinated, ungainly. *Opp* GRACEFUL.

gay adj 1 animated, bright, care-free, cheerful, colourful, festive, fun-loving, jolly, jovial, joyful, light-hearted, lively, merry, sparkling, sunny, vivacious. ▷ HAPPY. 2 ▷ HOMOSEXUAL.

gaze v contemplate, gape, look, regard, stare, view, wonder (at).

gear n accessories, accoutrements, apparatus, appliances, baggage, belongings, equipment, inf get-up, harness, kit, luggage, materials, paraphernalia, rig, stuff, tackle, things, tools, trappings. ▷ CLOTHES.

gem n gemstone, jewel, precious stone, sl sparkler.

general adj 1 accepted, accustomed, collective, common, communal, conventional, customary, everyday, familiar, habitual, normal, ordinary, popular, prevailing, public, regular, inf run-of-the-mill, shared, typical, usual. 2 general discussion. across-the-board, all-embracing, broad-based, catholic, comprehensive, encyclopaedic, extensive, far-reaching, global, heterogeneous, hybrid, inclusive, sweeping, universal, wholesale, wide-ranging, widespread, worldwide. 3 general idea. approximate, broad, ill-defined, imprecise, indefinite, inexact, loose, simplified, superficial, unclear, unspecific, vague. Opp SPECIFIC.

generally adv as a rule, broadly, chiefly, in the main, mainly, mostly, normally, on the whole, predominantly, principally, usually.

generate v beget, breed, bring about, cause, create, engender, father, give rise to, make, originate, procreate, produce, propagate, sire, spawn, inf whip up.

generosity n bounty, largesse, liberality, munificence, philanthropy.

generous adj 1 benevolent, big-hearted, bounteous, bountiful, charitable, forgiving, inf free, impartial, kind, liberal, magnanimous, munificent, noble, open, open-handed, philanthropic, public-spirited, unselfish, unsparing, unstinting. 2 generous gifts. handsome, princely, valuable. ▷ EXPENSIVE. 3 generous portions. abundant, ample, copious, lavish, plentiful, sizeable, substantial. ▷ BIG. Opp MEAN, SELFISH.

genial adj affable, agreeable, amiable, cheerful, convivial, easy-going, happy, jolly, jovial, kindly, pleasant, relaxed, sociable, sunny, warm, warmhearted. ▷ FRIENDLY. Opp UNFRIENDLY.

genitals pl n genitalia, inf private parts, pudenda, sex organs.

genius n 1 ability, aptitude, bent, brains, brilliance, flair, gift, intellect, intelligence, knack, talent, wit. 2 academic, inf egghead, expert, intellectual, derog know-all, mastermind, thinker, virtuoso.

genteel adj derog affected, courtly, ladylike, mannered, overpolite, inf posh, refined, stylish, inf upper-crust. ▷ POLITE.

gentle adj 1 amiable, compassionate, docile, easygoing, good-tempered, harmless, humane, kind, kindly, lenient, loving, meek, merciful, mild, moderate, passive, peaceful, placid, pleasant, quiet, soft-hearted, sweet-tempered, sympathetic, tame, tender. **2** *gentle music*. low, muted, reassuring, relaxing, soft, soothing. **3** *gentle wind*. balmy, faint, light, soft, warm. **4** *gentle hint*. indirect, polite, subtle, tactful. **5** *gentle hill*. easy, gradual, imperceptible, moderate, slight. *Opp* HARSH, SEVERE.

genuine *adj* **1** actual, authentic, authenticated, bona fide, legitimate, original, real, sterling, veritable. **2** *genuine feelings*. earnest, frank, heartfelt, honest, sincere, true, unaffected, unfeigned. *Opp* FALSE.

germ *n* **1** beginning, cause, embryo, genesis, nucleus, origin, root, seed, source. **2** bacterium, *inf* bug, microbe, microorganism, virus.

germinate *v* bud, develop, grow, root, shoot, spring up, sprout, start growing, take root.

gesture *n* action, flourish, gesticulation, indication, motion, movement, sign, signal. ● *v* gesticulate, indicate, motion, sign, signal.

get *v* **1** acquire, be given, bring, buy, come by, earn, fetch, gain, *inf* get hold of, inherit, *inf* land, *inf* lay hands on, obtain, pick up, procure, purchase, receive, retrieve, secure, take, win. **2** *get her by phone*. contact, reach, speak to. **3** *get a cold*. catch, come down with, contract, develop, fall ill with. **4** *get a criminal*. apprehend, arrest, capture, catch, *inf* collar, *inf* nab, *sl* pinch, seize. **5** *get him to help*. cajole, cause, induce, persuade, prevail on, *inf* twist someone's arm, wheedle. **6** *get tea*. cook, prepare. **7** *get what he means*. appreciate, comprehend, fathom,

follow, grasp, know, take in, understand, work out. **8** *get what he says*. catch, distinguish, hear, make out. **9** *get somewhere*. arrive, come, go, reach, travel. **10** *get cold*. become, grow, turn.
get across ▷ COMMUNICATE.
get ahead ▷ PROSPER. **get at** ▷ CRITICIZE. **get away** ▷ ESCAPE. **get down** ▷ DESCEND. **get in** ▷ ENTER. **get off** ▷ DESCEND. **get on** ▷ PROSPER. **get out** ▷ LEAVE. **get together** ▷ GATHER.

getaway *n* escape, flight, retreat.

ghastly *adj* appalling, awful, dreadful, frightful, grim, grisly, gruesome, hideous, horrible, macabre, nasty, shocking, terrible, upsetting. ▷ UNPLEASANT.

ghost *n* apparition, banshee, ghoul, hallucination, illusion, phantasm, phantom, poltergeist, shade, shadow, spectre, spirit, *inf* spook, vision, visitant, wraith. **give up the ghost** ▷ DIE.

ghostly *adj* creepy, disembodied, eerie, frightening, *inf* scary, sinister, spectral, *inf* spooky, supernatural, uncanny, unearthly, weird, wraith-like.

giant *adj* ▷ GIGANTIC.
● *n* colossus, Goliath, leviathan, monster, ogre, superhuman, titan, *inf* whopper.

giddiness *n* dizziness, faintness, unsteadiness, vertigo.

giddy *adj* dizzy, faint, lightheaded, reeling, silly, spinning, unbalanced, unsteady.

gift *n* **1** bequest, bounty, charity, contribution, donation, favour, *inf* give-away, grant, gratuity, handout, largesse, offering, present, tip. **2** ability, aptitude,

bent, capability, capacity, facility, flair, genius, knack, talent.

gifted *adj* expert, skilful, skilled, talented. ▷ CLEVER.

gigantic *adj* colossal, elephantine, enormous, gargantuan, giant, huge, immense, *inf* jumbo, *inf* king-size, mammoth, massive, mighty, monstrous, prodigious, titanic, towering, vast. ▷ BIG. *Opp* SMALL.

giggle *v* laugh, snicker, snigger, titter.

gimcrack *adj* cheap, *inf* cheap and nasty, flimsy, *inf* rubbishy, shoddy, tawdry, *inf* trashy, useless, worthless.

gimmick *n* device, ploy, ruse, stratagem, stunt, trick.

girder *n* bar, beam, joist, rafter.

girdle *n* band, belt, corset, waistband. ● *v* ▷ SURROUND.

girl *n sl* bird, daughter, debutante, girlfriend, fiancée, lass, *old use* maiden, *inf* miss, schoolgirl, tomboy, wench. ▷ WOMAN.

girth *n* circumference, measurement round, perimeter.

gist *n* core, direction, drift, essence, general sense, main idea, meaning, nub, pith, point.

give *v* 1 allocate, allot, allow, apportion, assign, award, bestow, confer, contribute, deal out, *inf* dish out, distribute, *inf* dole out, donate, endow, entrust, *inf* fork out, furnish, give away, give out, grant, hand over, lend, offer, pay, present, provide, render, share out, supply. 2 *give information.* deliver, display, express, impart, issue, notify, publish, put across, put into words, reveal, set out, show, tell, transmit. 3 *give a shout.* emit, let out, utter, voice.

4 *give treatment.* administer, dispense, dose with, impose, inflict, mete out, prescribe. **5** *give a party.* arrange, organize, provide, put on. **6** *give trouble.* cause, create, engender, occasion. **7** *give under pressure.* bend, buckle, collapse, distort, fail, fall apart, give way, warp, yield. *Opp* RECEIVE, TAKE. **give away** ▷ BETRAY. **give in** ▷ SURRENDER. **give off, give out** ▷ EMIT. **give up** ▷ ABANDON, SURRENDER.

glad *adj* 1 content, delighted, overjoyed, pleased. ▷ HAPPY. *Opp* GLOOMY. 2 *glad to help.* disposed, eager, inclined, keen, ready, willing. *Opp* RELUCTANT.

glamorize *v* idealize, romanticize.

glamorous *adj* alluring, appealing, colourful, dazzling, enviable, exciting, exotic, fascinating, glittering, prestigious, romantic, smart, spectacular, wealthy. ▷ BEAUTIFUL.

glamour *n* allure, appeal, attraction, brilliance, charm, excitement, fascination, glitter, magic, romance. ▷ BEAUTY.

glance *v* glimpse, have a quick look, peep, scan. ▷ LOOK.

glare *v* 1 frown, *inf* give a nasty look, glower, *inf* look daggers, scowl, stare angrily. 2 blaze, dazzle, flare, reflect, shine. **glaring** ▷ BRIGHT.

glass *n* 1 crystal, glassware. 2 glazing, pane, plate glass, window. 3 looking-glass, mirror, reflector. 4 beaker, goblet, tumbler, wineglass. **glasses** *inf* specs, spectacles.

glasshouse *n* conservatory, greenhouse, hothouse, orangery.

glassy adj 1 glazed, gleaming, glossy, icy, polished, shining, shiny, smooth. 2 glassy stare.
▷ EXPRESSIONLESS.

glaze v burnish, enamel, gloss, lacquer, polish, shine, varnish.

gleam v flash, glimmer, glint, glisten, glow, reflect, shine.
▷ LIGHT. **gleaming** ▷ BRIGHT.

gleeful adj delighted, ecstatic, exuberant, gay, jovial, joyful, jubilant, pleased, rapturous, triumphant. ▷ HAPPY. Opp SAD.

glib adj articulate, facile, fast-talking, fluent, insincere, plausible, quick, ready, slick, smooth, smooth-tongued, superficial.
▷ TALKATIVE.
Opp INARTICULATE, SINCERE.

glide v coast, drift, float, fly, free-wheel, move smoothly, sail, skate, ski, skid, skim, slide, slip, soar, stream.

glimpse n glance, look, peep, sight, view. ● v discern, distinguish, espy, get a glimpse of, make out, notice, observe, sight, spot, spy.

glisten v flash, gleam, glint, glitter, reflect, shine. ▷ LIGHT.

glitter v flash, scintillate, spark, sparkle, twinkle. ▷ LIGHT. **glittering** ▷ BRIGHT.

gloat v boast, brag, inf crow, exult, rejoice, inf rub it in, show off, triumph.

global adj broad, international, total, universal, wide-ranging, worldwide. Opp LOCAL.

globe n 1 ball, globule, orb, sphere. 2 earth, planet, world.

gloom n cloudiness, darkness, dimness, dullness, dusk, murk, obscurity, semi-darkness, shade, shadow, twilight. ▷ DEPRESSION.

gloomy adj 1 cheerless, cloudy, dark, depressing, dim, dingy, dismal, dreary, glum, grim, murky, obscure, overcast, shadowy, shady, sombre. 2 gloomy mood. depressed, downhearted, lugubrious, mournful, pessimistic, saturnine. ▷ SAD.
Opp CHEERFUL.

glorious adj 1 celebrated, distinguished, eminent, famous, heroic, illustrious, noble, noted, renowned, triumphant. 2 glorious weather. beautiful, bright, brilliant, dazzling, delightful, excellent, fine, gorgeous, grand, impressive, lovely, magnificent, marvellous, resplendent, spectacular, splendid, inf super, superb, wonderful. Opp ORDINARY.

glory n 1 credit, distinction, eminence, fame, honour, inf kudos, praise, prestige, renown, reputation, success, triumph. 2 glory to God. adoration, exaltation, glorification, homage, praise, thanksgiving, veneration, worship. 3 glory of sunrise. brightness, brilliance, grandeur, magnificence, majesty, radiance, splendour. ▷ BEAUTY.

gloss n 1 brightness, brilliance, burnish, finish, glaze, gleam, lustre, polish, sheen, shine, varnish. 2 annotation, comment, definition, elucidation, explanation, footnote, note, paraphrase. ● v annotate, comment on, define, elucidate, explain, interpret, paraphrase. **gloss over**
▷ CONCEAL.

glossary n dictionary, phrase-book, vocabulary, word-list.

glossy adj bright, burnished, glazed, gleaming, glistening, lus-

trous, polished, reflective, shiny,
silky, sleek, smooth, waxed.
Opp DULL.

glove *n* gauntlet, mitt, mitten.

glow *n* 1 burning, fieriness, heat,
incandescence, luminosity,
lustre, phosphorescence, radi-
ation, redness. 2 ardour, blush,
enthusiasm, fervour, flush, passion, rosiness, warmth.
• *v* blush, flush, gleam, light up,
radiate heat, redden, smoulder.
▷ LIGHT.

glower *v* frown, glare, lour,
scowl, stare angrily.

glowing *adj* 1 aglow, bright, hot,
incandescent, lambent, lumin-
ous, phosphorescent, radiant,
red, red-hot. 2 *glowing praise*.
enthusiastic, fervent, passionate,
warm.

glue *n* adhesive, cement, fixative,
gum, paste, size. • *v* affix, bond,
cement, fasten, fix, gum, paste,
seal, stick.

glum *adj* cheerless, gloomy, lugubrious, moody, mournful, *inf* out
of sorts, saturnine, sullen.
▷ SAD. *Opp* CHEERFUL.

glut *n* abundance, excess, overabundance, overflow, plenty,
superfluity, surfeit, surplus.
Opp SCARCITY.

glutton *n joc* gourmand,
inf greedy-guts, guzzler, *inf* pig.

gluttonous *adj* insatiable, voracious. ▷ GREEDY.

gnarled *adj* contorted, crooked,
distorted, knobbly, knotted,
lumpy, misshapen, rough,
rugged, twisted.

gnaw *v* bite, chew, erode, wear
away. ▷ EAT.

go *n* attempt, chance, *inf* crack,
opportunity, *inf* shot, *inf* stab,
try, turn. • *v* 1 advance, begin,

be off, depart, disappear,
embark, escape, *inf* get going,
get moving, get under way,
leave, make off, move, pass
along, pass on, proceed, retire,
retreat, set off, set out, start,
take off, take your leave, vanish,
wend your way, withdraw.
▷ RUN, TRAVEL, WALK. 2 die,
fade, fail, give way. 3 extend,
lead, reach, stretch. 4 *The car
won't go*. function, operate, perform, run, work. 5 *The days go
slowly*. elapse, lapse, pass. 7 *The
milk will go sour*. become, grow,
turn. 8 *Do the eggs go in the
fridge?* belong, live. **go away**
▷ DEPART. **go down**
▷ DESCEND, SINK. **go in for**
▷ LIKE. **go into** ▷ INVESTIGATE.
go off ▷ EXPLODE. **go on**
▷ CONTINUE. **go through**
▷ SUFFER. **go to** ▷ VISIT. **go
together** ▷ MATCH. **go with**
▷ ACCOMPANY. **go without**
▷ ABSTAIN.

goad *v* badger, chivvy, egg on,
inf needle, prod, prompt, spur,
urge. ▷ STIMULATE.

go-ahead *adj* ambitious, enterprising, forward-looking, progressive. • *n* approval, *inf* green
light, permission, sanction,
inf thumbs-up.

goal *n* aim, ambition, aspiration,
design, intention, object, objective, purpose, target.

gobble *v* bolt, devour, gulp,
guzzle. ▷ EAT.

go-between *n* agent, broker,
envoy, intermediary, mediator,
messenger, middleman, negotiator. **act as go-between**
▷ MEDIATE.

god, goddess *ns* deity, divinity,
godhead. **God** the Almighty, the
Creator, the supreme being. **the**

gods the immortals, the powers above.

godsend n blessing, boon, gift, miracle, stroke of good luck, windfall.

golden adj 1 gilded, gilt. 2 *golden hair.* blond(e), flaxen, yellow.

good adj 1 acceptable, admirable, agreeable, appropriate, commendable, delightful, enjoyable, esteemed, *inf* fabulous, fair, *inf* fantastic, fine, gratifying, happy, lovely, marvellous, nice, perfect, pleasant, pleasing, praiseworthy, proper, remarkable, right, satisfactory, *inf* sensational, sound, splendid, suitable, *inf* super, superb, useful, valid, valuable, wonderful, worthy. ▷ EXCELLENT. 2 *good person.* angelic, benevolent, caring, charitable, considerate, decent, dependable, dutiful, ethical, friendly, helpful, holy, honest, honourable, humane, incorruptible, innocent, just, law-abiding, loyal, merciful, moral, noble, obedient, pure, reliable, religious, righteous, saintly, sound, *inf* straight, thoughtful, true, trustworthy, upright, virtuous, well-behaved, well-mannered, worthy. ▷ KIND. 3 *good worker.* able, accomplished, capable, conscientious, efficient, gifted, proficient, skilful, skilled, talented. ▷ CLEVER. 4 *good work.* careful, competent, correct, creditable, efficient, neat, orderly, présentable, professional, thorough, well-done. 5 *good food.* delicious, healthy, nourishing, nutritious, tasty, well-cooked, wholesome. 6 *good book.* classic, exciting, great, interesting, readable, well-written. *Opp* BAD. **good-humoured** ▷ GOOD-TEMPERED.

good-looking ▷ HANDSOME.

good-natured ▷ GOOD-TEMPERED. **good person** *inf* angel, *inf* saint, Samaritan, worthy. **goods** 1 belongings, chattels, effects, possessions, property. 2 commodities, freight, load, merchandise, produce, stock, wares.

goodbye n departure, farewell, leave-taking, parting words, send-off, valediction.

good-tempered adj accommodating, amenable, amiable, bene volent, benign, cheerful, cheery, considerate, cooperative, cordial, friendly, genial, good-humoured, good-natured, helpful, obliging, patient, pleasant, relaxed, smiling, sympathetic, thoughtful, willing. ▷ KIND. *Opp* BAD-TEMPERED.

gorge v be greedy, fill up, guzzle, indulge yourself, *inf* make a pig of yourself, overeat, stuff yourself.

gorgeous adj dazzling, glorious, magnificent, resplendent, splendid, sumptuous. ▷ BEAUTIFUL.

gory adj bloodstained, bloody, grisly, gruesome, savage.

gospel n creed, doctrine, good news, good tidings, message, religion, revelation, teaching, testament.

gossip n 1 chatter, *inf* the grapevine, hearsay, rumour, scandal, small talk, *inf* tattle, *inf* tittle-tattle. 2 busybody, chatterbox, *inf* Nosey Parker, scandalmonger, tittle-tale. ● v *inf* blab, *inf* chat, chatter, *inf* natter, prattle, *inf* tattle, tell tales, *inf* tittle-tattle. ▷ TALK.

gouge v chisel, dig, gash, hollow, scoop. ▷ CUT.

gourmet n connoisseur, epicure, *derog* gourmand.

govern v 1 administer, be in charge of, command, conduct affairs, control, direct, guide, head, lead, look after, manage, oversee, preside over, reign, rule, run, steer, superintend, supervise. 2 *govern your anger*. bridle, check, control, curb, discipline, keep under control, master, regulate, restrain, tame.

government n administration, authority, bureaucracy, conduct of state affairs, constitution, control, direction, dominion, management, oversight, regime, regulation, rule, sovereignty, supervision, sway.

gown n dress, frock. ▷ CLOTHES.

grab v appropriate, *inf* bag, capture, catch, clutch, *inf* collar, commandeer, expropriate, get hold of, grasp, hold, *inf* nab, pluck, seize, snap up, snatch, usurp.

grace n 1 attractiveness, beauty, charm, ease, elegance, fluidity, gracefulness, loveliness, poise, refinement, tastefulness. 2 *God's grace*. beneficence, benevolence, compassion, favour, forgiveness, goodness, graciousness, kindness, love, mercy. 3 *grace before meals*. blessing, prayer, thanksgiving.

graceful adj 1 agile, deft, dignified, easy, elegant, flowing, fluid, natural, nimble, pliant, smooth, supple, willowy. ▷ BEAUTIFUL. 2 *graceful compliments*. courteous, courtly, kind, polite, refined, suave, tactful, urbane. *Opp* GRACELESS.

graceless adj 1 awkward, clumsy, gawky, inelegant, ungainly. ▷ CLUMSY.

Opp GRACEFUL. 2 *graceless manners*. boorish, gauche, inept, tactless, uncouth. ▷ RUDE.

gracious adj 1 affable, agreeable, civilized, cordial, courteous, dignified, elegant, friendly, good-natured, pleasant, polite.
▷ KIND. 2 clement, compassionate, forgiving, generous, indulgent, lenient, magnanimous, pitying, sympathetic.
▷ MERCIFUL. 3 *gracious living*. affluent, expensive, lavish, luxurious, opulent, sumptuous.

grade n category, class, condition, degree, echelon, estate, level, mark, notch, point, position, quality, rank, rung, situation, standard, standing, status, step. ● v 1 arrange, categorize, classify, differentiate, group, organize, range, size, sort. 2 *grade students' work*. assess, evaluate, mark, rank, rate.

gradient n ascent, bank, declivity, hill, incline, rise, slope.

gradual adj continuous, easy, even, gentle, leisurely, moderate, regular, slow, steady, unhurried. *Opp* SUDDEN.

graduate v 1 get a degree, pass, qualify. 2 *graduate a measuring rod*. calibrate, mark off, mark with a scale.

graft v implant, join, splice.

grain n 1 atom, bit, crumb, fleck, fragment, granule, iota, jot, mite, molecule, morsel, mote, particle, scrap, seed, speck, trace. 2 ▷ CEREAL.

grand adj 1 aristocratic, august, dignified, eminent, glorious, great, imposing, impressive, lordly, magnificent, majestic, noble, opulent, palatial, regal, royal, splendid, stately, sumptuous, superb. ▷ BIG. 2 [*derog*] haughty, *inf* high-and-mighty, lofty, patronizing, pompous, posh. ▷ GRANDIOSE. *Opp* MODEST.

grandiloquent *adj* bombastic, elaborate, florid, flowery, grandiose, high-flown, inflated, ornate, pompous, rhetorical, turgid. *Opp* SIMPLE.

grandiose *adj* affected, ambitious, exaggerated, extravagant, flamboyant, grand, ostentatious, *inf* over the top, pretentious, showy. ▷ GRANDILOQUENT. *Opp* MODEST.

grant *n* allocation, allowance, annuity, award, bequest, bursary, concession, contribution, donation, endowment, expenses, gift, investment, loan, pension, scholarship, sponsorship, subsidy. ● *v* 1 allocate, allot, allow, assign, award, bestow, confer, donate, give, pay, provide, supply. 2 *Grant that I'm right.* accept, acknowledge, admit, agree, concede, consent.

graph *n* chart, column-graph, diagram, grid, pie chart, table.

graphic *adj* clear, descriptive, detailed, lifelike, lucid, photographic, plain, realistic, representational, vivid, well-drawn.

grapple *v* clutch (at), tackle, wrestle. ▷ GRASP, FIGHT. **grapple with** attend to, come to grips with, contend with, cope with, deal with, get involved with, handle, *inf* have a go at, manage, try to solve.

grasp *v* catch, clasp, clutch, get hold of, grab, grapple with, grip, hang on to, hold, *inf* nab, seize, snatch, take hold of. 2 *grasp an idea.* appreciate, comprehend, *inf* cotton on to, follow, *inf* get the drift of, get the hang of,

learn, master, realize, take in, understand. ▷ GREEDY. **grasping** ▷ GREEDY.

grass *n* field, grassland, green, lawn, meadow, pasture, prairie, savannah, steppe, turf, veld. ● *v* ▷ INFORM.

grate *n* fireplace, hearth. ● *v* cut, grind, rasp, scrape, shred. **grate on** ▷ ANNOY. **grating** ▷ ANNOYING, HARSH.

grateful *adj* appreciative, beholden, gratified, indebted, obliged, thankful. *Opp* UNGRATEFUL.

gratify *v* delight, fulfil, indulge, please, satisfy.

gratis *adj* complimentary, free, free of charge, gratuitous.

gratitude *n* appreciation, gratefulness, thankfulness, thanks.

gratuitous *adj* 1 ▷ GRATIS. 2 *gratuitous insults.* baseless, groundless, inappropriate, needless, uncalled-for, undeserved, unjustifiable, unnecessary, unprovoked, unsolicited, unwarranted. *Opp* JUSTIFIABLE.

gratuity *n* bonus, *inf* perk, present, reward, tip.

grave *adj* 1 acute, critical, crucial, dangerous, *inf* life and death, major, momentous, pressing, serious, severe, significant, terminal (*illness*), threatening, urgent, vital, weighty, worrying. 2 *grave offence.* criminal, indictable, punishable. 3 *grave look.* dignified, earnest, grim, long-faced, pensive, serious, severe, sober, solemn, sombre, subdued, thoughtful, unsmiling. ▷ SAD. *Opp* CHEERFUL, TRIVIAL. ● *n* barrow, burial place, crypt, *inf* last resting place, mausoleum, sepulchre, tomb, vault. ▷ GRAVESTONE.

gravel n grit, pebbles, shingle, stones.

gravestone n headstone, memorial, monument, tombstone.

graveyard n burial ground, cemetery, churchyard.

gravity n 1 acuteness, danger, importance, magnitude, momentousness, seriousness, severity, significance. 2 *behave with gravity*. ceremony, dignity, earnestness, pomp, reserve, sedateness, sobriety, solemnity. 3 *force of gravity*. attraction, gravitation, heaviness, pull, weight.

graze n abrasion, laceration, raw spot, scrape, scratch. ▷ WOUND.

grease n fat, lubrication, oil.

greasy adj 1 buttery, fatty, oily, slippery, smeary, waxy. 2 *greasy manner*. fawning, flattering, fulsome, ingratiating, slick, *inf* smarmy, sycophantic, toadying, unctuous.

great adj 1 colossal, enormous, extensive, giant, gigantic, grand, huge, immense, massive, prodigious, *inf* tremendous, vast. ▷ BIG. 2 *great pain*. acute, considerable, excessive, extreme, intense, marked, pronounced. ▷ SEVERE. 3 *great events*. grand, imposing, momentous, serious, significant, spectacular. ▷ IMPORTANT. 4 *great music*. brilliant, *inf* fabulous, *inf* fantastic, fine, first-rate, outstanding, wonderful. ▷ EXCELLENT. 5 *great athlete*. able, celebrated, distinguished, eminent, gifted, noted, prominent, renowned, talented, well-known. ▷ FAMOUS. 6 *great friend*. close, dedicated, devoted, faithful, fast, loyal, true, valued. 7 *great reader*. active, ardent, assiduous, eager, enthusiastic,

habitual, keen, passionate, zealous. 8 ▷ GOOD. *Opp* SMALL, UNIMPORTANT.

greed n 1 appetite, craving, gluttony, hunger, insatiability, intemperance, ravenousness, self-indulgence, voracity. 2 *greed for wealth*. avarice, covetousness, cupidity, desire, rapacity, self-interest. ▷ SELFISHNESS.

greedy adj 1 famished, gluttonous, *inf* hoggish, hungry, insatiable, intemperate, *inf* piggish, ravenous, self-indulgent, starving, voracious. *Opp* ABSTEMIOUS. 2 *greedy for wealth*. acquisitive, avaricious, avid, covetous, desirous, eager, grasping, materialistic, mean, mercenary, rapacious, selfish. *Opp* UNSELFISH. **be greedy** ▷ GORGE. **greedy person** ▷ GLUTTON.

green adj 1 grassy, leafy, verdant. 2 emerald, jade, lime, olive.

greenery n foliage, leaves, plants, vegetation.

greet v accost, acknowledge, address, hail, receive, salute, *inf* say hello to, usher in, welcome.

greeting n salutation, reception, welcome. **greetings** compliments, congratulations, felicitations, good wishes, regards.

grey adj ashen, colourless, greying, grizzled, grizzly, hoary, leaden, livid, pearly, silvery, slate-grey, smoky, sooty. ▷ GLOOMY.

grid n framework, grating, grille, lattice, network.

grief n affliction, anguish, depression, desolation, distress, heartache, heartbreak, melancholy, misery, mourning, regret, remorse, sadness, sorrow, suffering, tragedy, unhappiness,

woe, wretchedness. ▷ PAIN.
Opp HAPPINESS. **come to grief**
▷ FAIL.

grievance *n* **1** calamity, damage,
hardship, harm, indignity,
injury, injustice. **2** allegation,
inf bone to pick, charge, complaint, *inf* gripe, objection.

grieve *v* **1** afflict, depress,
dismay, distress, hurt, pain,
sadden, upset, wound.
Opp PLEASE. **2** be in mourning,
inf eat your heart out, lament,
mourn, suffer, wail, weep.
Opp REJOICE.

grim *adj* appalling, cruel, dreadful, fearsome, fierce, forbidding,
formidable, frightful, frowning,
ghastly, grisly, gruesome, harsh,
hideous, horrible, horrid, inexorable, inflexible, menacing, merciless, ominous, relentless, ruthless, savage, severe, sinister,
stark, stern, sullen, surly, terrible, threatening, unattractive,
unfriendly, unpleasant, unrelenting, unsmiling, unyielding.
▷ GLOOMY. *Opp* CHEERFUL.

grime *n* dirt, dust, filth, grit,
muck, scum, soot.

grind *v* **1** crumble, crush, erode,
granulate, grate, mill, pound,
powder, pulverize, rasp. **2** file,
polish, sand, sandpaper, scrape,
sharpen, smooth, wear away,
whet. **3** *grind your teeth.* gnash,
grate, rasp. **grind away** ▷ WORK.
grind down ▷ OPPRESS.

grip *n* clasp, clutch, grasp, hold,
purchase, stranglehold.
▷ CONTROL. ● *v* **1** clasp, clutch,
grab, grasp, hold, seize, take
hold of. **2** *grip the imagination.*
absorb, compel, engage, engross,
enthral, fascinate, hypnotize,
mesmerize, rivet. **come to grips
with** ▷ TACKLE.

grisly *adj* ▷ GRUESOME.

gristly *adj* leathery, stringy,
tough, uneatable.

gritty *adj* abrasive, dusty,
grainy, granular, gravelly,
harsh, rasping, rough, sandy.

groan *v* **1** cry out, moan, sigh,
wail. **2** ▷ COMPLAIN.

groom *n* **1** ostler, stable-lad, sta-
bleman. **2** bridegroom, husband.
● *v* **1** brush, clean, neaten, preen,
smarten up, spruce up, tidy.
2 *groom someone for a job.*
coach, drill, educate, get ready,
prepare, prime, train up, tutor.

groove *n* channel, cut, fluting,
furrow, gutter, hollow, indentation, rut, scratch, slot, track.

grope *v* feel about, fish, flounder,
fumble, search blindly.

gross *adj* **1** bloated, massive,
obese, repellent, repulsive,
revolting. ▷ FAT. **2** churlish,
coarse, crude, rude, unrefined,
vulgar. **3** *gross injustice.* blatant,
flagrant, glaring, manifest, monstrous, obvious, outrageous,
shameful. **4** *gross income.* before
tax, inclusive, overall, total,
whole.

grotesque *adj* absurd, bizarre,
deformed, distorted, fantastic,
freakish, ludicrous, macabre,
malformed, misshapen, monstrous, outlandish, preposterous,
queer, ridiculous, strange, surreal, twisted, ugly, unnatural,
weird.

ground *n* **1** clay, dirt, earth,
loam, mud, soil. **2** area, land,
property, terrain. **3** campus,
estate, garden, park, surroundings. **4** *sports ground.* arena,
court, field, pitch, playing field,
stadium. **5** *grounds for complaint.* argument, base, basis,
case, cause, evidence, foundation, justification, motive,
reason. ● *v* **1** base, establish,

found, set, settle. 2 coach, educate, instruct, prepare, teach, train, tutor. 3 beach, run ashore, shipwreck, strand, wreck.

groundless *adj* baseless, false, gratuitous, hypothetical, illusory, imaginary, irrational, needless, speculative, uncalled-for, unfounded, unjustifiable, unjustified, unreasonable, unsubstantiated, unsupported, unwarranted.

group *n* 1 [*people*] alliance, assemblage, assembly, association, band, body, brotherhood, *inf* bunch, cartel, caste, caucus, circle, clan, class, clique, club, colony, committee, community, company, congregation, consortium, contingent, corps, coterie, crew, crowd, delegation, faction, family, federation, fraternity, gang, gathering, group, horde, host, knot, league, meeting, *derog* mob, multitude, number, organization, party, platoon, posse, *derog* rabble, ring, sect, *derog* shower, sisterhood, society, squad, swarm, team, throng, troop, troupe, union, unit. 2 [*things, animals*] accumulation, assemblage, assortment, batch, battery (*guns*), brood (*chicks*), bunch, bundle, category, class, clump, cluster, clutch (*eggs*), collection, combination, conglomeration, constellation, convoy, covey (*birds*), fleet, flock, gaggle (*geese*), galaxy, heap, herd, hoard, litter, mass, pack, pile, pride (*lions*), school, set, shoal (*fish*), species. 3 ▷ MUSICIAN. ● *v* 1 arrange, assemble, bring together, categorize, classify, collect, deploy, gather, herd, marshal, order, organize, put together, set out, sort. 2 associate, band, cluster,

come together, congregate, crowd, flock, gather, get together, herd, swarm, team up, throng.

grovel *v* abase yourself, cower, *inf* crawl, *inf* creep, cringe, demean yourself, fawn, flatter, kowtow, *inf* lick someone's boots, prostrate yourself, snivel, *inf* suck up, toady. **grovelling** ▷ OBSEQUIOUS.

grow *v* 1 augment, broaden, build up, burgeon, develop, emerge, enlarge, evolve, expand, extend, fill out, flourish, flower, germinate, improve, increase, lengthen, live, make progress, mature, multiply, mushroom, progress, proliferate, prosper, ripen, rise, shoot up, spread, spring up, sprout, swell, thicken, thrive. 2 *grow roses.* cultivate, farm, nurture, produce, propagate, raise. 3 *grow older.* become, get, turn.

grown-up *adj* adult, fully-grown, mature, well-developed.

growth *n* 1 advance, augmentation, development, enlargement, evolution, expansion, extension, flowering, improvement, increase, maturation, maturing, progress, proliferation, prosperity, spread, success. 2 crop, harvest, plants, produce, vegetation, yield. 3 cancer, cyst, excrescence, lump, swelling, tumour.

grub *n* 1 caterpillar, larva, maggot. 2 [*inf*] ▷ FOOD.
● *v* ▷ DIG.

grudge *n* ▷ RESENTMENT.
● *v* begrudge, envy, resent.

grudging *adj* cautious, envious, guarded, half-hearted, jealous, reluctant, resentful, unenthusiastic, ungracious, unwilling.
Opp ENTHUSIASTIC.

gruelling adj arduous, demanding, exhausting, laborious, severe, stiff, strenuous, tiring, tough, uphill, wearying. ▷ DIFFICULT. Opp EASY.

gruesome adj appalling, awful, dreadful, fearful, fearsome, frightful, ghastly, ghoulish, gory, grim, grisly, hair-raising, hideous, horrible, horrid, horrific, macabre, revolting, shocking, sickening, terrible.

gruff adj 1 guttural, harsh, hoarse, husky, rasping, rough, throaty. 2 ▷ BAD-TEMPERED.

grumble v fuss, inf gripe, inf grouch, inf grouse, make a fuss, object, protest, inf whinge. ▷ COMPLAIN.

guarantee n assurance, bond, oath, obligation, pledge, promise, surety, undertaking, warranty, word of honour.
● v 1 assure, certify, pledge, promise, swear, undertake, vouch, vow. 2 ensure, make sure of, reserve, secure.

guard n bodyguard, inf bouncer, custodian, escort, guardian, sl heavy, lookout, sl minder, patrol, picket, security guard, sentinel, sentry, warder, watchman. ● v care for, defend, keep safe, look after, mind, oversee, patrol, police, preserve, protect, safeguard, secure, shelter, shield, stand guard over, supervise, tend, watch, watch over.
on your guard ▷ ALERT.

guardian n 1 adoptive parent, foster-parent. 2 defender, keeper, protector, trustee, warden. ▷ GUARD.

guess n assumption, conjecture, estimate, feeling, sl guesstimate, guesswork, hunch, hypothesis, intuition, opinion, prediction, inf shot in the dark, speculation, supposition, surmise, suspicion, theory. ● v assume, conjecture, divine, estimate, expect, fancy, feel, have a hunch, inf hazard a guess, hypothesize, imagine, judge, predict, inf reckon, speculate, suppose, surmise, suspect, think likely.

guest n 1 caller, visitor. 2 boarder, lodger, patron, resident.

guidance n advice, briefing, counselling, direction, guidelines, help, instruction, leadership, management, spoonfeeding, teaching, tips.

guide n 1 courier, escort, leader, navigator, pilot. 2 adviser, counsellor, director, guru, mentor. 3 atlas, directory, gazetteer, guidebook, handbook.
● v 1 conduct, direct, escort, lead, manoeuvre, navigate, pilot, shepherd, show the way, steer, supervise, usher. 2 advise, brief, control, counsel, educate, govern, help along, influence, instruct, regulate, inf take by the hand, teach, train, tutor. Opp MISLEAD.

guilt n 1 blame, culpability, fault, guiltiness, liability, responsibility, sinfulness, wickedness, wrongdoing. 2 look of guilt. bad conscience, contrition, dishonour, penitence, regret, remorse, self-reproach, shame, sorrow. Opp INNOCENCE.

guiltless adj above suspicion, blameless, clear, faultless, free, innocent, in the right, irreproachable, pure, sinless, untarnished, virtuous. Opp GUILTY.

guilty adj 1 at fault, culpable, in the wrong, liable, reprehensible, responsible. 2 guilty look.

ashamed, conscience-stricken, contrite, penitent, *inf* red-faced, remorseful, repentant, rueful, shamefaced, sheepish, sorry. *Opp* GUILTLESS, SHAMELESS.

gullible *adj* credulous, easily taken in, *inf* green, impressionable, innocent, naive, trusting, unsuspecting. *Opp* SCEPTICAL.

gulp *n* mouthful, swallow, *inf* swig. ● *v* 1 bolt down, gobble, *inf* wolf. ▷ EAT. 2 *inf* knock back, quaff, *inf* swig. ▷ DRINK. 3 *gulp back tears.* choke back, stifle, suppress.

gumption *n* cleverness, common sense, enterprise, initiative, judgement, *inf* nous, resourcefulness, sense, wisdom.

gun *n* pl artillery, firearm, weapon. **gun down** ▷ SHOOT.

gunfire *n* cannonade, crossfire, firing, gunshots, salvo.

gunman *n* assassin, fighter, gangster, killer, marksman, sniper, terrorist.

gurgle *v* babble, bubble, burble, ripple, purl, splash.

gush *n* burst, cascade, eruption, flood, flow, jet, outpouring, overflow, rush, spout, spurt, squirt, stream, tide, torrent. ● *v* 1 cascade, flood, flow freely, overflow, pour, run, rush, spout, spurt, squirt, stream, well up. 2 be enthusiastic, be sentimental, fuss, prattle on, talk on. **gushing** ▷ EFFUSIVE, SENTIMENTAL.

gusto *n* delight, enjoyment, enthusiasm, excitement, liveliness, pleasure, relish, spirit, verve, vigour, zest.

gut *v* 1 clean, disembowel, eviscerate. 2 *gut a building.* clear, empty, loot, pillage, plunder,

ransack, remove the contents of, sack, strip.

guts *pl n* 1 bowels, entrails, *inf* innards, insides, intestines, stomach, viscera. 2 ▷ COURAGE.

gutter *n* channel, conduit, ditch, drain, duct, guttering, sewer, sluice, trench, trough.

gypsy *n* nomad, Romany, traveller, wanderer.

gyrate *v* circle, revolve, rotate, spin, spiral, swivel, turn, twirl, wheel, whirl.

H

habit *n* 1 convention, custom, pattern, policy, practice, routine, rule, usage, wont. 2 bent, disposition, inclination, manner, mannerism, penchant, predisposition, propensity, quirk, tendency, way. 3 *bad habit.* addiction, compulsion, craving, dependence, fixation, obsession, vice.

habitable *adj* in good repair, inhabitable, usable.

habitual *adj* 1 accustomed, common, conventional, customary, expected, familiar, fixed, frequent, natural, normal, ordinary, predictable, regular, ritual, routine, set, settled, standard, traditional, typical, usual, wonted. 2 addictive, besetting, chronic, established, ingrained, obsessive, persistent, recurrent. 3 *habitual smoker.* addicted, confirmed, dependent, hardened, *inf* hooked, inveterate, persistent.

hack v carve, chop, gash, hew, mangle, mutilate, slash. ▷ CUT.

hackneyed adj banal, clichéd, commonplace, conventional, inf corny, familiar, feeble, obvious, overused, pedestrian, platitudinous, predictable, stale, stereotyped, stock, tired, trite, uninspired, unoriginal. Opp NEW.

haggard adj careworn, drawn, emaciated, exhausted, gaunt, hollow-eyed, pinched, run-down, scraggy, scrawny, shrunken, thin, tired out, wasted, weary, worn out, inf worried to death. Opp HEALTHY.

haggle v bargain, barter, negotiate, quibble. ▷ QUARREL.

hail v 1 accost, address, call to, greet, signal to. 2 ▷ ACCLAIM.

hair n 1 beard, bristles, curls, fleece, fur, locks, mane, inf mop, moustache, shock, tresses, whiskers. 2 coiffure, cut, haircut, inf hairdo, hairstyle.

hairdresser n barber, coiffeur, coiffeuse, hairstylist.

hairless adj bald, bare, clean-shaven, naked, shaved, shaven, smooth. Opp HAIRY.

hairy adj bearded, bristly, downy, fleecy, furry, fuzzy, hirsute, shaggy, stubbly, woolly. Opp HAIRLESS.

half-hearted adj apathetic, cool, feeble, indifferent, ineffective, lackadaisical, listless, lukewarm, passive, perfunctory, phlegmatic, uncommitted, unconcerned, unenthusiastic, wavering, weak, inf wishy-washy. Opp ENTHUSIASTIC.

hall n 1 auditorium, concert hall, lecture room, theatre.

2 corridor, entrance hall, foyer, hallway, lobby, passage, passageway, vestibule.

hallowed adj blessed, consecrated, holy, honoured, revered, sacred, sacrosanct.

hallucinate v daydream, dream, fantasize, inf see things.

hallucination n chimera, daydream, delusion, dream, fantasy, figment of the imagination, illusion, mirage. ▷ GHOST.

halt n break, close, end, interruption, pause, standstill, stop, stoppage, termination. ● v 1 block, break off, cease, check, curb, end, impede, obstruct, stop, terminate. 2 come to a halt, come to rest, discontinue, draw up, pull up, stop, wait. Opp START. **halting** ▷ HESITANT, IRREGULAR.

halve v bisect, cut by half, cut in half, decrease, lessen, share equally, split in two.

hammer n mallet, sledgehammer. ● v batter, beat, pound, strike. ▷ DEFEAT, HIT.

hamper v block, curb, delay, encumber, entangle, fetter, foil, frustrate, handicap, hinder, hold up, impede, inhibit, interfere with, obstruct, prevent, restrain, restrict, shackle, slow down, thwart. Opp HELP.

hand n 1 fist, sl mitt, palm, inf paw. 2 hand on a dial. indicator, pointer. 3 ▷ WORKER. ● v convey, deliver, give, offer, pass, present, submit. **at hand** ▷ HANDY. **give a hand** ▷ HELP. **hand down** ▷ BEQUEATH. **hand over** ▷ SURRENDER. **hand round** ▷ DISTRIBUTE. **lend a hand** ▷ HELP. **to hand** ▷ HANDY.

handicap n 1 barrier, disadvantage, difficulty, drawback, encumbrance, hindrance, impediment, inconvenience, *inf* minus, nuisance, obstacle, problem, restriction, shortcoming, stumbling block. *Opp* ADVANTAGE. **2** defect, disability, impairment. ● *v* burden, check, curb, disable, disadvantage, encumber, hamper, hinder, hold back, impede, limit, restrain, restrict. *Opp* HELP.

handicapped *adj* **1** encumbered, hindered, impeded. **2** crippled, disabled, disadvantaged, paralysed.

handiwork *n* creation, doing, invention, production, responsibility, work.

handle *n* grip, haft, hilt, knob, stock (*of rifle*). ● *v* **1** feel, finger, fondle, grasp, hold, *inf* maul, *inf* paw, stroke, touch. **2** *handle situations, people*. contend with, control, cope with, deal with, direct, guide, look after, manage, manipulate, tackle, treat. ▷ ORGANIZE. **3** *car handles well*. manoeuvre, operate, respond, steer, work. **4** *handle goods*. deal in, market, sell, stock, touch, traffic in.

handsome *adj* **1** attractive, beautiful, *old use* comely, *old use* fair, good-looking, personable, tasteful. *Opp* UGLY. **2** *handsome gift*. big, bountiful, generous, gracious, large, liberal, magnanimous, sizeable, unselfish, valuable. *Opp* MEAN.

handy *adj* **1** convenient, easy to use, helpful, manageable, practical, serviceable, useful, well-designed, worth having. **2** *handy with tools*. adept, capable, clever, competent, practical, proficient, skilful. **3** *keep tools handy*. accessible, available, close at

hand, nearby, reachable, ready, to hand. *Opp* AWKWARD, INACCESSIBLE.

hang *v* **1** be suspended, dangle, droop, flap, flop, sway, swing, trail down. **2** attach, drape, fasten, fix, peg up, pin up. **3** *hang in the air*. drift, float, hover. **hang about** ▷ DAWDLE. **hang back** ▷ HESITATE. **hanging** ▷ PENDENT. **hangings** ▷ DRAPE. **hang on** ▷ WAIT. **hang on to** ▷ KEEP.

hank *n* coil, length, loop, skein.

hanker *v* hanker after crave, long for. ▷ DESIRE.

haphazard *adj* accidental, arbitrary, casual, chance, chaotic, confusing, disorderly, disorganized, fortuitous, *inf* higgledy-piggledy, *inf* hit-or-miss, illogical, irrational, random, unforeseen, unplanned, unstructured, unsystematic. *Opp* ORDERLY.

happen *v* arise, befall, chance, come about, *inf* crop up, emerge, follow, materialize, occur, result, take place, transpire. **happen on** ▷ FIND.

happening *n* accident, affair, chance, circumstance, episode, event, incident, occasion, occurrence, phenomenon.

happiness *n* bliss, cheerfulness, contentment, delight, ecstasy, elation, euphoria, exhilaration, exuberance, felicity, gaiety, gladness, glee, *inf* heaven, high spirits, joy, joyfulness, jubilation, light-heartedness, merriment, pleasure, rapture, well-being. *Opp* SADNESS.

happy *adj* **1** beatific, blessed, blissful, buoyant, cheerful, cheery, contented, delighted, ecstatic, elated, euphoric, exhilarated, exuberant, exultant, felicitous, festive, gay, glad, gleeful, good-humoured, halcyon (days), inf heavenly, high-spirited, idyllic, jocund, jolly, jovial, joyful, jubilant, laughing, light-hearted, lively, merry, inf on top of the world, overjoyed, inf over the moon, pleased, proud, radiant, rapturous, rejoicing, relaxed, satisfied, smiling, inf starry-eyed, sunny, thrilled. Opp SAD. 2 happy accident. advantageous, apt, auspicious, beneficial, convenient, favourable, fortuitous, fortunate, lucky, opportune, propitious, timely, welcome, well-timed.

harangue n diatribe, exhortation, inf pep talk. ▷ SPEECH.
● v exhort, inf hold forth, lecture, pontificate, preach, sermonize.

harass v annoy, attack, badger, bait, bother, disturb, inf hassle, hound, molest, nag, persecute, pester, inf pick on, plague, torment, trouble, vex, worry.

harassed adj inf at the end of your tether, careworn, distraught, distressed, exhausted, frayed, pressured, strained, stressed, tired, weary, worn out.

harbour n anchorage, dock, haven, jetty, landing stage, marina, mooring, pier, port, quay, safe haven, shelter, wharf.
● v 1 conceal, give asylum to, give refuge to, hide, protect, shelter, shield. 2 harbour a grudge. hold on to, keep in mind, maintain, nurse, nurture, retain.

hard adj 1 adamantine, compact, compressed, dense, firm, flinty, frozen, hardened, impenetrable, inflexible, rigid, rocky, solid, steely, stiff, stony, unyielding. 2 hard labour. arduous, back-breaking, exhausting, fatiguing, gruelling, harsh, heavy, laborious, onerous, rigorous, severe, strenuous, taxing, tiring, tough, uphill, wearying. 3 hard problem. baffling, complex, complicated, confusing, difficult, insoluble, intricate, involved, inf knotty, perplexing, puzzling, inf thorny. 4 hard person. callous, cold, cruel, harsh, heartless, hostile, inflexible, intolerant, merciless, obdurate, ruthless, severe, stern, strict, unbending, unfeeling, unkind. 5 hard blow. forceful, heavy, powerful, strong, violent. 6 hard times. austere, bad, calamitous, distressing, grim, intolerable, painful, unhappy, unpleasant. 7 hard worker. assiduous, conscientious, indefatigable, industrious, keen, unflagging, untiring, zealous. Opp EASY, SOFT.
hard-headed ▷ BUSINESSLIKE.
hard-hearted ▷ CRUEL. **hard up** ▷ POOR. **hard-wearing** ▷ DURABLE.

harden v bake, cake, clot, congeal, freeze, reinforce, set, solidify, stiffen, strengthen, toughen. Opp SOFTEN.

hardly adv barely, faintly, only just, rarely, scarcely, seldom.

hardship n adversity, affliction, austerity, bad luck, deprivation, destitution, difficulty, distress, misery, misfortune, need, privation, suffering, trouble, unhappiness, want.

hardware n equipment, implements, instruments, ironmongery, machinery, tools.

hardy adj 1 durable, fit, healthy, resilient, robust, rugged, strong, sturdy, tough. Opp TENDER.
2 ▷ BOLD.

harm n abuse, damage, detriment, disadvantage, disservice, havoc, hurt, inconvenience, injury, loss, mischief, pain, unhappiness, inf upset. ▷ EVIL. ● v abuse, damage, hurt, ill-treat, impair, injure, maltreat, misuse, ruin, spoil, wound. Opp BENEFIT.

harmful adj bad, baleful, damaging, dangerous, deadly, deleterious, destructive, detrimental, evil, fatal, hurtful, injurious, lethal, malign, noxious, pernicious, poisonous, prejudicial, ruinous, unhealthy, unpleasant, unwholesome. Opp BENEFICIAL, HARMLESS.

harmless adj acceptable, benign, gentle, innocent, innocuous, inoffensive, mild, non-addictive, non-toxic, safe, tame, unobjectionable. Opp HARMFUL.

harmonious adj 1 concordant, consonant, inf easy on the ear, euphonious, harmonizing, melodious, musical, sweetsounding, tuneful. Opp DISCORDANT. 2 harmonious group. amicable, compatible, congenial, cooperative, friendly, like-minded, sympathetic.

harmonize v agree, balance, be in harmony, blend, coordinate, correspond, go together, match, tally, tone in.

harmony n 1 assonance, consonance, euphony, tunefulness. 2 accord, agreement, amity, balance, compatibility, concord, conformity, cooperation, friendship, like-mindedness, peace, rapport, sympathy, understanding. Opp DISCORD.

harness n equipment, inf gear, straps, tackle. ● v control, domesticate, exploit, keep under control, make use of, mobilize, tame, use, utilize.

harsh adj 1 abrasive, bristly, coarse, hairy, rough, scratchy. 2 harsh sounds. cacophonous, croaking, disagreeable, discordant, dissonant, grating, gruff, guttural, hoarse, husky, irritating, jarring, rasping, raucous, rough, screeching, shrill, stertorous, strident, unpleasant. 3 harsh colours, light. bright, brilliant, dazzling, gaudy, glaring, lurid. 4 harsh smell. acrid, bitter, sour. 5 harsh conditions. arduous, austere, comfortless, difficult, hard, severe, tough. 6 harsh criticism, treatment. abusive, acerbic, bitter, blunt, brutal, cruel, draconian, frank, hard-hearted, hurtful, merciless, outspoken, pitiless, severe, sharp, stern, strict, unforgiving, unkind, unrelenting, unsympathetic. Opp GENTLE.

harvest n crop, gathering-in, produce, reaping, return, yield. ● v bring in, collect, garner, gather, glean, mow, pick, reap.

hash n 1 goulash, stew. 2 inf botch, confusion, inf hotchpotch, jumble, mess, inf mishmash, mixture, muddle. **make a hash of** ▷ BUNGLE.

hassle n argument, bother, confusion, difficulty, disagreement, disturbance, fuss, harassment, inconvenience, nuisance, problem, struggle, trouble, upset. ● v ▷ HARASS.

haste n impetuosity, precipitateness, rashness, recklessness, rush, urgency. ▷ SPEED.

hasty adj 1 abrupt, fast, foolhardy, headlong, hurried, ill-considered, impetuous, impulsive, incautious, inf pell-mell, precipitate, quick, rapid, rash, reckless, speedy, sudden, summary (*justice*), swift. **2** *hasty work.* brief, careless, cursory, perfunctory, rushed, slapdash, superficial, thoughtless, unthinking. *Opp* CAREFUL, SLOW.

hatch *v* **1** brood, incubate. **2** conceive, concoct, contrive, *inf* cook up, design, devise, dream up, formulate, invent, plan, plot, scheme, think up.

hate *n* **1** ▷ HATRED. **2** *pet hate.* abomination, aversion, *Fr* bête noire, dislike, loathing. ● *v* abhor, abominate, be hostile to, be revolted by, deplore, despise, detest, dislike, execrate, fear, find intolerable, loathe, object to, recoil from, resent, scorn, shudder at. *Opp* LIKE, LOVE.

hateful *adj* abhorrent, abominable, awful, contemptible, cursed, *inf* damnable, despicable, detestable, disgusting, distasteful, execrable, foul, hated, horrible, horrid, loathsome, nasty, nauseating, obnoxious, odious, offensive, repellent, repugnant, repulsive, revolting, vile. ▷ EVIL. *Opp* LOVABLE.

hatred *n* abhorrence, animosity, antipathy, aversion, contempt, detestation, dislike, enmity, hate, hostility, ill will, loathing, misanthropy, odium, repugnance, revulsion. *Opp* LOVE.

haughty *adj* arrogant, bumptious, cavalier, *inf* cocky, conceited, condescending, disdainful, egotistical, *inf* high-and-mighty, *inf* hoity-toity, imperious, lofty, offhand, pompous, presumptuous, pretentious, proud, self-important, snobbish, *inf* snooty,

inf stuck-up, supercilious, superior, vain. *Opp* MODEST.

haul *v* carry, cart, drag, draw, heave, lug, move, pull, tow, trail, tug.

haunt *v* **1** frequent, *inf* hang around, keep returning to, loiter about, patronize, visit regularly. **2** *haunt the mind.* beset, linger in, obsess, plague, prey on, torment.

have *v* **1** be in possession of, keep, maintain, own, possess, use, utilize. **2** *play has two themes.* comprise, consist of, contain, embody, hold, include, incorporate, involve. **3** *have fun, trouble.* endure, enjoy, experience, feel, go through, know, live through, put up with, suffer, tolerate, undergo. **4** *have a reward.* accept, acquire, be given, gain, get, obtain, receive. **5** *thieves had the lot. inf* get away with, remove, steal, take. **6** *have a snack.* consume, eat, drink, swallow. **7** *have a party.* arrange, hold, organize, prepare, set up. **8** *have guests.* be host to, cater for, entertain, put up. **have on** ▷ HOAX. **have to** be compelled to, be forced to, must, need to, ought to, should. **have up** ▷ ARREST.

haven *n* asylum, refuge, retreat, sanctuary. ▷ HARBOUR.

havoc *n* carnage, chaos, confusion, damage, destruction, devastation, disorder, disruption, *inf* mayhem, *inf* rack and ruin, ruin, *inf* shambles, waste, wreckage.

hazard *n* chance, danger, jeopardy, peril, risk, threat. ● *v* dare, gamble, jeopardize, risk, stake, venture.

hazardous adj inf chancy, dangerous, inf dicey, fraught with danger, perilous, precarious, risky, uncertain, unpredictable, unsafe. Opp SAFE.

haze n cloud, film, fog, mist, steam, vapour.

hazy adj 1 blurred, cloudy, dim, faint, foggy, fuzzy, indefinite, milky, misty, obscure, unclear. 2 ▷ VAGUE. Opp CLEAR.

head adj ▷ CHIEF. ● n 1 brain, cranium, skull. 2 head for figures. ability, brains, capacity, imagination, intelligence, intellect, mind, understanding. 3 head of a mountain. apex, crown, highest point, peak, summit, top. 4 director, leader, manager. ▷ CHIEF. 5 headmaster, headmistress, head teacher, principal. 6 head of a river. ▷ SOURCE. ● v 1 be in charge of, command, control, direct, govern, guide, lead, manage, rule, run, superintend, supervise. 2 head for home. aim, go, make, inf make a beeline, point, set out, start, steer, turn. **head off** ▷ DEFLECT. **lose your head** ▷ PANIC. **off your head** ▷ MAD.

heading n caption, headline, rubric, title.

headquarters n administration, base, depot, head office, inf HQ, main office, inf nerve-centre.

heal v 1 get better, improve, knit, mend, recover, recuperate. 2 cure, make better, minister to, nurse, rejuvenate, remedy, renew, restore, revitalize, tend, treat. 3 heal differences. patch up, put right, reconcile, repair, settle.

health n 1 condition, constitution, inf fettle, form, shape, trim.

2 picture of health. fitness, robustness, soundness, strength, vigour, well-being.

healthy adj 1 active, blooming, fine, fit, flourishing, good, hearty, inf in fine fettle, in good shape, lively, perky, robust, sound, strong, sturdy, vigorous, well. 2 bracing, hygienic, invigorating, salubrious, sanitary, wholesome. Opp ILL, UNHEALTHY.

heap n accumulation, assemblage, bank, collection, hill, hoard, mass, mound, mountain, pile, stack. ● v bank up, mass, pile, stack. ▷ COLLECT. **heaps** ▷ PLENTY.

hear v 1 attend to, catch, heed, listen to, overhear, pick up. 2 hear evidence. examine, investigate, judge, try. 3 hear news. discover, find out, gather, get, inf get wind of, learn, receive.

hearing n case, inquest, inquiry, trial.

heart n 1 sl ticker. 2 centre, core, crux, essence, focus, hub, kernel, marrow, middle, sl nitty-gritty, nub, nucleus, pith. 3 affection, compassion, concern, courage, humanity, kindness, love, pity, sensitivity, sympathy, tenderness, understanding, warmth.

heartbreaking adj bitter, distressing, grievous, heart-rending, pitiful, tragic.

heartbroken adj desolate, despairing, grieved, inconsolable, miserable, inf shattered. ▷ SAD.

hearten v boost, cheer up, encourage, strengthen, uplift.

heartless adj callous, cold, icy, inhuman, ruthless, steely, stony, unemotional, unkind, unsympathetic. ▷ CRUEL.

hearty adj 1 enthusiastic, exuberant, friendly, genuine, healthy, lively, positive, robust, sincere, strong, vigorous, warm. Opp HALF-HEARTED. 2 *hearty meal.* ▷ BIG.

heat n 1 fever, fieriness, glow, incandescence, warmth. 2 closeness, hot weather, humidity, sultriness, warmth. 3 *heat of the moment.* anger, eagerness, excitement, feverishness, impetuosity, violence. ▷ PASSION. Opp COLD. ● v bake, blister, boil, burn, cook, fry, grill, inflame, melt, roast, scald, scorch, simmer, sizzle, smoulder, steam, stew, toast, warm. Opp COOL. **heated** ▷ FERVENT, HOT.

heath n common land, moor, moorland, open country, wasteland.

heathen adj atheistic, barbaric, godless, idolatrous, infidel, irreligious, pagan, philistine, savage, unenlightened. ● n atheist, barbarian, heretic, idolater, infidel, pagan, philistine, savage, unbeliever.

heave v 1 drag, haul, hoist, lift, lug, move, pull, raise, tow. 2 ▷ THROW. **heave into sight** ▷ APPEAR. **heave up** ▷ VOMIT.

heaven n 1 afterlife, eternal rest, the next world, nirvana, paradise. 2 bliss, contentment, delight, ecstasy, felicity, happiness, joy, perfection, pleasure, rapture, Utopia. Opp HELL.

heavenly adj angelic, beautiful, blissful, celestial, delightful, divine, exquisite, glorious, lovely, other-worldly, inf out of this world, saintly, spiritual, sublime, wonderful.

heavy adj 1 bulky, burdensome, dense, hefty, large, leaden, massive, ponderous, unwieldy, weighty. ▷ BIG, FAT. 2 *heavy work.* arduous, demanding, difficult, hard, exhausting, laborious, onerous, strenuous, tough. 3 *heavy rain.* severe, torrential. 4 *heavy with fruit.* abundant, copious, laden, loaded, profuse, thick. 5 *heavy heart.* burdened, gloomy, miserable, sorrowful. ▷ SAD. 6 *heavy conversation.* dull, intellectual, intense, serious, tedious, wearisome. Opp LIGHT. **heavy-handed** ▷ CLUMSY. **heavy-hearted** ▷ SAD.

hectic adj animated, brisk, bustling, busy, chaotic, excited, feverish, frantic, frenetic, frenzied, hurried, hyperactive, lively, mad, restless, riotous, turbulent, wild. Opp LEISURELY.

hedge n barrier, fence, hedgerow, screen. ● v inf beat about the bush, be evasive, equivocate, inf hum and haw, stall, temporize. **hedge in** ▷ ENCLOSE.

hedonistic adj epicurean, extravagant, intemperate, luxurious, pleasure-loving, self-indulgent, sensual, sybaritic, voluptuous. Opp PURITANICAL.

heed v attend to, bear in mind, consider, follow, keep to, listen to, mark, mind, note, notice, obey, observe, pay attention to, regard, take notice of. Opp DISREGARD.

heedful adj attentive, careful, concerned, considerate, mindful, observant, vigilant, watchful. Opp HEEDLESS.

heedless adj blind, careless, deaf, inattentive, inconsiderate, neglectful, oblivious, reckless, thoughtless, unconcerned, unobservant, unsympathetic. *Opp* HEEDFUL.

hefty *adj inf* beefy, brawny, bulky, heavy, heavyweight, muscular, powerful, robust, rugged, solid, *inf* strapping, strong, tough. ▷ BIG. *Opp* SLIGHT.

height *n* 1 altitude, elevation, level. 2 crag, fell, hill, mound, mountain, peak, prominence, ridge, summit, top. 3 *height of your career.* acme, climax, crest, culmination, high point, peak, pinnacle, zenith.

heighten *v* add to, amplify, augment, boost, build up, elevate, enhance, improve, increase, intensify, magnify, maximize, raise, reinforce, sharpen, strengthen. *Opp* LOWER, REDUCE.

hell *n* 1 Hades, inferno, nether world, *sl* the other place, underworld. 2 ▷ MISERY. *Opp* HEAVEN.

help *n* advice, aid, assistance, backing, benefit, boost, collaboration, contribution, cooperation, encouragement, friendship, guidance, moral support, relief, remedy, succour, support. *Opp* HINDRANCE. ● *v* 1 advise, aid, aid and abet, assist, back, befriend, boost, collaborate, contribute, cooperate, encourage, facilitate, forward, further the interests of, *inf* give a hand, promote, prop up, *inf* rally round, serve, side with, spoonfeed, stand by, subsidize, succour, support, take pity on. *Opp* HINDER. 2 alleviate, benefit, cure, ease, improve, lessen, make easier, relieve, remedy. 3 *can't help it.* ▷ AVOID, PREVENT.

helper *n* accomplice, aide, ally, assistant, associate, collabor-

ator, colleague, deputy, *inf* henchman, partner, *inf* right-hand man, second, supporter.

helpful *adj* 1 accommodating, benevolent, caring, considerate, constructive, cooperative, favourable, friendly, kind, neighbourly, obliging, practical, supportive, sympathetic, thoughtful, willing. 2 *helpful comment.* advantageous, beneficial, informative, instructive, profitable, valuable, useful, worthwhile. 3 *helpful tool.* ▷ HANDY. *Opp* UNHELPFUL, USELESS.

helping *adj* ▷ HELPFUL. ● *n* amount, *inf* dollop, plateful, portion, ration, serving, share.

helpless *adj* abandoned, defenceless, dependent, deserted, destitute, disabled, exposed, feeble, handicapped, impotent, incapable, in difficulties, infirm, lame, marooned, powerless, stranded, unprotected, vulnerable. *Opp* INDEPENDENT.

herald *n* 1 announcer, courier, messenger. 2 *herald of spring.* forerunner, harbinger, omen, precursor, sign. ● *v* advertise, announce, indicate, proclaim, promise. ▷ FORETELL.

herd *n* bunch, flock, mob, pack, swarm, throng. ▷ GROUP. ● *v* assemble, collect, congregate, drive, gather, group together, round up, shepherd.

hereditary *adj* 1 ancestral, bequeathed, family, handed down, inherited, passed on, willed. 2 congenital, constitutional, genetic, inborn, inherent, innate, native, natural, transmissible.

heresy n blasphemy, dissent, idolatry, nonconformity, unorthodoxy.

heretic n blasphemer, dissenter, free thinker, iconoclast, nonconformist, rebel, renegade, unorthodox thinker. *Opp* BELIEVER.

heretical adj atheistic, blasphemous, dissenting, free-thinking, heathen, iconoclastic, idolatrous, impious, irreligious, nonconformist, pagan, rebellious, unorthodox. *Opp* ORTHODOX.

heritage n birthright, culture, history, inheritance, legacy, past, tradition.

hermit n monk, recluse, solitary.

hero, heroine ns champion, conqueror, exemplar, ideal, idol, luminary, protagonist, star, superman, *inf* superstar, superwoman, victor, winner.

heroic adj adventurous, bold, brave, chivalrous, courageous, daring, dauntless, epic, fearless, gallant, herculean, intrepid, noble, selfless, stout-hearted, superhuman, unafraid, valiant, valorous. *Opp* COWARDLY.

hesitant adj cautious, diffident, dithering, faltering, half-hearted, halting, hesitating, indecisive, irresolute, nervous, *inf* shilly-shallying, shy, stumbling, tentative, timid, uncertain, uncommitted, undecided, unsure, vacillating, wary, wavering. *Opp* DECISIVE, FLUENT.

hesitate v 1 be indecisive, *inf* be in two minds, delay, demur, *inf* dilly-dally, dither, equivocate, falter, halt, hang back, *inf* hum and haw, pause, *inf* shilly-shally, teeter, temporize, think twice, vacillate, wait,

waver. 2 stammer, stumble, stutter.

hesitation n caution, delay, dithering, doubt, indecision, irresolution, nervousness, reluctance, *inf* shilly-shallying, uncertainty, vacillation.

hidden adj 1 concealed, covered, disguised, enclosed, invisible, obscured, out of sight, private, shrouded, *inf* under wraps, unseen, veiled. *Opp* VISIBLE. 2 *hidden meaning*. arcane, coded, covert, cryptic, dark, esoteric, implicit, mysterious, obscure, occult, recondite, secret, unclear. *Opp* OBVIOUS.

hide n fur, leather, pelt, skin. ● v 1 blot out, bury, camouflage, cloak, conceal, cover, disguise, eclipse, mantle, mask, obscure, put out of sight, screen, secrete, shelter, shroud, veil, wrap up. 2 *inf* go to ground, *inf* hole up, keep hidden, *inf* lie low, lurk, take cover. 3 *hide facts*. censor, *inf* hush up, repress, silence, suppress, withhold.

hideous adj appalling, beastly, disgusting, ghastly, grotesque, macabre, odious, repulsive, revolting, sickening, terrible. ▷ UGLY. *Opp* BEAUTIFUL.

hiding-place n den, haven, hide-away, *inf* hideout, lair, refuge, retreat, sanctuary.

hierarchy n ladder, pecking order, ranking, scale, sequence, series, social order.

high adj 1 elevated, high-rise, lofty, raised, soaring, tall, towering. 2 aristocratic, chief, distinguished, eminent, exalted, important, leading, powerful, prominent, royal, superior, top. 3 *high prices*. dear, excessive, exorbitant, expensive, outra-

geous, *inf* steep, unreasonable.
4 *high winds.* extreme, great,
intense, *inf* stiff, stormy, strong.
5 *high reputation.* favourable,
good, noble, respected, virtuous.
6 *high voice.* acute, high-pitched,
penetrating, piercing, sharp,
shrill, soprano, squeaky, treble.
Opp LOW. **high-and-mighty**
▷ ARROGANT. **high-class**
▷ EXCELLENT. **high-handed**
▷ ARROGANT. **high-minded**
▷ MORAL. **high-powered**
▷ POWERFUL. **high-speed**
▷ FAST. **high-spirited**
▷ LIVELY.

highbrow *adj* **1** academic,
bookish, *inf* brainy, cultured,
intellectual, *derog* pretentious.
2 classical, cultural, deep,
difficult, improving, serious.
Opp LOWBROW.

highlight *n* best moment,
climax, high spot, peak.

hilarious *adj* amusing, entertaining, jolly, *inf* side-splitting,
uproarious. ▷ FUNNY.

hill *n* **1** elevation, eminence, foot-
hill, height, hillock, knoll,
mound, mount, mountain, peak,
prominence, ridge, summit.
2 ascent, declivity, drop, gradient, incline, ramp, rise, slope.

hinder *v* arrest, bar, be a hindrance to, check, curb, delay,
deter, frustrate, get in the way
of, hamper, handicap, hold back,
hold up, impede, limit, obstruct,
oppose, prevent, restrain,
restrict, retard, slow down,
stand in the way of, stop,
thwart. *Opp* HELP.

hindrance *n* bar, barrier, check,
curb, deterrent, difficulty, disadvantage, drawback, encum-
brance, handicap, impediment,
inconvenience, limitation, obs-

tacle, obstruction, restraint,
restriction, snag, stumbling
block. *Opp* HELP.

hinge *n* joint, pivot. ● *v* depend,
hang, rest, turn.

hint *n* **1** allusion, clue, idea,
implication, indication, inkling,
innuendo, insinuation, pointer,
sign, suggestion, tip, tip-off.
2 *hint of herbs.* dash, taste, tinge,
touch, trace, undertone, whiff.
● *v* allude, imply, indicate,
insinuate, intimate, mention,
suggest, tip off.

hire *v* book, charter, employ,
engage, lease, rent, take on. **hire
out** lease out, let, rent out.

hiss *v* **1** buzz, fizz, sizzle, whizz.
2 ▷ JEER.

historic *adj* celebrated, eminent,
epoch-making, famed, famous,
important, momentous, notable,
outstanding, remarkable,
renowned, significant, well-
known. *Opp* INSIGNIFICANT.

historical *adj* authentic, docu-
mented, factual, real, recorded,
true, verifiable. *Opp* FICTITIOUS.

history *n* **1** antiquity, bygone
days, heritage, historical events,
the past. **2** annals, chronicles,
memoirs, records.

histrionic *adj* actorish, dramatic, theatrical.

hit *n* **1** blow, bull's-eye, collision,
impact, shot, stroke. **2** success,
triumph, *inf* winner. ● *v* **1** bang,
bash, batter, beat, *sl* belt, box,
bludgeon, buffet, bump, butt,
cane, cannon into, clip,
inf clobber, clout, club, collide
with, crack, crash into, cuff,
deliver a blow, elbow, flog,
hammer, head, head-butt,
impact, jab, jar, kick, knee,
knock, lash, pound, pummel,
punch, punt, ram, rap, run into,

slam, slap, slog, slug, smack, smash, *inf* sock, spank, strike, stub, swat, *sl* tan, tap, thrash, thump, *sl* wallop, *inf* whack, whip. 2 *The slump hit sales.* affect, attack, check, damage, harm, have an effect on, hinder, hurt, ruin. **hit back** ▷ RETALIATE. **hit on** ▷ DISCOVER.

hoard *n* cache, collection, fund, heap, pile, reserve, stockpile, store, supply, treasure trove. ● *v* accumulate, amass, assemble, collect, gather, keep, lay up, mass, pile up, put by, save, stockpile, store, treasure. *Opp* SQUANDER, USE.

hoarse *adj* croaking, grating, gravelly, gruff, harsh, husky, rasping, raucous, rough, throaty.

hoax *n* cheat, *inf* con, confidence trick, deception, fake, fraud, joke, *inf* leg-pull, practical joke, *inf* spoof, swindle, trick. ● *v* bluff, cheat, *inf* con, deceive, delude, dupe, fool, gull, *inf* have on, hoodwink, lead on, mislead, swindle, *inf* take for a ride, take in, trick. ▷ TEASE.

hoaxer *n inf* con-man, joker, practical joker, trickster. ▷ CHEAT.

hobble *v* falter, limp, shuffle, stagger, stumble, totter.

hobby *n* diversion, interest, pastime, pursuit, recreation, relaxation, sideline.

hoist *n* block-and-tackle, crane, jack, lift, pulley, tackle, winch, windlass. ● *v* elevate, heave, lift, pull up, raise, winch up.

hold *n* 1 clasp, clutch, foothold, grasp, grip, purchase. 2 *hold over someone.* authority, control, dominance, influence, leverage,

mastery, power, sway. ● *v* 1 bear, carry, catch, clasp, cling to, clutch, cradle, embrace, enfold, grasp, grip, hang on to, have, hug, keep, possess, retain, seize, support, take. 2 *hold a suspect.* arrest, confine, detain, imprison, keep in custody. 3 *hold an opinion.* believe in, stick to, subscribe to. 4 *hold a pose.* continue, keep up, maintain, occupy, preserve, retain, sustain. 5 *hold a party.* conduct, convene, have, organize. 6 *jug holds a litre.* contain, enclose, have a capacity of, include. 7 *My offer holds.* continue, endure, hold out, keep on, last, persist, remain unchanged, stay. **hold back** ▷ RESTRAIN. **hold forth** ▷ SPEAK, TALK. **hold out** ▷ OFFER, PERSIST. **hold over, hold up** ▷ DELAY. **hold-up** ▷ ROBBERY.

hole *n* 1 abyss, burrow, cave, cavern, cavity, chamber, chasm, crater, dent, depression, excavation, fault, fissure, hollow, niche, pit, pot-hole, shaft, tunnel. 2 aperture, breach, break, chink, crack, cut, eyelet, fissure, gap, opening, orifice, perforation, puncture, rip, slot, split, tear, vent.

holiday *n* bank holiday, break, day off, furlough, half-term, leave, recess, respite, rest, sabbatical, time off, vacation.

holiness *n* devotion, divinity, faith, godliness, piety, *derog* religiosity, sacredness, saintliness, sanctity, venerability.

hollow *adj* 1 empty, unfilled, vacant, void. 2 cavernous, concave, deep, indented, recessed, sunken. 3 *hollow laugh, victory.* cynical, false, futile, insincere,

holocaust meaningless, pointless, value-less, worthless. ● *n* cavern, cavity, concavity, crater, dent, depression, dimple, dip, excavation, furrow, hole, indentation, pit, trough. ▷ VALLEY. **hollow out** ▷ EXCAVATE.

holocaust *n* 1 ▷ FIRE. 2 annihilation, bloodbath, destruction, devastation, extermination, genocide, massacre, pogrom.

holy *adj* 1 blessed, consecrated, dedicated, devoted, divine, hallowed, heavenly, revered, sacred, sacrosanct, venerable. 2 *holy pilgrims*: devout, faithful, God-fearing, godly, pious, pure, religious, reverent, reverential, righteous, saintly, *derog* sanctimonious, sinless. *Opp* IRRELIGIOUS.

home *n* 1 abode, accommodation, base, domicile, dwelling, dwelling place, habitation, house, household, lodging, *inf* pad, quarters, residence. 2 birthplace, native land. 3 *derog* institution.

homeless *adj* abandoned, destitute, dispossessed, down-and-out, evicted, exiled, itinerant, outcast, rootless, vagrant. ● *pl n* beggars, refugees, tramps, vagrants.

homely *adj* comfortable, congenial, cosy, easygoing, friendly, informal, natural, relaxed, simple, unaffected, unassuming, unpretentious, unsophisticated. ▷ FAMILIAR. *Opp* FORMAL, SOPHISTICATED.

homogeneous *adj* alike, comparable, compatible, consistent, identical, matching, similar, uniform, unvarying. *Opp* DIFFERENT.

homosexual *adj inf* camp, gay, lesbian, *derog* queer.

honest *adj* above-board, blunt, candid, conscientious, direct, equitable, fair, forthright, frank, genuine, good, honourable, impartial, incorruptible, just, law-abiding, legitimate, moral, *inf* on the level, open, outspoken, plain, principled, pure, reliable, respectable, scrupulous, sincere, straight, straightforward, trustworthy, trusty, truthful, unbiased, unequivocal, unprejudiced, upright, veracious, virtuous. *Opp* DISHONEST.

honesty *n* 1 fairness, honour, integrity, morality, probity, rectitude, reliability, scrupulousness, trustworthiness, truthfulness, uprightness, veracity, virtue. *Opp* DECEIT. 2 bluntness, candour, directness, frankness, outspokenness, plainness, sincerity, straightforwardness.

honorary *adj* nominal, titular, unofficial, unpaid.

honour *n* 1 acclaim, accolade, compliment, credit, esteem, fame, good name, *inf* kudos, regard, renown, repute, respect, reverence, veneration. 2 distinction, duty, importance, privilege. 3 *sense of honour*: decency, dignity, honesty, integrity, loyalty, morality, nobility, principle, rectitude, righteousness, sincerity, uprightness, virtue. ● *v* acclaim, admire, applaud, celebrate, commemorate, commend, dignify, esteem, give credit to, glorify, pay homage to, pay tribute to, praise, remember, respect, revere, reverence, value, venerate, worship.

honourable adj admirable, chivalrous, creditable, decent, estimable, ethical, high-minded, irreproachable, loyal, moral, noble, proper, reputable, respected, righteous, sincere, trustworthy, upright, venerable, virtuous, worthy. ▷ HONEST.
Opp DISHONOURABLE.

hoodwink v cheat, inf con, delude, dupe, fool, gull, inf have on, hoax, mislead, inf pull the wool over someone's eyes, swindle, take in, trick.
▷ DECEIVE.

hook n barb, catch, clasp, fastener, lock, peg. • v 1 ▷ FASTEN.
2 hook a fish. catch, take.

hooligan n delinquent, hoodlum, lout, ruffian, inf tearaway, thug, tough, troublemaker, vandal, inf yob.

hoop n band, circle, loop, ring.

hop v bound, caper, dance, jump, leap, skip, spring, vault.

hope n 1 ambition, aspiration, craving, desire, dream, longing, wish, yearning. 2 conviction, expectation, faith, likelihood, promise, prospect.
• v inf anticipate, aspire, be hopeful, believe, count on, desire, expect, foresee, have faith, trust, wish. Opp DESPAIR.

hopeful adj 1 confident, expectant, optimistic, positive, sanguine. 2 hopeful signs. auspicious, cheering, encouraging, heartening, promising, propitious, reassuring.
Opp HOPELESS.

hopefully adv 1 confidently, expectantly, optimistically, with hope. 2 [inf] Hopefully I'll be better by then. all being well, most likely, probably.

hopeless adj 1 defeatist, demoralized, despairing, desperate, disconsolate, pessimistic, wretched. 2 hopeless situation. impossible, incurable, irremediable, irreparable, irreversible. 3 [inf] He's hopeless! feeble, inadequate, incompetent, inefficient, useless.
Opp HOPEFUL.

horde n crowd, gang, mob, swarm, tribe. ▷ GROUP.

horizontal adj even, flat, level, lying down, prone, prostrate, supine. Opp VERTICAL.

horrible adj awful, beastly, disagreeable, ghastly, hateful, loathsome, nasty, odious, offensive, revolting, terrible, unkind.
▷ HORRIFIC, UNPLEASANT.
Opp PLEASANT.

horrific adj appalling, atrocious, blood-curdling, disgusting, dreadful, frightening, frightful, grisly, gruesome, hair-raising, harrowing, horrendous, horrifying, nauseating, shocking, sickening, spine-chilling, unnerving, unthinkable.

horrify v alarm, appal, disgust, frighten, outrage, scare, shock, sicken, stun, terrify, unnerve.
horrifying ▷ HORRIFIC.

horror n 1 abhorrence, antipathy, aversion, detestation, disgust, dread, fear, hatred, loathing, repugnance, revulsion, terror. 2 awfulness, frightfulness, ghastliness, gruesomeness, hideousness.

horse n bronco, carthorse, cob, colt, dun, filly, foal, gelding, grey, hack, hunter, mare, mount, mule, mustang, inf nag, piebald, pony, racehorse, roan, skewbald, stallion, steed, warhorse.

horseman, horsewoman ns equestrian, jockey, rider.

hospitable adj courteous, generous, sociable, welcoming.
▷ FRIENDLY. Opp INHOSPITABLE.

hospital n clinic, health centre, hospice, infirmary, medical centre, nursing home, sanatorium, sick bay.

hospitality n 1 accommodation, entertainment, 2 cordiality, courtesy, friendliness, sociability, warmth, welcome.

host n 1 army, crowd, mob, multitude, swarm, throng, troop.
▷ GROUP. 2 ▷ COMPÈRE.

hostage n captive, pawn, prisoner, surety.

hostile adj 1 aggressive, antagonistic, antipathetic, attacking, averse, bellicose, belligerent, confrontational, ill-disposed, inhospitable, inimical, malevolent, pugnacious, resentful, rival, unfriendly, unsympathetic, unwelcoming, warlike, warring.
▷ ANGRY. Opp FRIENDLY.
2 hostile conditions. adverse, contrary, opposing, unfavourable, unhelpful, unpropitious. ▷ BAD. Opp FAVOURABLE.

hostility n aggression, animus, antagonism, bad feeling, belligerence, dissension, enmity, estrangement, friction, incompatibility, malevolence, malice, opposition, rancour, resentment, strife, unfriendliness.
▷ HATRED. Opp FRIENDSHIP.

hostilities ▷ WAR.

hot adj 1 baking, blistering, boiling, burning, close, fiery, flaming, humid, oppressive, red-hot, roasting, scalding, scorching, searing, sizzling, steamy, stifling, sultry, sweltering, thermal, torrid, tropical, warm.

2 ardent, eager, emotional, excited, feverish, fierce, heated, hot-headed, impatient, impetuous, inflamed, intense, passionate, violent. 3 hot taste. gingery, peppery, piquant, pungent, spicy, strong. Opp COLD, COOL.
hot-tempered ▷ BAD-TEMPERED. **hot under the collar** ▷ ANGRY.

hotel n guest house, hostel, inn, lodge, motel.

hound n ▷ DOG. ● v annoy, chase, harass, harry, hunt, nag, persecute, pester, pursue.

house n 1 abode, domicile, dwelling, dwelling place, habitation, home, homestead, place, residence. 2 clan, dynasty, line, lineage. 3 business, company, firm. ● v accommodate, billet, board, harbour, keep, lodge, place, inf put up, quarter, shelter, take in.

household n establishment, family, home, ménage.

hovel n cottage, inf dump, hole, hut, shack, shanty, shed.

hover v 1 be suspended, drift, float, flutter, fly, hang. 2 dally, dither, hang about, hesitate, linger, loiter, pause, vacillate, wait about, waver.

howl v bay, bellow, cry, roar, scream, shout, wail, yowl.

hub n axis, centre, core, focal point, focus, heart, middle, nucleus, pivot.

huddle n ▷ GROUP. ● v 1 cluster, converge, crowd, flock, gather, group, heap, herd, jam, jumble, pile, press, squeeze, swarm, throng. 2 cuddle, curl up, hug, nestle, snuggle.

hue *n* cast, complexion, dye, nuance, shade, tone. ▷ COLOUR.
hue and cry ▷ OUTCRY.

hug *v* clasp, cling to, crush, cuddle, embrace, enfold, fold in your arms, hold close, nurse, snuggle against, squeeze.

huge *adj* **1** colossal, elephantine, enormous, gargantuan, giant, gigantic, *inf* hulking, immense, imposing, mammoth, massive, mighty, *inf* monster, monstrous, monumental, mountainous, prodigious, stupendous, titanic, towering, *inf* tremendous, vast, *inf* whopping. ▷ BIG. **2** *huge number*. ▷ INFINITE. *Opp* SMALL.

hulk *n* **1** body, frame, shell, wreck. **2** lout, lump, oaf.

hulking *adj* awkward, bulky, cumbersome, heavy, ungainly, unwieldy. ▷ BIG, CLUMSY.

hull *n* body, frame, framework, skeleton.

hum *v* buzz, drone, murmur, purr, sing, thrum, vibrate, whirr. **hum and haw** ▷ HESITATE.

human *adj* **1** anthropoid, hominoid, mortal. **2** kind, rational, reasonable, sensible, sensitive, thoughtful. ▷ HUMANE. *Opp* INHUMAN. **human beings** folk, humanity, mankind, men and women, mortals, people.

humane *adj* altruistic, benevolent, charitable, civilized, compassionate, feeling, forgiving, good, human, humanitarian, kindhearted, loving, magnanimous, merciful, pitying, sympathetic, tender, understanding, unselfish, warm-hearted. ▷ KIND. *Opp* INHUMANE.

humble *adj* **1** deferential, meek, modest, *derog* obsequious, respectful, self-effacing, *derog* servile, submissive, subservient, *derog* sycophantic, unassertive, unassuming, unpretentious. *Opp* PROUD. **2** *humble birth, lifestyle*. commonplace, insignificant, low, lowly, mean, obscure, ordinary, plebeian, poor, simple, undistinguished, unremarkable. ● *v* ▷ HUMILIATE.

humid *adj* clammy, close, damp, moist, muggy, steamy, sticky, sultry, sweaty.

humiliate *v* abase, abash, bring someone down, chasten, crush, deflate, degrade, demean, discredit, disgrace, embarrass, humble, make someone ashamed, *inf* make someone feel small, mortify, *inf* put someone in their place, shame, *inf* show someone up, *inf* take someone down a peg. **humiliating** ▷ SHAMEFUL.

humiliation *n* abasement, chagrin, degradation, discredit, disgrace, dishonour, embarrassment, ignominy, indignity, loss of face, mortification, shame.

humility *n* deference, humbleness, lowliness, meekness, modesty, self-abasement, self-effacement, *derog* servility. *Opp* PRIDE.

humorous *adj* absurd, amusing, comic, comical, diverting, droll, entertaining, facetious, farcical, funny, hilarious, *inf* hysterical, jocular, merry, *inf* priceless, satirical, *inf* side-splitting, slapstick, uproarious, whimsical, witty, zany. *opp* SERIOUS.

humour *n* **1** banter, comedy, facetiousness, fun, jesting, jocularity, jokes, joking, merriment, quips, raillery, repartee, satire, wit, witticism, wittiness. **2** *in a good humour*. disposition, frame of mind, mood, spirits, state of mind, temper.

hump n bulge, bump, curve, knob, lump, node, projection, protrusion, protuberance, swelling. 2 barrow, hillock, hummock, mound, rise. ● v 1 arch, bend, curl, curve, hunch, raise. 2 hump a load. drag, heave, hoist, lift, lug, raise, shoulder.

hunch n feeling, guess, idea, impression, inkling, intuition, premonition, presentiment, suspicion. ● v arch, bend, curl, curve, huddle, shrug.

hunger n 1 appetite, craving, greed, ravenousness, voracity. 2 famine, malnutrition, starvation, want. ● v ▷ DESIRE.

hungry adj avid, covetous, craving, eager, famished, greedy, longing, inf peckish, ravenous, starved, starving, undernourished, voracious.

hunt n chase, pursuit, quest, search. ▷ HUNTING. ● v 1 chase, course, ferret, hound, pursue, stalk, track, trail. 2 enquire after, inf ferret out, look for, rummage, search for, seek, trace, track down.

hunter n huntsman, huntswoman, predator, trapper.

hunting n blood sports, coursing, stalking, trapping.

hurdle n 1 barricade, barrier, fence, hedge, jump, obstacle, wall. 2 difficulty, handicap, hindrance, impediment, obstruction, problem, restraint, snag, stumbling block.

hurl v cast, catapult, inf chuck, dash, fire, fling, heave, launch, inf let fly, pitch, project, propel, send, shy, sling, throw, toss.

hurricane n cyclone, storm, tempest, tornado, typhoon, whirlwind.

hurry n ▷ HASTE. ● v 1 chase, dash, fly, inf get a move on, hasten, hurtle, hustle, make haste, rush, inf shift, speed, inf step on it. 2 hurry a process. accelerate, expedite, press on with, quicken, speed up. Opp DELAY. **hurried** ▷ HASTY.

hurt v 1 ache, be painful, burn, pinch, smart, sting, throb, tingle. 2 abuse, afflict, bruise, cripple, cut, disable, injure, maim, misuse, mutilate, torture, wound. 3 affect, aggrieve, be hurtful to, inf cut to the quick, distress, grieve, insult, offend, pain, sadden, torment, upset. 4 damage, harm, mar, ruin, sabotage, spoil.

hurtful adj cruel, cutting, damaging, derogatory, detrimental, distressing, hard to bear, harmful, injurious, malicious, nasty, painful, scathing, spiteful, uncharitable, unkind, upsetting, vicious, wounding. Opp KIND.

hurtle v charge, chase, dash, fly, plunge, race, rush, shoot, speed, inf tear.

hush int be quiet! inf hold your tongue! inf shut up! ● v ▷ SILENCE. **hush up** ▷ SUPPRESS.

hustle v 1 bustle, hasten, hurry, jostle. 2 hustle along. coerce, compel, force, push, shove, thrust.

hut n cabin, den, hovel, lean-to, shack, shanty, shed, shelter.

hybrid n combination, composite, compound, cross, crossbreed, mixture, mongrel.

hygiene n cleanliness, sanitariness, wholesomeness.

slight, snub, take no notice of, *inf* turn a blind eye to.

ill *adj* 1 ailing, bad, bedridden, diseased, feeble, frail, *inf* groggy, indisposed, infirm, invalid, nauseated, nauseous, *inf* off-colour, *inf* out of sorts, pasty, poorly, queasy, *inf* seedy, sick, sickly, suffering, *inf* under the weather, unhealthy, unwell, weak. *Opp* HEALTHY. 2 *ill effects.* bad, damaging, detrimental, evil, harmful, injurious, unfavourable, unfortunate, unlucky. *Opp* GOOD. ● *pl n* the infirm, invalids, patients, the sick, sufferers. **be ill** ail, languish, sicken. **ill-advised** ▷ MISGUIDED. **ill-bred** ▷ RUDE. **ill-fated** ▷ UNLUCKY. **ill-humoured** ▷ BAD-TEMPERED. **ill-mannered** ▷ RUDE. **ill-natured** ▷ UNKIND. **ill-omened** ▷ UNLUCKY. **ill-tempered** ▷ BAD-TEMPERED. **ill-treat** ▷ MISTREAT.

illegal *adj* actionable, against the law, banned, black-market, criminal, felonious, forbidden, illicit, prohibited, proscribed, unlawful, unlicensed, wrong, wrongful. ▷ ILLEGITIMATE. *Opp* LEGAL.

illegible *adj* indecipherable, indistinct, obscure, unclear, unreadable. *Opp* LEGIBLE.

illegitimate *adj* 1 against the rules, improper, inadmissible, incorrect, invalid, irregular, spurious, unauthorized, unjustifiable, unreasonable, unwarranted. ▷ ILLEGAL. 2 bastard, natural. *Opp* LEGITIMATE.

illiterate *adj* unable to read. ▷ IGNORANT. *Opp* LITERATE.

illness *n* abnormality, affliction, ailment, allergy, attack, blight,

inf bug, complaint, condition, disability, disease, disorder, epidemic, fever, health problem, indisposition, infection, infirmity, malady, malaise, pestilence, plague, sickness, *inf* trouble, *inf* upset.

illogical *adj* inconsequential, inconsistent, invalid, senseless, unreasonable. ▷ SILLY. *Opp* LOGICAL.

illuminate *v* 1 brighten, light up, make brighter, reveal. 2 clarify, clear up, elucidate, enlighten, explain, throw light on.

illusion *n* 1 apparition, conjuring trick, daydream, delusion, dream, fancy, fantasy, figment of the imagination, hallucination, mirage. 2 *under an illusion.* error, false impression, misapprehension, mistake.

illusory *adj* deceptive, deluding, fallacious, false, misleading, sham, unreal, untrue. ▷ IMAGINARY. *Opp* REAL.

illustrate *v* 1 demonstrate, elucidate, exemplify, explain, show. 2 adorn, decorate, depict, illuminate, picture, portray.

illustration *n* 1 case in point, demonstration, example, instance, sample, specimen. 2 depiction, diagram, drawing, figure, picture, sketch. ▷ IMAGE.

image *n* 1 imitation, likeness, reflection, representation. ▷ PICTURE. 2 carving, effigy, figure, icon, idol, statue. 3 *the image of her mother.* double, likeness, spitting image, twin.

imaginary *adj* fabulous, fanciful, fictional, fictitious, hypothetical, imagined, insubstantial, invented, legendary, made-up, mythical, mythological, non-existent, supposed, unreal, visionary. ▷ ILLUSORY. Opp REAL.

imagination n artistry, creativity, fancy, ingenuity, insight, inspiration, inventiveness, inf mind's eye, originality, sensitivity, thought, vision.

imaginative adj artistic, attractive, beautiful, clever, creative, fanciful, ingenious, innovative, inspired, inventive, original, poetic, resourceful, sensitive, thoughtful, visionary, vivid. Opp UNIMAGINATIVE.

imagine v 1 conceive, conjure up, create, dream up, envisage, fancy, fantasize, invent, make believe, picture, pretend, see, think of, think up, visualize. 2 assume, believe, guess, infer, judge, presume, suppose, surmise, suspect, think.

imitate v 1 ape, caricature, counterfeit, duplicate, echo, guy, mimic, parody, parrot, reproduce, satirize, inf send up, simulate, inf take off. ▷ IMPERSONATE. 2 copy, emulate, follow, match, model yourself on.

imitation adj artificial, copied, counterfeit, ersatz, man-made, mock, model, inf phoney, sham, simulated, synthetic. Opp REAL. ● n 1 copying, duplication, emulation, mimicry. 2 inf clone, copy, counterfeit, dummy, duplicate, fake, forgery, impersonation, impression, likeness, inf mock-up, model, parody, replica, reproduction, sham, simulation, inf take-off, travesty.

immature adj adolescent, babyish, callow, childish, inf green, inexperienced, infantile, juvenile, new, puerile, undeveloped, young. Opp MATURE.

immediate adj 1 instant, instantaneous, prompt, quick, speedy, sudden, swift, unhesitating. 2 immediate problem. current, present, pressing, urgent. 3 immediate neighbours. adjacent, closest, direct, nearest, next.

immediately adv at once, directly, forthwith, instantly, now, promptly, inf right away, straight away, unhesitatingly.

immense adj colossal, elephantine, enormous, gargantuan, giant, gigantic, great, huge, inf hulking, immeasurable, imposing, impressive, incalculable, inf jumbo, large, mammoth, massive, mighty, inf monster, monstrous, monumental, mountainous, prodigious, stupendous, titanic, towering, inf tremendous, vast, inf whopping. ▷ BIG. Opp SMALL.

immerse v bathe, dip, drench, drown, duck, dunk, lower, plunge, sink, submerge. **immersed** ▷ BUSY, INTERESTED.

immersion n baptism, dipping, ducking, submersion.

immigrant n incomer, newcomer, outsider, settler.

imminent adj about to happen, approaching, close, coming, forthcoming, impending, looming, near, inf on the horizon, threatening.

immobile adj 1 ▷ IMMOVABLE. 2 frozen, inexpressive, inflexible, rigid. Opp MOBILE.

immobilize v cripple, damage, disable, paralyse, put out of action, sabotage, stop.

immoral adj base, corrupt, debauched, degenerate, depraved, dishonest, dissipated, dissolute, impure, indecent, licentious, loose, low, profligate, promiscuous, *inf* rotten, sinful, unchaste, unethical, unprincipled, wanton, wrong. ▷ WICKED. Opp MORAL.

immoral person cheat, degenerate, liar, libertine, rake, reprobate, scoundrel, sinner, villain, wrongdoer.

immortal adj 1 ageless, deathless, endless, eternal, everlasting, incorruptible, indestructible, perpetual, timeless, unchanging, undying, unending, unfading. 2 *immortal beings*. divine, godlike, legendary, mythical. Opp MORTAL.

immortalize v commemorate, deify, enshrine, keep alive, make immortal, perpetuate.

immovable adj 1 anchored, fast, firm, fixed, immobile, immobilized, paralysed, riveted, rooted, secure, set, settled, solid, static, stationary, still, stuck.
2 ▷ IMMUTABLE.

immune adj exempt, free, immunized, invulnerable, protected, resistant, safe, unaffected. Opp VULNERABLE.

immunize v inoculate, vaccinate.

immutable adj constant, dependable, enduring, eternal, fixed, invariable, lasting, permanent, perpetual, reliable, settled, stable, unalterable, unchangeable, unvarying. ▷ RESOLUTE. Opp CHANGEABLE.

impact n 1 bang, blow, bump, collision, concussion, contact, crash, knock, smash.
2 consequence, effect, force, impression, influence, repercussions, reverberations, shock.
● v ▷ HIT.

impair v damage, harm, injure, mar, ruin, spoil, weaken.

impale v ▷ PIERCE.

impartial adj balanced, detached, disinterested, dispassionate, equitable, even-handed, fair, fair-minded, just, neutral, non-partisan, objective, open-minded, unbiased, uninvolved, unprejudiced. Opp BIASED.

impartiality n balance, detachment, disinterest, fairness, justice, neutrality, objectivity, open-mindedness. Opp BIAS.

impassable adj blocked, closed, obstructed, unusable.

impatient adj 1 anxious, eager, keen. 2 agitated, edgy, fidgety, fretful, irritable, nervous, restive, restless, uneasy. 3 *impatient manner*. abrupt, brusque, curt, hasty, intolerant, irascible, quick-tempered, short-tempered, snappish, snappy, testy. Opp APATHETIC, PATIENT.

impede v be an impediment to, obstruct. ▷ HINDER.

impediment n 1 bar, burden, check, curb, deterrent, *inf* drag, hindrance, inconvenience, limitation, obstacle, obstruction, restraint, snag, stumbling block. ▷ HANDICAP.

impending adj ▷ IMMINENT.

impenetrable adj 1 dense, resilient, solid, thick. ▷ IMPERVIOUS. 2 impregnable, invincible, inviolable, invulnerable, safe, secure, unassailable. Opp VULNERABLE. 3 *impenetrable language*. inaccessible, incomprehensible, inscrutable, unfathomable. Opp ACCESSIBLE.

imperceptible adj faint, gradual, inaudible, indistinguishable, insignificant, invisible, negligible, subtle, undetectable, unnoticeable. ▷ SMALL. Opp PERCEPTIBLE.

imperceptive adj undiscriminating, unobservant. ▷ STUPID. Opp PERCEPTIVE.

imperfect adj blemished, broken, damaged, defective, deficient, faulty, flawed, incomplete, marred, partial, shop-soiled, spoilt, unfinished, wanting. Opp PERFECT.

imperfection n blemish, defect, deficiency, error, failing, fault, flaw, frailty, inadequacy, shortcoming, weakness. Opp PERFECTION.

impermanent adj changing, ephemeral, evanescent, fleeting, momentary, passing, short-lived, temporary, transient, transitory. ▷ CHANGEABLE. Opp PERMANENT.

impersonal adj aloof, business-like, cold, cool, detached, disinterested, dispassionate, distant, formal, mechanical, objective, official, remote, unemotional, unfriendly, unprejudiced, unsympathetic, wooden. Opp FRIENDLY.

impersonate v disguise yourself as, masquerade as, pass yourself off as, portray, pose as, pretend to be. ▷ IMITATE.

impertinent adj brazen, cheeky, disrespectful, forward, inf fresh, impudent, insolent, insulting, irreverent, pert. ▷ RUDE. Opp RESPECTFUL.

impervious adj 1 hermetic, impenetrable, impermeable, non-porous, solid, waterproof, water-repellent, watertight. Opp POROUS. 2 ▷ RESISTANT.

impetuous adj eager, hasty, headlong, hot-headed, impulsive, incautious, precipitate, quick, rash, reckless, speedy, spontaneous, inf spur-of-the-moment, thoughtless, unplanned, unpremeditated. Opp CAUTIOUS.

impetus n boost, drive, encouragement, energy, fillip, force, impulse, incentive, inspiration, momentum, motivation, power, push, spur, stimulus, thrust.

impiety n blasphemy, irreverence, profanity, sacrilege, sinfulness, ungodliness, unrighteousness, wickedness. Opp PIETY.

impious adj blasphemous, godless, irreligious, irreverent, profane, sacrilegious, sinful, unholy. ▷ WICKED. Opp PIOUS.

implausible adj doubtful, dubious, far-fetched, feeble, improbable, suspect, unconvincing, unlikely. Opp PLAUSIBLE.

implement n apparatus, appliance, device, gadget, instrument, tool, utensil. ● v bring about, carry out, effect, enforce, execute, fulfil, perform, put into practice, realize, try out.

implicate v associate, connect, embroil, entangle, include, incriminate, involve.

implication n 1 hidden meaning, hint, innuendo, insinuation, overtone, significance. 2 association, connection, embroilment, entanglement, involvement.

implicit adj 1 hinted at, implied, indirect, tacit, undeclared, understood, unsaid, unspoken, unvoiced. Opp EXPLICIT. 2 implicit faith. ▷ ABSOLUTE.

imply v 1 hint, indicate, insinuate, intimate, mean, point to, suggest. 2 ▷ SIGNIFY.

impolite adj discourteous, disrespectful, ill-mannered.
▷ RUDE. Opp POLITE.

import v bring in, buy in, introduce, ship in. ▷ CONVEY.

important adj 1 basic, big, cardinal, central, chief, critical, epoch-making, essential, foremost, fundamental, grave, historic, key, main, major, momentous, noteworthy, once in a lifetime, outstanding, pressing, primary, principal, salient, serious, significant, urgent, vital, weighty. 2 celebrated, distinguished, eminent, famous, great, high-ranking, influential, leading, notable, noted, powerful, pre-eminent, prominent, renowned, well-known.
Opp UNIMPORTANT. **be important** ▷ MATTER.

importunate adj demanding, insistent, persistent, pressing, relentless, urgent.

importune v harass, hound, pester, plague, plead with, press, solicit, urge. ▷ ASK.

impose v decree, dictate, enforce, exact, fix, foist, inflict, insist on, lay, levy, prescribe, set. **impose on** ▷ BURDEN, EXPLOIT. **imposing** ▷ IMPRESSIVE.

impossible adj hopeless, impracticable, impractical, inconceivable, insoluble, insurmountable, inf not on, out of the question, unattainable, unimaginable, unobtainable, unthinkable, unviable, unworkable. Opp POSSIBLE.

impotent adj emasculated, helpless, inadequate, incapable, ineffective, ineffectual, inept, infirm,

powerless, unable. ▷ WEAK.
Opp POTENT.

impracticable adj not feasible, useless. ▷ IMPOSSIBLE.
Opp PRACTICABLE.

impractical adj idealistic, quixotic, romantic, unrealistic, visionary. Opp PRACTICAL.

imprecise adj ambiguous, approximate, careless, estimated, fuzzy, guessed, hazy, ill-defined, inaccurate, inexact, loose, inf sloppy, undefined, vague, inf waffly. Opp PRECISE.

impregnable adj impenetrable, invincible, invulnerable, safe, secure, strong, unassailable.
Opp VULNERABLE.

impress v 1 affect, excite, influence, inspire, leave its mark on, move, persuade, stir, touch. 2 emboss, engrave, imprint, mark, print, stamp.

impression n 1 effect, impact, influence, mark. 2 belief, fancy, feeling, hunch, idea, memory, notion, opinion, recollection, sense, suspicion, view. 3 dent, hollow, imprint, indentation, mark, print, stamp. 4 imitation, impersonation, parody, inf take-off. 5 edition, printing, reprint.

impressionable adj easily influenced, gullible, inexperienced, naive, receptive, suggestible, susceptible.

impressive adj affecting, awe-inspiring, awesome, commanding, formidable, grand, imposing, magnificent, majestic, memorable, moving, powerful, remarkable, splendid, stately, stirring, striking, touching.
▷ BIG. Opp INSIGNIFICANT.

imprison v cage, commit to prison, confine, detain, gaol, immure, incarcerate, intern, jail, keep in custody, *inf* keep under lock and key, lock up, *inf* put away, remand, *inf* send down, shut up. *Opp* FREE.

imprisonment *n* confinement, custody, detention, gaol, incarceration, internment, jail, remand.

improbable *adj* doubtful, dubious, far-fetched, *inf* hard to believe, implausible, incredible, unbelievable, unconvincing, unexpected, unlikely. *Opp* PROBABLE.

impromptu *adj inf* ad-lib, extempore, improvised, offhand, *inf* off the cuff, *inf* off the top of your head, spontaneous, unplanned, unpremeditated, unprepared, unrehearsed, unscripted. ▷ IMPULSIVE. *Opp* REHEARSED.

improper *adj* 1 inappropriate, irregular, mistaken, out of place, uncalled-for, unfit, unseemly, unsuitable, unwarranted. ▷ WRONG. 2 ▷ INDECENT. *Opp* PROPER.

impropriety *n* incorrectness, indecency, indelicacy, irregularity, rudeness, unseemliness. ▷ OBSCENITY. *Opp* PROPRIETY.

improve *v* 1 advance, develop, get better, grow, increase, *inf* look up, move on, progress. 2 *improve after illness*. convalesce, *inf* pick up, rally, recover, recuperate, revive, strengthen, *inf* turn the corner. 3 *improve your manners, finances*. ameliorate, amend, better, correct, enhance, mend, polish (up), rectify, refine, reform, revise. 4 *improve a home*. decorate, extend, modernize, rebuild, refurbish, renovate, repair, update. *Opp* WORSEN.

improvement *n* 1 advance, amelioration, correction, development, enhancement, gain, increase, progress, rally, recovery, reformation, upturn. 2 *home improvement*. alteration, extension, *inf* facelift, modernization, renovation.

improvise *v* 1 concoct, contrive, devise, invent, make do, make up, *inf* throw together. 2 *inf* ad-lib, extemporize, play by ear.

impudent *adj* bold, cheeky, disrespectful, forward, *inf* fresh, impertinent, insolent, pert, presumptuous, saucy. ▷ RUDE. *Opp* RESPECTFUL.

impulse *n* 1 drive, force, impetus, motive, pressure, push, stimulus, thrust. 2 caprice, desire, instinct, urge, whim.

impulsive *adj* emotional, hasty, headlong, hot-headed, impetuous, instinctive, intuitive, involuntary, madcap, precipitate, rash, reckless, spontaneous, *inf* spur-of-the-moment, sudden, thoughtless, unthinking, wild. ▷ IMPROMPTU. *Opp* DELIBERATE.

impure *adj* 1 adulterated, defiled, infected, polluted, tainted, unwholesome. ▷ DIRTY. 2 ▷ INDECENT.

impurity *n* contamination, defilement, taint. ▷ DIRT.

inaccessible *adj* cut off, desolate, godforsaken, impassable, impenetrable, isolated, lonely, outlying, out-of-the-way, private, remote, solitary, unattainable, unavailable, unfrequented, unobtainable. *Opp* ACCESSIBLE.

inaccurate *adj* erroneous, fallacious, false, faulty, imperfect, imprecise, incorrect, inexact, misleading, mistaken, unreliable, unsound, untrue, vague, wrong. *Opp* ACCURATE.

inactive *adj* asleep, dormant, hibernating, idle, immobile, inanimate, indolent, inert, languid, lazy, lethargic, passive, quiet, sedentary, sleepy, slothful, slow, sluggish, somnolent, torpid, unemployed, unoccupied. *Opp* ACTIVE.

inadequate *adj* deficient, imperfect, incompetent, incomplete, ineffective, insufficient, limited, meagre, niggardly, *inf* pathetic, scanty, scarce, skimpy, sparse, unsatisfactory. *Opp* ADEQUATE.

inadvisable *adj* misguided, unwise. ▷ SILLY. *Opp* WISE.

inanimate *adj* cold, dead, dormant, inactive, insentient, lifeless, motionless, unconscious. *Opp* ANIMATE.

inappropriate *adj* ill-judged, ill-timed, improper, inapplicable, inapposite, incongruous, incorrect, inopportune, irrelevant, out of place, tactless, tasteless, unbecoming, unfit, unseemly, unsuitable, untimely, wrong. *Opp* APPROPRIATE.

inarticulate *adj* dumb, faltering, halting, hesitant, mumbling, mute, shy, silent, speechless, stammering, stuttering, tongue-tied. ▷ INCOHERENT. *Opp* ARTICULATE.

inattentive *adj* absent-minded, abstracted, careless, daydreaming, distracted, dreaming, drifting, heedless, *inf* in a world of your own, negligent, preoccupied, unobservant, vague, wandering. *Opp* ATTENTIVE.

inaudible *adj* imperceptible, indistinct, quiet, silent, undistinguishable. ▷ FAINT. *Opp* AUDIBLE.

incapable *adj* 1 clumsy, helpless, impotent, incompetent, ineffective, ineffectual, inept, powerless, unable, unfit, unqualified, useless, weak. *Opp* CAPABLE. 2 ▷ DRUNK.

incentive *n* bait, *inf* carrot, encouragement, inducement, lure, motivation, reward, stimulus, *inf* sweetener.

incessant *adj* ceaseless, constant, continual, continuous, endless, eternal, everlasting, interminable, never-ending, nonstop, perennial, perpetual, persistent, relentless, unbroken, unending, unremitting. *Opp* INTERMITTENT, TEMPORARY.

incident *n* 1 affair, circumstance, episode, event, happening, occasion, occurrence. 2 accident, disturbance, scene, upset. ▷ COMMOTION.

incidental *adj* accidental, attendant, casual, chance, fortuitous, minor, odd, random, secondary, subordinate, subsidiary. *Opp* ESSENTIAL.

incipient *adj* beginning, developing, early, embryonic, growing, new, rudimentary.

incisive *adj* acute, clear, concise, cutting, decisive, direct, keen, penetrating, percipient, precise, sharp, telling, trenchant. *Opp* VAGUE.

incite *v* inflame, rouse, spur on, stir up, urge. ▷ PROVOKE.

inclination *n* affection, bent, bias, desire, disposition, fondness, habit, instinct, leaning, liking, partiality, penchant, predilection, predisposition, preference, proclivity, propensity, readiness, tendency, trend. ▷ DESIRE.

incline n ascent, declivity, descent, drop, gradient, hill, ramp, rise, slope. • v angle, ascend, bend, descend, drop, lean, rise, slant, slope, tend, tilt, tip, veer.

inclined (to) ▷ LIABLE.

include v 1 add in, combine, comprehend, comprise, consist of, contain, embody, embrace, encompass, incorporate, involve, subsume, take in. 2 *The price includes VAT.* allow for, cover, take into account. *Opp* EXCLUDE.

incoherent adj confused, disconnected, disjointed, disordered, disorganized, garbled, illogical, incomprehensible, inconsistent, jumbled, mixed up, muddled, rambling, scrambled, unclear, unconnected, unintelligible. ▷ INARTICULATE. *Opp* COHERENT.

incombustible adj fireproof, fire-resistant, flameproof, non-flammable. *Opp* COMBUSTIBLE.

income n earnings, interest, pay, proceeds, profits, receipts, revenue, salary, takings, wages. *Opp* EXPENSE.

incoming adj 1 approaching, arriving, entering, landing, new, next. 2 *incoming tide.* flowing, rising. *Opp* OUTGOING.

incompatible adj at variance, clashing, conflicting, contradictory, contrasting, different, discordant, incongruous, inconsistent, irreconcilable, mismatched, opposed, unsuited. *Opp* COMPATIBLE.

incompetent adj 1 bungling, clumsy, feckless, gauche, helpless, *inf* hopeless, incapable, ineffective, ineffectual, inefficient, unfit, unprofessional, untrained. 2 bungled, inadequate, unsatis-factory, unskilful, useless. *Opp* COMPETENT.

incomplete adj abbreviated, abridged, *inf* bitty, deficient, edited, expurgated, faulty, fragmentary, imperfect, insufficient, partial, selective, sketchy, unfinished, wanting. *Opp* COMPLETE.

incomprehensible adj abstruse, arcane, baffling, beyond comprehension, cryptic, enigmatic, illegible, impenetrable, indecipherable, meaningless, mysterious, mystifying, obscure, opaque, perplexing, puzzling, recondite, strange, unclear, unfathomable, unintelligible. *Opp* COMPREHENSIBLE.

inconceivable adj implausible, incredible, *inf* mind-boggling, staggering, unbelievable, undreamed-of, unimaginable, unthinkable. *Opp* CREDIBLE.

inconclusive adj ambiguous, equivocal, indefinite, open, open-ended, questionable, uncertain, unconvincing, unresolved, *inf* up in the air. *Opp* CONCLUSIVE.

incongruous adj clashing, conflicting, discordant, ill-matched, ill-suited, inappropriate, incompatible, inconsistent, irreconcilable, odd, out of place, surprising, uncoordinated, unsuited. ▷ ABSURD. *Opp* COMPATIBLE.

inconsiderate adj careless, heedless, insensitive, intolerant, negligent, rude, self-centred, selfish, tactless, thoughtless, uncaring, unconcerned, ungracious, unhelpful, unkind, unsympathetic, unthinking. *Opp* CONSIDERATE.

inconsistent adj capricious, changeable, erratic, fickle, patchy, unpredictable, unreliable, unstable, *inf* up-and-down,

variable. ▷ INCOMPATIBLE.
Opp CONSISTENT.

inconspicuous adj camouflaged,
discreet, hidden, insignificant,
in the background, invisible,
modest, ordinary, out of sight,
plain, retiring, unassuming,
unobtrusive. Opp CONSPICUOUS.

inconvenience n annoyance,
bother, discomfort, disruption,
drawback, hindrance, impediment, irritation, nuisance,
trouble. ● v annoy, bother,
disturb, irk, irritate, put out,
trouble.

inconvenient adj annoying,
awkward, bothersome, difficult,
embarrassing, ill-timed, inopportune, irksome, irritating, tiresome, troublesome, unsuitable,
untimely, unwieldy.
Opp CONVENIENT.

incorporate v ▷ INCLUDE.

incorrect adj erroneous, fallacious, false, faulty, imprecise,
inaccurate, inexact, misin-
formed, misleading, mistaken,
specious, untrue. Opp CORRECT.

incorrigible adj confirmed,
inf dyed-in-the-wool, habitual,
hardened, inf hopeless, impenitent, incurable, inveterate, irredeemable, obdurate, shameless,
unalterable, unreformable, unrepentant. ▷ WICKED.

incorruptible adj 1 honest, just,
moral, sound, inf straight, true,
trustworthy, upright.
Opp CORRUPT.
2 ▷ EVERLASTING.

increase n addition, amplifica-
tion, boost, build-up, crescendo,
development, enlargement,
escalation, expansion, extension,
gain, growth, increment, intensi-
fication, proliferation, rise,
spread, upsurge, upturn.

● v 1 add to, advance, amplify,
augment, boost, build up,
develop, enlarge, expand,
extend, lengthen, magnify, maximize, multiply, prolong, put up,
raise, inf step up, strengthen,
stretch, swell. 2 escalate, gain,
grow, intensify, proliferate,
inf snowball, spread.
Opp DECREASE.

incredible adj beyond belief, far-
fetched, implausible, impossible,
improbable, inconceivable,
unconvincing, unlikely,
untenable, unthinkable.
▷ EXTRAORDINARY.
Opp CREDIBLE.

incredulous adj disbelieving,
distrustful, doubtful, dubious,
questioning, sceptical, suspicious, uncertain, unconvinced.
Opp CREDULOUS.

incriminate v accuse, blame,
implicate, involve, inf point the
finger at. Opp EXCUSE.

incur v earn, expose yourself to,
get, lay yourself open to, provoke, run up, suffer.

incurable adj 1 fatal, hopeless,
inoperable, irremediable, irreparable, terminal, untreatable.
Opp CURABLE.
2 ▷ INCORRIGIBLE.

indebted adj beholden, bound,
grateful, obliged, thankful.

indecent adj blue, coarse, crude,
dirty, immodest, impolite,
improper, impure, indelicate,
inf naughty, obscene, offensive,
risqué, rude, smutty, suggestive,
unprintable, unrepeatable,
vulgar. ▷ INDECOROUS.
Opp DECENT.

indecisive adj doubtful, equivocal, inf in two minds, irresolute. ▷ HESITANT, INDEFINITE.

Opp DECISIVE. **be indecisive**
▷ HESITATE.

indecorous *adj* ill-bred, inappropriate, *inf* in bad taste, tasteless, unbecoming, uncouth, undignified, unseemly. ▷ INDECENT.
Opp DECOROUS.

indefensible *adj* insupportable, unjustifiable, unpardonable, untenable, vulnerable, weak.
▷ WRONG.

indefinite *adj* ambiguous, blurred, confused, dim, general, ill-defined, imprecise, indeterminate, inexact, obscure, uncertain, unclear, unsettled, unspecific, unsure, vague.
▷ INDECISIVE. *Opp* DEFINITE.

indelible *adj* ingrained, unfading, unforgettable.
▷ PERMANENT.

indentation *n* cut, dent, depression, dimple, dip, furrow, groove, hollow, nick, notch, pit.

independence *n* 1 autonomy, freedom, individualism, liberty, nonconformity, self-reliance, self-sufficiency. 2 home rule, self-determination, self-government, self-rule, sovereignty.

independent *adj* 1 carefree, *inf* footloose, free, freethinking, nonconformist, non-partisan, open-minded, private, self-reliant, separate, unbiased, unconventional, untrammelled, without ties. 2 autonomous, liberated, neutral, non-aligned, self-determining, self-governing, sovereign.

indescribable *adj* beyond words, indefinable, stunning, unspeakable, unutterable.

indestructible *adj* durable, enduring, eternal, everlasting, immortal, imperishable, lasting,

permanent, solid, strong, tough, unbreakable.

index *n* 1 catalogue, directory, guide, key, register, table (*of contents*). 2 ▷ INDICATOR.

indicate *v* announce, communicate, convey, denote, describe, designate, display, express, give notice of, imply, intimate, make known, manifest, mean, notify, point out, register, reveal, say, show, signal, signify, specify, spell, stand for, suggest, warn.

indication *n* augury, clue, evidence, forewarning, hint, inkling, intimation, omen, portent, sign, signal, suggestion, symptom, token, warning.

indicator *n* clock, dial, display, gauge, marker, meter, needle, pointer, sign, signal.

indifferent *adj* 1 aloof, apathetic, blasé, bored, casual, cold, cool, distant, half-hearted, impassive, insouciant, nonchalant, uncaring, unconcerned, unemotional, unenthusiastic, unimpressed, uninterested, unmoved. ▷ IMPARTIAL.
Opp ENTHUSIASTIC. 2 mediocre, *inf* nothing to write home about, undistinguished. ▷ ORDINARY.
Opp EXCELLENT.

indigestion *n* dyspepsia, flatulence, heartburn.

indignant *adj* annoyed, disgruntled, exasperated, infuriated, irritated, *inf* miffed, *inf* peeved, piqued, put out, upset, vexed. ▷ ANGRY.

indirect *adj* 1 circuitous, devious, long, meandering, oblique, rambling, roundabout, tortuous, twisting, winding, zigzag.
2 ambiguous, backhanded, circumlocutory, disguised, equivocal, euphemistic, evasive,

implicit, implied, oblique. *Opp* DIRECT.

indiscreet *adj* careless, foolish, ill-advised, ill-considered, ill-judged, incautious, injudicious, tactless, undiplomatic, unguarded, unthinking, unwise. *Opp* DISCREET.

indiscriminate *adj* aimless, careless, casual, desultory, general, haphazard, *inf* hit or miss, miscellaneous, mixed, random, uncritical, undifferentiated, undiscriminating, uninformed, unselective, unsystematic, wholesale. *Opp* SELECTIVE.

indispensable *adj* basic, central, compulsory, crucial, essential, imperative, key, necessary, needed, obligatory, required, requisite, vital. *Opp* UNNECESSARY.

indisputable *adj* absolute, accepted, acknowledged, axiomatic, beyond doubt, certain, clear, definite, evident, incontestable, incontrovertible, irrefutable, positive, proved, proven, self-evident, sure, unanswerable, undeniable, undoubted, unquestionable. *Opp* DEBATABLE.

indistinct *adj* bleary, blurred, confused, dim, dull, faint, fuzzy, hazy, ill-defined, indefinite, misty, obscure, shadowy, unclear, vague. **2** muffled, mumbled, muted, slurred, unintelligible. *Opp* DISTINCT.

indistinguishable *adj* alike, identical, interchangeable, the same, twin. *Opp* DIFFERENT.

individual *adj* characteristic, different, distinct, distinctive, exclusive, idiosyncratic, particular, peculiar, personal, private, separate, singular, special, specific, unique. *Opp* COLLECTIVE, GENERAL. ● *n* ▷ PERSON.

indoctrinate *v* brainwash, re-educate. ▷ TEACH.

induce *v* **1** coax, encourage, incite, motivate, persuade, press, prevail on, sway, *inf* talk into, tempt, urge. *Opp* DISCOURAGE. **2** induce *a fever*. bring on, cause, engender, generate, give rise to, lead to, occasion, produce, provoke.

inducement *n* ▷ INCENTIVE.

indulge *v* be indulgent to, cosset, favour, give in to, gratify, humour, mollycoddle, pamper, pander to, spoil, treat. *Opp* DEPRIVE. **indulge in** ▷ ENJOY. **indulge yourself** be self-indulgent, give in to temptation, overdo it, spoil yourself, succumb, yield.

indulgent *adj* compliant, easygoing, fond, forbearing, forgiving, genial, kind, lenient, liberal, patient, permissive, tolerant. *Opp* STRICT.

industrious *adj* assiduous, busy, conscientious, diligent, earnest, energetic, enterprising, hard-working, keen, persistent, productive, sedulous, tireless, unflagging, untiring, zealous. *Opp* LAZY.

industry *n* **1** business, commerce, manufacturing, production, trade. **2** activity, application, commitment, determination, diligence, energy, enterprise, keenness, perseverance, persistence, zeal. ▷ WORK. *Opp* LAZINESS.

inedible *adj* indigestible, nauseating, *inf* off, poisonous, rotten, tough, uneatable, unpalatable. *Opp* EDIBLE.

ineffective adj 1 fruitless, futile, inf hopeless, idle, inadequate, ineffectual, unproductive, unsuccessful, useless, vain, worthless. 2 feeble, incapable, incompetent, ineffectual, inefficient, powerless, shiftless, unenterprising, weak. Opp EFFECTIVE.

inefficient adj 1 uneconomic, wasteful. 2 ▷ INEFFECTIVE. Opp EFFICIENT.

inelegant adj awkward, clumsy, crude, gauche, graceless, inartistic, rough, ungainly, unpolished, unskilful, unstylish. Opp ELEGANT.

ineligible adj disqualified, inf ruled out, unacceptable, unfit, unqualified, unsuitable. Opp ELIGIBLE.

inept adj 1 awkward, bumbling, bungling, clumsy, gauche, incompetent, inexpert, maladroit, unskilful, unskilled. 2 ▷ INAPPROPRIATE.

inequality n contrast, difference, discrepancy, disparity, dissimilarity, imbalance, incongruity. Opp EQUALITY.

inert adj dormant, idle, immobile, inactive, inanimate, lifeless, passive, quiescent, quiet, sluggish, static, still, supine, torpid. Opp LIVELY.

inertia n apathy, idleness, immobility, inactivity, indolence, lassitude, laziness, lethargy, listlessness, numbness, passivity, sluggishness, torpor. Opp LIVELINESS.

inessential adj dispensable, expendable, minor, needless, optional, ornamental, spare, superfluous, unimportant, unnecessary. Opp ESSENTIAL.

inevitable adj inf bound to happen, certain, destined, fated,

inescapable, inexorable, ordained, sure, unavoidable. ▷ RELENTLESS.

inexcusable adj ▷ UNFORGIVABLE.

inexpensive adj ▷ CHEAP.

inexperienced adj inf born yesterday, callow, inf green, immature, inexpert, innocent, naive, new, probationary, raw, unskilled, unsophisticated, untried, inf wet behind the ears, young. Opp EXPERT.

inexplicable adj baffling, bewildering, enigmatic, incomprehensible, insoluble, mysterious, mystifying, perplexing, puzzling, strange, unaccountable, unfathomable, unsolvable. Opp STRAIGHTFORWARD.

infallible adj certain, dependable, faultless, foolproof, perfect, reliable, sound, sure, trustworthy, unerring, unfailing. Opp FALLIBLE.

infamous adj disgraceful, disreputable, notorious, outrageous, well-known. ▷ WICKED.

infant n baby, inf tot. ▷ CHILD.

infantile adj babyish, childish, immature, juvenile, puerile. ▷ SILLY. Opp MATURE.

infatuated adj besotted, in love, obsessed, inf smitten.

infatuation n inf crush, obsession, passion. ▷ LOVE.

infect v blight, contaminate, defile, poison, pollute, spoil, taint. infected ▷ SEPTIC.

infection n contagion, contamination, epidemic, pollution, virus. ▷ ILLNESS.

infectious adj ▷ CONTAGIOUS.

infer v assume, conclude, deduce, derive, draw a conclusion, gather, guess, surmise, understand, work out.

inferior *adj* 1 junior, lesser, lower, menial, secondary, servile, subordinate, unimportant. 2 cheap, indifferent, mediocre, poor, second-class, shoddy, tawdry. *Opp* SUPERIOR.
● *n* ▷ SUBORDINATE.

infertile *adj* barren, sterile, unfruitful, unproductive.

infest *v* infested alive, crawling, swarming, teeming, verminous.

infidelity *n* 1 adultery, unfaithfulness. 2 ▷ DISLOYALTY.

infiltrate *v* enter secretly, intrude, penetrate.

infinite *adj* boundless, countless, endless, eternal, everlasting, immeasurable, immense, incalculable, inexhaustible, innumerable, interminable, limitless, never-ending, numberless, perpetual, uncountable, undefined, unending, unfathomable, unlimited, untold. ▷ HUGE. *Opp* FINITE.

infinity *n* eternity, infinitude, perpetuity, space.

infirm *adj* feeble, frail, lame, old, poorly, sickly, unwell. ▷ ILL, WEAK. *Opp* HEALTHY.

inflame *v* arouse, encourage, excite, fire, foment, ignite, incense, kindle, rouse, stimulate, stir up, work up. ▷ ANGER. *Opp* COOL. **inflamed** ▷ PASSIONATE, SEPTIC.

inflammable *adj* burnable, combustible, flammable, volatile. *Opp* INCOMBUSTIBLE.

inflammation *n* abscess, boil, infection, irritation, redness, sore, soreness, swelling.

inflate *v* 1 blow up, dilate, distend, enlarge, puff up, pump up, swell. 2 ▷ EXAGGERATE.

inflexible *adj* 1 firm, hard, hardened, immovable, rigid, solid, stiff, unbending, unyielding. 2 adamant, entrenched, fixed, immutable, intractable, intransigent, obdurate, obstinate, *inf* pig-headed, resolute, rigorous, strict, stubborn, unchangeable, uncompromising. *Opp* FLEXIBLE.

inflict *v* administer, apply, deal out, enforce, force, impose, mete out, perpetrate, wreak.

influence *n* authority, control, direction, dominance, effect, guidance, hold, impact, leverage, power, pressure, pull, sway.
● *v* 1 affect, change, control, direct, dominate, guide, impinge on, impress, manipulate, modify, motivate, move, persuade, prejudice, prompt, stir, sway. 2 bribe, corrupt, lead astray, suborn, tempt.

influential *adj* authoritative, compelling, convincing, dominant, effective, far-reaching, forceful, guiding, important, inspiring, leading, persuasive, powerful, significant, strong, telling, weighty. *Opp* UNIMPORTANT.

influx *n* flood, flow, inflow, inundation, invasion, rush, stream.

inform *v* advise, apprise, brief, enlighten, *inf* fill in, give information to, instruct, leak, notify, *inf* put in the picture, teach, tell, tip off. **inform against** ▷ BETRAY. **informed** ▷ KNOWLEDGEABLE.

informal *adj* 1 casual, comfortable, cosy, easy, easygoing, everyday, familiar, *inf* free and

easy, friendly, homely, natural, ordinary, relaxed, simple, unceremonious, unofficial, unpretentious, unsophisticated.
2 *informal language*. chatty, colloquial, slangy, vernacular. *Opp* FORMAL.

information *n* 1 announcement, briefing, bulletin, communication, instruction, message, news, report, statement, tip-off, word. 2 data, evidence, facts, intelligence, knowledge, statistics.

informative *adj* communicative, edifying, educational, enlightening, factual, helpful, illuminating, instructive, meaningful, revealing, useful. *Opp* MEANINGLESS.

informer *n sl* grass, informant, spy, *inf* tell-tale, traitor.

infrequent *adj* exceptional, intermittent, irregular, occasional, *inf* once in a blue moon, rare, spasmodic, uncommon, unusual. *Opp* FREQUENT.

infringe *v* ▷ VIOLATE.

ingenious *adj* adroit, artful, astute, brilliant, clever, crafty, creative, cunning, deft, imaginative, inspired, intelligent, intricate, inventive, original, resourceful, shrewd, skilful, *inf* smart, subtle. *Opp* UNIMAGINATIVE.

ingenuous *adj* artless, childlike, frank, guileless, honest, innocent, naive, open, plain, simple, trusting, unaffected, unsophisticated. *Opp* SOPHISTICATED.

ingredient *n* component, constituent, element, factor, *pl* makings, part.

inhabit *v* colonize, dwell in, live in, occupy, people, populate, possess, reside in, settle in, set up home in.

inhabitable *adj* habitable, in good repair, usable.

inhabitant *n* citizen, denizen, dweller, inmate, native, occupant, occupier, *pl* population, resident, settler, tenant, *pl* townspeople.

inherent *adj* congenital, essential, fundamental, hereditary, inborn, ingrained, intrinsic, native, natural.

inherit *v* be left, *inf* come into, receive as an inheritance, succeed to. **inherited** ▷ HEREDITARY.

inheritance *n* bequest, birthright, estate, fortune, heritage, legacy, patrimony.

inhibit *v* check, curb, discourage, frustrate, hinder, hold back, prevent, repress, restrain. **inhibited** ▷ REPRESSED, SHY.

inhibition *n* 1 bar, barrier, check, constraint, curb, impediment, restraint. 2 diffidence, *inf* hang-up, repression, reserve, self-consciousness, shyness.

inhospitable *adj* standoffish, unsociable, unwelcoming. ▷ UNFRIENDLY. 2 bleak, cold, comfortless, desolate, hostile, lonely. *Opp* HOSPITABLE.

inhuman *adj* barbaric, bestial, bloodthirsty, brutish, diabolical, fiendish, merciless, pitiless, ruthless, savage, unnatural, vicious. ▷ INHUMANE. *Opp* HUMAN.

inhumane *adj* cruel, hardhearted, heartless, inconsiderate, insensitive, uncaring, uncharitable, uncivilized, unfeeling, unkind, unsympathetic. ▷ INHUMAN. *Opp* HUMANE.

initial *adj* beginning, first, inaugural, introductory, opening, ori-

ginal, primary, starting.
Opp FINAL.

initiate v ▷ BEGIN.

initiative n ambition, drive, dynamism, enterprise, inf get-up-and-go, inventiveness, lead, leadership, originality, resourcefulness. **take the initiative** ▷ INITIATE.

injection n inf fix, inoculation, inf jab, vaccination.

injure v break, crush, cut, damage, deface, disfigure, harm, hurt, ill-treat, mar, ruin, spoil. ▷ WOUND.

injurious adj 1 damaging, destructive, detrimental, harmful, ruinous. 2 ▷ ABUSIVE.

injury n damage, harm, hurt, mischief. ▷ WOUND.

injustice n bias, bigotry, discrimination, dishonesty, favouritism, inequality, inequity, onesidedness, oppression, partiality, partisanship, prejudice, unfairness, unlawfulness, wrong. Opp JUSTICE.

inn n hostelry, hotel, inf local, pub, tavern.

inner adj central, hidden, innermost, inside, interior, internal, inward, middle, private, secret. Opp OUTER.

innocence n 1 goodness, honesty, purity, righteousness, virtue. 2 [derog] gullibility, inexperience, naivety.

innocent adj 1 above suspicion, blameless, faultless, free from blame, guiltless. Opp GUILTY. 2 pure, righteous, sinless, virtuous. Opp CORRUPT. 3 artless, childlike, credulous, inf green, guileless, gullible, inexperienced, ingenuous, naive, simple, trusting, unsophisticated.

innovation n change, departure, new feature, novelty, reform.

innovator n discoverer, inventor, pioneer, reformer.

innumerable adj countless, many, numberless, uncountable, untold. ▷ INFINITE.

inquest n hearing. ▷ INQUIRY.

inquire v investigate, probe, search, seek information, survey. ▷ ENQUIRE.

inquiry n cross-examination, examination, inquest, inquisition, interrogation, investigation, inf post-mortem, probe, review, study, survey.

inquisitive adj curious, inquiring, interfering, intrusive, investigative, meddlesome, meddling, inf nosy, probing, prying, questioning, inf snooping, spying. **be inquisitive** ▷ PRY.

insane adj crazy, deranged, lunatic, inf mental, psychotic, unhinged. ▷ MAD. Opp SANE.

inscription n dedication, engraving, writing.

insect n inf bug, inf creepy-crawly.

insecure adj 1 dangerous, flimsy, loose, precarious, rickety, rocky, shaky, unsafe, unstable, unsteady, unsupported, weak, wobbly. 2 insecure feeling. anxious, apprehensive, defenceless, exposed, open, uncertain, unconfident, vulnerable, worried. Opp SECURE.

insensible adj anaesthetized, inf dead to the world, inert, insentient, knocked out, numb, inf out, unaware, unconscious. Opp CONSCIOUS.

insensitive adj 1 dead, numb, unresponsive. 2 boorish, callous, crass, cruel, obtuse, tactless,

inseparable *adj* 1 indissoluble, indivisible, integral. 2 close, devoted, intimate.

insert *v* embed, implant, introduce, place in, *inf* pop in, push in, put in, tuck in.

inside *adj* central, indoor, inner, interior, internal. ● *n* centre, contents, core, heart, indoors, interior, middle. *Opp* OUTSIDE.
    insides ▷ ENTRAILS.

insidious *adj* creeping, furtive, stealthy, subtle, surreptitious, treacherous. ▷ CRAFTY.

insignificant *adj* forgettable, irrelevant, insubstantial, lightweight, meaningless, minor, negligible, paltry, small, trifling, trivial, unimpressive, valueless, worthless, unimportant. *Opp* SIGNIFICANT.

insincere *adj* deceitful, deceptive, devious, dishonest, false, feigned, flattering, disingenuous, hollow, hypocritical, lying, *inf* mealy-mouthed, *inf* phoney, pretended, *inf* put on, *inf* smarmy, sycophantic, *inf* two-faced, untrue, untruthful. *Opp* SINCERE.

insist *v* 1 assert, aver, declare, emphasize, hold, maintain, state, stress, swear, vow. 2 assert yourself, persist, *inf* put your foot down, stand firm. **insist on** ▷ DEMAND.

insistent *adj* assertive, demanding, dogged, emphatic, firm, forceful, importunate, persistent, relentless, repeated, unremitting, urgent.

insolence *n* arrogance, boldness, cheek, disrespect, effrontery, impertinence, impudence, insub-ordination, *inf* lip, presumptuousness, rudeness, *inf* sauce.

insolent *adj* arrogant, audacious, bold, brazen, cheeky, contemptuous, defiant, disdainful, forward, *inf* fresh, impertinent, impudent, insubordinate, insulting, pert, presumptuous, sneering. ▷ RUDE. *Opp* POLITE.

insoluble *adj* baffling, enigmatic, incomprehensible, inexplicable, mystifying, puzzling, strange, unaccountable, unfathomable. *Opp* SOLUBLE.

insolvent *adj* bankrupt, *inf* bust, failed, ruined. ▷ POOR.

inspect *v* check, examine, *sl* give it the once over, investigate, peruse, scan, scrutinize, study, survey, vet.

inspection *n* check, examination, *inf* going-over, investigation, review, scrutiny, survey.

inspector *n* controller, examiner, investigator, official, superintendent, supervisor.

inspiration *n* 1 creativity, genius, imagination, muse. 2 enthusiasm, impulse, incitement, spur, stimulation, stimulus. 3 *sudden inspiration*. brainwave, idea, insight, revelation, thought.

inspire *v* activate, animate, arouse, awaken, encourage, energize, enthuse, fire, galvanize, influence, inspirit, instigate, kindle, motivate, prompt, set off, spark off, spur, stimulate, stir, support.

instability *n* capriciousness, change, fickleness, fluctuation, flux, impermanence, inconstancy, insecurity, precariousness, shakiness, transience, uncertainty, unpredictability, unreliability, unsteadiness, *inf* ups-and-downs, variability, variations, weakness. *Opp* STABILITY.

install *v* ensconce, establish, fit, fix, introduce, place, plant, position, put in, settle, set up, station. *Opp* REMOVE.

instalment *n* 1 payment, rent, rental. 2 chapter, episode, part.

instance *n* ▷ EXAMPLE.

instant *adj* direct, fast, immediate, instantaneous, on-the-spot, prompt, quick, rapid, speedy, swift, unhesitating, urgent.
● *n* ▷ MOMENT.

instigate *v* activate, begin, cause, encourage, foment, generate, incite, initiate, inspire, kindle, prompt, provoke, set up, start, stimulate, stir up, urge, *inf* whip up.

instigator *n* agitator, initiator, leader, mischief-maker, ringleader, troublemaker.

instil *v inf* din into, imbue, implant, inculcate, indoctrinate, introduce.

instinct *n* bent, faculty, feel, feeling, hunch, impulse, inclination, intuition, presentiment, sixth sense, tendency, urge.

instinctive *adj* automatic, *inf* gut, impulsive, inborn, inherent, innate, intuitive, involuntary, natural, reflex, spontaneous, unconscious, unreasoning, unthinking. *Opp* DELIBERATE.

institute *n* ▷ INSTITUTION.
● *v* begin, create, establish, found, inaugurate, initiate, introduce, launch, open, organize, originate, pioneer, set up, start.

institution *n* 1 creation, formation, inauguration, inception, initiation, introduction.

setting-up. 2 academy, asylum, college, establishment, foundation, home, hospital, institute, organization, school, *inf* set-up. 3 convention, custom, habit, practice, ritual, routine, rule, tradition.

instruct *v* 1 ▷ TEACH. 2 authorize, command, direct, enjoin, order, tell.

instruction *n* 1 briefing, coaching, demonstration, drill, education, guidance, indoctrination, lecture, schooling, teaching, training, tuition. 2 authorization, command, direction, directive, order.

instructive *adj* didactic, edifying, educational, enlightening, helpful, illuminating, improving, informative, revealing.

instructor *n* coach, teacher, trainer, tutor.

instrument *n* apparatus, appliance, contraption, device, gadget, implement, machine, mechanism, tool, utensil.

instrumental *adj* active, advantageous, beneficial, contributory, helpful, influential, supportive, useful, valuable.

insubordinate *adj* defiant, disobedient, mutinous, rebellious, undisciplined, unruly.
▷ IMPERTINENT. *Opp* OBEDIENT.

insufficient *adj* deficient, inadequate, meagre, mean, niggardly, *inf* pathetic, poor, scanty, scarce, short, sparse, unsatisfactory. *Opp* EXCESSIVE, SUFFICIENT.

insular *adj* closed, limited, narrow, narrow-minded, parochial, provincial. *Opp* BROAD-MINDED, COSMOPOLITAN.

insulate *v* 1 cocoon, cover, cushion, enclose, lag, protect, shield,

surround, wrap up.
2 ▷ ISOLATE.

insult n abuse, affront, aspersion, defamation, indignity, libel, inf put-down, slander, slight, slur, snub. • v abuse, be rude to, inf call names, defame, dishonour, disparage, libel, mock, offend, patronize, revile, slander, slight, sneer at, snub, vilify. Opp COMPLIMENT.

insulting ▷ RUDE.

insuperable adj insurmountable, overwhelming, unconquerable. ▷ IMPOSSIBLE.

insurance n assurance, cover, guarantee, indemnity, protection, security.

insure v cover yourself, protect, take out insurance.

intact adj complete, unbroken, undamaged, whole. ▷ PERFECT.

intangible adj abstract, airy, disembodied, elusive, ethereal, impalpable, incorporeal, indefinite, insubstantial, invisible, shadowy, unreal, vague. Opp TANGIBLE.

integral adj 1 basic, essential, fundamental, indispensable, intrinsic, requisite. 2 complete, full, indivisible, whole. Opp SEPARATE.

integrate v amalgamate, blend, bring together, combine; consolidate, desegregate, fuse, harmonize, join, knit, merge, mix, unify, unite, weld. Opp SEPARATE.

integrity n 1 decency, fidelity, goodness, honesty, honour, incorruptibility, loyalty, morality, principle, probity, rectitude, righteousness, sincerity, trustworthiness, uprightness, virtue. 2 ▷ UNITY.

intellect n ▷ INTELLIGENCE.

intellectual adj 1 academic, inf bookish, cerebral, cultured, educated, scholarly, studious, thoughtful. ▷ INTELLIGENT. 2 cultural, deep, difficult, highbrow, improving. • n academic, inf egghead, genius, highbrow, inf one of the intelligentsia, thinker.

intelligence n 1 ability, acumen, astuteness, brainpower, brains, brilliance, capacity, cleverness, discernment, genius, insight, intellect, judgement, mind, inf nous, perceptiveness, perspicacity, reason, sagacity, sense, sharpness, shrewdness, understanding, wisdom, wit, wits. 2 data, facts, information, knowledge, inf low-down, news, notification, report, tip-off, warning. 3 espionage, secret service, spying.

intelligent adj able, acute, alert, astute, inf brainy, bright, brilliant, canny, clever, discerning, intellectual, knowing, penetrating, perceptive, perspicacious, profound, quick, rational, sagacious, sharp, shrewd, inf smart, thoughtful, trenchant, wise, inf with it. Opp STUPID.

intelligible adj clear, comprehensible, decipherable, legible, logical, lucid, meaningful, plain, straightforward, unambiguous, understandable. Opp INCOMPREHENSIBLE.

intend v aim, contemplate, design, determine, have in mind, mean, plan, plot, propose, purpose, resolve, scheme.

intense adj 1 ardent, burning, consuming, deep, eager, earnest, fanatical, fervent, impassioned, passionate, powerful, profound

serious, strong, vehement, violent. *Opp* COOL, HALF-HEARTED.
2 *intense pain*. acute, agonizing, excruciating, extreme, fierce, great, harsh, keen, severe, sharp. *Opp* SLIGHT.

intensify *v* add to, aggravate, augment, boost, build up, deepen, emphasize, escalate, fire, fuel, heighten, *inf* hot up, increase, magnify, quicken, raise, redouble, reinforce, sharpen, *inf* step up, strengthen, whet. *Opp* REDUCE.

intensive *adj inf* all-out, concentrated, detailed, exhaustive, thorough, unremitting.

intent *adj* absorbed, attentive, committed, concentrating, determined, eager, engrossed, focused, keen, occupied, preoccupied, rapt, resolute, set, steadfast, watchful. *Opp* CASUAL.
● *n* ▷ INTENTION.

intention *n* aim, ambition, design, end, goal, intent, object, objective, plan, point, purpose.

intentional *adj* calculated, conscious, contrived, deliberate, designed, intended, planned, pre-arranged, premeditated, prepared, studied, wilful. *Opp* ACCIDENTAL.

intercept *v* ambush, arrest, block, catch, check, cut off, deflect, head off, impede, obstruct, stop, thwart, trap.

intercourse *n* **1** communication, conversation, dealings, interaction, traffic. **2** *sexual intercourse*. copulation, love-making. ▷ SEX.

interest *n* **1** attention, attentiveness, care, commitment, concern, curiosity, involvement, notice, regard. **2** *of no interest*. consequence, importance, note, significance, value. **3** *leisure*

interest. activity, diversion, hobby, pastime, pursuit, relaxation. ● *v* absorb, appeal to, attract, captivate, capture the imagination of, concern, divert, enchant, engage, engross, entertain, enthral, fascinate, intrigue, involve, preoccupy, *inf* turn on. ▷ EXCITE. *Opp* BORE.

interested *adj* **1** absorbed, attentive, curious, engrossed, enthusiastic, immersed, intent, keen, preoccupied, rapt, responsive, riveted. *Opp* UNINTERESTED. **2** concerned, involved. ▷ BIASED. *Opp* DISINTERESTED.

interesting *adj* absorbing, challenging, compelling, curious, engaging, engrossing, entertaining, enthralling, fascinating, gripping, intriguing, original, piquant, riveting, stimulating, unpredictable, unusual, varied. *Opp* BORING.

interfere *v* be a busybody, butt in, interrupt, intervene, intrude, meddle, *inf* poke your nose in, pry, tamper. **interfere with** ▷ OBSTRUCT. **interfering** ▷ NOSY.

interim *adj* half-time, provisional, stopgap, temporary.

interior *adj* ▷ INTERNAL.
● *n* centre, core, depths, heart, inside, middle, nucleus.

interlude *n* intermission. ▷ INTERVAL.

intermediary *n* go-between, spokesperson. ▷ MEDIATOR.

intermediate *adj* halfway, intermediary, intervening, middle, midway, transitional.

intermittent *adj* discontinuous, fitful, irregular, occasional, *inf* on and off, periodic, random, recurrent, spasmodic, sporadic. *Opp* CONTINUOUS.

internal *adj* 1 inner, inside, interior. *Opp* EXTERNAL.
2 confidential, personal, private, secret.

international *adj* cosmopolitan, global, universal, worldwide.

interpret *v* clarify, decipher, decode, define, elucidate, explain, expound, gloss, make sense of, paraphrase, rephrase, reword, simplify, sort out, translate, understand, unravel.

interpretation *n* clarification, definition, elucidation, explanation, gloss, paraphrase, reading, rendering, translation, understanding, version.

interrogation *n* cross-examination, debriefing, examination, grilling, inquisition, questioning, *inf* third degree.

interrupt *v* 1 break in, butt in, *inf* chip in, cut in, disrupt, disturb, heckle, hold up, interfere, intervene, intrude, obstruct, spoil. 2 break off, cut off, cut short, discontinue, halt, stop, suspend, terminate.

interruption *n* break, check, disruption, division, gap, halt, hiatus, interference, intrusion, stop, suspension. ▷ INTERVAL.

intersect *v* converge, criss-cross, cross, divide, meet.

interval *n* 1 adjournment, break, *inf* breather, breathing-space, delay, gap, hiatus, lapse, lull, opening, pause, recess, respite, rest, space, wait. 2 interlude, intermezzo, intermission.

intervene *v* 1 elapse, occur, pass. 2 arbitrate, butt in, intercede, interfere, interrupt, intrude, mediate, *inf* step in.

interview *n* appraisal, audience, meeting, selection procedure.
● *v* appraise, ask questions, evaluate, examine, interrogate, question, sound out, vet.

interweave *v* criss-cross, entwine, interlace, intertwine, knit, tangle, weave together.

intestines *pl n* bowels, entrails, *inf* innards, insides, offal.

intimate *adj* 1 close, familiar, informal, loving, sexual.
▷ FRIENDLY. 2 *intimate details*. confidential, detailed, personal, private, secret. ● *n* ▷ FRIEND.
● *v* ▷ INDICATE.

intimidate *v* browbeat, bully, coerce, cow, daunt, dismay, frighten, hector, menace, persecute, scare, terrify, terrorize, threaten, tyrannize.

intolerable *adj* impossible, insufferable, insupportable, unbearable, unendurable.
Opp TOLERABLE.

intolerant *adj* biased, bigoted, chauvinistic, discriminatory, dogmatic, narrow-minded, opinionated, prejudiced, racist, sexist, xenophobic.
Opp TOLERANT.

intonation *n* accent, inflection, modulation, pronunciation, sound, speech pattern, tone.

intoxicate *v* addle, inebriate, make drunk, stupefy. **intoxicated** ▷ DRUNK, EXCITED. **intoxicating** ▷ ALCOHOLIC, EXCITING.

intricate *adj* complex, complicated, convoluted, delicate, detailed, elaborate, *inf* fiddly, involved, *inf* knotty, labyrinthine, ornate, sophisticated, tangled, tortuous. *Opp* SIMPLE.

intrigue *n* ▷ PLOT. ● *v* 1 appeal to, arouse the curiosity of, attract, captivate, capture the interest of, engage, engross, fascinate, interest, stimulate. *Opp* BORE.

intrinsic *adj* basic, essential, fundamental, inborn, inbuilt, inherent, native, natural, proper, real.

introduce *v* 1 acquaint, make known, present. 2 announce, lead into, preface. 3 add, advance, bring in, broach, create, establish, inaugurate, initiate, inject, insert, interpose, launch, offer, phase in, pioneer, put forward, set up, start, suggest, usher in. ▷ BEGIN.

introduction *n* foreword, *inf* intro, *inf* lead-in, overture, preamble, preface, prologue. ▷ BEGINNING.

introductory *adj* basic, early, first, inaugural, initial, opening, preliminary, preparatory, starting. *Opp* FINAL.

introverted *adj* introspective, inward-looking, pensive, quiet, reserved, retiring, self-contained, shy, unsociable, withdrawn. *Opp* EXTROVERTED.

intrude *v* break in, butt in, eavesdrop, encroach, gatecrash, interfere, interrupt, intervene, *inf* snoop.

intruder *n* burglar, gatecrasher, interloper, invader, prowler, raider, robber, *inf* snooper, thief, trespasser, *inf* uninvited guest.

intuition *n* insight. ▷ INSTINCT.

invade *v* descend on, encroach on, enter, impinge on, infest, infringe, march into, occupy, overrun, penetrate, raid, subdue, violate. ▷ ATTACK.

invalid *adj* 1 null and void, out-of-date, unacceptable, unusable,

void, worthless. 2 false, illogical, incorrect, irrational, spurious, unfounded, unsound, untenable, untrue, wrong. *Opp* VALID. 3 ▷ ILL. ● *n* patient, sufferer.

invaluable *adj* incalculable, precious, priceless, useful. ▷ VALUABLE. *Opp* WORTHLESS.

invariable *adj* certain, constant, eternal, even, immutable, inflexible, predictable, regular, reliable, rigid, stable, steady, unalterable, unchangeable, unchanging, unfailing, uniform, unvarying, unwavering. *Opp* VARIABLE.

invasion *n* 1 encroachment, incursion, infiltration, inroad, intrusion, raid, violation. ▷ ATTACK. 2 infestation, spate, swarm.

invasive *adj* increasing, mushrooming, proliferating, relentless, unstoppable.

invent *v* coin, conceive, concoct, contrive, *inf* cook up, create, design, devise, discover, *inf* dream up, fabricate, formulate, *inf* hit upon, imagine, improvise, make up, originate, plan, think up.

invention *n* 1 brainchild, contrivance, creation, design, discovery. 2 contraption, device, gadget. 3 fabrication, falsehood, fantasy, fiction, lie. 4 ▷ INVENTIVENESS.

inventive *adj* clever, creative, fertile, imaginative, ingenious, innovative, inspired, original, resourceful. *Opp* BANAL.

inventiveness *n* creativity, genius, imagination, ingenuity, originality, resourcefulness.

inventor *n* architect, author, creator, designer, discoverer, maker, originator.

inverse *adj* opposite, reversed.

invert *v* capsize, overturn, reverse, transpose, upset.

invest *v* 1 buy stocks and shares, speculate. 2 lay out, use profitably, venture. **invest in** ▷ BUY.

investigate *v* consider, examine, explore, follow up, gather evidence about, *inf* go into, inquire into, look into, probe, research, scrutinize, study.

investigation *n* enquiry, examination, inquiry, inquisition, inspection, *inf* post-mortem, probe, research, review, scrutiny, study, survey.

invidious *adj* discriminatory, offensive, unfair, unjust.

invigorating *adj* bracing, enlivening, exhilarating, fresh, refreshing, rejuvenating, revitalizing, stimulating, tonic, vitalizing. *Opp* EXHAUSTING.

invincible *adj* impregnable, indestructible, indomitable, invulnerable, strong, unassailable, unbeatable, unconquerable, unstoppable.

invisible *adj* camouflaged, concealed, covered, disguised, hidden, imperceptible, inconspicuous, out of sight, secret, undetectable, unnoticed, unseen. *Opp* VISIBLE.

invite *v* 1 ask, encourage, request, summon, urge. 2 attract, entice, solicit, tempt. **inviting** ▷ ATTRACTIVE.

invoice *n* account, bill, statement.

invoke *v* appeal to, call for, cry out for, entreat, implore, pray for, solicit, supplicate.

involuntary *adj* automatic, instinctive, mechanical, reflex, spontaneous, unconscious, uncontrollable, unintentional, unthinking. *Opp* DELIBERATE.

involve *v* 1 comprise, contain, entail, hold, include, incorporate, take in. 2 affect, concern, interest, touch. 3 *involve in crime*. embroil, implicate, include, incriminate, *inf* mix up. **involved** ▷ BUSY, COMPLEX.

involvement *n* 1 interest, participation. 2 association, complicity, entanglement, partnership.

ironic *adj* derisive, double-edged, ironical, sarcastic, satirical, wry.

irony *n* double meaning, paradox, sarcasm, satire.

irrational *adj* absurd, arbitrary, crazy, emotional, illogical, nonsensical, senseless, subjective, surreal, unconvincing, unreasonable, unreasoning, unsound, unthinking, wild. ▷ SILLY. *Opp* RATIONAL.

irregular *adj* 1 erratic, fitful, fluctuating, haphazard, intermittent, occasional, random, spasmodic, sporadic, unequal, unpredictable, variable, varying, wavering. 2 abnormal, anomalous, eccentric, exceptional, extraordinary, improper, odd, peculiar, quirky, unconventional, unofficial, unplanned, unusual. 3 *irregular surface*. broken, bumpy, jagged, lumpy, patchy, pitted, ragged, rough, uneven. *Opp* REGULAR.

irrelevant *adj* *inf* beside the point, extraneous, immaterial, inapplicable, inapposite, inappropriate, inessential, *inf* neither here nor there, unnecessary, unrelated. *Opp* RELEVANT.

irreligious *adj* agnostic, atheistic, godless, heathen, humanist, impious, irreverent, pagan, uncommitted, ungodly, wicked. Opp RELIGIOUS.

irreparable *adj* hopeless, incurable, irremediable, irretrievable, irreversible, permanent.

irreplaceable *adj* inimitable, priceless, unique. ▷ RARE.

irrepressible *adj* bouncy, *inf* bubbling, buoyant, ebullient, uncontrollable, uninhibited, unmanageable, unstoppable. ▷ LIVELY. Opp LETHARGIC.

irresistible *adj* compelling, inescapable, inexorable, not to be denied, overpowering, overriding, overwhelming, persuasive, powerful, relentless, seductive, strong, unavoidable. Opp WEAK.

irresolute *adj* doubtful, indecisive, tentative, uncertain, undecided, vacillating, wavering, weak, weak-willed. ▷ HESITANT. Opp RESOLUTE.

irresponsible *adj* careless, devil-may-care, feckless, immature, inconsiderate, negligent, rash, reckless, shiftless, thoughtless, unethical, unreliable, unthinking, untrustworthy, wild. Opp RESPONSIBLE.

irreverent *adj* disrespectful, mocking, profane, sacrilegious. ▷ RUDE. Opp REVERENT.

irrevocable *adj* binding, final, fixed, hard and fast, permanent, settled, unalterable, unchangeable.

irrigate *v* flood, inundate, supply water to, water.

irritable *adj* cantankerous, crabby, cross, crotchety, curmud-

geonly, dyspeptic, edgy, fractious, grumpy, impatient, irascible, peevish, petulant, *inf* prickly, querulous, *inf* ratty, short-tempered, snappy, testy, tetchy, touchy, waspish. ▷ ANGRY. Opp EVEN-TEMPERED.

irritate *v* 1 chafe, itch, rub, tickle, tingle. 2 ▷ ANNOY.

island *n pl* archipelago, atoll, coral reef, isle, islet.

isolate *v* cordon off, cut off, detach, insulate, keep apart, quarantine, seclude, segregate, separate, set apart, shut off, shut out, single out. **isolated** ▷ SOLITARY.

issue *n* 1 affair, argument, controversy, dispute, matter, problem, question, subject, topic. 2 consequence, effect, end, impact, outcome, repercussions, result, upshot. 3 *issue of a magazine*. copy, edition, instalment, number, publication, version. ● *v* 1 appear, emerge, erupt, flow out, gush, leak, rise, spring. 2 bring out, broadcast, circulate, disseminate, distribute, give out, make public, print, produce, publish, put out, release, send out, supply.

itch *n* 1 irritation, prickling, tickle, tingling. 2 ache, craving, desire, hankering, hunger, impatience, impulse, longing, need, thirst, urge, wish, yearning, *inf* yen. ● *v* 1 prickle, tickle, tingle. 2 ▷ DESIRE.

item *n* 1 article, bit, component, entry, ingredient, lot, matter, object, particular, thing. 2 *item in a newspaper*. article, feature, notice, piece, report.

J

jab *v* dig, elbow, nudge, poke, prod, stab, thrust. ▷ HIT.

jacket *n* casing, cover, covering, envelope, folder, sheath, skin, wrapper, wrapping. ▷ COAT.

jaded *adj* 1 ▷ WEARY. 2 bored, fed up, gorged, listless, sated, satiated. *Opp* LIVELY.

jagged *adj* angular, barbed, broken, indented, irregular, ragged, rough, serrated, sharp, snagged, spiky, toothed, uneven, zigzag. *Opp* SMOOTH.

jail, jailer *ns* ▷ GAOL, GAOLER.

jam *n* 1 blockage, bottleneck, congestion, crush. ▷ CROWD. 2 difficulty, dilemma, *inf* fix, *inf* hole, *inf* pickle, plight, predicament, quandary, tight corner, trouble. 3 conserve, jelly, marmalade, preserve.
● *v* 1 block, *inf* bung up, clog, congest, cram, crowd, crush, force, pack, obstruct, ram, squash, squeeze, stop up, stuff. 2 prop, stick, wedge.

jar *n* carafe, crock, ewer, glass, jug, mug, pitcher, pot, receptacle, urn, vessel. ● *v* 1 jerk, jog, jolt, shake, shock. 2 *That noise jars on me.* grate. ▷ ANNOY.

jarring ▷ HARSH.

jargon *n* dialect, idiom, language, patois, slang, vernacular.

jaunt *n* excursion, expedition, outing, tour, trip. ▷ JOURNEY.

jaunty *adj* breezy, buoyant, carefree, debonair, frisky, lively, perky, spirited, sprightly. ▷ HAPPY.

jazzy *adj* 1 ▷ LIVELY. *Opp* SEDATE. 2 *jazzy colours.* bold, clashing, contrasting, flashy, gaudy, loud.

jealous *adj* 1 bitter, covetous, envious, *inf* green-eyed, *inf* green with envy, grudging, resentful. 2 *jealous of your reputation.* careful, possessive, protective, vigilant, watchful.

jeer *v* boo, deride, gibe, heckle, hiss, laugh, make fun (of), mock, scoff, sneer, taunt. ▷ RIDICULE. *Opp* CHEER.

jeopardize *v* gamble, venture. ▷ ENDANGER.

jerk *v* jar, jiggle, jog, jolt, lurch, move suddenly, pluck, pull, rattle, shake, tug, tweak, twitch, wrench, *inf* yank.

jerky *adj* bouncy, bumpy, convulsive, erratic, fitful, jolting, jumpy, rough, shaky, spasmodic, twitchy, uncontrolled, uneven. *Opp* STEADY.

jest *n*, *v* ▷ JOKE.

jester *n* ▷ CLOWN.

jet *adj* ▷ BLACK. ● *n* 1 flow, fountain, gush, rush, spout, spray, spurt, stream. 2 nozzle, sprinkler.

jetty *n* breakwater, landing stage, pier, quay, wharf.

jewel *n* brilliant, gem, gemstone, ornament, precious stone, *inf* rock, *inf* sparkler.

jeweller *n* goldsmith, silversmith.

jewellery *n* gems, jewels, ornaments, treasure, *inf* sparklers.

jilt *v* abandon, desert, *inf* ditch, drop, *inf* dump, forsake, *inf* leave in the lurch, renounce, repudiate, *inf* throw over.

jingle *n* 1 doggerel, rhyme, song, tune, verse. 2 chinking, clinking,

jangling, ringing, tinkling.
● v chime, chink, clink, jangle, ring, tinkle.

job n **1** activity, assignment, chore, duty, errand, function, mission, pursuit, responsibility, role, stint, task, undertaking, work. **2** appointment, calling, career, craft, employment, livelihood, métier, occupation, position, post, profession, situation, trade, vocation.

jobless adj out of work, redundant, unemployed, unwaged.

jocular adj cheerful, gay, glad, gleeful, happy, joking, jolly, jovial, merry, overjoyed.
Opp SAD, SERIOUS.

jog v **1** bounce, jar, jerk, joggle, jolt, knock, nudge, shake. ▷ HIT. **2** jog the memory. prompt, refresh, remind, set off, stimulate, stir. **3** run, trot.

join n connection, joint, knot, link, seam. ● v **1** add, amalgamate, attach, combine, connect, couple, dovetail, fit, fix, knit, link, marry, merge, put together, splice, tack on, unite, yoke.
▷ FASTEN. Opp SEPARATE.
2 adjoin, border on, come together, converge, meet, touch. **3** join a crowd. accompany, follow, go with, inf latch on to, tag along with, team up with. **4** join a club. become a member of, enlist in, enrol in, sign up for, subscribe to, volunteer for.
Opp LEAVE.

joint adj collaborative, collective, combined, common, communal, concerted, cooperative, corporate, general, mutual, shared, united. Opp SEPARATE.
● n connection, hinge, junction, union.

joist n beam, girder, rafter.

joke n inf crack, funny story, inf gag, jest, laugh, pleasantry, pun, quip, wisecrack, witticism.
● v banter, be facetious, have a laugh, jest, quip, tease.

jolly adj cheerful, gay, gleeful, grinning, high-spirited, jocular, jovial, laughing, merry, playful, smiling, sportive. ▷ HAPPY.
Opp SAD.

jolt v **1** bounce, bump, jar, jerk, jog, shake. ▷ HIT. **2** astonish, disturb, shake up, shock, startle, stun, surprise.

jostle v crowd in on, hustle, press, push, shove.

jot v jot down note, scribble, take down. ▷ WRITE.

journal n **1** daily, gazette, magazine, monthly, newsletter, newspaper, paper, periodical, review, weekly. **2** chronicle, diary, dossier, history, log, memoir, record, scrapbook.

journalist n broadcaster, columnist, contributor, correspondent, derog hack, inf newshound, reporter, writer.

journey n excursion, expedition, jaunt, mission, odyssey, outing, pilgrimage, progress, ride, route, tour, pl travels, trip, voyage, wandering. ● v ▷ TRAVEL.

joy n bliss, cheer, cheerfulness, delight, ecstasy, elation, euphoria, exhilaration, exultation, felicity, gaiety, gladness, glee, gratification, happiness, high spirits, joyfulness, jubilation, merriment, mirth, pleasure, rapture, rejoicing, triumph.
Opp SORROW.

joyful adj cheerful, ecstatic, elated, euphoric, exhilarated, exultant, gay, glad, gleeful, joyous, jubilant, merry, overjoyed, pleased, rapturous, rejoi-

cing, triumphant. ▷ HAPPY.
Opp SAD.

jubilee n anniversary, celebration, commemoration, festival.

judge n 1 sl beak, justice, magistrate. 2 adjudicator, arbiter, arbitrator, moderator, referee, umpire. 3 authority, connoisseur, critic, expert. • v 1 convict, examine, pass judgement on, sentence, try. 2 adjudicate, mediate, referee, umpire. 3 believe, conclude, consider, decide, decree, deem, determine, estimate, gauge, guess, reckon, rule, suppose. 4 appraise, assess, criticize, evaluate, rate, rebuke, scold, size up, weigh up.

judgement n 1 arbitration, conclusion, conviction, decision, decree, doom, finding, outcome, result, ruling, verdict. 2 use your judgement. common sense, discernment, discretion, discrimination, expertise, reason. ▷ INTELLIGENCE. 3 in my judgement. assessment, belief, estimation, evaluation, idea, impression, opinion, point of view.

judicial adj 1 forensic, legal, official. 2 ▷ JUDICIOUS.

judicious adj appropriate, astute, careful, circumspect, considered, diplomatic, discriminating, enlightened, expedient, judicial, politic, prudent, sensible, shrewd, well-judged. ▷ WISE.

jug n carafe, decanter, ewer, flagon, flask, jar, pitcher.

juggle v alter, falsify, inf fix, manipulate, move about, rearrange, rig.

juice n fluid, liquid, sap.

juicy adj lush, moist, soft, succulent, wet. Opp DRY.

jumble n chaos, clutter, confusion, disarray, disorder, inf hotchpotch, mess, muddle, tangle. • v confuse, disarrange, disorganize, inf mess up, mingle, mix up, muddle, shuffle. Opp ARRANGE.

jump n 1 bounce, bound, hop, leap, pounce, skip, spring, vault. 2 ditch, fence, gap, gate, hurdle, obstacle. 3 jump in prices. ▷ RISE. • v 1 bounce, bound, caper, dance, frisk, frolic, gambol, hop, leap, pounce, prance, skip, spring. 2 jump a fence. clear, hurdle, vault. 3 jump in surprise. flinch, recoil, start, wince. **jump on** ▷ ATTACK. **make someone jump** ▷ STARTLE.

junction n crossroads, interchange, intersection, joining, juncture, inf link-up, meeting, T-junction, union.

jungle n forest, rainforest, tangle, undergrowth, woods.

junior adj inferior, lesser, lower, secondary, subordinate, younger. Opp SENIOR.

junk n clutter, debris, flotsam and jetsam, garbage, litter, oddments, odds and ends, refuse, rubbish, scrap, trash, waste. • v ▷ DISCARD.

just adj apt, deserved, equitable, even-handed, fair, fair-minded, impartial, justified, lawful, legal, legitimate, reasonable, rightful, unbiased, unprejudiced. ▷ MORAL. Opp UNJUST.

justice n 1 equity, even-handedness, fair play, impartiality, integrity, legality, neutrality, objectivity, right. ▷ MORALITY. 2 amends, reparation, redress.

justifiable adj acceptable, defensible, excusable, forgivable, justified, legitimate, pardonable, reasonable, understandable, warranted. *Opp* UNJUSTIFIABLE.

justify v condone, defend, excuse, exonerate, explain, explain away, forgive, pardon, rationalize, substantiate, support, sustain, uphold, validate, vindicate, warrant.

jut v extend, overhang, project, protrude. *Opp* RECEDE.

juvenile adj 1 babyish, childish, immature, infantile, puerile. 2 adolescent, *inf* teenage, underage, young. *Opp* MATURE.

K

keen adj 1 ambitious, ardent, assiduous, avid, bright, clever, committed, dedicated, diligent, eager, enthusiastic, fervent, industrious, intelligent, intent, interested, motivated, quick, zealous. 2 *keen knife*. piercing, razor-sharp, sharp, sharpened. 3 *keen wit*. acute, biting, clever, cutting, discerning, incisive, lively, mordant, rapier-like, sarcastic, satirical, scathing, shrewd, stinging. 4 *keen eyesight*. acute, clear, perceptive. 5 *keen wind*. bitter, cold, icy, intense, penetrating, severe. 6 *keen prices*. competitive, low, rock-bottom. *Opp* APATHETIC, DULL.

keep v 1 conserve, guard, hang on to, hoard, hold, preserve, protect, put aside, retain, safeguard, save, store, stow away, withhold. 2 *keep going*. carry on, continue, keep on, persevere in, persist in. 3 *keep left*. remain, stay. 4 *keep a family*. be responsible for, care for, cherish, feed, foster, guard, have charge of, look after, maintain, manage, mind, own, protect, provide for, support, tend, watch over. 5 *keep a birthday*. celebrate, commemorate, mark, observe. 6 *food keeps in the fridge*. last, stay fresh. 7 *won't keep you*. delay, detain, deter, get in the way of, hamper, hinder, hold up, impede, obstruct, prevent, restrain. **keep still** ▷ STAY. **keep to** ▷ FOLLOW, OBEY. **keep up** ▷ PROLONG, SUSTAIN.

keeper n caretaker, curator, custodian, gaoler, guard, guardian, warden, warder.

kernel n centre, core, essence, heart, middle, nub, pith.

key n 1 answer, clue. explanation, indicator, pointer, secret, solution. 2 *key to a map*. glossary, guide, index.

kick v boot, heel. ▷ HIT.

kidnap v abduct, carry off, run away with, seize, snatch.

kill v annihilate, assassinate, *sl* bump off, butcher, cull, decimate, destroy, *inf* dispatch, *inf* do away with, *sl* do in, execute, exterminate, *inf* finish off, *inf* knock off, massacre, murder, put down, put to death, put to sleep, slaughter, slay, *inf* snuff out.

killer n assassin, butcher, cutthroat, destroyer, executioner, exterminator, gunman, *sl* hit man, murderer, slayer.

killing n annihilation, assassination, bloodbath, bloodshed, butchery, carnage, decimation, destruction, elimination, eradication, euthanasia, execution, extermination, extinction, genocide, homicide, infanticide, manslaughter, massacre, murder, pogrom, regicide, slaughter, suicide, unlawful killing.

kin n clan, family, inf folks, kindred, kith and kin, relations, relatives.

kind adj accommodating, affable, affectionate, agreeable, altruistic, amenable, amiable, amicable, approachable, benevolent, benign, bountiful, caring, charitable, compassionate, considerate, cordial, courteous, favourable, friendly, generous, genial, gentle, good-natured, good-tempered, gracious, helpful, hospitable, humane, indulgent, kindly, lenient, loving, merciful, mild, neighbourly, nice, obliging, patient, philanthropic, pleasant, polite, public-spirited, soft-hearted, sweet, sympathetic, tactful, tender, thoughtful, tolerant, understanding, unselfish, warm, warm-hearted, well-intentioned, well-meaning. *Opp* UNKIND. • n brand, breed, category, class, family, form, genre, genus, make, manner, nature, race, set, sort, species, style, type, variety.

kindle v 1 burn, fire, ignite, light, set alight, set fire to, spark off. 2 ▷ AROUSE.

king n 1 monarch, ruler, sovereign. 2 ▷ CHIEF.

kingdom n country, empire, land, monarchy, realm.

kink n 1 bend, coil, crimp, crinkle, curl, knot, loop, tangle, twist, wave. 2 ▷ QUIRK.

kiosk n booth, stall.

kiss v brush, caress, sl neck, peck, pet, inf smack.

kit n accoutrements, apparatus, baggage, effects, equipment, inf gear, implements, luggage, outfit, paraphernalia, rig, supplies, tackle, tools, utensils.

kitchen n cookhouse, galley, kitchenette, scullery.

knack n aptitude, art, dexterity, facility, flair, talent, trick, inf way. ▷ ABILITY.

knapsack n backpack, haversack, rucksack.

knead v massage, pound, press, pummel, squeeze. work.

kneel v bend, bow, crouch, fall to your knees, genuflect, stoop.

knickers pl n boxer-shorts, briefs, drawers, pants, shorts, trunks, underpants.

knife n blade. • v cut, pierce, slash, stab, wound.

knit v 1 crochet, weave. 2 bind, combine, fasten, heal, interweave, join, knot, link, marry, mend, tie, unite. **knit your brow** ▷ FROWN.

knob n bulge, bump, handle, lump, projection, protuberance, protrusion, swelling.

knock v 1 bang, bump, pound, rap, strike, tap, thump. ▷ HIT. 2 ▷ CRITICIZE. **knock off** ▷ DEMOLISH. **knock off** ▷ CEASE. **knock out** ▷ STUN.

knot n 1 bow, tangle, tie. 2 ▷ GROUP. • v entangle, entwine, tie, unite. ▷ FASTEN. *Opp* UNTIE.

know v 1 be certain, have no doubt. 2 *know facts*. be familiar with, comprehend, have experience of, remember, understand. 3 *know a person*. be acquainted with, be a friend of. 4 discern, distinguish, identify, make out, perceive, realize, recognize, see.

knowing adj astute, clever, conspiratorial, discerning, meaningful, perceptive, shrewd. ▷ CUNNING, KNOWLEDGEABLE. Opp INNOCENT.

knowledge n 1 data, facts, information. 2 acquaintance, awareness, consciousness, erudition, experience, expertise, familiarity, grasp, insight, inf know-how, learning, lore, scholarship, skill, training. Opp IGNORANCE.

knowledgeable adj Fr au fait, aware, conversant, educated, erudite, experienced, expert, familiar (with), learned, scholarly, versed (in), well-informed. Opp IGNORANT.

L

label n hallmark, identification, logo, marker, sticker, tag, ticket, trademark. ● v brand, call, categorize, class, classify, define, identify, mark, name, pigeonhole, stamp, tag.

laborious adj 1 arduous, back-breaking, difficult, exhausting, gruelling, hard, heavy, herculean, onerous, strenuous, taxing, tough, uphill, wearisome, wearying. Opp EASY. 2 laborious style. contrived, forced, laboured, overdone, overworked, ponderous, strained. Opp FLUENT.

labour n 1 inf donkey work, drudgery, effort, exertion, industry, inf pains, toil, work. 2 employees, old use hands, workers, workforce.

3 childbirth, contractions, delivery, labour pains. ● v inf slave, struggle, sweat, toil. ▷ WORK.

laboured ▷ LABORIOUS.

labourer n employee, old use hand, manual worker, inf navvy, wage-earner, worker.

labour-saving adj convenient, handy, helpful, time-saving.

labyrinth n complex, jungle, maze, network, tangle.

lace n 1 filigree, mesh, net, openwork, web. 2 cord, shoelace, string, thong. ● v ▷ FASTEN.

lacerate v claw, gash, mangle, rip, scratch, slash, tear.

lack n absence, dearth, deficiency, insufficiency, need, paucity, privation, scarcity, shortage, want. Opp PLENTY. ● v be short of, be without, miss, need, require, want.

lacking adj defective, deficient, inadequate, short, wanting. ▷ STUPID.

laden adj burdened, full, hampered, loaded, piled high, weighed down.

lady n 1 wife, woman. 2 aristocrat, peeress.

ladylike adj aristocratic, cultured, elegant, genteel, refined, well-bred. ▷ POLITE.

lag v 1 be slow, dally, dawdle, delay, fall behind, go too slow, hang back, idle, linger, loiter, saunter, straggle, trail. 2 lag pipes. insulate, wrap up.

lair n den, hiding-place, refuge, retreat, shelter.

lake n lagoon, lido, loch, mere, pool, reservoir, sea.

lame adj 1 crippled, disabled, hobbling, incapacitated, limping, maimed. 2 lame leg. dragging, game, inf gammy, injured, stiff.

3 *lame excuse.* feeble, flimsy, inadequate, poor, tame, thin, unconvincing, weak. ● *v* cripple, disable, hobble, incapacitate, maim. **be lame** ▷ LIMP.

lament *n* dirge, elegy, lamentation, moaning, mourning, requiem. ● *v* bemoan, complain, cry, deplore, grieve, keen, mourn, regret, shed tears, sorrow, wail, weep.

lamentable *adj* deplorable, regrettable. ▷ SAD.

lamentation *n* crying, grief, grieving, moaning, mourning, regrets, tears, wailing, weeping.

lamp *n* headlamp, lantern, light, standard lamp, street light, torch.

land *n* 1 coast, ground, shore, *joc* terra firma. 2 *lie of the land.* geography, landscape, terrain, topography. 3 country, homeland, nation, region, state, territory. 4 earth, farmland, soil. 5 estate, grounds, property. ● *v* 1 alight, arrive, berth, come ashore, come to rest, disembark, dock, go ashore, settle, touch down. 2 *land a job.* ▷ GET.

landing *n* 1 docking, re-entry, return, touchdown. 2 alighting, arrival, disembarkation. 3 ▷ LANDING STAGE.

landing stage *n* berth, dock, jetty, pier, quay, wharf.

landlady, landlord *ns* 1 host, hostess, hotelier, *old use* innkeeper, licensee, publican, restaurateur. 2 landowner, letter, owner, proprietor.

landmark *n* 1 feature, high point. 2 milestone, turning point, watershed.

landscape *n* countryside, panorama, prospect, scene, scenery, terrain, view, vista.

language *n* 1 dialect, jargon, parlance, speech, tongue, vernacular. 2 linguistics. 3 *computer language.* code, system of signs.

languid *adj* apathetic, *inf* droopy, feeble, inactive, lazy, lethargic, slow, sluggish, torpid, unenthusiastic. *Opp* ENERGETIC.

languish *v* decline, flag, lose momentum, mope, pine, stagnate, suffer, waste away, wither. *Opp* FLOURISH.

lank *adj* 1 drooping, lifeless, limp. 2 ▷ LANKY.

lanky *adj* angular, bony, gaunt, lank, lean, long, scraggy, scrawny, skinny, tall, thin, weedy. *Opp* STURDY.

lap *n* circuit, course, orbit, revolution. ● *v* ▷ DRINK.

lapse *n* 1 blunder, error, failing, fault, mistake, omission, relapse, shortcoming, slip, *inf* slip-up, temporary failure. 2 break, gap, hiatus, *inf* hold-up, interruption, interval, lull, pause.
● *v* 1 decline, deteriorate, drop, fall, sink, slide, slip. 2 become invalid, expire, finish, run out.

large *adj* above average, abundant, ample, big, bold, broad, bulky, capacious, colossal, considerable, copious, enormous, extensive, fat, formidable, generous, giant, gigantic, great, heavy, hefty, high, huge, immense, impressive, *inf* jumbo, *inf* king-sized, lofty, long, mammoth, massive, mighty, monumental, outsize, overgrown, oversized, prodigious, roomy, sizeable, spacious, substantial, tall, thick, *inf* tidy (*sum*), titanic, towering, *inf* tremendous, vast, voluminous, weighty, *inf* whopping. *Opp* SMALL.

larva *n* caterpillar, grub.

lash *n* ▷ WHIP. • *v* 1 cane, flog, scourge, thrash, whip. ▷ HIT. 2 ▷ CRITICIZE.

last *adj* closing, concluding, final, furthest, hindmost, latest, most recent, rearmost, ultimate. *Opp* FIRST. • *v* carry on, continue, endure, hold out, keep on, linger, live, persist, remain, stay, survive, *inf* wear well. *Opp* DIE, FINISH. **lasting** ▷ PERMANENT.

late *adj* 1 belated, delayed, overdue, slow, tardy, unpunctual. 2 *the late king.* dead, deceased, departed, ex-, former, past, previous.

latent *adj* dormant, hidden, invisible, potential, undeveloped, undiscovered.

latitude *n* freedom, leeway. ▷ SCOPE.

latter *adj* closing, concluding, last, last-mentioned, later, recent, second. *Opp* FORMER.

lattice *n* framework, grid, mesh, trellis.

laugh *v* chortle, chuckle, *sl* fall about, giggle, guffaw, roar with laughter, simper, smirk, sneer, snicker, snigger, titter. **laugh at** ▷ RIDICULE.

laughable *adj* derisory, ludicrous, ridiculous. ▷ FUNNY.

laughter *n* chuckling, giggling, guffawing, hilarity, *inf* hysterics, merriment, mirth, sniggering. ▷ RIDICULE.

launch *v* 1 begin, embark on, establish, found, inaugurate, initiate, open, set in motion, set up, start. 2 catapult, fire, propel, send off, set off, shoot.

lavatory *n* bathroom, cloak-room, convenience, *inf* Gents, *inf* Ladies, latrine, *inf* loo, *inf* men's room, public convenience, toilet, urinal, WC, *inf* women's room.

lavish *adj* 1 abundant, bountiful, copious, generous, liberal, luxuriant, munificent, opulent, plentiful, profuse, sumptuous, unselfish, unsparing, unstinting. 2 excessive, extravagant, prodigal, self-indulgent, wasteful. *Opp* ECONOMICAL.

law *n* 1 act, commandment, decree, directive, edict, injunction, mandate, measure, order, ordinance, regulation, rule, statute. 2 code, convention, practice. 3 *law of science.* formula, principle, proposition, theory.

law-abiding *adj* decent, good, honest, obedient, orderly, peaceable, peaceful, respectable, well-behaved. *Opp* LAWLESS.

lawful *adj* allowable, allowed, authorized, just, justifiable, legal, legitimate, permitted, proper, recognized, regular, right, rightful, valid. *Opp* ILLEGAL.

lawless *adj* anarchic, chaotic, disobedient, disorderly, insubordinate, mutinous, rebellious, rowdy, turbulent, uncontrolled, undisciplined, unrestrained, unruly, wild. ▷ WICKED. *Opp* LAW-ABIDING.

lawlessness *n* anarchy, chaos, disorder, mob-rule, rebellion, rioting. *Opp* ORDER.

lawyer *n* advocate, barrister, counsel, legal representative, solicitor.

lax *adj* careless, casual, easygoing, lenient, loose, negligent, permissive, remiss, slack, slip-

shod, unreliable, vague.
Opp STRICT.

laxative n purgative, purge.

lay v 1 apply, arrange, deposit, leave, place, position, put down, rest, set down, set out, spread. 2 *lay foundations.* build, construct, establish. 3 *lay the blame on me.* assign, attribute, burden, plant, *inf* saddle. 4 *lay plans.* concoct, create, design, organize, plan, set up. **lay bare** ▷ REVEAL. **lay bets** ▷ GAMBLE. **lay by** ▷ STORE. **lay down the law** ▷ DICTATE. **lay in** ▷ STORE. **lay into** ▷ ATTACK. **lay low** ▷ DEFEAT. **lay off something** ▷ CEASE. **lay someone off** ▷ DISMISS. **lay to rest** ▷ BURY. **lay up** ▷ STORE. **lay waste** ▷ DESTROY.

layer n 1 coat, coating, covering, film, sheet, skin, surface, thickness. 2 *layer of rock.* seam, stratum. **in layers** laminated, layered, sandwiched, stratified.

layman n 1 amateur, nonspecialist, untrained person. Opp PROFESSIONAL. 2 [*church*] layperson, member of the congregation, parishioner. Opp CLERGYMAN.

laze v do nothing, idle, lie about, loaf, lounge, relax, unwind.

laziness n idleness, inactivity, indolence, lethargy, sloth, sluggishness, torpor. Opp INDUSTRY.

lazy adj 1 idle, inactive, indolent, languid, lethargic, listless, shiftless, *sl* skiving, slack, slothful, slow, sluggish, torpid, work-shy. 2 peaceful, quiet, relaxing. Opp ENERGETIC, INDUSTRIOUS. **be lazy** ▷ LAZE. **lazy person** ▷ SLACKER.

lead n 1 direction, example, guidance, leadership. 2 *lead on a*

crime. clue, hint, line, tip, tip-off. 3 *in the lead.* first place, front, vanguard. 4 *lead in a play.* chief part, hero, heroine, protagonist, starring role, title role. 5 cable, flex, wire. 6 *dog's lead.* chain, leash, strap. ● v 1 conduct, draw, escort, guide, influence, pilot, prompt, show the way, steer, usher. 2 be in charge of, captain, command, direct, govern, head, preside over, rule, supervise. 3 be in front, excel, go first, head the field, outdo, outstrip, surpass. Opp FOLLOW. **lead astray** ▷ MISLEAD. **leading** ▷ CHIEF, INFLUENTIAL. **lead off** ▷ BEGIN.

leader n 1 ayatollah, captain, commander, conductor, director, figure-head, *inf* godfather, guide, head, patriarch, premier, prime minister, ringleader, superior. ▷ CHIEF, RULER. 2 *leader in a newspaper.* editorial, leading article.

leaf n 1 *pl* foliage, frond, *pl* greenery. 2 folio, page, sheet.

leaflet n advertisement, booklet, brochure, circular, flyer, handbill, notice, pamphlet.

league n alliance, association, coalition, confederation, guild, society, union. ▷ GROUP. **be in league with** ▷ CONSPIRE.

leak n 1 discharge, drip, emission, escape, leakage, oozing, seepage, trickle. 2 chink, crack, crevice, fissure, flaw, hole, opening, perforation, puncture. 3 *security leak.* disclosure, revelation. ● v 1 discharge, drip, escape, exude, ooze, seep, spill, trickle. 2 *leak secrets.* disclose, divulge, give away, let out, let slip, pass on, reveal, *inf* spill the beans.

leaky *adj* cracked, dripping, perforated, punctured.

lean *adj* angular, bony, emaciated, gaunt, lanky, long, rangy, skinny, slender, slim, spare, thin, wiry. *Opp* FAT. • *v* 1 bank, incline, keel over, list, slant, slope, tilt, tip. 2 loll, recline, rest, support yourself.

leaning *n* bent, bias, inclination, instinct, liking, partiality, penchant, preference, propensity, taste, tendency, trend.

leap *v* 1 bound, hop over, hurdle, jump, skip over, spring, vault. 2 caper, dance, frolic, gambol, hop, prance. 3 *leap on someone*. ambush, attack, pounce.

learn *v* acquire, ascertain, become aware of, be taught, *inf* catch on, discover, find out, gain, gather, grasp, master, memorize, *inf* mug up, pick up, remember, study, *inf* swot up.
• **learned** ▷ ACADEMIC, EDUCATED.

learner *n* apprentice, beginner, cadet, novice, pupil, starter, student, trainee.

learning *n* culture, education, erudition, information, knowledge, lore, scholarship, wisdom.

lease *n* agreement, contract.
• *v* charter, hire out, let, rent out, sublet.

least *adj* fewest, lowest, minimum, negligible, slightest, smallest, tiniest.

leave *n* 1 authorization, consent, dispensation, liberty, permission, sanction. 2 *leave from work*. absence, free time, holiday, sabbatical, time off, vacation. • *v* 1 *inf* be off, *inf* check out, decamp, depart, disappear, escape, go away, go out, *sl* hop it, *inf* pull out, retire, retreat, run away, say goodbye, set off, *inf* take off, take your leave, vacate, withdraw. 2 abandon, desert, forsake. 3 *leave your job*. *inf* chuck in, *inf* drop out, give up, quit, relinquish, resign from, retire from, *inf* walk out. 4 *leave it as it is*. *inf* let alone, let be. 5 *leave it here*. deposit, place, put down. 6 *I left my keys somewhere*. forget, lose, mislay. 7 *leave it to me*. consign, entrust, refer, relinquish. 8 *leave in a will*. bequeath, hand down, will.
leave off ▷ STOP. **leave out** ▷ OMIT.

lecture *n* 1 address, discourse, lesson, paper, speech, talk, treatise. 2 *lecture on bad manners*. diatribe, harangue, sermon.
▷ REPRIMAND. • *v* 1 discourse, harangue, *inf* hold forth, pontificate, preach, speak.
2 ▷ REPRIMAND.

lecturer *n* don, fellow, professor, speaker, teacher, tutor.

ledge *n* mantel, ridge, shelf, sill, step, window-sill.

left *adj*. *n* 1 left-hand, port [= *left facing bow of ship*]. 2 *left wing in politics*. communist, Labour, liberal, progressive, radical, *derog* red, revolutionary, socialist. *Opp* RIGHT.

leg *n* 1 limb, *inf* peg, *inf* pin, shank. 2 prop, support, upright. 3 *leg of a journey*. lap, part, section, stage, stretch. **pull someone's leg** ▷ HOAX.

legacy *n* bequest, endowment, estate, inheritance.

legal *adj* 1 above-board, admissible, allowable, allowed, authorized, just, lawful, licensed, permitted, permissible, proper, regular, rightful, valid.

Opp ILLEGAL. 2 *legal proceedings.* judicial, judiciary.

legalize *v* allow, authorize, legitimize, license, permit, regularize, validate. Opp BAN.

legend *n* epic, folk tale, myth, saga, story, tradition.

legendary *adj* 1 apocryphal, fabled, fabulous, fictional, fictitious, imaginary, mythical, non-existent. 2 *legendary name.* ▷ FAMOUS.

legible *adj* clear, decipherable, distinct, neat, plain, readable. Opp ILLEGIBLE.

legitimate *adj* 1 authentic, genuine, proper, true. ▷ LEGAL. 2 ethical, just, justifiable, moral, proper, reasonable, right. Opp ILLEGITIMATE.

leisure *n* ease, freedom, holiday, liberty, quiet, recreation, relaxation, repose, respite, rest, spare time.

leisurely *adj* easy, gentle, lingering, peaceful, relaxed, relaxing, restful, unhurried. ▷ SLOW. Opp BRISK.

lend *v* advance, loan. Opp BORROW.

length *n* 1 distance, extent, measurement, mileage, reach, size. 2 duration, period, stretch, term.

lengthen *v* continue, drag out, draw out, elongate, expand, extend, increase, *inf* pad out, prolong, protract, pull out, stretch. Opp SHORTEN.

lenient *adj* easygoing, forbearing, forgiving, indulgent, merciful, mild, soft, soft-hearted, sparing, tolerant. ▷ KIND. Opp STRICT.

less *adj* fewer, reduced, shorter, smaller. Opp MORE.

lessen *v* 1 assuage, cut, deaden, decrease, ease, lighten, lower, minimize, mitigate, reduce, relieve, tone down. 2 abate, decline, die away, diminish, dwindle, ease off, let up, moderate, slacken, subside, tail off, weaken. Opp INCREASE.

lesson *n* 1 class, drill, instruction, lecture, practical, seminar, session, task, teaching, tutorial. 2 example, moral, warning.

let *v* 1 agree to, allow, consent to, give permission to, permit, sanction. 2 charter, contract out, hire, lease, rent. **let alone, let be** ▷ LEAVE. **let go, let loose** ▷ LIBERATE. **let off** ▷ FIRE. **let out** ▷ LIBERATE. **let someone off** ▷ ACQUIT. **let up** ▷ LESSEN.

letdown *n* anti-climax, disappointment, *inf* wash-out.

lethal *adj* deadly, fatal, mortal, poisonous.

lethargic *adj* apathetic, heavy, inactive, indolent, languid, lazy, listless, phlegmatic, sleepy, slow, sluggish, torpid. ▷ WEARY. Opp ENERGETIC.

lethargy *n* apathy, inactivity, indolence, inertia, laziness, listlessness, sluggishness, torpor, weariness. Opp ENERGY.

letter *n* 1 character, consonant, vowel. 2 card, communication, dispatch, epistle, message, missive, note, postcard. **letters** correspondence, mail, post.

level *adj* 1 even, flat, flush, horizontal, plane, regular, smooth, straight, true, uniform. 2 *level scores.* balanced, even, equal, *inf* neck-and-neck, the same. Opp UNEVEN. • *n* 1 altitude, depth, elevation, height, value. 2 degree, echelon, grade, position, rank, *inf* rung on the ladder, stage, standard, standing, status. 3 *level in a building*. floor, storey. ● v 1 even out, flatten, rake, smooth. 2 bulldoze, demolish, destroy, devastate, knock down, lay low, raze, wreck. **level-headed** ▷ SENSIBLE.

lever v force, prise, wrench.

liable adj 1 accountable, answerable, responsible. 2 apt, disposed, inclined, in the habit of, likely, minded, predisposed, prone, ready, susceptible, tempted, willing.

liaison n 1 communication, contact, cooperation, mediation, tie. 2 ▷ AFFAIR.

liar n deceiver, *inf* fibber, perjurer, *inf* story-teller.

libel n defamation, insult, lie, misrepresentation, slander, slur, smear, vilification. ● v defame, denigrate, disparage, malign, misrepresent, slander, slur, smear, write lies about, vilify.

libellous adj cruel, damaging, defamatory, disparaging, false, insulting, lying, malicious, scurrilous, slanderous, untrue, vicious.

liberal adj 1 abundant, ample, bounteous, bountiful, copious, free, generous, lavish, munificent, open-handed, plentiful, unstinting. 2 *liberal attitudes*. broad-minded, charitable, easygoing, enlightened, fair-minded, humanitarian, indulgent, lenient, magnanimous, openminded, permissive, tolerant, unbiased, unprejudiced. *Opp* NARROW-MINDED. 3 *liberal politics*. progressive, radical, reformist. *Opp* CONSERVATIVE.

liberalize v ease, make more liberal, open up, relax, soften, widen.

liberate v discharge, emancipate, enfranchise, free, let go, let loose, let out, release, rescue, save, set free, untie. *Opp* CAPTURE, SUBJUGATE.

liberty n autonomy, emancipation, independence, liberation, release. ▷ FREEDOM. **at liberty** ▷ FREE.

licence n 1 certificate, document, papers, permit, warrant. 2 ▷ FREEDOM.

license v 1 allow, authorize, certify, entitle, give a licence to, permit, sanction. 2 buy a licence for, make legal.

lid n cap, cover, covering, top.

lie n deceit, dishonesty, disinformation, fabrication, falsehood, falsification, *inf* fib, fiction, invention, untruth, *inf* whopper. *Opp* TRUTH. ● v 1 *inf* be economical with the truth, bluff, falsify the facts, *inf* fib, perjure yourself, tell lies. 2 be recumbent, lean back, lounge, recline, repose, rest, sprawl, stretch out. 3 be, be found, be located, be situated. **lie low** ▷ HIDE.

life n 1 being, existence, living. 2 activity, animation, energy, enthusiasm, exuberance, *inf* go, liveliness, sparkle, spirit, verve, vigour, vitality, vivacity, zest. 3 autobiography, biography, memoir, story.

lifeless adj 1 comatose, dead, deceased, inanimate, inert, insensible, motionless, unconscious. 2 *lifeless desert*. arid, bare, barren, desolate, empty, sterile, waste. 3 *lifeless performance*. apathetic, boring, dull, flat, lacklustre, lethargic, slow, unexciting, wooden. Opp LIVELY, LIVING.

lifelike adj authentic, convincing, faithful, natural, photographic, realistic, true-to-life, vivid. Opp UNREALISTIC.

lift n elevator, hoist. • v 1 buoy up, carry, elevate, hoist, pick up, pull up, raise, rear. 2 ascend, fly, lift off, rise, soar. 3 boost, cheer, enhance, improve. 4 ▷ STEAL.

light adj 1 lightweight, portable, weightless. Opp HEAVY. 2 bright, illuminated, lit-up, well-lit. Opp DARK. 3 light work. ▷ EASY. 4 light wind. ▷ GENTLE. 5 light touch. ▷ DELICATE. 6 light colours. ▷ PALE. 7 light heart. ▷ CHEERFUL. 8 light traffic. ▷ SPARSE. • n 1 beam, blaze, brightness, brilliance, flare, flash, glare, gleam, glint, glitter, glow, halo, illumination, incandescence, luminosity, lustre, radiance, ray, reflection, shine, sparkle, twinkle. 2 beacon, candle, lamp, lantern, torch. • v 1 fire, ignite, kindle, put a match to, set alight, set fire to, switch on. Opp EXTINGUISH. 2 ▷ LIGHTEN. **bring to light** ▷ DISCOVER. **give light, reflect light** be luminous, blaze, dazzle, flash, flicker, glare, gleam, glimmer, glint, glisten, glitter, glow, radiate, reflect, scintillate, shimmer, shine, spark, sparkle, twinkle. **light-headed** ▷ DIZZY. **light-hearted** ▷ CHEERFUL. **light up** ▷ LIGHTEN. **shed light on** ▷ EXPLAIN.

lighten v 1 cast light on, floodlight, illuminate, irradiate, light up, shed light on, shine on. 2 become lighter, brighten, cheer up, clear. 3 ▷ LESSEN.

lighthouse n beacon, light, lightship, warning-light.

like adj akin to, analogous to, close to, comparable to, corresponding to, equal to, equivalent to, identical to, parallel to, similar to. • v admire, approve of, appreciate, be attracted to, be fond of, be interested in, be keen on, be partial to, delight in, enjoy, sl go for, inf go in for, inf have a weakness for, prefer, relish, revel in, take pleasure in, inf take to, welcome. ▷ LOVE. Opp HATE.

likeable adj admirable, attractive, charming, congenial, endearing, interesting, lovable, nice, personable, pleasant, pleasing. ▷ FRIENDLY. Opp HATEFUL.

likelihood n chance, hope, possibility, probability, prospect.

likely adj 1 anticipated, expected, feasible, foreseeable, plausible, possible, predictable, probable, unsurprising. 2 likely candidate. acceptable, appropriate, convincing, favourite, hopeful, promising, qualified, suitable. 3 likely to help. apt, disposed, inclined, liable, prone, ready, tempted, willing. Opp UNLIKELY.

liken v ▷ COMPARE.

likeness n 1 affinity, analogy, compatibility, correspondence, resemblance, similarity. Opp DIFFERENCE. 2 copy, drawing, duplicate, image, model, picture, portrait, replica, representation, reproduction.

liking n affection, affinity, appetite, eye, fondness, inclination, partiality, penchant, predilection, predisposition, preference, propensity, inf soft spot, taste, weakness. ▷ LOVE. Opp HATRED.

limb n appendage, member, off-shoot, projection

limber v limber up exercise, loosen up, prepare, warm up.

limbo n in limbo abandoned, forgotten, left out, neglected, neither one thing nor the other, inf on hold, unattached.

limit n 1 border, boundary, bounds, brink, confines, demarcation line, edge, end, extent, frontier, perimeter. 2 ceiling, check, curb, cut-off point, limitation, maximum, restraint, restriction, stop, threshold. ● v circumscribe, confine, control, curb, define, fix, hold in check, ration, restrain, restrict. **limited** ▷ FINITE, INADEQUATE.

limitation n 1 ▷ LIMIT. 2 defect, deficiency, fault, inadequacy, shortcoming, weakness.

limitless adj boundless, countless, endless, immeasurable, incalculable, inexhaustible, infinite, innumerable, never-ending, perpetual, renewable, unbounded, unconfined, unending, unimaginable, unlimited, unrestricted. ▷ VAST. Opp FINITE.

limp adj inf bendy, drooping, flaccid, inf floppy, loose, sagging, slack, soft, weak, wilting. ▷ WEARY. Opp RIGID. ● v be lame, hobble, hop.

line n 1 band, borderline, boundary, contour, mark, streak, strip, stripe, stroke, trail. 2 corrugation, crease, fold, furrow, groove, wrinkle. 3 cable, cord, flex, hawser, lead, rope, string, thread, wire. 4 chain, column, cordon, crocodile, file, procession, queue, rank, row, series. 5 railway line. route, ser-

vice, track. ● v 1 rule, score, streak, underline. 2 line the street. border, edge, fringe. **line up** ▷ ALIGN, QUEUE.

linger v dally, dawdle, delay, dither, endure, hang about, hover, idle, lag, last, loiter, pause, persist, remain, inf shilly-shally, stay, stay behind, survive, wait about. Opp HURRY.

link n 1 bond, connection, coupling, join, joint, tie, yoke. ▷ FASTENER. 2 affiliation, alliance, association, communication, liaison, partnership, relationship, inf tie-up, union. ● v 1 amalgamate, associate, attach, compare, connect, couple, interlink, join, juxtapose, merge, relate, unite, yoke. ▷ FASTEN.

lip n brim, brink, edge, rim.

liquefy v become liquid, dissolve, liquidize, melt, run, thaw. Opp SOLIDIFY.

liquid adj aqueous, flowing, fluid, liquefied, molten, running, inf runny, sloppy, inf sloshy, thin, watery, wet. Opp SOLID. ● n fluid, juice, liquid, solution.

liquidate v annihilate, destroy, inf get rid of, remove, silence, wipe out. ▷ KILL.

liquor n 1 alcohol, inf booze, sl hard stuff, spirits, strong drink. 2 ▷ LIQUID.

list n catalogue, column, directory, file, index, inventory, register, roll, roster, rota, schedule. ● v 1 catalogue, enumerate, file, index, itemize, note, record, register, write down. 2 bank, incline, keel over, lean, slant, slope, tilt, tip.

listen v attend, concentrate, eavesdrop, hear, heed, inf keep your ears open, overhear, pay attention, take notice.

listless *adj* apathetic, enervated, feeble, heavy, languid, lazy, lethargic, lifeless, phlegmatic, sluggish, tired, torpid, unenthusiastic, uninterested, weak.
▷ WEARY. *Opp* LIVELY.

literal *adj* exact, faithful, matter of fact, strict, unimaginative, verbatim, word for word.

literary *adj* **1** cultured, educated, erudite, imaginative, learned, refined, scholarly, well-read. **2** *literary style.* ornate, poetic, polished, rhetorical, *derog* self-conscious.

literate *adj* cultured, educated, learned, well-read.

literature *n* books, brochures, circulars, creative writing, handbills, leaflets, pamphlets, papers, writings.

lithe *adj* agile, flexible, lissom, loose-jointed, pliable, pliant, supple. *Opp* STIFF.

litter *n* bits and pieces, clutter, debris, garbage, jumble, junk, mess, odds and ends, refuse, rubbish, trash, waste. ● *v* clutter, *inf* mess up, scatter, strew.

little *adj* **1** *inf* baby, bantam, diminutive, *inf* dinky, dwarf, infinitesimal, microscopic, midget, *inf* mini, miniature, minuscule, minute, petite, *inf* pint-sized, *inf* pocket-sized, *inf* poky, pygmy, short, slight, small, *inf* teeny, tiny, toy, under-sized, *inf* wee, *inf* weeny. *Opp* BIG. **2** *little helping.* inadequate, insufficient, meagre, *inf* measly, miserly, modest, *inf* piddling, scanty, skimpy, stingy. **3** *of little importance.* inconsequential, insignificant,

minor, negligible, slight, trifling, trivial, unimportant.

live *adj* **1** ▷ LIVING. **2** *live fire.* ▷ ALIGHT. **3** *live issue.* contemporary, current, important, pressing, relevant, topical, vital. *Opp* DEAD. ● *v* **1** breathe, continue, endure, exist, function, last, remain, stay alive, survive. *Opp* DIE. **2** dwell, lodge, reside, room, stay. **3** *live on £20 a week.* fare, *inf* get along, keep going, pay the bills, subsist. **live in** ▷ INHABIT. **live on** ▷ EAT.

liveliness *n* activity, animation, bustle, dynamism, energy, enthusiasm, exuberance, *inf* go, gusto, high spirits, spirit, verve, vigour, vitality, vivacity, zeal. *Opp* APATHY.

lively *adj* active, alert, animated, boisterous, bubbly, busy, cheerful, colourful, dashing, eager, energetic, enthusiastic, exciting, exuberant, frisky, gay, high-spirited, irrepressible, jaunty, jazzy, jolly, merry, *inf* perky, playful, quick, spirited, sprightly, stimulating, vigorous, vital, vivacious, vivid. ▷ HAPPY. *Opp* APATHETIC.

livestock *n* cattle, farm animals.

living *adj* active, actual, alive, animate, breathing, existing, extant, flourishing, functioning, live, *old use* quick, sentient, surviving. ▷ LIVELY. *Opp* DEAD, EXTINCT. ● *n* income, livelihood, occupation, subsistence, way of life.

load *n* **1** burden, cargo, consignment, freight, shipment. **2** anxiety, care, *inf* cross, millstone, onus, trouble, weight, worry. ● *v* **1** burden, encumber, fill, heap, pack, pile, saddle, stack, stow, weigh down. **2** *load*

a gun. charge, prime. **loaded**
▷ BIASED, LADEN, WEALTHY.

loafer *n* idler, *inf* good-for-nothing, layabout, *inf* lazybones, shirker, *sl* skiver.

loan *n* advance, credit, mortgage.
● *v* advance, lend.

loathe *v* abhor, abominate, be revolted by, despise, detest, dislike, find intolerable, hate, recoil from, resent, scorn, shudder at. *Opp* LOVE.

lobby *n* **1** ante-room, entrance hall, entry, foyer, hall, hallway, porch, reception.
2 *environmental lobby.* campaign, campaigners, pressure group, supporters. ● *v* petition, pressurize, try to influence, urge.

local *adj* **1** adjacent, adjoining, nearby, neighbouring. **2** *local politics.* community, neighbourhood, parochial, particular, provincial, regional. *Opp* GENERAL, NATIONAL. ● *n* **1** inhabitant, resident. **2** [*inf*] ▷ PUB.

locality *n* area, community, district, location, neighbourhood, parish, region, town, vicinity, zone.

localize *v* concentrate, confine, contain, enclose, keep within bounds, limit, narrow down, pin down, restrict. *Opp* SPREAD.

locate *v* **1** detect, discover, find, identify, *inf* lay your hands on, track down, unearth. **2** build, establish, find a place for, place, position, put, set up, site, situate, station.

location *n* **1** locale, locality, place, point, position, site, situation, spot, venue, whereabouts. **2** *film location.* background, scene, setting.

lock *n* bar, bolt, catch, clasp, fastening, hasp, latch, padlock.
● *v* bolt, close, fasten, padlock, seal, secure, shut. **lock away** ▷ IMPRISON. **lock out** ▷ EXCLUDE. **lock up** ▷ IMPRISON.

lodge *n* cabin, chalet, cottage, house, hut, shelter.
● *v* **1** accommodate, billet, board, house, *inf* put up. **2** dwell, live, *inf* put up, reside, stay, stop. **3** *lodge a complaint.* enter, file, put on record, register, submit.

lodger *n* boarder, guest, inmate, paying guest, resident, tenant.

lodgings *n* accommodation, apartment, billet, boarding house, *inf* digs, *inf* pad, quarters, rooms, shelter.

lofty *adj* **1** elevated, high, imposing, majestic, noble, soaring, tall, towering. **2** ▷ ARROGANT.

log *n* **1** timber, wood. **2** account, diary, journal, record.

logic *n* clarity, logical thinking, rationality, reasoning, sense, validity.

logical *adj* clear, cogent, coherent, consistent, intelligent, methodical, rational, reasonable, sensible, sound, structured, systematic, valid, well-reasoned, well-thought-out, wise.
Opp ILLOGICAL.

loiter *v* dally, dawdle, hang back, linger, loaf about, *inf* mess about, skulk, stand about, straggle.

lone *adj* isolated, separate, single, solitary, solo, unaccompanied. ▷ LONELY.

lonely *adj* **1** abandoned, alone, forlorn, forsaken, friendless, outcast, reclusive, retiring, solitary, withdrawn. ▷ SAD. **2** *inf* cut off, deserted, desolate, isolated, *inf* off the beaten track, out of the way, remote, secluded, unfrequented, uninhabited.

long *adj* drawn out, elongated, endless, extended, extensive, interminable, lasting, lengthy, prolonged, protracted, slow, stretched, sustained, time-consuming, unending. • *v* crave, desire, hanker, have a longing (for), hunger, pine, thirst, wish, yearn. **long-lasting, long-lived** ▷ PERMANENT. **long-standing** ▷ OLD. **long-suffering** ▷ PATIENT. **long-winded** ▷ TEDIOUS.

longing *n* appetite, craving, desire, hankering, hunger, itch, need, thirst, urge, wish, yearning, *inf* yen.

look *n* 1 gaze, glance, glimpse, peek, peep, *inf* squint, view. 2 air, appearance, aspect, bearing, complexion, countenance, demeanour, expression, face, looks, manner, mien.
• *v* 1 behold, *inf* cast your eye, consider, contemplate, examine, eye, gape, *inf* gawp, gaze, glance, glimpse, goggle, inspect, observe, ogle, peek, peep, peer, read, regard, scan, scrutinize, skim through, squint, stare, study, survey, view, watch. 2 *The windows look south.* face, overlook. 3 **look pleased.** appear, seem. **look after** ▷ TEND. **look down on** ▷ DESPISE. **look for** ▷ SEEK. **look into** ▷ INVESTIGATE. **look out** ▷ BEWARE. **look up to** ▷ ADMIRE.

lookout *n* guard, sentry.

loom *v* arise, appear, emerge, hover, materialize, menace, rise,

stand out, take shape, threaten, tower.

loop *n* bend, bow, circle, coil, curl, eye, hoop, kink, noose, ring, turn, twist, whorl. • *v* bend, coil, curl, entwine, make a loop, turn, twist, wind.

loophole *n* escape, *inf* get out, *inf* let-out, outlet, way out.

loose *adj* 1 detached, disconnected, insecure, loosened, movable, scattered, shaky, unattached, unconnected, unfastened, unsteady, wobbly. 2 *loose animals.* at large, escaped, free, released, roaming, uncaged, unconfined, unrestricted, untied. 3 *loose hair.* hanging, spread out, straggling, trailing. 4 *loose clothing.* baggy, *inf* floppy, loose-fitting. 5 *loose agreement, translation.* broad, careless, casual, diffuse, general, ill-defined, imprecise, inexact, informal, lax, rambling, rough, *inf* sloppy, vague. *Opp* PRECISE, SECURE, TIGHT. 6 ▷ IMMORAL.
• *v* ▷ FREE, LOOSEN.

loosen *v* 1 free, let go, loose, relax, release, slacken, unfasten, untie. ▷ UNDO. 2 become loose, come adrift. *Opp* TIGHTEN.

loot *n* booty, contraband, haul, *inf* ill-gotten gains, plunder, prize, spoils, *inf* swag, takings.
• *v* pillage, plunder, raid, ransack, rob, steal from.

lopsided *adj* askew, asymmetrical, awry, crooked, tilting, uneven.

lord *n* aristocrat, noble, peer.

lose *v* 1 be deprived of, drop, forfeit, forget, leave (somewhere), mislay, misplace, miss, stray from. *Opp* FIND. 2 be defeated, capitulate, fail, succumb. *Opp* WIN. 3 *lose your chance.* let slip, squander, waste. 4 *lose pursuers*: escape from, evade, give the slip, leave behind, outrun, shake off, throw off. **losing** ▷ UNSUCCESSFUL.

loser n also-ran, *sl* no-hoper, runner-up, underdog. *Opp* WINNER.

loss n bereavement, defeat, deficit, depletion, deprivation, destruction, disappearance, erosion, failure, privation, reduction, sacrifice. *Opp* GAIN. **losses** casualties, deaths, death toll, fatalities.

lost adj 1 abandoned, disappeared, forgotten, gone, irretrievable, left behind, mislaid, misplaced, missing, strayed, untraceable, vanished. 2 absorbed, daydreaming, distracted, engrossed, preoccupied, rapt. 3 corrupt, damned, fallen. ▷ WICKED.

lot n *lot in a sale*. ▷ ITEM. **a lot of, lots of** ▷ PLENTY. **draw lots** ▷ GAMBLE. **the lot** all (of), everything, the whole thing, *inf* the works.

lotion n balm, cream, liniment, ointment, salve.

lottery n 1 raffle, sweepstake. 2 gamble, speculation, venture.

loud adj 1 audible, blaring, booming, clamorous, deafening, earsplitting, echoing, high, noisy, penetrating, piercing, raucous, resounding, reverberating, roaring, shrieking, shrill, sonorous, strident, thundering, vociferous. 2 *loud colours*. ▷ GAUDY. *Opp* QUIET.

lounge n drawing room, living room, salon, sitting room. ● v be idle, be lazy, dawdle, hang about, idle, laze, loaf, lie around, loiter, *inf* loll about, *inf* mess

about, relax, sprawl, stand about, take it easy, waste time.

lout n hooligan, oaf, *inf* yob.

lovable adj adorable, appealing, charming, cuddly, *inf* cute, *inf* darling, dear, enchanting, endearing, engaging, fetching, likeable, lovely, pleasing, winning. *Opp* HATEFUL.

love n 1 admiration, adoration, affection, ardour, attachment, desire, devotion, fervour, fondness, infatuation, passion, tenderness, warmth. ▷ FRIENDSHIP. 2 beloved, darling, dear, dearest, loved one. ▷ LOVER. ● v 1 admire, adore, be fond of, be infatuated with, be in love with, care for, cherish, desire, dote on, fancy, *inf* have a crush on, have a passion for, idolize, lose your heart to, lust after, treasure, value, worship. ▷ LIKE. *Opp* HATE. **in love** besotted, enamoured, fond, *inf* head over heels, infatuated. **love affair** courtship, liaison, relationship, romance. **make love** *inf* canoodle, caress, embrace, have sex, pet. ▷ SEX.

loved adj beloved, cherished, darling, dear, dearest, esteemed, favourite, precious, treasured, valued, wanted.

loveless adj cold, frigid, heartless, passionless, unfeeling, unloving. *Opp* LOVING. ▷ UNLOVED.

lovely adj appealing, charming, delightful, enjoyable, nice, pleasant, pretty, sweet. ▷ BEAUTIFUL. *Opp* NASTY.

lover n admirer, boyfriend, companion, fiancé(e), friend, gigolo, girlfriend, *inf* intended, mate, mistress, suitor, sweetheart, *sl* toy boy, valentine.

lovesick *adj* frustrated, languishing, lovelorn, pining.

loving *adj* admiring, adoring, affectionate, amorous, ardent, attached, brotherly, caring, close, concerned, dear, demonstrative, devoted, doting, fatherly, fond, inseparable, kind, maternal, motherly, passionate, paternal, sisterly, tender, warm. ▷ FRIENDLY. *Opp* LOVELESS.

low *adj* 1 flat, low-lying, sunken. 2 *low trees.* short, stumpy, stunted. 3 *low status.* abject, base, degraded, humble, inferior, junior, lesser, lower, lowly, menial, modest. 4 *low behaviour.* churlish, coarse, common, cowardly, crude, disreputable, ignoble, mean, nasty, vulgar, wicked. ▷ IMMORAL. 5 *low sounds.* gentle, indistinct, muffled, muted, quiet, soft, subdued, whispered. 6 *low notes.* bass, deep, reverberant. *Opp* HIGH. **in low spirits** ▷ SAD. **low point** ▷ NADIR.

lowbrow *adj* easy, pop, popular, *derog* rubbishy, simple, *derog* trashy, *derog* uncultured, undemanding, unsophisticated. *Opp* HIGHBROW.

lower *v* 1 dip, drop, let down, take down. 2 *lower prices.* bring down, cut, decrease, discount, lessen, reduce, *inf* slash. 3 *lower the volume.* diminish, quieten, turn down. 4 *lower yourself.* abase, degrade, demean, discredit, disgrace, humble, humiliate, stoop. *Opp* RAISE.

lowly *adj* base, humble, insignificant, meek, modest, obscure, unimportant. ▷ ORDINARY. *Opp* EMINENT.

loyal *adj* constant, dedicated, devoted, dutiful, faithful, honest, patriotic, reliable, staunch, steadfast, true, trustworthy, trusty, unswerving, unwavering. *Opp* DISLOYAL.

loyalty *n* allegiance, constancy, dedication, devotion, duty, faithfulness, fidelity, honesty, patriotism, reliability, steadfastness, trustworthiness. *Opp* DISLOYALTY.

lubricate *v* grease, oil.

luck *n* 1 accident, chance, coincidence, destiny, fate, fluke, fortune, serendipity. 2 *wish her luck.* good fortune, happiness, prosperity, success.

lucky *adj* 1 accidental, chance, *inf* fluky, fortuitous, opportune, providential, timely, unplanned, welcome. 2 blessed, favoured, fortunate, successful. ▷ HAPPY. 3 *lucky number.* auspicious. *Opp* UNLUCKY.

luggage *n* bags, baggage, belongings, cases, *inf* gear, paraphernalia, suitcases, *inf* things, trunks.

lukewarm *adj* 1 tepid, warm. 2 apathetic, cool, half-hearted, indifferent, unenthusiastic.

lull *n* break, calm, gap, hiatus, interlude, interval, lapse, *inf* let-up, pause, respite, rest, silence. ● *v* calm, hush, pacify, quell, quieten, soothe, subdue.

lumber *n* 1 planks, timber, wood. 2 clutter, junk, odds and ends, rubbish, *inf* white elephants. ● *v* 1 blunder, move clumsily, shamble, trudge. 2 ▷ BURDEN.

luminous *adj* bright, glowing, lustrous, phosphorescent, radiant, shining.

lump *n* 1 ball, bar, bit, block, cake, chunk, clod, clot, cube, *inf* dollop, gobbet, hunk, mass,

nugget, piece, slab, wad,
inf wodge. 2 boil, bulge, bump,
cyst, excrescence, growth, hump,
knob, node, nodule, protrusion,
protuberance, spot, swelling,
tumour. ● *v* lump together
▷ COMBINE.

lunacy *n* delirium, dementia,
derangement, frenzy, hysteria,
insanity, madness, mania, psychosis. ▷ STUPIDITY.

lunatic *adj* ▷ MAD.
● *n* ▷ MADMAN.

lunge *v* 1 jab, stab, strike, thrust.
2 charge, lurch, plunge, throw
yourself.

lurch *v* list, lunge, pitch, plunge,
reel, roll, stagger, stumble,
sway, totter. **leave in the lurch**
▷ ABANDON.

lure *v* attract, coax, decoy, draw,
entice, inveigle, lead on, persuade, seduce, tempt.

lurid *adj* 1 gaudy, glaring, striking, vivid. 2 ▷ SENSATIONAL.

lurk *v* crouch, hide, lie in wait,
lie low, prowl, skulk, steal.

luscious *adj* delectable, delicious, juicy, mouth-watering,
rich, succulent.

lust *n* 1 desire, lasciviousness,
lechery, libido, passion, sensual-
ity, sexuality. 2 appetite, craving, greed, hunger, itch, longing.

lustful *adj* carnal, lascivious,
lecherous, lewd, libidinous, on
heat, passionate, *sl* randy, sensual, *sl* turned on. ▷ SEXY.

lustrous *adj* burnished, gleaming, glossy, metallic, polished,
reflective, shiny.

luxuriant *adj* 1 abundant,
ample, copious, dense, exuberant, fertile, flourishing, green,
lush, opulent, plentiful, profuse,
prolific, rich, teeming, thick,

thriving, verdant. 2 ▷ ORNATE.
Opp SPARSE.

luxurious *adj* comfortable,
costly, expensive, grand, hedonistic, lavish, lush, magnificent,
palatial, opulent, *inf* plush,
inf posh, rich, self-indulgent,
splendid, sumptuous, voluptuous. *Opp* SPARTAN.

luxury *n* affluence, comfort,
ease, enjoyment, extravagance,
hedonism, high living, indulgence, opulence, pleasure, self-
indulgence, splendour, sumptuousness, voluptuousness.

lying *adj* crooked, deceitful,
deceptive, dishonest, double-
dealing, duplicitous, false, hypocritical, insincere, mendacious,
perfidious, untruthful.
Opp TRUTHFUL. ● *n* deceit, deception, dishonesty, duplicity, falsehood, *inf* fibbing, hypocrisy,
mendacity, perjury, prevarica-
tion.

lyrical *adj* emotional, impassioned, melodious, musical,
poetic, rapturous, rhapsodic,
song-like, tuneful. *Opp* PROSAIC.

M

macabre *adj* eerie, frightful,
ghoulish, grim, grisly, gruesome, morbid, *inf* sick, weird.

machine *n* appliance, contraption, device, engine, gadget,
instrument, mechanism, robot,
tool. ▷ MACHINERY.

machinery *n* 1 apparatus, equipment, gear, machines, plant.
2 procedure, system.

mackintosh n anorak, cape, mac, sou'wester, waterproof.

mad adj 1 berserk, inf bonkers, crazed, crazy, inf daft, delirious, demented, deranged, distracted, inf dotty, fanatical, frenzied, insane, lunatic, maniacal, manic, inf nutty, inf off your head, inf out of your mind, possessed, inf potty, psychotic, inf round the bend, inf touched, unbalanced, unhinged, unstable. Opp SANE. 2 mad comedy. ▷ ABSURD. 3 ▷ ANGRY. 4 ▷ ENTHUSIASTIC.

madden v anger, craze, derange, inf drive crazy, enrage, exasperate, incense, inflame, infuriate, irritate, inf make you see red, provoke, unhinge, vex.

madman, madwoman ns inf crackpot, lunatic, maniac, inf nutcase, inf nutter, psychopath.

madness n delirium, dementia, derangement, folly, frenzy, hysteria, insanity, lunacy, mania, mental illness, psychosis. ▷ STUPIDITY.

magazine n 1 comic, journal, monthly, paper, periodical, publication, quarterly, weekly. 2 magazine of weapons. armoury, arsenal, storehouse.

magic adj bewitching, charming, enchanting, entrancing, magical, miraculous, spellbinding, supernatural. ● n 1 black magic, . enchantment, inf hocus-pocus, incantations, inf mumbo-jumbo, necromancy, the occult, sorcery, spells, voodoo, witchcraft, wizardry. 2 conjuring, illusion, sleight of hand, tricks.

magician n conjuror, magus, necromancer, sorcerer, witch, wizard.

magnetic adj alluring, attractive, bewitching, captivating, charismatic, charming, compelling, entrancing, fascinating, hypnotic, inviting, irresistible, seductive, spellbinding. Opp REPULSIVE.

magnetism n allure, appeal, attractiveness, charisma, charm, fascination, lure, power, pull, seductiveness.

magnificent adj awe-inspiring, beautiful, excellent, fine, glorious, gorgeous, grand, grandiose, imposing, impressive, majestic, marvellous, noble, opulent, inf posh, regal, rich, spectacular, splendid, stately, sumptuous, superb, wonderful. Opp ORDINARY.

magnify v 1 amplify, augment, inf blow up, enlarge, expand, increase, intensify, make larger. Opp SHRINK. 2 magnify difficulties. dramatize, exaggerate, heighten, inflate, make too much of, maximize, overdo, overestimate, overstate. Opp MINIMIZE.

magnitude n extent, immensity, importance, size.

mail n correspondence, letters, parcels, post. ● v dispatch, forward, post, send.

maim v cripple, disable, incapacitate, lame, mutilate.

main adj basic, cardinal, central, chief, critical, crucial, dominant, essential, first, foremost, fundamental, leading, major, most important, paramount, predominant, pre-eminent, primary, prime, principal, special, supreme, vital. Opp MINOR.

mainly adv above all, chiefly, especially, essentially, generally, largely, mostly, on the whole, predominantly, primarily, principally, usually.

maintain v 1 carry on, continue, hold to, keep going, keep up, perpetuate, preserve, retain, stick to, sustain. 2 *maintain a car*. keep in good condition, look after, service, take care of 3 *maintain a family*. feed, keep, provide for, support. 4 *maintain your innocence*. affirm, allege, argue, assert, claim, contend, declare, defend, insist, proclaim, profess, uphold.

maintenance n 1 care, conservation, preservation, repairs, servicing, upkeep. 2 alimony, allowance, subsistence.

majestic adj august, awe-inspiring, dignified, distinguished, glorious, grand, imperial, imposing, impressive, kingly, lofty, magnificent, monumental, noble, pompous, princely, queenly, regal, royal, splendid, stately, sublime.

majesty n dignity, glory, grandeur, magnificence, nobility, pomp, royalty, splendour, stateliness, sublimity.

major adj bigger, extensive, greater, important, key, larger, leading, outstanding, serious, significant. ▷ MAIN. *Opp* MINOR.

majority n 1 *inf* best part, *inf* better part, bulk, greater number, mass, preponderance. 2 adulthood, coming of age, maturity. **be in the majority** ▷ DOMINATE.

make n brand, kind, model, sort, type, variety. ● v 1 assemble, beget, bring about, build, compose, constitute, construct, create, devise, do, engender, erect, execute, fabricate, fashion, forge, form, frame, generate,

invent, make up, manufacture, originate, produce, put together. 2 *make dinner*. cook, *inf* fix, prepare. 3 *make clothes*. knit, *inf* run up, sew, weave. 4 *make an effigy*. carve, cast, model, mould, shape. 5 *make a speech*. deliver, pronounce, utter. ▷ SPEAK. 6 *make her director*. appoint, elect, nominate, ordain. 7 *make P into B*. alter, change, convert, transform, turn. 8 *make a fortune*. earn, gain, get, obtain. 9 *make a good employee*. become, grow into, turn into. 10 *make your objective*. accomplish, achieve, arrive at, attain, reach, win. 11 *2 and 2 make 4*. add up to, amount to, come to, total. 12 *make rules*. agree, arrange, establish, decide on, draw up, fix, write. 13 *make trouble*. cause, give rise to, provoke. 14 *make them obey*. coerce, compel, constrain, force, induce, oblige, order, pressurize, prevail on, require. **make amends** ▷ COMPENSATE. **make believe** ▷ IMAGINE. **make fun of** ▷ RIDICULE. **make good** ▷ PROSPER. **make love** ▷ LOVE. **make off** ▷ DEPART. **make off with** ▷ STEAL. **make out** ▷ UNDERSTAND. **make up** ▷ INVENT. **make up for** ▷ COMPENSATE. **make up your mind** ▷ DECIDE.

make-believe adj fanciful, imaginary, made-up, *inf* pretend, pretended, unreal. ● n dream, fantasy, play-acting, pretence, self-deception, unreality.

maker n architect, author, builder, creator, manufacturer, originator, producer.

makeshift adj provisional, stop-gap, temporary.

maladjusted adj disturbed, muddled, neurotic, unbalanced.

male adj ▷ MASCULINE.
- n ▷ MAN. Opp FEMALE.

malefactor n ▷ WRONGDOER.

malice n animosity, inf bitchiness, bitterness, enmity, hatred, hostility, ill will, malevolence, maliciousness, rancour, spite, spitefulness, venom, viciousness, vindictiveness.

malicious adj inf bitchy, bitter, inf catty, evil, hateful, malevolent, malignant, nasty, rancorous, sly, spiteful, venomous, vicious, villainous, vindictive, wicked. Opp KIND.

malignant adj dangerous, deadly, destructive, fatal, harmful, injurious, life-threatening, inf terminal, virulent.
▷ MALICIOUS.

malleable adj ductile, plastic, pliable, soft, tractable, workable. Opp BRITTLE.

malnutrition n famine, hunger, starvation, undernourishment.

man n 1 ▷ MANKIND. 2 bachelor, boy, boyfriend, brother, chap, father, fellow, gentleman, groom, inf guy, husband, lad, son, inf squire, widower.
- v cover, crew, staff.

manage v 1 administer, be in charge of, conduct, control, direct, govern, head, lead, look after, mastermind, organize, oversee, preside over, regulate, rule, run, superintend, supervise, take care of. 2 Can you manage that horse? cope with, deal with, handle. 3 I can manage 2 essays this week. accomplish, achieve, carry out, do, finish, get through, perform, undertake. 4 I can manage on my own. cope, muddle through,

scrape by, shift for yourself, succeed, survive. 4 I can manage £10. afford, spare.

manageable adj 1 convenient, handy, reasonable.
Opp AWKWARD. 2 amenable, compliant, controllable, docile, submissive, tame, tractable.
▷ OBEDIENT. Opp DISOBEDIENT.

manager, manageress ns administrator, inf boss, chief, controller, director, executive, governor, head, organizer, overseer, proprietor, ruler, supervisor. ▷ CHIEF.

mandatory adj ▷ COMPULSORY.

mangle v crush, damage, deform, hack, injure, lacerate, maim, maul, mutilate, squash, tear, wound.

mangy adj moth-eaten, scabby, inf scruffy, shabby, squalid, inf tatty, unkempt, wretched.

manhandle v 1 haul, heave, hump, manoeuvre, pull, push. 2 abuse, inf beat up, ill-treat, knock about, mistreat, misuse, inf rough up.

mania n craze, enthusiasm, fad, fetish, frenzy, infatuation, obsession, passion, rage. ▷ MADNESS.

maniac n ▷ MADMAN.

manifest adj apparent, clear, conspicuous, evident, explicit, glaring, noticeable, obvious, patent, plain, visible.
- v ▷ SHOW.

manifesto n declaration, policy statement.

manipulate v 1 feel, massage, rub. 2 manipulate people, events. control, direct, exploit, guide, handle, influence, manage, manoeuvre, steer.

mankind n Lat homo sapiens, human beings, humanity, the

human race, man, men and women, people.

manly *adj* chivalrous, gallant, heroic, *inf* macho, male, masculine, strong, virile. ▷ BRAVE. *Opp* EFFEMINATE.

man-made *adj* artificial, imitation, manufactured, simulated, synthetic, unnatural. *Opp* NATURAL.

manner *n* 1 fashion, means, method, mode, procedure, process, style, technique, way. 2 air, aspect, attitude, bearing, behaviour, character, conduct, demeanour, disposition, look, mien. 3 *all manner of things.* kind, sort, type, variety.

manners *pl n* behaviour, conduct, courtesy, etiquette, politeness, protocol, refinement, social graces.

mannerism *n* characteristic, habit, peculiarity, quirk, trait.

manoeuvre *n* device, dodge, gambit, move, operation, plan, plot, ploy, ruse, scheme, stratagem, strategy, tactic, trick. ● *v* contrive, engineer, guide, jockey, manipulate, move, navigate, pilot, steer.

manoeuvres *pl n* army exercises, operations, training.

mansion *n* manor, manor house, palace, stately home.

mantle *n* cape, cloak, hood, shroud, wrap. ● *v* ▷ COVER.

manufacture *v* assemble, build, create, fabricate, make, mass-produce, process, *inf* turn out. **manufactured** ▷ MAN-MADE.

manufacturer *n* factory-owner, industrialist, maker, producer.

manure *n* compost, dung, fertilizer, *inf* muck.

manuscript *n* document, papers, script.

many *adj* abundant, copious, countless, diverse, frequent, innumerable, multifarious, myriad, numerous, profuse, *inf* umpteen, various. *Opp* FEW.

map *n* chart, diagram, plan.

mar *v* damage, hurt, impair, stain, tarnish. ▷ SPOIL.

marauder *n* bandit, invader, pirate, plunderer, raider.

march *n* demonstration, march-past, parade, procession, progress. ● *v* file, pace, parade, step, stride, troop.

margin *n* 1 border, boundary, brink, edge, frieze, perimeter, rim, side, verge. 2 latitude, leeway, room, scope, space.

marginal *adj* borderline, doubtful, minimal, negligible, peripheral.

marital *adj* conjugal, matrimonial, nuptial.

mark *n* 1 blemish, blot, blotch, dot, *pl* graffiti, line, pockmark, print, scar, scratch, scribble, smear, smudge, smut, *inf* splotch, spot, stain, *pl* stigmata, streak, trace, vestige. 2 *mark of breeding.* characteristic, feature, indication, token. 3 *identifying mark.* badge, brand, device, emblem, hallmark, label, seal, sign, stamp, standard, symbol, trademark. ● *v* 1 blemish, blot, brand, bruise, damage, deface, dirty, disfigure, draw on, mar, scar, scratch, smudge, spot, stain, stamp, streak, tattoo. 2 *mark pupils' work.* appraise, assess, correct, evaluate, grade. 3 *mark my words.* attend to, heed, listen to, mind, note, notice, observe, take note of, *inf* take to heart, watch.

market *n* auction, bazaar, exchange, fair, market place, sale. ▷ SHOP. ● *v* advertise, deal in, peddle, promote, put on the market, retail, sell, *inf* tout, trade, trade in, vend.

marksman *n* crack shot, gunman, sharpshooter, sniper.

maroon *v* abandon, cast away, desert, isolate, leave, strand.

marriage *n* 1 matrimony, partnership, union, wedlock. 2 nuptials, wedding.

marriageable *adj* adult, mature, nubile.

marry *v* espouse, *inf* get hitched, join in matrimony, *inf* tie the knot, unite, wed.

marsh *n* bog, fen, marshland, morass, mud, mudflats, quagmire, swamp, wetland.

marshal *v* arrange, assemble, deploy, gather, group, line up, muster, organize.

martial *adj* aggressive, belligerent, military, pugnacious, warlike. *Opp* PEACEABLE.

marvel *n* miracle, phenomenon, wonder. ● *v* marvel at admire, be amazed by, gape at, wonder at.

marvellous *adj* amazing, astonishing, astounding, breathtaking, excellent, extraordinary, *inf* fabulous, *inf* fantastic, glorious, incredible, magnificent, miraculous, phenomenal, prodigious, remarkable, *inf* sensational, spectacular, splendid, stupendous, *inf* super, superb, *inf* terrific, unbelievable, wonderful. *Opp* ORDINARY.

masculine *adj* boyish, *inf* butch, gentlemanly, heroic, *inf* macho,

male, manly, powerful, strong, virile. *Opp* FEMININE.

mash *v* beat, crush, grind, pound, pulp, pulverize, squash.

mask *n* camouflage, cloak, cover, cover-up, disguise, façade, front, guise, screen, shield, veil, visor. ● *v* blot out, camouflage, cloak, conceal, cover, disguise, hide, obscure, screen, shield, shroud, veil.

masonry *n* bricks, brickwork, stone, stonework.

mass *adj* general, popular, universal, wholesale, widespread. ● *n* 1 accumulation, body, bulk, collection, conglomeration, *inf* dollop, heap, hoard, *inf* load, lot, lump, mound, mountain, pile, profusion, quantity, stack, volume. 2 ▷ GROUP. ● *v* accumulate, amass, assemble, collect, congregate, convene, flock together, gather, marshal, meet, mobilize, muster, pile up, rally.

massacre *v* annihilate, slaughter. ▷ KILL.

massage *v* knead, manipulate, rub.

mast *n* aerial, flagpole, maypole, pylon, transmitter.

master *n* 1 keeper, owner, person in charge, proprietor. ▷ CHIEF. 2 captain, skipper. 3 *master of an art*. *inf* ace, authority, expert, genius, mastermind, maestro, virtuoso. 4 ▷ TEACHER. ● *v* 1 become expert in, *inf* get the hang of, grasp, learn, understand. 2 conquer, control, curb, defeat, dominate, *inf* get the better of, overcome, overpower, quell, repress, subdue, subjugate, suppress, tame, triumph over, vanquish.

masterly *adj* ▷ SKILFUL.

mastermind *n* architect, brains, creator, engineer, expert, genius, intellectual, inventor, manager, originator, prime mover. ● *v* carry through, conceive, devise, direct, engineer, execute, organize, originate, plan, plot. ▷ MANAGE.

masterpiece *n* best work, classic, magnum opus, masterwork, *Fr* pièce de résistance.

match *n* 1 bout, competition, contest, duel, game, tournament. 2 counterpart, double, equal, equivalent, twin. 3 *love match*. marriage, partnership, relationship, union. ● *v* 1 agree, accord, be compatible, be similar, blend, coincide, compare, coordinate, correspond, fit, *inf* go together, harmonize, suit, tally, tone in. *Opp* CONTRAST. 2 ally, combine, fit, join, link up, marry, mate, pair off, put together, team up. *Opp* SPLIT. **matching** ▷ SIMILAR.

mate *n* 1 *inf* better half, companion, consort, husband, partner, spouse, wife. ▷ FRIEND. 2 assistant, associate, colleague, helper. ● *v* copulate, couple, have intercourse, *inf* have sex, marry, *inf* pair up, unite.

material *adj* concrete, corporeal, palpable, physical, solid, substantial, tangible. ● *n* 1 cloth, fabric, stuff, textile. 2 content, data, facts, ideas, information, matter, statistics, subject matter, substance, supplies.

materialize *v* become visible, take shape. ▷ APPEAR.

mathematics *pl n* arithmetic, *inf* maths, number work.

matted *adj* knotted, tangled, uncombed, unkempt. ▷ DISHEVELLED.

matter *n* 1 body, material, stuff, substance. 2 discharge, pus, suppuration. 3 *matter of life and death*. affair, business, concern, incident, issue, occurrence, question, situation, subject, topic. 4 *What's the matter?* difficulty, problem, trouble, upset, worry. ● *v* be important, be significant, count, make a difference, signify. **matter-of-fact** ▷ PROSAIC.

mature *adj* 1 adult, experienced, full-grown, grown-up, nubile, of age. 2 mellow, ready, ripe. *Opp* IMMATURE. ● *v* age, develop, grow up, mellow, reach maturity, ripen.

maturity *n* adulthood, completion, majority, mellowness, perfection, readiness, ripeness.

maul *v* claw, lacerate, mangle, manhandle, mutilate, paw, savage, treat roughly, wound.

maximize *v* 1 build up, make the most of. ▷ INCREASE. 2 inflate, magnify, overdo, overstate. ▷ EXAGGERATE. *Opp* MINIMIZE.

maximum *adj* biggest, extreme, full, greatest, highest, largest, most, peak, supreme, top, topmost, utmost. ● *n* apex, ceiling, climax, highest point, peak, pinnacle, top, upper limit, zenith. *Opp* MINIMUM.

maybe *adv* conceivably, perhaps, possibly.

maze *n* complex, labyrinth, network, tangle, web.

meadow *n* field, paddock, pasture.

meagre *adj* deficient, inadequate, mean, paltry, poor,

puny, scanty, slight, sparse, thin. *Opp* SMALL. *Opp* GENEROUS.

meal *n* banquet, *inf* blow-out, breakfast, dinner, *inf* elevenses, feast, lunch, repast, snack, *inf* spread, supper, tea.

mean *adj* **1** close, close-fisted, *inf* mingy, miserly, niggardly, parsimonious, *inf* penny-pinching, selfish, sparing, stingy, *inf* tight, tight-fisted, ungenerous. **2** *mean disposition.* callous, contemptible, cruel, despicable, ignoble, malicious, nasty, spiteful, unkind, vicious. **3** *mean dwelling.* humble, inferior, lowly, miserable, poor, shabby, squalid, wretched. *Opp* GENEROUS, VALUABLE.
● *v* **1** betoken, connote, convey, denote, express, foretell, hint at, imply, indicate, intimate, portend, represent, say, signify, stand for, suggest, symbolize. **2** *I mean to succeed.* aim, desire, hope, intend, plan, propose, want, wish. **3** *The job means long hours.* entail, involve, necessitate.

meander *v* ramble, rove, snake, wander, wind, zigzag. **meandering** ▷ TWISTY.

meaning *n* connotation, definition, drift, explanation, force, gist, idea, implication, import, interpretation, message, point, purport, purpose, relevance, sense, significance, substance, thrust, value.

meaningful *adj* eloquent, expressive, pointed, positive, pregnant, serious, significant, suggestive, telling, weighty, worthwhile. *Opp* MEANINGLESS.

meaningless *adj* **1** absurd, incomprehensible, incoherent, nonsensical, pointless, senseless.

2 *meaningless compliments.* empty, flattering, hollow, insincere, shallow, sycophantic, worthless. *Opp* MEANINGFUL.

means *n* **1** ability, capacity, channel, course, medium, method, mode, process, way. **2** *private means.* ▷ WEALTH.

measurable *adj* appreciable, discernible, significant. *Opp* NEGLIGIBLE.

measure *n* **1** allocation, allowance, amount, extent, magnitude, portion, quantity, quota, ration, size, unit.
▷ MEASUREMENT. **2** criterion, *inf* litmus test, standard, test, yardstick. **3** course of action, expedient, means, procedure, step. **4** act, bill, law, statute.
● *v* assess, calculate, calibrate, compute, count, determine, estimate, gauge, judge, mark out, meter, plumb (*depth*), quantify, rate, reckon, survey. **measure out** ▷ DISPENSE.

measurement *n* assessment, calculation, dimension, evaluation, extent, size. ▷ MEASURE.

meat *n* flesh. ▷ FOOD.

mechanic *n* engineer, technician.

mechanical *adj* **1** automatic, machine-driven. **2** cold, habitual, impersonal, instinctive, lifeless, perfunctory, reflex, routine, soulless, unconscious, unemotional, unfeeling, unthinking. *Opp* HUMAN.

mechanize *v* automate, equip with machines, modernize.

medal *n* award, decoration, honour, medallion, prize, reward, trophy.

meddle *v* ▷ INTERFERE.

mediate *v* act as mediator, arbitrate, liaise, negotiate.

mediator *n* arbitrator, broker, go-between, intermediary, judge, liaison officer, middleman, moderator, negotiator, peacemaker, referee, umpire.

medicinal *adj* curative, healing, restorative, therapeutic.

medicine *n* 1 healing, surgery, therapy. 2 drug, medicament, medication, panacea, prescription, remedy, treatment.

mediocre *adj* average, commonplace, fair, indifferent, inferior, middling, moderate, ordinary, passable, pedestrian, *inf* run-of-the-mill, second-rate, *inf* so-so, undistinguished, unexceptional, uninspired, unremarkable. *Opp* OUTSTANDING.

meditate *v* be lost in thought, brood, cogitate, consider, contemplate, deliberate, mull things over, muse, ponder, pray, reflect, ruminate, think.

meditation *n* contemplation, deliberation, prayer, reflection, rumination, thought.

meditative *adj* ▷ THOUGHTFUL.

medium *adj* average, intermediate, mean, mid, middle, middling, moderate, normal, ordinary, standard, usual.
● *n* 1 average, compromise, mean, middle, midpoint. 2 agency, channel, form, means, method, mode, vehicle, way. 3 clairvoyant, seer, spiritualist. **the media, mass media** ▷ COMMUNICATION.

meek *adj* acquiescent, compliant, deferential, docile, forbearing, gentle, humble, long-suffering, lowly, mild, modest, obedient, patient, quiet, resigned, retiring, self-effacing, shy, soft, spineless, submissive, tame, timid, tractable, unassuming, weak, *inf* wimpish. *Opp* AGGRESSIVE.

meet *v* 1 *inf* bump into, chance upon, come across, confront, encounter, face, happen on, run into, see. 2 be introduced to, make the acquaintance of. 3 greet, *inf* pick up, rendezvous with. 4 assemble, collect, come together, congregate, convene, gather, muster, rally, rendezvous. 5 *The roads don't meet.* come together, connect, converge, cross, intersect, join, link up, merge, touch, unite. 6 *meet a demand.* acquiesce in, agree to, answer, comply with, deal with, fulfil, *inf* measure up to, pay, satisfy, settle, take care of. 7 *meet difficulties.* endure, experience, suffer, undergo.

meeting *n* 1 assembly, audience, conference, congregation, convention, council, gathering, *inf* get-together, forum, rally. 2 appointment, assignation, date, engagement, rendezvous. 3 *chance meeting.* confrontation, encounter. 4 *meeting of lines, roads.* confluence (*of rivers*), convergence, crossing, crossroads, intersection, junction, union.

melancholy *adj* dejected, depressed, depressing, despondent, disconsolate, dismal, dispiriting, *inf* down, forlorn, gloomy, glum, low, lugubrious, miserable, mournful, sombre, sorrowful, unhappy, woebegone. ▷ SAD. *Opp* CHEERFUL. ● *n* ▷ SADNESS.

mellow *adj* 1 mature, rich, ripe, sweet. 2 *mellow mood.* agreeable, easygoing, genial, gentle, happy, mild, peaceful, pleasant, subdued, warm. *Opp* HARSH. ● *v* age, develop, improve with age, mature, ripen, soften, sweeten.

melodious *adj* dulcet, harmonious, lyrical, mellifluous, melodic, sweet, tuneful.

melodramatic *adj* emotional, exaggerated, histrionic, overdone, *inf* over the top, sensationalized, theatrical.

melody *n* air, song, strain, subject, theme, tune.

melt *v* dissolve, liquefy, soften, thaw, unfreeze. **melt away** ▷ DISAPPEAR.

member *n* 1 associate, colleague, fellow. 2 ▷ LIMB.

memorable *adj* catchy (*tune*), distinguished, extraordinary, haunting, impressive, indelible, outstanding, remarkable, striking, unforgettable.

memorial *n* cenotaph, gravestone, headstone, monument, plaque, statue, tablet, tomb.

memorize *n* commit to memory, learn, learn by heart, remember, retain.

memory *n* 1 recall, retention. 2 impression, recollection, reminder, reminiscence, souvenir. 3 *memory of the dead.* honour, remembrance.

menace *n* danger, peril, threat, warning. ● *v* intimidate, threaten. ▷ FRIGHTEN.

mend *v* 1 fix, patch up, put right, rectify, remedy, renew, renovate, repair, restore. 2 *mend your ways.* amend, correct, improve, reform, revise. 3 *mend after illness.* convalesce, heal, improve, recover, recuperate.

menial *adj* degrading, demeaning, humble, inferior, lowly, subservient, unskilled.

● *n* lackey, minion, slave, underling. ▷ SERVANT.

mental *adj* 1 abstract, cerebral, cognitive, conceptual, intellectual, rational, theoretical. 2 [*inf*] ▷ MAD. **mental illness** ▷ MADNESS.

mentality *n* attitude, bent, character, disposition, frame of mind, *inf* make-up, outlook, personality, predisposition, propensity, psychology, temperament.

mention *v* acknowledge, allude to, bring up, broach, cite, comment on, disclose, draw attention to, enumerate, hint at, *inf* let drop, make known, name, note, observe, pay tribute to, point out, refer to, remark, reveal, say, speak about, touch on.

mercenary *adj* acquisitive, avaricious, covetous, grasping, greedy. ● *n* fighter, soldier.

merchandise *n* commodities, goods, produce, products, stock. ● *v* ▷ ADVERTISE.

merchant *n* broker, dealer, distributor, retailer, seller, shopkeeper, stockist, supplier, trader, vendor, wholesaler.

merciful *adj* benevolent, charitable, clement, compassionate, forbearing, forgiving, generous, gracious, humane, humanitarian, kind, kindly, lenient, liberal, mild, pitying, *inf* soft, softhearted, sympathetic, tolerant. *Opp* MERCILESS.

merciless *adj* barbaric, brutal, callous, cruel, hard, hardhearted, harsh, heartless, inexorable, inflexible, inhuman, intolerant, pitiless, relentless, remorseless, ruthless, savage, severe, stern, strict, tyrannical, unbending, unforgiving, unkind, unrelenting, unremitting, vicious. *Opp* MERCIFUL.

mercy *n* charity, clemency, compassion, feeling, forbearance, forgiveness, generosity, grace, humanity, kindness, leniency, love, pity, quarter, sympathy, understanding.

merge *v* 1 amalgamate, blend, coalesce, combine, consolidate, fuse, integrate, link up, mingle, mix, pool, put together, unite. 2 *motorways merge.* converge, join, meet. *Opp* SEPARATE.

merit *n* credit, distinction, excellence, importance, quality, strength, talent, value, virtue, worth, worthiness. ● *v* be entitled to, be worthy of, deserve, earn, justify, rate, warrant.

meritorious *adj* ▷ PRAISEWORTHY.

merriment *n* amusement, conviviality, gaiety, glee, high spirits, hilarity, jollity, joviality, laughter, levity, light-heartedness, liveliness, mirth, vivacity. ▷ MERRYMAKING.

merry *adj* bright, *inf* bubbly, carefree, cheerful, cheery, convivial, festive, fun-loving, gay, glad, jocular, jolly, jovial, joyful, light-hearted, lively, spirited, vivacious. ▷ HAPPY. *Opp* SERIOUS.

merrymaking *n* carousing, celebration, conviviality, festivity, frolic, fun, fun and games, merriment, revelry. ▷ PARTY.

mesh *n* grid, lace, lattice, net, netting, network, sieve, tangle, tracery, trellis, web, webbing.

mess *n* 1 chaos, clutter, disarray, disorder, *inf* hotchpotch, jumble, litter, *inf* mishmash, muddle, *inf* shambles, tangle, untidiness.

▷ CONFUSION, DIRT. 2 *got into a mess.* difficulty, dilemma, *inf* fix, *inf* jam, *inf* pickle, plight, predicament, trouble. ● *v* **mess about** amuse yourself, loaf, loiter, lounge about, *inf* play about. **make a mess of, mess up** ▷ BUNGLE, MUDDLE.

message *n* announcement, bulletin, cable, communication, communiqué, dispatch, information, letter, memo, memorandum, missive, news, note, notice, report, statement.

messenger *n* bearer, carrier, courier, dispatch-rider, emissary, envoy, go-between, herald, intermediary, runner.

messy *adj* careless, chaotic, cluttered, dirty, dishevelled, disorderly, grubby, mucky, muddled, *inf* shambolic, slapdash, *inf* sloppy, slovenly, unkempt, untidy. *Opp* NEAT.

metallic *adj* gleaming, lustrous, shiny.

metaphorical *adj* allegorical, figurative, symbolic. *Opp* LITERAL.

method *n* 1 approach, fashion, *inf* knack, manner, means, mode, plan, procedure, process, programme, recipe, scheme, style, technique, trick, way. 2 arrangement, design, discipline, order, orderliness, organization, pattern, routine, structure, system.

methodical *adj* businesslike, careful, deliberate, disciplined, logical, meticulous, neat, orderly, organized, painstaking, precise, regular, routine, structured, systematic, tidy. *Opp* DISORGANIZED.

meticulous *adj* accurate, careful, exact, fastidious, painstaking, particular, precise, punctilious, scrupulous, thorough. Opp CARELESS.

microbe n bacterium, inf bug, germ, micro-organism, virus.

middle adj central, centre, halfway, inner, inside, intermediate, intervening, mean, mid, midway, neutral. ● n bull's-eye, centre, core, focus, heart, hub, inside, midpoint, midst, nucleus.

middling adj average, fair, inf fair to middling, indifferent, mediocre, moderate, modest, ordinary, passable, inf run-of-the-mill, inf so-so, unremarkable. Opp OUTSTANDING.

might n energy, force, muscle, power, strength, vigour.

mighty adj forceful, great, hefty, muscular, potent, powerful, robust, inf strapping, strong, sturdy, vigorous, weighty. ▷ BIG. Opp WEAK.

migrate v move, relocate, resettle, settle, travel.

mild adj 1 affable, amiable, docile, easygoing, equable, forbearing, forgiving, gentle, good-tempered, harmless, indulgent, inoffensive, kind, kindly, lenient, meek, merciful, modest, peaceable, placid, quiet, inf soft, soft-hearted, submissive, tractable, unassuming. 2 mild weather. balmy, calm, clement, fair, peaceful, pleasant, serene, temperate, warm. 3 mild illness. insignificant, minor, slight, trivial, unimportant. 4 mild flavour. bland, delicate, faint, mellow, subtle. Opp SEVERE, STRONG.

mildness n affability, amiability, clemency, docility, forbearance, gentleness, kindness, leniency,

placidity, softness, tenderness. Opp ASPERITY.

militant adj active, aggressive, assertive, attacking, combative, fierce, hostile. Opp PASSIVE. ● n activist, extremist, inf hawk, partisan.

militaristic adj ▷ WARLIKE. Opp PEACEABLE.

military adj armed, combatant, fighting, martial, uniformed, warlike.

militate against v cancel out, counteract, oppose, prevent, resist.

milk v bleed, drain, exploit, extract, tap, wring.

milky adj chalky, cloudy, misty, opaque, whitish. Opp CLEAR.

mill n 1 factory, foundry, plant, works. 2 crusher, grinder, watermill, windmill. ● v ▷ GRIND. **mill about** move aimlessly, seethe, swarm, throng.

mimic n impersonator, impressionist. ● v ape, caricature, copy, echo, imitate, impersonate, make fun of, mirror, mock, parody, parrot, pretend to be, reproduce, ridicule, satirize, simulate, inf take off.

mind n 1 astuteness, brain, brainpower, brains, inf grey matter, head, insight, intellect, intelligence, judgement, mental power, perception, psyche, reason, sense, shrewdness, wisdom, wit, wits. 2 attitude, belief, bias, disposition, humour, inclination, intention, opinion, outlook, point of view, position, viewpoint. ● v 1 attend to, guard, keep an eye on, look after, take care of, watch. 2 mind the warning. beware of, heed, listen to, look out for, mark, note, obey, pay attention to, remember, watch out for. **3** *won't mind if he's late.* be annoyed, bother, care, object, take offence, worry. **be in two minds** ▷ HESITATE. **make up your mind** ▷ DECIDE. **out of your mind** ▷ MAD.

mindful *adj* alert, attentive, aware, conscious, heedful, vigilant, watchful. ▷ CAREFUL. *Opp* CARELESS.

mindless *adj* fatuous, idiotic, senseless, thoughtless, unthinking, witless. ▷ STUPID. *Opp* INTELLIGENT.

mine *n* **1** coalfield, colliery, excavation, pit, quarry, shaft, tunnel, working. **2** *mine of information.* fund, repository, source, store, storehouse, supply, wealth. • *v* dig, excavate, extract, quarry, remove.

mineral *n* metal, ore, rock.

mingle *v* amalgamate, associate, blend, circulate, combine, fraternize, *inf* hobnob, intermingle, merge, mix, *inf* rub shoulders, socialize.

miniature *adj inf* baby, diminutive, dwarf, pocket, pygmy, scaled-down, tiny, toy. ▷ SMALL.

minimal *adj* least, minimum, negligible, nominal, slightest, smallest, token.

minimize *v* **1** cut down, decrease, diminish, lessen, prune, reduce. **2** *minimize problems.* belittle, decry, gloss over, make light of, play down, underestimate, undervalue. *Opp* MAXIMIZE.

minimum *adj* bottom, least, lowest, minimal, minutest, nominal, *inf* rock bottom, slightest, smallest. • *n* least, lowest, minimum amount. *Opp* MAXIMUM.

minister *n* ▷ CLERGYMAN, OFFICIAL. • *v* **minister** to aid, assist, attend to, care for, help, look after, nurse, see to, support, wait on.

minor *adj* inconsequential, inferior, lesser, negligible, petty, secondary, subordinate, subsidiary, trivial, unimportant. ▷ SMALL. *Opp* MAJOR. • *n* ▷ ADOLESCENT, CHILD.

minstrel *n* entertainer, musician, singer, troubadour.

mint *adj* brand-new, first-class, fresh, immaculate, new, perfect, unblemished, unmarked, unused. • *n* fortune, heap, *inf* packet, pile, stack. • *v* cast, coin, forge, make, manufacture, produce, stamp out, strike.

minute *adj* diminutive, dwarf, infinitesimal, insignificant, microscopic, *inf* mini, miniature, minuscule, *inf* pint-sized, pocket, pygmy, tiny. ▷ SMALL.

minutes *pl n* log, notes, proceedings, record, résumé, summary, transactions.

miracle *n* marvel, miraculous event, mystery, wonder.

miraculous *adj* extraordinary, incredible, inexplicable, magic, magical, mysterious, supernatural, unaccountable, unbelievable. ▷ MARVELLOUS.

mirage *n* delusion, hallucination, illusion, vision.

mire *n* bog, fen, marsh, morass, mud, ooze, quagmire, slime, swamp. ▷ DIRT.

mirror *n* glass, looking-glass, reflector. • *v* ▷ REFLECT.

misadventure *n* accident, calamity, disaster, mischance, misfortune, mishap.

misanthropic adj antisocial, unfriendly, unpleasant, unsociable. Opp PHILANTHROPIC.

misappropriate v embezzle, expropriate. ▷ STEAL.

misbehave v behave badly, be mischievous, inf blot your copybook, disobey, do wrong, err, fool about, make mischief, inf play about, play up, sin, transgress.

misbehaviour n delinquency, disobedience, insubordination, mischief, mischief-making, misconduct, misdemeanour, naughtiness, rudeness, vandalism, wrongdoing.

miscalculate v sl boob, err, inf get it wrong, go wrong, make a mistake, misjudge, misread, overestimate, inf slip up, underestimate.

miscarriage n 1 abortion, premature birth, termination. 2 miscarriage of justice. breakdown, defeat, failure, perversion.

miscarry v 1 abort, inf lose a baby. 2 break down, inf come to grief, come to nothing, fail, fall through, go wrong, misfire. Opp SUCCEED.

miscellaneous adj assorted, different, diverse, heterogeneous, mixed, motley, multifarious, sundry, varied, various.

miscellany n jumble, inf mixed bag, variety. ▷ MIXTURE.

mischief n 1 devilry, misbehaviour, misconduct, naughtiness, playfulness, inf shenanigans, trouble. 2 damage, harm, hurt, injury, misfortune.

mischievous adj badly behaved, disobedient, full of mischief, impish, naughty, playful,

roguish, inf up to no good, wayward. ▷ WICKED. Opp WELL-BEHAVED.

miser n inf Scrooge, inf skinflint. Opp SPENDTHRIFT.

miserable adj 1 crestfallen, dejected, depressed, desolate, despairing, despondent, disconsolate, dismayed, dispirited, distressed, doleful, inf down, downcast, forlorn, gloomy, glum, grief-stricken, heartbroken, hopeless, in low spirits, languishing, lonely, low, melancholy, moping, mournful, sad, sorrowful, tearful, unfortunate, unhappy, unlucky, woebegone, wretched. 2 churlish, cross, disagreeable, grumpy, mean, miserly, morose, pessimistic, sour, sulky, sullen, surly, unhelpful, unsociable. 3 miserable living conditions. abject, awful, deplorable, disgraceful, distressing, hopeless, impoverished, inadequate, inhuman, lamentable, pathetic, pitiful, poor, shameful, sordid, soul-destroying, squalid, vile, wretched. 4 miserable weather. damp, depressing, dismal, dreary, grey, unpleasant, wet. Opp HAPPY, PLEASANT.

miserly adj avaricious, inf cheese-paring, inf close, covetous, economical, grasping, greedy, mean, inf mingy, niggardly, parsimonious, penny-pinching, sparing, stingy, inf tight, inf tight-fisted. Opp GENEROUS.

misery n 1 angst, anguish, bitterness, despair, desperation, despondency, distress, gloom, grief, heartache, heartbreak, inf hell, hopelessness, melancholy, sadness, sorrow, suffering, unhappi-

ness, woe, wretchedness.
Opp HAPPINESS. **2** adversity,
affliction, deprivation, destitution, hardship, misfortune, need,
oppression, penury, poverty, privation, squalor, suffering, tribulation, trouble, want.

misfire *v* abort, fail, fall through,
inf flop, founder, go wrong, miscarry. *Opp* SUCCEED.

misfortune *n* accident, adversity, affliction, bad luck, blow,
calamity, catastrophe, curse, disappointment, disaster, evil, hardship, misadventure, mischance,
mishap, reverse, set-back, tragedy, trouble, vicissitude.

misguided *adj* foolish, ill-
advised, inappropriate, misin-
formed, misjudged, misled, mistaken, unfounded, unjust,
unwise. ▷ WRONG.

misjudge *v* get wrong, guess
wrongly, make a mistake, misinterpret, overestimate, underestimate. ▷ MISCALCULATE.

mislay *v* ▷ LOSE.

mislead *v* bluff, confuse, delude,
fool, give a wrong impression to,
lead astray, lie to, misguide, mis-
inform, outwit, take in,
inf throw off the scent, trick.
▷ DECEIVE. **misleading**
▷ DECEPTIVE, PUZZLING.

miss *v* **1** avoid, be absent from,
be too late for, dodge, escape,
evade, forget, lose, play truant
from, skip, *sl* skive off. **2** *miss a
target*. be wide of, fail to hit, fall
short of. **3** *miss absent friends*.
grieve for, long for, need, pine
for, want, yearn for. **miss out**
▷ OMIT.

misshapen *adj* bent, contorted,
crooked, deformed, disfigured,
distorted, gnarled, grotesque,
knotted, malformed, monstrous,

twisted, twisty, ugly, warped.
Opp PERFECT.

missile *n* projectile, rocket,
weapon.

missing *adj* absent, disappeared,
lost, mislaid, straying, truant,
unaccounted for. *Opp* PRESENT.

mission *n* **1** delegation, deputation, task-force. **2** *mission in life*.
aim, assignment, calling, duty,
goal, job, life's work, métier,
objective, occupation, profession, purpose, quest, undertaking, vocation. **3** *evangelical mission*. campaign, crusade, holy
war.

missionary *n* crusader, evangelist, minister, preacher.

mist *n* **1** cloud, drizzle, fog, haze,
vapour. **2** condensation, film,
steam.

mistake *n* *inf* bloomer, blunder,
sl boob, error, fault, *Fr* faux pas,
gaffe, *inf* howler, inaccuracy,
indiscretion, lapse, misapprehension, miscalculation, misconception, misjudgement, misprint,
misunderstanding, omission,
oversight, slip, *inf* slip-up.
● *v* confuse, get wrong, misconstrue, misinterpret, misjudge,
misread, misunderstand, mix
up, *inf* take the wrong way.

mistaken *adj* erroneous, distorted, false, ill-judged, inappropriate, incorrect, misguided, mis-
informed, unfounded, unjust.
▷ WRONG. *Opp* CORRECT.

mistimed *adj* early, inconvenient, inopportune, late, untimely.
Opp OPPORTUNE.

mistreat *v* abuse, damage, harm,
hurt, ill-treat, injure, maltreat,
manhandle, misuse, molest,
treat roughly.

mistress *n* **1** keeper, owner, person in charge. **2** ▷ TEACHER. **3** ▷ LOVER.

mistrust *n* apprehension, distrust, doubt, misgiving, reservation, scepticism, suspicion, uncertainty, wariness. ● *v* be suspicious of, be wary of, disbelieve, distrust, doubt, fear, have misgivings about, question, suspect. *Opp* TRUST.

misty *adj* bleary, blurred, clouded, cloudy, dim, faint, foggy, fuzzy, hazy, indistinct, murky, obscure, opaque, shadowy, steamy, vague. *Opp* CLEAR.

misunderstand *v inf* get the wrong end of the stick, get wrong, misconstrue, mishear, misinterpret, misjudge, misread, mistake. *Opp* UNDERSTAND.

misunderstanding *n* **1** error, false impression, misapprehension, misconception, misinterpretation, misjudgement, misreading, mistake, *inf* mix up, wrong idea. **2** disagreement, dispute. ▷ QUARREL.

misuse *n* abuse, corruption, illtreatment, maltreatment, misappropriation. ● *v* **1** damage, harm, mishandle, treat carelessly. **2** *misuse an animal.* ▷ MISTREAT. **3** *misuse funds.* fritter away, misappropriate, squander, waste.

mitigate *v* abate, allay, alleviate, decrease, ease, extenuate, lessen, lighten, moderate, qualify, reduce, relieve, soften, temper, tone down. *Opp* AGGRAVATE.

mix *n* amalgam, assortment, blend, combination, compound, range, variety. ● *v* **1** alloy, amalgamate, blend, coalesce, combine, compound, confuse, diffuse, fuse, integrate, intermingle, join, jumble up, merge, mingle, mix up, muddle, shuffle, stir together, unite. *Opp* SEPARATE. **2** *mix with people.* ▷ SOCIALIZE.

mixed *adj* **1** assorted, different, diverse, heterogeneous, miscellaneous, varied, various. **2** amalgamated, combined, composite, diluted, integrated, joint, united. **3** *mixed feelings.* ambiguous, ambivalent, confused, equivocal, muddled, uncertain.

mixture *n* **1** alloy, amalgam, amalgamation, assortment, blend, collection, combination, composite, compound, concoction, conglomeration, fusion, *inf* hotchpotch, intermingling, jumble, medley, miscellany, *inf* mishmash, mix, *inf* motley collection, pot-pourri, selection, synthesis, variety. **2** cross-breed, hybrid, mongrel.

moan *n* complaint, grievance, lament, lamentation. ● *v* **1** complain, *inf* grouse, grumble, whine. **2** cry, groan, keen, lament, sigh, ululate, wail, weep, whimper.

mob *n inf* bunch, crowd, gang, herd, horde, host, multitude, pack, press, rabble, riot, *inf* shower, swarm, throng. ▷ GROUP. ● *v* besiege, crowd round, hem in, jostle, surround.

mobile *adj* **1** itinerant, movable, portable, travelling. **2** able to move, active, *inf* up and about. **3** *mobile features.* animated, changeable, changing, expressive, flexible, fluid. *Opp* IMMOVABLE.

mobilize *v* activate, assemble, call up, enlist, enrol, gather, get together, marshal, muster, organize, rally, stir up, summon.

mock adj artificial, fake, false, inf pretend, substitute.
▷ IMITATION. ● v decry, deride, disparage, insult, jeer at, laugh at, make fun of, parody, poke fun at, ridicule, scoff at, scorn, inf send up, sneer at, taunt, tease. ▷ MIMIC.

mockery n 1 derision, insults, jeering, laughter, ridicule, scorn. 2 caricature, parody, inf send-up, travesty.

mocking adj contemptuous, derisive, disparaging, disrespectful, insulting, irreverent, jeering, rude, sarcastic, satirical, scornful, taunting, teasing, unkind. Opp RESPECTFUL.

mode n 1 approach, manner, medium, method, procedure, set-up, system, technique, way. 2 ▷ FASHION.

model adj 1 imitation, miniature, scaled-down, toy. 2 model pupil. exemplary, ideal, perfect, unequalled. ● n 1 archetype, copy, dummy, effigy, image, imitation, likeness, miniature, inf mock-up, prototype, replica, representation, toy. 2 model of excellence. byword, epitome, example, exemplar, ideal, paragon, pattern, standard, yardstick. 3 artist's model. sitter, subject. 4 latest model. brand, design, kind, type, version. 5 fashion model. mannequin. ● v carve, fashion, form, make, mould, inf sculpt, sculpture, shape. **model yourself on** ▷ IMITATE.

moderate adj 1 average, balanced, calm, cautious, fair, judicious, medium, middling, modest, ordinary, reasonable, respectable, sensible, sober, steady, temperate, unexcep-tional, usual. Opp EXTREME. 2 moderate winds. gentle, light, mild. ● v 1 abate, decline, decrease, die down, ease off, subside. 2 calm, check, keep down, lessen, mitigate, modify, modulate, reduce, regulate, restrain, slacken, subdue, temper, tone down.

moderately adv comparatively, fairly, passably, quite, rather, reasonably, somewhat.

moderation n balance, caution, common sense, fairness, reasonableness, restraint, reticence, sobriety, temperance.

modern adj advanced, avant-garde, contemporary, current, fashionable, forward-looking, fresh, futuristic, in vogue, latest, new, newfangled, novel, present, present-day, progressive, recent, stylish, inf trendy, up-to-date. Opp OLD.

modernize v bring up-to-date, inf do up, improve, rebuild, redesign, redo, refurbish, renovate, revamp, update.

modest adj 1 bashful, coy, diffident, discreet, humble, meek, quiet, reserved, restrained, reticent, retiring, self-conscious, self-effacing, shy, unassuming, unobtrusive, unpretentious. Opp CONCEITED. 2 modest dress. chaste, decent, demure, proper, simple. 3 modest house. inconspicuous, lowly, ordinary, plain, 4 modest income. moderate, ordinary, reasonable, unexceptional. Opp EXCESSIVE.

modesty n 1 bashfulness, coyness, discretion, humility, meekness, reserve, restraint, reticence, self-consciousness, shyness. Opp OSTENTATION.

2 decorum, decency, propriety, seemliness.

modify *v* adapt, adjust, alter, amend, change, improve, redesign, remake, remodel, reorganize, revise, reword, transform, vary. ▷ MODERATE.

modulate *v* adjust, balance, change key, change the tone, moderate, regulate, soften.

moist *adj* clammy, damp, dank, dewy, humid, muggy, rainy, steamy, watery. ▷ WET. *Opp* DRY.

moisten *v* dampen, soak, spray, wet. *Opp* DRY.

moisture *n* condensation, damp, dampness, dew, humidity, liquid, precipitation, spray, steam, vapour, water.

molest *v* abuse, accost, annoy, assault, badger, bother, disturb, harass, interfere with, manhandle, mistreat, persecute, pester, plague, torment, vex, worry.

molten *adj* fluid, liquid, liquefied, melted, soft.

moment *n* **1** flash, instant, *inf* jiffy, minute, second, split second, *inf* tick, *inf* twinkling of an eye. **2** *historic moment*. hour, juncture, occasion, opportunity, time.

momentary *adj* brief, ephemeral, evanescent, fleeting, fugitive, passing, short-lived, temporary, transient, transitory. *Opp* PERMANENT.

momentous *adj* critical, crucial, decisive, epoch-making, fateful, grave, historic, important, serious, significant, weighty. *Opp* UNIMPORTANT.

monarch *n* emperor, empress, king, queen, ruler, tsar.

monarchy *n* empire, domain, kingdom, realm.

money *n* affluence, assets, banknotes, *inf* bread, capital, cash, change, coins, currency, *inf* dough, earnings, finances, fortune, funds, legal tender, *inf* lolly, *old use* lucre, *inf* nest-egg, notes, pocket-money, proceeds, profit, *inf* the ready, resources, revenue, riches, savings, sterling, takings, wage, wealth, *inf* the wherewithal, winnings.

mongrel *n* cross-breed, hybrid.

monitor *n* **1** prefect, supervisor, watchdog. **2** *TV monitor*. screen, set, television, VDU, visual display unit. ● *v* check, *inf* keep an eye on, oversee, record, supervise, trace, track, watch.

monk *n* brother, friar, hermit.

monkey *n* ape, primate, simian.

monopolize *v* control, corner, dominate, *inf* hog, keep for yourself, take over. *Opp* SHARE.

monotonous *adj* boring, dreary, dull, featureless, flat, level, repetitive, soporific, tedious, tiresome, uneventful, uniform, uninteresting, unvarying, wearisome. *Opp* INTERESTING.

monster *n* beast, bogey-man, brute, demon, devil, fiend, giant, horror, monstrosity, mutant, ogre, troll.

monstrous *adj* **1** colossal, enormous, gargantuan, giant, gigantic, huge, *inf* hulking, immense, mammoth, mighty, prodigious, titanic, towering, tremendous, vast. ▷ BIG. **2** *monstrous crime*. abhorrent, atrocious, awful, beastly, brutal, cruel, dreadful, disgusting, evil, grisly, gross, gruesome, heinous, hideous, horrendous, horrible, horrific, inhuman, nightmarish, obscene, outrageous, repulsive, shocking, terrible, villainous, wicked. ▷ EVIL.

monument n cenotaph, cross, gravestone, headstone, mausoleum, memorial, obelisk, pillar, relic, reminder, shrine, tomb, tombstone.

monumental adj 1 awe-inspiring, awesome, enduring, epoch-making, grand, historic, impressive, lasting, major, memorable, unforgettable. ▷ BIG. 2 commemorative, memorial.

mood n 1 attitude, disposition, frame of mind, humour, spirit, state of mind, temper, vein. 2 atmosphere, feeling, tone. **in the mood** ▷ READY.

moody adj bad-tempered, cantankerous, capricious, changeable, crabby, cross, crotchety, depressed, disgruntled, erratic, gloomy, grumpy, irritable, melancholy, miserable, morose, peevish, petulant, short-tempered, snappy, sulky, sullen, temperamental, touchy, unpredictable, unstable, volatile. ▷ SAD.

moor n fell, heath, moorland. • v anchor, berth, dock, make fast, secure, tie up. ▷ FASTEN.

mope v languish, inf moon, pine, sulk.

moral adj blameless, chaste, decent, ethical, good, high-minded, honest, honourable, incorruptible, innocent, irreproachable, just, moralistic, noble, principled, proper, pure, respectable, responsible, right, righteous, sinless, trustworthy, truthful, upright, virtuous. Opp IMMORAL. • n lesson,

maxim, meaning, message, point, precept, principle. **morals** ▷ MORALITY. **moral tale** allegory, cautionary tale, fable, parable.

morale n cheerfulness, confidence, inf heart, self-confidence, self-esteem, spirit, state of mind.

morality n decency, ethics, ethos, goodness, honesty, integrity, justice, morals, principles, rectitude, righteousness, scruples, standards, uprightness, virtue.

moralize v lecture, philosophize, pontificate, preach, sermonize.

morbid adj black (humour), brooding, ghoulish, gloomy, grim, lugubrious, macabre, pessimistic, inf sick, sombre, unhealthy, unpleasant, unwholesome. Opp CHEERFUL.

more adj added, additional, extra, further, increased, new, other, renewed, supplementary. Opp LESS.

moreover adv also, as well, besides, further, furthermore, in addition, too.

morose adj bad-tempered, depressed, gloomy, glum, grim, humourless, melancholy, moody, mournful, pessimistic, saturnine, sour, sulky, sullen, surly, taciturn, unhappy, unsociable. ▷ SAD. Opp CHEERFUL.

morsel n bite, crumb, fragment, mouthful, nibble, piece, sample, scrap, small amount, taste, titbit. ▷ BIT.

mortal adj 1 ephemeral, human, passing, transient. Opp IMMORTAL. 2 mortal illness. deadly, fatal, lethal, terminal. 3 mortal enemies. deadly, implacable, irreconcilable, sworn, unrelenting. • n creature, human being, man, person, woman.

mortality n 1 humanity, impermanence, transience. 2 *infant mortality*. death rate, loss of life.

mortify v ▷ HUMILIATE.

mostly adv chiefly, generally, largely, mainly, predominantly, primarily, principally, typically, usually.

moth-eaten adj antiquated, decrepit, holey, mangy, ragged, shabby, *inf* tatty. ▷ OLD.

mother n *inf* ma, *inf* mamma, *old use* mater, *inf* mum, *inf* mummy, parent. • v care for, cherish, comfort, cuddle, fuss over, indulge, look after, love, nurse, pamper, protect, take care of.

motherly adj caring, kind, maternal, protective. ▷ LOVING.

motif n decoration, design, device, figure, idea, ornament, pattern, symbol, theme.

motion n action, activity, agitation, change, commotion, movement, progress, rise and fall, shift, stir, travel, travelling. • v ▷ GESTURE.

motionless adj at rest, calm, frozen, immobile, lifeless, paralysed, resting, stagnant, static, stationary, still, stock-still, unmoving. *Opp* MOVING.

motivate v activate, arouse, cause, drive, egg on, encourage, galvanize, goad, incite, induce, influence, inspire, instigate, move, persuade, prompt, provoke, push, rouse, spur, stimulate, stir, urge.

motive n aim, ambition, cause, drive, end, grounds, impulse, incentive, inducement, inspiration, instigation, intention, motivation, object, purpose, rationale, reason, spur, stimulus, thinking.

motor n engine, mechanism. ▷ CAR. • v drive, go by car.

mottled adj blotchy, patchy, speckled, spotty. ▷ DAPPLED.

motto n ▷ SAYING.

mould n blight, fungus, growth, mildew. • v cast, fashion, forge, form, model, *inf* sculpt, shape, stamp, work.

mouldy adj damp, decaying, fusty, mildewed, musty, rotten, stale.

mound n bank, dune, heap, hill, hillock, hummock, hump, knoll, pile, stack.

mount n ▷ MOUNTAIN.
• v 1 ascend, clamber up, climb, go up, rise, scale. *Opp* DESCEND. 2 *mount a horse*. get astride, jump onto. 3 *savings mount*. accumulate, build up, escalate, expand, grow, increase, intensify, multiply, pile up, swell. *Opp* DECREASE. 4 *mount a picture*. display, exhibit, frame, install, put in place, set up.

mountain n alp, eminence, height, mount, peak, prominence, range, ridge, sierra, summit, tor, volcano.

mountainous adj alpine, craggy, high, hilly, precipitous, rocky, rugged, steep, towering. ▷ BIG.

mourn v bemoan, bewail, grieve, keen, lament, pine, regret, wail, weep. *Opp* REJOICE.

mournful adj dismal, distressing, doleful, funereal, gloomy, grief-stricken, grieving, heartbreaking, lamenting, lugubrious, melancholy, plaintive, plangent, sad, sorrowful, tearful,

tragic, unhappy, woeful.
Opp CHEERFUL.

mouth *n* 1 *inf* chops, *sl* gob, jaws,
lips, maw, muzzle. 2 *mouth of a
cave*. aperture, door, entrance,
exit, gateway, inlet, opening, orifice, outlet, way in. 3 *mouth of a
river*. delta, estuary, outflow.
● *v* articulate, enunciate, form,
pronounce. ▷ SAY.

mouthful *n* bite, gulp, morsel,
sip, spoonful, swallow, taste.

movable *adj* adjustable, changeable, detachable, floating,
mobile, portable, transferable,
transportable, unfixed, variable.
Opp IMMOVABLE.

move *n* 1 act, action, deed,
device, dodge, gambit, manoeuvre, measure, movement,
ploy, ruse, step, stratagem,
inf tack, tactic. 2 *career move*.
change, relocation, shift, transfer. 3 *your move*. chance, go,
opportunity, turn. ● *v* 1 *move
about*. be astir, budge, fidget,
roll, shake, shift, stir, swing,
toss, tremble, turn, twist, twitch,
wag, wave. 2 *move along*. cruise,
fly, jog, journey, make progress,
march, pass, proceed, travel,
walk. 3 *move quickly*. bolt,
canter, career, dash, dart, flit,
fly, gallop, hasten, hurry, hurtle,
hustle, *inf* nip, race, run, rush,
shoot, speed, stampede, streak,
sweep along, *inf* tear, *inf* zip,
zoom. 4 *move slowly*. amble,
crawl, dawdle, drift, stroll.
5 *move gracefully*. dance, flow,
glide, skate, skim, slide, sweep.
6 *move awkwardly*. falter, flounder, lumber, lurch, pitch,
shuffle, stagger, stumble, totter,
trip, trundle. 7 *move stealthily*.
crawl, creep, edge, slink, slither.
8 *move things*. carry, export,

import, shift, ship, relocate,
transfer, transplant, transport,
transpose. 9 *move him to action*.
encourage, impel, influence,
inspire, persuade, prompt, stimulate, urge. 10 *move one's feelings*.
affect, arouse, fire, impassion,
rouse, stir, touch. 11 *move on a
problem*. act, make a move, take
action. **move away** ▷ DEPART.
move back ▷ RETREAT. **move
down** ▷ DESCEND. **move in**
▷ ENTER. **move round**
▷ CIRCULATE, ROTATE. **move
towards** ▷ APPROACH. **move
up** ▷ ASCEND.

movement *n* 1 action, activity,
migration, motion, shifting, stirring. ▷ GESTURE, MOVE.
2 *movement towards green issues*.
change, development, drift,
evolution, progress, shift, swing,
tendency, trend. 3 *political movement*. campaign, crusade, faction, group, organization, party.
4 *military movements*. exercises,
operations.

movie *n* film, *inf* flick, motion
picture.

moving *adj* 1 active, alive, astir,
dynamic, flowing, mobile, on the
move, travelling, under way.
Opp MOTIONLESS. 2 *moving tale*.
affecting, emotional, emotive,
heart-rending, heart-warming,
inspiring, pathetic, poignant,
stirring, *inf* tear-jerking,
touching.

mow *v* clip, cut, scythe, shear.

muck *n* dirt, filth, grime,
inf gunge, mess, mire, mud,
ooze, ordure, rubbish, scum,
sewage, slime, sludge.
▷ EXCRETA.

mucky *adj* dirty, filthy, foul,
grimy, grubby, messy, muddy,

scummy, slimy, soiled, sordid, squalid. *Opp* CLEAN.

mud *n* dirt, mire, muck, ooze, silt, slime, sludge, slurry, soil.

muddle *n* chaos, clutter, confusion, disorder, *inf* hotchpotch, jumble, mess, *inf* mishmash, *inf* mix up, *inf* shambles, tangle, untidiness. ● *v* 1 bemuse, bewilder, confound, confuse, disorientate, mislead, perplex, puzzle. *Opp* CLARIFY. 2 disarrange, disorder, entangle, *inf* foul up, jumble, make a mess of, *inf* mess up, mix up, shuffle, tangle. *Opp* TIDY.

muddy *adj* 1 caked, dirty, filthy, messy, soiled. 2 *muddy water.* cloudy, opaque. 3 *muddy ground.* boggy, marshy, sodden, soft, spongy, waterlogged, wet. *Opp* CLEAN, FIRM.

muffle *v* 1 cloak, conceal, cover, enclose, enfold, envelop, shroud, swathe, wrap up. 2 *muffle noise.* dampen, deaden, disguise, dull, hush, mask, mute, quieten, silence, soften, stifle, still, suppress.

muffled *adj* deadened, dull, fuzzy, indistinct, muted, silenced, stifled, suppressed, unclear. *Opp* CLEAR.

mug *n* beaker, cup, pot, tankard. ● *v* assault, rob, steal from. ▷ ATTACK. **mug up** ▷ LEARN.

mugger *n* attacker, hooligan, robber, ruffian, thief, thug.

mugging *n* attack, robbery, street crime.

muggy *adj* clammy, close, damp, humid, moist, oppressive, steamy, sticky, stuffy, sultry.

multiple *adj* collective, compound, many, numerous, several, various.

multiplicity *n* abundance, array, number, profusion, variety.

multiply *v* 1 double, quadruple, triple. 2 breed, increase, proliferate, propagate, reproduce, spread.

multitude *n* crowd, host, mass, myriad, swarm, throng. ▷ GROUP.

mumble *v* murmur, mutter, speak indistinctly.

munch *v* bite, chew, champ, chomp, crunch, gnaw.

mundane *adj* banal, common, commonplace, dull, everyday, familiar, pedestrian, prosaic, routine, worldly. ▷ ORDINARY. *Opp* EXTRAORDINARY, SPIRITUAL.

municipal *adj* borough, city, civic, community, district, local, public, town, urban.

murder *n* assassination, genocide, homicide, infanticide, killing, manslaughter, regicide, unlawful killing. ● *v* ▷ KILL.

murderer *n* assassin, butcher, cut-throat, gunman, *sl* hit man, killer, slayer.

murderous *adj* barbarous, bloodthirsty, bloody, brutal, cruel, deadly, ferocious, fierce, homicidal, pitiless, ruthless, savage, vicious, violent.

murky *adj* clouded, cloudy, dark, dim, dull, foggy, funereal, gloomy, grey, misty, muddy, obscure, overcast, shadowy, sombre. *Opp* CLEAR.

murmur *n* background noise, buzz, drone, hum, mutter, rumble, undertone, whisper. ● *v* drone, hum, mumble, mutter, rumble, speak in an undertone, whisper.

muscular *adj* athletic, *inf* beefy, brawny, burly, hefty, powerful, robust, sinewy, *inf* strapping, strong, sturdy, tough, well-built, wiry. *Opp* WEAK.

muse *v* cogitate, consider, contemplate, deliberate, meditate, mull over, ponder, reflect, ruminate, study, think.

mushy *adj* pulpy, spongy, squashy. ▷ SOFT.

musical *adj* euphonious, harmonious, lyrical, melodious, pleasant, sweet-sounding, tuneful.

musician *n* composer, music-maker, performer, player, singer. **musicians** band, ensemble, group, orchestra.

muster *v* assemble, call together, collect, convene, convoke, gather, get together, group, marshal, mobilize, rally, round up, summon.

musty *adj* airless, damp, dank, fusty, mildewed, mouldy, stale, stuffy, unventilated.

mutant *n* deviant, freak, monster, monstrosity, variant.

mutation *n* alteration, evolution, metamorphosis, modification, transfiguration, transformation, variation. ▷ CHANGE.

mute *adj* dumb, quiet, silent, speechless, tongue-tied.
● *v* ▷ MUFFLE.

mutilate *v* cripple, damage, deface, disfigure, dismember, injure, lame, maim, mangle, mar, spoil, vandalize, wound.

mutinous *adj* defiant, disobedient, insubordinate, insurgent, rebellious, refractory, revolutionary, seditious, subversive, ungovernable, unmanageable, unruly. *Opp* OBEDIENT.

mutiny *n* defiance, disobedience, insubordination, insurrection, rebellion, revolt, revolution, sedition, subversion, uprising.
● *v* agitate, be mutinous, disobey, rebel, revolt, rise up, strike.

mutter *v* grumble, mumble, murmur, speak in an undertone, whisper.

mutual *adj* common, joint, reciprocal, requited, shared.

muzzle *n* jaws, mouth, nose, snout. ● *v* censor, gag, restrain, silence, stifle, suppress.

mysterious *adj* arcane, baffling, cryptic, curious, enigmatic, incomprehensible, inexplicable, inscrutable, magical, miraculous, mystical, mystifying, obscure, perplexing, puzzling, secret, strange, uncanny, unfathomable, unknown, weird. *Opp* STRAIGHTFORWARD.

mystery *n* conundrum, enigma, miracle, problem, puzzle, question, riddle, secret.

mystical *adj* arcane, mysterious, occult, other-worldly, religious, spiritual, supernatural. *Opp* MUNDANE.

mystify *v* baffle, *inf* bamboozle, bewilder, confound, confuse, *inf* flummox, perplex, puzzle.

myth *n* 1 allegory, fable, legend, mythology. 2 fabrication, fiction, invention, pretence, untruth.

mythical *adj* 1 allegorical, fabled, fabulous, legendary, mythological, symbolic. 2 fanciful, fictional, imaginary, invented, make-believe, non-existent, unreal. *Opp* REAL.

N

nadir n bottom, depths, low point, zero. *Opp* ZENITH.

nag n ▷ HORSE. ● v annoy, badger, chivvy, goad, harass, hector, *inf* henpeck, keep complaining, pester, *inf* plague, scold, worry.

nail n pin, spike, stud, tack. ● v ▷ FASTEN.

naive adj artless, *inf* born yesterday, childlike, credulous, *inf* green, guileless, gullible, inexperienced, ingenuous, innocent, simple, trustful, trusting, unsophisticated, unsuspecting. *Opp* ARTFUL.

naked adj bare, denuded, exposed, in the nude, nude, stark-naked, stripped, unclothed, uncovered, undressed.

name n 1 alias, Christian name, first name, forename, given name, *inf* handle, identity, nickname, pen name, pseudonym, surname, title. 2 designation, epithet, term. ● v 1 baptize, call, christen, dub, style. 2 *name a book*. entitle, label. 3 *name him man of the match*. appoint, choose, designate, elect, nominate, select, single out, specify. **named** ▷ SPECIFIC.

nameless adj 1 anonymous, incognito, unidentified, unnamed, unsung. 2 *nameless horrors*. dreadful, horrible. ▷ UNSPEAKABLE.

nap n catnap, doze, rest, siesta, sleep, snooze.

narrate v chronicle, describe, detail, recount, relate, report, tell, unfold.

narration n commentary, reading, recital, recitation, relation, storytelling, voice-over.

narrative n account, chronicle, description, history, report, story, tale, *inf* yarn.

narrator n author, reporter, storyteller.

narrow adj close, confined, cramped, enclosed, fine, limited, restricted, slender, slim, thin, tight. *Opp* WIDE.

narrow-minded adj biased, bigoted, conservative, conventional, hidebound, illiberal, inflexible, insular, intolerant, narrow, parochial, petty, prejudiced, prim, puritanical, reactionary, rigid, strait-laced, *inf* stuffy. *Opp* BROAD-MINDED.

nasty adj bad, beastly, dirty, disagreeable, disgusting, distasteful, foul, hateful, horrible, loathsome, objectionable, obnoxious, obscene, *inf* off-putting, repulsive, revolting, sickening, unkind, unpleasant. *Opp* NICE.

nation n civilization, community, country, domain, land, people, population, power, race, realm, society, state.

national adj 1 domestic, internal. 2 *national emergency*. countrywide, general, nationwide, widespread. ● n citizen, inhabitant, native, resident, subject.

nationalism n ▷ PATRIOTISM.

native adj 1 indigenous, local, original. 2 *native wit*. congenital, hereditary, inborn, inherent, inherited, innate, mother (*tongue*), natural. ● *n* citizen, local inhabitant.

natural *adj* **1** common, everyday, habitual, normal, ordinary, predictable, regular, routine, standard, typical, usual. **2** *natural feelings*. healthy, human, inborn, inherent, innate, instinctive, intuitive, maternal, paternal. **3** *natural smile*. artless, genuine, guileless, sincere, spontaneous, unaffected, unselfconscious. **4** *natural resources*. crude (*oil*), raw, unadulterated, unprocessed, unrefined. **5** *natural leader*. born, untaught. Opp UNNATURAL.

nature *n* **1** countryside, creation, environment, natural world. **2** attributes, character, constitution, disposition, essence, humour, *inf* make-up, manner, personality, properties, temperament, traits. **3** category, kind, sort, species, type, variety.

naughty *adj* **1** bad, badly-behaved, bad-mannered, contrary, delinquent, disobedient, disruptive, fractious, head-strong, impish, incorrigible, insubordinate, intractable, mischievous, obstinate, obstreperous, perverse, playful, rebellious, roguish, rude, self-willed, stubborn, troublesome, uncontrollable, undisciplined, unmanageable, unruly, wayward, wicked, wild, wilful. **2** [*inf*] cheeky, improper, ribald, risqué, smutty, vulgar. ▷ OBSCENE. Opp POLITE, WELL BEHAVED.

nauseate *v* disgust, offend, repel, revolt, sicken.

nauseating *adj* disgusting, offensive, repulsive, revolting, sickening.

nautical *adj* marine, maritime, naval, seafaring, seagoing.

navigate *v* direct, drive, guide, handle, manoeuvre, map-read, pilot, sail, steer.

navy *n* armada, convoy, fleet, flotilla.

near *adj* **1** adjacent, adjoining, bordering, close, connected, nearby, neighbouring. **2** *Christmas is near*. approaching, coming, forthcoming, imminent, impending, looming, *inf* round the corner. **3** *near friends*. close, dear, familiar, intimate. Opp DISTANT.

nearly *adv* about, all but, almost, approaching, approximately, around, as good as, close to, just about, not quite, practically, roughly, virtually.

neat *adj* **1** *neat room*. clean, orderly, shipshape, *inf* spick and span, tidy, uncluttered, well-kept. **2** *neat dress*. dainty, smart, spruce, trim. **3** *neat work*. accurate, deft, dexterous, methodical, meticulous, precise. **4** *neat alcohol*. pure, straight, unadulterated, undiluted. Opp CLUMSY, UNTIDY.

necessary *adj* compulsory, essential, imperative, important, indispensable, inescapable, inevitable, mandatory, needed, obligatory, required, requisite, unavoidable, vital. Opp UNNECESSARY.

necessity *n* **1** essential, inevitability, *inf* must, need, obligation, prerequisite, requirement, requisite. **2** destitution, hardship, need, penury, poverty, privation, shortage, suffering, want.

need *n* call, demand, lack, requirement, want.

▷ NECESSITY. ● *v* be short of, call for, demand, depend on, lack, miss, rely on, require, want.

needless *adj* excessive, gratuitous. ▷ UNNECESSARY.

needy *adj* destitute, *inf* hard up, impecunious, impoverished, indigent, penurious, poverty-stricken. ▷ POOR.

negate *v* deny, disprove. ▷ NULLIFY.

negative *adj inf* anti, contradictory, destructive, grudging, obstructive, pessimistic, uncooperative, unenthusiastic, unhelpful, unwilling. ● *n* denial, no, refusal, rejection, veto. *Opp* POSITIVE.

neglect *n* carelessness, inattention, indifference, negligence, oversight. ● *v* be remiss about, disregard, forget, ignore, let slide, omit, overlook, pay no attention to, shirk, skip. **neglected** ▷ DERELICT.

negligent *adj* careless, forgetful, heedless, inattentive, irresponsible, lax, offhand, reckless, remiss, slack, thoughtless, uncaring, unthinking. *Opp* CAREFUL.

negligible *adj* imperceptible, inconsequential, insignificant, paltry, petty, slight, small, tiny, trifling, trivial, unimportant. *Opp* CONSIDERABLE.

negotiate *v* arbitrate, bargain, confer, deal, discuss terms, haggle, make arrangements, mediate, parley.

negotiation *n* arbitration, bargaining, conciliation, debate, diplomacy, discussion, mediation, transaction.

negotiator *n* agent, ambassador, arbitrator, broker, conciliator,

diplomat, go-between, intermediary, mediator, middleman.

neighbourhood *n* area, community, district, environs, locality, place, quarter, region, surroundings, vicinity, zone.

neighbouring *adj* adjacent, adjoining, attached, bordering, close, closest, connecting, near, nearby, nearest, next-door, surrounding.

neighbourly *adj* civil, considerate, friendly, helpful, kind, sociable, well-disposed.

nerve *n* coolness, resolution, resolve, will-power. ▷ COURAGE.

nervous *adj* afraid, agitated, anxious, apprehensive, edgy, excitable, fidgety, flustered, fretful, highly-strung, ill-at-ease, insecure, *inf* jittery, *inf* jumpy, neurotic, on edge, *inf* on tenterhooks, restless, shaky, shy, tense, timid, *inf* twitchy, uneasy, unnerved, unsettled, *inf* uptight, worried. ▷ FRIGHTENED. *Opp* CALM.

nestle *v* cuddle, curl up, huddle, nuzzle, snuggle.

net *n* lace, mesh, netting, network, web. ● *v* 1 catch, capture, ensnare, trap. 2 *net £40 a day*. bring in, clear, earn, get, make, realize, receive, *inf* take home.

network *n* 1 *inf* criss-cross, grid, labyrinth, lattice, maze, mesh, net, tracery, web. 2 complex, organization, system.

neurosis *n* anxiety, obsession, phobia.

neurotic *adj* anxious, distraught, irrational, nervous, obsessive, overwrought, unbalanced, unstable.

neuter adj asexual, sterile.
- v castrate, inf doctor, emasculate, geld, spay, sterilize.

neutral adj 1 detached, disinterested, dispassionate, fair, impartial, indifferent, non-aligned, non-partisan, objective, unbiased, uncommitted, uninvolved, unprejudiced. Opp BIASED. 2 neutral colours. colourless, dull, drab, indeterminate, intermediate, pale, vague. Opp DISTINCTIVE.

neutralize v cancel out, counteract, invalidate, make ineffective, negate, nullify, offset, wipe out.

new adj 1 brand-new, clean, fresh, mint, strange, unfamiliar, untried, unused. 2 new ideas. advanced, contemporary, current, different, fashionable, latest, modern, newfangled, novel, original, recent, revolutionary, inf trendy, up-to-date. 3 new data. additional, changed, extra, further, supplementary, unexpected. Opp OLD.

newcomer n arrival, immigrant, outsider, settler, stranger.

news n account, advice, announcement, bulletin, communication, communiqué, dispatch, headlines, information, intelligence, inf the latest, message, newsflash, notice, press release, report, rumour, statement, word.

newspaper n inf daily, gazette, journal, paper, periodical, inf rag, tabloid.

next adj 1 adjacent, adjoining, closest, nearest, neighbouring. 2 the next moment. following, subsequent, succeeding.

nice adj 1 accurate, careful, delicate, discriminating, exact, fine, hair-splitting, meticulous, pre-

cise, punctilious, scrupulous, subtle. 2 nice manners. dainty, elegant, fastidious, fussy, particular, inf pernickety, polished, refined. 3 [inf] acceptable, agreeable, amiable, attractive, beautiful, delicious, delightful, friendly, good, gratifying, kind, likeable, pleasant, satisfactory, welcome. Opp NASTY.

niche n alcove, corner, hollow, nook, recess.

nickname n alias, sobriquet.

niggardly adj mean, miserly, parsimonious, stingy.

nimble adj acrobatic, active, adroit, agile, brisk, deft, lithe, lively, inf nippy, sprightly, spry, swift. Opp CLUMSY.

nip v bite, clip, pinch, snap at, squeeze.

nobility n 1 dignity, grandeur, greatness, high-mindedness, integrity, magnanimity, morality, uprightness, virtue, worthiness. 2 the nobility. aristocracy, elite, peerage, the ruling classes, inf the upper crust.

noble adj 1 aristocratic, inf blue-blooded, courtly, distinguished, elite, gentle, patrician, princely, royal, thoroughbred, titled, upper-class. 2 noble deeds. brave, chivalrous, courageous, gallant, glorious, heroic. 3 noble thoughts. elevated, honourable, lofty, magnanimous, moral, upright, virtuous, worthy. 4 noble edifice. dignified, elegant, grand, great, imposing, magnificent, majestic, splendid, stately. Opp BASE, COMMON.
- n ▷ ARISTOCRAT.

nod v bend, bob, bow. **nod off** ▷ SLEEP.

noise n babel, babble, bedlam, blare, cacophony, caterwauling, clamour, clatter, commotion, din, discord, fracas, hubbub, hullabaloo, outcry, pandemonium, racket, *inf* row, *inf* rumpus, screaming, shouting, tumult, uproar. ▷ SOUND. *Opp* SILENCE.

noiseless *adj* inaudible, mute, muted, quiet, silent, soft, soundless, still. *Opp* NOISY.

noisy *adj* blaring, booming, cacophonous, clamorous, deafening, discordant, dissonant, earsplitting, harsh, loud, raucous, resounding, reverberating, rowdy, screaming, screeching, shrieking, shrill, strident, talkative, thunderous, unmusical, uproarious, vociferous. *Opp* NOISELESS.

nomadic *adj* itinerant, roving, travelling, vagrant, wandering.

nominal *adj* 1 formal, in name only, ostensible, *inf* so-called, supposed, theoretical, titular. 2 *nominal sum.* insignificant, minimal, minor, small, token.

nominate *v* propose, put forward, recommend. ▷ NAME.

non-existent *adj* fictional, fictitious, hypothetical, imaginary, legendary, made-up, mythical, unreal. *Opp* REAL.

nonplus *v* amaze, baffle, disconcert, dumbfound, *inf* flummox, perplex, puzzle.

nonsense *n* 1 [Most synonyms *inf*] balderdash, bosh, bunkum, claptrap, codswallop, double Dutch, drivel, eyewash, foolishness, gibberish, gobbledegook, mumbo-jumbo, piffle, poppycock, rot, rubbish, silliness, trash, tripe, twaddle. 2 *The plan was a nonsense.* absurdity, mistake, nonsensical idea.

nonsensical *adj* absurd, crazy, *inf* daft, fatuous, foolish, idiotic, illogical, impractical, incomprehensible, irrational, laughable, ludicrous, mad, meaningless, ridiculous, senseless, stupid. ▷ SILLY. *Opp* SENSIBLE.

non-stop *adj* ceaseless, constant, continual, continuous, endless, eternal, incessant, interminable, perpetual, persistent, unbroken, unending, uninterrupted, unremitting.

norm *n* criterion, measure, model, pattern, rule, standard, type, yardstick.

normal *adj* 1 accustomed, average, common, commonplace, conventional, customary, established, everyday, familiar, general, habitual, natural, ordinary, orthodox, predictable, prosaic, regular, routine, *inf* run-of-the-mill, standard, typical, unsurprising, usual. 2 *normal person.* balanced, rational, reasonable, sane, stable, *inf* straight, well-adjusted. *Opp* ABNORMAL.

nose *n* 1 snout. 2 *nose of a boat.* bow, front, prow. ● *v* insinuate yourself, interfere, intrude, nudge your way, penetrate, probe, push, shove. **nose about** ▷ PRY.

nostalgia *n* longing, memory, pining, regret, reminiscence, sentimentality, yearning.

nostalgic *adj* emotional, maudlin, regretful, romantic, sentimental, wistful, yearning.

nosy *adj* curious, inquisitive, interfering, meddlesome, prying.

notable *adj* celebrated, conspicuous, distinguished, eminent, evident, extraordinary, famous, important, impressive, memorable, noted, noteworthy, noticeable, obvious, outstanding, pre-

note *n* 1 chit, communication, correspondence, jotting, letter, *inf* memo, memorandum, message. 2 annotation, comment, explanation, footnote, jotting. 3 *note of frustration.* quality, sound, tone. 4 *£5 note.* banknote, bill, draft. • *v* 1 enter, jot down, record, scribble, write down. 2 detect, discern, discover, feel, find, heed, mark, notice, observe, pay attention to, register, remark, see, spy. **noted** ▷ FAMOUS.

noteworthy *adj* exceptional, extraordinary, rare, remarkable, uncommon, unique, unusual. *Opp* ORDINARY.

nothing *n* nil, nought, zero, *sl* zilch.

notice *n* 1 advertisement, announcement, handbill, leaflet, message, note, notification, placard, poster, sign, warning. 2 attention, awareness, heed, note, regard. • *v* be aware, detect, discern, discover, feel, find, heed, mark, note, observe, pay attention to, perceive, register, remark, see, spy, take note. **give notice** ▷ NOTIFY, WARN.

noticeable *adj* appreciable, audible, clear, conspicuous, detectable, discernible, distinct, distinguishable, manifest, marked, measurable, notable, obtrusive, obvious, overt, palpable, perceptible, plain, prominent, pronounced, salient, significant, striking, unconcealed, unmistakable, visible. *Opp* IMPERCEPTIBLE.

eminent, prominent, remarkable, renowned, striking, uncommon, unusual, well-known. *Opp* ORDINARY.

notify *v* acquaint, advise, alert, announce, give notice, inform, proclaim, report, tell, warn.

notion *n* belief, concept, conception, fancy, hypothesis, idea, impression, inkling, opinion, theory, thought, understanding, view.

notorious *adj* disgraceful, disreputable, flagrant, infamous, outrageous, scandalous, shocking, undisputed, well-known. ▷ FAMOUS.

nourish *v* feed, maintain, nurse, nurture, provide for, strengthen, support, sustain. **nourishing** ▷ NUTRITIOUS.

nourishment *n* diet, food, goodness, nutrient, nutriment, nutrition, sustenance.

novel *adj* different, fresh, imaginative, innovative, new, odd, original, singular, startling, strange, surprising, uncommon, unconventional, unfamiliar, unusual. *Opp* FAMILIAR. • *n* best-seller, *inf* blockbuster, fiction, romance, story.

novelty *n* 1 freshness, oddity, originality, strangeness, surprise, unfamiliarity, uniqueness. 2 bauble, curiosity, knick-knack, souvenir, trifle, trinket.

novice *n* amateur, apprentice, beginner, initiate, learner, probationer, trainee.

now *adv* at once, at present, immediately, instantly, just now, nowadays, promptly, straight away, today.

noxious *adj* corrosive, foul, harmful, nasty, noisome, objectionable, poisonous, polluting, unwholesome.

nub n centre, core, crux, essence, gist, heart, kernel, nucleus, pith, point.

nucleus n centre, core, heart, kernel, middle.

nude adj bare, exposed, inf in the altogether, in the nude, naked, stark-naked, stripped, unclothed, uncovered, undressed.

nudge v bump, dig, elbow, jog, poke, prod, push, touch.

nuisance n annoyance, bother, inconvenience, irritation, inf pain, pest, trouble, worry.

nullify v abolish, annul, cancel, invalidate, negate, quash, repeal, rescind, revoke.

numb adj anaesthetized, inf asleep, cold, dead, deadened, frozen, insensible, insensitive, paralysed, senseless. Opp SENSITIVE. ● v anaesthetize, deaden, desensitize, drug, dull, freeze, paralyse, stun, stupefy.

number n 1 digit, figure, integer, numeral, unit. 2 aggregate, amount, collection, quantity, sum, total. ▷ GROUP. 3 musical number. item, piece, song. 4 back number. copy, edition, impression, issue, printing, publication. ● v add up to, total, work out at. ▷ COUNT.

numerous adj abundant, copious, countless, incalculable, infinite, innumerable, many, myriad, plentiful, several, untold. Opp FEW.

nun n abbess, mother superior, novice, prioress, sister.

nurse n 1 district nurse, sister. 2 nanny, nursemaid. ● v 1 care for, look after, minister to, nurture, tend, treat. 2 breast-feed, feed, suckle. 3 cherish, cradle,

cuddle, hold, hug, mother, pamper.

nursery n 1 crèche, kindergarten, nursery school. 2 garden centre, market garden.

nurture v bring up, cultivate, educate, feed, promise, nourish, nurse, rear, tend, train.

nutriment n food, nourishment, nutrient, nutrition, sustenance.

nutritious adj beneficial, health-giving, healthy, nourishing, sustaining, wholesome.

O

oasis n 1 spring, well. 2 asylum, haven, refuge, retreat, safe harbour, sanctuary.

oath n 1 assurance, avowal, guarantee, pledge, promise, undertaking, vow, word of honour. 2 blasphemy, curse, expletive, inf four-letter word, imprecation, obscenity, profanity, swear word.

obedient adj acquiescent, amenable, biddable, compliant, deferential, disciplined, docile, dutiful, law-abiding, manageable, submissive, subservient, tractable, well-behaved. Opp DISOBEDIENT.

obese adj corpulent, gross, overweight. ▷ FAT.

obey v abide by, accept, acquiesce in, act in accordance with, adhere to, agree to, bow to, carry out, comply with, conform to, defer to, execute, follow, fulfil, give in to, heed, honour, keep to, mind, observe, perform,

inf stick to, submit to.
Opp DISOBEY.

object *n* 1 article, body, item, thing. 2 aim, end, goal, intention, objective, point, purpose, reason. 3 *object of ridicule.* butt, target. • *v* argue, be opposed, carp, cavil, complain, demur, disapprove, dispute, dissent, expostulate, *inf* grouse, grumble, *inf* mind, oppose, protest, quibble, raise objections, remonstrate, take a stand, take exception. Opp ACCEPT, AGREE.

objection *n* argument, cavil, challenge, complaint, disapproval, opposition, outcry, protest, query, question, quibble, remonstration.

objectionable *adj* abhorrent, disagreeable, disgusting, distasteful, foul, hateful, insufferable, intolerable, loathsome, nasty, noisome, obnoxious, offensive, *inf* off-putting, repellent, repugnant, repulsive, revolting, sickening, unacceptable. ▷ UNPLEASANT. Opp ACCEPTABLE.

objective *adj* 1 detached, disinterested, dispassionate, factual, impartial, impersonal, neutral, open-minded, rational, scientific, unbiased, unemotional, unprejudiced. 2 *objective evidence.* empirical, existing, observable, real. Opp SUBJECTIVE. • *n* ambition, aspiration, destination, goal, target. ▷ OBJECT.

obligation *n* commitment, compulsion, constraint, contract, duty, liability, need, requirement, responsibility.
▷ PROMISE. Opp OPTION.

obligatory *adj* essential, required. ▷ COMPULSORY. Opp OPTIONAL.

oblige *v* 1 coerce, compel, constrain, force, make, require. 2 *Please oblige me.* accommodate, gratify, indulge, please.
obliged ▷ BOUND, GRATEFUL.
obliging ▷ HELPFUL, POLITE.

oblique *adj* 1 angled, askew, diagonal, inclined, leaning, listing, slanted, slanting, sloping, tilted. 2 *oblique insult.* backhanded, implied, implicit, indirect.
▷ EVASIVE. Opp DIRECT.

obliterate *v* blot out, cancel, delete, destroy, efface, eliminate, eradicate, erase, expunge, leave no trace of, wipe out.

oblivion *n* 1 anonymity, darkness, disregard, extinction, obscurity. 2 forgetfulness, insensibility, unawareness, unconsciousness.

oblivious *adj* forgetful, heedless, ignorant, insensible, insensitive, unaware, unconscious, unfeeling, uninformed, unmindful.
Opp AWARE.

obscene *adj* abominable, bawdy, blue, coarse, crude, debauched, degenerate, depraved, dirty, disgusting, filthy, foul, foulmouthed, gross, immodest, immoral, improper, impure, indecent, indelicate, *inf* kinky, lecherous, lewd, offensive, outrageous, perverted, pornographic, prurient, ribald, risqué, rude, salacious, scurrilous, shameless, shocking, *inf* sick, smutty, suggestive, vile, vulgar.
▷ OBJECTIONABLE. Opp DECENT.

obscenity *n* abomination, blasphemy, coarseness, dirt, evil, filth, immorality, impropriety, indecency, licentiousness, offensiveness, outrage, perversion, pornography, profanity, vulgarity.
▷ SWEAR WORD.

obscure adj 1 blurred, clouded, dark, dim, faint, hazy, inconspicuous, indefinite, indistinct, misty, murky, nebulous, shadowy, shady, shrouded, unclear, unlit, unrecognizable, vague, veiled. Opp CLEAR. 2 obscure subject. arcane, baffling, complex, cryptic, enigmatic, esoteric, incomprehensible, mystifying, perplexing, puzzling, recondite, strange. Opp OBVIOUS. 3 obscure poet. forgotten, minor, undistinguished, unimportant, unknown, unnoticed. Opp FAMOUS.

• v blur, cloak, cloud, conceal, cover, darken, disguise, eclipse, envelop, hide, mask, overshadow, screen, shade, shroud, veil. Opp CLARIFY.

obsequious adj abject, crawling, cringing, deferential, fawning, flattering, fulsome, inf greasy, grovelling, ingratiating, insincere, mealy-mouthed, inf oily, servile, inf smarmy, submissive, sycophantic, unctuous. **be obsequious** ▷ GROVEL.

observant adj alert, attentive, aware, careful, eagle-eyed, heedful, mindful, on the lookout, perceptive, percipient, quick, vigilant, watchful, with eyes peeled. Opp INATTENTIVE.

observation n 1 examination, inspection, monitoring, scrutiny, study, surveillance. 2 comment, reaction, reflection, remark, response, statement, thought, utterance.

observe v 1 contemplate, detect, discern, examine, inf keep an eye on, look at, monitor, note, notice, perceive, regard, scrutinize, see, spot, spy, study, view, watch, witness. 2 observe rules. abide by, adhere to, comply

with, conform to, follow, heed, keep, obey, pay attention to, respect. 3 observe Easter. celebrate, commemorate, keep, mark, recognize, remember. 4 comment, declare, explain, make an observation, mention, reflect, remark, say, state.

observer n commentator, onlooker, witness. ▷ SPECTATOR.

obsess v consume, control, dominate, grip, haunt, monopolize, plague, possess, preoccupy, rule, take hold of.

obsession n inf bee in your bonnet, fetish, fixation, inf hang-up, Fr idée fixe, infatuation, mania, passion, phobia, preoccupation, sl thing.

obsessive adj addictive, compulsive, consuming, controlling, dominating, haunting.

obsolescent adj ageing, declining, dying out, fading, losing popularity, moribund, inf on the way out, waning.

obsolete adj anachronistic, antiquated, archaic, dated, discarded, disused, extinct, old-fashioned, inf old hat, out-of-date, outmoded, passé, superannuated, unfashionable. ▷ OLD. Opp CURRENT.

obstacle n bar, barricade, barrier, blockage, catch, difficulty, hindrance, hurdle, impediment, obstruction, problem, snag, stumbling block.

obstinate adj adamant, inf bloody-minded, defiant, determined, dogged, firm, headstrong, inflexible, intractable, intransigent, inf mulish, obdurate, persistent, pertinacious, inf pigheaded, refractory, resolute, rigid, self-willed, single-minded, stubborn, tenacious, uncooperative, unreasonable, unyielding, wilful. *Opp* AMENABLE.

obstreperous *adj* boisterous, disorderly, irrepressible, naughty, rowdy, turbulent, uncontrollable, undisciplined, unmanageable, unruly, wild. ▷ NOISY. *Opp* WELL-BEHAVED.

obstruct *v* arrest, bar, block, check, curb, delay, deter, frustrate, halt, hamper, hinder, hold up, impede, inhibit, interfere with, interrupt, prevent, restrict, retard, slow down, stand in the way of, stop, *inf* stymie, thwart. *Opp* HELP.

obtain *v* 1 acquire, attain, be given, buy, capture, come by, come into possession of, earn, enlist (*help*), extort, extract, find, gain, get, *inf* get hold of, *inf* lay your hands on, *inf* pick up, procure, purchase, receive, secure, seize, win. 2 *rules still obtain.* apply, be in force, be relevant, be valid, exist, prevail, stand.

obtrusive *adj* blatant, conspicuous, inescapable, intrusive, noticeable, out of place, prominent, unwanted, unwelcome. ▷ OBVIOUS. *Opp* INCONSPICUOUS.

obtuse *adj* dense, dull, slow, slow-witted. ▷ STUPID. *Opp* CLEVER.

obviate *v* make unnecessary, preclude, prevent, remove.

obvious *adj* apparent, blatant, clear, clear-cut, conspicuous, distinct, evident, eye-catching, flagrant, glaring, manifest, notable, noticeable, obtrusive, open, overt, palpable, patent, perceptible, plain, prominent, pronounced, recognizable, self-evident, self-explanatory,

straightforward, unconcealed, undisguised, unmistakable, visible. *Opp* HIDDEN, OBSCURE.

occasion *n* 1 chance, moment, opportunity, time. 2 *no occasion for rudeness.* call, cause, excuse, grounds, justification, need, reason. 3 *happy occasion.* celebration, ceremony, event, function, *inf* get-together, happening, incident, occurrence, party.

occasional *adj* desultory, fitful, infrequent, intermittent, irregular, odd, *inf* once in a while, periodic, random, rare, spasmodic, sporadic, unpredictable. *Opp* FREQUENT, REGULAR.

occult *adj* ▷ SUPERNATURAL. ● *n* black arts, black magic, sorcery, the supernatural, witchcraft.

occupant *n* denizen, householder, inhabitant, occupier, owner, resident, tenant.

occupation *n* 1 lease, occupancy, possession, tenancy, tenure, use. 2 colonization, conquest, invasion, oppression, seizure, subjection, subjugation, *inf* takeover, usurpation. 3 business, calling, career, employment, job, *inf* line, métier, position, post, profession, situation, trade, vocation, work. 4 *leisure occupation.* activity, entertainment, hobby, interest, pastime, pursuit, recreation.

occupy *v* 1 dwell in, inhabit, live in, move into, reside in. 2 *occupy space.* fill, take up, use, utilize. 3 capture, colonize, conquer, invade, overrun, subjugate, take over, take possession of. 4 *occupy your time.* absorb, divert, engage, engross, involve, preoccupy. **occupied** ▷ BUSY.

occur *v* appear, arise, befall, be found, chance, come about, *inf* crop up, develop, exist, happen, materialize, *inf* show up, take place, transpire, *inf* turn out, *inf* turn up.

occurrence *n* affair, case, circumstance, development, event, happening, incident, manifestation, matter, occasion, phenomenon, proceeding.

odd *adj* 1 *odd numbers.* uneven. *Opp* EVEN. 2 *odd socks.* extra, left over, remaining, single, spare, superfluous, surplus. 3 *odd jobs.* casual, irregular, miscellaneous, occasional, random, sundry, varied, various. 4 *odd behaviour.* abnormal, anomalous, atypical, bizarre, curious, deviant, different, eccentric, extraordinary, freak, funny, incongruous, inexplicable, outlandish, out of the ordinary, peculiar, puzzling, queer, rare, singular, strange, uncharacteristic, uncommon, unconventional, unexpected, unusual, weird. *Opp* NORMAL.

oddments *pl n* bits, bits and pieces, fragments, junk, leftovers, litter, odds and ends, remnants, scraps, shreds.

odious *adj* detestable, execrable, loathsome, offensive, repugnant, repulsive. ▷ HATEFUL.

odorous *adj* fragrant, perfumed, scented. ▷ SMELLING.

odour *n* aroma, bouquet, fragrance, nose, redolence, scent, smell, stench, *inf* stink.

odourless *adj* deodorized, unscented. *Opp* ODOROUS.

offence *n* 1 crime, fault, infringement, lapse, misdeed, misdemeanour, outrage, peccadillo, sin, transgression, violation, wrong, wrongdoing. 2 anger, annoyance, disgust, displeasure, hard feelings, indignation, irritation, pique, resentment. **give offence** ▷ OFFEND.

offend *v* 1 affront, anger, annoy, disgust, displease, embarrass, give offence, insult, irritate, *inf* miff, outrage, provoke, *inf* put your back up, sicken, snub, upset, vex. 2 *offend against the law.* do wrong, transgress. **be offended** be annoyed, *inf* take umbrage.

offender *n* criminal, culprit, delinquent, guilty party, malefactor, miscreant, sinner, transgressor, wrongdoer.

offensive *adj* 1 abusive, annoying, antisocial, coarse, detestable, disagreeable, displeasing, disrespectful, embarrassing, impolite, indecent, insulting, loathsome, nasty, nauseating, noxious, objectionable, obnoxious, *inf* off-putting, repugnant, revolting, rude, sickening, unpleasant, unsavoury. ▷ OBSCENE. *Opp* PLEASANT. 2 *offensive action.* aggressive, antagonistic, hostile, threatening, warlike. *Opp* PEACEABLE. ● *n* ▷ ATTACK.

offer *n* bid, proposal, proposition, suggestion, tender. ● *v* 1 bid, extend, give the opportunity of, hold out, make an offer of, make available, proffer, put forward, put up, suggest. 2 *offer to help.* come forward, propose, *inf* show willing, volunteer.

offering *n* contribution, donation, gift, present, sacrifice.

offhand *adj* 1 abrupt, aloof, careless, cavalier, cool, curt, perfunctory, unceremonious, uninter-

ested. ▷ CASUAL.
2 ▷ IMPROMPTU.

office n 1 bureau, workplace.
2 appointment, duty, function,
job, occupation, place, position,
post, responsibility, role, situation, work.

officer n 1 adjutant, aide-de-
camp, CO, commanding officer.
2 constable, PC, policeman,
policewoman, WPC.
3 ▷ OFFICIAL.

official adj accredited, approved,
authentic, authoritative, authorized, bona fide, certified, formal,
lawful, legal, legitimate,
licensed, organized, recognized,
valid. ▷ FORMAL.
● n administrator, agent,
appointee, authorized person,
bureaucrat, commissioner, dignitary, diplomat, executive, functionary, inspector, mandarin,
minister, officer, organizer, representative, steward, umpire.

officiate v adjudicate, be in
charge, be responsible, chair (a
meeting), conduct, manage, preside, referee, umpire.

officious adj inf bossy, bumptious, dictatorial, forward, interfering, over-zealous, inf pushy,
self-important.

offset v cancel out, compensate
for, counteract, make amends
for, make good, make up for,
redress. ▷ BALANCE.

offshoot n branch, by-product,
development, inf spin-off.

offspring n [sing] baby, child,
descendant, heir, successor. [pl]
brood, family, issue, litter, progeny, young.

often adv commonly, frequently,
generally, habitually, regularly,
repeatedly, time after time, time
and again, usually.

oil v grease, lubricate.

oily adj 1 buttery, fatty, greasy.
2 oily manner. ▷ OBSEQUIOUS.

ointment n balm, cream,
embrocation, liniment, lotion,
salve.

old adj 1 ancient, antediluvian,
antiquated, antique, crumbling,
decaying, decrepit, dilapidated,
early, historic, medieval, primitive, ruined, superannuated,
time-worn, venerable, veteran,
vintage. ▷ OLD-FASHIONED. 2 old
times. bygone, former, (time)
immemorial, olden (days), past,
prehistoric, previous, remote.
3 old people. advanced in years,
aged, inf doddery, elderly, geriat-
ric, inf getting on, grey-haired,
hoary, inf in your dotage,
inf past it, senile. 4 old customs.
age-old, established, lasting,
long-standing, time-honoured,
traditional. 5 old clothes. moth-
eaten, ragged, inf scruffy,
shabby, threadbare, worn, worn-
out. 6 old bread. dry, stale. 7 old
tickets. expired, invalid, used.
8 old hand. experienced, expert,
familiar, practised, skilled, veteran. Opp NEW, YOUNG. **old age**
inf declining years, decrepitude,
dotage, senility.

old-fashioned adj anachronistic, antiquated, archaic,
backward-looking, conven-
tional, dated, narrow-minded,
obsolete, old, inf old hat,
out-of-date, out-of-touch, outmoded, passé, prudish, reactionary, time-honoured, traditional,
unfashionable. Opp MODERN.
old-fashioned person inf fogey,
inf fuddy-duddy, reactionary,
inf square.

omen n augury, foreboding, forewarning, harbinger, indication,

portent, premonition, presage, sign, token, warning.

ominous *adj* baleful, dire, fateful, forbidding, foreboding, grim, ill-omened, ill-starred, inauspicious, menacing, portentous, prophetic, sinister, threatening, unfavourable, unlucky, unpromising, unpropitious. *Opp* AUSPICIOUS.

omission *n* 1 deletion, elimination, exclusion. 2 failure, oversight.

omit *v* 1 cut, dispense with, drop, eliminate, erase, exclude, ignore, jump, leave out, miss out, overlook, pass over, reject, skip. 2 fail, forget, neglect.

omnipotent *adj* all-powerful, almighty, invincible, supreme.

oncoming *adj* advancing, approaching, looming.

onerous *adj* burdensome, demanding, heavy, laborious, taxing. ▷ DIFFICULT.

one-sided *adj* 1 biased, bigoted, partial, partisan, prejudiced. 2 *one-sided game.* unbalanced, unequal, uneven.

onlooker *n* bystander, eyewitness, looker-on, observer, spectator, watcher, witness.

only *adj* lone, single, sole, solitary, unique. ● *adv* just, merely, simply, solely.

ooze *v* bleed, discharge, emit, exude, leak, secrete, seep.

opaque *adj* cloudy, dark, dim, dull, filmy, muddy, murky, unclear. *Opp* CLEAR.

open *adj* ajar, gaping, unfastened, unlocked, unsealed, wide-open, yawning. 2 accessible, available, exposed, free, public, revealed, unprotected, unrestricted. 3 *open space.*

broad, clear, empty, extensive, spacious, treeless, uncrowded, undefended, vacant. 4 *open arms.* extended, outstretched. 5 *open nature.* artless, candid, communicative, frank, generous, guileless, honest, innocent, open-minded, sincere, straightforward, uninhibited. 6 *open defiance.* barefaced, blatant, conspicuous, downright, evident, flagrant, obvious, outspoken, overt, plain, unconcealed, undisguised, visible. 7 *open question.* arguable, debatable, moot, unanswered, undecided, unresolved. *Opp* CLOSED, HIDDEN. ● *v* 1 unblock, uncork, undo, unfasten, unfold, unfurl, unlatch, unlock, unseal, untie, unwrap. 2 *open proceedings.* begin, commence, establish, *inf* get going, inaugurate, initiate, *inf* kick off, launch, set in motion, set up, start. *Opp* CLOSE.

opening *adj* first, inaugural, initial, introductory. *Opp* FINAL. ● *n* 1 aperture, breach, break, chink, cleft, crack, crevice, doorway, fissure, gap, gateway, hatch, hole, leak, mouth, orifice, outlet, rift, slit, slot, space, split, tear, vent. 2 beginning, birth, dawn, inauguration, inception, initiation, launch, outset, start. 3 *business opening. inf* break, chance, opportunity, way in.

operate *v* 1 act, function, go, perform, run, work. 2 *operate a machine.* control, drive, handle, manage, use, work. 3 perform surgery.

operation *n* 1 control, direction, management. 2 action, activity, business, campaign, effort, enterprise, exercise, manoeuvre, movement, procedure, proceeding, process, transaction, undertaking, venture. 3 [*medical*] biopsy, surgery, transplant.

operational *adj* functioning, going, in operation, in working order, operating, *inf* up and running, usable, working.

operative *adj* ▷ OPERATIONAL. ● *n* ▷ WORKER.

opinion *n* assessment, belief, conclusion, conjecture, conviction, estimate, feeling, guess, idea, impression, judgement, notion, perception, point of view, sentiment, theory, thought, view, viewpoint.

opponent *n* adversary, antagonist, competitor, contender, contestant, enemy, foe, opposition, rival. *Opp* ALLY.

opportune *adj* advantageous, appropriate, auspicious, convenient, favourable, felicitous, fortunate, good, happy, lucky, propitious, suitable, timely, well-timed. *Opp* INCONVENIENT.

opportunity *n inf* break, chance, moment, occasion, opening, possibility, time.

oppose *v* argue with, attack, challenge, combat, compete against, confront, contend with, contest, contradict, counter, counter-attack, defy, disagree with, face, fight, object to, obstruct, quarrel with, resist, rival, stand up to, *inf* take a stand against, take issue with, withstand. *Opp* SUPPORT. **opposed** ▷ HOSTILE, OPPOSITE.

opposite *adj* 1 antithetical, conflicting, contradictory, contrasting, converse, different, hostile, incompatible, opposed, opposing, rival. 2 contrary, reverse. 3 *your opposite number.* corresponding, equivalent,

facing, matching. ● *n* antithesis, contrary, converse, reverse.

opposition *n* antagonism, antipathy, competition, defiance, enmity, hostility, objection, resistance. ▷ OPPONENT. *Opp* SUPPORT.

oppress *v* abuse, afflict, burden, crush, depress, enslave, exploit, grind down, harass, intimidate, keep under, maltreat, persecute, subdue, subjugate, terrorize, *inf* trample on, tyrannize, weigh down.

oppressed *adj* browbeaten, downtrodden, enslaved, exploited, persecuted.

oppression *n* abuse, exploitation, harassment, injustice, maltreatment, persecution, pressure, repression, suppression, tyranny.

oppressive *adj* 1 brutal, cruel, despotic, harsh, repressive, tyrannical, unjust. 2 airless, close, heavy, hot, humid, muggy, stifling, stuffy, suffocating, sultry.

optimism *n* buoyancy, cheerfulness, confidence, hope, idealism, positiveness. *Opp* PESSIMISM.

optimistic *adj* buoyant, cheerful, confident, expectant, hopeful, idealistic, positive, sanguine. *Opp* PESSIMISTIC.

optimum *adj* highest, ideal, maximum, most favourable, perfect, prime. ▷ BEST.

option *n* alternative, chance, choice, possibility, selection.

optional *adj* discretionary, dispensable, inessential, possible, unforced, unnecessary, voluntary. *Opp* COMPULSORY.

oral *adj* by mouth, said, spoken, unwritten, verbal, vocal.

oratory n declamation, eloquence, fluency, inf gift of the gab, grandiloquence, rhetoric, speaking, speech making.

orbit n circuit, course, path, revolution, trajectory. • v circle, travel round.

orchestrate v 1 arrange, compose. 2 ▷ ORGANIZE.

ordeal n difficulty, distress, hardship, misery, inf nightmare, suffering, test, torture, trial, tribulation, trouble.

order n 1 arrangement, array, classification, disposition, layout, inf line-up, neatness, organization, pattern, progression, sequence, series, succession, system, tidiness. 2 calm, control, discipline, government, harmony, law and order, obedience, orderliness, peace, quiet, rule. 3 social order. caste, category, class, degree, group, hierarchy, level, rank, status. 4 in good order. condition, repair, state. 5 command, decree, direction, directive, edict, fiat, injunction, instruction, law, mandate, ordinance, regulation, requirement, rule. 6 application, booking, commission, demand, request, requisition. 7 religious order. association, brotherhood, community, group, lodge, sect, sisterhood, society.
Opp DISORDER. • v 1 arrange, categorize, classify, inf lay out, organize, put in order, sort out, tidy up. 2 command, compel, decree, demand, direct, enjoin, instruct, require, tell. 3 book, reserve, requisition, send away for.

orderly adj 1 careful, methodical, neat, organized, regular, symmetrical, systematic, tidy,

well-organized. Opp CONFUSED, DISORGANIZED. 2 civilized, controlled, decorous, disciplined, law-abiding, peaceable, restrained, well-behaved.
Opp UNDISCIPLINED.

ordinary adj accustomed, average, common, inf common or garden, commonplace, conventional, customary, established, everyday, familiar, habitual, humble, humdrum, indifferent, mediocre, moderate, modest, mundane, nondescript, normal, orthodox, passable, pedestrian, plain, prosaic, regular, routine, inf run-of-the-mill, satisfactory, simple, inf so-so, standard, stock, typical, undistinguished, unexceptional, unexciting, unimpressive, uninteresting, unremarkable, unsurprising, usual, workaday. Opp EXTRAORDINARY.

organic adj 1 animate, biological, growing, live, living, natural. 2 organic whole. coherent, coordinated, evolving, integral, integrated, organized, structured, systematic.

organism n animal, being, cell, creature, living thing.

organization n 1 arrangement, categorization, classification, codification, composition, coordination, planning, inf running, structuring. 2 alliance, association, body, business, club, company, concern, confederation, consortium, corporation, federation, firm, group, institute, institution, league, network, inf outfit, party, society, syndicate, union.

organize v 1 arrange, catalogue, categorize, classify, codify, coordinate, group, order, pigeonhole, put in order, rearrange,

regiment, sort, sort out, structure, systematize, tidy up.
2 coordinate, deal with, establish, make arrangements for, manage, mobilize, orchestrate, plan, put together, run, *inf* see to, set up. **organized** ▷ OFFICIAL, SYSTEMATIC.

orgy *n inf* binge, *inf* fling, party, revel, revelry, *inf* splurge, *inf* spree.

orient *v* acclimatize, accustom, adapt, adjust, familiarize, orientate, position.

oriental *adj* Asiatic, eastern, far-eastern.

origin *n* **1** basis, beginning, birth, cause, commencement, cradle, creation, dawn, derivation, foundation, fount, genesis, inauguration, inception, provenance, root, source, start.
Opp END. **2** *humble origin.* ancestry, background, descent, extraction, family, parentage, pedigree, start in life, stock.

original *adj* **1** archetypal, earliest, first, initial, native, primitive. **2** *original antiques.* authentic, genuine, real, true, unique. **3** *original ideas.* creative, fresh, imaginative, ingenious, innovative, inspired, inventive, new, novel, resourceful, unconventional, unfamiliar, unique, unusual. *Opp* HACKNEYED.

originate *v* **1** arise, be born, be derived, be descended, begin, commence, derive, emanate, emerge, issue, proceed, start, stem. **2** coin, conceive, create, design, discover, engender, found, give birth to, inaugurate, initiate, inspire, institute, introduce, invent, launch, pioneer, produce, think up.

ornament *n* accessory, adornment, bauble, decoration, embellishment, embroidery, filigree, frill, frippery, garnish, ornamentation, tracery, trimming, trinket. ▷ JEWELLERY.
● *v* adorn, beautify, deck, decorate, dress up, elaborate, embellish, embroider, festoon, garnish, prettify, trim.

ornamental *adj* attractive, decorative, fancy, pretty, showy.

ornate *adj* baroque, *inf* busy, decorated, elaborate, fancy, florid, flowery, fussy, luxuriant, overdone, pretentious, rococo.
Opp PLAIN.

orphan *n* foundling, stray, waif.

orthodox *adj* accepted, approved, authorized, conservative, conventional, customary, established, mainstream, normal, official, ordinary, prevailing, recognized, regular, standard, traditional, usual.
Opp UNCONVENTIONAL.

ostensible *adj* alleged, apparent, outward, pretended, professed, seeming, supposed. *Opp* REAL.

ostentation *n* affectation, display, exhibitionism, flamboyance, flaunting, parade, pretentiousness, show, showing-off, *inf* swank. *Opp* MODESTY.

ostentatious *adj* flamboyant, *inf* flashy, pretentious, showy, *inf* swanky, vulgar.
▷ BOASTFUL. *Opp* MODEST.

ostracize *v* avoid, banish, blacklist, boycott, cast out, cold-shoulder, *inf* cut, *inf* cut dead, exclude, expel, isolate, reject, *inf* send to Coventry, shun, shut out, snub.

oust *v* banish, drive out, eject, expel, *inf* kick out, remove, replace, supplant, unseat.

outbreak n epidemic, inf flare-up, plague, rash, upsurge.

outburst n attack, eruption, explosion, fit, flood, outbreak, outpouring, paroxysm, rush, spasm, surge, upsurge.

outcast n displaced person, exile, leper, outlaw, outsider, pariah, refugee.

outcome n ▷ RESULT.

outcry n clamour, complaint, hue and cry, objection, protest, protestation, uproar.

outdo v beat, defeat, exceed, excel, inf get the better of, outdistance, outshine, outstrip, overcome, surpass, top.

outdoor adj alfresco, open-air, out of doors, outside.

outer adj 1 exterior, external, outside, outward, superficial, surface. 2 distant, outlying, peripheral, remote. Opp INNER.

outfit n 1 accoutrements, clothes, costume, equipment, garb, inf gear, inf get-up, suit, trappings. 2 ▷ ORGANIZATION.

outgoing adj 1 outgoing president. departing, ex-, former, last, past, retiring. 2 outgoing tide. ebbing, falling, retreating. 3 ▷ SOCIABLE. Opp INCOMING.

outgoings ▷ EXPENSE.

outing n excursion, expedition, jaunt, ride, tour, trip.

outlast v outlive, survive.

outlaw n bandit, brigand, criminal, deserter, desperado, fugitive, highwayman, marauder, outcast, renegade, robber. • v ban, exclude, forbid, prohibit, proscribe. ▷ BANISH.

outlet n 1 channel, duct, exit, mouth, opening, orifice, safety valve, vent, way out. 2 ▷ SHOP.

outline n 1 inf bare bones, diagram, draft, framework, plan, précis, résumé, inf rough idea, scenario, skeleton, sketch, summary, synopsis. 2 contour, figure, form, profile, shadow, shape, silhouette. • v delineate, draft, give the gist of, plan out, rough out, sketch out, summarize.

outlook n 1 ▷ VISTA. 2 mental outlook. attitude, frame of mind, opinion, perspective, point of view, position, slant, viewpoint. 3 outlook for the future. forecast, prediction, prognosis, prospect.

outlying adj distant, far-away, far-flung, far-off, outer, outermost, remote. Opp CENTRAL.

output n achievement, crop, harvest, production, yield.

outrage n 1 atrocity, crime, inf disgrace, enormity, indignity, scandal, inf sensation. 2 anger, disgust, fury, horror, indignation, resentment, revulsion, shock, wrath. • v ▷ ANGER.

outrageous adj 1 abominable, atrocious, barbaric, beastly, cruel, disgraceful, disgusting, infamous, monstrous, nefarious, notorious, offensive, preposterous, scandalous, shocking, unspeakable, unthinkable, wicked. 2 outrageous prices. excessive, extortionate, extravagant, unreasonable. Opp REASONABLE.

outside adj 1 exterior, external, facing, outer, outward, superficial, surface, visible. 2 outside interference. extraneous, foreign. 3 outside chance. ▷ REMOTE. • n casing, exterior, façade, face, front, shell, skin, surface.

outsider n alien, foreigner, gatecrasher, guest, immigrant, interloper, newcomer, non-resident, outcast, stranger, trespasser, visitor.

outskirts pl n borders, edge, fringe, margin, periphery, suburbs. Opp CENTRE.

outspoken adj blunt, candid, direct, explicit, forthright, frank, tactless, unambiguous, undiplomatic. ▷ HONEST. Opp EVASIVE.

outstanding adj 1 conspicuous, distinguished, dominant, eminent, excellent, exceptional, extraordinary, first-class, first-rate, important, impressive, memorable, noteworthy, noticeable, pre-eminent, remarkable, singular, special, striking, superior, unrivalled. ▷ FAMOUS. Opp ORDINARY. 2 ▷ OVERDUE.

outward adj apparent, evident, exterior, external, manifest, noticeable, observable, obvious, ostensible, outer, outside, superficial, surface, visible.

outwit v deceive, dupe, fool, inf get the better of, make a fool of, outmanoeuvre, inf outsmart, inf put one over on, trick. ▷ CHEAT.

oval adj egg-shaped, ovoid.

ovation n acclamation, applause, cheering, clapping, plaudits, praise.

overcast adj black, cloudy, dark, dismal, dull, gloomy, grey, leaden, lowering, murky, sombre, stormy, sunless, threatening. Opp CLOUDLESS.

overcoat n greatcoat, mackintosh, topcoat, trench coat.

overcome adj beaten, inf done in, exhausted, overwhelmed, prostrate, speechless.
● v ▷ OVERTHROW.

overcrowded adj congested, crammed, jammed, inf jam-packed, overloaded, packed.

overdue adj 1 belated, delayed, late, slow, unpunctual. Opp EARLY. 2 overdue bills. outstanding, owing, unpaid, unsettled.

overeat v be greedy, feast, gorge, guzzle, inf make a pig of yourself, overindulge, stuff yourself.

overflow v brim over, flood, pour over, run over, spill.

overgrown adj 1 outsize, oversized. ▷ BIG. 2 overgrown garden. overrun, rank, tangled, uncut, unkempt, untidy, unweeded, wild.

overhang v bulge, jut, project, protrude, stick out.

overhaul v check over, examine, inf fix, inspect, mend, recondition, renovate, repair, restore, service.

overhead adj aerial, elevated, overhanging, raised, upper.

overlook v 1 fail to notice, forget, miss, neglect, omit. 2 condone, disregard, excuse, gloss over, ignore, pardon, pass over, pay no attention to, inf shut your eyes to, inf turn a blind eye to, inf write off. 3 overlook a lake. face, front, have a view of, look on to.

overpower v ▷ OVERTHROW.

overpowering adj compelling, consuming, irresistible, overriding, overwhelming, powerful, strong, unbearable, uncontrollable, unendurable.

oversee v be in charge of, direct. ▷ SUPERVISE.

oversight n 1 carelessness, error, failure, fault, mistake, omission. 2 control, direction, management, supervision, surveillance.

overstate v inf blow up out of proportion, embroider, exaggerate, magnify, make too much of, maximize.

overt adj apparent, blatant, clear, evident, manifest, obvious, open, patent, plain, unconcealed, undisguised, visible. Opp SECRET.

overtake v catch up with, gain on, leave behind, outdistance, outpace, outstrip, pass.

overthrow n conquest, defeat, destruction, rout, subjugation, suppression. ● v beat, bring down, conquer, crush, deal with, defeat, depose, dethrone, get the better of, master, oust, overcome, overpower, overturn, overwhelm, rout, subdue, inf topple, triumph over, unseat, vanquish.

overtone n association, connotation, implication, suggestion, undertone.

overturn v 1 capsize, flip, invert, keel over, spill, tip over, topple, inf turn turtle, turn upside down, up-end, upset. 2 ▷ OVERTHROW.

overwhelm v 1 engulf, flood, immerse, inundate, submerge, swamp. 2 ▷ OVERTHROW. **overwhelming** ▷ OVERPOWERING.

owe v be in debt, be indebted to, have debts.

owing adj due, outstanding, overdue, owed, payable, unpaid, unsettled. **owing to** because of, caused by, resulting from, thanks to, through.

own v have, hold, keep, possess. **own up** ▷ CONFESS.

owner n holder, landlady, landlord, possessor, proprietor.

P

pace n 1 step, stride. 2 fast pace. gait, movement, rate, speed, tempo. ● v ▷ WALK.

pacify v appease, assuage, calm, conciliate, humour, mollify, placate, quell, quieten, soothe, subdue, tame. Opp ANGER.

pack n 1 bale, box, bundle, package, packet, parcel. 2 backpack, haversack, kitbag, knapsack, rucksack. 3 ▷ GROUP. ● v 1 bundle (up), fill, load, package, parcel up, put, put together, store, stow, wrap up. 2 compress, cram, crowd, jam, press, ram, squeeze, stuff, tamp down, wedge. **pack off** ▷ DISMISS. **pack up** ▷ FINISH.

pact n agreement, alliance, arrangement, bargain, concord, contract, covenant, deal, entente, league, peace, settlement, treaty, truce, understanding.

pad n 1 cushion, hassock, kneeler, padding, pillow, wad. 2 jotter, notebook, writing pad. ● v cushion, fill, pack, protect, stuff. **pad out** ▷ EXTEND.

padding n 1 filling, protection, stuffing, wadding. 2 verbiage, verbosity, inf waffle, wordiness.

paddle n oar, scull. ● v 1 propel, row, scull. 2 dabble, splash about, wade.

paddock n enclosure, field, meadow, pasture.

pagan *adj* atheistic, godless, heathen, idolatrous, infidel, irreligious, unchristian. ● *n* atheist, heathen, infidel, unbeliever.

page *n* 1 folio, leaf, sheet, side. 2 messenger, page-boy.

pageant *n* display, parade, procession, spectacle, tableau.

pageantry *n* ceremony, display, formality, grandeur, magnificence, pomp, ritual, show, spectacle, splendour.

pain *n* ache, affliction, agony, anguish, cramp, discomfort, distress, headache, hurt, irritation, ordeal, pang, smart, soreness, spasm, stab, sting, suffering, tenderness, throb, *pl* throes, toothache, torment, torture, twinge. ● *v* ▷ HURT.

painful *adj* 1 aching, *inf* achy, agonizing, burning, excruciating, hard to bear, hurting, inflamed, piercing, raw, severe, sharp, smarting, sore, *inf* splitting (*head*), stabbing, stinging, tender, throbbing. 2 distressing, harrowing, hurtful, traumatic, trying, unpleasant, upsetting. 3 *painful decision.* difficult, hard, troublesome. *Opp* PAINLESS. **be painful** ▷ HURT.

painkiller *n* anaesthetic, analgesic, anodyne, sedative.

painless *adj* comfortable, easy, effortless, simple, trouble-free. *Opp* PAINFUL.

paint *n* colour, colouring, dye, pigment, stain, tint. ● *v* 1 coat, colour, cover, daub, decorate, enamel, gild, lacquer, redecorate, stain, tint, touch up, varnish, whitewash. 2 delineate, depict, describe, picture, portray, represent.

painter *n* artist, decorator, illustrator, miniaturist.

painting *n* fresco, landscape, miniature, mural, oil painting, portrait, still life, water colour.

pair *n* brace, couple, duet, duo, set of two, twins, twosome. ● *v* **pair off**, **pair up** find a partner, get together, *inf* make a twosome, match up, mate, *inf* pal up, team up.

palace *n* castle, chateau, mansion, official residence, stately home.

palatable *adj* acceptable, agreeable, appetizing, easy to take, eatable, edible, pleasant, tasty. *Opp* UNPALATABLE.

palatial *adj* aristocratic, grand, luxurious, majestic, opulent, *inf* posh, splendid, stately, up-market.

pale *adj* 1 anaemic, ashen, blanched, bloodless, colourless, *inf* deathly, drained, etiolated, ghastly, ghostly, pallid, pasty, *inf* peaky, sallow, sickly, unhealthy, wan, *inf* washed-out, *inf* whey-faced, white, whitish. 2 *pale colours.* bleached, faded, faint, light, pastel, subtle, weak. *Opp* BRIGHT. ● *v* blanch, fade, lighten, lose colour, whiten.

pall *n* cloth, mantle, shroud, veil. ▷ COVERING. ● *v* become boring, cloy, irritate, jade, sate, satiate, weary.

palliative *adj* calming, reassuring, sedative, soothing. ● *n* sedative, tranquillizer.

palpable *adj* apparent, corporeal, evident, manifest, obvious, patent, physical, real, solid, substantial, tangible, visible. *Opp* INTANGIBLE.

palpitate v beat, flutter, pound, pulsate, quiver, throb, vibrate.

paltry adj contemptible, inconsequential, insignificant, petty, inf piddling, pitiful, puny, trifling, unimportant, worthless. ▷ SMALL. Opp IMPORTANT.

pamper v cosset, indulge, mollycoddle, overindulge, pet, spoil, spoonfeed.

pamphlet n booklet, brochure, bulletin, catalogue, circular, flyer, folder, handbill, leaflet, notice, tract.

pan n container, pan, saucepan, utensil. ● v ▷ CRITICIZE.

panache n confidence, dash, élan, flair, flamboyance, flourish, Fr savoir faire, self-assurance, spirit, style, verve, zest.

pandemonium n babel, bedlam, chaos, hubbub, inf rumpus, turmoil, uproar. ▷ COMMOTION.

pander n go-between, inf pimp. ● v pander to cater for, fulfil, gratify, humour, indulge, please, satisfy.

pane n glass, panel, sheet of glass, window-pane.

panel n 1 insert, pane, panelling, rectangular piece. 2 committee, group, jury, team.

panic n alarm, consternation, inf flap, horror, hysteria, stampede, terror. ▷ FEAR. ● v become panic-stricken, inf flap, inf go to pieces, inf lose your head, over-react, stampede.

panic-stricken adj alarmed, inf beside yourself, frantic, frenzied, horrified, hysterical, inf in a cold sweat, inf in a tizzy, jumpy, panicky, terror-stricken, unnerved, worked up. ▷ FRIGHTENED. Opp CALM.

panorama n landscape, prospect, scene, view, vista.

panoramic adj extensive, scenic, sweeping, wide.

pant v breathe quickly, gasp, inf huff and puff, puff, wheeze. **panting** ▷ BREATHLESS.

pants n 1 boxer shorts, briefs, camiknickers, drawers, knickers, shorts, inf smalls, underpants, inf undies, Y-fronts. 2 [Amer] trousers.

paper n 1 folio, leaf, sheet. 2 [often pl] certificate, deed, document, form, licence, record. 3 daily paper, inf daily, journal, newspaper, inf rag, tabloid. 4 academic paper. article, discourse, dissertation, essay, thesis, treatise.

parable n allegory, fable, moral tale.

parade n cavalcade, ceremony, column, cortège, display, file, march-past, motorcade, pageant, procession, show, spectacle. ● v 1 assemble, file past, form up, line up, march past, process. 2 ▷ DISPLAY.

paradise n bliss, Eden, heaven, nirvana, Utopia.

paradox n absurdity, anomaly, contradiction, incongruity, inconsistency.

paradoxical adj absurd, anomalous, conflicting, contradictory, illogical, incongruous.

parallel adj 1 equidistant. 2 parallel events. analogous, contemporary, corresponding, equivalent, like, matching, similar. ● n 1 counterpart, equal, likeness, match. 2 analogy, comparison, correspondence, equivalence, resemblance, similarity. ● v be parallel with, correspond to, equate with, keep pace with, match, run alongside.

paralyse v 1 cripple, disable, incapacitate. 2 anaesthetize, deaden, desensitize, freeze, halt, immobilize, numb, stop, stun.

paralysed adj 1 crippled, disabled, incapacitated, palsied. 2 dead, desensitized, frozen, immobile, numb, unusable, useless.

paralysis n 1 immobility, numbness, palsy. 2 breakdown, halt, standstill.

paraphernalia pl n accessories, baggage, belongings, effects, equipment, materials, inf odds and ends, possessions, property, stuff, tackle, things, trappings.

paraphrase v explain, interpret, put into other words, rephrase, translate.

parcel n bale, box, bundle, carton, case, pack, package, packet. **parcel out** ▷ DIVIDE. **parcel up** ▷ PACK.

parch v bake, burn, dehydrate, desiccate, dry, scorch, shrivel, wither. **parched** ▷ DRY, THIRSTY.

pardon n absolution, amnesty, discharge, exoneration, forgiveness, indulgence, mercy, release, reprieve. ● v absolve, condone, exculpate, excuse, exonerate, forgive, free, let off, overlook, release, reprieve, set free, spare.

pardonable adj allowable, excusable, forgivable, justifiable, minor, negligible, petty, understandable, venial (sin). Opp UNFORGIVABLE.

parent n begetter, father, guardian, mother, procreator.

parentage n ancestry, birth, descent, extraction, family, line, lineage, pedigree, stock.

park n common, estate, gardens, grounds, nature reserve, parkland, recreation ground. ● v deposit, leave, place, position, put, station, store. **park yourself** ▷ SETTLE.

parliament n assembly, congress, convocation, council, government, legislature, lower house, upper house.

parody n burlesque, caricature, imitation, lampoon, mimicry, satire, inf send-up, inf spoof, inf take-off, travesty. ● v ape, burlesque, caricature, imitate, lampoon, mimic, satirize, inf send up, inf take off. ▷ RIDICULE.

parry v avert, block, deflect, evade, fend off, push away, repel, stave off, ward off.

part n 1 bit, branch, component, constituent, division, element, fraction, fragment, ingredient, particle, percentage, piece, portion, ramification, scrap, section, segment, shard, share, single item, subdivision, unit. 2 department, faction, party. 3 part of a book. chapter, episode. 4 part of a town. area, district, neighbourhood, quarter, region, sector. 5 part of the body. limb, member, organ. 6 part in a play. cameo, character, role. ● v 1 detach, disconnect, divide, pull apart, separate, sever, split, sunder. Opp JOIN. 2 depart, go away, leave, part company, quit, say goodbye, separate, split up, take leave. Opp MEET. **part with** ▷ RELINQUISH. **take part** ▷ PARTICIPATE.

partial adj 1 incomplete, limited, qualified. Opp COMPLETE.

2 *partial judge.* biased, one-sided, partisan, prejudiced, unfair. *Opp* IMPARTIAL. **be partial to** ▷ LIKE.

participate *v* assist, be involved, contribute, cooperate, engage, enter, help, join in, share, take part.

participation *n* assistance, complicity, contribution, cooperation, engagement, involvement, partnership, sharing.

particle *n* **1** bit, crumb, dot, drop, fragment, grain, hint, iota, jot, mite, morsel, piece, scrap, shred, sliver, *inf* smidgen, speck, trace. **2** atom, molecule.

particular *adj* **1** distinct, idiosyncratic, individual, personal, singular, specific, unique, unmistakable. **2** *particular with detail.* exact, meticulous, nice, painstaking, precise, rigorous, scrupulous, thorough. **3** *gave particular pleasure.* especial, exceptional, marked, notable, outstanding, significant, special, unusual. **4** *particular about food.* *inf* choosy, discriminating, fastidious, finicky, fussy, *inf* pernickety, selective. *Opp* GENERAL, EASYGOING. **particulars** circumstances, details, facts, information, *inf* low-down.

parting *n* departure, farewell, leave-taking, leaving, saying goodbye, separation.

partisan *adj* biased, bigoted, blinkered, devoted, factional, fanatical, narrow-minded, one-sided, partial, prejudiced, sectarian, unfair. *Opp* IMPARTIAL.
● *n* adherent, devotee, fanatic, freedom fighter, guerrilla, zealot.

partition *n* **1** break-up, division, separation, splitting up.

2 barrier, panel, room-divider, screen, wall. ● *v* cut up, divide, parcel out, separate off, share out, split up, subdivide.

partner *n* **1** accomplice, ally, assistant, associate, *inf* bedfellow, collaborator, colleague, companion, comrade, confederate, helper, *inf* mate. **2** consort, husband, mate, spouse, wife.

partnership *n* **1** affiliation, alliance, association, combination, company, confederation, syndicate. **2** collaboration, complicity, cooperation. **3** marriage, relationship, union.

party *n* **1** celebration, dance, *inf* do, festivity, function, gathering, *inf* get-together, *inf* jollification, *inf* knees-up, merrymaking, *inf* rave-up, reception, *inf* shindig, social gathering. **2** *political party.* alliance, association, *inf* camp, caucus, clique, coalition, faction, league, sect, side. ▷ GROUP.

pass *n* **1** canyon, cut, gap, gorge, gully, opening, passage, ravine, valley, way through. **2** *identity pass.* authorization, clearance, *inf* ID, licence, passport, permission, permit, ticket, warrant.
● *v* **1** go beyond, go by, move on, move past, outstrip, overtake, overshoot, proceed, progress. **2** disappear, elapse, fade, go away, tick by, vanish. **3** *pass drinks.* circulate, deliver, give, hand round, offer, present, share, supply. **4** *pass a resolution.* agree, approve, authorize, confirm, decree, enact, establish, ratify. **5** *pass exams* get through, qualify, succeed. **pass away** ▷ DIE. **pass on** ▷ TRANSFER.

pass out ▷ FAINT. **pass over** ▷ IGNORE.

passable *adj* 1 acceptable, adequate, allowable, all right, fair, indifferent, mediocre, middling, moderate, ordinary, satisfactory, *inf* so-so, tolerable. *Opp* UNACCEPTABLE. 2 clear, navigable, open, unobstructed, usable. *Opp* IMPASSABLE.

passage *n* 1 corridor, entrance, hall, hallway, lobby, passageway, vestibule. 2 *passage of time.* advance, flow, lapse, march, movement, passing, progress, transition. 3 *sea passage.* crossing, cruise, journey, voyage. 4 *through passage.* pass, route, thoroughfare, tunnel, way through. 5 *passage from a book.* citation, episode, excerpt, extract, paragraph, piece, quotation, scene, section, selection.

passenger *n* commuter, rider, traveller, voyager.

passer-by *n* bystander, onlooker, witness.

passion *n* appetite, ardour, craving, craze, desire, drive, eagerness, emotion, enthusiasm, fervour, fire, flame, frenzy, greed, heat, hunger, infatuation, intensity, keenness, love, lust, mania, obsession, strong feeling, thirst, urge, vehemence, warmth, zeal, zest.

passionate *adj* ardent, aroused, avid, burning, eager, emotional, enthusiastic, excited, fervent, fiery, frenzied, greedy, heated, hot, hungry, impassioned, infatuated, inflamed, intense, lustful, obsessive, sexy, strong, urgent, vehement, warm, worked up, zealous. *Opp* APATHETIC.

passive *adj* apathetic, complaisant, compliant, docile, inert, inactive, long-suffering, malleable, non-violent, patient, phlegmatic, pliable, quiescent, resigned, submissive, supine, tame, tractable, unassertive, unmoved, yielding. ▷ CALM. *Opp* ACTIVE.

past *adj* bygone, *inf* dead and buried, earlier, ended, finished, forgotten, former, historical, late, *inf* over and done with, previous, recent, sometime. ● *n* antiquity, days gone by, days of yore, former times, history, old days, olden days. *Opp* FUTURE.

paste *n* 1 adhesive, fixative, glue, gum. 2 pâté, spread. ● *v* fix, glue, stick. ▷ FASTEN.

pastiche *n* blend, *inf* hotchpotch, miscellany, mixture, *inf* motley collection, patchwork, selection.

pastime *n* activity, amusement, diversion, entertainment, fun, game, hobby, leisure activity, occupation, play, recreation, relaxation, sport.

pastoral *adj* 1 bucolic, country, idyllic, outdoor, provincial, rural, rustic. ▷ PEACEFUL. *Opp* URBAN. 2 *pastoral duties.* clerical, ecclesiastical, parochial, priestly.

pasture *n* field, grassland, grazing, mead, meadow, paddock.

pat *v* caress, stroke, tap. ▷ TOUCH.

patch *n* 1 darn, mend, repair. 2 area, garden, plot. ● *v* cover, darn, fix, mend, reinforce, repair, sew up, stitch up.

patchy *adj inf* bitty, blotchy, changing, dappled, erratic, inconsistent, irregular, speckled, spotty, uneven, unpredictable, variable, varied, varying. *Opp* UNIFORM.

patent adj apparent, evident, manifest, plain, transparent. ▷ OBVIOUS.

path n 1 alley, bridle path, footpath, pathway, pavement, road, Amer sidewalk, towpath, track, trail, walkway. 2 approach, course, direction, flight path, orbit, route, trajectory, way.

pathetic adj 1 affecting, emotional, emotive, heartbreaking, heart-rending, moving, piteous, pitiful, plaintive, poignant, stirring, touching, tragic. ▷ SAD. 2 ▷ INADEQUATE.

pathos n pity, poignancy, sadness, tragedy.

patience n 1 calmness, composure, endurance, equanimity, forbearance, fortitude, resignation, restraint, self-control, serenity, stoicism, toleration, inf unflappability. 2 determination, diligence, doggedness, endurance, firmness, perseverance, persistence, tenacity.

patient adj 1 accommodating, acquiescent, calm, composed, docile, easygoing, eventempered, forbearing, forgiving, lenient, long-suffering, mild, philosophical, quiet, resigned, serene, stoical, tolerant, uncomplaining. 2 patient worker. determined, diligent, dogged, persevering, persistent, steady, tenacious, untiring. Opp IMPATIENT. ● n case, invalid, outpatient, sufferer.

patriot n derog chauvinist, loyalist, nationalist, derog xenophobe.

patriotic adj derog chauvinistic, derog jingoistic, loyal, nationalistic, derog xenophobic.

patriotism n derog chauvinism, derog jingoism, loyalty, nationalism, derog xenophobia.

patrol n 1 beat, guard, policing, sentry duty, surveillance, watch. 2 guard, lookout, patrolman, sentinel, sentry, watchman. ● v be on patrol, defend, guard, keep a lookout, make the rounds, police, protect, tour.

patron n 1 inf angel, backer, benefactor, champion, defender, helper, philanthropist, promoter, sponsor, subscriber, supporter. 2 patron of a shop. client, customer, frequenter, inf regular.

patronage n backing, custom, sponsorship, support, trade.

patronize v 1 back, be a patron of, buy from, deal with, encourage, frequent, shop at, support. 2 Don't patronize me! inf put down, talk down to. **patronizing** ▷ SUPERIOR.

pattern n 1 arrangement, decoration, design, device, figure, motif, ornamentation, sequence, shape. 2 archetype, criterion, example, exemplar, guide, ideal, model, norm, original, precedent, prototype, sample, specimen, standard.

pause n break, inf breather, breathing-space, delay, gap, halt, hesitation, hiatus, hold-up, interlude, intermission, interruption, interval, inf let-up, lull, respite, rest, standstill, stop, suspension, wait. ● v break off, delay, falter, halt, hang back, hesitate, mark time, rest, stop, inf take a breather, wait.

pave v asphalt, concrete, surface, tarmac, tile. **pave the way** ▷ PREPARE.

pavement n footpath, *Amer* sidewalk. ▷ PATH.

pay n dividend, earnings, fee, income, money, payment, profit, recompense, reimbursement, remittance, return, salary, settlement, stipend, take-home pay, wages. • v 1 *inf* cough up, *inf* fork out, give, grant, hand over, recompense, remunerate, spend, *inf* stump up. 2 *pay debts*. bear the cost of, clear, compensate, *inf* foot, honour, meet, pay back, pay off, refund, reimburse, repay, settle. 3 *crime doesn't pay*. be profitable, pay off, produce results. 4 *pay for mistakes*. be punished, suffer. ▷ ATONE. **pay back** ▷ RETALIATE.

payment n advance, alimony, allowance, charge, commission, compensation, contribution, cost, deposit, donation, expenditure, fare, fee, fine, instalment, loan, outgoings, outlay, premium, price, rate, remittance, reward, royalty, *inf* sub, subscription, surcharge, tip, toll, wage. *Opp* INCOME.

peace n 1 accord, agreement, amity, conciliation, concord, friendliness, harmony, order. *Opp* CONFLICT. 2 alliance, armistice, ceasefire, pact, treaty, truce. *Opp* WAR. 3 calmness, peace and quiet, peacefulness, placidity, quiet, repose, serenity, silence, stillness, tranquillity. *Opp* ANXIETY.

peaceable adj amicable, civil, conciliatory, cooperative, easygoing, friendly, gentle, harmonious, inoffensive, mild, nonviolent, placid, temperate, understanding. *Opp* QUARRELSOME.

peaceful adj balmy, calm, easy, gentle, pacific, placid, pleasant, quiet, relaxing, restful, serene, soothing, still, tranquil, undisturbed, unruffled, untroubled. *Opp* NOISY, STORMY.

peacemaker n adjudicator, arbitrator, conciliator, diplomat, intermediary, mediator, referee, umpire.

peak n 1 apex, brow, cap, crest, crown, eminence, hill, mountain, pinnacle, point, summit, tip, top. 2 *peak of your career*. acme, climax, crisis, crown, culmination, height, highest point, zenith.

peal n chime, chiming, knell, reverberation, ringing, tintinnabulation, toll. • v chime, clang, resonate, ring, sound, toll.

peasant n bumpkin, countryman, rustic, yokel.

pebbles pl n cobbles, gravel, stones.

peculiar adj 1 aberrant, abnormal, anomalous, atypical, bizarre, curious, deviant, eccentric, exceptional, funny, odd, offbeat, outlandish, out of the ordinary, queer, quirky, surprising, strange, uncommon, unconventional, unusual, weird. 2 *a style peculiar to her*. characteristic, distinctive, identifiable, idiosyncratic, individual, particular, personal, singular, special, unique, unmistakable. *Opp* COMMON, ORDINARY.

peculiarity n abnormality, characteristic, distinctiveness, eccentricity, foible, idiosyncrasy, individuality, mannerism, oddity, quirk, singularity, speciality, trait, uniqueness.

pedantic adj 1 academic, bookish, dry, formal, learned, old-fashioned, pompous, scholarly, stiff, stilted, *inf* stuffy. **2** *inf* by the book, exact, fastidious, fussy, inflexible, *inf* nit-picking, precise, punctilious, strict, unimaginative. *Opp* INFORMAL, LAX.

peddle *v inf* flog, hawk, market, *inf* push, sell, traffic in, vend.

pedestrian *adj* **1** pedestrianized, traffic-free. **2** banal, boring, dull, commonplace, flat-footed, mundane, prosaic, *inf* run-of-the-mill, tedious, unimaginative.
▷ ORDINARY. ● *n* foot-traveller, walker.

pedigree *adj* pure-bred, thoroughbred. ● *n* ancestry, blood, descent, extraction, family history, genealogy, line, lineage, parentage, roots, stock, strain.

pedlar *n* door-to-door salesman, hawker, *inf* pusher, seller, street trader, trafficker, vendor.

peel *n* coating, rind, skin.
● *v* denude, flay, pare, skin, strip. ▷ UNDRESS.

peep *v* glance, have a look, peek, squint.

peer *n* aristocrat, countess, duchess, duke, earl, grandee, lady, lord, marquis, nobleman, noblewoman, viscount. ● *v* look earnestly, spy, squint. ▷ LOOK.

peers 1 aristocracy, nobility, peerage. **2** colleagues, equals, fellows, peer-group.

peevish *adj* cantankerous, crabby, grumpy, irritable, petulant, querulous, testy, touchy, waspish. ▷ BAD-TEMPERED.

peg *n* bolt, dowel, pin, rod, stick.
● *v* ▷ FASTEN.

pelt *n* coat, fur, hide, skin.
● *v* bombard, shower. ▷ THROW.

pen *n* **1** coop, corral, enclosure, fold, hutch, pound. **2** ballpoint, biro, felt-tip, fountain pen.

penalize *v* discipline, fine, impose a penalty on, punish.

penalty *n* fine, forfeit, price, punishment. **pay the penalty**
▷ ATONE.

penance *n* amends, atonement, reparation. **do penance**
▷ ATONE.

pendent *adj* dangling, hanging, loose, pendulous, suspended, swaying, swinging, trailing.

pending *adj* about to happen, imminent, impending, *inf* in the offing, undecided, waiting.

penetrate *v* **1** bore through, break through, drill into, enter, get into, get through, infiltrate, lance, perforate, pierce, puncture, stab. **2** *damp penetrates.* filter through, impregnate, permeate, pervade, seep into, suffuse.

penitent *adj* apologetic, conscience-stricken, contrite, regretful, remorseful, repentant, rueful, shamefaced, sorry.
Opp UNREPENTANT.

pennon *n* ▷ FLAG.

pension *n* annuity, benefit, old age pension, superannuation.

pensive *adj* brooding, contemplative, daydreaming, *inf* far-away, lost in thought, meditative, reflective, ruminative, thoughtful.

penury *n* destitution, impoverishment, lack, need, poverty, scarcity, want.

people *n* **1** folk, human beings, humanity, humans, individuals, mankind, men and women, mortals, persons. **2** citizens, community, electorate, *inf* grass roots, nation, populace, population, the public, society, subjects. 3 *your own people*. clan, family, kinsmen, kith and kin, race, relations, relatives, tribe. ● *v* colonize, fill, inhabit, occupy, overrun, populate, settle.

perceive *v* 1 become aware of, catch sight of, detect, discern, distinguish, glimpse, identify, make out, notice, note, observe, recognize, see, spot. 2 appreciate, apprehend, comprehend, deduce, feel, figure out, gather, grasp, infer, realize, sense, understand.

perceptible *adj* appreciable, audible, detectable, discernible, distinct, distinguishable, evident, identifiable, manifest, marked, notable, noticeable, obvious, palpable, plain, recognizable, unmistakable, visible. *Opp* IMPERCEPTIBLE.

perception *n* appreciation, awareness, comprehension, consciousness, discernment, insight, instinct, intuition, observation, recognition, sensation, sense, understanding, view.

perceptive *adj* acute, alert, astute, attentive, aware, clever, discerning, discriminating, observant, percipient, quick, responsive, sensitive, sharp, sharp-eyed, shrewd, sympathetic, understanding. ▷ INTELLIGENT.

perch *n* rest, resting place, roost. ● *v* balance, rest, settle, sit.

perdition *n* ▷ DAMNATION.

perfect *adj* 1 absolute, complete, consummate, excellent, exemplary, faultless, flawless, ideal, immaculate, incomparable, matchless, mint, superlative, unbeatable, undamaged, unqualified, whole. 2 blameless, irreproachable, pure, sinless, spotless, unimpeachable. 3 accurate, authentic, correct, exact, faithful, impeccable, precise, true. *Opp* IMPERFECT. ● *v* bring to fruition, carry through, complete, consummate, effect, execute, finish, fulfil, realize.

perfection *n* 1 beauty, completeness, excellence, flawlessness, ideal, precision, purity, wholeness. *Opp* IMPERFECTION. 2 *the perfection of a plan*. achievement, completion, consummation, end, fruition, fulfilment, realization.

perforate *v* bore through, drill, penetrate, pierce, prick, punch, puncture, riddle.

perform *v* 1 accomplish, achieve, bring about, carry out, commit, complete, discharge, dispatch, do, effect, execute, finish, fulfil. 2 behave, function, go, operate, run, work. 3 *perform on stage*. act, appear, dance, feature, figure, take part. 4 *perform a play, song*. enact, mount, present, produce, put on, render, represent, sing, stage.

performance *n* 1 accomplishment, achievement, carrying out, completion, execution, fulfilment. 2 behaviour, conduct, exhibition, exploit, feat, play-acting, pretence. 3 *stage performance*. acting, debut, interpretation, play, playing, portrayal, presentation, production, rendition, representation, show, turn.

performer *n* actor, actress, artist, artiste, entertainer, player, singer, star, *inf* superstar.

perfume n 1 aroma, bouquet, fragrance, odour, scent, smell. 2 aftershave, eau de Cologne, scent, toilet water.

perfunctory adj apathetic, brief, cursory, dutiful, fleeting, half-hearted, hurried, indifferent, mechanical, offhand, routine, superficial, unenthusiastic. Opp ENTHUSIASTIC.

perhaps adv conceivably, maybe, possibly.

peril n danger, hazard, insecurity, jeopardy, risk, threat.

perilous adj dangerous, hazardous, insecure, risky, uncertain, unsafe. Opp SAFE.

perimeter n border, borderline, boundary, bounds, circumference, confines, edge, fringe, frontier, limit, margin, periphery, verge.

period n 1 duration, interval, phase, season, session, span, spell, stage, stint, stretch, term, while. 2 age, epoch, era, time.

periodic adj recurrent, repeated. ▷ OCCASIONAL.

peripheral adj 1 distant, on the perimeter, outer, outermost, outlying. 2 borderline, incidental, inessential, irrelevant, marginal, nonessential, unimportant. Opp CENTRAL.

perish v 1 be destroyed, be killed, die, expire. 2 decay, decompose, disintegrate, go bad, rot.

perjury n ▷ LYING.

permanent adj abiding, changeless, chronic, constant, continual, continuous, durable, enduring, eternal, everlasting, fixed, immutable, incessant, incurable, indestructible, ineradicable, invariable, irreparable,

irreversible, lasting, lifelong, long-lasting, never-ending, nonstop, ongoing, perennial, perpetual, persistent, stable, steady, unalterable, unchanging, undying, unending. Opp TEMPORARY.

permeate v diffuse, filter through, impregnate, infiltrate, penetrate, pervade, saturate, spread through.

permissible adj acceptable, admissible, allowed, lawful, legal, legitimate, permitted, proper, right, sanctioned, tolerable, valid, venial (sin). Opp UNACCEPTABLE.

permission n agreement, approbation, approval, assent, consent, dispensation, franchise, inf go-ahead, inf green light, leave, licence, inf rubber stamp, sanction, seal of approval, support. ▷ PERMIT.

permissive adj easygoing, indulgent, lenient, liberal, libertarian, tolerant.

permit n authority, authorization, charter, licence, order, pass, passport, ticket, visa, warrant. • v admit, agree to, allow, approve of, authorize, consent to, endorse, give permission for, give your blessing to, legalize, license, sanction, support, tolerate.

perpendicular adj at right angles, upright, vertical.

perpetual adj abiding, ceaseless, chronic, constant, continual, continuous, endless, enduring, eternal, everlasting, immutable, incessant, incurable, indestructible, interminable, lasting, long-lasting, never-ending, non-stop, ongoing, perennial, permanent, persistent, protracted, recurrent, repeated, timeless, unceasing, unchanging, undying, unending, unremitting. *Opp* TEMPORARY.

perpetuate *v* extend, immortalize, keep going, maintain, preserve.

perplex *v* baffle, *inf* bamboozle, bewilder, confound, confuse, disconcert, dumbfound, muddle, mystify, nonplus, puzzle, *inf* stump, worry.

perquisite *n* benefit, bonus, extra, fringe benefit, gratuity, *inf* perk, tip.

persecute *v* annoy, badger, bother, bully, discriminate against, harass, ill-treat, intimidate, maltreat, molest, oppress, pester, *inf* put the screws on, suppress, terrorize, torment, torture, tyrannize, victimize, worry.

persist *v* carry on, continue, endure, go on, *inf* hang on, hold out, keep going, keep on, last, linger, persevere, remain, *inf* soldier on, stand firm, stay, *inf* stick at it. *Opp* CEASE.

persistent *adj* 1 ceaseless, chronic, constant, continual, continuous, endless, eternal, everlasting, incessant, interminable, lasting, long-lasting, neverending, permanent, perpetual, recurrent, recurring, unending, unrelenting, unrelieved, unremitting. *Opp* BRIEF, INTERMITTENT. 2 assiduous, determined, dogged, hard-working, indefatigable, patient, persevering, relentless, resolute, steadfast, steady, stubborn, tenacious, tireless, unflagging, untiring, unwavering, zealous.

person *n* adolescent, adult, being, *inf* body, character, child, figure, human, human being, individual, infant, mortal, personage, *inf* soul, *inf* type. ▷ MAN, PEOPLE, WOMAN.

persona *n* character, façade, guise, identity, image, personality, role, self-image.

personal *adj* 1 distinct, distinctive, exclusive, idiosyncratic, individual, inimitable, particular, peculiar, private, special, unique, your own. *Opp* GENERAL. 2 *personal appearance*. in person, in the flesh, live, physical. 3 *personal letters*. confidential, informal, intimate, private, secret. *Opp* PUBLIC. 4 *personal friends*. close, dear, familiar, intimate. 5 *personal remarks*. belittling, critical, derogatory, disparaging, insulting, offensive, pejorative, rude, slighting. 6 *personal knowledge*. direct, empirical, experiential.

personality *n* 1 character, disposition, identity, individuality, *inf* make-up, nature, persona, temperament. 2 *inf* big name, celebrity, idol, luminary, name, public figure, star, *inf* superstar.

personification *n* embodiment, epitome, incarnation, living image, manifestation.

personify *v* embody, epitomize, exemplify, incarnate, manifest, represent, stand for, symbolize, typify.

personnel *n* employees, people, staff, workforce, workers.

perspective *n* angle, approach, attitude, outlook, point of view, position, slant, standpoint, view, viewpoint.

persuade *v* bring round, cajole, coax, convert, convince, entice, induce, influence, inveigle, press, prevail upon, talk into, tempt, urge, use persuasion,

wheedle (into), win over.
Opp DISSUADE.

persuasion *n* **1** argument, blandishment, cajolery, coaxing, enticement, inducement, persuading. **2** affiliation, belief, conviction, creed, denomination, faith, religion, sect.

persuasive *adj* cogent, compelling, convincing, credible, effective, eloquent, forceful, influential, logical, plausible, potent, reasonable, sound, strong, telling, valid. *Opp* UNCONVINCING.

pertain *v* apply, be relevant, have bearing, relate, refer.
pertain to affect, concern.

pertinent *adj* ▷ RELEVANT.

perturb *v* agitate, bother, confuse, discomfort, disconcert, disquiet, distress, disturb, fluster, make anxious, ruffle, shake, trouble, unnerve, unsettle, upset, worry. *Opp* REASSURE.

peruse *v* inspect, look over, read, scan, scrutinize, study.

pervade *v* diffuse, fill, filter through, flow through, penetrate, permeate, saturate, spread through, suffuse.

pervasive *adj* general, pervading, prevalent, rife, ubiquitous, universal, widespread.

perverse *adj* contradictory, contrary, disobedient, illogical, intractable, intransigent, obdurate, obstinate, pig-headed, *inf* rebellious, refractory, selfwilled, stubborn, tiresome, uncooperative, unreasonable, wayward, wilful, wrong-headed.
Opp REASONABLE.

perversion *n* **1** corruption, distortion, falsification, misrepresentation, misuse, twisting.
2 abnormality, depravity, deviance, immorality, impropriety, vice, wickedness.

pervert *n* degenerate, deviant.
● *v* **1** bend, distort, falsify, misrepresent, perjure, subvert, twist, undermine. **2** *pervert a witness*. bribe, corrupt.

perverted *adj* abnormal, amoral, bad, corrupt, degenerate, depraved, deviant, evil, immoral, profligate, twisted, unnatural, warped, wicked, wrong. ▷ OBSCENE.
Opp NATURAL.

pessimism *n* cynicism, despair, despondency, gloom, hopelessness, resignation, unhappiness. *Opp* OPTIMISM.

pessimistic *adj* bleak, cynical, defeatist, despairing, fatalistic, gloomy, hopeless, morbid, negative, resigned. ▷ SAD.
Opp OPTIMISTIC.

pest *n* **1** annoyance, bane, bother, curse, irritation, nuisance, *inf* pain in the neck. **2** *inf* bug, insect, parasite, *pl* vermin.

pester *v* annoy, badger, bait, besiege, bother, harass, *inf* hassle, irritate, molest, nag, plague, torment, trouble, worry.

pestilence *n* blight, epidemic, illness, plague, scourge.

pet *n inf* apple of your eye, darling, favourite, idol. ● *v* caress, cuddle, fondle, kiss, nuzzle, pat, stroke. ▷ TOUCH.

petition *n* appeal, entreaty, list of signatures, plea, request, supplication. ● *v* appeal to, call upon, entreat, importune, supplicate. ▷ ASK.

petty *adj* **1** insignificant, minor, niggling, small, trivial, trifling.
▷ UNIMPORTANT.
Opp IMPORTANT. **2** *petty com-*

plaints. grudging, *inf* nit-picking, small-minded. *Opp* GENEROUS.

phase *n* development, period, season, spell, stage, state, step. ▷ TIME. **phase in** ▷ INTRODUCE. **phase out** ▷ FINISH.

phenomenal *adj* amazing, astonishing, astounding, exceptional, extraordinary, *inf* fantastic, incredible, marvellous, *inf* mind-boggling, outstanding, prodigious, rare, remarkable, *inf* sensational, singular, staggering, unbelievable, wonderful. *Opp* ORDINARY.

phenomenon *n* **1** circumstance, event, fact, happening, incident, occasion, occurrence, sight. **2** curiosity, marvel, miracle, prodigy, rarity.

philanthropic *adj* altruistic, beneficent, bountiful, charitable, generous, humanitarian, magnanimous, munificent, public-spirited. ▷ KIND. *Opp* MISANTHROPIC.

philanthropist *n* altruist, benefactor, donor, giver, *inf* Good Samaritan, humanitarian, patron, provider, sponsor.

philistine *adj* ignorant, low-brow, uncivilized, uncultured, unenlightened.

philosopher *n* sage, thinker.

philosophical *adj* **1** abstract, analytical, erudite, ideological, intellectual, learned, logical, metaphysical, rational, reasoned, theoretical, thoughtful, wise. **2** calm, collected, composed, patient, reasonable, resigned, serene, sober, stoical, unemotional, unruffled. *Opp* EMOTIONAL.

philosophize *v* analyse, moralize, pontificate, preach, reason, theorize, think things out.

philosophy *n* **1** ideology, logic, metaphysics, thinking, thought. **2** *philosophy of life*. convictions, outlook, set of beliefs, tenets, values, viewpoint, wisdom.

phlegmatic *adj* apathetic, impassive, imperturbable, lethargic, passive, placid, slow, sluggish, stolid, torpid, undemonstrative, unemotional, unenthusiastic, unresponsive. *Opp* EXCITABLE.

phobia *n* anxiety, aversion, dislike, dread, *inf* hang-up, hatred, horror, loathing, neurosis, obsession, repugnance, revulsion. ▷ FEAR.

phone *v* ▷ TELEPHONE.

phoney *adj* affected, artificial, assumed, bogus, cheating, contrived, counterfeit, deceitful, ersatz, fake, faked, false, fraudulent, hypocritical, imitation, insincere, mock, pretended, *inf* pseudo, *inf* put-on, sham, spurious, synthetic, trick. *Opp* REAL.

photograph *n* enlargement, exposure, negative, *inf* photo, picture, plate, print, shot, slide, *inf* snap, snapshot, transparency. *v* film, shoot, snap.

photographic *adj* **1** accurate, exact, faithful, graphic, lifelike, realistic, true to life. **2** *photographic memory*. pictorial, retentive, visual.

phrase *n* clause, expression. ▷ SAYING. *v* ▷ SAY.

phraseology *n* expression, idiom, language, parlance, phrasing, turn of phrase, wording.

physical *adj* actual, bodily, carnal, concrete, corporeal, earthly, fleshly, material, palpable, physiological, real, solid,

substantial, tangible.
Opp INTANGIBLE, SPIRITUAL.

physician *n* consultant, general practitioner, *inf* GP, specialist.
▷ DOCTOR.

physiological *adj* anatomical, bodily, physical.
Opp PSYCHOLOGICAL.

physique *n* body, build, figure, form, frame, shape.

pick *n* 1 choice, election, option, preference, selection. 2 best, cream, elite, favourite, flower, pride. • *v* 1 choose, decide on, elect, fix on, name, nominate, opt for, prefer, select, settle on, single out, vote for. 2 *pick flowers.* collect, cut, gather, harvest, pluck, pull off. **pick on** ▷ BULLY. **pick up** ▷ GET, IMPROVE.

pictorial *adj* diagrammatic, graphic, illustrated, representational.

picture *n* 1 delineation, depiction, design, drawing, engraving, illustration, image, likeness, outline, painting, portrait, print, portrayal, profile, representation, reproduction, sketch. 2 film, movie, video. • *v* 1 delineate, depict, display, draw, engrave, illustrate, outline, paint, portray, represent, show, sketch. 2 *picture the future.* conceive, describe, envisage, fancy, imagine, see in your mind's eye, think up, visualize.

picturesque *adj* 1 charming, idyllic, lovely, pleasant, pretty, quaint, scenic, *inf* story-book.
▷ BEAUTIFUL. *Opp* UNATTRACTIVE. 2 *picturesque language.* colourful, descriptive, expressive, graphic, poetic, vivid.

pie *n* flan, pasty, quiche, tart, turnover.

piece *n* 1 bar, bit, bite, block, chip, chunk, crumb, dollop, fraction, fragment, grain, helping, hunk, length, lump, morsel, part, particle, portion, quantity, sample, scrap, section, segment, shard, share, shred, slab, slice, sliver, snippet, speck, stick, *inf* titbit, wedge. 2 component, constituent, element, spare part, unit. 3 *piece of music, writing.* article, composition, example, item, passage, specimen, work. **piece together** ▷ ASSEMBLE.

pied *adj* dappled, flecked, piebald, spotted, variegated.

pier *n* 1 breakwater, jetty, landing stage, quay, wharf. ▷ DOCK. 2 buttress, column, pile, pillar, post, support, upright.

pierce *v* bore through, cut, drill, enter, go through, impale, jab, lance, make a hole in, penetrate, perforate, prick, punch, puncture, skewer, spear, spike, spit, stab, stick into, transfix, wound.
piercing ▷ SHARP.

piety *n* devotion, devoutness, faith, godliness, holiness, piousness, religion, *derog* religiosity, saintliness, sanctity.
Opp IMPIETY.

pig *n* boar, hog, piglet, runt, sow, swine.

pile *n* 1 abundance, accumulation, collection, conglomeration, deposit, heap, hoard, mass, mound, *inf* plethora, quantity, stack, stockpile, *inf* tons. 2 column, post, support, upright. • *v* accumulate, amass, assemble, build up, collect, concentrate, gather, heap, hoard, load, mass, stack up, stockpile, store.

pilfer *v inf* filch, *inf* pinch, rob, shoplift. ▷ STEAL.

pilgrim *n* ▷ TRAVELLER.

pill *n* capsule, lozenge, tablet.

pillage *n* depredation, devastation, looting, marauding, piracy, plunder, ransacking, rape, robbery, robbing, stealing.
● *v* devastate, raid, ransack.
▷ PLUNDER.

pillar *n* baluster, column, pilaster, pile, post, prop, shaft, support, upright.

pilot *n* 1 airman, *old use* aviator, captain, flier. 2 helmsman, leader, navigator. ● *v* conduct, direct, drive, fly, guide, lead, navigate, shepherd, steer.

pimple *n* blackhead, boil, eruption, pustule, spot, swelling, *sl* zit. **pimples** acne, rash.

pin *n* brooch, clip, drawing-pin, nail, peg, rivet, safety pin, spike, staple. ● *v* clip, nail, pierce, staple, tack, transfix. ▷ FASTEN.

pinch *v* 1 crush, hurt, nip, squeeze. 2 ▷ STEAL.

pine *v* mope, mourn, sicken, waste away. **pine for** ▷ WANT.

pinnacle *n* 1 acme, apex, cap, climax, crest, crown, height, highest point, peak, summit, top, zenith. 2 spire, steeple, turret.

pioneer *n* 1 colonist, discoverer, explorer, pathfinder, settler, trail-blazer. 2 innovator, inventor, originator, trend-setter. ● *v* begin, *inf* bring out, create, develop, discover, establish, found, inaugurate, initiate, institute, introduce, invent, launch, originate, set up, start.

pious *adj* 1 devout, faithful, God-fearing, godly, holy, moral, religious, reverent, reverential, saintly, sincere, spiritual, virtuous. *Opp* IMPIOUS. 2 [*derog*] *inf* goody-goody, *inf* holier-than-thou, hypocritical, mealy-mouthed, sanctimonious, self-righteous, self-satisfied, unctuous. *Opp* SINCERE.

pip *n* 1 pit, seed, stone. 2 spot, star. 3 bleep, sound, stroke.

pipe *n* conduit, channel, duct, hose, hydrant, line, main, pipeline, tube. ● *v* 1 carry along a pipe, channel, convey, supply, transmit. 2 *pipe a tune.* blow, play, sound, whistle. **pipe up** ▷ SPEAK. **piping** ▷ HOT, SHRILL.

piquant *adj* 1 appetizing, pungent, salty, sharp, spicy, tangy, tart, tasty. *Opp* BLAND. 2 *piquant notion.* exciting, provocative, stimulating. *Opp* BANAL.

pirate *n* buccaneer, marauder, privateer, raider. ▷ THIEF.
● *v* ▷ PLAGIARIZE.

pit *n* 1 abyss, chasm, crater, depression, excavation, hole, hollow, pothole, well. 2 coal mine, colliery, mine, quarry, shaft, working.

pitch *n* 1 bitumen, tar. 2 angle, gradient, incline, slope, tilt. 3 *musical pitch.* sound, timbre, tone. 4 *soccer pitch.* arena, ground, playing field. ● *v* 1 erect, put up, raise, set up. 2 *pitch stones.* bowl, *inf* bung, cast, *inf* chuck, fling, heave, hurl, lob, sling, throw, toss. 3 *pitch into the water.* dive, drop, fall headlong, plunge, plummet, topple. **pitch about** ▷ TOSS. **pitch in** ▷ COOPERATE. **pitch into** ▷ ATTACK.

piteous *adj* affecting, distressing, heartbreaking, heart-rending, lamentable, moving, pathetic, pitiable, pitiful, plaintive, poignant, wretched. ▷ SAD.

pitfall n catch, danger, difficulty, hazard, peril, snag, trap.

pitiful adj 1 abject, contemptible, hopeless, inadequate, incompetent, laughable, inf miserable, inf pathetic, ridiculous, sorry, trifling, useless, worthless. Opp ADMIRABLE. 2 ▷ PITEOUS.

pitiless adj bloodthirsty, brutal, cruel, ferocious, heartless, inhuman, merciless, relentless, ruthless, sadistic, unrelenting, unremitting, unsympathetic. Opp MERCIFUL.

pitted adj dented, inf holey, pock-marked, rough, scarred, uneven. Opp SMOOTH.

pity n charity, clemency, commiseration, compassion, condolence, forbearance, forgiveness, grace, humanity, kindness, mercy, sympathy, tenderness, understanding. Opp CRUELTY.
● v commiserate with, inf feel for, feel sorry for, sympathize with.

pivot n axis, axle, centre, fulcrum, hinge, hub, pin, point of balance, swivel. ● v hinge, revolve, rotate, spin, swivel, turn, whirl.

placard n advert, advertisement, bill, notice, poster, sign.

placate v ▷ PACIFY.

place n 1 area, country, district, location, locality, neighbourhood, part, point, position, region, scene, setting, site, situation, inf spot, town, venue, whereabouts. 2 place in society. function, niche, office, position, rank, role, standing, station, status. 3 place to live. accommodation, inf digs, room, home, house. ● v 1 deposit, inf dump, lay, leave, locate, pinpoint, plant, position, put down, rest,

set down, settle, situate, stand, station. 2 categorize, class, classify, grade, order, position, put in order, rank, sort. 3 can't place it. identify, put a name to, recognize, remember.

placid adj 1 collected, composed, cool, equable, even-tempered, imperturbable, mild, phlegmatic, stable, unexcitable. 2 calm, motionless, peaceful, quiet, tranquil, unruffled. Opp EXCITABLE, STORMY.

plagiarize v borrow, copy, inf crib, imitate, inf lift, pirate, reproduce, steal.

plague n 1 affliction, bane, blight, calamity, contagion, epidemic, illness, infection, outbreak, pestilence, scourge. 2 infestation, invasion, swarm. ● v afflict, annoy, be a nuisance to, bother, disturb, harass, hound, irritate, molest, nag, persecute, pester, torment, torture, trouble, vex, worry.

plain adj 1 apparent, audible, clear, comprehensible, definite, distinct, evident, intelligible, legible, lucid, manifest, obvious, patent, transparent, unambiguous, understandable, unmistakable, visible, well-defined. Opp OBSCURE. 2 plain speech. blunt, candid, direct, explicit, forthright, frank, honest, outspoken, prosaic, sincere, straightforward, unequivocal, unvarnished. 3 plain dress, food. austere, everyday, frugal, homely, modest, ordinary, simple, spartan, unattractive, unexciting, unprepossessing, unremarkable, workaday. Opp SOPHISTICATED.
● n grassland, pasture, pampas,

prairie, savannah, steppe, tundra, veld.

plaintive adj doleful, melancholy, mournful, plangent, sorrowful, wistful. ▷ SAD.

plan n 1 blueprint, chart, design, diagram, drawing, layout, map, representation, sketch-map. 2 *plan of action*. design, formula, idea, intention, method, plot, policy, procedure, programme, project, proposal, scheme, strategy, system. • v 1 arrange, concoct, contrive, design, devise, formulate, invent, map out, organize, outline, plot, prepare, think out, work out. 2 *I plan to leave*. aim, contemplate, envisage, expect, intend, mean, propose. **planned** ▷ DELIBERATE.

plane adj even, flat, flush, level, smooth, uniform. • n 1 flat surface, level surface. 2 aeroplane, aircraft, glider.

planet n globe, orb, satellite, sphere, world.

plank n beam, board, timber.

planning n arrangement, design, drafting, forethought, organization, preparation, setting up, thinking out.

plant n [sing] flower, herb, shrub, tree, weed. [pl] greenery, growth, undergrowth, vegetation. 2 *manufacturing plant*. factory, foundry, mill, shop, works. 3 *industrial plant*. apparatus, equipment, machinery. • v 1 bed out, sow, transplant. 2 locate, place, position, put, situate, station.

plaster n 1 mortar, stucco. 2 dressing, sticking plaster. • v coat, cover, daub, smear, spread.

plastic adj ductile, flexible, malleable, pliable, shapable, soft, supple, workable.

plate n 1 dinner-plate, dish, platter, salver, side-plate. 2 lamina, layer, leaf, pane, panel, sheet, slab, stratum. 3 illustration, picture, print. 4 *dental plate*. dentures, false teeth. • v coat, cover, electroplate, gild (*with gold*).

platform n 1 dais, podium, rostrum, stage, stand. 2 *political platform*. ▷ POLICY.

platitude n banality, cliché, commonplace, truism.

plausible adj acceptable, believable, conceivable, credible, feasible, glib, likely, logical, persuasive, possible, probable, reasonable, *derog* specious, tenable. *Opp* IMPLAUSIBLE.

play n 1 amusement, diversion, entertainment, frivolity, fun, fun and games, horseplay, joking, make-believe, merrymaking, recreation, revelry, *inf* skylarking, sport. 2 flexibility, freedom, *inf* give, leeway, looseness, movement. 3 ▷ DRAMA. • v 1 caper, enjoy yourself, fool about, frisk, frolic, gambol, have fun, *inf* mess about, romp, sport. 2 *play a game*. join in, participate, take part. 3 *play an opponent*. challenge, compete against, take on. 4 *play a role*. act, depict, perform, portray, pretend to be, represent, take the part of. **play along, play ball** ▷ COOPERATE. **play down** ▷ MINIMIZE. **play for time** ▷ DELAY. **play it by ear** ▷ IMPROVISE. **play up** ▷ MISBEHAVE. **play up to** ▷ FLATTER.

player n 1 competitor, contestant, participant, sportsman, sportswoman. 2 actor, actress, artiste, entertainer, instrumentalist, musician, performer, soloist.

playful adj cheerful, flirtatious, frisky, frolicsome, fun-loving, high-spirited, humorous, impish, inf jokey, joking, light-hearted, lively, mischievous, roguish, skittish, spirited, sportive, sprightly, inf tongue-in-cheek, vivacious. Opp SERIOUS.

plea n 1 appeal, entreaty, invocation, petition, prayer, request, suit, supplication. 2 excuse, explanation, justification, reason.

plead v 1 appeal, ask, beg, beseech, entreat, implore, importune, petition, request, seek, solicit, supplicate. 2 argue, maintain. ▷ ALLEGE.

pleasant adj acceptable, affable, agreeable, amiable, attractive, balmy, beautiful, charming, cheerful, congenial, delightful, enjoyable, entertaining, fine, friendly, genial, gentle, good, gratifying, hospitable, kind, likeable, lovely, mellow, mild, nice, palatable, pleasing, pleasurable, relaxed, satisfying, soothing, sympathetic, warm, welcome, welcoming. Opp UNPLEASANT.

please v 1 amuse, content, delight, divert, entertain, give pleasure to, gladden, gratify, make happy, satisfy, suit. 2 Do what you please. ▷ WANT. **pleasing** ▷ PLEASANT.

pleased adj inf chuffed, contented, delighted, elated, euphoric, glad, gratified, satisfied, thankful, thrilled. ▷ HAPPY. Opp ANNOYED.

pleasure n 1 bliss, comfort, contentment, delight, ecstasy, enjoyment, euphoria, fulfilment, gratification, happiness, joy, rapture, satisfaction. 2 amusement, diversion, entertainment, fun, luxury, recreation, self-indulgence.

pleat n crease, fold, gather, tuck.

plebiscite n ballot, poll, referendum, vote.

pledge n 1 assurance, covenant, guarantee, oath, pact, promise, undertaking, vow, warranty, word. 2 bail, bond, collateral, deposit, pawn, security, surety. • v agree, commit yourself, contract, give your word, guarantee, promise, swear, undertake, vow.

plenary adj full, general, open.

plentiful adj abundant, ample, bountiful, bristling, bumper (crop), copious, generous, lavish, liberal, overflowing, profuse. Opp SCARCE. **be plentiful** ▷ ABOUND.

plenty n abundance, affluence, cornucopia, excess, fertility, fruitfulness, glut, inf heaps, inf loads, inf lots, inf masses, much, more than enough, inf oodles, inf piles, plethora, profusion, prosperity, quantities, inf stacks, surfeit, surplus, inf tons, wealth. Opp SCARCITY.

pliable adj 1 bendable, inf bendy, ductile, flexible, plastic, pliant, springy, supple. 2 pliable character. adaptable, compliant, easily led, impressionable, manageable, persuadable, responsive, suggestible, susceptible, tractable, yielding.

plod v 1 slog, tramp, trudge. 2 grind on, labour, persevere, inf plug away, toil. ▷ WORK.

plot n 1 acreage, allotment, area, estate, garden, lot, patch, smallholding, tract. 2 *plot of a novel.* chain of events, narrative, outline, scenario, story, storyline, thread. 3 *subversive plot.* conspiracy, intrigue, machination, plan, scheme. • *v* 1 chart, draw, map out, mark, outline, plan, project. 2 collude, conspire, intrigue, scheme. 3 *inf* brew, concoct, *inf* cook up, design, devise, dream up, hatch.

pluck *n* ▷ COURAGE. *v* 1 collect, gather, harvest, pick, pull off, remove. 2 grab, pull, seize, snatch, tweak, yank. 3 *pluck a guitar.* strum, twang.

plug *n* 1 bung, cork, stopper. 2 ▷ ADVERTISEMENT. • *v* 1 block up, *inf* bung up, close, cork, fill, jam, seal, stop up. 2 advertise, mention frequently, promote, publicize. **plug away** ▷ WORK.

plumb *adv* 1 *inf* dead, exactly, precisely, *inf* slap. 2 vertically. • *v* fathom, measure, probe, sound.

plume *n* feather, *pl* plumage, quill.

plump *adj* ample, buxom, chubby, dumpy, podgy, pudgy, *inf* roly-poly, rotund, round, tubby, *inf* well-upholstered. ▷ FAT. *Opp* THIN. **plump for** ▷ CHOOSE.

plunder *n* booty, contraband, loot, pickings, pillage, prize, spoils, *inf* swag, takings. • *v* devastate, lay waste, loot, maraud, pillage, raid, ransack, ravage, rifle, rob, seize, spoil, strip, vandalize.

plunge *v* 1 dive, drop, fall, fall headlong, hurtle, immerse, jump, leap, nosedive, pitch, plummet, sink, submerge, swoop, tumble. 2 force, push, thrust.

poach *v* 1 hunt, steal, trap. 2 boil, cook, steam.

pocket *n* bag, container, pouch, receptacle. • *v* ▷ TAKE.

pod *n* case, hull, shell.

poem *n* ballad, *inf* ditty, limerick, lyric, ode, piece of poetry, rhyme, sonnet, verse.

poet *n* bard, lyricist, minstrel, rhymer, versifier, writer.

poetic *adj* emotive, *derog* flowery, imaginative, lyrical, metrical, poetical. *Opp* PROSAIC.

poignant *adj* affecting, distressing, heartbreaking, heart-rending, moving, pathetic, pitiful, tender, touching, upsetting. ▷ SAD.

point *n* 1 apex, peak, prong, spike, spur, tip. 2 *point on a map.* location, place, position, site, situation, spot. 3 *point in time.* instant, juncture, moment, second, stage, time. 4 *decimal point.* dot, full stop. 5 *point of an argument.* aim, crux, drift, end, essence, gist, goal, heart, import, intention, meaning, motive, nub, object, pith, purpose, relevance, significance, subject, substance, theme, thrust, use. 6 *points to raise.* detail, idea, item, matter, particular, question, thought, topic. 7 *She has many good points.* attribute, characteristic, facet, feature, property, quality, trait. • *v* 1 draw attention to, indicate, point out, show, signal. 2 aim, direct, guide, lead, steer. **pointed** ▷ SHARP. **to the point** ▷ RELEVANT.

pointer *n* arrow, hand (*of clock*), indicator.

pointless *adj* aimless, fruitless, futile, ineffective, senseless, unproductive, useless, vain, worthless. ▷ STUPID.

poise n aplomb, assurance, balance, calmness, composure, coolness, dignity, equanimity, equilibrium, equipoise, imperturbability, presence, sang-froid, self-confidence, self-control, self-possession, serenity, steadiness. • v balance, be poised, hover, keep in balance, support, suspend.

poised adj 1 balanced, hovering, in equilibrium, standing, steady, teetering, wavering. 2 poised to begin. keyed up, prepared, ready, set, standing by, waiting. 3 poised performer. assured, calm, composed, cool, level-headed, dignified, self-confident, self-possessed, serene, suave, inf unflappable, unruffled, urbane.

poison n toxin, venom. • v 1 adulterate, contaminate, infect, pollute, taint. 2 poison the mind. corrupt, defile, deprave, pervert, prejudice, subvert, warp. **poisoned** ▷ DIRTY, POISONOUS.

poisonous adj deadly, fatal, lethal, noxious, poisoned, toxic, venomous, virulent.

poke v butt, dig, elbow, jab, jog, nudge, prod, stab, thrust. **poke about** ▷ SEARCH. **poke fun at** ▷ RIDICULE. **poke out** ▷ PROTRUDE.

poky adj confined, cramped, restrictive, small, uncomfortable. Opp SPACIOUS.

polar adj arctic, freezing, glacial, icy, Siberian. ▷ COLD.

polarize v divide, move to opposite positions, split.

pole n 1 bar, column, flagpole, mast, post, rod, shaft, spar, staff, stake, standard, stick, stilt, upright. 2 opposite poles. end,

extreme, limit. **poles apart** ▷ DIFFERENT.

police n sl the Bill, sl the fuzz, constabulary, inf the law, police force. • v control, guard, keep in order, patrol, protect, supervise, watch over.

policeman, policewoman ns inf bobby, constable, sl cop, sl copper, detective, inspector, officer, (W)PC, (woman) police constable.

policy n 1 approach, code of conduct, custom, guidelines, inf line, method, practice, procedure, protocol, rules, stance, strategy, tactics. 2 manifesto, plan of action, platform, programme, proposals.

polish n 1 brightness, brilliance, finish, glaze, gleam, gloss, lustre, sheen, shine, sparkle. 2 beeswax, varnish, wax. 3 His manners show polish. inf class, elegance, finesse, grace, refinement, sophistication, style, urbanity. • v brighten, brush up, buff up, burnish, gloss, rub up, shine, smooth, wax. **polish off** ▷ FINISH. **polish up** ▷ IMPROVE.

polished adj 1 bright, burnished, gleaming, glossy, lustrous, shining, shiny. 2 polished manners. civilized, inf classy, cultured, elegant, faultless, fine, flawless, genteel, gracious, impeccable, perfect, polite, inf posh, refined, sophisticated, suave, urbane. Opp ROUGH.

polite adj agreeable, attentive, chivalrous, civil, considerate, correct, courteous, deferential, diplomatic, formal, gallant, genteel, gentlemanly, gracious, lady-like, obliging, polished, proper, respectful, tactful, thoughtful, well-bred, well-mannered, well-spoken. Opp RUDE.

political adj 1 administrative, diplomatic, governmental, legislative, parliamentary, state. 2 factional, partisan, party-political.

politics n diplomacy, government, political affairs, public affairs, statesmanship.

poll n 1 go to the polls. ballot, election, vote. 2 opinion poll. plebiscite, referendum, survey. ● v ballot, canvass, question, sample, survey.

pollute v adulterate, blight, contaminate, corrupt, defile, dirty, foul, infect, poison, taint.

pomp n ceremony, display, formality, grandeur, magnificence, ostentation, pageantry, ritual, show, solemnity, spectacle, splendour.

pompous adj affected, arrogant, bombastic, grandiose, haughty, imperious, long-winded, ostentatious, pedantic, pretentious, self-important, sententious, showy, snobbish, inf snooty, inf stuck-up, inf stuffy, supercilious, turgid, vain. ▷ PROUD. Opp MODEST.

ponderous adj 1 awkward, clumsy, cumbersome, heavy, hefty, huge, massive, unwieldy, weighty. Opp LIGHT. 2 ponderous style. dull, heavy-handed, humourless, laboured, lifeless, long-winded, pedestrian, plodding, slow, stilted, stodgy, tedious, tiresome, verbose. Opp LIVELY.

pool n lagoon, lake, mere, pond, puddle, swimming pool. ● v ▷ COMBINE.

poor adj 1 badly off, bankrupt, inf broke, deprived, destitute,

disadvantaged, inf down-and-out, inf hard up, impecunious, impoverished, in debt, indigent, insolvent, needy, inf on your uppers, penniless, penurious, poverty-stricken, sl skint, under-privileged. 2 poor soil. barren, exhausted, infertile, unfruitful, unproductive. 3 poor salary. inadequate, insufficient, low, meagre, mean, small. 4 poor in health. inf below par, poorly. ▷ ILL. 5 poor quality. bad, cheap, defective, disappointing, faulty, imperfect, inferior, low-grade, mediocre, second-rate, shoddy, substandard, unacceptable, unsatisfactory, useless, worthless. 6 poor child! hapless, luckless, miserable, pathetic, pitiable, unfortunate, unlucky, wretched. Opp GOOD, LARGE, LUCKY, RICH. ● pl n beggars, the destitute, down-and-outs, the homeless, tramps, the under-privileged, vagrants.

populace n masses, people, public, derog rabble, derog riff-raff.

popular adj 1 accepted, inf all the rage, approved, celebrated, famous, fashionable, favoured, favourite, inf in, in demand, liked, loved, renowned, sought-after, inf trendy, well-known, well-liked. Opp UNPOPULAR. 2 popular opinion. common, conventional, current, general, predominant, prevailing, representative, standard, universal.

popularize v 1 make popular, promote, spread. 2 popularize classics. make easy, simplify.

populate v colonize, dwell in, inhabit, live in, occupy, people, reside in, settle.

population n citizens, community, denizens, inhabitants, natives, occupants, people, populace, public, residents.

populous adj crowded, full, heavily populated, jammed, packed, swarming, teeming.

porch n doorway, entrance, lobby, portico.

pore v pore over examine, peruse, read, scrutinize, study.

pornographic adj arousing, blue, erotic, explicit, exploitative, titillating. ▷ OBSCENE.

porous adj absorbent, penetrable, permeable, pervious, spongy. Opp IMPERVIOUS.

port n anchorage, dock, harbour, haven, marina, mooring.

portable adj compact, convenient, easy to carry, handy, light, lightweight, manageable, mobile, pocket, pocket-sized, small, transportable.
Opp UNWIELDY.

porter n 1 caretaker, concierge, doorman, gatekeeper, janitor, security guard. 2 baggage-handler, bearer, carrier.

portion n allocation, allowance, bit, division, fraction, fragment, helping, measure, part, percentage, piece, quantity, quota, ration, section, segment, serving, share, slice, wedge. **portion out** ▷ SHARE.

portrait n depiction, image, likeness, picture, portrayal, profile, representation, self-portrait.

portray v delineate, depict, describe, evoke, illustrate, paint, picture, represent, show.

pose n 1 attitude, position, posture, stance. 2 act, affectation, façade, masquerade, pretence.

● v 1 model, sit, strike a pose. 2 posture, inf put on airs, show off. 3 pose a question. advance, ask, posit, postulate, put forward, submit, suggest. **pose as** ▷ IMPERSONATE.

poser n 1 dilemma, enigma, problem, puzzle, question, riddle. 2 ▷ POSEUR.

poseur n exhibitionist, fraud, impostor, masquerader, inf phoney, inf poser, inf show-off.

posh adj inf classy, elegant, formal, grand, luxurious, showy, smart, stylish, sumptuous, inf swanky, inf swish.

position n 1 locality, location, place, point, site, situation, spot, whereabouts. 2 awkward position. circumstances, condition, predicament, state. 3 position of the body. posture, stance. 4 intellectual position. attitude, contention, hypothesis, opinion, outlook, perspective, proposition, standpoint, view, viewpoint. 5 position in a firm. appointment, employment, function, grade, job, level, niche, occupation, place, post, rank, role, standing, station, status.

● v arrange, deploy, fix, locate, place, put, settle, site, situate, stand, station.

positive adj 1 affirmative, categorical, certain, clear, conclusive, confident, convinced, decided, definite, emphatic, explicit, firm, incontestable, incontrovertible, irrefutable, sure. 2 positive advice. beneficial, constructive, helpful, practical, useful, worthwhile.
Opp NEGATIVE.

possess v 1 enjoy, have, hold, own. 2 possess territory. acquire, control, dominate, invade, occupy, seize, seize, take over. **3** *possess a person.* bewitch, captivate, cast a spell over, charm, enthral, haunt, obsess.

possessions *pl n* assets, belongings, chattels, effects, estate, fortune, goods, property, riches, things, wealth, worldly goods.

possessive *adj* clinging, domineering, jealous, proprietorial, protective, selfish.

possibility *n* chance, danger, feasibility, likelihood, odds, opportunity, potential, practicality, probability, risk.

possible *adj* achievable, attainable, conceivable, credible, feasible, imaginable, likely, obtainable, *inf* on, plausible, potential, practicable, practical, probable, prospective, thinkable, viable, workable. *Opp* IMPOSSIBLE.

possibly *adv* God willing, *inf* hopefully, if possible, maybe, perhaps.

post *n* **1** baluster, column, leg, paling, picket, pile, pillar, pole, prop, pylon, shaft, stake, stanchard, starting post, strut, support, upright, winning post. **2** *He returned to his usual post.* location, position, station. **3** appointment, assignment, employment, job, occupation, office, place, position, situation, work. **4** airmail, cards, junk mail, letters, mail, parcels, postcards. • *v* **1** advertise, announce, display, pin up, proclaim, put up, stick up. **2** dispatch, mail, send. **3** *A guard was posted at the gate.* assign, place, postion, set, situate, station.

poster *n* advertisement, announcement, bill, display, flyer, notice, placard, sign.

posterity *n* descendants, future generations, heirs, issue, offspring, progeny, successors.

postpone *v* adjourn, defer, delay, hold over, put back, put off, *inf* put on ice, *inf* shelve, suspend.

postscript *n* addendum, addition, afterthought, codicil (*to will*), epilogue, *inf* PS.

postulate *v* assume, posit. ▷ SUPPOSE.

posture *n* **1** bearing, carriage, deportment, pose, position, stance. **2** ▷ ATTITUDE.

posy *n* bouquet, bunch of flowers, buttonhole, corsage, nosegay, spray.

pot *n* basin, bowl, casserole, container, dish, jar, pan, saucepan, vessel.

potent *adj* **1** effective, forceful, formidable, influential, intoxicating (*drink*), mighty, overpowering, overwhelming, powerful, puissant, strong, vigorous. ▷ STRONG. **2** *potent argument.* ▷ PERSUASIVE. *Opp* WEAK.

potential *adj* aspiring, budding, embryonic, future, imminent, latent, likely, possible, probable, prospective, *inf* would-be. • *n* aptitude, capability, capacity, possibility, power, resources.

potion *n* brew, concoction, dose, draught, drink, drug, elixir, liquid, medicine, mixture, tonic.

potter *v* dabble, fiddle about, *inf* mess about, tinker.

pottery *n* ceramics, china, crockery, earthenware, porcelain, stoneware.

pouch *n* bag, pocket, purse, sack, wallet.

pounce v ambush, attack, jump on, leap on, spring at, swoop down on, take by surprise.

pound n compound, corral, enclosure, pen. ● v batter, beat, crush, grind, hammer, knead, mash, pulp, pulverize, smash. ▷ HIT.

pour v 1 cascade, course, flood, flow, gush, run, spill, spout, spurt, stream. 2 *pour wine.* decant, serve, tip.

poverty n 1 beggary, bankruptcy, destitution, hardship, indigence, insolvency, necessity, need, penury, privation, want. 2 *poverty of talent.* absence, dearth, insufficiency, lack, paucity, scarcity, shortage. *Opp* WEALTH.

powder n dust, particles, talc. ● v 1 crush, granulate, grind, pound, pulverize, reduce to powder. 2 dredge, dust, sprinkle.

powdered adj 1 ▷ POWDERY. 2 dehydrated, dried.

powdery adj chalky, crumbly, disintegrating, dry, dusty, fine, friable, granular, granulated, ground, loose, powdered, pulverized, sandy.

power n 1 ability, capability, capacity, competence, faculty, force, might, muscle, potential, vigour. 2 *power to arrest.* authority, privilege, right. 3 *power of a tyrant.* inf clout, command, control, dominance, dominion, influence, omnipotence, potency, rule, sovereignty, supremacy, sway. ▷ STRENGTH. *Opp* WEAKNESS.

powerful adj authoritative, cogent, commanding, compelling, convincing, dominant, dynamic, effective, energetic, forceful, high-powered, influen-tial, invincible, irresistible, mighty, omnipotent, over-powering, overwhelming, persuasive, potent, vigorous, weighty. ▷ STRONG. *Opp* POWERLESS.

powerless adj defenceless, helpless, impotent, incapable, incapacitated, ineffective, paralysed, unable, unfit. ▷ WEAK. *Opp* POWERFUL.

practicable adj achievable, attainable, feasible, possible, practical, realistic, sensible, viable, workable. *Opp* IMPRACTICABLE.

practical adj 1 applied, empirical, experimental. 2 businesslike, capable, competent, down-to-earth, efficient, expert, hard-headed, matter-of-fact, inf no-nonsense, pragmatic, realistic, sensible. 3 convenient, functional, handy, useful. 4 ▷ PRACTICABLE. *Opp* IMPRACTICAL, THEORETICAL. **practical joke** ▷ TRICK.

practically adv almost, close to, just about, nearly, to all intents and purposes, virtually.

practice n 1 action, actuality, application, effect, operation, reality, use. 2 inf dummy-run, exercise, preparation, rehearsal, inf run-through, training, inf try-out. 3 *common practice.* convention, custom, habit, routine, tradition, way, wont. 4 *doctor's practice.* business, office, work.

practise v 1 drill, exercise, prepare, rehearse, train, inf work out. 2 *practise what you preach.* carry out, do, follow, make a practice of, perform, put into practice.

praise n **1** acclaim, accolade, admiration, applause, approbation, approval, commendation, compliments, congratulations, encomium, eulogy, homage, honour, ovation, panegyric, plaudits, tribute. **2** *praise to God*. adoration, devotion, glorification, worship. ● v **1** acclaim, admire, applaud, cheer, commend, compliment, congratulate, eulogize, extol, give a good review of, pay tribute to, *inf* rave about, recommend, sing the praises of. *Opp* CRITICIZE. **2** *praise God*. exalt, glorify, honour, worship. *Opp* CURSE.

praiseworthy adj admirable, commendable, creditable, deserving, laudable, meritorious, worthy. ▷ GOOD. *Opp* BAD.

prance v bound, caper, cavort, dance, frisk, frolic, gambol, hop, jig about, jump, leap, play, romp, skip, spring.

prattle v babble, chatter, gabble, *inf* rattle on, *inf* witter on.

pray v beseech, say prayers, supplicate. ▷ ASK.

prayer n entreaty, invocation, litany, meditation, petition, supplication.

preach v **1** deliver a sermon, evangelize. **2** give moral advice, *inf* lay down the law, lecture, moralize, pontificate, sermonize.

preacher n divine, ecclesiastic, evangelist, minister, missionary, moralist, pastor. ▷ CLERGYMAN.

pre-arranged adj arranged beforehand, planned, predetermined, prepared. *Opp* SPONTANEOUS.

precarious adj dangerous, *inf* dicey, *inf* dodgy, hazardous, insecure, perilous, risky, treacherous, uncertain, unreliable,

unsafe, unstable, unsteady, vulnerable. *Opp* SAFE.

precaution n preventive measure, provision, safeguard, safety measure.

precede v come before, go in front, herald, introduce, lead, lead into, pave the way for, preface, start. *Opp* FOLLOW.

precious adj **1** expensive, irreplaceable, priceless, valuable. *Opp* WORTHLESS. **2** adored, beloved, darling, dear, loved, prized, treasured, valued.

precipice n bluff, cliff, crag, drop, height, escarpment.

precipitate adj hasty, headlong, meteoric, premature. ▷ QUICK. ● v accelerate, bring on, cause, encourage, hasten, hurry, induce, instigate, occasion, provoke, spark off, trigger off.

precipitation n condensation, moisture, rain.

precipitous adj abrupt, perpendicular, sharp, sheer, steep.

precise adj **1** accurate, clear-cut, correct, defined, definite, distinct, exact, explicit, fixed, measured, right, specific, unambiguous, well-defined. *Opp* IMPRECISE. **2** *precise work*. careful, fastidious, faultless, flawless, meticulous, perfect, punctilious, rigorous, scrupulous. *Opp* CARELESS.

preclude v avert, debar, exclude, forestall, make impossible, obviate, pre-empt, prevent, prohibit, rule out.

precocious adj advanced, forward, gifted, mature, quick. ▷ CLEVER. *Opp* BACKWARD.

preconception n assumption, expectation, preconceived idea, predisposition.

predatory adj avaricious, greedy, hunting, marauding, plundering, preying, rapacious, ravenous, voracious.

predecessor n ancestor, antecedent, forebear, forefather, forerunner, precursor.

predetermined adj 1 ▷ FATED. 2 agreed, pre-arranged, preplanned, recognized, inf set up.

predicament n crisis, difficulty, dilemma, emergency, inf fix, inf jam, inf mess, inf pickle, plight, problem, quandary, situation.

predict v augur, forebode, forecast, foreshadow, foretell, forewarn, intimate, presage, prophesy.

predictable adj anticipated, expected, foreseeable, foreseen, likely, inf on the cards, probable, unsurprising.
Opp UNPREDICTABLE.

predominant adj chief, dominating, leading, main, prevalent, primary, ruling.

predominate v be in the majority, dominate, hold sway, lead, outnumber, outweigh, prevail.

pre-eminent adj distinguished, excellent, matchless, unsurpassed. ▷ OUTSTANDING.

pre-empt v anticipate, forestall.

preface n foreword, introduction, inf lead-in, overture, preamble, prelude, prologue.
● v begin, introduce, lead into, open, precede, start.

prefer v inf back, be partial to, choose, fancy, favour, inf go for, incline towards, like, like better, opt for, pick out, inf plump for, recommend, select, single out, vote for, want.

preferable adj better, desirable, favoured, likely, preferred, recommended, right.
Opp OBJECTIONABLE.

preference n 1 choice, fancy, favourite, liking, option, pick, selection, wish. 2 favouritism, inclination, partiality, predilection, prejudice, proclivity.

preferential adj advantageous, better, biased, favourable, privileged, special, superior.

pregnant adj 1 carrying a child, expectant, inf expecting, inf in the club, in the family way, old use with child. 2 pregnant remark. ▷ MEANINGFUL.

prejudice n bias, bigotry, chauvinism, discrimination, favouritism, intolerance, leaning, partiality, partisanship, predisposition, racism, sexism, unfairness, xenophobia. Opp TOLERANCE.
● v 1 bias, colour, incline, influence, make prejudiced, predispose, sway. 2 prejudice your chances. damage, harm, injure, ruin, spoil, undermine.

prejudiced adj biased, bigoted, chauvinist, discriminatory, illiberal, intolerant, narrow-minded, one-sided, parochial, partial, partisan, racist, sexist, unfair, xenophobic. Opp IMPARTIAL. **prejudiced person** bigot, chauvinist, fanatic, racist, sexist, zealot.

prejudicial adj damaging, detrimental, harmful, injurious, unfavourable.

preliminary adj advance, early, experimental, exploratory, first, inaugural, initial, introductory, opening, preparatory, tentative, trial. ● n ▷ PRELUDE.

prelude n beginning, inf curtain-raiser, introduction, opener, opening, overture, preamble,

precursor, preface, pre-liminary, preparation, prologue, start, starter. *Opp* CONCLUSION.

premature *adj* before time, early, hasty, precipitate, *inf* previous, too soon, undeveloped, untimely. *Opp* LATE.

premeditated *adj* calculated, conscious, considered, deliberate, intended, intentional, planned, pre-arranged, pre-conceived, wilful. *Opp* SPONTANEOUS.

premiss *n* assertion, assumption, basis, grounds, hypothesis, proposition, supposition.

premonition *n* fear, foreboding, forewarning, *inf* hunch, intuition, misgiving, omen, portent, presentiment, suspicion, warning.

preoccupied *adj* 1 absorbed, engrossed, immersed, involved, intent, wrapped up. 2 absent-minded, abstracted, day-dreaming, distracted, inattentive, lost in thought, musing, pensive, rapt, thoughtful.

preparation *n* arrangements, briefing, getting ready, groundwork, organization, plans, practice, preparing, setting up, spadework, training.

prepare *v* 1 arrange, *inf* fix up, get ready, make arrangements, make ready, organize, pave the way, plan, set up. ▷ MAKE. 2 *prepare for exams*. *inf* cram, practise, revise, study, *inf* swot. 3 *prepare pupils for exams*. coach, educate, equip, groom, instruct, teach, train, tutor. **prepared** ▷ PRE-ARRANGED, READY. **prepare yourself** be prepared, be ready, brace yourself, steel yourself.

preposterous *adj* bizarre, excessive, extreme, monstrous, outrageous, unthinkable. ▷ ABSURD.

prerequisite *adj* compulsory, essential, indispensable, mandatory, necessary, obligatory, prescribed, required, requisite, specified, stipulated. *Opp* OPTIONAL. ● *n* condition, necessity, precondition, proviso, qualification, requirement, stipulation.

prescribe *n* assign, command, dictate, direct, fix, impose, lay down, ordain, order, recommend, require, specify, stipulate.

presence *n* 1 attendance, closeness, companionship, company, proximity, society. 2 air, appearance, aura, bearing, demeanour, mien, personality, poise, self-assurance, self-possession.

present *adj* 1 adjacent, at hand, close, here, in attendance. 2 contemporary, current, existing, extant. ● *n* 1 *inf* here and now, today. 2 bonus, contribution, donation, endowment, gift, grant, gratuity, handout, offering, tip. ● *v* 1 award, bestow, confer, donate, give, hand over, offer. 2 *present evidence*. demonstrate, display, exhibit, furnish, proffer, put forward, reveal, set out, show, submit. 3 *present a guest*. announce, introduce. 4 *present a play*. perform, put on, stage. **present yourself** ▷ ATTEND, REPORT.

presentable *adj* acceptable, clean, decent, good enough, neat, passable, proper, respectable, satisfactory, tidy, tolerable, *inf* up to scratch.

presently adv old use anon, before long, by and by, inf in a jiffy, shortly, soon.

preserve n 1 conserve, jam, jelly, marmalade. 2 wildlife preserve. reservation, reserve, sanctuary. • v conserve, defend, guard, keep, look after, maintain, perpetuate, protect, retain, safeguard, save, secure, stockpile, store, sustain, uphold. Opp DESTROY. 2 preserve food. can, cure, freeze, irradiate, pickle, refrigerate, salt. 3 preserve a corpse. embalm, mummify.

preside v be in charge, chair, officiate, take charge, take the chair. **preside over** ▷ GOVERN.

press n newspapers, magazines, the media. • v 1 apply pressure to, compress, condense, crowd, crush, force, inf jam, push, shove, squash, squeeze. 2 press laundry. iron. 3 press someone to stay. ask, beg, bully, coerce, constrain, entreat, implore, importune, induce, inf lean on, persuade, pressurize, put pressure on, request, urge. **pressing** ▷ URGENT.

pressure n 1 force, heaviness, load, power, strength, weight. 2 pressure of modern life. constraints, demands, difficulties, exigencies, inf hassle, hurry, strain, stress. • v coerce, entreat, implore, persuade. ▷ PRESS.

prestige n cachet, credit, distinction, esteem, fame, glory, good name, honour, importance, influence, inf kudos, renown, reputation, respect, standing, status.

prestigious adj acclaimed, celebrated, distinguished, eminent, esteemed, famed, famous, highly regarded, honourable, honoured, important, influential, preeminent, renowned, reputable, respected. Opp INSIGNIFICANT.

presume v 1 assume, believe, conjecture, gather, guess, imagine, infer, suppose, surmise, suspect, inf think, think. 2 He presumed to correct me. be presumptuous enough, dare, have the effrontery, take the liberty, venture.

presumptuous adj arrogant, bold, cheeky, forward, impertinent, impudent, over-confident, inf pushy. ▷ PROUD.

pretence n act, acting, affectation, artifice, charade, deception, disguise, display, dissembling, dissimulation, fabrication, façade, front, guise, hoax, inf humbug, hypocrisy, invention, make-believe, masquerade, pretext, pose, posturing, ruse, sham, show, simulation, trickery.

pretend v 1 act, affect, bluff, dissemble, fake, feign, imitate, impersonate, inf kid, inf make out, play-act, play a part, pose, put on an act, sham, simulate. 2 imagine, make believe, suppose.

pretender n aspirant, claimant.

pretentious adj affected, conceited, exaggerated, extravagant, grandiose, immodest, inflated, ostentatious, inf over the top, pompous, showy, inf snobbish. Opp UNPRETENTIOUS.

pretext n cover, disguise, excuse, pretence.

pretty adj appealing, attractive, charming, inf cute, dainty, inf easy on the eye, fetching, good-looking, lovely, nice, pleasing. ▷ BEAUTIFUL. Opp UGLY.

• adv [inf] fairly, moderately, quite, rather, somewhat. Opp VERY.

prevail v be prevalent, hold sway, predominate, triumph, inf win the day. ▷ WIN. **prevailing** ▷ PREVALENT.

prevalent adj accepted, common, current, customary, dominant, established, extensive, fashionable, general, governing, ordinary, pervasive, popular, predominant, prevailing, ubiquitous, universal, usual, widespread. Opp UNUSUAL.

prevaricate v inf beat about the bush, be evasive, equivocate, inf hum and haw, hedge, mislead, temporize.

prevent v anticipate, avert, avoid, curb, deter, foil, forestall, frustrate, hamper, inf head off, inf help (can't help it), hinder, impede, inhibit, intercept, inf nip in the bud, obstruct, obviate, preclude, pre-empt, restrain, stave off, stop, take precautions against, thwart. ▷ FORBID. Opp ENCOURAGE.

preventive adj obstructive, precautionary, pre-emptive, preventative.

previous adj 1 above-mentioned, aforementioned, earlier, erstwhile, former, past, preceding, prior. Opp SUBSEQUENT. 2 ▷ PREMATURE.

prey n kill, quarry, victim.
• v **prey on** eat, feed on, hunt, kill, live off. ▷ EXPLOIT.

price n 1 amount, charge, cost, inf damage, expenditure, expense, fare, fee, figure, outlay, payment, rate, sum, terms, toll, value, worth. 2 Give me a price. estimate, offer, quotation, valu-

ation. **pay the price for** ▷ ATONE.

priceless adj 1 costly, dear, expensive, incalculable, invaluable, irreplaceable, precious, rare, valuable. Opp WORTHLESS. 2 ▷ FUNNY.

prick v 1 bore into, jab, perforate, pierce, puncture, stab, sting. 2 ▷ SPUR.

prickle n 1 barb, bristle, needle, spike, spine, thorn. 2 irritation, itch, prickling, tingle, tingling.
• v irritate, itch, make your skin crawl, scratch, sting, tingle.

prickly adj 1 bristly, rough, scratchy, spiky, spiny, stubbly, thorny, unshaven. Opp SMOOTH. 2 ▷ IRRITABLE.

pride n 1 honour, self-esteem. self-respect. ▷ DIGNITY. 2 her pride and joy. jewel, treasure, treasured possession. 3 pride before a fall. arrogance, conceit, egotism, haughtiness, narcissism, overconfidence, presumption, self-admiration, self-importance, self-love, smugness, snobbishness, vanity. Opp HUMILITY.

priest n confessor, minister, preacher. ▷ CLERGYMAN.

priggish adj inf goody-goody, moralistic, prudish, self-righteous, sententious, stiff-necked, inf stuffy. ▷ PRIM.

prim adj demure, fastidious, formal, inhibited, precise, inf prissy, proper, prudish, inf starchy, strait-laced. Opp BROAD-MINDED.

primal adj early, earliest, first, original, primeval, primordial.

primarily adv basically, chiefly, especially, essentially, firstly, fundamentally, generally, mainly, mostly, predominantly, principally.

primary *adj* basic, cardinal, chief, dominant, first, foremost, fundamental, leading, main, major, paramount, predominant, pre-eminent, prime, principal, supreme, top.

prime *adj* 1 best, first-class, first-rate, foremost, select, superior, top, top-quality. ▷ EXCELLENT. 2 ▷ PRIMARY. • *v* get ready, prepare.

primitive *adj* 1 ancient, early, prehistoric, primeval, savage, uncivilized, uncultivated. 2 *primitive technology.* basic, *inf* behind the times, crude, elementary, obsolete, rough, rudimentary, simple, undeveloped. ▷ OLD. 3 *primitive art.* childlike, crude, naive, unsophisticated. *Opp* ADVANCED, SOPHISTICATED.

principal *adj* cardinal, chief, dominant, first, foremost, fundamental, highest, important, key, leading, main, major, outstanding, paramount, pre-eminent, predominant, prevailing, primary, prime, starring, supreme, top. • *n* 1 ▷ CHIEF. 2 *principal in a play.* diva, hero, heroine, lead, leading role, prima ballerina, star.

principle *n* 1 axiom, belief, creed, criterion, doctrine, dogma, ethic, idea, ideal, maxim, notion, precept, proposition, rule, standard, teaching, tenet, truth, value. 2 *person of principle.* conscience, high-mindedness, honesty, honour, ideals, integrity, morality, probity, scruples, standards, uprightness, virtue.

print *n* 1 impression, imprint, indentation, mark, stamp.

2 characters, lettering, letters, printing, text, type, typeface. 3 copy, duplicate, engraving, etching, facsimile, photograph, picture, reproduction, woodcut. • *v* 1 copy, issue, publish, run off, stamp. 2 ▷ WRITE.

prior *adj* ▷ PREVIOUS.

priority *n* first place, greater importance, precedence, preference, right-of-way, seniority.

prise *v* force, lever, wrench.

prison *n* cell, *sl* clink, custody, detention centre, dungeon, gaol, house of correction, jail, *inf* lock-up, *Amer* penitentiary, reformatory, *sl* slammer. ▷ CAPTIVITY.

prisoner *n* captive, convict, detainee, *inf* gaolbird, hostage, inmate, *sl* lifer.

privacy *n* isolation, quietness, retirement, retreat, seclusion, secrecy, solitude.

private *adj* 1 exclusive, individual, particular, personal, reserved. 2 classified, confidential, *inf* hush-hush, *inf* off the record, secret, top secret. 3 *private meeting.* clandestine, covert, intimate, surreptitious. 4 *private hideaway.* concealed, hidden, isolated, little-known, quiet, secluded, solitary, unknown. *Opp* PUBLIC.

privilege *n* advantage, benefit, concession, entitlement, exemption, freedom, immunity, licence, prerogative, right.

privileged *adj* 1 authorized, elite, entitled, favoured, honoured, immune, licensed, protected, sanctioned, special. 2 ▷ WEALTHY.

prize *n* award, jackpot, *inf* purse, reward, trophy, winnings.

● *v* appreciate, cherish, esteem, hold dear, like, rate highly, revere, treasure, value.

probable *adj* believable, convincing, credible, expected, feasible, likely, *inf* odds-on, plausible, possible, predictable.
Opp IMPROBABLE.

probationer *n* learner, novice.
▷ APPRENTICE.

probe *n* examination, exploration, inquiry, investigation, research, scrutiny, study.
● *v* 1 feel around, poke, prod. 2 examine, explore, go into, investigate, look into, scrutinize, study.

problem *n* 1 *inf* brain-teaser, conundrum, enigma, mystery, *inf* poser, puzzle, question, riddle. 2 complication, difficulty, dilemma, dispute, *inf* headache, *inf* hornet's nest, predicament, quandary, set-back, snag, trouble, worry.

problematic *adj* complicated, controversial, debatable, difficult, enigmatic, hard to deal with, *inf* iffy, intractable, problematical, puzzling, questionable, taxing, tricky, worrying.
Opp STRAIGHTFORWARD.

procedure *n* approach, course of action, *inf* drill, formula, method, plan of action, policy, practice, process, routine, scheme, strategy, system, technique, way.

proceed *v* 1 advance, carry on, continue, follow, go ahead, make headway, make progress, move forward, press on, progress. 2 arise, be derived, begin, develop, emerge, grow, originate, spring up, start. ▷ RESULT.

proceedings *pl n* 1 events, *inf* goings-on, happenings.

2 *legal proceedings*. action, lawsuit, procedure, process. 3 *proceedings of a meeting*. business, matters, minutes, records, report, transactions.

proceeds *pl n* earnings, gain, income, profit, receipts, returns, revenue, takings.

process *n* 1 method, operation, procedure, proceeding, system, technique. 2 *process of ageing*. course, development, evolution, progression. ● *v* 1 alter, change, convert, deal with, make usable, modify, prepare, refine, transform, treat. 2 ▷ PARADE.

procession *n* cavalcade, chain, column, cortège, file, line, march, march-past, motorcade, pageant, parade, sequence, string, succession, train.

proclaim *v* 1 announce, assert, declare, give out, make known, profess, pronounce. 2 ▷ DECREE.

procrastinate *v* be indecisive, dally, delay, *inf* dilly-dally, dither, drag your feet, equivocate, evade the issue, hesitate, *inf* hum and haw, pause, *inf* play for time, prevaricate, *inf* shilly-shally, stall, temporize.

procure *v* acquire, buy, come by, find, get, *inf* get hold of, *inf* lay your hands on, obtain, purchase.

prod *v* dig, elbow, goad, jab, nudge, poke, push. ▷ URGE.

prodigal *adj* extravagant, improvident, irresponsible, lavish, profligate, reckless, self-indulgent, wasteful.
Opp THRIFTY.

prodigy *n* genius, marvel, miracle, phenomenon, rarity, sensation, talent, virtuoso, *inf* whizz kid, wonder.

produce n crop, harvest, output, yield. ▷ PRODUCT.
● v 1 assemble, bring out, cause, compose, conjure up, construct, create, cultivate, develop, fabricate, form, generate, give rise to, grow, invent, make, manufacture, originate, provoke, result in, supply, turn out, yield. 2 *produce evidence*. advance, bring out, disclose, display, exhibit, furnish, introduce, offer, present, provide, put forward, reveal, show, supply. 3 *produce children*. bear, breed, give birth to. 4 *produce a play*. mount, present, put on, stage.

product n 1 artefact, by-product, commodity, end-product, goods, merchandise, output, produce. 2 consequence, fruit, issue, outcome, result, upshot.

productive adj 1 beneficial, constructive, creative, effective, efficient, gainful (*employment*), profitable, remunerative, rewarding, useful, valuable, worthwhile. 2 *productive garden*. abundant, fecund, fertile, fruitful, lush, prolific.
Opp UNPRODUCTIVE.

profess v 1 affirm, announce, assert, declare, maintain, state, vow. 2 *profess to be an expert*. allege, claim, make out, pretend, purport.

profession n 1 business, calling, career, craft, employment, job, line of work, métier, occupation, trade, vocation, work. 2 *profession of love*. affirmation, assertion, avowal, confession, declaration, statement, testimony.

professional adj 1 educated, experienced, expert, knowledgeable, licensed, official, proficient, qualified, skilled, trained.
Opp AMATEUR. 2 *professional work*. businesslike, competent, conscientious, efficient, skilful, thorough, well-done.
Opp UNPROFESSIONAL.
● n ▷ EXPERT.

proficient adj able, accomplished, adept, capable, competent, efficient, expert, gifted, professional, skilled, talented.
Opp INCOMPETENT.

profile n 1 outline, shape, side view, silhouette. 2 *personal profile*. account, biography, *inf* CV, sketch, study.

profit n advantage, benefit, excess, gain, interest, proceeds, return, revenue, surplus, yield.
● v 1 avail, benefit, pay, serve.
▷ HELP. 2 *profit from a sale*. capitalize (on), *inf* cash in on, gain, make a profit, make money.
profit by, profit from
▷ EXPLOIT.

profitable adj advantageous, beneficial, commercial, fruitful, gainful, lucrative, money-making, paying, productive, profit-making, remunerative, rewarding, useful, valuable, well-paid, worthwhile.
Opp UNPROFITABLE.

profiteer n black-marketeer, extortioner, racketeer.
● v exploit, extort, overcharge.

profligate adj 1 debauched, degenerate, depraved, dissolute, immoral, licentious, perverted, promiscuous, sinful, unprincipled, wanton. ▷ WICKED.
2 ▷ PRODIGAL.

profound adj 1 deep, extreme, heartfelt, intense, strong.
2 *profound ideas*. abstruse, erudite, esoteric, informed, intellectual, knowledgeable, learned,

penetrating, philosophical, recondite, sagacious, scholarly, serious, thoughtful, wise. **3** *profound silence.* absolute, complete, perfect, thorough, total, unqualified. *Opp* SUPERFICIAL.

profuse *adj* abundant, ample, bountiful, copious, extravagant, exuberant, generous, lavish, luxuriant, plentiful, productive, prolific. *Opp* MEAN, SPARSE.

programme *n* **1** agenda, curriculum, *inf* line-up, listing, plan, prospectus, schedule, scheme, syllabus, timetable. **2** *TV programme.* broadcast, performance, presentation, production, show, transmission.

progress *n* **1** advance, breakthrough, development, evolution, gain, growth, headway, improvement, march (*of time*), progression, *inf* step forward. **2** journey, route, travels, way. **3** *progress in a career.* advancement, elevation, promotion, rise, *inf* step up. ● *v* advance, *inf* come on, develop, forge ahead, make headway, make progress, move forward, press on, proceed, prosper. ▷ IMPROVE. *Opp* REGRESS, STAGNATE.

progression *n* **1** ▷ PROGRESS. **2** chain, course, flow, order, row, sequence, series, string, succession.

progressive *adj* **1** advancing, continuing, continuous, developing, escalating, gradual, growing, increasing, ongoing, steady. **2** *progressive ideas.* advanced, avant-garde, dynamic, enterprising, forward-looking, *inf* go-ahead, radical, reformist, revolutionary. *Opp* CONSERVATIVE.

prohibit *v* ban, bar, block, censor, debar, disallow, exclude, forbid, impede, inhibit, make illegal, outlaw, place an embargo on, preclude, prevent, proscribe, restrict, rule out, shut out, stop, veto. *Opp* ALLOW.

prohibitive *adj* excessive, exorbitant, impossible, *inf* out of reach, out of the question, unreasonable.

project *n* activity, assignment, design, enterprise, idea, job, piece of research, plan, programme, proposal, scheme, task, undertaking, venture. ● *v* **1** concoct, contrive, design, devise, scheme, think up. **2** bulge, extend, jut out, overhang, protrude, stand out, stick out. **3** *project into space.* fling, launch, shoot. ▷ HURL. **4** *project light.* cast, shine, throw out. **5** *project future profits.* estimate, forecast, predict.

proliferate *v* burgeon, flourish, grow, increase, multiply, mushroom, reproduce, thrive.

prolific *adj* **1** abundant, bountiful, copious, fruitful, numerous, plenteous, profuse, rich. **2** *prolific writer.* fertile, productive. *Opp* UNPRODUCTIVE.

prolong *v* drag out, draw out, extend, lengthen, *inf* pad out, protract, *inf* spin out, stretch out. *Opp* SHORTEN.

prominent *adj* **1** conspicuous, discernible, distinguishable, evident, eye-catching, large, noticeable, obtrusive, obvious, pronounced, recognizable, salient, significant, striking. *Opp* INCONSPICUOUS. **2** jutting out, projecting, protruding, protuberant, sticking out. **3** celebrated, distinguished, eminent, familiar, foremost, important, leading, major, outstanding, public, renowned. ▷ FAMOUS. *Opp* UNKNOWN.

promiscuous *adj* **1** casual, haphazard, indiscriminate, irresponsible, random. **2** ▷ IMMORAL.

promise *n* **1** assurance, commitment, contract, covenant, guarantee, oath, pledge, undertaking, vow, word, word of honour. **2** *actor with promise.* capability, potential, promising qualities, talent. ● *v* **1** agree, assure, commit yourself, consent, contract, engage, give your word, guarantee, pledge, swear, take an oath, undertake, vow. **2** *The clouds promise rain.* augur, forebode, foretell, hint at, indicate, presage, prophesy, show signs of, suggest.

promising *adj* auspicious, encouraging, favourable, hopeful, likely, optimistic, propitious, talented, *inf* up-and-coming.

promontory *n* cape, headland, point, projection, spit, spur.

promote *v* **1** advance, elevate, give promotion, move up, prefer, raise, upgrade. **2** *promote a product.* advertise, back, boost, champion, encourage, endorse, further, market, *inf* plug, popularize, publicize, *inf* push, recommend, sell, speak for, sponsor, support. ▷ HELP.

promoter *n* backer, champion, patron, sponsor, supporter.

promotion *n* **1** advancement, elevation, preferment, rise, upgrading. **2** *promotion of a product.* advertising, backing, marketing, publicity, recommendation, selling, sponsorship.

prompt *adj* eager, immediate, instantaneous, on time, punctual, timely, unhesitating, willing. ▷ QUICK. *Opp* UNPUNCTUAL. ● *n* cue, line, reminder. ● *v* egg on, encourage, help, incite, influence, inspire, jog the memory, motivate, nudge, persuade, prod, provoke, remind, spur, stimulate, urge.

prone *adj* **1** face down, horizontal, on your front, prostrate, stretched out. *Opp* SUPINE. **2** *prone to colds.* apt, disposed, given, inclined, liable, likely, predisposed, susceptible, vulnerable. *Opp* IMMUNE.

prong *n* point, spike, spur, tine.

pronounce *v* **1** articulate, enunciate, express, put into words, say, sound, speak, utter, voice. **2** *pronounce judgement.* announce, assert, declare, decree, proclaim, state.

pronounced *adj* clear, conspicuous, decided, definite, distinct, evident, marked, noticeable, obvious, prominent, recognizable, striking, unmistakable.

pronunciation *n* accent, articulation, delivery, diction, elocution, enunciation, inflection, intonation, modulation, speech.

proof *n* **1** confirmation, corroboration, demonstration, evidence, facts, grounds, substantiation, testimony, validation, verification. **2** *the proof of the pudding.* criterion, measure, test, trial.

prop *n* buttress, crutch, post, stay, strut, support, truss, upright. ● *v* **1** bolster, buttress, hold up, reinforce, shore up, support, sustain. **2** lean, rest, stand.

propaganda *n* advertising, *sl* hype, promotion, publicity.

propagate *v* 1 breed, generate, increase, multiply, produce, proliferate, reproduce. 2 *propagate ideas*. circulate, disseminate, publish, spread, transmit. 3 *propagate plants*. grow from seed, sow, take cuttings.

propel *v* drive, force, impel, launch, push, send, shoot, spur, thrust, urge.

proper *adj* 1 becoming, conventional, decent, decorous, delicate, dignified, formal, genteel, gentlemanly, in good taste, ladylike, modest, polite, *derog* prim, respectable, sedate, seemly, tactful, tasteful. 2 acceptable, accepted, advisable, apposite, appropriate, apt, deserved, fair, fitting, just, lawful, legal, normal, orthodox, sensible, suitable, usual, valid. 3 *the proper time*. accurate, correct, exact, precise, right. 4 *the proper place*. individual, own, particular, reserved, separate, special, unique. *Opp* IMPROPER.

property *n* 1 assets, belongings, capital, chattels, effects, fortune, goods, holdings, patrimony, possessions, resources, riches, wealth. 2 buildings, estate, land, premises. 3 attribute, characteristic, feature, hallmark, idiosyncrasy, peculiarity, quality, quirk, trait.

prophecy *n* augury, divination, forecast, foretelling, fortune-telling, prediction, prognosis.

prophesy *v* augur, bode, divine, forecast, foresee, foreshadow, foretell, portend, predict, presage, promise.

prophet *n* clairvoyant, forecaster, fortune-teller, oracle, seer, sibyl, soothsayer.

prophetic *adj* inspired, oracular, predictive, prescient, visionary.

propitious *adj* advantageous, auspicious, favourable, fortunate, happy, lucky, opportune, promising, timely, well-timed.

proportion *n* 1 balance, correlation, correspondence, ratio, symmetry. 2 allocation, fraction, part, percentage, piece, quota, ration, section, share.
▷ NUMBER, QUANTITY. **proportions** dimensions, extent, magnitude, measurements, size, volume.

proportional *adj* balanced, commensurate, comparable, corresponding, in proportion, proportionate, relative, symmetrical. *Opp* DISPROPORTIONATE.

proposal *n* bid, motion, offer, plan, project, proposition, recommendation, scheme, suggestion, tender.

propose *v* 1 advance, *inf* come up with, present, propound, put forward, recommend, submit, suggest. 2 aim, have in mind, intend, mean, offer, plan. 3 *propose a candidate*. nominate, put up, sponsor.

propriety *n* aptness, correctness, courtesy, decency, decorum, delicacy, dignity, etiquette, fairness, fitness, formality, gentility, good manners, modesty, politeness, *derog* prudishness, refinement, respectability, seemliness, sensitivity, suitability, tact, tastefulness. *Opp* IMPROPRIETY.

prosaic *adj* 1 clear, direct, down to earth, factual, matter-of-fact, plain, simple, straightforward, to the point, unadorned, unvarnished. 2 [*derog*] characterless,

cliched, commonplace, dry, dull, flat, hackneyed, lifeless, mundane, pedestrian, routine, stereotyped, trite, unimaginative, uninspired, uninspiring.
▷ ORDINARY. Opp POETIC.

prosecute v 1 accuse, bring an action against, bring to trial, charge, indict, prefer charges against, put on trial, sue, take to court. 2 ▷ PURSUE.

prospect n 1 aspect, landscape, outlook, panorama, perspective, scene, sight, spectacle, view, vista. 2 *prospect of fine weather*. chance, expectation, hope, likelihood, possibility, promise. ● v explore, search, survey.

prospective adj anticipated, awaited, expected, forthcoming, future, imminent, impending, intended, likely, pending, possible, potential, probable.

prospectus n brochure, catalogue, leaflet, manifesto, pamphlet, programme, syllabus.

prosper v become prosperous, be successful, *inf* boom, burgeon, do well, flourish, *inf* get ahead, *inf* get on, *inf* go from strength to strength, grow, *inf* make good, profit, progress, succeed, thrive.
Opp FAIL.

prosperity n affluence, *inf* boom, good fortune, growth, plenty, profitability, riches, success, wealth.

prosperous adj affluent, *inf* blooming, *inf* booming, buoyant; expanding, flourishing, healthy, moneyed, productive, profitable, rich, successful, thriving, vigorous, wealthy, *inf* well-heeled, well-off, well-to-do. Opp UNSUCCESSFUL.

prostitute n call girl, *old use* courtesan, *old use* harlot, *inf* hooker, streetwalker, *inf* tart, whore. ● v cheapen, debase, degrade, demean, devalue, misuse.

prostrate adj ▷ OVERCOME, PRONE. ● v *prostrate yourself* abase yourself, bow, kowtow, lie flat. ▷ GROVEL.

protagonist n chief actor, contender, contestant, hero, heroine, lead, leading figure, principal.

protect v care for, cherish, conserve, defend, guard, insulate, keep, keep safe, look after, mind, preserve, safeguard, screen, secure, shield, stand up for, support, take care of, tend, watch over. Opp ENDANGER, NEGLECT.

protection n 1 care, conservation, custody, defence, guardianship, safekeeping, safety, security. 2 barrier, buffer, bulwark, cloak, cover, guard, insulation, screen, shelter, shield.

protective adj 1 fireproof, insulating, protecting, sheltering, shielding, waterproof. 2 *protective parents*. careful, defensive, heedful, possessive, solicitous, vigilant, watchful.

protector n benefactor, bodyguard, champion, defender, guard, guardian, *sl* minder, patron.

protest n 1 complaint, cry of disapproval, exception, grievance, *inf* gripe, *inf* grouse, grumble, objection, opposition, outcry, protestation, remonstrance. 2 *inf* demo, demonstration, march, rally. ● v 1 appeal, argue, challenge a decision, complain, cry out, expostulate, express disapproval, *inf* gripe, *inf* grouse, grumble, *inf* moan, object, remonstrate, take exception. **2** demonstrate, march. **3** *protest your innocence.* affirm, assert, declare, insist on, profess, swear.

protracted *adj* endless, extended, interminable, long-winded, never-ending, prolonged. ▷ LONG. *Opp* SHORT.

protrude *v* bulge, extend, overhang, poke out, project, stand out, stick out, stick up.

protruding *adj* bulbous, bulging, jutting, overhanging, projecting, prominent, protuberant, swollen.

proud *adj* **1** content, glad, gratified, happy, honoured, pleased, satisfied. **2** *a proud history.* august, dignified, distinguished, glorious, great, honourable, illustrious, noble, reputable, respected, splendid, worthy. **3** [*derog*] arrogant, *inf* big-headed, boastful, bumptious, *inf* cocksure, *inf* cocky, conceited, disdainful, egotistical, haughty, *inf* high and mighty, narcissistic, self-centred, self-important, self-satisfied, smug, snobbish, *inf* snooty, *inf* stuck-up, supercilious, *inf* swollen-headed, *inf* toffee-nosed, vain. *Opp* MODEST.

provable *adj* demonstrable, verifiable.

prove *v* ascertain, attest, authenticate, *inf* bear out, certify, check, confirm, corroborate, demonstrate, establish, explain, justify, show to be true, substantiate, verify. *Opp* DISPROVE.

proven *adj* accepted, proved, reliable, tried and tested, trustworthy, undoubted, unquestion-able, valid, verified. *Opp* DOUBTFUL, THEORETICAL.

proverb *n* adage, maxim, *old use* saw. ▷ SAYING.

proverbial *adj* axiomatic, conventional, famous, legendary, time-honoured, traditional, well-known.

provide *v* afford, allot, allow, arrange for, cater, contribute, donate, endow, equip, *inf* fix up with, *inf* fork out, furnish, give, grant, lay on, lend, offer, produce, spare, stock, supply, yield.

providence *n* ▷ FATE.

provident *adj* careful, economical, far-sighted, frugal, judicious, prudent, thrifty.

providential *adj* fortunate, happy, lucky, opportune, timely.

provincial *adj* **1** local, regional. *Opp* NATIONAL. **2** [*derog*] insular, narrow-minded, parochial, small-minded, uncultured, unsophisticated. *Opp* COSMOPOLITAN.

provisional *adj* conditional, interim, stopgap, temporary, tentative, transitional. *Opp* DEFINITIVE, PERMANENT.

provisions *pl n* food, foodstuffs, groceries, rations, requirements, stocks, stores, subsistence, supplies.

proviso *n* condition, exception, limitation, qualification, requirement, restriction, stipulation.

provocation *n* [*derog*] aggravation, cause, challenge, grievance, grounds, incitement, motivation, motive, reason, stimulus, taunts, teasing.

provocative *adj* **1** alluring, arousing, erotic, exciting, *inf* raunchy, seductive, sexy, tantalizing, tempting.

2 *inf* aggravating, annoying, infuriating, irksome, irritating, maddening, vexing.

provoke *v* 1 arouse, awaken, bring about, call forth, cause, elicit, encourage, evoke, foment, generate, give rise to, induce, inspire, instigate, kindle, motivate, prompt, spark off, start, stimulate, stir up.
2 *inf* aggravate, anger, annoy, enrage, exasperate, *inf* get on your nerves, goad, incense, incite, inflame, infuriate, irk, irritate, madden, offend, outrage, pique, rouse, tease, torment, upset, vex, *inf* wind up, worry. *Opp* PACIFY.

prowess *n* 1 ability, adroitness, aptitude, cleverness, competence, dexterity, excellence, expertise, flair, genius, proficiency, skill, talent: 2 *prowess in battle.* boldness, bravery, courage, daring, gallantry, heroism, mettle, spirit, valour.

prowl *v* creep, lurk, roam, rove, skulk, slink, sneak.

proximity *n* 1 closeness, propinquity. 2 locality, neighbourhood, vicinity.

prudent *adj* advisable, careful, cautious, circumspect, discreet, economical, far-sighted, frugal, judicious, politic, proper, provident, sagacious, sage, sensible, shrewd, thrifty, vigilant, watchful, wise. *Opp* UNWISE.

prudish *adj* easily shocked, intolerant, narrow-minded, old-fashioned, priggish, prim, *inf* prissy, proper, puritanical, rigid, strait-laced, strict. *Opp* BROAD-MINDED.

prune *v* clip, cut back, lop, pare down, trim. ▷ CUT.

pry *v inf* be nosy, delve, *inf* ferret, interfere, intrude, meddle, nose about, peer, poke about, *inf* poke your nose in, search, *inf* snoop. **prying** ▷ INQUISITIVE.

pseudonym *n* alias, assumed name, false name, nickname, pen-name, sobriquet, stage name.

psychic *adj* clairvoyant, extrasensory, mystic, occult, preternatural, spiritual, supernatural, telepathic. ● *n* astrologer, clairvoyant, crystal-gazer, fortuneteller, medium, mind-reader, spiritualist, telepathist.

psychological *adj* emotional, mental, subconscious, subjective, unconscious. *Opp* PHYSIOLOGICAL.

pub *n* bar, *inf* boozer, hostelry, inn, *inf* local, public house, saloon, tavern, wine bar.

puberty *n* adolescence, growing-up, pubescence, *inf* teens.

public *adj* 1 accessible, available, common, familiar, known, open, shared, unrestricted, visible, well-known. 2 *public support.* collective, communal, democratic, general, majority, national, popular, social, universal. 3 *public figure.* ▷ PROMINENT. *Opp* PRIVATE.
● *n* citizens, the community, the country, the nation, people, the populace, society, voters.

publication *n* 1 appearance, issuing, printing, production. ▷ BOOK, MAGAZINE.
2 announcement, broadcasting, disclosure, dissemination, proclamation, reporting.

publicity *n* 1 attention, fame, limelight, notoriety.

2 advertising, *sl* hype, marketing, promotion.

publicize *v* advertise, *sl* hype, *inf* plug, promote. ▷ PUBLISH.

publish *v* **1** bring out, circulate, issue, print, produce, release. **2** *publish secrets*. advertise, announce, broadcast, communicate, declare, disclose, divulge, *inf* leak, make known, make public, proclaim, publicize, *inf* put about, report, reveal, spread.

pucker *v* contract, crease, crinkle, draw together, purse, screw up, tighten, wrinkle.

puerile *adj* babyish, boyish, childish, immature, infantile, juvenile. ▷ SILLY.

puff *n* **1** blast, breath, draught, flurry, gust, whiff, wind. **2** *puff of smoke*. cloud, wisp. ● *v* **1** blow, breathe heavily, gasp, pant, wheeze. **2** *puff at a cigar*. *inf* drag, draw, inhale, pull, smoke. **3** *sails puffed by the wind*. balloon, billow, distend, enlarge, inflate, swell.

pugnacious *adj* aggressive, antagonistic, argumentative, bellicose, belligerent, combative, contentious, hostile, hot-tempered, militant, unfriendly, warlike. ▷ QUARRELSOME. *Opp* PEACEABLE.

pull *v* **1** drag, draw, haul, lug, tow, trail. *Opp* PUSH. **2** jerk, tug, pluck, wrench, *inf* yank. **3** *pull a tooth*. extract, pull out, remove. **pull off** ▷ DETACH. **pull out** ▷ WITHDRAW. **pull round** ▷ RECOVER. **pull someone's leg** ▷ TEASE. **pull through** ▷ RECOVER. **pull together** ▷ COOPERATE. **pull up** ▷ HALT.

pulp *n* mash, pap, paste, purée. ● *v* crush, liquidize, mash, pound, pulverize, purée, squash.

pulsate *v* beat, drum, palpitate, pound, quiver, reverberate, throb, tick, vibrate.

pulse *n* beat, drumming, pounding, pulsation, rhythm, throb, ticking, vibration.

pump *v* drain, draw off, empty, force, raise, siphon. **pump up** blow up, fill, inflate.

punch *v* **1** beat, *sl* biff, box, clout, cuff, pummel, slog, slug, *inf* sock, strike, thump. ▷ HIT. **2** ▷ PIERCE.

punctual *adj* in good time, *inf* on the dot, on time, prompt. *Opp* UNPUNCTUAL.

punctuate *v* **1** accentuate, emphasize, stress. **2** *punctuated by applause*. break, interrupt, intersperse, *inf* pepper.

puncture *n* blow-out, *inf* flat tyre, hole, leak, perforation, pinprick, rupture. ● *v* deflate, go through, let down, penetrate, perforate, pierce, prick, rupture.

pungent *adj* **1** aromatic, hot, peppery, piquant, sharp, spicy, strong, tangy. **2** acid, acrid, astringent, caustic, harsh, sour, stinging. **3** *pungent criticism*. biting, incisive, mordant, sarcastic, scathing, trenchant.

punish *v* castigate, chastise, discipline, exact retribution from, *inf* make an example of, pay back, penalize, *inf* rap over the knuckles, scold, *inf* teach someone a lesson.

punishment *n* **1** chastisement, correction, discipline, *inf* just deserts, penalty, punitive measure, retribution, revenge, sentence. **2** abuse, battering, beating, maltreatment, torture.

punitive adj disciplinary, retaliatory, severe, stiff.

puny adj diminutive, feeble, frail, sickly, undernourished, weak. ▷ SMALL. Opp LARGE, STRONG.

pupil n apprentice, disciple, follower, learner, novice, protégé(e), scholar, schoolboy, schoolgirl, student.

puppet n doll, dummy, finger puppet, glove puppet, marionette.

purchase n **1** acquisition, inf buy (a good buy). **2** grasp, grip, hold, leverage. ● v acquire, buy, get, obtain, pay for, procure, secure.

pure adj **1** genuine, neat, real, solid, sterling, straight, unadulterated, unalloyed, undiluted. **2** pure food. hygienic, uncontaminated, untainted, wholesome. **3** pure water. clean, clear, distilled, drinkable, fresh, sterile, unpolluted. **4** pure in morals. blameless, chaste, decent, good, impeccable, innocent, irreproachable, modest, moral, proper, sinless, virginal, virtuous. **5** pure genius. absolute, complete, downright, out and out, perfect, sheer, total, true, unmitigated, unqualified, utter. **6** pure science. abstract, conceptual, hypothetical, speculative, theoretical. Opp IMPURE, PRACTICAL.

purgative n enema, laxative, purge.

purge v **1** clean out, cleanse, clear, empty, purify, wash out. **2** eject, eliminate, eradicate, expel, get rid of, oust, remove, root out.

purify v clean, cleanse, decontaminate, disinfect, distil, filter, make pure, purge, refine, sterilize.

puritan n fanatic, killjoy, moralist, prig, prude, zealot.

puritanical adj ascetic, austere, moralistic, narrow-minded, pietistic, priggish, prim, proper, prudish, rigid, self-denying, self-disciplined, severe, stern, stiff-necked, strait-laced, strict. Opp HEDONISTIC.

purpose n **1** aim, ambition, aspiration, design, end, goal, hope, intention, motive, object, objective, outcome, plan, result, target, wish. **2** determination, devotion, drive, firmness, persistence, resolution, resolve, steadfastness, tenacity, will, zeal. **3** purpose of a tool. application, benefit, good (what's the good of it?), point, use, usefulness, utility, value. ● v ▷ INTEND.

purposeful adj decided, decisive, deliberate, determined, firm, persistent, positive, resolute, steadfast, unfaltering, unwavering. ▷ INTENTIONAL. Opp HESITANT.

purposeless adj aimless, empty, gratuitous, meaningless, pointless, senseless, unnecessary, useless, wanton. Opp MEANINGFUL, USEFUL.

purposely adv deliberately, intentionally, knowingly, on purpose, wilfully.

purse n bag, handbag, pocketbook, pouch, wallet.

pursue v **1** chase, follow, go in pursuit of, hound, hunt, run after, shadow, stalk, inf tail, trace, track down, trail. **2** aim for, aspire to, be committed to, carry on, conduct, continue, engage in, follow up, *inf* go for, persevere in, persist in, proceed with, prosecute, *inf* stick with, strive for, try for. 3 *pursue truth.* inquire into, investigate, search for, seek.

pursuit *n* 1 chase, chasing, following, *inf* hue and cry, hunt, hunting, shadowing, stalking, tracking down. 2 *leisure pursuit.* activity, employment, enthusiasm, hobby, interest, occupation, pastime, pleasure.

push *v* 1 drive, force, impel, jostle, move, nudge, poke, press, prod, propel, set in motion, shove, thrust. 2 *push a button.* depress, press. 3 *push into a space.* compress, cram, crowd, crush, insert, jam, pack, ram, squash, squeeze. 4 *push someone to act.* bully, coerce, compel, constrain, encourage, force, hurry, incite, induce, influence, *inf* lean on, motivate, nag, persuade, pressurize, prompt, put pressure on, spur, urge. 5 *push a new product.* advertise, boost, market, *inf* plug, promote, publicize. *Opp* PULL. **push around** ▷ BULLY. **push off** ▷ DEPART. **push on** ▷ ADVANCE.

put *v* 1 arrange, assign, consign, deploy, deposit, dispose, fix, lay, leave, locate, park, place, *inf* plonk, position, rest, set down, settle, situate, stand, station. 2 *put a question.* express, frame, phrase, say, state, utter, voice, word, write. 3 *put a proposal.* advance, bring forward, offer, outline, present, propose, submit, suggest, tender. 4 *put blame on someone.* attach, attribute, cast, fix, impose, inflict, lay, *inf* pin. **put across** ▷ COMMUNICATE. **put back** ▷ RETURN. **put by** ▷ SAVE. **put**

down ▷ KILL, SUPPRESS. **put in** ▷ INSERT, INSTALL. **put off** ▷ POSTPONE. **put out** ▷ EJECT, EXTINGUISH. **put over** ▷ COMMUNICATE. **put right** ▷ REPAIR. **put someone up** ▷ ACCOMMODATE. **put up** ▷ RAISE. **put your foot down** ▷ INSIST. **put your foot in it** ▷ BLUNDER.

putative *adj* alleged, conjectural, hypothetical, presumed, reputed, rumoured, supposed.

putrefy *v* decay, decompose, *inf* go off, moulder, rot, spoil.

putrid *adj* bad, decaying, decomposing, fetid, foul, mouldy, putrefying, rotten, rotting.

puzzle *n* brain-teaser, conundrum, difficulty, dilemma, enigma, mystery, paradox, *inf* poser, problem, quandary, question, riddle. ● *v* baffle, bewilder, confound, confuse, *inf* floor, *inf* flummox, mystify, perplex, *inf* stump, worry. **puzzle out** ▷ SOLVE. **puzzle over** ▷ CONSIDER.

puzzling *adj* baffling, bewildering, confusing, cryptic, enigmatic, impenetrable, inexplicable, insoluble, *inf* mind-boggling, mysterious, mystifying, perplexing, strange, unaccountable, unfathomable. *Opp* STRAIGHTFORWARD.

pygmy *adj* dwarf, midget, tiny. ▷ SMALL.

Q

quadrangle *n* cloisters, courtyard, enclosure, *inf* quad.

quagmire *n* bog, fen, marsh, mire, morass, mud, quicksand, swamp.

quail *v* back away, blench, cower, cringe, falter, flinch, quake, recoil, shrink, tremble, wince.

quaint *adj* antiquated, charming, curious, eccentric, fanciful, fantastic, odd, offbeat, old-fashioned, outlandish, picturesque, strange, *inf* twee, unusual, whimsical.

quake *v* convulse, heave, move, quaver, quiver, rock, shake, shiver, shudder, sway, tremble, vibrate, wobble.

qualification *n* 1 ability, aptitude, capability, capacity, competence, eligibility, experience, fitness, *inf* know-how, knowledge, proficiency, skill, suitability. 2 certificate, degree, diploma, doctorate. 3 *agree without qualification.* condition, exception, limitation, modification, proviso, reservation, restriction.

qualified *adj* 1 able, capable, competent, eligible, equipped, experienced, expert, fit, practised, professional, proficient, skilled, suitable, trained, well-informed. *Opp* UNSKILLED. 2 *qualified praise.* cautious, conditional, equivocal, guarded, half-hearted, limited, modified, provisional, restricted. *Opp* UNCONDITIONAL.

qualify *v* 1 authorize, entitle, equip, fit, make eligible, permit, sanction. 2 be eligible, get through, *inf* make the grade, meet requirements, pass. 3 *qualify your praise.* lessen, limit, mitigate, moderate, modify, restrict, temper.

quality *n* 1 calibre, class, condition, grade, rank, sort, standard, status, value, worth. 2 *personal quality.* attribute, characteristic, feature, mark, peculiarity, property, trait.

quandary *n inf* catch-22, *inf* cleft stick, confusion, difficulty, dilemma, plight, predicament, uncertainty.

quantity *n* aggregate, amount, bulk, consignment, dosage, dose, extent, length, load, lot, magnitude, mass, measurement, number, part, portion, proportion, sum, total, volume, weight. ▷ MEASURE.

quarrel *n* altercation, argument, bickering, clash, conflict, confrontation, controversy, debate, difference, disagreement, discord, disharmony, dispute, dissension, division, feud, *inf* hassle, misunderstanding, *inf* row, *inf* ructions, *inf* scene, *inf* slanging match, split, squabble, strife, *inf* tiff, vendetta, wrangle. ● *v* argue, *inf* be at loggerheads, bicker, clash, conflict, contend, *inf* cross swords, differ, disagree, dissent, *inf* fall out, feud, haggle, *inf* row, squabble, wrangle. ▷ FIGHT.

quarrel with ▷ DISPUTE.

quarrelsome *adj* aggressive, argumentative, bad-tempered, cantankerous, contrary, defiant, disagreeable, dyspeptic, fractious, impatient, irascible, irritable, petulant, peevish, querulous, quick-tempered, *inf* stroppy, testy, truculent, unfriendly, volatile. ▷ PUGNACIOUS. *Opp* PEACEABLE.

quarry *n* 1 game, kill, object, prey, victim. 2 excavation, mine, pit, working. ● *v* dig out, excavate, extract, mine.

quarter *n* area, district, locality, neighbourhood, part, region, section, sector, territory, vicinity, zone. ● *v* accommodate, billet, board, house, lodge, *inf* put up.

quarters accommodation, barracks, dwelling place, home, housing, living quarters, lodgings, residence, rooms.

quash *v* 1 abolish, annul, cancel, invalidate, overrule, overthrow, reject, rescind, reverse, revoke. 2 ▷ QUELL.

quaver *v* falter, quake, quiver, shake, shiver, shudder, tremble, vibrate, waver.

quay *n* berth, dock, harbour, jetty, landing stage, pier, wharf.

queasy *adj* bilious, *inf* green, nauseated, nauseous, poorly, *inf* queer, sick. ▷ ILL.

queer *adj* 1 abnormal, anomalous, atypical, bizarre, curious, different, eerie, exceptional, extraordinary, *inf* fishy, freakish, *inf* funny, incongruous, inexplicable, irrational, mysterious, odd, offbeat, outlandish, peculiar, puzzling, quaint, *inf* rum, singular, strange, uncanny, uncommon, unnatural, unorthodox, unusual, weird. 2 *inf* cranky, eccentric, *inf* shady (*customer*), *inf* shifty, suspect, suspicious. ▷ ILL. 3 ▷ ILL. 4 ▷ HOMOSEXUAL.

quell *v* 1 crush, overcome, put down, quash, repress, subdue, suppress. 2 *quell fears.* allay, alleviate, calm, mitigate, mollify, pacify, soothe.

quench *v* 1 allay, appease, sate, satisfy, slake. 2 *quench a fire.* damp down, douse, extinguish, put out, smother, snuff out.

quest *n* crusade, expedition, hunt, mission, pilgrimage, search, voyage of discovery. ● *v* quest after ▷ SEEK.

question *n* 1 demand, enquiry, inquiry, *inf* poser, query. 2 argument, controversy, debate, difficulty, dispute, doubt, misgiving, mystery, problem, puzzle, uncertainty. ● *v* 1 ask, catechize, cross-examine, cross-question, examine, *inf* grill, inquire of, interrogate, interview, probe, *inf* pump, quiz. 2 *question a decision.* be sceptical about, call into question, cast doubt upon, challenge, dispute, inquire about, object to, oppose, quarrel with, query.

questionable *adj* arguable, borderline, debatable, disputable, doubtful, dubious, *inf* iffy, moot, suspect, suspicious, uncertain, unclear, unprovable, unreliable.

questionnaire *n* opinion poll, quiz, survey, test.

queue *n* chain, column, *inf* crocodile, file, line, line-up, procession, row, string, tailback, train. ● *v* fall in, form a queue, line up.

quibble *n* ▷ OBJECTION. ● *v* be evasive, carp, cavil, equivocate, *inf* nit-pick, object, *inf* split hairs, wrangle.

quick *adj* 1 breakneck, brisk, fast, headlong, high-speed, *inf* nippy, rapid, *inf* smart (*pace*), *inf* spanking, speedy, swift. 2 *quick steps.* agile, animated, brisk, deft, dexterous, energetic, lively, nimble, spirited, spry, vivacious. 3 *quick response.* abrupt, hasty, hurried, immediate, instant, instantaneous, perfunctory, precipitate, prompt, punctual, ready, sudden, summary, unhesitating. 4 *quick mind.* acute, alert, astute, bright, clever, intelligent, perceptive, quick-witted, sharp, shrewd, smart. *Opp* SLOW. 5 *quick visit.* brief, fleeting, momentary, passing, short, temporary, transitory. 6 [*old use*] *the quick and the dead.* ▷ ALIVE. *Opp* SLOW.

quicken *v* 1 accelerate, expedite, hasten, hurry, go faster, speed up. 2 ▷ AROUSE.

quiet *adj* 1 inaudible, noiseless, silent, soundless. 2 *quiet music.* hushed, low, soft. 3 *quiet person.* contemplative, gentle, introverted, meditative, meek, mild, modest, peaceable, placid, reserved, retiring, shy, taciturn, thoughtful, uncommunicative, unforthcoming, unsociable, withdrawn. 4 *quiet life.* cloistered, sheltered, tranquil, unadventurous, untroubled. 5 *quiet place.* isolated, lonely, peaceful, private, secluded, undisturbed, unfrequented. 6 *quiet sea.* calm, motionless, serene, still. *Opp* BUSY, NOISY, RESTLESS.

quieten *v* 1 calm, compose, hush, lull, pacify, sedate, soothe, subdue. 2 deaden, dull, muffle, mute, silence, soften, stifle, suppress, tone down.

quirk *n* aberration, caprice, eccentricity, idiosyncrasy, kink, oddity, peculiarity, whim.

quit *v* 1 abandon, decamp from, depart from, desert, forsake, leave, walk out (on), withdraw. 2 abdicate, discontinue, drop, give up, leave, *inf* pack in, relinquish, renounce, resign from, retire from, withdraw from. 3 [*inf*] *Quit pushing!* cease, desist from, leave off, stop.

quite *adv* [NB: senses are almost opposite.] 1 *I've quite finished.* absolutely, altogether, completely, entirely, perfectly, thoroughly, totally, utterly, wholly. 2 *quite good.* comparatively, fairly, moderately, *inf* pretty, rather, relatively, somewhat.

quits *adj* equal, even, level, repaid, revenged, square.

quiver *v* flicker, fluctuate, flutter, palpitate, pulsate, quake, quaver, shake, shiver, shudder, tremble, vibrate, wobble.

quixotic *adj* fanciful, idealistic, impracticable, impractical, romantic, *inf* starry-eyed, unrealistic, Utopian, visionary. *Opp* REALISTIC.

quiz *n* competition, exam, questioning, questionnaire, test. ● *v* ▷ QUESTION.

quizzical *adj* amused, curious, perplexed, puzzled, questioning.

quota *n* allocation, allowance, *inf* cut, part, portion, proportion, ration, share.

quotation *n* 1 allusion, citation, excerpt, extract, passage, piece, reference, selection. 2 estimate, price, tender, valuation.

quote *v* 1 cite, instance, mention, refer to, repeat, reproduce. 2 *quote a price.* estimate, tender.

R

rabble *n* crowd, gang, herd, horde, mob, *inf* riff-raff, swarm, throng. ▷ GROUP.

race *n* 1 breed, ethnic group, family, folk, genus, kind, lin-

eage, nation, people, species, stock, tribe, variety. 2 chase, competition, contest, heat, marathon, rally, rivalry.
• v 1 compete with, have a race with, try to beat. 2 *race along*. career, dash, fly, gallop, hasten, hurry, run, rush, speed, sprint, *inf* tear, *inf* zip, zoom.

racial *adj* ethnic, folk, genetic, national, tribal.

racism *n* anti-Semitism, apartheid, bias, bigotry, chauvinism, discrimination, prejudice, xenophobia.

racist *adj* biased, bigoted, chauvinist, discriminatory, intolerant, prejudiced, xenophobic.

rack *n* frame, framework, holder, shelf, stand, support.
• v ▷ TORTURE.

radiant *adj* 1 bright, brilliant, gleaming, glorious, glowing, incandescent, luminous, phosphorescent, shining. 2 *The bride was radiant.* ▷ HAPPY.

radiate *v* beam, diffuse, emanate, emit, give off, gleam, glow, send out, shed, shine, spread, transmit.

radical *adj* 1 basic, deep-seated, elementary, essential, fundamental, primary, principal, profound. 2 complete, comprehensive, drastic, entire, exhaustive, thorough, thoroughgoing. 3 *radical politics*. extremist, fanatical, revolutionary, subversive. *Opp* MODERATE, SUPERFICIAL.

radio *n* CB, *sl* ghettoblaster, receiver, set, transistor, transmitter, walkie-talkie, *old use* wireless. • v broadcast, send out, transmit.

rafter *n* beam, girder, joist.

rage *n* ▷ ANGER. • v fume, go berserk, lose control, rave, *inf* see red, seethe, storm.

ragged *adj* 1 frayed, in ribbons, old, patched, patchy, ripped, rough, rough-edged, shabby, tattered, *inf* tatty, threadbare, torn, unkempt, unravelled, untidy, worn out. 2 *ragged line*. erratic, irregular, jagged, serrated, uneven, zigzag.

rags *pl n* bits and pieces, fragments, old clothes, remnants, scraps, shreds, tatters.

raid *n* assault, attack, blitz, foray, incursion, inroad, invasion, onslaught, sortie, strike, surprise attack, swoop.
• v 1 assault, attack, descend on, invade, rush, storm, swoop down on. 2 loot, pillage, plunder, ransack, rifle, rob, sack, steal from, strip.

raider *n* attacker, invader, looter, marauder, outlaw, pirate, ransacker, robber, rustler, thief.

railway *n* branch line, line, main line, metro, monorail, overground, *Amer* railroad, rails, track, tramway, tube, underground.

rain *n* cloudburst, deluge, downpour, drizzle, precipitation, raindrops, rainfall, shower, squall.
• v *inf* bucket down, drizzle, pelt, pour, *inf* rain cats and dogs, spit, teem.

rainy *adj* damp, drizzly, showery, wet.

raise *v* 1 elevate, hoist, hold up, jack up, lift, pick up, put up, rear. 2 *raise prices*. augment, increase, put up, *inf* up. 3 *raise to a higher rank*. exalt, promote, upgrade. 4 *raise a monument*. build, construct, create, erect, set up. 5 *raise hopes*. arouse, awaken, build up, buoy up, encourage, engender, excite, foment, foster, heighten, incite, kindle, provoke, rouse, stimulate, uplift. 6 *raise animals, children, crops.* breed, bring up, care for, cultivate, educate, farm, grow, look after, nurture, produce, propagate, rear. 7 *raise money.* collect, get, make, receive. 8 *raise questions.* advance, bring up, broach, express, instigate, introduce, mention, moot, pose, present, put forward, suggest. *Opp* LOWER, REDUCE. **raise from the dead** ▷ RESURRECT. **raise the alarm** ▷ WARN.

rally *n* 1 assembly, *inf* demo, demonstration, gathering, march, mass meeting. 2 ▷ COMPETITION. ● *v* 1 assemble, congregate, convene, get together, group, marshal, muster, organize, round up, summon. 2 *rally after illness.* ▷ RECOVER.

ram *v* 1 bump, butt, collide with, crash into, slam into, strike. ▷ HIT. 2 compress, cram, crowd, crush, drive, force, jam, pack, press, push, squash, squeeze, wedge.

ramble *n* hike, tramp, trek, walk. ● *v* 1 hike, range, roam, rove, stroll, tramp, trek, walk, wander. 2 digress, drift, *inf* lose the thread, *inf* rattle on, talk aimlessly, wander, *inf* witter on.

rambling *adj* 1 circuitous, indirect, labyrinthine, meandering, roundabout, tortuous, twisting, wandering, winding, zigzag. *Opp* DIRECT. 2 aimless, circumlocutory, confused, digressive, disconnected, discursive, disjointed, illogical, incoherent, jumbled, muddled, periphrastic, verbose, wordy. *Opp* COHERENT. 3 *rambling house.* irregular, large, sprawling, straggling. *Opp* COMPACT.

ramification *n* branch, byproduct, complication, consequence, division, effect, extension, implication, offshoot, result, subdivision, upshot.

ramp *n* gradient, incline, rise, slope.

rampage *n* frenzy, riot, tumult, uproar, violence. ● *v* go berserk, go wild, lose control, run amok, run riot, storm about. **on the rampage** ▷ WILD.

ramshackle *adj* broken-down, crumbling, decrepit, derelict, dilapidated, rickety, ruined, rundown, shaky, tottering, tumbledown, unsafe, unstable, unsteady. *Opp* SOLID.

random *adj* accidental, aimless, arbitrary, casual, chance, fortuitous, haphazard, *inf* hit-or-miss, indiscriminate, irregular, stray, unplanned, unpremeditated, unsystematic. *Opp* DELIBERATE, SYSTEMATIC.

range *n* 1 area, compass, distance, extent, field, limit, orbit, radius, reach, scope, span, spectrum, sphere, spread, sweep. 2 *wide range of goods.* diversity, selection, variety. 3 *range of mountains.* chain, file, line, rank, row, series, string. ● *v* 1 differ, extend, fluctuate, reach, run the gamut, spread, stretch, vary. 2 ▷ RANK. 3 ▷ ROAM.

rank *adj* 1 *rank growth.* ▷ ABUNDANT. 2 *rank odour.* ▷ SMELLING. ● *n* 1 column, file, formation, line, order, queue, row, series, tier. 2 caste, class, condition, degree, echelon, estate, grade, level, position, standing, station, status, title. ● *v* arrange, array, categorize, class, classify, grade, line up, order, organize, range, rate, set out in order, sort.

ransack *v* 1 go through, rummage through, scour, search, *inf* turn upside down. 2 *ransack a shop.* despoil, loot, pillage, plunder, raid, rob, sack, strip, wreck.

ransom *n* payment, *inf* pay-off, price, redemption. ● *v* deliver, redeem, rescue.

rap *v* 1 knock, strike, tap. ▷ HIT. 2 ▷ CRITICIZE.

rape *n* 1 assault, sexual attack. 2 ▷ PILLAGE. ● *v* assault, defile, force yourself on, ravish, violate.

rapid *adj* breakneck, brisk, express, fast, hasty, headlong, high-speed, hurried, immediate, impetuous, instant, instantaneous, *inf* lightning, *inf* nippy, precipitate, prompt, quick, smooth, speedy, swift. *Opp* SLOW.

rapids *pl n* cataract, current, waterfall, white water.

rapture *n* bliss, delight, ecstasy, elation, euphoria, exaltation, happiness, joy, pleasure.

rare *adj* abnormal, atypical, exceptional, extraordinary, *inf* few and far between, infrequent, irreplaceable, occasional, out of the ordinary, peculiar, scarce, singular, special, strange, surprising, uncommon, unfamiliar, unusual. *Opp* COMMON.

rascal *n* good-for-nothing, knave, mischief-maker, miscreant, ne'er-do-well, rogue, scallywag,

scamp, scoundrel, troublemaker, villain, wretch.

rash *adj* careless, foolhardy, hare-brained, hasty, heedless, hot-headed, ill-advised, ill-considered, impetuous, imprudent, impulsive, incautious, indiscreet, injudicious, madcap, precipitate, reckless, risky, thoughtless, unthinking, wild. *Opp* CAREFUL. ● *n* 1 eruption, spots. 2 *rash of thefts.* ▷ OUTBREAK.

rasp *v* 1 file, grate, rub, scrape. 2 *rasp orders.* croak, screech, speak hoarsely. **rasping** ▷ HARSH.

rate *n* 1 gait, pace, speed, tempo, velocity. 2 amount, charge, cost, fare, fee, figure, payment, price, tariff, wage. ● *v* 1 appraise, assess, consider, estimate, evaluate, gauge, grade, judge, measure, put a price on, rank, reckon, regard, value, weigh. 2 be worthy of, deserve, merit. 3 ▷ REPRIMAND.

rather *adv* 1 fairly, moderately, *inf* pretty, quite, relatively, slightly, somewhat. 2 *I'd rather have coffee.* preferably, sooner.

ratify *v* approve, authorize, confirm, endorse, sanction, sign, validate, verify.

rating *n* classification, evaluation, grade, grading, mark, order, placing, ranking.

ratio *n* balance, correlation, fraction, percentage, proportion, relationship.

ration *n* allocation, allotment, allowance, amount, helping, measure, percentage, portion, quota, share. ● *v* allocate, allot, apportion, conserve, control, distribute fairly, limit, restrict, share equally. **rations** food, necessities, provisions, stores, supplies.

rational *adj* balanced, clear-headed, enlightened, intelligent, judicious, logical, lucid, normal, reasonable, reasoned, sane, sensible, sound, thoughtful, wise. *Opp* IRRATIONAL.

rationale *n* argument, case, cause, excuse, explanation, grounds, justification, logical basis, principle, reason, reasoning, theory.

rationalize *v* 1 account for, be rational about, excuse, explain, justify, make rational, think through, vindicate.
2 ▷ REORGANIZE.

rattle *v* 1 clatter, vibrate. 2 agitate, jar, joggle, jiggle about, jolt, shake about. 3 [*inf*] discomfit, discompose, disconcert, disturb, fluster, frighten, make nervous, put off, unnerve, upset, worry. **rattle off** ▷ RECITE. **rattle on** ▷ RAMBLE.

raucous *adj* ear-splitting, grating, harsh, jarring, noisy, rasping, rough, screeching, shrill, squawking, strident.

ravage *v* damage, despoil, destroy, devastate, lay waste, loot, pillage, plunder, raid, ransack, ruin, sack, spoil, wreak havoc on, wreck.

rave *v* 1 be angry, fulminate, fume, rage, rant, roar, storm, thunder. 2 be enthusiastic, enthuse, *inf* go into raptures, *inf* gush, rhapsodize.

ravenous *adj* famished, hungry, insatiable, ravening, starved, starving, voracious. ▷ GREEDY.

ravish *v* 1 bewitch, captivate, charm, delight, enchant, entrance, transport. 2 ▷ RAPE.
ravishing ▷ BEAUTIFUL.

raw *adj* 1 fresh, uncooked, underdone, unprepared. 2 *raw materials.* crude, natural, unprocessed, unrefined, untreated. 3 *raw recruits. inf* green, ignorant, immature, inexperienced, innocent, new, untrained. 4 *raw skin.* bloody, chafed, grazed, inflamed, painful, red, rough, scraped, scratched, sensitive, sore, tender. 5 *raw wind.* ▷ COLD.

ray *n* 1 bar, beam, laser, shaft, streak, stream. 2 *ray of hope.* flicker, gleam, glimmer, hint, indication, sign, trace.

raze *v* bulldoze, demolish, destroy, flatten, tear down.

reach *n* compass, distance, orbit, range, scope, sphere. • *v* 1 arrive at, come to, get to, go as far as. 2 *reach the semifinals.* achieve, attain, *inf* make. 3 *reach me by phone.* contact, *inf* get hold of, get in touch with. **reach out** ▷ EXTEND.

react *v* act, answer, behave, reciprocate, reply, respond, retaliate, retort. **react to** ▷ COUNTER.

reaction *n* answer, backlash, *inf* comeback, effect, feedback, reflex, rejoinder, reply, reprisal, response, retaliation, retort, revenge, riposte.

reactionary *adj* conservative, die-hard, old-fashioned, rightwing, *inf* stick-in-the-mud, traditionalist. *Opp* PROGRESSIVE.

read *v* 1 devour, dip into, glance at, look over, peruse, pore over, scan, skim, study. 2 *can't read his writing.* decipher, decode, interpret, make out, understand.

readable *adj* 1 absorbing, compulsive, easy, enjoyable, enter-

taining, gripping, interesting, well-written. *Opp* BORING.
2 clear, decipherable, distinct, intelligible, legible, neat, plain. *Opp* ILLEGIBLE.

readily *adv* cheerfully, eagerly, easily, freely, gladly, happily, promptly, quickly, voluntarily, willingly.

ready *adj* **1** *inf* all set, arranged, at hand, available, complete, convenient, done, finalized, finished, obtainable, prepared, ripe, set, set up, waiting. *2 ready to help.* agreeable, content, disposed, eager, equipped, *inf* game, glad, inclined, in the mood, keen, keyed up, likely, minded, open, organized, pleased, poised, predisposed, primed, *inf* psyched up, raring (*to go*), trained, willing. *3 ready reply, wit.* acute, alert, apt, immediate, prompt, quick, quick-witted, rapid, sharp, smart, speedy. *Opp* SLOW, UNPREPARED.

real *adj* **1** actual, authentic, certain, everyday, existing, factual, genuine, material, natural, ordinary, palpable, physical, pure, realistic, tangible, visible. **2** authenticated, legal, legitimate, official, valid, verifiable. *3 real friends.* dependable, reliable, sound, true, trustworthy, worthy. *4 real grief.* earnest, heartfelt, honest, sincere, undoubted, unfeigned. *Opp* FALSE.

realism *n* **1** authenticity, fidelity, verisimilitude. **2** clearsightedness, common sense, objectivity, practicality, pragmatism.

realistic *adj* **1** businesslike, clear-sighted, commonsense, down-to-earth, feasible, level-

headed, logical, matter-of-fact, *inf* no-nonsense, objective, possible, practicable, practical, pragmatic, rational, sensible, tough, unemotional, unsentimental, viable, workable. *2 realistic pictures.* authentic, convincing, faithful, lifelike, natural, recognizable, true-to-life, truthful, vivid. *3 realistic prices.* acceptable, fair, justifiable, moderate, reasonable. *Opp* UNREALISTIC.

reality *n* actuality, authenticity, certainty, experience, *sl* nitty-gritty, real life, the real world, truth, verity. *Opp* FANTASY.

realize *v* **1** accept, appreciate, be aware of, become conscious of, *inf* catch on to, comprehend, conceive of, *inf* cotton on to, grasp, know, perceive, recognize, see, sense, understand, *inf* wake up to. *2 realize an ambition.* accomplish, achieve, bring about, complete, effect, fulfil, implement, obtain, perform, put into effect. *3 realize a price. inf* clear, earn, fetch, make, net, obtain, produce.

realm *n* country, domain, empire, kingdom, monarchy.

reap *v* **1** cut, garner, gather in, glean, harvest, mow. *2 reap a reward.* acquire, collect, get, obtain, receive, win.

rear *adj* back, end, hind, hindmost, last, rearmost. *Opp* FRONT. ▪ *n* **1** back, end, stern (*of ship*), tail-end. **2** ▷ BUTTOCKS.
● *v* **1** breed, bring up, care for, educate, feed, look after, nurse, nurture, produce, raise, train. *2 rear your head.* hold up, lift, raise. **3** ▷ BUILD.

rearrange *v* change round, regroup, reorganize, switch round, transpose. ▷ CHANGE.

rearrangement n reorganization. ▷ CHANGE.

reason n 1 apology, argument, case, cause, defense, excuse, explanation, grounds, incentive, justification, motive, occasion, pretext, rationale, vindication. 2 brains, common sense, *inf* gumption, intelligence, judgement, logic, mind, *inf* nous, sanity, sense, understanding, wisdom, wit. ▷ REASONING. 3 *reason for living.* aim, motivation, motive, object, objective, point, purpose, stimulus. ● v 1 calculate, conclude, consider, deduce, estimate, figure out, hypothesize, infer, judge, *inf* put two and two together, theorize, think, use your head, work out. 2 *I reasoned with her.* argue, debate, discuss, remonstrate.

reasonable adj 1 calm, honest, intelligent, rational, realistic, sane, sensible, sober, thinking, thoughtful, unemotional, wise. 2 *reasonable argument.* arguable, believable, credible, defensible, justifiable, logical, plausible, practical, reasoned, sound, tenable, viable. 3 *reasonable prices.* acceptable, appropriate, average, cheap, competitive, fair, inexpensive, moderate, ordinary, proper, right, suitable, tolerable. *Opp* IRRATIONAL.

reasoning n analysis, argument, case, deduction, hypothesis, line of thought, logic, proof, *derog* sophistry, theorizing, thinking.

reassure v assure, bolster, buoy up, calm, cheer, comfort, encourage, give confidence to, hearten, *inf* set someone's mind at rest, support, uplift. *Opp* ALARM, THREATEN. **reassuring** ▷ SOOTHING, SUPPORTIVE.

rebel adj ▷ REBELLIOUS. ● n anarchist, dissenter, freedom fighter, heretic, iconoclast, insurgent, malcontent, maverick, mutineer, nonconformist, revolutionary. ● v disobey, dissent, fight, *inf* kick over the traces, mutiny, refuse to obey, revolt, rise up, *inf* run riot, *inf* take a stand. *Opp* CONFORM. **rebel against** ▷ DEFY.

rebellion n defiance, disobedience, insubordination, insurrection, mutiny, rebelliousness, resistance, revolt, revolution, rising, sedition, uprising.

rebellious adj *inf* bolshie, breakaway, defiant, difficult, disaffected, disloyal, disobedient, insubordinate, insurgent, intractable, malcontent, mutinous, obstinate, quarrelsome, rebel, recalcitrant, refractory, resistant, revolutionary, seditious, uncontrollable, unmanageable, unruly, wild. *Opp* OBEDIENT.

rebirth n reawakening, regeneration, renaissance, renewal, resurgence, resurrection, return, revival.

rebound v backfire, bounce, misfire, ricochet, spring back.

rebuff n *inf* brush-off, discouragement, refusal, rejection, slight, snub. ● v cold-shoulder, discourage, refuse, reject, repulse, slight, snub, spurn, turn down.

rebuild n reassemble, reconstruct, recreate, redevelop, remake. ▷ RECONDITION.

rebuke v admonish, castigate, censure, reprehend, reproach, reprove, scold, upbraid. ▷ REPRIMAND.

recall v 1 bring back, call in, summon, withdraw. 2 ▷ REMEMBER.

recede v decline, dwindle, ebb, fall back, go back, lessen, retire, retreat, sink, subside, wane, withdraw.

receipt n 1 account, acknowledgement, bill, proof of purchase, ticket. 2 *receipt of goods*. acceptance, delivery. **receipts** gains, income, proceeds, profits, return, takings.

receive v 1 accept, acquire, be given, be sent, collect, come by, come into, derive, earn, gain, get, gross, inherit, make, net, obtain, take. 2 *receive an injury*. be subjected to, endure, experience, meet with, suffer, sustain, undergo. 3 *receive visitors*. admit, entertain, greet, meet, show in, welcome. *Opp* GIVE.

recent adj contemporary, current, fresh, just out, latest, modern, new, novel, present-day, up-to-date. *Opp* OLD.

reception n 1 greeting, response, welcome. 2 ▷ PARTY.

receptive adj amenable, favourable, interested, open, open-minded, responsive, susceptible, sympathetic, welcoming, well-disposed. *Opp* RESISTANT.

recess n 1 alcove, bay, corner, cranny, hollow, niche, nook. 2 adjournment, break, *inf* breather, breathing-space, interlude, interval, respite, rest, time off.

recession n decline, depression, downturn, slump.

recipe n directions, formula, instructions, method, procedure, technique.

reciprocal adj corresponding, exchanged, joint, mutual, requited, returned, shared.

reciprocate v exchange, match, repay, requite, return.

recital n 1 concert, performance, programme. 2 *recital of events*. account, description, narrative, recounting, relation, story, telling. ▷ RECITATION.

recitation n declamation, delivery, monologue, narration, performance, presentation, reading, speaking, telling.

recite v articulate, declaim, deliver, narrate, perform, present, quote, *inf* rattle off, recount, reel off, rehearse, relate, repeat, speak, tell.

reckless adj 1 careless, crazy, daredevil, devil-may-care, foolhardy, harebrained, hasty, heedless, impetuous, imprudent, impulsive, incautious, indiscreet, injudicious, irresponsible, *inf* mad, madcap, negligent, rash, thoughtless, unconsidered, unwise, wild. *Opp* CAREFUL. 2 *reckless criminals*. dangerous, desperate, violent.

reckon v 1 add up, assess, calculate, count, enumerate, estimate, evaluate, figure out, gauge, tally, total, value, work out. 2 ▷ THINK.

reclaim v 1 get back, recapture, recover, regain. 2 *reclaim land*. make usable, regenerate, rescue, restore, salvage, save.

recline v lean back, lie, lounge, rest, sprawl, stretch out.

recluse n hermit, loner, monk, nun, solitary.

recognizable adj detectable, distinctive, distinguishable, identifiable, known, noticeable, perceptible, undisguised, unmistakable, visible.

recognize v 1 detect, diagnose, discern, distinguish, identify, know, name, notice, perceive, pick out, place (*can't place him*), *inf* put a name to, recall, recollect, remember, see, spot. 2 *recognize your faults.* accept, acknowledge, admit to, appreciate, be aware of, concede, confess, grant, realize, understand. 3 *recognize someone's rights.* endorse, ratify, sanction, support.

recoil v blench, draw back, falter, flinch, jump, quail, shrink, shy away, start, wince.

recollect v recall, think back to. ▷ REMEMBER.

recommend v 1 advise, advocate, counsel, prescribe, propose, put forward, suggest, urge. 2 approve of, *inf* back, commend, favour, praise, *inf* push, *inf* put in a good word for, speak well of, support, vouch for. ▷ ADVERTISE.

recommendation n advice, advocacy, approbation, approval, *inf* backing, commendation, counsel, favourable mention, reference, seal of approval, support, testimonial.

reconcile v bring together, harmonize, placate, reunite, settle differences between. **be reconciled to** accept, adjust to, resign yourself to, submit to.

recondition v make good, overhaul, rebuild, renew, renovate, repair, restore.

reconnaissance n examination, exploration, inspection, investigation, observation, *inf* recce, reconnoitring, survey.

reconnoitre v *inf* check out, examine, explore, gather intelligence (about), inspect, investigate, patrol, scout, scrutinize, spy, survey.

reconsider v be converted, change your mind, come round, reappraise, reassess, re-examine, rethink, review your position, think better of.

reconstruct v act out, mock up, recreate, rerun. ▷ REBUILD.

record n 1 account, annals, archives, catalogue, chronicle, diary, documentation, dossier, file, journal, log, minutes, narrative, note, register, report, transactions. 2 best performance, best time. 3 ▷ RECORDING.
• v 1 chronicle, document, enter, inscribe, list, log, note, register, set down, transcribe, write down. 2 keep, tape, tape-record, video.

recording n album, cassette, CD, compact disc, disc, performance, record, release, single, tape, video, videotape.

record player n CD player, gramophone, midi system, record deck, turntable.

recount v communicate, describe, impart, narrate, recite, relate, report, tell, unfold.

recover v 1 find, get back, make good, recapture, reclaim, recoup, regain, repossess, restore, retrieve, salvage, trace, track down, win back. 2 *inf* be on the mend, come round, convalesce, get better, heal, improve, mend, *inf* pull round, *inf* pull through, rally, recuperate, regain your strength, revive, survive, *inf* take a turn for the better.

recovery n 1 recapture, reclamation, repossession, restoration,

retrieval, salvage, salvaging.
2 *recovery from illness.* convalescence, cure, healing, improvement, rally, recuperation, revival, upturn.

recreation *n* amusement, diversion, enjoyment, entertainment, fun, games, hobby, leisure, pastime, play, pleasure, relaxation, sport.

recrimination *n* accusation, *inf* comeback, reprisal, retaliation, retort.

recruit *n* apprentice, beginner, conscript, initiate, learner, new boy or girl, novice, trainee. *Opp* VETERAN. ● *v* advertise for, conscript, draft in, engage, enlist, enrol, mobilize, muster, register, sign on, sign up, take on.

rectify *v* amend, correct, cure, *inf* fix, make good, put right, repair, revise.

recumbent *adj* flat, flat on your back, horizontal, lying down, prone, reclining, stretched out, supine. *Opp* UPRIGHT.

recuperate *v* convalesce, get better, heal, mend, rally, regain strength. ▷ RECOVER.

recur *v* be repeated, happen again, persist, reappear, return.

recurrent *adj* chronic, frequent, intermittent, periodic, persistent, recurring, regular, repeated. ▷ CONTINUAL.

recycle *v* retrieve, reuse, salvage, use again.

red *adj* 1 bloodshot, blushing, embarrassed, fiery, flaming, florid, flushed, glowing, inflamed, rosy, ruddy. 2 auburn, crimson, magenta, maroon, ruby, scarlet, vermilion, wine-coloured. **red herring** ▷ DECOY.

redden *v* blush, colour, flush, glow.

redeem *v* buy back, cash in, reclaim, recover, trade in, win back. ▷ LIBERATE. **redeem yourself** ▷ ATONE.

redolent *adj* 1 aromatic, fragrant, perfumed, scented, smelling. 2 *redolent of the past.* reminiscent, suggestive.

reduce *v* 1 abbreviate, abridge, clip, compress, curtail, cut back, decimate, decrease, detract from, devalue, dilute, diminish, *inf* dock (*wages*), *inf* ease up on, halve, lessen, limit, lower, minimize, moderate, narrow, prune, shorten, shrink, simplify, *inf* slash, slim down, trim, truncate, weaken, whittle. 2 contract, dwindle, shrink. 3 *reduce a liquid.* concentrate, condense, thicken. 4 *reduce to rubble.* break up, destroy, grind, pulp, pulverize. 5 *reduce to poverty.* degrade, humble, impoverish, ruin. *Opp* INCREASE, RAISE.

reduction *n* 1 contraction, curtailment, cutback, decimation, decline, decrease, diminution, drop, lessening, limitation, loss, moderation, narrowing, remission, shortening, shrinkage, weakening. 2 *reduction in price.* concession, cut, depreciation, devaluation, discount, rebate, refund. *Opp* INCREASE.

redundant *adj* excessive, inessential, non-essential, superfluous, surplus, unnecessary, unneeded, unwanted. *Opp* NECESSARY.

reek *n* stench, stink. ▷ SMELL.

reel *n* bobbin, spool. ● *v* lurch, pitch, rock, roll, spin, stagger, stumble, sway, totter, whirl, wobble. **reel off** ▷ RECITE.

refer v **refer to 1** allude to, bring up, cite, comment on, draw attention to, mention, name, point to, quote, speak of, touch on. **2** *refer one person to another.* direct to, hand over to, pass on to, recommend to, send to. **3** *refer to the dictionary.* consult, resort to, study, turn to.

referee n arbiter, arbitrator, judge, mediator, umpire.

reference n **1** allusion, citation, example, illustration, instance, mention, note, quotation, referral, remark. **2** recommendation, testimonial.

refill v fill up, refuel, renew, replenish, top up.

refine v **1** clarify, cleanse, clear, decontaminate, distil, process, purify, treat. **2** *refine manners.* civilize, improve, perfect, polish.

refined adj **1** aristocratic, civilized, courteous, courtly, cultured, delicate, dignified, discriminating, elegant, fastidious, genteel, gentlemanly, gracious, ladylike, polished, polite, *inf* posh, *derog* pretentious, *derog* prissy, sensitive, sophisticated, subtle, tasteful, *inf* uppercrust, urbane, well-bred, well brought-up. *Opp* RUDE. **2** *refined oil.* distilled, processed, purified, treated. *Opp* CRUDE.

refinement n **1** breeding, *inf* class, courtesy, cultivation, delicacy, discrimination, elegance, finesse, gentility, graciousness, polish, *derog* pretentiousness, sophistication, style, subtlety, taste, urbanity. **2** *refinement in design.* enhancement, improvement, modification.

reflect v **1** echo, mirror, return, shine back, throw back. **2** brood,

inf chew things over, consider, contemplate, deliberate, meditate, ponder, reminisce, ruminate. ▷ THINK. **3** *Her success reflects her hard work.* bear witness to, demonstrate, illustrate, indicate, match, point to, reveal, show.

reflection n **1** echo, image, likeness. **2** *reflection of hard work.* demonstration, evidence, indication, result. **3** *no reflection on you.* criticism, discredit, reproach, shame, slur. **4** *time for reflection.* cogitation, contemplation, deliberation, meditation, pondering, rumination, self-examination, study, thinking, thought.

reflective adj **1** glittering, lustrous, reflecting, shiny, silvery. **2** ▷ THOUGHTFUL.

reform v **1** ameliorate, amend, better, change, convert, correct, improve, mend, put right, rectify. **2** *reform a system.* reconstruct, regenerate, remodel, reorganize, revolutionize.

refrain v **refrain from** abstain from, avoid, cease, desist from, do without, eschew, forbear, leave off, *inf* quit, renounce, stop.

refresh v **1** cool, energize, enliven, freshen, invigorate, *inf* perk up, quench the thirst of, rejuvenate, renew, restore, resuscitate, revitalize, revive, slake (*thirst*). **2** *refresh the memory.* awaken, jog, remind, prod, prompt, stimulate.

refreshing adj **1** bracing, cool, enlivening, exhilarating, invigorating, restorative, reviving, stimulating, thirst-quenching, tonic. *Opp* EXHAUSTING. **2** *refreshing change.* fresh, interesting, new, novel, original, unexpected, unfamiliar, unforeseen, welcome. *Opp* BORING.

refreshments *pl n* drinks, *inf* eats, *inf* nibbles, snacks.

refrigerate *v* chill, cool, freeze, ice, keep cold.

refuge *n* asylum, *inf* bolt-hole, cover, harbour, haven, hideaway, *inf* hideout, hiding-place, protection, retreat, safety, sanctuary, security, shelter, stronghold.

refugee *n* displaced person, exile, fugitive, outcast.

refund *n* rebate, repayment. ● *v* give back, pay back, reimburse, repay, return.

refusal *n* *inf* brush-off, denial, rebuff, rejection, veto. *Opp* ACCEPTANCE.

refuse *n* detritus, dirt, garbage, junk, litter, rubbish, trash, waste. ● *v* baulk at, decline, disallow, *inf* pass up, rebuff, reject, repudiate, spurn, turn down, veto, withhold. *Opp* ACCEPT, GRANT.

refute *v* counter, discredit, disprove, negate, prove wrong.

regain *v* be reunited with, find, get back, recapture, reclaim, recoup, recover, retake, retrieve, win back.

regal *adj derog* haughty, imperial, kingly, lordly, majestic, noble, palatial, princely, queenly, royal, stately.
▷ SPLENDID.

regard *n* 1 gaze, look, scrutiny, stare. 2 attention, care, concern, consideration, deference, heed, notice, reference, thought. 3 admiration, affection, appreciation, approval, esteem, favour, honour, love, respect, reverence,

veneration. ● *v* 1 behold, contemplate, eye, gaze at, keep an eye on, look at, note, observe, scrutinize, view, watch. 2 *regarded me as a liability*. consider, deem, esteem, judge, look upon, perceive, rate, reckon, respect, think of, value, view.

regarding *prep* about, apropos, concerning, connected with, involving, on the subject of, with reference to, with regard to.

regardless *adj regardless of* despite, heedless of, indifferent to, neglectful of, notwithstanding, unmindful of.

regime *n* administration, government, leadership, management, order, reign, rule, system.

regiment *v* arrange, control, discipline, organize, regulate.

region *n* area, country, department, district, division, expanse, land, locality, neighbourhood, part, place, province, quarter, sector, territory, tract, vicinity, zone.

register *n* catalogue, diary, directory, file, index, inventory, journal, ledger, list, record, roll. ● *v* 1 enlist, enrol, enter your name, join, sign on. 2 *register a complaint*. enter, list, log, make official, present, record, set down, submit, write down. 3 *register emotion*. display, express, indicate, manifest, reflect, reveal, show. 4 *register in a hotel*. check in, sign in. 5 *register what someone says*. make a note of, mark, notice, take account of.

regress *v* backslide, degenerate, deteriorate, go back, retreat, retrogress, revert, slip back. *Opp* PROGRESS.

regret n 1 compunction, contrition, guilt, penitence, pang of conscience, remorse, repentance, self-reproach, shame. 2 disappointment, grief, sadness, sorrow, sympathy. • v bemoan, deplore, deprecate, feel remorse, grieve (about), lament, mourn, repent (of), reproach yourself, rue, weep (over).

regretful adj apologetic, ashamed, conscience-stricken, contrite, disappointed, penitent, remorseful, repentant, rueful, sorry. ▷ SAD.
Opp UNREPENTANT.

regrettable adj deplorable, disappointing, distressing, lamentable, reprehensible, sad, shameful, undesirable, unfortunate, unlucky, upsetting, woeful, wrong.

regular adj 1 consistent, constant, daily, equal, even, fixed, hourly, measured, monthly, ordered, predictable, recurring, repeated, rhythmic, steady, systematic, weekly, yearly. 2 regular procedure. accustomed, common, conventional, customary, established, everyday, familiar, frequent, habitual, normal, ordinary, proper, routine, scheduled, standard, traditional, typical, usual. 3 regular supporter. dependable, faithful, reliable.
Opp IRREGULAR. • n habitué, regular customer, patron.

regulate v 1 administer, control, direct, manage, order, organize, oversee, restrict, supervise. 2 regulate temperature. adjust, alter, change, get right, moderate, set, vary.

regulation n by-law, decree, dictate, directive, edict, law, order, ordinance, requirement, rule, ruling, statute.

rehearsal n dress rehearsal, inf dry run, practice, inf run-through, trial, inf try-out.

rehearse v drill, go over, practise, prepare, inf run over, inf run through, try out.

rehearsed adj practised, prearranged, prepared, scripted, studied, thought out.
Opp IMPROMPTU.

reign n ascendancy, command, empire, jurisdiction, monarchy, power, rule, sovereignty. • v be on the throne, command, govern, have power, hold sway, rule, inf wear the crown.

reincarnation n rebirth, return to life.

reinforce v 1 back up, bolster, buttress, fortify, give strength to, hold up, prop up, stiffen, strengthen, support, toughen. 2 reinforce an army. add to, augment, help, provide reinforcements for, supplement.

reinforcements pl n additional troops, auxiliaries, backup, help, reserves, support.

reinstate v recall, rehabilitate, restore, take back, welcome back. Opp DISMISS.

reject v 1 discard, discount, dismiss, eliminate, exclude, jettison, inf junk, put aside, scrap, throw away, throw out. 2 reject friends. disown, inf drop, inf give (someone) the cold shoulder, jilt, rebuff, renounce, repel, repudiate, repulse, shun, spurn, turn your back on. 3 reject an invitation. decline, refuse, turn down, veto. Opp ACCEPT, ADOPT.

rejoice v be happy, celebrate, delight, exult, glory, revel, triumph. Opp GRIEVE.

relapse n degeneration, deterioration, recurrence (of illness), regression, worsening. • v backslide, degenerate, deteriorate, lapse, regress, revert, sink back, slip back, weaken.

relate v 1 communicate, describe, detail, divulge, impart, narrate, present, recite, recount, report, reveal, tell. 2 ally, associate, compare, connect, correlate, couple, join, link. **relate to** 1 apply to, be relevant to, concern, pertain to, refer to. 2 relate to other people. empathize with, handle, identify with, socialize with, understand.

related adj affiliated, akin, allied, associated, comparable, connected, interdependent, interrelated, joined, joint, linked, mutual, parallel, reciprocal, relative, similar. ▷ RELEVANT. Opp UNRELATED.

relation n 1 pl kith and kin, member of the family, relative. ▷ FAMILY. 2 relation of a story. ▷ NARRATION.

relationship n 1 affiliation, affinity, association, attachment, bond, closeness, connection, correlation, correspondence, interdependence, kinship, link, parallel, rapport, ratio, tie, understanding. ▷ SIMILARITY. Opp CONTRAST. 2 affair, inf intrigue, inf liaison, love affair, romance. ▷ FRIENDSHIP.

relative adj ▷ RELATED, RELEVANT. **relative to** commensurate (with), comparative, proportional, proportionate.

Opp UNRELATED.
• n ▷ RELATION.

relax v 1 be relaxed, calm down, feel at home, inf let go, inf put your feet up, rest, inf slow down, inf take it easy, unbend, unwind. Opp TENSION. 2 decrease, diminish, ease off, lessen, loosen, mitigate, moderate, reduce, release, relieve, slacken, soften, temper, inf tone down, unclench, unfasten, weaken. Opp INCREASE.

relaxation n 1 ease, informality, loosening up, relaxing, rest, unwinding. ▷ RECREATION. Opp TENSION. 2 alleviation, diminution, lessening, inf let-up, moderation, remission, slackening. Opp INCREASE.

relaxed adj derog blasé, calm, carefree, casual, comfortable, contented, cool, easygoing, inf free and easy, friendly, good-humoured, happy, inf happy-go-lucky, informal, inf laid-back, leisurely, nonchalant, peaceful, restful, serene, derog slack, tranquil, unconcerned, unhurried, untroubled. Opp TENSE.

relay n 1 shift, turn. 2 live relay. broadcast, programme, transmission. • v broadcast, communicate, pass on, send out, spread, televise, transmit.

release v 1 acquit, allow out, discharge, dismiss, emancipate, excuse, exonerate, free, let go, liberate, loose, pardon, rescue, save, set free, set loose, unfasten, unfetter, unleash, untie. Opp DETAIN. 2 fire off, launch, let off. 3 release information. circulate, disseminate, distribute, issue, make available, present, publish, send out.

relegate *v* consign to a lower position, demote, downgrade.

relent *v* acquiesce, be merciful, capitulate, give in, give way, relax, show pity, soften, weaken, yield.

relentless *adj* 1 dogged, fierce, hard-hearted, implacable, inexorable, intransigent, merciless, obdurate, obstinate, pitiless, remorseless, ruthless, uncompromising, unforgiving, unmerciful, unyielding. ▷ CRUEL. 2 unceasing, unrelieved, unstoppable. ▷ CONTINUAL.

relevant *adj* applicable, apposite, appropriate, apt, connected, essential, fitting, linked, material, pertinent, proper, related, relative, significant, suitable, suited, to the point. *Opp* IRRELEVANT.

reliable *adj* certain, consistent, constant, dependable, devoted, efficient, faithful, honest, loyal, predictable, proven, punctilious, regular, reputable, responsible, safe, solid, sound, stable, staunch, steady, sure, trusted, trustworthy, unchanging, unfailing. *Opp* UNRELIABLE.

relic *n* heirloom, keepsake, memento, remains, reminder, remnant, souvenir, token, vestige.

relief *n* abatement, aid, alleviation, assistance, comfort, cure, deliverance, diversion, ease, help, *inf* let-up, mitigation, relaxation, release, remedy, remission, respite, rest.

relieve *v* abate, alleviate, anaesthetize, assuage, bring relief to, calm, comfort, console, cure, diminish, dull, ease, lessen, lift, lighten, mitigate, moderate, palliate, reduce, relax, release,

soften, soothe, unburden. ▷ HELP. *Opp* INTENSIFY.

religion *n* 1 belief, creed, divinity, doctrine, dogma, theology. 2 creed, cult, denomination, faith, persuasion, sect.

religious *adj* 1 devotional, divine, holy, sacramental, sacred, scriptural, theological. *Opp* SECULAR. 2 church-going, committed, dedicated, devout, God-fearing, godly, *derog* pietistic, pious, reverent, righteous, saintly, *derog* sanctimonious, spiritual. *Opp* IRRELIGIOUS. 3 *religious wars.* doctrinal, sectarian.

relinquish *v* concede, hand over, part with, surrender, yield.

relish *n* 1 appetite, delight, enjoyment, enthusiasm, gusto, pleasure, zest. 2 flavour, piquancy, savour, tang, taste. • *v* appreciate, delight in, enjoy, like, love, revel in, savour, take pleasure in.

reluctant *adj* averse, disinclined, grudging, hesitant, loath, unenthusiastic, unwilling. *Opp* EAGER.

rely *v* **rely on** *inf* bank on, count on, depend on, have confidence in, lean on, put your faith in, *inf* swear by, trust.

remain *v* be left, carry on, continue, endure, keep on, linger, live on, persist, stay, *inf* stay put, survive, wait. **remaining** ▷ RESIDUAL.

remainder *n* balance, excess, extra, remnant, rest, surplus. ▷ REMAINS.

remains *pl n* 1 crumbs, debris, detritus, dregs, fragments, leftovers, oddments, *inf* odds and ends, remainder, remnants, residue, rubble, ruins, scraps,

traces, vestiges, wreckage.
2 historic remains. heirloom,
keepsake, memento, monument,
relic, reminder, souvenir.
3 human remains. ashes, body,
bones, carcass, corpse.

remake v piece together,
rebuild, reconstitute, reconstruct, redo. ▷ RENEW.

remark n comment, mention,
observation, reflection, statement, thought, utterance, word.
● v 1 assert, comment, declare,
mention, note, observe, reflect,
say, state. **2** perceive, see.
▷ NOTICE.

remarkable adj amazing, astonishing, astounding, curious,
different, distinguished,
exceptional, extraordinary,
impressive, marvellous, memorable, notable, noteworthy, odd,
out of the ordinary, outstanding,
peculiar, phenomenal, prominent, signal, significant, singular,
special, strange, striking, surprising, inf terrific, tremendous,
uncommon, unusual, wonderful.
Opp ORDINARY.

remedy n inf answer, antidote,
corrective, countermeasure,
cure, drug, elixir, medicament,
medication, medicine, palliative,
panacea, prescription, redress,
relief, restorative, solution,
therapy, treatment. ● v alleviate,
correct, counteract, inf fix, heal,
help, mend, mitigate, palliate,
put right, rectify, redress,
relieve, repair, solve, treat.
▷ CURE.

remember v 1 be mindful of,
have in mind, keep in mind,
recognize. **2** learn, memorize,
retain. **3 remember old times.** be
nostalgic about, hark back to,
recall, recollect, reminisce

about, review, summon up,
think back to. **4 remember an**
anniversary. celebrate, commemorate, observe. Opp FORGET.

remind v cause to remember, jog
the memory, prompt.

reminder n 1 cue, hint,
inf memo, memorandum, note,
inf nudge, prompt, inf shopping
list. **2** keepsake, memento, relic,
souvenir.

reminisce v be nostalgic, hark
back, look back, recall, remember, review, think back.

reminiscence n account, anecdote, memoir, memory, recollection, remembrance.

reminiscent adj evocative,
nostalgic, redolent, suggestive.

remiss adj dilatory, forgetful, irresponsible, lax, negligent, slack, thoughtless.
Opp CAREFUL.

remit v 1 remit a debt. cancel, let
off, pay, settle. **2** decrease, ease
off, lessen, relax, slacken.
3 dispatch, forward, send.

remittance n allowance, fee,
payment.

remnants pl n bits, fragments,
leftovers, oddments, offcuts, residue, scraps, traces, vestiges.
▷ REMAINS.

remodel v ▷ RENEW.

remorse n compunction, contrition, grief, guilt, mortification,
pangs of conscience, penitence,
regret, repentance, sadness, self-
reproach, shame, sorrow.

remorseful adj ashamed,
conscience-stricken, contrite,
guilt-ridden, penitent, regretful,
repentant, rueful, sorry.
Opp UNREPENTANT.

remorseless adj dogged, implacable, inexorable, merciless,

obdurate, pitiless, relentless, ruthless, unkind, unmerciful, unremitting. ▷ CRUEL.

remote *adj* 1 cut off, desolate, distant, far-away, foreign, godforsaken, hard to find, inaccessible, isolated, lonely, outlying, out of reach, out of the way, secluded, solitary, unfamiliar, unfrequented, unreachable. *Opp* CLOSE. 2 *remote chance*. doubtful, improbable, outside, poor, slender, slight, small, unlikely. *Opp* SURE. 3 *remote manner*. abstracted, aloof, cold, cool, detached, haughty, preoccupied, reserved, standoffish, withdrawn. *Opp* FRIENDLY.

removal *n* 1 relocation, transfer, transportation. 2 elimination, eradication, extermination, liquidation, purge. ▷ KILLING. 3 *removal from a position*. deposition, dethronement, dislodgement, dismissal, displacement, ejection, expulsion, *inf* firing, *inf* sacking, transference, unseating. 4 *removal of teeth*. drawing, extraction, pulling, taking out.

remove *v* 1 abolish, amputate (*limb*), banish, clear away, cut off, cut out, delete, depose, detach, disconnect, dismiss, dispense with, displace, dispose of, do away with, eject, eliminate, eradicate, erase, evict, exile, expel, *inf* fire, *inf* get rid of, *inf* kick out, kill, oust, purge, root out, *inf* sack, sweep away, take out, throw out, turn out, uproot, wash off, wipe out. 2 *remove furniture*. carry away, convey, move, transfer, transport. 3 *remove a tooth*. draw out, extract, pull out. 4 *remove clothes*. doff (*a hat*), peel off, strip off, take off.

rend *v* cleave, pull apart, rip, rupture, shred, split, tear.

render *v* 1 cede, deliver, furnish, give, hand over, offer, present, proffer, provide, tender, yield. 2 *render a song*. ▷ PERFORM. 3 *render speechless*. cause to be, make.

rendezvous *n* appointment, assignation, date, engagement, meeting, meeting place.

renegade *n* backslider, defector, deserter, fugitive, heretic, mutineer, outlaw, rebel, runaway, traitor, turncoat.

renege *v* *renege on* *inf* back out of, break, default on, fail to keep, go back on, repudiate.

renew *v* 1 bring up to date, *inf* do up, *inf* give a facelift to, improve, mend, modernize, overhaul, recondition, reconstitute, recreate, redecorate, redesign, redevelop, redo, refit, refresh, refurbish, reintroduce, remake, remodel, renovate, repaint, repair, replace, replenish, restore, resurrect, revamp, revive, transform, update. 2 *renew an activity*. come back to, pick up again, restart, resume, return to. 3 *renew vows*. confirm, reaffirm, repeat, restate.

renounce *v* 1 abandon, abstain from, deny, discard, disown, eschew, forgo, forsake, forswear, give up, reject, repudiate, spurn. 2 *renounce the throne*. abdicate, quit, relinquish, resign, surrender.

renovate *v* ▷ RENEW.

renovation *n* improvement, modernization, overhaul, redevelopment, refit, refurbishment, renewal, repair, restoration, transformation, updating.

renowned adj celebrated, eminent, illustrious, prominent, well-known. ▷ FAMOUS.

rent n 1 fee, instalment, payment, rental. 2 rent in a garment. ▷ SPLIT. ● v charter, hire, lease, let.

reorganize v rationalize, rearrange, reshuffle, restructure.

repair v 1 inf fix, mend, overhaul, patch up, put right, rectify, service. ▷ RENEW. 2 darn, patch, sew up.

repay v 1 compensate, pay back, recompense, refund, reimburse, remunerate, settle. 2 avenge, get even, inf get your own back, requite, retaliate, return, revenge.

repeal v abolish, annul, cancel, nullify, rescind, reverse, revoke.

repeat v 1 do again, duplicate, redo, rehearse, replicate, reproduce, re-run. 2 echo, quote, recapitulate, re-echo, reiterate, restate, retell, say again.

repel v 1 drive away, fend off, fight off, inf keep at bay, parry, push away, rebuff, repulse, ward off. 2 repel water. be impermeable to, exclude, keep out. 3 cruelty repels us. alienate, be repellent to, disgust, nauseate, offend, inf put off, revolt, sicken, inf turn off. Opp ATTRACT.

repellent adj 1 impermeable, impervious, resistant. 2 ▷ REPULSIVE.

repent v bemoan, be repentant about, bewail, feel repentance for, lament, regret, rue.

repentance n contrition, guilt, penitence, regret, remorse, self-reproach, shame, sorrow.

repentant adj apologetic, ashamed, conscience-stricken, contrite, guilt-ridden, penitent, regretful, remorseful, rueful, sorry. Opp UNREPENTANT.

repertory n collection, repertoire, stock, store, supply.

repetitive adj boring, monotonous, recurrent, repeated, repetitious, tautologous, tedious, unvaried. ▷ CONTINUAL.

replace v 1 put back, reinstate, restore, return. 2 come after, follow, oust, succeed, supersede, supplant, take over from, take the place of. ▷ DEPUTIZE. 3 replace worn parts. change, renew, substitute.

replacement n inf fill-in, proxy, stand-in, substitute, successor, understudy.

replenish v fill up, refill, renew, restock, top up.

replete adj inf bursting, gorged, inf jam-packed, sated, stuffed. ▷ FULL.

replica n inf carbon copy, clone, copy, duplicate, facsimile, imitation, likeness, model, reproduction.

reply n acknowledgement, answer, inf comeback, reaction, rejoinder, response, retort, riposte. ● v answer, react, rejoin, respond. **reply to** ▷ ACKNOWLEDGE, COUNTER.

report n 1 account, announcement, article, communication, communiqué, description, dispatch, narrative, news, record, statement, story, inf write-up. 2 bang, blast, boom, crack, detonation, explosion, noise.

• *v* 1 announce, broadcast, circulate, communicate, declare, describe, document, give an account of, notify, proclaim, publish, put out, record, recount, reveal, state, tell. 2 *report for duty.* check in, clock in, introduce yourself, present yourself, sign in. 3 *report someone to the police.* complain about, denounce, inform against, *inf* tell on.

reporter *n* columnist, commentator, correspondent, *inf* hack, journalist, news presenter, newsreader, photojournalist, writer.

repose *n* calm, calmness, comfort, ease, inactivity, peace, peacefulness, quiet, quietness, relaxation, respite, rest, serenity, tranquillity. ▷ SLEEP. *Opp* ACTIVITY.

reprehensible *adj* culpable, deplorable, disgraceful, immoral, objectionable, regrettable, shameful, unworthy, wicked. ▷ GUILTY. *Opp* INNOCENT.

represent *v* 1 act out, be an example of, embody, enact, epitomize, exemplify, exhibit, illustrate, impersonate, masquerade as, personify, pose as, present, stand for, symbolize, typify. 2 characterize, define, delineate, depict, describe, draw, paint, picture, portray, reflect, show, sketch. 3 act for, speak for, stand up for.

representation *n* depiction, figure, image, imitation, likeness, model, picture, portrait, portrayal, semblance, statue.

representative *adj* 1 archetypal, average, characteristic, illustrative, normal, typical. *Opp* ABNORMAL.

2 *representative government.* chosen, democratic, elected. • *n* 1 delegate, deputy, proxy, spokesman, spokeswoman, stand-in, substitute. 2 agent, *inf* rep, salesman, saleswoman. 3 ambassador, consul, diplomat, emissary, envoy. 4 *Amer* congressman, councillor, MP, ombudsman.

repress *v* 1 control, crush, curb, keep down, put down, quell, restrain, subdue, subjugate. 2 *repress emotion.* *inf* bottle up, inhibit, stifle, suppress.

repressed *adj* 1 cold, frustrated, inhibited, neurotic, *inf* prim and proper, tense, undemonstrative, *inf* uptight. *Opp* UNINHIBITED. 2 *repressed emotion.* *inf* bottled up, hidden, latent, subconscious, suppressed, unconscious.

repression *n* 1 censorship, coercion, control, dictatorship, oppression, restraint, subjugation, tyranny. 2 *repression of emotion.* *inf* bottling up, inhibition, suffocation, suppression.

repressive *adj* authoritarian, autocratic, brutal, cruel, despotic, dictatorial, harsh, oppressive, restricting, severe, totalitarian, tyrannical, undemocratic. *Opp* LIBERAL.

reprieve *n* amnesty, pardon, respite, stay of execution. • *v* forgive, let off, pardon, postpone execution, set free, spare.

reprimand *n* admonition, castigation, censure, condemnation, criticism, *inf* dressing-down, lecture, lesson, *inf* rap on the knuckles, rebuke, remonstration, reproach, reproof, scolding, *inf* slap on the wrist, *inf* slating, *inf* talking-to, *inf* telling-off, *inf* ticking-off. • *v* admonish, berate, blame, *inf* carpet, castigate, censure, condemn, criticize, find fault with, *inf* haul over the coals, lecture, *inf* rap, rate, rebuke, reprehend, reproach, reprove, scold, *inf* slate, take to task, *inf* teach a lesson, *inf* tell off, *inf* tick off, upbraid. *Opp* PRAISE.

reprisal *n* counter-attack, redress, repayment, retaliation, retribution, revenge, vengeance.

reproach *n* blame, disapproval, disgrace, scorn. ● *v* censure, criticize, scold, upbraid. ▷ REPRIMAND. *Opp* PRAISE.

reproachful *adj* censorious, critical, disapproving, disparaging, reproving, withering.

reproduce *v* 1 copy, counterfeit, duplicate, forge, imitate, mimic, photocopy, print, reissue, reprint. ▷ REPEAT. 2 breed, increase, multiply, procreate, produce offspring, propagate, regenerate, spawn.

reproduction *n* 1 breeding, cloning, increase, multiplying, procreation, proliferation, propagation, spawning. 2 *inf* carbon copy, clone, copy, duplicate, facsimile, fake, forgery, imitation, likeness, print, replica.

repudiate *v* 1 deny, dispute, rebuff, refute, reject, scorn, turn down. *Opp* ACKNOWLEDGE. 2 *repudiate an agreement*. discard, go back on, recant, renounce, rescind, retract, reverse, revoke.

repugnant *adj* ▷ REPULSIVE.

repulsive *adj* abhorrent, abominable, beastly, disagreeable, disgusting, distasteful, foul, gross, hateful, hideous, loathsome, nasty, nauseating, obnoxious, odious, offensive, *inf* off-putting,

repellent, repugnant, revolting, *inf* sick, sickening, unpalatable, unpleasant, unsavoury, unsightly, vile. ▷ UGLY. *Opp* ATTRACTIVE.

reputable *adj* creditable, dependable, good, highly regarded, honourable, prestigious, reliable, respectable, respected, trustworthy, up-market, well-thought-of, worthy. *Opp* DISREPUTABLE.

reputation *n* character, fame, name, prestige, renown, repute, standing, stature, status.

reputed *adj* alleged, believed, considered, deemed, judged, reckoned, regarded, rumoured, said, supposed, thought.

request *n* appeal, application, call, demand, entreaty, petition, plea, prayer, requisition, solicitation, suit, supplication. ● *v* appeal, apply (for), ask, beg, beseech, call for, claim, demand, entreat, implore, importune, invite, petition, pray for, require, requisition, seek, solicit, supplicate.

require *v* 1 be short of, lack, need, want. 2 *require a response*. call for, command, compel, direct, force, insist, instruct, make, oblige, order, put pressure on. ▷ REQUEST. **required** ▷ REQUISITE.

requirement *n* condition, demand, necessity, need, precondition, prerequisite, provision, proviso, qualification, stipulation.

requisite *adj* compulsory, essential, mandatory, necessary, needed, obligatory, prescribed, required, set, stipulated. *Opp* OPTIONAL.

requisition n application, authorization, demand, order, request. • v 1 demand, order, inf put in for, request. 2 appropriate, commandeer, confiscate, occupy, seize, take over, take possession of.

rescue n deliverance, emancipation, freeing, liberation, recovery, release, relief, salvage. • v 1 deliver, emancipate, extricate, free, let go, liberate, loose, ransom, release, save, set free. 2 get back, recover, retrieve, salvage.

research n analysis, examination, experimentation, exploration, fact-finding, investigation, probe, scrutiny, study. • v inf check out, experiment, investigate, probe, search, study.

resemblance n affinity, closeness, coincidence, comparison, conformity, congruity, correspondence, equivalence, likeness, similarity.

resemble v approximate to, bear resemblance to, be similar to, compare with, look like, mirror, inf take after.

resent v begrudge, be resentful about, envy, feel bitter about, grudge, object to, take exception to, inf take umbrage at.

resentful adj aggrieved, annoyed, begrudging, bitter, disgruntled, displeased, embittered, envious, grudging, irked, jaundiced, jealous, offended, inf peeved, put out, spiteful, unfriendly, vexed, vindictive. ▷ ANGRY.

resentment n animosity, bitterness, discontent, envy, grudge, hatred, hurt, ill will, irritation, jealousy, pique, rancour, spite,

unfriendliness, vexation, vindictiveness. ▷ ANGER.

reservation n 1 condition, doubt, hesitation, misgiving, proviso, qualification, qualm, reluctance, reticence, scruple. 2 hotel reservation. booking. 3 wildlife reservation. ▷ RESERVE.

reserve n 1 cache, fund, hoard, inf nest-egg, reservoir, savings, stock, stockpile, store, supply. 2 backup, deputy, pl reinforcements, replacement, stand-by, stand-in, substitute, understudy. 3 wildlife reserve. game park, preserve, protected area, reservation, safari park, sanctuary. 4 aloofness, caution, modesty, quietness, reluctance, reticence, self-consciousness, self-effacement, shyness, timidity. • v 1 earmark, hoard, hold back, keep, keep back, preserve, put aside, retain, save, set aside, stockpile, store up. 2 reserve seats. inf bag, book, order.
reserved ▷ RETICENT.

reside v reside in dwell in, inhabit, live in, lodge in, occupy, settle in.

residence n abode, address, domicile, dwelling, dwelling place, habitation, home, house, quarters, seat.

resident adj in residence, living in, permanent, staying. • n citizen, denizen, householder, inhabitant, inf local, native.

residual adj continuing, left over, persisting, remaining, spare, surplus.

resign v abandon, abdicate, inf chuck in, forsake, give up, leave, quit, relinquish, renounce, retire, stand down, step down, surrender, vacate.

resigned ▷ PATIENT. **resign yourself to** ▷ ACCEPT.

resilient adj 1 bouncy, elastic, firm, plastic, pliable, rubbery, springy, supple. Opp BRITTLE. 2 resilient person. adaptable, buoyant, irrepressible, strong, tough. Opp VULNERABLE.

resist v avoid, be resistant to, confront, counteract, defy, face up to, hinder, hold out against, impede, inhibit, keep at bay, oppose, prevent, rebuff, refuse, stand up to, withstand. ▷ FIGHT. Opp ASSIST, YIELD.

resistant adj defiant, hostile, intransigent, obstinate, opposed, stubborn, uncooperative, unresponsive, unyielding. **resistant to** impervious to, invulnerable to, opposed to, proof against, unaffected by, unsusceptible to. Opp SUSCEPTIBLE.

resolute adj adamant, bold, committed, constant, courageous, decided, decisive, determined, dogged, firm, immovable, immutable, indefatigable, derog inflexible, derog obstinate, persevering, persistent, relentless, resolved, single-minded, staunch, steadfast, strong-willed, derog stubborn, tireless, unbending, undaunted, unflinching, unswerving, untiring, unwavering. Opp IRRESOLUTE.

resolution n 1 boldness, constancy, determination, devotion, doggedness, firmness, derog obstinacy, perseverance, persistence, purposefulness, resolve, single-mindedness, steadfastness, derog stubbornness, tenacity, will-power. ▷ COURAGE. 2 commitment, oath, pledge, promise, undertaking, vow. 3 resolution at a meeting. decision, motion, proposal, statement. 4 resolution of a problem. answer, settlement, solution, sorting out.

resolve n ▷ RESOLUTION. ● v 1 agree, conclude, decide, determine, elect, fix, make a decision, opt, pass a resolution, settle, undertake, vote. 2 resolve a problem. answer, clear up, figure out, settle, solve, sort out, work out.

resonant adj booming, resounding, reverberant, reverberating, rich, ringing, sonorous, vibrant, vibrating.

resort n 1 alternative, course of action, expedient, option, recourse. 2 seaside resort. holiday town, retreat, spot. ● v resort to adopt, inf fall back on, have recourse to, make use of, turn to, use.

resound v boom, echo, resonate, reverberate, ring, rumble, vibrate. **resounding** ▷ RESONANT.

resourceful adj clever, creative, enterprising, imaginative, ingenious, innovative, inspired, inventive, original, inf smart, talented. Opp SHIFTLESS.

resources pl n 1 assets, capital, funds, money, possessions, property, reserves, riches, wealth. 2 natural resources. materials, raw materials.

respect n 1 admiration, appreciation, consideration, courtesy, deference, esteem, honour, liking, love, regard, reverence, tribute, veneration. 2 perfect in every respect. aspect, attribute, characteristic, detail, element, facet, feature, particular, point, property, quality, trait, way.

● *v* admire, appreciate, esteem, have high regard for, honour, look up to, revere, show respect to, think well of, value, venerate. *Opp* DESPISE.

respectable *adj* 1 decent, genteel, honest, honourable, law-abiding, respected, upright, virtuous, worthy. 2 *respectable clothes.* clean, decorous, modest, presentable, proper, seemly. *Opp* DISREPUTABLE. 3 *respectable sum.* ▷ CONSIDERABLE.

respectful *adj* admiring, civil, considerate, cordial, courteous, deferential, dutiful, gracious, humble, obliging, polite, proper, reverent, *derog* servile, thoughtful, well-mannered. *Opp* DISRESPECTFUL.

respective *adj* individual, own, particular, personal, separate, specific.

respite *n* break, *inf* breather, delay, hiatus, holiday, interval, *inf* let-up, lull, pause, recess, relaxation, relief, remission, rest, time off, vacation.

resplendent *adj* brilliant, dazzling, glittering, shining, splendid. ▷ BRIGHT.

respond *v* 1 answer, come back, counter, react, reciprocate, reply, retort. 2 *respond to a need.* ▷ SYMPATHIZE.

response *n* acknowledgement, answer, *inf* comeback, feedback, reaction, rejoinder, reply, retort, riposte.

responsible *adj* 1 at fault, culpable, guilty, liable, to blame. 2 *responsible person.* accountable, answerable, concerned, conscientious, dependable, diligent, dutiful, ethical, honest, in charge, law-abiding, loyal, mature, moral, reliable, sens-

ible, sober, steady, thinking, trustworthy. *Opp* IRRESPONSIBLE. 3 *responsible job.* executive, *inf* front-line, important, managerial, *inf* top. *Opp* MENIAL.

responsive *adj* alert, alive, aware, interested, open, perceptive, receptive, sensitive, sharp, sympathetic, willing. *Opp* UNINTERESTED.

rest *n* 1 break, *inf* breather, breathing-space, ease, hiatus, holiday, inactivity, interlude, intermission, interval, leisure, *inf* let-up, *inf* lie-down, lull, *inf* nap, pause, recess, relaxation, relief, remission, repose, respite, siesta, tea-break, time off, vacation. ▷ SLEEP. 2 base, holder, prop, stand, support, trestle, tripod. 3 ▷ REMAINDER.
● *v* 1 doze, have a rest, idle, laze, lie back, lie down, lounge, nod off, *inf* put your feet up, recline, relax, snooze, *inf* take it easy, unwind. ▷ SLEEP. 2 lean, place, position, prop, set, stand, support. 3 *It rests on the weather.* depend, hang, hinge, rely, turn. **come to rest** ▷ HALT.

restaurant *n* bistro, brasserie, buffet, café, cafeteria, canteen, carvery, diner, dining room, refectory, snack bar.

restful *adj* calm, calming, comfortable, leisurely, peaceful, quiet, relaxed, relaxing, soothing, still, tranquil, undisturbed, unhurried, untroubled. *Opp* EXHAUSTING.

restless *adj* 1 agitated, anxious, edgy, excitable, fidgety, highly-strung, impatient, *inf* jittery, jumpy, nervous, *inf* on tenterhooks, uneasy, worried. ▷ ACTIVE. 2 *restless night.* dis-

turbed, interrupted, sleepless,
inf tossing and turning,
troubled, uncomfortable,
unsettled. Opp RESTFUL.

restore v 1 bring back, give
back, put back, reinstate,
replace, return. 2 restore
antiques. clean, inf do up, fix,
inf make good, mend, rebuild,
recondition, refurbish, renew,
renovate, repair, touch up.
3 restore good relations. re-
establish, reinstate, reintroduce,
rekindle, revive. 4 restore to
health. cure, nurse, rejuvenate,
resuscitate, revitalize.

restrain v 1 check, control, curb,
govern, hold back, inhibit, keep
under control, limit, regulate,
rein in, repress, restrict, stifle,
stop, subdue, suppress. 2 arrest,
confine, detain, handcuff, harness, imprison, incarcerate, jail,
inf keep under lock and key,
lock up, muzzle, pinion, tie up.
restrained ▷ CALM, DISCREET.

restrict v circumscribe, confine,
control, cramp, enclose, impede,
imprison, inhibit, keep within
bounds, limit, regulate, shut.
▷ RESTRAIN. Opp FREE.

restriction n ban, constraint,
control, curb, curfew, inhibition,
limit, limitation, proviso, qualification, regulation, restraint,
rule, stipulation.

result n 1 conclusion, consequence, effect, end-product,
fruit, issue, outcome, repercussion, sequel, upshot. 2 result of a
trial. decision, judgement, verdict. 3 result of a game, sum.
answer, score, total. ● v arise, be
produced, come about, develop,
emerge, ensue, follow, happen,
issue, occur, proceed, spring,

stem, turn out. **result in**
▷ CAUSE.

resume v begin again, carry
on, continue, inf pick up the
threads, proceed, recommence,
reconvene, re-open, restart.

resumption n continuation,
re-opening, restart.

resurrect v breathe new life
into, bring back, raise (from the
dead), reawaken, restore, resuscitate, revive. ▷ RENEW.

retain v 1 inf hang on to, hold,
hold back, keep, maintain, preserve, reserve, save. Opp LOSE.
2 retain moisture. absorb, soak
up. 3 retain facts. keep in mind,
learn, memorize, remember.
Opp FORGET.

retaliate v avenge yourself, be
revenged, counter-attack, exact
retribution, inf get even, inf get
your own back, inf give tit for
tat, hit back, pay back, repay,
inf settle a score, strike back,
take revenge, wreak vengeance.

retaliation n counter-attack,
reprisal, retribution, revenge,
vengeance.

retard v hold back, obstruct,
slow down. ▷ DELAY. **retarded**
▷ BACKWARD.

reticent adj aloof, bashful, cautious, derog cold, cool, demure,
diffident, distant, modest, quiet,
remote, reserved, restrained,
retiring, secretive, self-effacing,
shy, silent, derog standoffish,
taciturn, timid, uncommunicative, undemonstrative, unforthcoming, unsociable, withdrawn.
Opp DEMONSTRATIVE.

retinue n attendants, company,
entourage, followers,
inf hangers-on, servants.

retire v 1 give up, leave, quit, resign. 2 *retire from society.* become reclusive, go away, go into retreat, withdraw. 3 go to bed. ▷ SLEEP.

retort n answer, *inf* comeback, rejoinder, reply, response, retaliation, riposte. ● v answer, counter, react, rejoin, reply, respond, retaliate, return.

retract v 1 draw in, pull back, pull in. 2 cancel, disclaim, *inf* have second thoughts about, recant, renounce, repeal, rescind, reverse, revoke, withdraw.

retreat n 1 departure, escape, evacuation, exit, flight, withdrawal. 2 *secluded retreat.* asylum, den, haven, hideaway, *inf* hideout, hiding-place, refuge, resort, sanctuary, shelter.
● v 1 back away, back down, decamp, depart, fall back, flee, give ground, leave, move back, pull back, retire, run away, take flight, *inf* take to your heels, *inf* turn tail, withdraw. 2 *the floods retreated.* ebb, flow back, recede, shrink back.
Opp ADVANCE.

retribution n compensation, recompense, redress, reprisal, retaliation, revenge, vengeance. *Opp* FORGIVENESS.

retrieve v bring back, find, get back, recapture, recoup, recover, regain, repossess, rescue, restore, return, salvage, save, take back, trace, track down.

retrograde adj backward, regressive, retreating, reverse.

retrospective adj backward-looking, looking back, nostalgic, with hindsight.

return n 1 arrival, homecoming, reappearance, re-entry. 2 *return to normality.* re-establishment (of), reversion. 3 *return of a problem.* recurrence, re-emergence, repetition. 4 *return of stolen goods.* replacing, restitution, restoration. 5 *return on an investment.* earnings, gain, income, interest, proceeds, profit, yield.
● v 1 backtrack, come back, do a U-turn, double back, go back, reassemble, reconvene, re-enter, retrace your steps, revert, turn back. 2 put back, readdress, replace, restore, send back. 3 *return money.* give back, refund, reimburse, repay. 4 *return a verdict. inf* come up with, deliver, give, report. 5 *The problem returned. inf* crop up again, happen again, reappear, recur, resurface.

reveal v announce, bare, betray, bring to light, confess, declare, dig up, disclose, display, divulge, exhibit, expose, *inf* give the game away, lay bare, leak, let out, let slip, make known, proclaim, produce, publish, show, show up, *inf* spill the beans, tell, uncover, unearth, unfold, unmask, unveil. *Opp* HIDE.

revel n carnival, festival, fête, *inf* jamboree, *inf* rave-up, *inf* spree. ▷ REVELRY.
● v carouse, celebrate, have fun, *inf* live it up, make merry, *inf* paint the town red. **revel in** ▷ ENJOY.

revelation n admission, announcement, confession, declaration, disclosure, discovery, exposé, exposure, *inf* leak, news, publication, unmasking, unveiling.

revelry n carousing, celebration, conviviality, festivity, fun, gaiety, *inf* high jinks, *inf* jollification, jollity, *inf* living it up, party, merrymaking, revelling, revels, *inf* spree.

revenge *n* reprisal, retaliation, retribution, vengeance.
• *v* avenge, repay. **be revenged**
▷ RETALIATE.

revenue *n* gain, income, interest, money, proceeds, profits, receipts, returns, takings, yield.

reverberate *v* boom, echo, pulsate, resonate, resound, ring, rumble, thunder, vibrate.

revere *v* admire, adore, esteem, feel reverence for, glorify, honour, idolize, pay homage to, praise, respect, venerate, worship. *Opp* DESPISE.

reverence *n* admiration, adoration, awe, deference, devotion, esteem, glorification, homage, honour, praise, respect, veneration, worship.

reverent *adj* adoring, awed, deferential, devoted, devout, pious, religious, respectful, reverential, solemn.
Opp IRREVERENT.

reverie *n* brown study, daydream, dream, fantasy, thought.

reverse *adj* back, backward, contrary, inverse, inverted, opposite, rear. • *n* 1 antithesis, contrary, converse, opposite. 2 back, rear, underside, wrong side. 3 defeat, difficulty, disaster, failure, mishap, misfortune, problem, reversal, set-back, *inf* upset, vicissitude. • *v* 1 change, invert, overturn, transpose, turn upside down. 2 *reverse a car.* back, drive backwards, go into reverse. 3 *reverse a decision.* annul, cancel, countermand, invalidate, negate, nullify, overturn, quash, repeal, rescind, retract, revoke, undo.

review *n* 1 *inf* post-mortem, reappraisal, reassessment, recapitulation, reconsideration, re-examination, report, retrospective, study, survey. 2 *book review.* appreciation, assessment, commentary, criticism, critique, evaluation, notice, *inf* write-up.
• *v* 1 appraise, assess, consider, evaluate, *inf* go over, inspect, reassess, recapitulate, reconsider, re-examine, scrutinize, study, survey, take stock, *inf* weigh up. 2 *review a book.* criticize, write a review of.

revise *v* 1 adapt, alter, change, correct, edit, improve, modify, overhaul, *inf* polish up, reconsider, rectify, *inf* redo, rephrase, revamp, reword, rewrite, update. 2 *revise for exams.* brush up, *inf* cram, study, *inf* swot.

revival *n* reawakening, rebirth, recovery, renaissance, renewal, restoration, resurgence, resurrection, return, revitalization, upsurge.

revive *v* 1 awaken, *inf* come round, *inf* come to, rally, reawaken, recover, rouse, waken. *Opp* RELAPSE. 2 bring back to life, *inf* cheer up, freshen, invigorate, refresh, renew, restore, resurrect, resuscitate, revitalize, strengthen.

revolt *n* civil war, coup, coup d'état, insurrection, mutiny, rebellion, revolution, rising, *inf* takeover, uprising.
• *v* 1 disobey, mutiny, rebel, riot, rise up. 2 appal, disgust, nauseate, offend, outrage, repel, sicken. **revolting** ▷ OFFENSIVE.

revolution *n* 1 ▷ REVOLT. 2 circuit, cycle, orbit, rotation, spin, turn. 3 change, reorganization, shift, transformation, *inf* turn-about, upheaval, U-turn.

revolutionary *adj* 1 insurgent, mutinous, rebel, rebellious, seditious, subversive.
2 *revolutionary ideas*. avant-garde, different, experimental, extremist, innovative, new, novel, progressive, radical, unheard-of. *Opp* CONSERVATIVE.
● *n* anarchist, extremist, freedom fighter, insurgent, mutineer, rebel, terrorist.

revolve *v* circle, go round, gyrate, orbit, pirouette, pivot, reel, rotate, spin, swivel, turn, twirl, wheel, whirl.

revulsion *n* abhorrence, aversion, disgust, hatred, loathing, nausea, outrage, repugnance.

reward *n* award, bonus, compensation, decoration, favour, honour, medal, payment, prize, recompense, remuneration, tribute. *Opp* PUNISHMENT.
● *v* compensate, decorate, honour, recompense, remunerate, repay. *Opp* PENALIZE, PUNISH. **rewarding**
▷ PROFITABLE, WORTHWHILE.

rhapsodize *v* be expansive, effuse, enthuse, *inf* go into raptures.

rhetoric *n* eloquence, expressiveness, *inf* gift of the gab, grandiloquence, oratory, rhetorical language, *derog* speechifying.

rhetorical *adj* [*most synonyms derog*] bombastic, florid, *inf* flowery, grandiloquent, grandiose, high-flown, oratorical, ornate, pretentious, verbose, wordy.

rhyme *n* doggerel, jingle.
▷ POEM.

rhythm *n* accent, beat, metre, movement, pattern, pulse, stress, tempo, time.

rhythmic *adj* beating, measured, metrical, regular, repeated, steady. *Opp* IRREGULAR.

ribald *adj* bawdy, coarse, earthy, *inf* naughty, racy, rude, smutty, vulgar. ▷ OBSCENE.

ribbon *n* band, braid, line, strip, stripe, tape, trimming. **in ribbons** ▷ RAGGED.

rich *adj* 1 affluent, *inf* flush, *inf* loaded, moneyed, prosperous, wealthy, *inf* well-heeled, well-off, well-to-do. *Opp* POOR. 2 *rich furnishings*. costly, elaborate, expensive, luxurious, luxurious, opulent, priceless, splendid, sumptuous, valuable. 3 *rich land*. fecund, fertile, fruitful, lush, productive. 4 *rich harvest*. abundant, ample, bountiful, copious, plentiful, profuse, prolific, teeming. 5 *rich colours*. deep, full, intense, strong, vibrant, vivid, warm. 6 *rich food*. cloying, creamy, fat, fattening, filling, heavy, luscious, sweet. **rich person** billionaire, capitalist, millionaire, plutocrat, tycoon.

riches *pl n* affluence, fortune, resources. ▷ WEALTH.

rickety *adj* dilapidated, flimsy, frail, insecure, ramshackle, shaky, tottering, tumbledown, unsteady, wobbly. ▷ WEAK.

rid *v* clear, deliver (from), free, purge. **get rid of** ▷ DESTROY, REMOVE.

riddle *n* 1 *inf* brain-teaser, conundrum, enigma, mystery, *inf* poser, problem, puzzle, question. 2 filter, sieve. ● *v* 1 filter, sieve, sift, strain. 2 *riddle with holes*. *inf* pepper, perforate, pierce, puncture.

ride n ▷ JOURNEY. ● v 1 *ride a bike.* control, freewheel, handle, pedal, sit on, steer. 2 *ride a horse.* canter, gallop, trot.

ridge n bank, crest, edge, embankment. ▷ HILL.

ridicule n badinage, banter, caricature, derision, jeering, laughter, mockery, parody, raillery, *inf* ribbing, sarcasm, satire, scorn, sneers, taunts, teasing. ● v be sarcastic, caricature, chaff, deride, guy, hold up to ridicule, jeer at, joke about, lampoon, laugh at, make fun of, mimic, mock, parody, pillory, *inf* poke fun at, *inf* rib, satirize, scoff at, *inf* send up, *inf* take the mickey, taunt, tease.

ridiculous adj absurd, amusing, comic, comical, crazy, *inf* daft, farcical, foolish, idiotic, illogical, irrational, laughable, ludicrous, mad, nonsensical, preposterous, senseless, silly, unbelievable. ▷ FUNNY, STUPID. *Opp* SENSIBLE.

rife adj abundant, common, endemic, prevalent, widespread.

rift n 1 break, chink, cleft, crack, fracture, gap, gulf, opening, split. 2 *rift between friends.* alienation, breach, difference, disagreement, separation.

rig n 1 *oil rig.* platform. 2 *sporting rig.* clothes, equipment, *inf* gear, kit, outfit, tackle. ● v **rig out** equip, fit out, kit out, supply.

right adj 1 decent, ethical, fair, good, honest, honourable, just, law-abiding, lawful, moral, principled, responsible, righteous, right-minded, upright, virtuous. 2 *right answers.* accurate, appropriate, correct, exact, faultless, fitting, perfect, precise, proper, suitable, true, truthful, valid,

veracious. 3 *the right way.* best, convenient, normal, preferable, preferred, recommended, sensible, usual. 4 *your right side.* right-hand, starboard [= *right facing bow of ship*]. 5 *right wing in politics.* conservative, fascist, reactionary, Tory. *Opp* LEFT, WRONG. ● n 1 decency, equity, fairness, goodness, honesty, integrity, justice, morality, propriety, reason, truth, virtue. 2 *right to free speech.* entitlement, freedom, liberty, prerogative, privilege. 3 *right to give orders.* authority, licence, position, power, title. ● v 1 correct, make amends for, put right, rectify, redress, remedy, repair, set right. 2 set upright, stand upright, straighten up.

righteous adj blameless, God-fearing, good, guiltless, *derog* holier-than-thou, just, law-abiding, moral, pious, *derog* sanctimonious, upright, virtuous. *Opp* SINFUL.

rightful adj authorized, bona fide, correct, just, lawful, legal, legitimate, licensed, proper, real, true, valid. *Opp* ILLEGAL.

rigid adj 1 adamantine, firm, hard, inelastic, inflexible, set, solid, steely, stiff, strong, unbending, wooden. ▷ OBSTINATE. 2 *rigid discipline.* austere, harsh, intransigent, stern, strict, unkind, unrelenting, unyielding. ▷ RIGOROUS. *Opp* FLEXIBLE.

rigorous adj 1 conscientious, demanding, exact, exacting, meticulous, painstaking, precise, punctilious, rigid, scrupulous, strict, stringent, thorough, tough, uncompromising, undeviating, unsparing, unswerving,

Opp LAX. **2** *rigorous climate.*
extreme, hard, harsh, inhospitable, severe, unfriendly, unpleasant. *Opp* MILD.

rim *n* brim, brink, circumference, edge, lip, perimeter.

rind *n* crust, husk, peel, skin.

ring *n* **1** band, bracelet, circle, circlet, collar, corona, eyelet, girdle, halo, hoop, loop, ringlet. **2** *boxing ring.* arena, enclosure, rink. **3** *drugs ring.* association, band, gang, organization, syndicate. ▷ GROUP. **4** *ring of a bell.* buzz, chime, clang, clink, jangle, jingle, knell, peal, ping, reverberation, tinkle, tintinnabulation, tolling. **5** *give me a ring.* *inf* bell, *inf* buzz, call. ● *v* **1** circle, encircle, enclose, encompass, surround. **2** boom, buzz, chime, clang, clink, jangle, jingle, peal, ping, resound, reverberate, sound (the knell), tinkle, toll. **3** call, *inf* give someone a buzz, phone, ring up, telephone.

rinse *v* bathe, clean, flush, sluice, swill, wash.

riot *n* affray, anarchy, brawl, chaos, commotion, disorder, disturbance, fracas, fray, hubbub, insurrection, lawlessness, mass protest, mêlée, mutiny, pandemonium, *inf* punch-up, revolt, rioting, rising, *inf* rumpus, strife, tumult, turmoil, unrest, uproar, violence. ● *v* brawl, *inf* go on the rampage, *inf* go wild, mutiny, rampage, rebel, revolt, rise up, run riot, *inf* take to the streets. ▷ FIGHT.

riotous *adj* anarchic, boisterous, chaotic, disorderly, lawless, mutinous, noisy, obstreperous, rebellious, rowdy, uncivilized, uncontrollable, undisciplined,

unrestrained, unruly, uproarious, violent, wild. *Opp* ORDERLY.

rip *v* gash, lacerate, pull apart, rend, shred, slit, split, tear.

ripe *adj* mature, mellow, ready to eat, seasoned.

ripen *v* age, come to maturity, develop, mature, mellow.

ripple *n* ▷ WAVE. ● *v* agitate, disturb, make waves, purl, ruffle, stir.

rise *n* **1** ascent, bank, climb, elevation, hill, hump, incline, ramp, ridge, slope. **2** *rise in prices.* escalation, gain, increase, increment, jump, leap, upsurge, upturn, upward movement. ● *v* **1** arise, ascend, climb, fly up, jump, leap, lift, lift off, mount, soar, spring, take off. **2** get to your feet, get up, stand up. **3** *prices rise each year.* escalate, grow, increase, spiral. **4** *cliffs rise above us.* loom, stand out, tower. **rise up** ▷ REBEL.

risk *n* **1** chance, likelihood, possibility. **2** danger, gamble, hazard, peril, speculation, uncertainty. ● *v* **1** chance, dare, endanger, hazard, jeopardize. **2** *risk money.* gamble, speculate, venture.

risky *adj inf* chancy, *inf* dicey, hazardous, *inf* iffy, perilous, precarious, unsafe. ▷ DANGEROUS. *Opp* SAFE.

ritual *n* ceremonial, ceremony, custom, formality, observance, practice, rite, routine, service, set procedure, tradition.

rival *n* adversary, antagonist, challenger, competitor, contender, contestant, enemy, opponent. ● *v* **1** challenge, compete with, contend with, contest, emulate, oppose, struggle with, undercut, vie with.

Opp COOPERATE. 2 compare with, equal, match, measure up to.

rivalry *n* antagonism, competition, conflict, contention, feuding, opposition, strife. *Opp* COOPERATION.

river *n* brook, channel, rivulet, stream, tributary, watercourse, waterway.

road *n* alley, avenue, boulevard, bypass, crescent, dual carriageway, *Amer* freeway, highway, lane, motorway, path, ring road, roadway, route, side-street, sliproad, street, thoroughfare, trunk road, way.

roam *v* amble, drift, meander, prowl, ramble, range, rove, saunter, stray, stroll, traipse, travel, walk, wander.

roar *v* bellow, cry out, growl, howl, shout, snarl, thunder, yell, yowl.

rob *v* burgle, *inf* con, defraud, hold up, loot, mug, pilfer from, plunder, ransack, rifle, steal from. ▷ STEAL.

robber *n* bandit, brigand, burglar, *inf* con-man, defrauder, embezzler, housebreaker, looter, mugger, pickpocket, raider, shoplifter, swindler, thief.

robbery *n* breaking and entering, burglary, *inf* con-fidence trick, embezzlement, fraud, *inf* hold-up, larceny, looting, mugging, pilfering, plunder, shoplifting, stealing, theft, thieving.

robe *n* bathrobe, caftan, cassock, cloak, dress, dressing gown, frock, gown, habit, kimono, surplice, vestment. ● *v* ▷ DRESS.

robust *adj* 1 athletic, brawny, fit, *inf* hale and hearty, hardy,

healthy, hearty, muscular, powerful, rugged, sound, strong, sturdy, tough, vigorous. 2 durable, serviceable, well-made. *Opp* WEAK.

rock *n* boulder, crag, flint, granite, limestone, marble, ore, outcrop, quartz, sandstone, scree, shale, slate, stone. ● *v* 1 lurch, move to and fro, pitch, reel, roll, shake, sway, swing, totter, wobble. 2 ▷ SHOCK.

rocky *adj* 1 barren, craggy, pebbly, rough, rugged, stony. 2 ▷ UNSTEADY.

rod *n* bar, baton, cane, pole, rail, shaft, spoke, staff, stick, strut, wand.

rogue *n* blackguard, charlatan, cheat, *inf* con-man, fraud, mischief-maker, rascal, ruffian, scoundrel, swindler, trickster, villain, wretch.

role *n* 1 character, impersonation, part, portrayal. 2 *role in a business.* contribution, duty, function, job, position, post, task.

roll *n* 1 cylinder, drum, reel, scroll, spool, tube. 2 catalogue, directory, index, inventory, list, listing, record, register. ● *v* 1 gyrate, move round, revolve, rotate, spin, turn, twirl, whirl. 2 coil, curl, furl, twist, wind, wrap. 3 *roll the lawn.* flatten, level out, smooth. 4 *roll in a storm.* lumber, lurch, pitch, reel, rock, stagger, sway, toss, totter, wallow, welter. **rolling** ▷ WAVY. **roll in, roll up** ▷ ARRIVE.

romance *n* 1 fantasy, legend, story, tale. 2 adventure, excitement, fascination, glamour, mystery. 3 amour, attachment, intrigue, liaison, love affair, relationship.

romantic adj 1 exotic, fairy-tale, glamorous, idealized, idyllic, imaginary, picturesque. 2 *romantic feelings*. affectionate, amorous, loving, passionate, tender. 3 *romantic fiction*. emotional, escapist, heart-warming, nostalgic, sentimental, *inf* soppy. 4 *romantic ideals*. *inf* head in the clouds, idealistic, illusory, impractical, quixotic, starry-eyed, unrealistic, Utopian, visionary. *Opp* REALISTIC.

room n 1 *inf* elbow-room, freedom, latitude, leeway, margin, scope, space. 2 apartment, cell, chamber, cubicle, office. **rooms** accommodation, dwelling, lodgings, quarters.

roomy adj capacious, commodious, large, sizeable, spacious, voluminous. ▷ BIG. *Opp* SMALL.

root n 1 rhizome, rootlet, tuber. 2 *root of a problem*. base, basis, bottom, cause, foundation, origin, seat, source, starting point. ● v **root out** ▷ REMOVE.

rope n cable, cord, hawser, lasso, line, strand, string, tether. ● v bind, hitch, lash, moor, tether, tie. ▷ FASTEN.

rot n 1 corrosion, decay, decomposition, deterioration, disintegration, dry rot, mould, putrefaction, wet rot. 2 *What rot!* ▷ NONSENSE. ● v become rotten, corrode, decay, decompose, degenerate, deteriorate, disintegrate, fester, go bad, *inf* go off, perish, putrefy, spoil.

rota n list, roster, schedule, timetable.

rotary adj revolving, rotating, spinning, turning.

rotate v 1 gyrate, move round, pirouette, pivot, reel, revolve, roll, spin, swivel, turn, turn anti-clockwise *or* clockwise, twiddle, twirl, twist, wheel, whirl. 2 *rotate duties*. alternate, take in turn, take turns.

rotten adj 1 bad, corroded, crumbling, decayed, decaying, decomposed, disintegrating, foul, mouldering, mouldy, *inf* off, overripe, putrid, tainted, unfit for consumption. 2 ▷ IMMORAL.

rough adj 1 broken, bumpy, coarse, craggy, irregular, knobbly, jagged, lumpy, pitted, ragged, rocky, rugged, rutted, stony, uneven. 2 *rough skin*. bristly, callused, chapped, coarse, leathery, scratchy, unshaven. 3 *rough sea*. agitated, choppy, stormy, tempestuous, turbulent, violent, wild. 4 *rough voice*. discordant, grating, gruff, harsh, hoarse, husky, rasping, raucous, strident. 5 *rough crowd, manners*. badly-behaved, blunt, brusque, churlish, ill-bred, impolite, loutish, rowdy, rude, surly, *inf* ugly, uncivil, uncivilized, undisciplined, unfriendly. 6 *rough treatment*. brutal, cruel, painful, violent. 7 *rough work*. amateurish, careless, crude, hasty, imperfect, inept, *inf* rough and ready, unfinished, unpolished, unskilful. 8 *rough estimate*. approximate, general, imprecise, inexact, sketchy, vague. *Opp* EXACT, GENTLE, SMOOTH.

roughly adv about, approximately, around, close to, nearly.

round adj 1 [*two-dimensional*] circular, curved, disc-shaped, ring-shaped. 2 [*three-dimensional*] bulbous, cylindrical, globe-shaped, globular, spherical. 3 *round stomach*. ample, full, plump, rotund, roun-

ded, well-padded. ▷ FAT.
● *n* bout, contest, game, heat,
stage. ● *v* skirt, travel round,
turn. **round off** ▷ COMPLETE.
round on ▷ ATTACK. **round
the bend** ▷ MAD. **round the
clock** ▷ CONTINUOUS. **round
up** ▷ ASSEMBLE.

roundabout *adj* circuitous, circular, devious, indirect, long,
meandering, oblique, rambling,
tortuous, twisting, winding.
Opp DIRECT. ● *n* 1 carousel,
merry-go-round. 2 traffic island.

rouse *v* 1 arouse, awaken, call,
get up, wake up. 2 *rouse to a
frenzy*. animate, excite, galvanize, goad, incite, inflame, provoke, stimulate, stir up, *inf* wind
up, work up.

rout *v* conquer, crush, overwhelm, put to flight, *inf* send
packing. ▷ DEFEAT.

route *n* course, direction, itinerary, journey, path, road, way.

routine *adj* accustomed, commonplace, customary, everyday,
familiar, habitual, normal, ordinary, planned, *inf* run-of-the-mill,
scheduled, uneventful, well-
rehearsed. ● *n* 1 course of action,
custom, *inf* drill, habit, method,
pattern, practice, procedure,
schedule, system, way. 2 *comedy
routine*. act, number, performance, programme, set piece.

row *n* 1 chain, column, cordon,
file, line, queue, rank, sequence,
series, string, tier. 2 ado, commotion, fracas, hubbub, hullabaloo,
racket, *inf* rumpus, tumult,
uproar. ▷ NOISE. 3 altercation,
argument, disagreement, dispute, fight, *inf* ructions,
inf slanging match, squabble.
▷ QUARREL. ● *v* 1 *row a boat*.

move, propel, scull.
2 ▷ QUARREL.

rowdy *adj* badly-behaved, boisterous, disorderly, irrepressible,
obstreperous, riotous, rough, turbulent, undisciplined, unruly,
violent, wild. ▷ NOISY.
Opp QUIET.

royal *adj* imperial, kingly,
majestic, princely, queenly,
regal, stately, sovereign.
● *n* [*inf*] member of royal family.

rub *v* 1 knead, massage, smooth,
stroke. 2 chafe, graze, scrape,
wear away. 3 *rub clean*. buff,
burnish, polish, scour, scrub,
shine, wipe. **rub it in**
▷ EMPHASIZE. **rub out**
▷ ERASE. **rub up the wrong
way** ▷ ANNOY.

rubbish *n* 1 debris, detritus,
dregs, dross, filth, flotsam and
jetsam, garbage, junk, leavings,
leftovers, litter, lumber, *inf* odds
and ends, refuse, rubble, scrap,
sweepings, trash, waste.
2 ▷ NONSENSE.

rubble *n* broken bricks, debris,
fragments, remains, ruins,
wreckage.

ruddy *adj* fresh, flushed, glowing, healthy, red, sunburnt.

rude *adj* 1 abrupt, abusive, bad-
mannered, blunt, boorish,
brusque, cheeky, churlish,
coarse, contemptuous, curt, discourteous, disparaging, disrespectful, graceless, ill-bred, ill-
mannered, impertinent,
impolite, improper, impudent,
in bad taste, inconsiderate,
indecent, insolent, insulting,
mocking, *inf* naughty, oafish,
offensive, offhand, peremptory,
personal (*remarks*), saucy,
scurrilous, shameless, tactless,
unchivalrous, uncivil, uncompli-

mentary, uncouth, ungracious, unprintable, vulgar. ▷ OBSCENE. **2** rude workmanship. basic, clumsy, crude, inartistic, primitive, rough, rough-hewn, simple, unpolished, unskilful, unsophisticated. Opp SOPHISTICATED. **be rude to** ▷ INSULT.

rudeness n abuse, inf backchat, bad manners, cheek, contempt, discourtesy, disrespect, ill-breeding, impertinence, impudence, incivility, insolence, insults, oafishness, tactlessness, vulgarity.

rudiments pl n basic principles, basics, elements, essentials, first principles, foundations, fundamentals.

rudimentary adj basic, crude, elementary, embryonic, initial, preliminary, primitive, provisional, undeveloped. Opp ADVANCED.

ruffian n inf brute, bully, hoodlum, hooligan, lout, rogue, scoundrel, thug, inf tough, villain, inf yob.

ruffle v **1** disturb, ripple, stir. **2** ruffle your hair. disarrange, dishevel, disorder, inf mess up, rumple, tangle, tousle. **3** ruffle your composure. agitate, confuse, disconcert, disquiet, fluster, irritate, inf nettle, inf rattle, inf throw, unnerve, unsettle, upset, worry. Opp SMOOTH.

rug n blanket, coverlet, mat, matting.

rugged adj **1** bumpy, craggy, irregular, jagged, pitted, rocky, rough, stony, uneven. **2** rugged conditions. arduous, difficult, hard, harsh, rough, severe, tough. **3** rugged good looks. burly, hardy, muscular, robust, rough, strong, sturdy, weather-beaten.

ruin n bankruptcy, collapse, inf crash, destruction, downfall, end, failure, fall, ruination, undoing, wreck. • v damage, demolish, destroy, devastate, flatten, overthrow, shatter, spoil, wreck. **ruins** debris, remains, rubble, wreckage.

ruined adj crumbling, derelict, dilapidated, fallen down, in ruins, ramshackle, tumbledown, uninhabitable, wrecked.

ruinous adj calamitous, cataclysmic, catastrophic, crushing, destructive, devastating, dire, disastrous, fatal, harmful, injurious, pernicious, shattering.

rule n **1** code, decree, pl guidelines, law, ordinance, precept, principle, regulation, ruling, statute. **2** administration, ascendancy, authority, command, control, domination, dominion, empire, government, influence, jurisdiction, management, mastery, power, regime, reign, sovereignty, supremacy, supremacy, sway. **3** as a general rule. convention, custom, norm, standard. • v **1** administer, command, control, direct, dominate, govern, hold sway, lead, manage, predominate, reign, run, superintend. **2** decide, decree, deem, determine, find, judge, pronounce, resolve. **rule out** ▷ EXCLUDE.

ruler n administrator, despot, dictator, emir, emperor, empress, governor, king, leader, lord, leader, manager, monarch, potentate, president, prince, princess, queen, regent, sovereign, sultan, tsar, viceroy. ▷ CHIEF.

rumour *n* gossip, hearsay, *inf* low-down, news, report, scandal, *inf* tittle-tattle, whisper.

run *n* 1 dash, gallop, jog, marathon, race, sprint, trot. 2 *run in the car*. drive, excursion, jaunt, journey, ride, *inf* spin, trip. 3 *run of bad luck*. chain, sequence, series, stretch. 4 *chicken run*. compound, coop, enclosure, pen. ● *v* 1 bolt, career, dash, gallop, hare, hurry, jog, race, rush, scamper, scurry, scuttle, speed, sprint, tear, trot. 2 *buses run hourly*. go, operate, provide a service, travel. 3 *car runs well*. function, perform, work. 4 *water runs downhill*. cascade, dribble, flow, gush, leak, pour, spill, stream, trickle. 5 *run a business* administer, conduct, control, direct, govern, look after, manage, rule, supervise. **run across** ▷ MEET. **run after** ▷ PURSUE. **run away** ▷ ESCAPE. **run into** ▷ MEET.

runner *n* 1 athlete, competitor, entrant, hurdler, jogger, participant, sprinter. 2 courier, dispatch-rider, messenger. 3 shoot, sprout, sucker, tendril.

runny *adj* fluid, free-flowing, liquid, thin, watery. *Opp* SOLID, VISCOUS.

rupture *n* 1 breach, break, burst, fracture, puncture, rift, split. 2 *rupture between friends*. break-up, separation. 3 [*medical*] hernia. ● *v* break, burst, fracture, part, separate, split.

rural *adj* agrarian, agricultural, bucolic, countrified, pastoral, rustic. *Opp* URBAN.

rush *n* 1 bustle, dash, haste, hurry, panic, race, scramble, speed, urgency. 2 *rush of water*. flood, gush, spate, surge. 3 *rush of people*. charge, onslaught, stampede. ● *v* bolt, burst, bustle, canter, career, charge, dash, fly, gallop, *inf* get a move on, hare, hasten, hurry, make haste, race, run, scamper, *inf* scoot, scramble, scurry, scuttle, shoot, speed, sprint, stampede, *inf* step on it, *inf* tear, zoom.

rust *v* become rusty, corrode, crumble away, oxidize, rot.

rustic *adj* 1 ▷ RURAL. 2 *rustic simplicity*. artless, naive, plain, rough, simple, uncomplicated, unsophisticated.

rusty *adj* 1 corroded, oxidized, tarnished. 2 [*inf*] *My French is rusty*. out of practice, unused, unpractised.

rut *n* 1 channel, furrow, groove, indentation, pothole, track, trough. 2 *in a rut*. dead end, pattern, routine, treadmill.

ruthless *adj* bloodthirsty, brutal, callous, cruel, fierce, hard, heartless, inhuman, merciless, pitiless, relentless, sadistic, unfeeling, unrelenting, unsympathetic, vicious, violent. *Opp* MERCIFUL.

S

sabotage *n* vandalism, wilful damage, wrecking. ● *v* cripple, damage, destroy, disable, disrupt, incapacitate, put out of action, vandalize, wreck.

sack *n* 1 bag, pouch. 2 *inf* the boot, *inf* the chop, dismissal, *inf* your cards. ● *v* 1 *inf* axe, discharge, dismiss, *inf* fire, give someone notice, *inf* give someone the boot, lay off, make redundant. 2 ▷ DESTROY, PLUN-DER. **get the sack** be dismissed, be sacked, *inf* get your cards, get your marching orders, lose your job.

sacred *adj* blessed, consecrated, dedicated, divine, godly, hallowed, holy, religious, revered, sacrosanct, sanctified, venerable, venerated. *Opp* SECULAR.

sacrifice *n* offering, propitiation, votive offering. ● *v* 1 kill, offer up, slaughter. 2 abandon, forfeit, forgo, give up, lose, relinquish, renounce, surrender.

sacrilege *n* blasphemy, desecration, heresy, impiety, irreverence.

sacrilegious *adj* blasphemous, disrespectful, heretical, impious, irreligious, irreverent, profane, ungodly. ▷ WICKED.

sacrosanct *adj* inviolable, inviolate, protected, untouchable. ▷ SACRED.

sad *adj* 1 abject, blue, broken-hearted, cheerless, crestfallen, dejected, depressed, desolate, despairing, despondent, disappointed, disconsolate, disheartened, dismal, dispirited, distressed, doleful, *inf* down, downcast, downhearted, dreary, forlorn, friendless, funereal, gloomy, glum, grave, grief-stricken, grieving, grim, heart-broken, *inf* heavy, heavy-hearted, homesick, in low spirits, *inf* in the doldrums, joyless, lachrymose, lonely, *inf* long-faced, *inf* low, lugubrious, melancholy, miserable, moody, moping, morose, mournful, pathetic, pessimistic, piteous, pitiable, pitiful, plaintive, poignant, regretful, rueful, saddened, sombre, sorrowful, sorry,

tearful, troubled, unhappy, upset, wistful, woebegone, woeful, wretched. 2 *sad news*. calamitous, depressing, dispiriting, distressing, grievous, heart-breaking, heart-rending, lamentable, moving, painful, regrettable, *inf* tear-jerking, touching, tragic, unfortunate, unwelcome, upsetting. 3 *sad state of disrepair*. ▷ UNSATISFACTORY. *Opp* HAPPY.

sadden *v inf* break someone's heart, depress, disappoint, discourage, dishearten, dismay, dispirit, distress, grieve, upset. *Opp* CHEER.

sadistic *adj* brutal, inhuman, monstrous, perverted, ruthless, vicious. ▷ CRUEL.

sadness *n* dejection, depression, desolation, despair, despondency, disappointment, disillusionment, distress, gloom, grief, heartbreak, heaviness, homesickness, hopelessness, loneliness, melancholy, misery, mournfulness, pessimism, poignancy, regret, sorrow, tearfulness, unhappiness, wistfulness, woe. *Opp* HAPPINESS.

safe *adj* 1 defended, foolproof, guarded, immune, impregnable, invulnerable, protected, secured, shielded. ▷ SECURE. *Opp* VULNERABLE. 2 *inf* alive and well, *inf* in one piece, intact, sound, undamaged, unharmed, unhurt, uninjured, unscathed. 3 *safe drivers*. cautious, circumspect, reliable, trustworthy. 4 *safe pets*. docile, friendly, harmless, tame. 5 *safe to drink*. drinkable, eatable, fit for human consumption, fresh, good, innocuous, non-toxic, pure, purified, uncontaminated, unpol-

luted, wholesome. **6** *safe vehicle.*
airworthy, roadworthy, seaworthy, tried and tested.
Opp DANGEROUS. **make safe**
▷ SECURE. **safe keeping** care,
charge, custody, guardianship,
protection.

safeguard *v* defend, look after,
protect, shelter, shield.

safety *n* **1** cover, immunity, protection, refuge, sanctuary, security, shelter. **2** *safety of air travel.*
dependability, reliability.

sag *v* be limp, bend, dip, droop,
fall, flop, hang down, sink,
slump. ▷ DROP.

sail *n* **1** canvas, mainsail, mizzen,
spinnaker. **2** cruise, sea-passage,
voyage. ● *v* **1** navigate, paddle,
pilot, punt, row, skipper, steer.
2 cruise, go sailing, put to sea,
set sail, steam.

sailor *n* boatman, captain,
pl crew, helmsman, mariner,
navigator, pilot, seafarer,
seaman, skipper, yachtsman,
yachtswoman.

saintly *adj* angelic, blessed,
godly, holy, innocent, moral,
pious, pure, religious, righteous,
sinless, virtuous. ▷ GOOD.
Opp SATANIC.

sake *n* account, advantage,
behalf, benefit, gain, good,
interest, welfare.

salary *n* earnings, income, pay,
payment, remuneration, stipend,
wages.

sale *n* **1** marketing, selling, trade,
traffic, transaction, vending.
2 auction, bazaar, car-boot sale,
jumble sale, mark-down.

salesperson *n* assistant, representative, salesman, saleswoman,
shopkeeper.

saliva *n inf* dribble, *inf* spit,
spittle, sputum.

sallow *adj* anaemic, colourless,
pale, pallid, pasty, unhealthy,
wan, yellowish.

salt *adj* brackish, briny, saline,
salted, salty, savoury.

salubrious *adj* health-giving,
healthy, hygienic, nice, pleasant,
sanitary, wholesome.

salute *n* acknowledgement, gesture, greeting, salutation, wave.
● *v* **1** address, greet, hail.
2 honour, pay respects to,
recognize.

salvage *n* **1** reclamation, recovery, rescue, retrieval, salvation,
saving. **2** recyclable material,
waste. ● *v* conserve, preserve,
reclaim, recover, recycle,
rescue, retrieve, reuse, save.

salvation *n* deliverance, escape,
redemption, rescue, saving, way
out. *Opp* DAMNATION.

salve *n* balm, cream, embrocation, liniment, lotion, ointment.
● *v* appease, comfort, ease, mitigate, mollify. ▷ SOOTHE.

same *adj* **1** actual, identical, self-same. **2** comparable, consistent,
corresponding, duplicate, equal,
equivalent, indistinguishable,
interchangeable, matching, parallel, similar, synonymous [=
having same meaning], twin,
unaltered, unchanged, uniform,
unvaried. *Opp* DIFFERENT.

sample *n* bit, demonstration,
example, foretaste, illustration,
indication, model, selection,
snippet, specimen, taste, trailer
(*of film*), trial offer.
● *v* experience, inspect, taste,
test, try.

sanatorium n clinic, convalescent home, hospital, nursing home, rest-home.

sanctify v beatify, bless, consecrate, hallow, purify.

sanctimonious adj holier-than-thou, hypocritical, moralizing, pietistic, pious, self-righteous, smug, superior, unctuous.

sanction n agreement, approval, authorization, inf blessing, confirmation, consent, endorsement, licence, permission, ratification, support, validation. • v agree to, allow, approve, authorize, confirm, consent to, endorse, inf give your blessing to, give permission for, licence, permit, ratify, support, validate.

sanctity adj godliness, piety. ▷ HOLINESS.

sanctuary n 1 asylum, haven, protection, refuge, retreat, safety, shelter. 2 wildlife sanctuary. conservation area, park, preserve, reservation, reserve. 3 holy sanctuary. chapel, church, holy place, sanctum, shrine, temple.

sands pl n beach, seaside, shore.

sane adj balanced, compos mentis, level-headed, lucid, normal, of sound mind, rational, reasonable, sensible, sound, stable, well-balanced. Opp MAD.

sanguine adj buoyant, cheerful, confident, hopeful, inf looking on the bright side, optimistic, positive. Opp PESSIMISTIC.

sanitary adj aseptic, clean, disinfected, germfree, healthy, hygienic, pure, salubrious, sterile, sterilized, uncontaminated, unpolluted, wholesome. Opp UNHEALTHY.

sanitation n drains, lavatories, sewage disposal, sewers.

sap n fluid, life-blood, moisture, vigour, vitality, vital juices. • v bleed, drain. ▷ EXHAUST.

sarcasm n derision, irony, mockery, ridicule, satire, scorn.

sarcastic adj biting, caustic, contemptuous, cutting, cynical, derisive, disparaging, ironic, mocking, sardonic, satirical, scathing, scornful, sharp, taunting.

sardonic adj bitter, black (comedy), cruel, cynical, malicious, mordant, sarcastic, wry.

sash n band, belt, cummerbund, girdle, waistband.

satanic adj demonic, devilish, diabolical, fiendish, infernal. ▷ WICKED. Opp SAINTLY.

satellite n 1 moon, planet, spacecraft, sputnik. 2 attendant, follower, inf hanger-on.

satire n burlesque, caricature, irony, lampoon, mockery, parody, ridicule, sarcasm, inf send-up, inf spoof, inf take-off, travesty.

satirical adj critical, derisive, disparaging, ironic, irreverent, mocking, scornful. ▷ SARCASTIC.

satirize v caricature, criticize, deride, hold up to ridicule, lampoon, laugh at, make fun of, mimic, mock, parody, pillory, inf send up, inf take off. ▷ RIDICULE.

satisfaction n comfort, content, contentment, delight, enjoyment, fulfilment, gratification, happiness, joy, pleasure, pride. Opp DISSATISFACTION.

satisfactory adj acceptable, adequate, inf all right, competent, fair, good enough, passable, satisfying, sufficient, suitable,

tolerable, *inf* up to scratch.
Opp UNSATISFACTORY.

satisfy *v* appease, assuage, comfort, comply with, content, fill, fulfil, gratify, meet, pacify, placate, please, quench, sate, satiate, serve (*a need*), settle, slake (*thirst*). *Opp* FRUSTRATE.
satisfied ▷ CONTENT.

saturate *v* drench, permeate, soak, souse, steep, suffuse, waterlog, wet.

sauce *n* 1 gravy, ketchup, relish. 2 ▷ INSOLENCE.

saucepan *n* cauldron, pan, pot, skillet, stockpot.

savage *adj* 1 barbarian, heathen, pagan, primitive, uncivilized, uneducated. *Opp* CIVILIZED. 2 *savage beasts.* feral, fierce, undomesticated, untamed, wild. *Opp* TAME. 3 *savage attack.* atrocious, barbarous, beastly, bestial, blistering, bloodthirsty, bloody, brutal, callous, cold-blooded, cruel, ferocious, fierce, heartless, inhuman, merciless, murderous, pitiless, ruthless, sadistic, unfeeling, vicious, violent. ● *n* barbarian, brute, heathen, wild man *or* woman. ● *v* attack, bite, claw, lacerate, maul, mutilate.

save *v* 1 be sparing with, collect, conserve, economize, hoard, hold back, keep, lay aside, put by, put in a safe place, reserve, retain, scrape together, set aside, *inf* stash away, store up. *Opp* WASTE. 2 bail out, deliver, free, liberate, ransom, recover, redeem, release, rescue, retrieve, salvage, set free. 3 *save from danger.* defend, deliver, guard, keep safe, preserve, protect, safeguard, screen, shelter, shield. 4 *saved me from looking a fool.*

prevent, spare, stop.
Opp ABANDON.

saving *n* economizing, frugality, parsimony, prudence, *inf* scrimping and scraping, thrift. **savings** funds, investments, *inf* nest-egg, reserves, resources, riches, wealth.

saviour *n* champion, defender, deliverer, *inf* friend in need, guardian, liberator, rescuer.

savour *n* flavour, piquancy, smell, tang, taste, zest.
● *v* appreciate, delight in, enjoy, relish, smell, taste.

savoury *adj* appetizing, delicious, flavoursome, piquant, salty. ▷ TASTY. *Opp* SWEET.

saw *n* 1 chainsaw, hacksaw. 2 [*old use*] just an old saw.
▷ SAYING. ● *v* ▷ CUT.

say *v* affirm, allege, announce, answer, articulate, *inf* come out with, comment, communicate, convey, declare, disclose, divulge, enunciate, exclaim, express, intimate, maintain, mention, mouth, phrase, pronounce, read out, recite, rejoin, remark, repeat, reply, report, respond, retort, reveal, signify, state, suggest, tell, utter.
▷ SPEAK, TALK.

saying *n* adage, aphorism, axiom, catchphrase, catchword, cliché, epigram, expression, formula, maxim, motto, phrase, precept, proverb, quotation, remark, *old use* saw, slogan, statement, tag, truism, watchword.

scale *n* 1 *scale forms in a kettle.* caking, coating, crust, deposit, encrustation, *inf* fur. 2 *scale on a thermometer.* calibration, gradation, graduation. 3 *the social scale.* hierarchy, ladder, order, ranking, spectrum. 4 *scale of a map*. proportion, ratio. ▷ SIZE. 5 *musical scale*. sequence, series. ● v ascend, clamber up, climb, go up, mount. **scales** balance, weighing machine.

scamper v dash, frisk, frolic, gambol, hasten, hurry, play, romp, run, rush, scuttle.

scan v 1 check, examine, eye, gaze at, investigate, look at, pore over, search, stare at, study, survey, view, watch. 2 *scan the papers*. flip through, glance at, read quickly, skim.

scandal n 1 discredit, disgrace, dishonour, disrepute, embarrassment, ignominy, infamy, notoriety, outrage, shame. 2 defamation, innuendo, libel, slander, slur, smear.

scandalize v affront, appal, disgust, horrify, offend, outrage, shock, upset.

scandalous adj 1 disgraceful, disgusting, dishonourable, disreputable, ignominious, immoral, indecent, infamous, licentious, notorious, outrageous, shameful, shocking, sinful, sordid, unmentionable, unspeakable, wicked. 2 *scandalous lie*. defamatory, libellous, scurrilous, slanderous, untrue.

scanty adj 1 inadequate, insufficient, meagre, mean, *inf* measly, minimal, scant, scarce, sparing, sparse, stingy. ▷ SMALL. *Opp* PLENTIFUL. 2 *scanty clothes*. revealing, *inf* see-through, skimpy, thin.

scapegoat n dupe, *sl* fall guy, *inf* front, whipping-boy, victim.

scar n blemish, brand, burn, cut, disfigurement, injury, mark, scab, scratch, wound. ● v brand,

burn, damage, deface, disfigure, injure, leave a scar on, mark, scratch, spoil.

scarce adj *inf* few and far between, inadequate, infrequent, in short supply, insufficient, lacking, meagre, rare, scant, scanty, sparse, *inf* thin on the ground, uncommon. *Opp* PLENTIFUL.

scarcely adv barely, hardly, only just.

scarcity n dearth, famine, insufficiency, lack, paucity, poverty, rarity, shortage, want. *Opp* PLENTY.

scare n alarm, jolt, shock, start. ▷ FRIGHT. ● v alarm, intimidate, make someone afraid, *inf* make someone jump, panic, shock, startle, terrorize, threaten, unnerve. ▷ FRIGHTEN. *Opp* REASSURE.

scarf n headscarf, muffler, shawl, stole.

scary adj [*inf*] creepy, eerie, hair-raising, unnerving. ▷ FRIGHTENING.

scathing adj biting, caustic, critical, mordant, satirical, savage, scornful, tart, withering. *Opp* COMPLIMENTARY.

scatter v 1 break up, disband, disintegrate, disperse, divide, send in all directions, separate. 2 *scatter seeds*. disseminate, shed, shower, sow, spread, sprinkle, strew, throw about. *Opp* GATHER.

scatterbrained adj absent-minded, careless, disorganized, forgetful, muddled, *inf* not with it, *inf* scatty, thoughtless, unreliable, unsystematic, vague. ▷ SILLY.

scavenge v forage, rummage, scrounge, search.

scenario n framework, outline, plan, scheme, storyline, summary.

scene n 1 area, background, context, locality, location, place, position, setting, site, situation, spot, whereabouts. 2 *beautiful scene*. picture, sight, spectacle. ▷ SCENERY. 3 *scene from a film*. *inf* clip, episode, part, section, sequence. 4 *nasty scene*. altercation, argument, *inf* carry-on, commotion, disturbance, furore, fuss, quarrel, *inf* row, tantrum, *inf* to-do.

scenery n 1 landscape, outlook, panorama, prospect, scene, terrain, view, vista. 2 *stage scenery*. backdrop, flats, set.

scenic adj attractive, beautiful, breathtaking, grand, impressive, lovely, panoramic, picturesque, pretty, spectacular.

scent n 1 aroma, bouquet, fragrance, nose, odour, perfume, redolence, smell. 2 eau de cologne, toilet water, perfume. 3 *animal's scent*. spoor, track, trail. • v ▷ SMELL. scented ▷ SMELLING.

sceptic n agnostic, cynic, doubter, *inf* doubting Thomas, unbeliever. *Opp* BELIEVER.

sceptical adj agnostic, cynical, disbelieving, distrustful, dubious, incredulous, mistrustful, questioning, suspicious, uncertain, unconvinced, unsure. *Opp* CONFIDENT.

scepticism n agnosticism, cynicism, disbelief, distrust, doubt, incredulity, mistrust, suspicion. *Opp* FAITH.

schedule n agenda, calendar, diary, itinerary, list, plan, programme, scheme, timetable. • v appoint, arrange, book, earmark, fix a time, organize, plan, programme, time.

scheme n 1 blueprint, design, draft, idea, method, plan, procedure, programme, project, proposal, strategy, system. 2 *dishonest scheme*. conspiracy, intrigue, machinations, manoeuvre, plot, ploy, *inf* racket, ruse, stratagem, subterfuge, tactic. 3 *colour scheme*. arrangement, design. • v collude, connive, conspire, *inf* cook up, hatch a plot, intrigue, manoeuvre, plan, plot.

scholar n academic, *inf* egghead, highbrow, intellectual, professor. ▷ PUPIL.

scholarly adj 1 academic, bookish, *inf* brainy, erudite, highbrow, intellectual, knowledgeable, learned, widely-read. 2 *scholarly treatise*. scientific, well-argued, well-informed.

scholarship n 1 academic achievement, education, erudition, intellectual attainment, knowledge, learning, research, wisdom. 2 *scholarship to Oxford*. award, bursary, endowment, grant.

school n 1 academy, boarding school, college, comprehensive, educational institution, high school, infant school, institute, junior school, kindergarten, nursery school, primary school, public school, secondary school, seminary. 2 adherents, circle, disciples, group, set. • v ▷ EDUCATE.

science n (body of) knowledge, discipline, field, subject, systematic study.

scientific *adj* analytical, methodical, orderly, organized, precise,
rational, systematic.

scientist *n inf* boffin, researcher,
scientific expert, technologist.

scintillating *adj* brilliant,
clever, dazzling, lively, sparkling, vivacious, witty. *Opp* DULL.

scoff *v* 1 belittle, be scornful,
deride, disparage, gibe, jeer,
laugh, mock, *inf* poke fun, ridicule, sneer, taunt. 2 ▷ EAT.

scold *v* admonish, berate, blame,
inf carpet, castigate, censure,
criticize, find fault with, lecture,
nag, rate, rebuke, reprehend,
reprimand, reproach, reprove,
inf slate, *inf* tell off, *inf* tick off,
upbraid.

scoop *n* 1 bailer, ladle, shovel,
spoon. 2 *news scoop.* exclusive,
inside story, *inf* latest, revelation. ● *v* dig, gouge, hollow,
scrape, shovel, spoon.

scope *n* 1 area, capacity, compass, competence, extent, field,
limit, range, reach, span, sphere,
terms of reference. 2 *scope for
expansion.* *inf* elbow-room, freedom, latitude, leeway, liberty,
opportunity, outlet, room, space.

scorch *v* blacken, burn, char,
heat, roast, sear, singe.

score *n* 1 amount, count, marks,
points, reckoning, result, sum,
tally, total. 2 cut, groove,
incision, line, mark, nick,
scrape, scratch. ● *v* 1 achieve,
add up, *inf* chalk up, earn, gain,
inf knock up, make, tally, win.
2 *score a groove.* engrave, scrape,
scratch. ▷ CUT. 3 *score music.*
orchestrate, write out. **settle a
score** ▷ RETALIATE.

scorn *n* contempt, derision,
detestation, disdain, disgust, dislike, disparagement, disrespect,

mockery, rejection, ridicule,
scoffing, taunting.
Opp ADMIRATION. ● *v* be scornful
about, deride, despise, disdain,
dislike, dismiss, disparage,
insult, jeer at, laugh at, look
down on, make fun of, mock,
reject, ridicule, scoff at, sneer at,
spurn, *inf* turn up your nose at.
Opp ADMIRE.

scornful *adj* condescending, contemptuous, derisive, disdainful,
dismissive, disparaging, disrespectful, insulting, jeering,
mocking, patronizing, sarcastic,
satirical, scathing, sneering,
inf snooty, *inf* snotty, supercilious, superior, taunting,
withering. *Opp* RESPECTFUL.

scoundrel *n* blackguard, good-
for-nothing, knave, rascal,
rogue, ruffian, scallywag, scamp,
villain, wretch.

scour *v* 1 clean, polish, rub,
scrape, scrub, shine, wash.
2 *scour the house.* comb, hunt
through, ransack, rummage
through, search, *inf* turn upside
down.

scourge *n* 1 affliction, bane,
curse, evil, misery, misfortune,
plague, torment, woe. 2 ▷ WHIP.
● *v* beat, *sl* belt, flog, lash, whip.

scout *n* lookout, spy. ● *v* explore,
hunt around, investigate, look
about, reconnoitre, search, spy.

scowl *v* frown, glower, grimace,
inf look daggers.

scraggy *adj* bony, emaciated,
gaunt, scrawny, skinny, starved,
thin. *Opp* PLUMP.

scramble *n* commotion, confusion, *inf* free-for-all, hurry,
mêlée, race, rush, scrimmage,
struggle. ● *v* 1 clamber, climb,
crawl, grope, scrabble.
2 *scramble for gold.* compete,

dash, fight, hasten, hurry, jostle, push, run, rush, scuffle, struggle, tussle, vie. 3 *scramble a message.* confuse, jumble, mix up.

scrap n 1 atom, bit, crumb, fraction. fragment, grain, iota, jot, mite, molecule, morsel, particle, piece, rag, shard, shred, sliver, snippet, speck, trace. 3 junk, leavings, litter, odds and ends, offcuts, refuse, remains, remnants, residue, rubbish, salvage, waste. 3 argument, quarrel, scuffle, *inf* set-to, squabble, tiff, tussle, wrangle. ▷ FIGHT.
• v 1 abandon, cancel, discard, *inf* ditch, drop, give up, jettison, throw away, write off. 2 argue, bicker, flare up, quarrel, spar, squabble, tussle, wrangle.
▷ FIGHT.

scrape n 1 abrasion, graze, injury, laceration, scratch, scuff, wound. 2 *awkward scrape.* difficulty, escapade, mischief, plight, prank, predicament, trouble.
• v 1 bark, bruise, damage, graze, injure, lacerate, scratch, scuff, skin, wound. 2 *scrape clean.* file, rasp, rub, scour, scrub. **scrape together** ▷ COLLECT.

scrappy *adj inf* bitty, careless, disjointed, fragmentary, imperfect, incomplete, inconclusive, sketchy, slipshod, unfinished, unsatisfactory. *Opp* PERFECT.

scratch n abrasion, dent, gash, gouge, graze, groove, indentation, injury, laceration, line, mark, score, scoring, scrape, scuff, wound. • v claw at, cut, damage the surface of, dent, gash, gouge, graze, groove, injure, lacerate, mark, score,

scrape, scuff, wound. **up to scratch** ▷ SATISFACTORY.

scrawl v doodle, scribble, write hurriedly. ▷ WRITE.

scream n & v bawl, caterwaul, cry, howl, roar, screech, shout, shriek, squeal, wail, yell, yowl.

screen n 1 blind, curtain, divider, partition. 2 camouflage, concealment, cover, disguise, protection, shelter, shield, smokescreen. 3 *sift through a screen.* filter, mesh, riddle, sieve, strainer. • v 1 divide, partition off. 2 camouflage, cloak, conceal, cover, disguise, guard, hide, mask, protect, safeguard, shade, shelter, shield, shroud, veil. 3 *screen employees. inf* check out, examine, investigate, vet.

screw n 1 bolt, screw-bolt. 2 rotation, spiral, turn, twist. • v rotate, turn, twist. **screw down** ▷ FASTEN. **screw up** ▷ BUNGLE, TIGHTEN.

scribble v ▷ SCRAWL.

scribe n clerk, copyist, secretary, writer.

script n 1 calligraphy, handwriting. 2 *script of a play.* libretto, screenplay, text, words.

scripture n bible, holy writ, sacred writings.

scrounge v beg, cadge, sponge on.

scrub v 1 brush, clean, rub, scour, wash. 2 ▷ CANCEL.

scruffy *adj* bedraggled, dirty, dishevelled, disordered, messy, ragged, scrappy, shabby, slovenly, *inf* tatty, unkempt, untidy, worn out. *Opp* SMART.

scruple n compunction, conscience, doubt, misgiving, qualm, reluctance, *inf* second thought. • v *He didn't scruple* *about taking the money.* be reluctant, have a conscience (about), have scruples (about), hesitate, *inf* think twice (about).

scrupulous *adj* 1 careful, conscientious, diligent, exacting, fastidious, finicky, meticulous, neat, painstaking, precise, punctilious, rigorous, strict, systematic, thorough. 2 *scrupulous honesty.* ethical, fair-minded, honest, honourable, just, moral, principled, proper, upright. *Opp* UNSCRUPULOUS.

scrutinize *v* analyse, check, examine, inspect, investigate, look closely at, observe, probe, sift, study, survey.

scrutiny *n* analysis, examination, inspection, investigation, probing, search, study.

sculpture *n* bust, carving, cast, effigy, figure, figurine, moulding, statue, statuette. ● *v* carve, cast, chisel, fashion, form, hew, model, mould, *inf* sculpt, shape.

scum *n* dirt, film, foam, froth, muck, suds.

scurrilous *adj* abusive, coarse, defamatory, derogatory, disparaging, indecent, insulting, libellous, low, obscene, offensive, shameful, slanderous, vile, vulgar.

sea *adj* marine, maritime, nautical, naval, ocean-going, oceanic, salt-water, seafaring, seagoing. ● *n inf* briny, *poet* deep, lake, ocean.

seal *n* 1 sea lion, walrus. 2 *royal seal.* badge, coat of arms, crest, emblem, impression, imprint, mark, monogram, sign, stamp, symbol. ● *v* 1 close, fasten, lock, make airtight, make watertight, plug, secure, shut, stick down, stop up. 2 *seal an agreement.*

clinch, conclude, confirm, decide, endorse, finalize, guarantee, ratify, settle, sign, validate.

seam *n* 1 join, stitching. 2 *seam of coal.* bed, layer, lode, stratum, thickness, vein.

seamy *adj* disreputable, distasteful, sordid, squalid, unpleasant, unsavoury, unwholesome.

search *n* check, enquiry, examination, hunt, inspection, investigation, look, probe, quest, scrutiny. ● *v* 1 explore, ferret about, hunt, investigate, *inf* leave no stone unturned, look, nose about, poke about, pry, seek. 2 *search suspects.* check, examine, *inf* frisk, inspect, scrutinize. 3 *search a house.* comb, go through, ransack, rifle, rummage through, scour. **searching** ▷ INQUISITIVE, THOROUGH.

seaside *n* beach, coast, coastal resort, sands, seashore, shore.

season *n* period, phase, time. ● *v* 1 add seasoning to, flavour, *inf* pep up, salt, spice. 2 age, mature, ripen.

seasonable *adj* convenient, favourable, opportune, suitable, timely. ▷ APPROPRIATE.

seasoning *n* condiments, dressing, flavouring, relish, spice.

seat *n* 1 armchair, bench, chair, couch, deckchair, easy chair, form, pew, place, rocking-chair, saddle, settee, sofa, stool, throne. 2 *country seat.* ▷ RESIDENCE. 3 ▷ BUTTOCKS. **seat yourself** ▷ SIT.

secluded *adj* cloistered, concealed, cut off, hidden, isolated, lonely, *inf* off the beaten track, private, remote, screened, sheltered, solitary, unfrequented, unvisited. *Opp* PUBLIC.

seclusion n concealment, hiding, isolation, privacy, remoteness, retirement, separation, solitude.

second adj added, additional, alternative, another, duplicate, extra, following, further, later, next, other, repeated, subsequent, twin. ● n 1 flash, instant, inf jiffy, moment, inf tick, inf twinkling. 2 second in a fight. assistant, deputy, helper, inf right-hand man or woman, second-in-command, stand-in, subordinate, supporter, understudy. ● v 1 aid, assist, back, encourage, give approval to, help, promote, side with, sponsor, support. 2 second to another job. move, reassign, relocate, transfer.

secondary adj 1 alternative, auxiliary, backup, extra, inessential, inferior, lesser, lower, minor, non-essential, reserve, second, spare, subordinate, subsidiary, supplementary, supporting, unimportant. 2 secondary sources. derivative, second-hand, unoriginal.

second-hand adj 1 inf hand-me-down, old, used, worn. Opp NEW. 2 second-hand experience. indirect, vicarious. Opp DIRECT.

second-rate adj indifferent, inferior, low-grade, mediocre, middling, ordinary, poor, second-best, second-class, undistinguished.

secret adj 1 clandestine, concealed, covert, disguised, hidden, inf hush-hush, invisible, private, secluded, shrouded, stealthy, undercover, underground, unknown. 2 secret papers. classified, confidential, intimate, personal, restricted,

sensitive, top secret, undisclosed, unpublished. 3 secret meanings. arcane, cryptic, esoteric, incomprehensible, mysterious, recondite. 4 secret about his private life. ▷ SECRETIVE. Opp OPEN, PUBLIC.

secretary n clerk, personal assistant, scribe, typist, word-processor operator.

secrete v 1 cloak, conceal, cover up, disguise, hide, mask, put away. 2 secrete fluid. emit, excrete, exude, leak, ooze. ▷ DISCHARGE.

secretion n discharge, emission, leakage.

secretive adj enigmatic, furtive, mysterious, quiet, reserved, reticent, secret, inf shifty, tight-lipped, uncommunicative, unforthcoming, withdrawn. Opp COMMUNICATIVE.

sect n cult, denomination, faction, party. ▷ GROUP.

sectarian adj bigoted, clannish, dogmatic, factional, inflexible, narrow, narrow-minded, partial, partisan, prejudiced.

section n bit, branch, chapter, compartment, component, department, division, element, fraction, fragment, group, instalment, part, passage, piece, portion, quarter, sample, sector, segment, slice, stage, subdivision, subsection.

sector n area, district, division, part, quarter, region, zone. ▷ SECTION.

secular adj earthly, lay, non-religious, temporal, worldly. Opp RELIGIOUS.

secure adj 1 cosy, defended, guarded, immune, impregnable, invulnerable, protected, safe, sheltered, shielded, snug, unharmed, unhurt, unscathed. **2** *the doors are secure.* bolted, burglar-proof, closed, fast, fastened, fixed, locked, shut, solid, tight, unyielding. **3** *secure faith.* certain, confident, firm, stable, steady, strong, sure. ● *v* **1** defend, guard, make safe, preserve, protect, shelter, shield. **2** anchor, attach, bolt, close, fix, lock, make fast. ▷ FASTEN. **3** *secure a loan.* acquire, gain, get, obtain, procure, win.

sedate *adj* calm, collected, composed, cool, decorous, deliberate, dignified, grave, level-headed, peaceful, proper, quiet, sensible, serene, serious, slow, sober, solemn, staid, tranquil, unruffled. *Opp* LIVELY. ● *v* calm, put to sleep, tranquillize, treat with sedatives.

sedative *adj* calming, narcotic, relaxing, soothing, soporific, tranquillizing. ● *n* anodyne, barbiturate, narcotic, opiate, sleeping-pill, tranquillizer.

sedentary *adj* desk-bound, inactive, seated, sitting down. *Opp* ACTIVE.

sediment *n* deposit, dregs, grounds, lees, precipitate, remains, residue, *inf* sludge.

sedition *n* agitation, incitement, rabble-rousing. ▷ REBELLION.

seduce *v* **1** allure, beguile, charm, deceive, ensnare, entice, inveigle, lure, mislead, tempt. **2** corrupt, deflower, dishonour, lead astray, ravish.

seduction *n* captivation, enticement, lure, temptation.

seductive *adj* alluring, appealing, attractive, bewitching, captivating, charming, enchanting, enticing, inviting, irresistible,

persuasive, provocative, tantalizing, tempting, sexy. *Opp* REPULSIVE.

see *v* **1** behold, catch sight of, discern, discover, distinguish, espy, glimpse, identify, look at, make out, mark, note, notice, observe, perceive, recognize, regard, sight, spot, spy, view, watch, witness. **2** *I see what you mean.* appreciate, comprehend, fathom, follow, *inf* get the hang of, grasp, know, realize, take in, understand. **3** *see problems ahead.* anticipate, envisage, foresee, foretell, imagine, picture, visualize. **4** *see what can be done.* consider, decide, mull over, think about, weigh up. **5** *see a play.* attend, watch. **6** *Are you still seeing him?* court, go out with, *inf* date, socialize with. **7** *see you home.* accompany, conduct, escort. **8** *saw fighting in the war.* endure, experience, go through, undergo. **9** *I saw Joe today.* encounter, meet, run into, talk to, visit. **see to** ▷ ORGANIZE.

seed *n* **1** egg, embryo, germ, ovule, ovum, semen, spawn, sperm, spore. **2** *seed in fruit.* pip, pit, stone. ● *v* ▷ SOW.

seek *v* aim at, ask for, aspire to, beg for, desire, go after, hunt for, inquire after, look for, pursue, request, search for, solicit, strive after, try for, want, wish for.

seem *v* appear, feel, give an impression of being, look, pretend to be, sound.

seep *v* dribble, drip, exude, flow, leak, ooze, percolate, run, soak, trickle.

seer *n* clairvoyant, fortune-teller, oracle, prophet, prophetess, psychic, sibyl, soothsayer.

seethe v 1 boil, bubble, foam, simmer. 2 be angry, fume, rage.

segment n bit, division, fragment, part, piece, portion, slice, wedge. ▷ SECTION.

segregate v compartmentalize, cut off, isolate, keep apart, put apart, separate, set apart.

segregation n 1 apartheid, discrimination. 2 isolation, quarantine, separation.

seize v 1 abduct, apprehend, arrest, capture, catch, clutch, *inf* collar, detain, grab, grasp, grip, hold, *inf* nab, snatch, take, take prisoner. 2 *seize a country*. annex, invade. 3 *seize property*. appropriate, commandeer, confiscate, hijack, impound, steal. *Opp* RELEASE. **seize up** ▷ STICK.

seizure n 1 abduction, annexation, appropriation, arrest, capture, confiscation, hijacking, theft, usurpation. 2 [*medical*] attack, convulsion, epileptic fit, fit, paroxysm, spasm, stroke.

seldom adv infrequently, occasionally, rarely.

select adj choice, chosen, elite, exceptional, exclusive, favoured, finest, first-class, *inf* handpicked, prime, privileged, rare, selected, special, topquality. *Opp* ORDINARY. ● v appoint, cast (*an actor*), choose, decide on, elect, nominate, opt for, pick, prefer, settle on, single out, vote for.

selection n 1 choice, option, pick, preference. 2 *selection of goods*. assortment, range, variety. 3 *selection from the classics*. excerpts, extracts, passages.

selective adj careful, *inf* choosy, discerning, discriminating, particular, specialized. *Opp* INDISCRIMINATE.

self-confident adj assertive, assured, collected, cool, outgoing, poised, positive, selfassured, self-possessed, sure of yourself. ▷ BOLD. *Opp* SELF-CONSCIOUS.

self-conscious adj awkward, bashful, blushing, diffident, embarrassed, ill at ease, insecure, nervous, self-effacing, shy, uncomfortable. ▷ TIMID. *Opp* SELF-CONFIDENT.

self-contained adj 1 complete, independent, separate. 2 aloof, cold, reserved, self-reliant, undemonstrative, unemotional.

self-control n calmness, composure, coolness, patience, restraint, self-discipline, selfpossession, will-power.

self-denial n abstemiousness, fasting, moderation, selfsacrifice, temperance, unselfishness. *Opp* SELF-INDULGENCE.

self-employed adj freelance, independent.

self-esteem n 1 ▷ SELF-RESPECT. 2 arrogance, conceit, egotism, self-importance, self-love, smugness, vanity.

self-explanatory adj apparent, clear, patent, plain, self-evident. ▷ OBVIOUS.

self-governing adj autonomous, free, independent, sovereign.

self-important adj arrogant, bombastic, conceited, haughty, officious, pompous, pretentious, smug, *inf* snooty, *inf* stuck-up, supercilious, superior.

self-indulgence n extravagance, gluttony, greed, hedonism, pleasure, profligacy, self-gratification. ▷ SELFISHNESS. *Opp* SELF-DENIAL.

self-indulgent adj dissipated, extravagant, gluttonous, greedy, hedonistic, immoderate, pleasure-loving, profligate. ▷ HEDONISTIC. *Opp* ABSTEMIOUS.

selfish adj acquisitive, avaricious, covetous, demanding, egocentric, egotistical, grasping, greedy, inconsiderate, mean, mercenary, miserly, self-centred, self-indulgent, self-interested, self-seeking, thoughtless, ungenerous. *Opp* UNSELFISH.

selfishness n avarice, covetousness, egotism, greed, meanness, miserliness, self-indulgence, self-interest, self-love, thoughtlessness.

self-reliant adj ▷ SELF-SUFFICIENT.

self-respect n dignity, honour, integrity, morale, pride, self-esteem.

self-righteous adj complacent, *inf* goody-goody, *inf* holier-than-thou, mealy-mouthed, pietistic, pious, pompous, priggish, sanctimonious, self-satisfied, smug, superior.

self-sufficient adj autonomous, independent, self-contained, self-reliant, self-supporting.

self-willed adj determined, dogged, forceful, headstrong, inflexible, intractable, intransigent, *inf* mulish, obstinate, *inf* pig-headed, stubborn, uncontrollable, uncooperative, wilful.

sell v 1 auction, barter, deal in, *inf* keep, offer for sale, peddle, *inf* put under the hammer, retail, sell off, stock, tout, trade, *inf* trade in, traffic in, vend. 2 advertise, market, promote, *inf* push.

seller n agent, dealer, merchant, pedlar, purveyor, *inf* rep, representative, retailer, salesman, saleswoman, shop assistant, shopkeeper, stockist, supplier, trader, tradesman, vendor, wholesaler.

seminal adj basic, creative, formative, important, influential, innovative, new, original, primary.

send v 1 address, consign, convey, deliver, direct, dispatch, fax, forward, mail, post, remit, ship, transmit. 2 fire, launch, project, release, shoot. **send away** ▷ DISMISS. **send down** ▷ IMPRISON. **send for** ▷ SUMMON. **send-off** ▷ GOODBYE. **send out** ▷ EMIT. **send round** ▷ CIRCULATE. **send up** ▷ PARODY.

senile adj *inf* in your dotage, old, *derog* past it.

senior adj chief, elder, higher, major, older, principal, revered, superior, well-established. *Opp* JUNIOR.

sensation n 1 awareness, feeling, perception, sense. 2 *She caused a sensation.* commotion, excitement, furore, outrage, scandal, stir, thrill.

sensational adj 1 electrifying, exciting, hair-raising, lurid, melodramatic, shocking, spine-tingling, startling, thrilling. 2 [*inf*] *sensational result.* amazing, astonishing, astounding, breathtaking, electrifying, exciting, extraordinary, *inf* fabulous, *inf* fantastic, *inf* great, incredible, marvellous, remarkable, spectacular, superb, surprising, unbelievable, unexpected, wonderful.

sense *n* **1** awareness, consciousness, faculty, feeling, sensation. **2** hearing, sight, smell, taste, touch. **3** gumption, intelligence, intuition, judgement, logic, *inf* nous, perception, reason, reasoning, understanding, wisdom, wit. **4** *the sense of a message.* coherence, connotations, *inf* drift, gist, import, intelligibility, meaning, message, point, purport, significance, substance. ● *v* be aware (of), detect, discern, divine, feel, guess, *inf* have a hunch, hear, notice, perceive, *inf* pick up vibes, realize, respond to, see, suspect, understand. **make sense of** ▷ UNDERSTAND.

senseless *adj* **1** anaesthetized, comatose, numb, stunned, unconscious. **2** absurd, crazy, fatuous, meaningless, pointless, purposeless, silly. ▷ STUPID.

sensible *adj* **1** calm, commonsense, cool, discriminating, intelligent, judicious, levelheaded, logical, prudent, rational, realistic, reasonable, sage, sane, serious-minded, sound, straightforward, thoughtful, wise. *Opp* STUPID. **2** *sensible phenomena.* ▷ TANGIBLE. **3** *sensible clothes.* comfortable, functional, *inf* no-nonsense, practical, useful. *Opp* IMPRACTICAL. **sensible of** alert to, alive to, appreciative of, aware of, in touch with, mindful of, responsive to, *inf* wise to.

sensitive *adj* **1** considerate, perceptive, receptive, responsive, susceptible, sympathetic, tactful, thoughtful, understanding. **2** *sensitive temperament.* emotional, hypersensitive, thin-skinned, touchy. **3** *sensitive skin.* delicate, fine, fragile, painful,

soft, sore, tender. **4** *sensitive topic.* confidential, controversial, delicate, secret, tricky. *Opp* INSENSITIVE. **sensitive to** affected by, aware of, considerate of, perceptive about, receptive to, responsive to.

sensual *adj* animal, bodily, carnal, fleshly, physical, pleasure-loving, self-indulgent, voluptuous. ▷ SEXY. *Opp* ASCETIC.

sensuous *adj* hedonistic, luxurious, rich, sumptuous. ▷ SENSUAL.

sentence *n* decision, judgement, pronouncement, punishment, ruling. ● *v* condemn, pass judgement on, pronounce sentence on.

sentiment *n* **1** attitude, belief, idea, judgement, opinion, outlook, thought, view. **2** *sentiment of a poem.* emotion, feeling.

sentimental *adj* **1** emotional, nostalgic, romantic, soft-hearted, sympathetic, tearful, tender, warm-hearted, *inf* weepy. **2** [*derog*] gushing, insincere, maudlin, mawkish, *inf* mushy, over-emotional, *inf* sloppy, *inf* soppy, *inf* sugary, treacly, unrealistic. *Opp* CYNICAL.

sentimentality *n* emotionalism, insincerity, mawkishness, nostalgia, *inf* slush.

sentry *n* guard, lookout, patrol, sentinel, watch, watchman.

separable *adj* detachable, distinguishable, removable.

separate *adj* apart, autonomous, cut off, detached, different, disjoined, distinct, divided, divorced, fenced off, free-standing, independent, individual, isolated, particular, secluded, segregated, separated, shut off, unattached, unconnected, unique, unrelated, withdrawn. ● *v* 1 break up, cut off, detach, disconnect, disengage, disentangle, dismember, dissociate, divide, fence off, hive off, isolate, keep apart, part, pull apart, segregate, sever, split, sunder, take apart, unfasten, unhook, unravel. 2 *The paths separate here.* branch, diverge, fork. 3 *separate the men from the boys.* distinguish, filter out, remove, single out, sort out. 4 *His parents separated.* become estranged, divorce, part company, *inf* split up. *Opp* COMBINE, UNITE.

separation *n* 1 cutting off, detachment, disconnection, dissociation, division, fragmentation, parting, rift, severance, splitting. *Opp* CONNECTION. 2 *separation of partners.* break, *inf* break-up, divorce, estrangement, rift, split. *Opp* UNION.

septic *adj* festering, infected, inflamed, poisoned, putrefying, putrid, suppurating.

sequel *n* consequence, continuation, development, *inf* follow-up, issue, outcome, result, upshot.

sequence *n* 1 chain, concatenation, course, cycle, line, order, procession, progression, range, row, run, series, set, string, succession, train. 2 *sequence from a film. inf* clip, episode, excerpt, extract, scene.

serene *adj* 1 calm, idyllic, peaceful, placid, quiet, restful, still, tranquil, undisturbed, unperturbed, unruffled, untroubled. 2 *serene temperament.* composed, contented, cool, easygoing, equable, even-tempered, imperturbable, peaceable, poised, self-possessed, *inf* unflappable. *Opp* BOISTEROUS, EXCITABLE.

series *n* 1 chain, concatenation, course, cycle, line, order, procession, programme, progression, range, row, run, sequence, set, string, succession, train. 2 *TV series.* mini-series, serial, *inf* soap, soap opera.

serious *adj* 1 dignified, earnest, grave, grim, humourless, long-faced, pensive, sedate, sober, solemn, sombre, staid, stern, straight-faced, thoughtful, unsmiling. *Opp* CHEERFUL. 2 grave, important, *inf* life-and-death, momentous, significant, urgent, weighty. 3 *serious illness.* acute, alarming, awful, calamitous, critical, dangerous, dreadful, ghastly, grievous, life-threatening, nasty, severe, terrible, unfortunate, unpleasant, violent. *Opp* TRIVIAL. 4 *serious offer.* genuine, honest, in earnest, sincere.

sermon *n* address, discourse, homily, lecture, lesson, talk.

serpentine *adj* labyrinthine, meandering, roundabout, sinuous, tortuous, twisting, winding. *Opp* STRAIGHT.

serrated *adj* indented, jagged, notched, saw-like, toothed, zigzag. *Opp* STRAIGHT.

servant *n* assistant, attendant, *derog* dogsbody, *inf* domestic, *derog* drudge, *derog* flunkey, helper, *derog* hireling, *derog* lackey, *derog* menial, *pl* retinue, *inf* skivvy, slave.

serve *v* 1 aid, assist, *inf* be at someone's beck and call, further, help, look after, minister to, wait upon, work for. 2 *serve in the forces.* be employed, do your duty, fight. 3 *serve goods.* distribute, dole out, give out, provide,

sell, supply. 4 *serve at table*.
carve, *inf* dish up, wait. 5 *serve a
sentence*. complete, go through,
pass, spend.

service *n* 1 aid, assistance,
benefit, favour, help, kindness.
2 *service of the community*.
attendance (on), employment
(by), ministering (to), work (for).
3 *bus service*. organization, provision, system, timetable. 4 *My car
needs a service*. check-over, maintenance, overhaul, repair, servicing. 5 *church service*. ceremony,
meeting, rite, ritual, worship.
● *v* check, maintain, mend, overhaul, repair, tune.

serviceable *adj* dependable, durable, functional, hard-wearing,
lasting, practical, strong, tough,
usable.

servile *adj* abject, *inf* boot-
licking, cringing, fawning,
flattering, grovelling, humble,
ingratiating, menial, obsequious, slavish, submissive, subservient, sycophantic, toadying,
unctuous. *Opp* BOSSY. **be servile**
▷ GROVEL.

serving *n* helping, plateful,
portion, ration.

session *n* 1 assembly, conference, hearing, meeting, sitting.
2 period, term, time.

set *adj* 1 *set price*. advertised,
agreed, arranged, definite, fixed,
pre-arranged, scheduled, standard. 2 *set in your ways*. predictable, regular, unchanging,
unvarying. ▷ STUBBORN.
● *n* 1 batch, category, class,
clique, collection, kind, series,
sort. ▷ GROUP. 2 *TV set*. apparatus, receiver. 3 *set for a play*.
scene, scenery, setting, stage.
● *v* 1 arrange, deploy, deposit,
lay, leave, locate, lodge, park,

place, plant, *inf* plonk, put, position, rest, set down, set out,
settle, situate, stand, station.
2 *set a clock*. adjust, correct, put
right, regulate. 3 *set a post in concrete*. embed, fasten, fix. 4 *set like
concrete*. congeal, harden, *inf* jell,
stiffen. 5 *set a question*. ask, formulate, frame, phrase, pose, present, put forward, suggest. 6 *set
a date*. allocate, allot, appoint,
decide, designate, determine,
establish, name, prescribe,
settle. **set about** ▷ ATTACK,
BEGIN. **set free** ▷ LIBERATE. **set
off** ▷ DEPART, EXPLODE. **set on**
▷ ATTACK. **set on fire**
▷ IGNITE. **set out** ▷ DEPART.
set up ▷ ESTABLISH.

set-back *n* *inf* blow, complication, delay, difficulty, disappointment, *inf* hitch, hold-up, impediment, misfortune, obstacle,
problem, reverse, snag, upset.

settee *n* chaise longue, couch,
sofa.

setting *n* 1 background, context,
environment, frame, habitat,
location, place, position, site,
surroundings. 2 *setting for a
play*. backdrop, scene, scenery,
set.

settle *v* 1 arrange, conclude, deal
with, organize, put in order,
straighten out. 2 alight, come to
rest, land, *inf* make yourself comfortable, *inf* park yourself,
pause, rest, sit down. 3 *settle
things in place*. deploy, deposit,
lay, lodge, park, place, position,
put, rest, set, situate. ▷ SET.
4 *the dust settled*. calm down,
clear, sink, subside. 5 *settle what
to do*. agree, decide, establish,
fix. 6 *settle differences*. end, put
an end to, reconcile, resolve,
sort out, square. 7 *settle debts*.

clear, discharge, pay, pay off.
8 *settle new territory.* colonize,
occupy, populate, set up home
in, stay in.

settlement *n* **1** camp, colony,
community, kibbutz, outpost,
town, village. **2** agreement,
arrangement, contract, payment.

settler *n* colonist, immigrant,
newcomer, pioneer.

sever *v* **1** amputate, break, cut
off, detach, disconnect, part, separate, split. ▷ CUT. **2** *sever a
relationship.* abandon, break off,
discontinue, end, put an end to,
terminate.

several *adj* assorted, different, a
few, a handful of, many, miscellaneous, a number of, some,
sundry, various.

severe *adj* **1** brutal, cold, cold-
hearted, cruel, dour, exacting,
forbidding, glowering, grave,
grim, hard, harsh, inexorable,
merciless, obdurate, relentless,
rigorous, stern, stony, strict,
unbending, uncompromising,
unkind, unsympathetic, unyielding. **2** *severe illness.* acute, critical, dangerous, drastic, fatal,
great, intense, keen, life-
threatening, mortal, nasty, serious, sharp, terminal. **3** *severe
penalties.* draconian, extreme,
maximum, stringent. **4** *severe
weather.* adverse, bad, inclement, violent. ▷ COLD, STORMY.
5 *severe challenge.* arduous,
demanding, difficult, onerous,
punishing, taxing, tough.
6 *severe style.* austere, bare,
chaste, plain, simple, spartan,
stark, unadorned.
Opp FRIENDLY, MILD, ORNATE.

sew *v* darn, hem, mend, repair,
stitch.

sewer *n* drain, drainage, *pl* sanitation, septic tank.

sewing *n* dressmaking, embroidery, mending, needlepoint,
needlework, tapestry.

sex *n* **1** gender. **2** carnal knowledge, coitus, copulation, coup-
ling, fornication, *inf* going to
bed, intercourse, intimacy, love-
making, mating, seduction,
sexual intercourse, sexual relations, union. **have sex (with)**
be intimate (with), copulate
(with), fornicate (with), have
sexual intercourse (with), make
love (to), mate (with), *sl* screw,
seduce.

sexism *n inf* chauvinism,
discrimination, prejudice.

sexual *adj* arousing, earthy,
erotic, physical, sensual, sexy,
voluptuous.

sexy *adj* **1** arousing, desirable,
erotic, flirtatious, provocative,
seductive, sensual, sensuous,
suggestive, sultry, tempting,
voluptuous. **2** aroused, lecherous, lustful, passionate, *sl* randy.
3 dirty, indecent, *inf* naughty,
obscene, pornographic,
inf raunchy, risqué, rude,
smutty, *inf* steamy, titillating,
vulgar.

shabby *adj* **1** dilapidated, dingy,
dirty, dowdy, drab, faded,
frayed, grubby, mangy,
inf moth-eaten, ragged, run-
down, *inf* scruffy, seedy,
tattered, *inf* tatty, threadbare,
worn, worn-out. *Opp* SMART.
2 *shabby behaviour.* contemptible, despicable, discreditable,
dishonest, dishonourable, disreputable, ignoble, mean, shameful,
shoddy, unfair, unkind,
unworthy. *Opp* HONOURABLE.

shack n cabin, hovel, hut, lean-to, shanty, shed.

shade n 1 ▷ SHADOW. 2 awning, blind, canopy, covering, curtain, parasol, screen, shelter, shield, umbrella. 3 colour, hue, tinge, tint, tone. 4 *shades of meaning*. degree, nicety, nuance, variation. • v 1 camouflage, conceal, cover, hide, mask, obscure, protect, screen, shield, shroud, veil. 2 *shade with pencil*. block in, darken, fill in.

shadow n 1 darkness, dimness, dusk, gloom, gloomy, semi-darkness, shade. 2 *The sun casts shadows*. outline, silhouette. 3 *shadow of doubt*. ▷ HINT. • v follow, inf keep tabs on, keep watch on, pursue, stalk, inf tail, track, trail, watch.

shadowy adj 1 faint, hazy, indistinct, nebulous, obscure, unrecognizable, vague. ▷ GHOSTLY. 2 ▷ SHADY.

shady adj 1 cool, dark, dim, dusky, gloomy, leafy, shaded, shadowy, sheltered, sunless. Opp SUNNY. 2 *shady character*. dishonest, disreputable, dubious, inf fishy, inf shifty, suspicious, untrustworthy. Opp HONEST.

shaft n 1 arrow, column, handle, pillar, pole, post, rod, stem, stick, upright. 2 mine, pit, tunnel, well, working. 3 *shaft of light*. beam, gleam, ray, streak.

shaggy adj bushy, dishevelled, fleecy, hairy, hirsute, rough, tousled, unkempt, untidy, woolly. Opp SMOOTH.

shake v 1 convulse, heave, jump, quake, quiver, rattle, rock, shiver, shudder, sway, totter, tremble, vibrate, waver, wobble. 2 agitate, flourish, gyrate, jerk, jiggle, joggle, sway, swing, twirl,

twitch, vibrate, wag, inf waggle, wave, inf wiggle. 3 distress, disturb, frighten, perturb, inf rattle, shock, startle, inf throw, unnerve, unsettle, upset. ▷ SURPRISE.

shaky adj 1 decrepit, dilapidated, feeble, flimsy, frail, insecure, precarious, ramshackle, rickety, rocky, unsteady, weak, wobbly. 2 *shaky voice*. faltering, quavering, quivering, trembling, tremulous. 3 *shaky start*. nervous, tentative, uncertain, unimpressive, unpromising. Opp STEADY, STRONG.

shallow adj empty, facile, foolish, frivolous, glib, insincere, puerile, silly, skin-deep, slight, superficial, trivial, unconvincing. Opp DEEP.

sham adj artificial, bogus, counterfeit, ersatz, fake, false, fraudulent, imitation, mock, inf pretend, pretended, simulated, synthetic. • n counterfeit, fake, fraud, hoax, imitation, pretence, inf put-up job, simulation. • v counterfeit, fake, feign, imitate, pretend, simulate.

shambles pl n [inf] chaos, confusion, devastation, disorder, mess, muddle, inf pigsty, inf tip.

shame n 1 chagrin, degradation, discredit, disgrace, dishonour, distress, embarrassment, guilt, humiliation, ignominy, infamy, loss of face, mortification, opprobrium, remorse, stain, stigma. 2 *What a shame!* outrage, pity, scandal. • v abash, chagrin, chasten, disgrace, embarrass, humble, humiliate, make someone ashamed, mortify, inf put someone in their place, inf show someone up.

shamefaced *adj* 1 ashamed, chagrined, *inf* hang-dog, humiliated, mortified, penitent, *inf* red-faced, remorseful, repentant, sorry. 2 modest, self-conscious, sheepish, shy. ▷ BASHFUL. *Opp* SHAMELESS.

shameful *adj* base, contemptible, degrading, demeaning, deplorable, discreditable, disgraceful, dishonourable, embarrassing, humiliating, ignominious, infamous, inglorious, low, mean, mortifying, outrageous, scandalous, unworthy. *Opp* HONOURABLE.

shameless *adj* barefaced, bold, brazen, flagrant, immodest, impudent, insolent, rude, shocking, unabashed, unashamed, unblushing, unrepentant, unselfconscious, wanton. *Opp* SHAMEFACED.

shape *n* 1 body, build, figure, physique, profile, silhouette. 2 *geometrical shape.* configuration, figure, form, model, mould, outline, pattern. ● *v* adapt, adjust, carve, cast, cut, fashion, form, frame, give shape to, model, mould, *inf* sculpt, sculpture, whittle.

shapeless *adj* 1 amorphous, formless, indeterminate, nebulous, undefined, unformed, unstructured, vague. 2 *shapeless figure.* dumpy, misshapen, unattractive. *Opp* SHAPELY.

shapely *adj* attractive, *inf* curvaceous, good-looking, graceful, neat, voluptuous, well-proportioned. *Opp* SHAPELESS.

share *n* allocation, allowance, bit, cut, division, due, fraction, helping, part, percentage, piece, portion, proportion, quota, ration, serving. ● *v* 1 allocate, allot, apportion, deal out, distribute, divide, dole out, *inf* go halves or shares (with), halve, portion out, ration out, split. 2 cooperate, join, participate, take part. **shared** ▷ JOINT.

sharp *adj* 1 cutting, fine, jagged, keen, knife-edged, needle-sharp, pointed, razor-sharp, sharpened, spiky. 2 *sharp bend, drop.* abrupt, acute, angular, hairpin, precipitous, sheer, steep, sudden, surprising, unexpected. 3 *sharp focus.* clear, distinct, well-defined. 4 *sharp storm.* heavy, intense, severe, sudden, violent. 5 *sharp frost.* biting, bitter, keen. ▷ COLD. 6 *sharp pain.* acute, excruciating, stabbing, stinging. 7 *sharp reply.* acerbic, acid, barbed, biting, caustic, critical, cutting, hurtful, mocking, mordant, sarcastic, sardonic, scathing, tart, trenchant, unkind, vitriolic. 8 *sharp mind.* acute, agile, alert, astute, bright, clever, crafty, *inf* cute, discerning, incisive, intelligent, penetrating, perceptive, probing, quick-witted, shrewd, *inf* smart. 9 *sharp eyes.* observant, *inf* peeled (*keep your eyes peeled*), watchful, wide-open. 10 *sharp taste, smell.* acid, acrid, bitter, piquant, pungent, sour, spicy, tangy, tart. 11 *sharp sound.* clear, ear-splitting, high, high-pitched, penetrating, piercing, shrill, staccato, strident. *Opp* BLUNT, DULL, SLIGHT.

sharpen *v* file, grind, hone, make sharp, whet. *Opp* BLUNT.

shatter *v* blast, break, break up, burst, crack, dash to pieces, destroy, disintegrate, explode, pulverize, smash, *inf* smash to smithereens, splinter, wreck. **shattered** ▷ SURPRISED, WEARY.

sheaf n bunch, bundle, file, ream.

shear v clip, strip, trim. ▷ CUT.

sheath n casing, covering, scabbard, sleeve.

sheathe v cocoon, cover, encase, enclose, put away, wrap.

shed n hut, lean-to, outhouse, potting-shed, shack, shelter, storehouse. ● v abandon, cast off, discard, drop, let fall, moult, scatter, shower, spill. **shed light** ▷ SHINE.

sheen n brightness, burnish, glaze, gleam, gloss, lustre, patina, polish, radiance, shine.

sheep n ewe, lamb, ram.

sheepish adj abashed, ashamed, bashful, coy, embarrassed, guilty, meek, shamefaced, shy, timid. Opp SHAMELESS.

sheer adj 1 absolute, complete, downright, out and out, pure, thoroughgoing, total, unadulterated, unmitigated, unqualified, utter. 2 sheer cliff. perpendicular, precipitous, steep, vertical. 3 sheer silk. diaphanous, filmy, fine, flimsy, gauzy, gossamer, inf see-through, thin, translucent, transparent.

sheet n 1 [paper] folio, leaf, page. 2 [glass, etc] pane, panel, plate. 3 [ice, etc] area, blanket, coating, covering, expanse, film, layer, skin, stretch, surface, veneer. 4 [rock] lamina, stratum.

shell n 1 carapace (of tortoise), case, casing, covering, crust, exterior, façade, hull, husk, outside, pod. 2 cartridge, projectile. ● v attack, blitz, bomb, bombard, fire at, shoot at, strafe.

shellfish n bivalve, crustacean, mollusc.

shelter n 1 asylum, cover, haven, lee, protection, refuge, safety, sanctuary, security. 2 barrier, cover, fence, hut, roof, screen, shield. 3 accommodation, lodging, home, housing, resting place. 4 air-raid shelter. bunker. ● v 1 defend, guard, keep safe, protect, safeguard, screen, shade, shield. 2 shelter a runaway. give shelter to, harbour, hide, inf put up. **sheltered** ▷ QUIET.

shelve v 1 defer, lay aside, postpone, put off, put on ice. 2 ▷ SLOPE.

shield n barrier, defence, guard, protection, safeguard, screen, shelter. ● v cover, defend, guard, keep safe, protect, safeguard, screen, shade, shelter.

shift n 1 adjustment, alteration, change, move, switch, transfer. 2 night shift. crew, gang, group, inf stint, team. ● v adjust, alter, budge, change, reposition, switch, transfer, transpose. ▷ MOVE. **shift for yourself** ▷ MANAGE.

shiftless adj idle, indolent, inefficient, irresponsible, lazy, unenterprising. Opp RESOURCEFUL.

shifty adj crafty, cunning, deceitful, devious, dishonest, evasive, inf foxy, furtive, scheming, secretive, inf shady, slippery, sly, tricky, untrustworthy, wily. Opp STRAIGHTFORWARD.

shimmer v flicker, glimmer, glisten, ripple. ▷ SHINE.

shine n brightness, burnish, glaze, gleam, glint, gloss, lustre, patina, phosphorescence, polish, radiance, reflection, sheen, shimmer, sparkle. ● v 1 beam, be luminous, blaze, dazzle, flare, flash, glare, gleam, glint, glisten, glitter, radiate, reflect, scintillate, shed light, shimmer, sparkle, twinkle. 2 *shine at maths.* be clever, do well, excel, stand out. 3 *shine your shoes.* brush, buff up, clean, polish, rub up. **shining** ▷ BRIGHT, CONSPICUOUS.

shingle *n* gravel, pebbles, stones.

shiny *adj* bright, brilliant, burnished, gleaming, glistening, glossy, luminous, lustrous, phosphorescent, polished, reflective, shining, sleek, smooth. *Opp* DULL.

ship *n* boat, craft, vessel. ● *v* carry, convey, deliver, ferry, move, send, transport.

shirk *v* avoid, dodge, duck, evade, get out of, neglect, shun, *sl* skive, sidestep.

shiver *n* flutter, frisson, quiver, rattle, shake, shudder, tremor, vibration. ● *v* chatter, flap, flutter, quake, quaver, quiver, rattle, shake, shudder, tremble, twitch, vibrate.

shock *n* 1 blow, collision, impact, jolt, thud. 2 *came as a shock.* *inf* bombshell, surprise, *inf* thunderbolt. 3 *state of shock.* dismay, distress, fright, trauma, upset. ● *v* 1 alarm, amaze, astonish, astound, daze, dismay, distress, dumbfound, frighten, *inf* give someone a turn, jolt, numb, paralyse, rock, scare, shake, stagger, startle, stun, stupefy, surprise, *inf* throw, traumatize, unnerve. 2 *Cruelty shocks us.* appal, disgust, horrify, offend, outrage, revolt, scandalize, sicken.

shoddy *adj* 1 cheap, flimsy, gimcrack, inferior, poor quality, *inf* rubbishy, second-rate, *sl* tacky, *inf* tatty, tawdry,

inf trashy. 2 *shoddy work.* careless, messy, slipshod, *inf* sloppy, slovenly, untidy. *Opp* SUPERIOR, CAREFUL.

shoe *n* boot, clog, *pl* footwear, moccasin, plimsoll, sandal, slipper, trainer, wellington.

shoemaker *n* bootmaker, cobbler.

shoot *n* branch, bud, new growth, offshoot, sucker, twig. ● *v* 1 *shoot a gun.* discharge, fire. 2 *shoot someone.* bombard, fire at, gun down, hit, kill, *inf* let fly at, open fire on, shell, strafe, *inf* take pot-shots at. 3 *shoot out of bed.* bolt, dart, dash, fly, hurtle, leap, race, run, rush, speed, spring, streak. 4 *plants shoot in the spring.* bud, burgeon, flourish, grow, put out shoots, spring up, sprout.

shop *n* boutique, cash-and-carry, department store, emporium, establishment, hypermarket, market, minimarket, outlet, store, supermarket.

shopkeeper *n* dealer, merchant, retailer, salesman, saleswoman, storekeeper, tradesman, tradeswoman.

shopper *n* buyer, customer, patron.

shopping *n* 1 buying, *inf* spending-spree. 2 goods, purchases.

shopping centre *n* arcade, complex, hypermarket, mall, precinct.

shore *n* 1 beach, coast, sands, seashore, seaside, shingle, strand. ● *v* **shore up** ▷ SUPPORT.

short *adj* 1 diminutive, dumpy, little, midget, petite, *inf* pint-sized, slight, small, squat, stubby, stumpy, stunted, tiny, *inf* wee. **2** *short visit*. brief, cursory, curtailed, fleeting, momentary, passing, quick, short-lived, temporary, transient. **3** *short book*. abbreviated, abridged, compact, concise, shortened, succinct. **4** *in short supply*. deficient, inadequate, insufficient, lacking, limited, low, meagre, scanty, scarce, sparse, wanting. **5** *a short manner*. abrupt, bad-tempered, blunt, brusque, cross, curt, gruff, grumpy, impolite, irritable, sharp, snappy, taciturn, terse, testy, unfriendly, unkind. *Opp* EXPANSIVE, LONG, PLENTIFUL, TALL. **cut short** ▷ SHORTEN.

shortage *n* absence, dearth, deficiency, deficit, insufficiency, lack, paucity, poverty, scarcity, shortfall, want. *Opp* PLENTY.

shortcoming *n* bad habit, defect, drawback, failing, fault, foible, imperfection, vice, weakness, weak point.

shorten *v* abbreviate, abridge, compress, condense, curtail, cut, cut down, cut short, précis, prune, reduce, summarize, take up *(clothes)*, trim, truncate. *Opp* LENGTHEN.

shortly *adv* old use anon, before long, by and by, presently, soon.

short-sighted *adj* **1** myopic, near-sighted. **2** unadventurous, unimaginative, without vision.

short-tempered *adj* abrupt, crabby, cross, crusty, curt, gruff, irascible, irritable, peevish, shrewish, snappy, testy, touchy, waspish.

shot *n* **1** ball, bullet, missile, pellet, projectile, round, slug. **2** *heard a shot*. bang, blast, crack, explosion, report.

3 *first-class shot*. marksman, markswoman, sharpshooter. **4** *give it a shot*. attempt, chance, *inf* crack, endeavour, *inf* go, *inf* stab, try. **5** *photographic shot*. photograph, picture, scene, snap, snapshot.

shout *v* bawl, bellow, call, cheer, clamour, cry out, exclaim, howl, rant, roar, scream, screech, shriek, whoop, yell. *Opp* WHISPER.

shove *v* *inf* barge, crowd, drive, elbow, hustle, jostle, press, push, shoulder, thrust.

shovel *v* clear, dig, scoop, shift.

show *n* **1** drama, entertainment, performance, play, presentation, production. **2** *flower show*. competition, demonstration, display, exhibition, *inf* expo. **3** *show of strength*. appearance, demonstration, illusion, impression, pose, pretence, threat. **4** *just for show*. affectation, exhibitionism, flamboyance, ostentation, showing off. ● *v* **1** bare, demonstrate, display, divulge, exhibit, expose, make public, make visible, manifest, present, produce, reveal, uncover. **2** appear, be seen, be visible, catch the eye, come out, emerge, materialize, *inf* peep through, stand out, stick out. **3** *show the way*. conduct, direct, escort, guide, indicate, lead, point out. **4** *show kindness*. bestow, confer, grant, treat with. **5** *The graph shows the results of the survey*. depict, illustrate, picture, portray, represent. **6** *Show me how*. describe, explain, instruct, make clear, teach, tell. **7** *Tests show I was right*. attest, bear out, confirm, demonstrate, evince, manifest, prove, substantiate, verify, witness. **show off**

▷ BOAST. **show up** ▷ ARRIVE, HUMILIATE.

showdown n confrontation, crisis, inf decider, inf moment of truth.

shower n cloudburst, downpour, sprinkling. ▷ RAIN. ● v 1 rain, spatter, splash, spray, sprinkle. 2 shower with gifts. heap, inundate, load, overwhelm.

show-off n inf big-head, boaster, conceited person, egotist, exhibitionist, inf poser, poseur, swaggerer.

showy adj bright, conspicuous, elaborate, fancy, flamboyant, inf flashy, fussy, garish, gaudy, loud, lurid, ornate, ostentatious, inf over the top, pretentious, vulgar. Opp DISCREET.

shred n atom, bit, fragment, grain, hint, iota, jot, piece, scrap, sliver, snippet, speck, trace. ● v cut to shreds, destroy, grate, rip up. **shreds** rags, ribbons, tatters.

shrewd adj acute, artful, astute, calculating, canny, clever, crafty, cunning, discerning, discriminating, intelligent, knowing, observant, perceptive, perspicacious, quick-witted, sharp, sly, smart, wily, wise. Opp STUPID.

shriek v cry, scream, screech, squawk, squeal.

shrill adj ear-splitting, harsh, high, high-pitched, jarring, piercing, raucous, screaming, screeching, sharp, shrieking, strident, treble. Opp GENTLE, SONOROUS.

shrine n altar, chapel, holy of holies, holy place, place of worship, sanctum, tomb.

shrink v 1 contract, decrease, diminish, dwindle, lessen, narrow, reduce, shorten. ▷ SHRIVEL. Opp EXPAND. 2 shrink with fear. cower, cringe, flinch, quail, recoil, retire, shy away, wince, withdraw. Opp ADVANCE.

shrivel v become parched, dehydrate, droop, dry out, dry up, wilt, wither, wrinkle. ▷ SHRINK.

shroud n blanket, cloak, cover, mantle, mask, pall, veil. ● v camouflage, cloak, conceal, cover, enshroud, envelop, hide, mask, screen, swathe, veil.

shrub n bush, plant, tree.

shudder v be horrified, quake, quiver, shake, shiver, squirm, tremble, vibrate.

shuffle v 1 disorganize, jumble, mix, mix up, rearrange, reorganize. 2 shuffle along. drag your feet, limp, shamble.

shun v avoid, disdain, flee, give (someone) the cold shoulder, rebuff, reject, shy away from, spurn, steer clear of. Opp SEEK.

shut v bolt, close, fasten, latch, lock, seal, secure, slam. **shut in** ▷ CONFINE, IMPRISON. **shut off** ▷ ISOLATE. **shut out** ▷ EXCLUDE. **shut up** ▷ CONFINE, IMPRISON, SILENCE.

shutter n blind, louvre, screen.

shy adj apprehensive, bashful, cautious, coy, diffident, hesitant, inhibited, introverted, modest, inf mousy, nervous, reserved, reticent, retiring, self-conscious, self-effacing, sheepish, timid, timorous, withdrawn. Opp ASSERTIVE, UNINHIBITED. ● v ▷ THROW.

sibling n brother, sister, twin.

sick adj **1** afflicted, ailing, bed-ridden, diseased, indisposed, infirm, inf laid up, poorly, sickly, inf under the weather, unwell. ▷ ILL. **2** airsick, bilious, carsick, nauseated, nauseous, queasy, seasick. **3** sick of rudeness. annoyed (by), bored (with), disgusted (by), inf fed up (with), nauseated (by), sickened (by), tired, weary. **4** [inf] sick joke. ▷ MORBID. **be sick** ▷ VOMIT.

sicken v **1** fall ill, take sick. **2** appal, disgust, nauseate, offend, repel, revolt, inf turn someone off, inf turn someone's stomach. **sickening** ▷ REPULSIVE.

sickly adj **1** ailing, anaemic, delicate, feeble, frail, pale, pallid, inf peaky, unhealthy, wan, weak. ▷ ILL. Opp HEALTHY. **2** sickly sentiment. cloying, maudlin, mawkish, nauseating, obnoxious, syrupy, treacly, unpleasant. Opp REFRESHING.

sickness n nausea, queasiness, vomiting. ▷ ILLNESS.

side n **1** sides of a cube. face, facet, flank, surface. **2** side of the road. border, boundary, brim, brink, edge, fringe, margin, perimeter, rim, verge. **3** sides in a debate. angle, aspect, attitude, perspective, point of view, position, slant, standpoint, view, viewpoint. **4** sides in a quarrel. army, camp, faction, interest, party, team. ● v **side with** ally with, favour, inf go along with, join up with, prefer, support, team up with. ▷ HELP.

sidestep v avoid, dodge, inf duck, evade, skirt round.

sidetrack v deflect, distract, divert.

sideways adj **1** indirect, oblique. **2** sideways glance. covert, side-long, sly, sneaky, unobtrusive.

siege n blockade. ● v ▷ BESIEGE.

sieve n colander, riddle, screen, strainer. ● v ▷ SIFT.

sift v **1** filter, riddle, separate, sieve, strain. **2** sift evidence. analyse, examine, investigate, review, select, sort out, weed out.

sigh n breath, exhalation, moan, murmur.

sight n **1** eyesight, seeing, vision. **2** within sight. field of vision, gaze, range, view, visibility. **3** brief sight of it. glimpse, look. **4** impressive sight. display, exhibition, scene, show, spectacle. ● v behold, discern, distinguish, glimpse, make out, notice, observe, perceive, recognize, see, spot. **catch sight of** ▷ SEE.

sightseer n globe-trotter, holidaymaker, tourist, tripper, visitor.

sign n **1** augury, forewarning, hint, indicator, intimation, omen, pointer, portent, presage, warning. ▷ SIGNAL. **2** sign of his presence. clue, inf give-away, indication, manifestation, marker, proof, reminder, spoor (of animal), symptom, token, trace, vestige. **3** put up a sign. advertisement, notice, placard, poster. **4** identifying sign. badge, cipher, device, emblem, flag, insignia, logo, mark, monogram, symbol, trademark. ● v **1** autograph, countersign, endorse, inscribe, write. **2** ▷ SIGNAL. **sign off** ▷ FINISH. **sign on** ▷ ENLIST. **sign over** ▷ TRANSFER.

signal n **1** communication, cue, gesticulation, gesture, *inf* go ahead, indication, sign, signal, tip-off, warning. **2** beacon, bell, buoy, flag, flare, siren, whistle. • *v* beckon, communicate, flag, gesticulate, gesture, indicate, motion, notify, sign, wave.

signature *n* autograph, endorsement, mark, name.

signet *n* seal, stamp.

significance *n* force, idea, implication, import, importance, message, point, purport, relevance, sense, value, weight. ▷ MEANING.

significant *adj* **1** eloquent, expressive, indicative, informative, knowing, meaningful, pregnant, revealing, suggestive, symbolic, *inf* tell-tale. **2** *significant event.* consequential, considerable, influential, memorable, relevant, serious, valuable, worthwhile. *Opp* INSIGNIFICANT.

signify *v* **1** announce, be a sign of, connote, convey, denote, express, imply, indicate, intimate, make known, reflect, reveal, signal, suggest, symbolize, tell, transmit. **2** *It doesn't signify.* be significant, count, matter.

signpost *n* pointer, road sign, sign.

silence *n* **1** calm, calmness, hush, peace, quiet, quietness, stillness, tranquillity. *Opp* NOISE. **2** *Her silence puzzled us.* reticence, speechlessness, taciturnity. • *v* **1** gag, hush, keep quiet, make silent, muzzle, shut up, suppress. **2** *silence engine noise.* deaden, muffle, mute, quieten, smother, stifle. Silence! Be quiet! *inf* Hold your tongue! Hush! *inf* Pipe down! Shut up! Stop talking!

silent *adj* **1** inaudible, muffled, muted, noiseless, quiet, soundless. **2** dumb, *inf* mum, reticent, speechless, taciturn, tight-lipped, tongue-tied, uncommunicative, unforthcoming, voiceless. **3** *silent listeners.* attentive, rapt, restrained, still. **4** *silent agreement.* implicit, implied, mute, tacit, understood, unspoken. *Opp* EXPLICIT, NOISY, TALKATIVE. **be silent** keep quiet, *inf* pipe down, say nothing, *inf* shut up.

silhouette *n* contour, form, outline, profile, shadow, shape.

silky *adj* fine, glossy, lustrous, satiny, silken, sleek, smooth, soft, velvety.

silly *adj* **1** absurd, asinine, brainless, childish, crazy, *inf* daft, *inf* dopey, *inf* dotty, fatuous, feather-brained, foolish, frivolous, *inf* half-baked, hare-brained, idiotic, ill-advised, illogical, immature, inane, infantile, irrational, laughable, light-hearted, ludicrous, mad, meaningless, mindless, misguided, nonsensical, playful, pointless, ridiculous, scatterbrained, *inf* scatty, senseless, simple-minded, simplistic, *inf* soppy, stupid, thoughtless, unintelligent, unwise, witless. *Opp* SERIOUS, WISE. **2** [*inf*] *knocked silly.* ▷ UNCONSCIOUS.

silt *n* deposit, mud, ooze, sediment, slime, sludge.

similar *adj* akin, alike, analogous, comparable, compatible, congruous, corresponding, equal, equivalent, harmonious, homogeneous, identical, indistinguishable, like, matching, parallel, related, resembling, the same, uniform, well-matched. *Opp* DIFFERENT.

similarity n affinity, closeness, congruity, correspondence, kinship, likeness, match, relationship, resemblance, sameness. *Opp* DIFFERENCE.

simmer v boil, bubble, cook, seethe, stew.

simple adj 1 artless, basic, candid, childlike, elementary, frank, guileless, homely, humble, ingenuous, innocent, lowly, modest, *derog* naive, natural, *derog* silly, simple-minded, unaffected, unassuming, unpretentious, unsophisticated. *Opp* SOPHISTICATED. 2 *simple instructions.* clear, comprehensible, direct, easy, foolproof, intelligible, lucid, straightforward, uncomplicated, understandable. *Opp* COMPLEX. 3 *simple dress.* austere, classical, plain, severe, stark, unadorned. *Opp* ORNATE.

simplify v clarify, explain, paraphrase, *inf* put in words of one syllable, streamline, untangle. *Opp* COMPLICATE.

simplistic adj [*derog*] facile, naive, oversimplified, shallow, silly, superficial.

simulate v act, counterfeit, fake, feign, imitate, *inf* mock up, pretend, reproduce, sham.

simultaneous adj coinciding, concurrent, contemporary, synchronous.

sin n blasphemy, corruption, depravity, desecration, error, evil, fault, guilt, immorality, impiety, iniquity, irreverence, misdeed, offence, peccadillo, sacrilege, sinfulness, transgression, ungodliness, vice, wickedness, wrong, wrongdoing.
  ● v blaspheme, do wrong, err, fall from grace, go astray, lapse, misbehave, offend, transgress.

sincere adj candid, direct, earnest, frank, genuine, guileless, heartfelt, honest, open, real, serious, straight, straightforward, true, truthful, unaffected, unfeigned, upright, whole-hearted. *Opp* INSINCERE.

sincerity n candour, directness, earnestness, frankness, honesty, honour, integrity, openness, straightforwardness, truthfulness.

sinewy adj brawny, muscular, tough, wiry. ▷ STRONG.

sinful adj bad, blasphemous, corrupt, depraved, erring, evil, fallen, guilty, immoral, impious, iniquitous, irreligious, irreverent, profane, sacrilegious, ungodly, unholy, unrighteous, wicked, wrong. *Opp* RIGHTEOUS.

sing v carol, chant, chirp, chorus, croon, hum, serenade, trill, warble, yodel.

singe v blacken, burn, char, scorch, sear.

singer n pl choir, chorister, pl chorus, entertainer, minstrel, performer, soloist, songster, vocalist.

single adj 1 exclusive, individual, isolated, lone, odd, one, only, personal, separate, singular, sole, solitary, unique. 2 *single person. inf* free, unattached, unmarried. ● v **single out** ▷ CHOOSE.

single-handed adj alone, independent, solitary, unaided, unassisted, without help.

single-minded adj dedicated, devoted, dogged, *derog* fanatical, *derog* obsessive, persevering, resolute, tireless. ▷ DETERMINED.

singular adj 1 ▷ SINGLE.
2 abnormal, curious, exceptional, extraordinary, odd, outstanding, rare, remarkable, strange, unusual.
▷ DISTINCTIVE. *Opp* COMMON.

sinister adj 1 dark, disquieting, disturbing, evil, forbidding, frightening, gloomy, inauspicious, malevolent, menacing, ominous, threatening, upsetting.
2 *sinister motives*. bad, corrupt, criminal, dishonest, illegal, nefarious, questionable, *inf* shady, suspect, treacherous, villainous.

sink v 1 collapse, decline, descend, diminish, disappear, drop, dwindle, ebb, fade, fail, fall, plunge, set (*sun sets*), slip down, subside. 2 be engulfed, be submerged, founder, go down, go under. 3 *sink a ship*. scupper, scuttle. 4 *sink a well*. bore, dig, drill, excavate.

sinner n evil-doer, malefactor, miscreant, offender, reprobate, transgressor, wrongdoer.

sip v drink, lap, sample, taste.

sit v 1 be seated, perch, rest, seat (yourself), settle, take a seat, *inf* take the weight off your feet. 2 *sit for a portrait*. pose. 3 *sit an exam*. take, write. 4 *Parliament sat for 12 hours*. assemble, be in session, convene, gather, meet.

site n area, campus, ground, location, place, plot, position, setting, situation, spot.
● v ▷ SITUATE.

sitting room n drawing room, living room, lounge.

situate v build, establish, locate, place, position, put, set up, site, station.

situation n 1 area, locale, locality, location, place, position, set-
ting, site, spot. 2 *awkward situation*. circumstances, condition, *inf* kettle of fish, plight, position, predicament, state of affairs.
3 *situations vacant*. job, place, position, post.

size n amount, area, breadth, bulk, capacity, depth, dimensions, extent, height, immensity, length, magnitude, mass, measurement, proportions, scale, scope, volume, weight, width.
▷ MEASURE. ● v **size up**
▷ ASSESS.

sizeable adj considerable, decent, generous, significant, worthwhile. ▷ BIG.

skate v glide, skim, slide.

skeleton n bones, frame, framework, structure.

sketch n 1 description, design, diagram, draft, drawing, outline, picture, plan, *inf* rough, skeleton. 2 *comic sketch*. performance, scene, skit, turn.
● v depict, draw, indicate, portray, represent. **sketch out**
▷ OUTLINE.

sketchy adj cursory, hasty, hurried, imperfect, incomplete, perfunctory, rough, scrappy, unfinished, unpolished.
Opp DETAILED, PERFECT.

skid v aquaplane, glide, go out of control, slide, slip.

skilful adj able, accomplished, adept, adroit, apt, capable, competent, crafty, cunning, deft, dexterous, expert, handy, ingenious, masterly, practised, professional, proficient, talented, trained, versatile, workmanlike.
▷ CLEVER. *Opp* UNSKILFUL.

skill n ability, accomplishment, adroitness, aptitude, art, artistry, capability, cleverness, competence, craft, cunning, dexterity, expertise, facility, flair, gift, ingenuity, knack, mastery, professionalism, proficiency, prowess, talent, technique, versatility, workmanship.

skilled adj experienced, expert, qualified, trained, versed. ▷ SKILFUL.

skim v 1 coast, glide, sail, skate, skid, slide, slip. 2 *skim through a book*. dip into, leaf through, look through, read quickly, scan, skip.

skin n casing, coat, coating, complexion, covering, epidermis, exterior, film, fur, hide, husk, membrane, outside, peel, pelt, rind, shell, surface. ● v flay, pare, peel, shell, strip.

skin-deep adj ▷ SUPERFICIAL.

skinny adj bony, gaunt, lanky, scraggy. ▷ THIN.

skip v 1 bound, caper, cavort, dance, frisk, gambol, hop, jump, leap, prance, romp, spring. 2 *skip the boring bits*. forget, ignore, leave out, miss out, omit, pass over, skim through. 3 *skip lessons*. cut, miss, play truant from.

skirmish n brush, fight, *inf* set-to, tussle. ● v ▷ FIGHT.

skirt v avoid, border, bypass, circle, go round, *inf* steer clear of, surround.

skit n burlesque, parody, satire, sketch, *inf* spoof, *inf* take-off.

sky n air, atmosphere, *poet* firmament, *poet* heavens, stratosphere.

slab n block, chunk, hunk, lump, piece, slice, wedge, *inf* wodge.

slack adj 1 limp, loose, sagging, soft. Opp TIGHT. 2 *slack attitude*. careless, dilatory, disorganized, easygoing, idle, inattentive,

indolent, lax, lazy, neglectful, negligent, relaxed, remiss, slothful, unbusinesslike, undisciplined. Opp RIGOROUS. 3 *slack trade*. quiet, slow, slow-moving, sluggish. Opp BUSY. ● v be lazy, idle, malinger, neglect your duty, shirk, *sl* skive.

slacken v 1 loosen, relax, release. 2 *slacken speed*. abate, decrease, ease, lessen, lower, moderate, reduce, slow down.

slacker n *inf* good-for-nothing, lazy person, *sl* skiver. ▷ IDLER.

slake v allay, assuage, cool, ease, quench, relieve, satisfy.

slam v 1 bang, shut. 2 [*inf*] ▷ CRITICIZE.

slander n backbiting, calumny, defamation, denigration, insult, libel, lie, misrepresentation, slur, smear, vilification.
● v blacken the name of, defame, denigrate, disparage, libel, malign, misrepresent, slur, smear, tell lies about, vilify.

slanderous adj abusive, damaging, defamatory, disparaging, false, libellous, lying, mendacious, scurrilous, untrue, vicious.

slang n argot, cant, jargon.
● v ▷ INSULT. **slanging match** ▷ QUARREL.

slant n 1 angle, diagonal, gradient, incline, list, pitch, ramp, slope, tilt. 2 *slant on a problem*. approach, attitude, perspective, point of view, standpoint, view, viewpoint. 3 *slant to the news*. bias, distortion, emphasis, imbalance, one-sidedness. ● v 1 be at an angle, incline, lean, slope, tilt. 2 *slant the news*. bias, colour, distort, twist, weight.

slanting ▷ OBLIQUE.

slap v smack, spank. ▷ HIT.

slash v gash, slit. ▷ CUT.

slaughter n carnage, massacre, murder. ▷ KILLING. ● v butcher, massacre, murder, slay. ▷ KILL.

slave n drudge, serf, servant, vassal. ● v drudge, grind away, labour, sweat, toil, *inf* work your fingers to the bone. ▷ WORK.

slave-driver n despot, hard taskmaster, tyrant.

slaver v dribble, drool, foam at the mouth, salivate, slobber.

slavery n bondage, captivity, enslavement, servitude, subjugation. *Opp* FREEDOM.

slavish adj 1 abject, cringing, fawning, grovelling, humiliating, menial, obsequious, servile, submissive. 2 *slavish imitation.* close, flattering, strict, sycophantic, unimaginative, unoriginal. *Opp* INDEPENDENT.

slay v assassinate, butcher, destroy, execute, exterminate, martyr, massacre, murder, put to death, slaughter. ▷ KILL.

sleazy adj dirty, disreputable, mean, run-down, seedy, slovenly, sordid, squalid, unprepossessing.

sledge n bob-sleigh, sled, sleigh, toboggan.

sleek adj 1 brushed, glossy, graceful, lustrous, shining, shiny, silken, silky, smooth, soft, trim, velvety, well-groomed. 2 complacent, contented, fawning, self-satisfied, *inf* smarmy, smug, suave, unctuous, well-fed.

sleep n *inf* beauty sleep, catnap, doze, *inf* forty winks, hibernation, *sl* kip, *inf* nap, repose, rest, *inf* shut-eye, siesta, slumber, snooze. ● v catnap, *inf* doss down, doze, *inf* drop off, drowse, fall asleep, *inf* have forty winks,

hibernate, *sl* kip, *inf* nod off, rest, slumber, snooze, *inf* take a nap. **sleeping** ▷ ASLEEP.

sleepiness n drowsiness, lassitude, lethargy, somnolence, tiredness, torpor.

sleepless adj awake, conscious, restless, *inf* tossing and turning, wakeful, watchful, wide awake. *Opp* ASLEEP.

sleepy adj 1 *inf* dopey, drowsy, heavy, lethargic, sluggish, somnolent, tired, weary. 2 *sleepy village.* boring, dull, inactive, quiet, restful, torpid, unexciting. *Opp* LIVELY.

slender adj 1 graceful, lean, narrow, slender, slight, svelte, sylphlike, thin, trim. 2 *slender thread.* fragile, tenuous. 3 *slender means.* inadequate, meagre, scanty, small. *Opp* FAT, LARGE.

slice n carving, layer, piece, rasher, shaving, sliver, wedge. ● v carve, sever, split. ▷ CUT.

slick adj 1 adroit, artful, clever, cunning, deft, dexterous, quick, skilful, smart. 2 *slick talker.* glib, plausible, *inf* smarmy, smooth, smug, suave, superficial, unctuous, urbane, wily. 3 *slick hair.* glossy, oiled, plastered down, shiny, sleek, smooth.

slide n 1 avalanche, landslide, landslip. 2 *photographic slide.* transparency. ● v coast, glide, skate, skid, skim, slip, slither, toboggan.

slight adj 1 imperceptible, inconsequential, inconsiderable, insignificant, little, minor, negligible, scanty, slim (*chance*), small, superficial, trifling, trivial, unimportant. 2 *slight build.* delicate, diminutive, fragile, frail, petite, slender, slim, svelte,

sylphlike, thin, weak. *Opp* BIG.
• *n*, *v* ▷ INSULT.

slightly *adv* hardly, moderately,
only just, scarcely. *Opp* VERY.

slim *adj* 1 graceful, lean, narrow,
slender, svelte, sylphlike, trim.
▷ THIN. 2 *slim chance*. little, negligible, remote, slight, unlikely.
• *v* diet, lose weight, reduce.

slime *n* muck, mucus, mud, ooze,
sludge.

slimy *adj* clammy, greasy, oily,
oozy, slippery, *inf* slippy, slithery, wet.

sling *v* cast, *inf* chuck, fling,
heave, hurl, launch, *inf* let fly,
lob, pelt, pitch, propel, shoot,
shy, throw, toss.

slink *v* creep, edge, move guilt-
ily, prowl, skulk, slither, sneak,
steal.

slinky *adj* [*inf*] clinging, close-
fitting, sexy, sinuous, sleek.

slip *n* 1 accident, *inf* bloomer,
blunder, error, fault, *Fr* faux
pas, inaccuracy, indiscretion,
lapse, miscalculation, mistake,
oversight, *inf* slip-up. 2 *slip of paper*. note,
piece, sheet, strip. • *v* 1 coast,
glide, skate, skid, skim, slide,
slip, slither, stumble, trip. 2 *slip
into the room*. creep, edge, slink,
sneak, steal. **give someone the
slip** ▷ ESCAPE. **let slip**
▷ REVEAL. **slip away, slip the
net** ▷ ESCAPE. **slip up**
▷ BLUNDER.

slippery *adj* 1 glassy, greasy,
icy, lubricated, oily, slimy,
inf slippy, slithery, smooth, wet.
2 *slippery customer*. crafty, cunning, devious, evasive, *inf* hard
to pin down, *inf* shifty, sly, specious, tricky, unreliable, untrustworthy, wily.

slipshod *adj* careless, disorganized, lax, messy, slapdash,
inf sloppy, slovenly, untidy.

slit *n* aperture, breach, break,
chink, cleft, crack, cut, fissure,
gap, gash, hole, incision, opening, rift, slot, split, tear, vent.
• *v* cut, gash, slice, split, tear.

slither *v* creep, glide, slide, slip,
snake, worm.

sliver *n* flake, shard, shaving,
snippet, splinter. ▷ PIECE.

slobber *v* ▷ SLAVER.

slogan *n* catchphrase, catchword, jingle, motto, watchword.
▷ SAYING.

slope *n* angle, ascent, bank, descent, dip, drop, gradient, fall,
hill, incline, pitch, ramp, rise,
slant, tilt. • *v* ascend, bank,
decline, descend, dip, fall,
incline, lean, pitch, rise, shelve,
slant, tilt, tip. **sloping**
▷ OBLIQUE.

sloppy *adj* 1 liquid, runny,
inf sloshy, slushy, squelchy,
watery, wet. 2 *sloppy work*.
careless, disorganized, lax,
messy, slapdash, slipshod,
slovenly, unsystematic, untidy.
3 ▷ SENTIMENTAL.

slot *n* 1 aperture, breach, break,
chink, cleft, cut, gap,
gash, groove, hole, incision,
opening, rift, slit, split, vent.
2 *slot on a schedule*. place, space,
spot, time.

sloth *n* apathy, idleness, indolence, inertia, laziness, lethargy,
sluggishness, torpor.

slouch *v* droop, hunch, loaf, loll,
lounge, sag, shamble, slump,
stoop.

slovenly *adj* careless,
inf couldn't-care-less, disorganized, messy, shoddy, slapdash,

sleazy, *inf* sloppy, untidy.
Opp CAREFUL.

slow *adj* **1** careful, cautious, crawling, delayed, deliberate, dilatory, gradual, lazy, leisurely, lingering, loitering, measured, moderate, painstaking, plodding, protracted, slow-moving, sluggish, steady, unhurried. **2** *slow learner*. dense, dim, dull, obtuse, *inf* thick. ▷ STUPID. **3** *slow worker*. reluctant, unenthusiastic, unwilling. ▷ SLUGGISH. *Opp* FAST. ● *v* slow down brake, decelerate, *inf* ease up, hold back, reduce speed. **be slow** ▷ DAWDLE, DELAY.

sludge *n* mire, muck, mud, ooze, precipitate, sediment, silt, slime, slurry, slush.

sluggish *adj* apathetic, dull, idle, inactive, lazy, lethargic, lifeless, listless, phlegmatic, slothful, torpid, unresponsive. ▷ SLOW. *Opp* LIVELY.

sluice *v* flush, rinse, swill, wash.

slumber *n*, *v* ▷ SLEEP.

slump *n* collapse, crash, decline, dip, downturn, drop, fall, falling-off, recession, trough. *Opp* BOOM. ● *v* **1** collapse, crash, decline, dive, drop, fall off, plummet, plunge, sink, slip, *inf* take a nosedive, worsen. *Opp* PROSPER. **2** *slump in a chair*. collapse, droop, flop, hunch, loll, lounge, sag, slouch, subside.

slur *n* affront, aspersion, innuendo, insinuation, insult, libel, slander, smear. ● *v* garble, mumble.

sly *adj* artful, canny, conniving, crafty, cunning, deceitful, designing, devious, *inf* foxy, furtive, guileful, insidious, knowing, scheming, secretive, *inf* shifty, shrewd, sneaky, stealthy, surreptitious, tricky, underhand, wily. *Opp* CANDID, OPEN.

smack *v* pat, slap, spank. ▷ HIT.

small *adj* **1** *inf* baby, compact, concise, cramped, diminutive, *inf* dinky, dwarf, infinitesimal, little, microscopic, midget, *inf* mini, miniature, minuscule, minute, narrow, petite, *inf* pint-sized, *inf* pocket-sized, *inf* poky, portable, pygmy, short, slight, *inf* teeny, tiny, toy, undersized, *inf* wee, *inf* weeny. **2** *small helpings*. inadequate, insufficient, meagre, mean, *inf* measly, miserly, modest, *inf* piddling, scanty, skimpy, stingy, ungenerous. **3** *small problem*. inconsequential, insignificant, minor, negligible, slight, trifling, trivial, unimportant. *Opp* BIG. **small arms** ▷ WEAPON.

small-minded *adj* bigoted, hidebound, intolerant, narrow-minded, parochial, petty, prejudiced, rigid, unimaginative. ▷ MEAN. *Opp* BROAD-MINDED.

smart *adj* **1** acute, artful, astute, bright, clever, crafty, *inf* cute, discerning, ingenious, intelligent, perceptive, perspicacious, quick, quick-witted, shrewd, *sl* streetwise. *Opp* DULL. **2** *smart appearance*. bright, chic, clean, dapper, *inf* dashing, elegant, fashionable, fresh, *inf* natty, neat, *inf* snazzy, spruce, stylish, tidy, trim, well-dressed, well-groomed. *Opp* SCRUFFY. **3** *smart pace*. brisk, *inf* cracking, fast, quick, rapid, *inf* rattling, speedy, swift. **4** *smart blow*. painful, sharp, stinging. ● *v* ▷ HURT.

smash *v* **1** crumple, crush, demolish, destroy, shatter, wreck. ▷ BREAK. **2** bang, bash, batter, bump, collide, crash, hammer, knock, pound, ram, slam, strike, thump. ▷ HIT.

smear n 1 blot, daub, mark, smudge, stain, streak. 2 *smear on your name*. aspersion, imputation, innuendo, insinuation, libel, slander, slur, vilification. ● v 1 dab, daub, plaster, rub, smudge, spread, wipe. 2 *smear a reputation*. blacken, defame, discredit, libel, slander, slander, stigmatize, tarnish, vilify.

smell n aroma, bouquet, fragrance, miasma, nose, odour, *inf* pong, redolence, reek, scent, stench, stink. ● v 1 *inf* get a whiff of, scent, sniff. 2 *onions smell*. *inf* hum, *inf* pong, reek, stink.

smelling adj 1 *pleasant-smelling*. aromatic, fragrant, musky, odorous, perfumed, redolent, scented. 2 *unpleasant-smelling*. fetid, foul, gamy, *inf* high, miasmic, musty, noisome, *inf* off, *inf* pongy, pungent, rank, reeking, smelly, stinking, *inf* whiffy. *Opp* ODOURLESS.

smelly adj ▷ SMELLING.

smile n, v beam, grin, simper, smirk.

smoke n 1 exhaust, fog, fumes, gas, smog, vapour. 2 cigar, cigarette, *inf* fag, pipe. ● v 1 fume, smoulder. 2 *smoke cigars*. inhale, puff at.

smoky adj clouded, foggy, hazy, sooty. *Opp* CLEAR.

smooth adj 1 even, flat, horizontal, level, plane, unbroken. 2 *smooth sea*. calm, peaceful, placid, quiet. 3 *smooth finish*. glassy, glossy, polished, satiny, shiny, silken, silky, sleek, soft, velvety. 4 *smooth progress*. comfortable, easy, effortless, steady, uneventful, uninterrupted, unobstructed. 5 *smooth taste*. agree-

able, bland, mellow, mild, pleasant. 6 *smooth mixture*. creamy, runny. 7 *smooth talker*. convincing, facile, glib, plausible, polite, self-assured, self-satisfied, slick, smug, sophisticated, suave, urbane. *Opp* ROUGH. ● v even out, file, flatten, iron, level, level off, plane, polish, press, roll out, sand down.

smother v 1 asphyxiate, choke, cover, kill, snuff out, stifle, strangle, suffocate, throttle. 2 ▷ SUPPRESS.

smoulder v burn, smoke.

smouldering ▷ ANGRY.

smudge v blot, blur, dirty, mark, smear, stain, streak.

smug adj complacent, conceited, *inf* holier-than-thou, self-righteous, self-satisfied, sleek, superior. *Opp* HUMBLE.

snack n bite, *inf* elevenses, light meal, *inf* nibble, refreshments.

snack bar n buffet, café, cafeteria, fast-food restaurant.

snag n catch, complication, difficulty, drawback, hindrance, hitch, obstacle, problem, stumbling block. ● v catch, jag, rip, tear.

snake n serpent. ● v crawl, creep, meander, twist and turn, wander, worm, zigzag. **snaking** ▷ TWISTY.

snap adj ▷ SUDDEN. ● v 1 crack, fracture, split. 2 ▷ BREAK. 2 *snap your fingers*. click, crack. 3 *The dog snapped at his heels*. bite, gnash, nip. 4 *Don't snap at me!* bark, growl, *inf* jump down someone's throat, snarl, speak angrily.

snare n ambush, booby-trap, noose, trap. ● v capture, catch, ensnare, entrap, net, trap.

snarl v 1 bare the teeth, growl. 2 *snarl up rope.* confuse, knot, tangle, twist.

snatch v 1 catch, clutch, grab, grasp, lay hold of, pluck, seize, take. 2 abduct, kidnap, steal.

sneak v 1 creep, move stealthily, prowl, skulk, slink, stalk, steal. 2 [*inf*] *sl* grass, inform (against), report, *sl* snitch, *inf* tell tales (about).

sneaking *adj* half-formed, intuitive, nagging, *inf* niggling, private, uncomfortable, worrying.

sneaky *adj* cheating, contemptible, crafty, deceitful, despicable, devious, dishonest, furtive, nasty, *inf* shady, *inf* shifty, sly, treacherous, underhand, unscrupulous, untrustworthy. *Opp* STRAIGHTFORWARD.

sneer v be contemptuous, be scornful, hiss, jeer, scoff. **sneer at** ▷ DENIGRATE, RIDICULE.

sniff v 1 *inf* get a whiff of, scent, smell. 2 ▷ SNIVEL. 3 ▷ SNEER.

snigger v chuckle, giggle, laugh, snicker, titter.

snip v clip, nick, nip. ▷ CUT.

snipe v fire, shoot, *inf* take potshots. **snipe at** ▷ CRITICIZE.

snippet n fragment, morsel, scrap, shred, snatch. ▷ PIECE.

snivel v *inf* grizzle, sniff, sniffle, snuffle, whimper, whine, *inf* whinge. ▷ WEEP.

snobbish *adj* affected, condescending, disdainful, highfalutin, *inf* hoity-toity, patronizing, pompous, *inf* posh, pretentious, *inf* snooty, *inf* stuck-up, supercilious, superior, *inf* toffee-nosed. ▷ CONCEITED. *Opp* UNPRETENTIOUS.

snoop v be inquisitive, interfere, intrude, investigate, meddle,

nose about, pry, sneak, spy, *inf* stick your nose in.

snooper n busybody, detective, investigator, meddler, spy.

snout n face, muzzle, nose, nozzle, proboscis, trunk.

snub v be rude to, brush off, cold-shoulder, disdain, humiliate, insult, offend, *inf* put someone down, rebuff, reject, scorn, *inf* squash.

snuff v extinguish, put out. **snuff it** ▷ DIE. **snuff out** ▷ KILL.

snug *adj* 1 comfortable, *inf* comfy, cosy, enclosed, friendly, intimate, protected, reassuring, relaxed, relaxing, restful, safe, secure, sheltered, soft, warm. 2 *snug fit.* close-fitting, exact, well-tailored.

soak v bathe, drench, dunk, immerse, marinate, permeate, saturate, souse, steep, submerge, wet thoroughly. **soaked, soaking** ▷ WET. **soak up** ▷ ABSORB.

soar v 1 ascend, climb, float, fly, glide, rise, tower. 2 *prices soared.* escalate, increase, rise, rocket, shoot up, spiral.

sob v cry, howl, snivel, *inf* sob your heart out. ▷ WEEP.

sober *adj* 1 calm, clear-headed, composed, dignified, grave, in control, level-headed, quiet, rational, sedate, sensible, serious, solemn, steady, subdued, unexciting. *Opp* SILLY. 2 *sober habits.* abstemious, moderate, restrained, self-controlled, staid, teetotal, temperate. *Opp* DRUNK. 3 *sober dress.* drab, dull, plain, sombre.

sociable *adj* affable, approachable, companionable, convivial, extroverted, friendly, gregarious, hospitable, neighbourly, outgoing, warm, welcoming. *Opp* UNFRIENDLY, WITHDRAWN.

social *adj* 1 *social events.* collective, communal, community, group, popular, public. 2 *social person.* ▷ SOCIABLE. *Opp* SOLITARY. ● *n* dance, disco, *inf* do, gathering, *inf* get-together, party, reception, reunion, soirée.

socialize *v* associate, be sociable, entertain, fraternize, get together, *inf* go out together, mix.

society *n* 1 civilization, the community, culture, mankind, nation, people, the public. 2 *the society of our friends.* camaraderie, companionship, company, fellowship, friendship. 3 *secret society.* alliance, association, circle, club, group, guild, league, organization, union.

sofa *n* chaise longue, couch, seat, settee.

soft *adj* 1 crumbly, cushiony, flexible, floppy, limp, malleable, mushy, plastic, pliable, pliant, pulpy, spongy, springy, squashy, supple, yielding. 2 *soft ground.* boggy, marshy, muddy, sodden, waterlogged. 3 *soft bed.* comfortable, cosy. 4 *soft texture.* downy, feathery, fleecy, fluffy, furry, satiny, silky, sleek, smooth, velvety. 5 *soft music, light.* dim, faint, low, muted, quiet, relaxing, restful, soothing, subdued. 6 *soft breeze.* balmy, delicate, gentle, light, mild, pleasant. 7 [*inf*] *soft option.* easy, undemanding. 8 *soft feelings.* ▷ SOFT-HEARTED. *Opp* HARD, HARSH, VIOLENT.

soften *v* 1 *soften the blow.* abate, alleviate, cushion, moderate, mit-

igate, reduce, temper. 2 *soften the high notes* deaden, lower, muffle, quell, quieten, tone down, turn down. 3 *soften in attitude.* concur, ease up, give in, give way, *inf* let up, relax, succumb, weaken, yield. 4 *soften him up.* appease, mellow, mollify, pacify. *Opp* HARDEN, INTENSIFY.

soft-hearted *adj* compassionate, easygoing, generous, gentle, indulgent, *derog* lax, lenient, mild, sentimental, *inf* soft, sympathetic, tender, tender-hearted, understanding. ▷ KIND. *Opp* CRUEL.

soggy *adj* drenched, dripping, heavy (*soil*), saturated, soaked, sodden, sopping, wet through. ▷ WET. *Opp* DRY.

soil *n* clay, dirt, earth, ground, humus, land, loam, topsoil. ● *v* blacken, contaminate, defile, dirty, pollute, smear, stain, sully, tarnish.

solace *n* comfort, consolation, reassurance. ● *v* ▷ CONSOLE.

soldier *n* fighter, mercenary, serviceman, servicewoman, trooper, *pl* troops, veteran, warrior. ● *v* **soldier on** ▷ PERSIST.

sole *adj* exclusive, individual, lone, one, only, single, singular, solitary, unique.

solemn *adj* 1 earnest, gloomy, glum, grave, grim, long-faced, reserved, sedate, serious, sober, sombre, staid, thoughtful, unsmiling. *Opp* CHEERFUL. 2 *solemn occasion.* august, awe-inspiring, ceremonial, ceremonious, dignified, formal, grand, important, imposing, impressive, momentous, ritualistic, stately. *Opp* FRIVOLOUS.

solicit v appeal for, ask for, beg, entreat, importune, petition, seek.

solicitous adj **1** attentive, caring, concerned, considerate, sympathetic. **2** ▷ ANXIOUS.

solid adj **1** solid ground. compact, concrete, hard, impenetrable, impermeable. **2** solid with people. crammed, crowded, jammed, packed. **3** solid gold. authentic, genuine, pure, real, unadulterated, unalloyed. **4** ten solid hours. continuous, unbroken, uninterrupted, unrelieved, whole. **5** solid foundations. firm, fixed, robust, sound, stable, steady, stout, strong, sturdy, substantial, well-made. **6** solid shape. cubic, rounded, spherical, three-dimensional. **7** solid evidence. authoritative, cogent, coherent, convincing, genuine, indisputable, irrefutable, proven, real, sound, tangible, weighty. **8** solid support. dependable, reliable, stalwart, strong, trustworthy, unanimous, united, unwavering, vigorous. Opp FLUID, FRAGMENTARY, WEAK.

solidarity n accord, agreement, coherence, concord, harmony, like-mindedness, unanimity, unity. Opp DISUNITY.

solidify v cake, clot, coagulate, congeal, crystallize, freeze, harden, inf jell, set, thicken. Opp LIQUEFY.

soliloquy n monologue, speech.

solitary adj **1** alone, friendless, isolated, lonely, reclusive, unsociable, withdrawn. **2** solitary survivor. individual, one, only, single, sole. **3** solitary place. desolate, distant, hidden, isolated, out-of-the-way, private, remote, secluded, unfrequented. Opp NUMEROUS, PUBLIC, SOCIAL. ● n anchorite, hermit, inf loner, recluse.

solitude n isolation, loneliness, privacy, remoteness, retirement, seclusion.

solo adv alone, individually, on your own, unaccompanied.

soloist n musician, performer, player, singer.

soluble adj explicable, solvable, understandable. Opp INSOLUBLE.

solution n **1** answer, conclusion, elucidation, explanation, key, resolution, solving, unravelling, working out. **2** chemical solution. compound, mixture, suspension.

solve v answer, clear up, inf crack, explain, figure out, find the solution to, puzzle out, resolve, unravel, work out.

solvent adj creditworthy, in credit, profitable, solid, sound, viable. Opp BANKRUPT.

sombre adj bleak, cheerless, dark, dim, dismal, doleful, drab, dull, funereal, gloomy, grave, grey, lugubrious, melancholy, morose, mournful, serious, sober. ▷ SAD. Opp CHEERFUL.

somewhat adv fairly, moderately, inf pretty, quite, rather.

song n air, anthem, ballad, carol, chant, inf ditty, folk song, inf hit, hymn, jingle, lullaby, lyric, number, psalm, serenade, tune.

sonorous adj deep, full, loud, powerful, resonant, resounding, reverberant, rich, ringing. Opp SHRILL.

soon adv old use anon, inf any minute now, before long, inf in a minute, presently, quickly, shortly.

sooner adv 1 before, earlier. 2 preferably, rather.

soothe v allay, appease, assuage, calm, comfort, ease, mollify, pacify, quiet, relieve, salve, settle, still.

soothing adj 1 *soothing lotion*. comforting, emollient, healing, mild, palliative. 2 *soothing music*. calming, gentle, peaceful, pleasant, reassuring, relaxing, restful.

sophisticated adj 1 adult, sl cool, cosmopolitan, cultivated, cultured, elegant, fashionable, inf grown-up, mature, polished, inf posh, refined, stylish, urbane, worldly. Opp UNSOPHISTICATED. 2 *sophisticated ideas*. advanced, clever, complex, complicated, elaborate, ingenious, intricate, involved, subtle. Opp PRIMITIVE, SIMPLE.

soporific adj boring, hypnotic, sleep-inducing, tedious. Opp LIVELY.

sorcerer n enchanter, enchantress, magician, magus, medicine man, necromancer, sorceress, old use warlock, witch, witchdoctor, wizard.

sorcery n black magic, charms, incantations, magic, inf mumbojumbo, necromancy, the occult, spells, voodoo, witchcraft, wizardry.

sordid adj 1 dingy, dirty, disreputable, filthy, foul, miserable, nasty, seamy, seedy, sleazy, inf slummy, squalid, ugly, unclean, undignified, unpleasant, unsanitary, wretched. Opp CLEAN. 2 *sordid dealings*. base, corrupt, despicable, dishonourable, ignoble, ignominious, immoral, mean, mercenary, selfish, shabby, shameful,

unethical, unscrupulous. Opp HONOURABLE.

sore adj 1 aching, burning, chafing, hurting, inflamed, painful, raw, red, sensitive, smarting, stinging, tender. 2 aggrieved, hurt, irked, inf peeved, inf put out, resentful, upset. ▷ ANNOYED. ● n abrasion, abscess, boil, bruise, burn, graze, inflammation, injury, laceration, rawness, scrape, spot, swelling, ulcer, wound. **make sore** burn, bruise, chafe, graze, hurt, inflame, redden, rub.

sorrow n 1 anguish, dejection, depression, desolation, despair, despondency, disappointment, dissatisfaction, distress, gloom, glumness, grief, heartache, heartbreak, heaviness, homesickness, hopelessness, loneliness, melancholy, misery, misfortune, mourning, sadness, suffering, tearfulness, trouble, unhappiness, wistfulness, woe, wretchedness. Opp HAPPINESS. 2 guilt, penitence, regret, remorse, repentance. ● v agonize, be sorrowful, bewail, grieve, lament, mourn, weep. Opp REJOICE.

sorrowful adj broken-hearted, dejected, disconsolate, doleful, grief-stricken, heartbroken, lugubrious, melancholy, miserable, mournful, rueful, saddened, sombre, tearful, unhappy, upset, woebegone, woeful, wretched. ▷ SAD, SORRY. Opp HAPPY.

sorry adj 1 apologetic, ashamed, conscience-stricken, contrite, guilt-ridden, penitent, regretful, remorseful, repentant, shamefaced. 2 *sorry for the homeless*.

compassionate, concerned, pitying, sympathetic.

sort n 1 brand, category, class, classification, description, form, genre, group, kind, make, mark, nature, quality, set, type, variety. 2 breed, class, family, genus, race, species, stock, strain, variety. ● v arrange, catalogue, categorize, classify, divide, file, grade, group, order, organize, put in order, rank, systematize, tidy. *Opp* MIX. **sort out** 1 choose, *inf* put on one side, select, separate, set aside. 2 *sort out a problem*. attend to, clear up, cope with, deal with, handle, manage, organize, put right, resolve, solve, straighten out, tackle.

soul n 1 psyche, spirit. 2 [*inf*] *poor soul!* ▷ PERSON.

soulful adj deeply felt, emotional, expressive, fervent, inspiring, moving, passionate, profound, sincere, uplifting, warm.

soulless adj cold, inhuman, mechanical, perfunctory, routine, superficial, trite, unemotional, unfeeling, uninspiring.

sound adj 1 durable, healthy, hearty, *inf* in good shape, robust, secure, solid, strong, sturdy, tough, undamaged, uninjured, unscathed, vigorous, well, whole. 2 *sound food*. eatable, edible, fit for human consumption, good, wholesome. 3 *sound ideas*. balanced, coherent, commonsense, convincing, correct, judicious, logical, prudent, rational, reasonable, reasoned, sane, sensible, well-founded, wise. 4 *a sound business*. dependable, established, profitable, recognized, reliable, reputable, safe, secure, trustworthy, viable.

Opp BAD, WEAK. ● n bang, clamour, clatter, din, echo, murmur, noise, resonance, reverberation, ring, rumble, thunder, timbre, tone. ● v 1 become audible, be heard, echo, make a noise, resonate, resound, reverberate. 2 *sound an alarm*. activate, make, produce, set off. **sound out** check, examine, investigate, measure, plumb, probe, research, survey, test, try.

soup n broth, consommé, stock.

sour n 1 acid, acidic, bitter, citrus, lemony, sharp, tangy, tart, unripe, vinegary. 2 *sour milk*. bad, curdled, *inf* off, rancid, stale, turned. 3 *sour remarks*. acerbic, bad-tempered, bitter, caustic, curmudgeonly, cynical, disaffected, disagreeable, grudging, grumpy, ill-natured, irritable, jaundiced, peevish, snappy, testy, unpleasant.

source n 1 author, cause, creator, derivation, informant, initiator, originator, root, starting point. 2 *source of river*. head, origin, spring, start, well-spring. ▷ BEGINNING.

souvenir n heirloom, keepsake, memento, relic, reminder.

sovereign adj 1 absolute, all-powerful, dominant, highest, royal, supreme. 2 *sovereign state*. autonomous, independent, self-governing. ● n emperor, empress, king, monarch, prince, princess, queen. ▷ RULER.

sow v broadcast, disseminate, plant, scatter, seed, spread.

space adj extraterrestrial, interplanetary, interstellar. ● n 1 emptiness, infinity, ionosphere, stratosphere, the universe. 2 *space to move*.

inf elbow-room, expanse, freedom, latitude, leeway, margin, room, scope, spaciousness. **3** *an empty space*. area, blank, break, distance, duration, gap, hiatus, intermission, interval, lacuna, lapse, opening, place, spell, stretch, time, vacuum, wait.
● *v* space things out. ▷ ARRANGE.

spacious *adj* ample, broad, capacious, commodious, extensive, large, open, roomy, sizeable, vast, wide. ▷ BIG. *Opp* SMALL.

span *n* breadth, compass, distance, duration, extent, interval, length, period, reach, scope, stretch, term, width. ● *v* arch over, bridge, cross, extend across, reach over, straddle, stretch over, traverse.

spank *v* slap, slipper, smack. ▷ HIT, PUNISH.

spar *v* box, exchange blows, scrap. ▷ FIGHT.

spare *adj* **1** additional, auxiliary, extra, free, inessential, in reserve, leftover, odd, remaining, superfluous, supplementary, surplus, unnecessary, unneeded, unused, unwanted. *Opp* NECESSARY. **2** *a spare figure*. ▷ THIN. ● *v* **1** be merciful to, forgive, free, have mercy on, let go, let off, pardon, release, reprieve, save. **2** *spare money, time*. afford, allow, donate, give, give up, manage, part with, provide, sacrifice. **sparing** ▷ ECONOMICAL, MISERLY.

spark *n* flash, flicker, gleam, glint, sparkle. ● *v* spark off ignite, kindle. ▷ PROVOKE.

sparkle *v* flash, flicker, gleam, glint, glitter, reflect, scintillate, shine, spark, twinkle, wink.

sparkling *adj* **1** brilliant, flashing, glinting, glittering, scintillating, shining, shiny, twinkling. ▷ BRIGHT. *Opp* DULL. **2** bubbling, bubbly, carbonated, effervescent, fizzy, foaming.

sparse *adj inf* few and far between, inadequate, light, little, meagre, scanty, scarce, scattered, thin, *inf* thin on the ground. *Opp* PLENTIFUL.

spartan *adj* abstemious, ascetic, austere, bare, bleak, frugal, hard, harsh, plain, rigorous, severe, simple, stern, strict. *Opp* LUXURIOUS.

spasm *n* attack, convulsion, eruption, fit, jerk, paroxysm, seizure, *pl* throes, twitch.

spasmodic *adj* erratic, fitful, intermittent, irregular, jerky, occasional, *inf* on and off, periodic, sporadic. *Opp* CONTINUOUS, REGULAR.

spate *n* cataract, flood, flow, gush, inundation, outpouring, rush, torrent.

spatter *v* bespatter, daub, pepper, scatter, shower, slop, speckle, splash, splatter, spray, sprinkle.

speak *v* answer, articulate, communicate, converse, declaim, declare, deliver a speech, discourse, enunciate, express yourself, harangue, hold a conversation, *inf* hold forth, *inf* pipe up, recite, say something, soliloquize, tell, utter, verbalize, vocalize, voice. ▷ SAY, TALK. **speak about** ▷ MENTION. **speak to** ▷ ADDRESS. **speak your mind** be honest, say what you think, speak honestly, speak out, state your opinion, voice your thoughts.

speaker *n* lecturer, orator, spokesperson.

spear n assegai, harpoon, javelin, lance, pike.

special adj 1 distinguished, exceptional, extraordinary, important, memorable, momentous, notable, noteworthy, out of the ordinary, rare, red-letter (day), remarkable, significant, uncommon, unconventional, unusual. Opp ORDINARY. 2 She has a special style. characteristic, distinctive, idiosyncratic, peculiar, singular, unique, unmistakable. 3 my special chair. especial, individual, particular, personal. 4 He's a special friend of mine. close, dear, intimate, particular, valued.

specialist n 1 authority, connoisseur, expert, master, professional, pundit. 2 [medical] consultant.

speciality n expertise, field, forte, genius, inf line, specialization, special skill, strength, strong point, talent.

specialize v specialize in be a specialist in, concentrate on, devote yourself to, have a reputation for.

specialized adj esoteric, expert, specialist, technical.

species n breed, class, genus, kind, race, sort, type, variety.

specific adj clear-cut, defined, definite, detailed, exact, explicit, express, individual, named, particular, peculiar, precise, predetermined, special, specified, unequivocal. Opp GENERAL.

specify v be specific about, define, detail, enumerate, identify, itemize, list, name, spell out, stipulate.

specimen n example, illustration, instance, model, pattern, representative, sample.

specious adj deceptive, misleading, plausible.

speck n bit, crumb, dot, fleck, grain, mark, mite, mote, particle, speckle, spot, trace.

speckled adj brindled, dappled, dotted, flecked, freckled, mottled, patchy, spattered (with), spotted, spotty, sprinkled (with), stippled.

spectacle n ceremony, display, exhibition, extravaganza, grandeur, magnificence, ostentation, pageantry, parade, pomp, show, sight, splendour. **spectacles** glasses, inf specs.

spectacular adj breathtaking, colourful, dramatic, eye-catching, impressive, magnificent, sensational, showy, splendid, stunning.

spectator n pl audience, bystander, pl crowd, eyewitness, looker-on, observer, onlooker, viewer, watcher, witness.

spectre n apparition, ghost, phantom, spirit, vision, wraith.

spectrum n scale, scope, variety. ▷ RANGE.

speculate v 1 conjecture, consider, hypothesize, meditate, ponder, reflect, ruminate, surmise, theorize, wonder. ▷ THINK. 2 speculate in shares. gamble, invest speculatively, inf play the market, take a chance, wager.

speculative adj 1 abstract, based on guesswork, conjectural, doubtful, hypothetical, notional, theoretical, unfounded, unproven, untested. Opp PROVEN. 2 speculative investments. inf chancy, inf dicey, inf dodgy, hazardous, inf iffy, risky, uncertain, unpredictable, unreliable. Opp SAFE.

speech n 1 articulation, communication, delivery, diction, elocution, enunciation, expression, pronunciation, speaking, talking, utterance. 2 dialect, idiom, jargon, language, parlance, register, tongue. 3 *public speech*. address, discourse, disquisition, harangue, homily, lecture, oration, paper, presentation, sermon, sl spiel, talk, tirade. 4 *speech in a play*. dialogue, lines, monologue, soliloquy.

speechless adj dumb, dumbfounded, thunderstruck, mute, silent, thunderstruck, tonguetied, voiceless. Opp TALKATIVE.

speed n 1 pace, rate, tempo, velocity. 2 alacrity, briskness, haste, hurry, quickness, rapidity, speediness, swiftness.
● v 1 bolt, inf bowl along, career, dash, dart, flash, fly, gallop, inf go like the wind, hasten, hurry, hurtle, make haste, inf nip, inf put your foot down, race, run, rush, shoot, sprint, stampede, streak, tear, inf zoom. 2 break the speed limit, go too fast. **speed up** ▷ ACCELERATE.

speedy adj 1 fast, nimble, quick, rapid, swift. 2 *speedy exit*. hasty, hurried, immediate, precipitate, prompt. Opp SLOW.

spell n 1 bewitchment, charm, enchantment, incantation, magic formula, sorcery, witchcraft. 2 *I fell under his spell*. allure, captivation, charm, fascination, glamour, magic. 3 *spell of rain*. interval, period, phase, season. 4 *spell at the wheel*. session, stint, stretch, term, time, turn, watch. ● v augur, bode, foretell, indicate, mean, portend, presage, signal, signify. **spell out** ▷ CLARIFY.

spellbound adj bewitched, captivated, charmed, enchanted, enthralled, entranced, fascinated, hypnotized, mesmerized.

spend v 1 sl blue, consume, inf cough up, exhaust, expend, inf fork out, fritter, inf get through, pay out, inf shell out, inf splash out, inf splurge, squander. 2 *spend time*. devote, fill, occupy, pass, use up, waste.

spendthrift n inf big spender, wasteful person. Opp MISER.
● adj extravagant, prodigal, profligate.

sphere n 1 ball, globe, globule, orb. 2 *sphere of influence*. area, department, domain, field, province, range, scope, speciality, subject, territory. 3 *social sphere*. caste, class, domain, milieu, position, rank, society, station, stratum, walk of life.

spherical adj globe-shaped, globular, rotund, round.

spice n 1 flavouring, piquancy, relish, seasoning. 2 *add spice to life*. colour, excitement, gusto, interest, inf lift, inf pep, vigour, zest.

spicy adj aromatic, fragrant, gingery, hot, peppery, piquant, seasoned, spiced, tangy, zestful. Opp BLAND.

spike n barb, nail, pin, point, prong, skewer, spine, stake, tine.
● v impale, perforate, pierce, skewer, spear, stab.

spill v 1 overturn, slop, tip over, upset. 2 brim, flow, overflow, run, pour. 3 *lorry spilled its load*. discharge, drop, shed, tip.

spin v 1 gyrate, pirouette, revolve, rotate, swirl, turn, twirl, twist, wheel, whirl. **2** be giddy, reel, swim. **spin out** ▷ PROLONG.

spindle *n* axle, pin, rod, shaft.

spine *n* **1** backbone, spinal column, vertebrae. **2** barb, bristle, needle, point, prickle, quill, spike, thorn.

spineless *adj* cowardly, craven, faint-hearted, feeble, irresolute, *inf* lily-livered, pusillanimous, timid, *inf* wimpish. ▷ WEAK. *Opp* BRAVE.

spiral *adj* coiled, corkscrew, turning, whorled. ● *n* coil, curl, helix, whorl. ● *v* **1** turn, twist. **2** *spiralling prices.* ▷ FALL, RISE.

spire *n* pinnacle, steeple, tower.

spirit *n* **1** mind, psyche, soul. **2** *supernatural spirits.* apparition, demon, devil, genie, ghost, ghoul, gremlin, hobgoblin, imp, phantasm, phantom, poltergeist, *poet* shade, spectre, *inf* spook, vision, visitant, wraith, zombie. **3** *spirit of the times.* atmosphere, feeling, mood. **4** *spirit of the law.* aim, essence, heart, intention, meaning, sense, **5** *fighting spirit.* bravery, cheerfulness, confidence, courage, daring, determination, dynamism, energy, enthusiasm, *inf* get-up-and-go, *inf* go, *inf* guts, heroism, liveliness, mettle, morale, motivation, optimism, pluck, valour, willpower, zest. **6** ▷ ALCOHOL.

spirited *adj* active, animated, assertive, brave, buoyant, courageous, daring, determined, dynamic, energetic, enterprising, enthusiastic, gallant, *inf* gutsy, intrepid, lively, plucky, positive, sparkling, sprightly, vigorous, vivacious. *Opp* SPIRITLESS.

spiritless *adj* apathetic, despondent, dispirited, dull, lacklustre, lethargic, lifeless, listless, negative, passive, slow, unenthusiastic. *Opp* SPIRITED.

spiritual *adj* devotional, divine, eternal, heavenly, holy, incorporeal, inspired, other-worldly, religious, sacred, unworldly, visionary. *Opp* TEMPORAL.

spit *n* **1** dribble, saliva, spittle, sputum. ● *v* dribble, expectorate, salivate, splutter. **spit out** ▷ DISCHARGE. **spitting image** ▷ TWIN.

spite *n* animosity, animus, *inf* bitchiness, bitterness, grudge, hate, hatred, hostility, ill feeling, ill will, malevolence, malice, maliciousness, rancour, resentment, venom, vindictiveness. ● *v* ▷ ANNOY.

spiteful *adj* acid, acrimonious, *inf* bitchy, bitter, *inf* catty, cruel, cutting, hateful, hostile, hurtful, ill-natured, malevolent, malicious, nasty, poisonous, rancorous, resentful, sharp, *inf* snide, sour, venomous, vicious, vindictive. *Opp* KIND.

splash *v* **1** bespatter, shower, slop, *inf* slosh, spatter, spill, splatter, spray, sprinkle, squirt, wash. **2** bathe, dabble, paddle, wade. **3** *splash across the front page.* blazon, display, flaunt, *inf* plaster, show, spread. **splash out** ▷ SPEND.

splendid *adj* admirable, awe-inspiring, beautiful, brilliant, costly, dazzling, dignified, elegant, fine, first-class, glittering, glorious, gorgeous, grand, great, handsome, imposing, impressive, lavish, luxurious, magnificent, majestic, marvellous, noble, ornate, palatial, *inf* posh,

regal, resplendent, rich, royal, spectacular, stately, sublime, sumptuous, *inf* super, superb, supreme, wonderful.
▷ EXCELLENT.

splendour *n* beauty, brilliance, ceremony, display, elegance, *inf* glitter, glory, grandeur, luxury, magnificence, majesty, nobility, pomp and circumstance, richness, show, spectacle, stateliness, sumptuousness.

splice *v* bind, entwine, join, knit, marry, tie together, unite.

splinter *n* chip, flake, fragment, shard, shaving, sliver. ● *v* chip, crack, fracture, shatter, smash, split. ▷ BREAK.

split *n* 1 break, chink, cleavage, cleft, crack, cranny, crevice, fissure, gash, leak, opening, rent, rift, rip, rupture, slash, slit, tear. 2 breach, difference, dissension, divergence of opinion, division, divorce, estrangement, schism, separation. ▷ QUARREL.
● *v* 1 break up, disintegrate, divide, divorce, go separate ways, separate. 2 burst, chop, cleave, crack, rend, rip apart, rip open, slash, slice, slit, splinter, tear. ▷ CUT. 3 *split profits.* distribute, divide, halve, share. 4 *road splits.* branch, diverge, fork. **split on** ▷ INFORM.

spoil *v* 1 blight, blot, bungle, damage, deface, destroy, disfigure, harm, injure, *inf* make a mess of, mar, *inf* mess up, ruin, stain, undermine, undo, upset, vitiate, wreck. *Opp* IMPROVE.
2 curdle, decay, decompose, go bad, *inf* go off, moulder, perish, putrefy, rot, *inf* turn. 3 *spoil children.* cosset, dote on, indulge,

make a fuss of, mollycoddle, overindulge, pamper.

spoken *adj* oral, unwritten, verbal. *Opp* WRITTEN.

spokesperson *n* mouthpiece, representative, spokesman, spokeswoman.

sponge *v* 1 clean, mop, rinse, wash, wipe. 2 *sponge on friends.* cadge (from), scrounge (from).

spongy *adj* absorbent, elastic, porous, soft, springy, yielding. *Opp* SOLID.

sponsor *n inf* angel, backer, benefactor, donor, patron, promoter, supporter. ● *v* back, finance, fund, help, promote, subsidize, support, underwrite.

sponsorship *n* auspices, backing, funding, guarantee, patronage, promotion, support.

spontaneous *adj* 1 *inf* ad lib, extempore, impromptu, impulsive, *inf* off-the-cuff, unplanned, unpremeditated, unprepared, unrehearsed, voluntary.
2 *spontaneous reaction.* automatic, instinctive, involuntary, natural, reflex, unconscious, unthinking. *Opp* PREMEDITATED.

spooky *adj* creepy, eerie, frightening, ghostly, haunted, mysterious, *inf* scary, uncanny, unearthly, weird.

spool *n* bobbin, reel.

spoon *n* dessertspoon, ladle, tablespoon, teaspoon.

spoonfeed *v* cosset, help, mollycoddle, pamper, spoil.

spoor *n* footprints, scent, traces, track, trail.

sporadic *adj* erratic, fitful, intermittent, irregular, occasional, periodic, scattered, unpredictable.

sport n 1 activity, amusement, diversion, entertainment, exercise, fun, games, pastime, play, pleasure, recreation. 2 badinage, banter, humour, jesting, joking, merriment, raillery, teasing. • v 1 caper, cavort, frisk about, frolic, gambol, lark about, romp, skip about. 2 *sport new clothes*. display, exhibit, flaunt, show off, wear.

sporting adj considerate, fair, generous, good-humoured, honourable, sportsmanlike.

sportive adj coltish, frisky, light-hearted. ▷ PLAYFUL.

sportsperson n contestant, participant, player, sportsman, sportswoman.

sporty adj 1 active, athletic, energetic, fit, vigorous. 2 *sporty clothes*. casual, informal, *inf* snazzy.

spot n 1 blemish, blot, blotch, discoloration, dot, fleck, mark, patch, smudge, speck, speckle, stain. 2 *spot on the skin*. birthmark, boil, freckle, mole, pimple, pock-mark, *pl* rash, sty, *sl* zit. 3 *spots of rain*. bead, blob, drop. 4 *spot for a picnic*. locality, location, place, point, position, setting, site, situation. 5 *awkward spot*. difficulty, dilemma, embarrassment, mess, predicament, quandary, situation. 6 *spot of bother*. bit, small amount, *inf* smidgen. • v 1 blot, fleck, mark, mottle, smudge, spatter, speckle, splash, spray, stain. 2 ▷ SEE.

spotless adj 1 clean, fresh, immaculate, laundered, unmarked. 2 *spotless reputation*. blameless, flawless, immaculate, innocent, irreproachable, pure,

unblemished, unsullied, untarnished, *inf* whiter than white.

spotty adj blotchy, flecked, freckled, mottled, pimply, pockmarked, spattered, speckled, speckly, *inf* splodgy.

spouse n *inf* better half, husband, partner, wife.

spout n duct, fountain, geyser, jet, lip, nozzle, outlet, spray, waterspout. • v 1 emit, erupt, flow, gush, jet, pour, shoot, spew, spit, spurt, squirt, stream. 2 *inf* hold forth, ramble on, rave, talk.

sprawl v 1 flop, lean back, lie, loll, lounge, recline, relax, slouch, slump, spread out, stretch out. 2 be scattered, spread, straggle.

spray n 1 droplets, fountain, mist, shower, splash, sprinkling. 2 *spray of flowers*. arrangement, bouquet, bunch, corsage, posy, sprig. 3 *paint spray*. aerosol, atomizer, spray-gun, sprinkler. • v diffuse, disperse, scatter, shower, spatter, splash, sprinkle.

spread n 1 broadcasting, broadening, development, diffusion, dispensing, dispersal, dissemination, distribution, expansion, extension, growth, increase, passing on, proliferation. 2 *spread of a bird's wings*. breadth, compass, extent, size, span, stretch, sweep. 3 ▷ MEAL. • v 1 arrange, display, lay out, open out, unfold. 2 broaden, enlarge, expand, extend, fan out, lengthen, mushroom, proliferate, straggle, widen. 3 *spread news*. broadcast, circulate, diffuse, dispense, disperse, disseminate, distribute, divulge, give out, make known, pass on, proclaim, promote, promulgate, publicize, publish, scatter, transmit. **4** *spread butter.* apply, cover with, smear, smooth.

spree *n inf* binge, escapade, *inf* fling, *inf* orgy, outing, *inf* splurge. ▷ REVELRY.

sprightly *adj* active, agile, animated, brisk, energetic, jaunty, lively, nimble, *inf* perky, playful, spirited, sportive, spry, vivacious. *Opp* LETHARGIC.

spring *n* **1** bounce, buoyancy, elasticity, give, liveliness, resilience. **2** bound, jump, leap, skip. **3** *spring of water.* fount, fountain, source (*of river*), spa, well-spring. ● *v* bounce, bound, hop, jump, leap, pounce, vault. **spring from** derive from, proceed from, stem from. **spring up** appear, develop, emerge, germinate, grow, shoot up, sprout.

springy *adj inf* bendy, elastic, flexible, pliable, resilient, spongy, stretchy, supple. *Opp* RIGID.

sprinkle *v* drip, dust, pepper, scatter, shower, spatter, splash, spray, strew.

sprint *v* dash, *inf* hare, race, speed, *inf* tear. ▷ RUN.

sprout *n* bud, shoot. ● *v* bud, develop, germinate, grow, shoot up, spring up.

spruce *adj* clean, dapper, elegant, *inf* natty, neat, smart, tidy, trim, well-dressed, well-groomed, *inf* well-turned-out. *Opp* SCRUFFY. ● *v* **spruce up** ▷ TIDY.

spur *n* encouragement, goad, impetus, incentive, incitement, inducement, motivation, motive, prod, prompting, stimulus, urging. ● *v* egg on, encourage, impel, incite, motivate, pressure,

pressurize, prick, prod, prompt, stimulate, urge.

spurn *v* disown, give (someone) the cold shoulder, jilt, rebuff, reject, shun, snub, turn your back on.

spy *n* contact, double agent, *sl* grass, infiltrator, informant, informer, *inf* mole, private detective, secret agent, *inf* snooper, undercover agent. ● *v* **1** be a spy, eavesdrop, gather intelligence, inform, *inf* snoop. **2** ▷ SEE. **spy on** keep under surveillance, *inf* tail, trail, watch.

spying *n* counter-espionage, detective work, eavesdropping, espionage, intelligence, *inf* snooping, surveillance.

squabble *v* argue, bicker, *inf* row, wrangle. ▷ QUARREL.

squalid *adj* **1** dingy, dirty, disgusting, filthy, foul, insalubrious, mean, mucky, nasty, repulsive, run-down, sleazy, *inf* slummy, sordid, ugly, unpleasant, wretched. *Opp* CLEAN. **2** *squalid behaviour.* degrading, dishonest, dishonourable, disreputable, shabby, scandalous, shabby, shameful, unethical, unworthy. *Opp* HONOURABLE.

squander *v inf* blow, *sl* blue, dissipate, fritter, misuse, spend unwisely, *inf* splurge, use up, waste. *Opp* SAVE.

square *adj* **1** *square deal.* *inf* above-board, decent, equitable, ethical, fair, honest, honourable, proper, *inf* straight. **2** [*inf*] *Don't be so square!* conservative, conventional, old-fashioned, *inf* stuffy. ● *n* **1** piazza, plaza. **2** [*inf*] *He's an old square.* die-hard, *inf* fuddy-duddy, *inf* old fogey, *inf* stick-in-the-mud, tradi-

tionalist. • v square an account.
▷ SETTLE. **squared** chequered,
criss-crossed.

squash v 1 compress, crumple,
crush, flatten, mangle, mash,
pound, press, pulp, stamp on,
tread on. 2 squash into a room.
cram, crowd, pack, push, shove,
squeeze, wedge. 3 squash an
uprising. control, put down,
quash, quell, repress, suppress.
4 squash with a look. humiliate,
inf put down, silence.

squashy adj mushy, pulpy,
shapeless, soft, spongy,
squelchy, yielding. Opp FIRM.

squat adj dumpy, short, stocky,
thick, thickset. Opp TALL.
• v crouch, sit.

squeamish adj inf choosy,
fastidious, finicky, particular,
inf pernickety, prim, inf prissy,
prudish.

squeeze v 1 clasp, compress,
crush, embrace, enfold, exert
pressure on, grip, hug, mangle,
pinch, press, squash, wring.
2 cram, crowd, pack, push, ram,
shove, squash, stuff, thrust,
wedge. 3 squeeze money out of
someone. extort, extract, wrest.

squirm v twist, wriggle, writhe.

squirt v gush, jet, send out,
shoot, spit, splash, spout, spray,
spurt.

stab n 1 blow, cut, jab, prick,
thrust, wound. 2 stab of pain.
pang, sting, throb, twinge.
• v cut, injure, jab, perforate,
pierce, puncture, skewer, spike,
thrust, wound. **have a stab at**
▷ TRY.

stability n balance, durability,
equilibrium, firmness, perman-
ence, reliability, solidity, steadiness, strength. Opp INSTABILITY.

stabilize v balance, become
stable, give stability to, make
stable, settle. Opp UPSET.

stable adj 1 balanced, firm, fixed,
solid, steady, strong. 2 constant,
continuing, durable, established,
lasting, long-lasting, permanent,
predictable, reliable, steadfast,
unchanging, unwavering.
3 stable personality. balanced,
even-tempered, sane, sensible.
Opp UNSTABLE.

stack n 1 accumulation, heap,
hoard, mound, mountain, pile,
quantity, stockpile, store.
2 chimney, pillar, smokestack.
3 stack of hay. haystack, rick,
stook. • v accumulate, amass,
assemble, collect, gather, heap,
load, mass, pile, inf stash away,
stockpile.

stadium n amphitheatre, arena,
ground, sports ground.

staff n 1 baton, crook, crosier,
flagstaff, pole, rod, sceptre, shaft,
stake, standard, stick, wand.
2 assistants, crew, employees,
old use hands, personnel, team,
workers, workforce. • v man,
provide with staff, run.

stage n 1 dais, performing area,
platform, podium, rostrum.
2 stage of a journey. juncture,
leg, phase, point, time.
• v arrange, inf get up, mount,
organize, perform, present,
produce, put on, set up,
stage-manage.

stagger v 1 falter, lurch, reel,
rock, stumble, sway, teeter,
totter, walk unsteadily, waver,
wobble. 2 price staggered us.
amaze, astonish, astound,
dismay, dumbfound, flabbergast,
shake, shock, startle, stun, stupefy, surprise.

stagnant *adj* motionless, sluggish, stale, standing, static, still. *Opp* MOVING.

stagnate *v* become stale, be stagnant, degenerate, deteriorate, idle, languish, vegetate. *Opp* PROGRESS.

stain *n* 1 blemish, blot, blotch, discoloration, mark, smear, speck, spot. 2 *wood stain*. colouring, dye, paint, pigment, tinge, tint, varnish.
• *v* 1 blacken, blemish, blot, contaminate, dirty, discolour, mark, smudge, soil, tarnish. 2 *stain your reputation*. damage, defile, disgrace, dishonour, spoil, sully, taint. 3 *stain wood*. colour, dye, paint, tinge, tint, varnish.

stair *n* riser, step, tread. **stairs** escalator, flight of stairs, staircase, stairway, steps.

stake *n* 1 paling, pole, post, rod, shaft, stick. 2 bet, pledge, wager.
• *v* 1 fasten, hitch, tether, tie up. 2 *stake a claim*. establish, put on record, state. 3 *stake my life on it*. bet, chance, gamble, hazard, risk, venture, wager. **stake out** define, demarcate, enclose, fence in, mark off, outline.

stale *adj* 1 dry, hard, mouldy, musty, *inf* off, old, *inf* past its best, tasteless. 2 *stale ideas*. banal, clichéd, hackneyed, old-fashioned, overused, stock, *inf* tired, trite, uninteresting, unoriginal, worn out. *Opp* FRESH.

stalemate *n* deadlock, impasse, standstill.

stalk *n* branch, shoot, stem, trunk, twig. • *v* 1 follow, hunt, pursue, shadow, *inf* tail, track, trail. 2 *stalk about*. prowl, rove, stride, strut.

stall *n* booth, compartment, kiosk, stand, table. • *v* delay,

hang back, hesitate, pause, *inf* play for time, postpone, prevaricate, procrastinate, put off, stop, temporize, waste time.

stalwart *adj* dependable, determined, faithful, indomitable, intrepid, reliable, resolute, robust, staunch, steadfast, sturdy, tough, trustworthy, valiant. ▷ BRAVE, STRONG. *Opp* WEAK.

stamina *n* endurance, energy, *inf* grit, resilience, staying power, strength.

stammer *v* falter, hesitate, splutter, stumble, stutter.

stamp *n* 1 brand, hallmark, impression, imprint, print, seal. 2 franking, postage stamp. 3 *stamp of genius*. characteristic, mark, sign. • *v* 1 squash, *inf* stomp, trample, tread. 2 *stamp a mark*. brand, emboss, engrave, impress, imprint, label, mark, print. **stamp on** ▷ SUPPRESS. **stamp out** ▷ ELIMINATE.

stampede *n* charge, dash, rout, rush, sprint. • *v* 1 bolt, career, charge, dash, gallop, run, rush, sprint, *inf* tear. 2 *stampede cattle*. frighten, panic, scatter.

stand *n* 1 base, pedestal, rack, support, tripod. 2 booth, kiosk, stall. 3 grandstand, terraces. • *v* 1 arise, get to your feet, get up, rise. 2 *Stand it on the floor*. arrange, deposit, locate, place, position, put up, set up, situate, station. 3 *My offer stands*. be unchanged, continue, remain valid, stay. 4 *I can't stand it any longer*. abide, bear, endure, put up with, suffer, tolerate, *inf* wear. **stand by** ▷ SUPPORT. **stand for** ▷ SYMBOLIZE. **stand in for** ▷ DEPUTIZE. **stand out**

▷ SHOW. **stand up for**
▷ PROTECT, SUPPORT. **stand up to** ▷ RESIST.

standard adj accepted, accustomed, approved, average, basic, classic, common, conventional, customary, definitive, established, everyday, familiar, habitual, normal, official, ordinary, orthodox, popular, prevailing, prevalent, recognized, regular, routine, set, staple (diet), stock, traditional, typical, universal, usual. Opp UNUSUAL.
● n 1 archetype, benchmark, criterion, example, gauge, grade, guide, guideline, ideal, level of achievement, measure, model, paradigm, pattern, requirement, rule, sample, touchstone, yardstick. 2 average, level, mean, norm. 3 standard of a regiment.
▷ FLAG. 4 lamp standard. column, pillar, pole, post, support, upright. **standards**
▷ MORALITY.

standardize v average out, equalize, normalize, stereotype, systematize.

standoffish adj aloof, antisocial, cold, cool, distant, frosty, haughty, remote, reserved, reticent, secretive, inf snooty, taciturn, unapproachable, unforthcoming, unfriendly, unsociable, withdrawn. Opp FRIENDLY.

standpoint n angle, attitude, belief, opinion, perspective, point of view, position, stance, vantage point, view, viewpoint.

standstill n inf dead end, deadlock, halt, impasse, stalemate, stop, stoppage.

staple adj basic, chief, important, main, principal.
▷ STANDARD.

star n 1 celestial body, comet, evening star, falling star, morning star, shooting star.
2 asterisk, pentagram. 3 TV star. attraction, big name, celebrity, diva, inf draw, idol, leading lady, leading man, personage, starlet, inf superstar. ▷ PERFORMER.

starchy adj conventional, formal, prim, stiff.
▷ UNFRIENDLY.

stare v gape, inf gawp, gaze, glare, goggle, look fixedly, peer. **stare at** contemplate, examine, eye, scrutinize, study, watch.

stark adj 1 austere, bare, bleak, depressing, desolate, dreary, gloomy, grim. 2 stark contrast. absolute, clear, complete, perfect, plain, sharp, sheer, total, unqualified, utter.

start n 1 beginning, birth, commencement, creation, dawn, establishment, founding, inauguration, inception, initiation, institution, introduction, launch, onset, opening, origin, outset, point of departure, setting out. Opp FINISH. 2 unfair start. advantage, edge, head start, opportunity. 3 The loan gave me a start. assistance, backing, inf break, financing, help, sponsorship. 4 I woke with a start. jump, shock, surprise.
● v 1 depart, inf get going, get under way, sl hit the road, leave, move off, proceed, set off, set out. 2 activate, begin, commence, create, embark on, engender, establish, found, inf get off the ground, inf get the ball rolling, inaugurate, initiate, instigate, institute, introduce, launch, open, originate, pioneer, set in motion, set up. Opp FINISH.
3 blench, draw back, flinch, jerk,

jump, quail, recoil, shy, twitch, wince. **make someone start** ▷ STARTLE.

startle v alarm, catch unawares, disturb, frighten, jolt, make you jump, scare, shake, shock, surprise, take aback, take by surprise, upset. **startling** ▷ SURPRISING.

starvation n deprivation, famine, hunger, malnutrition, undernourishment, want.

starve v die of starvation, go hungry, go without, perish. **starve yourself** diet, fast, go on hunger strike, refuse food. **starving** ▷ HUNGRY.

state n 1 pl circumstances, condition, health, mood, inf shape, situation. 2 agitation, excitement, inf flap, panic, plight, predicament, inf tizzy. 3 sovereign state. land, nation. ▷ COUNTRY.
● v affirm, announce, assert, communicate, declare, express, formulate, proclaim, put into words, report, submit, testify, voice. ▷ SAY, SPEAK.

stately adj august, dignified, distinguished, formal, grand, imperial, imposing, impressive, lofty, majestic, noble, regal, royal, solemn, splendid. Opp INFORMAL. **stately home** ▷ MANSION.

statement n account, affirmation, announcement, assertion, bulletin, comment, communiqué, declaration, disclosure, explanation, message, notice, proclamation, proposition, report, testimony, utterance.

statesman n diplomat, politician.

static adj fixed, immobile, immovable, inert, invariable, motionless, passive, stable, stag-

nant, stationary, still, unchanging, unmoving. Opp MOBILE, VARIABLE.

station n 1 calling, class, level, location, occupation, place, position, post, rank, situation, standing, status. 2 fire station. base, depot, headquarters, office. 3 radio station. channel, company, wavelength. 4 railway station. halt, platform, terminus, train station. ● v assign, garrison, locate, place, position, put, site, situate, spot, stand.

stationary adj at a standstill, halted, immobile, motionless, parked, standing, static, still, stock-still, unmoving. Opp MOVING.

stationery n paper, office supplies, writing materials.

statistics n data, figures, information, numbers.

statue n carving, figure, statuette. ▷ SCULPTURE.

statuesque adj dignified, imposing, impressive, stately.

stature n 1 build, height, size. 2 artist of international stature. importance, reputation, standing. ▷ STATUS.

status n class, degree, eminence, grade, importance, level, position, prestige, prominence, rank, reputation, significance, standing, station, stature, title.

staunch adj ▷ STEADFAST.

stay n 1 holiday, stop, stopover, visit. 2 stay of execution. ▷ DELAY. 3 ▷ SUPPORT.
● v 1 carry on, continue, endure, hang about, hold out, keep on, last, linger, live on, loiter, persist, remain, survive, wait. 2 stay in a hotel. abide, be a guest, be housed, board, dwell,

live, lodge, reside, stop, visit. **3** *stay judgement*. ▷ DELAY.

steadfast *adj* committed, constant, dedicated, dependable, devoted, faithful, firm, loyal, patient, persevering, reliable, resolute, single-minded, sound, stalwart, staunch, steady, true, trustworthy, trusty, unchanging, unflinching, unswerving, unwavering. *Opp* UNRELIABLE.

steady *adj* **1** balanced, fast, firm, poised, safe, secure, settled, solid, stable. **2** *steady flow*. ceaseless, consistent, constant, continuous, endless, even, incessant, invariable, never-ending, non-stop, persistent, regular, reliable, repeated, rhythmic, *inf* round-the-clock, unbroken, unchanging, unhurried, uniform, uninterrupted, unrelieved, unremitting, unvarying. *Opp* UNSTEADY. **3** ▷ STEADFAST. ● *v* **1** balance, brace, keep still, secure, stabilize, support. **2** *steady your nerves*. calm, control, soothe.

steal *v* **1** appropriate, burgle, commandeer, confiscate, embezzle, expropriate, *inf* filch, hijack, *inf* lift, loot, *inf* make off with, misappropriate, *inf* nick, pick pockets, pilfer, pillage, plunder, poach, purloin, *inf* rip off, rob, seize, shoplift, *sl* snitch, *inf* swipe, take, thieve, walk off with. **2** *steal quietly upstairs*. creep, move stealthily, slink, slip, sneak, tiptoe.

stealing *n* pilfering, *inf* pinching, robbery, thieving. ▷ THEFT.

stealthy *adj* clandestine, covert, disguised, furtive, inconspicu-

ous, quiet, secret, secretive, sly, sneaky, surreptitious, underhand, unobtrusive. *Opp* BLATANT.

steam *n* condensation, haze, mist, moisture, vapour.

steamy *adj* **1** blurred, clouded, cloudy, fogged over, foggy, hazy, misted over, misty. **2** close, damp, humid, moist, muggy, *inf* sticky, sultry, sweaty, sweltering. **3** [*inf*] *steamy sex scenes*. ▷ SEXY.

steep *adj* **1** abrupt, headlong, perpendicular, precipitous, sharp, sheer, sudden, vertical. *Opp* GRADUAL. **2** *steep prices*. ▷ EXPENSIVE. ● *v* ▷ SOAK.

steeple *n* pinnacle, point, spire.

steer *v* be at the wheel, control, direct, drive, guide, navigate, pilot. **steer clear of** ▷ AVOID.

stem *n*, shoot, stalk, trunk, twig. ● *v* arise, derive, develop, flow, issue, originate, proceed, result, spring, sprout. **2** *stem the flow*. ▷ CHECK.

stench *n inf* pong, reek, stink. ▷ SMELL.

step *n* **1** footfall, footstep, pace, stride, tread. **2** doorstep, rung, stair, tread. **3** advance, move, movement, progress, progression. **4** *step in a process*. action, initiative, measure, phase, procedure, stage. ● *v* move, pace, stride, tread, walk. **steps** ladder, stairs, staircase, stairway, stepladder. **step down** ▷ RESIGN. **step in** ▷ ENTER, INTERVENE. **step on it** ▷ HURRY. **step up** ▷ INCREASE. **take steps** ▷ BEGIN.

stereotype *n* formula, model, pattern, stereotyped idea.

stereotyped adj clichéd, conventional, hackneyed, predictable, standard, stock, typecast, unoriginal.

sterile adj 1 arid, barren, childless, fruitless, infertile, lifeless, unfruitful, unproductive. 2 *sterile bandage*. antiseptic, aseptic, clean, disinfected, germfree, hygienic, pure, sterilized, uncontaminated, uninfected, unpolluted. *Opp* FERTILE, FRUITFUL, SEPTIC.

sterilize v 1 clean, cleanse, decontaminate, disinfect, fumigate, make sterile, purify. 2 *sterilize animals*. castrate, emasculate, geld, neuter, spay.

stern adj austere, authoritarian, dour, forbidding, frowning, grim, hard, harsh, inflexible, obdurate, rigid, rigorous, severe, strict, tough, unbending, uncompromising, unrelenting, unremitting. ▷ SERIOUS. *Opp* LENIENT.
• n *stern of ship*. aft, back, rear end.

stew n casserole, goulash, hotpot.
• v braise, casserole, simmer.

steward, stewardess ns 1 attendant, waiter. 2 marshal, officer, official.

stick n baton, cane, pole, stake, stalk, twig, walking stick, wand.
• v 1 dig, jab, pierce, pin, poke, prick, prod, puncture, stab, thrust. 2 *stick with glue*. adhere, affix, bind, bond, cement, fasten, glue, gum, paste, solder, weld. 3 *stick in your mind*. be fixed, continue, endure, last, linger, persist, remain, stay. 4 *the gears stuck*. seize up, jam, freeze. 5 ▷ TOLERATE. **stick at** ▷ PERSIST. **stick out** ▷ PROTRUDE. **stick together** ▷ UNITE. **stick up** ▷ PROTRUDE. **stick up**

for ▷ DEFEND. **stick with** ▷ SUPPORT.

sticky adj 1 adhesive, gummed, self-adhesive. 2 *sticky paint*. gluey, glutinous, *inf* gooey, gummy, tacky, viscous. 3 *sticky weather*. clammy, close, damp, humid, muggy, steamy, sultry, sweaty. *Opp* DRY.

stiff adj 1 firm, hard, inelastic, inflexible, rigid, solid, solidified, stiffened, taut, thick, tough, unbendable. 2 *stiff joints*. arthritic, painful, rheumatic, tight. 3 *stiff task*. arduous, challenging, difficult, exacting, exhausting, hard, laborious, tiring, tough, uphill. 4 *stiff opposition*. determined, dogged, resolute, stubborn, unyielding, vigorous. 5 *stiff manner*. artificial, awkward, cold, forced, formal, graceless, haughty, inelegant, laboured, mannered, pedantic, self-conscious, standoffish, starchy, stilted, *inf* stuffy, tense, turgid, unnatural, wooden. 6 *stiff penalties*. cruel, drastic, excessive, harsh, merciless, pitiless, punitive, rigorous, severe, strict. 7 *stiff wind*. brisk, fresh, strong. 8 *stiff drink*. alcoholic, potent, strong. *Opp* EASY, RELAXED, SOFT.

stiffen v become stiff, clot, coagulate, congeal, dry out, harden, *inf* jell, set, solidify, thicken, tighten, toughen.

stifle v 1 asphyxiate, choke, smother, strangle, suffocate, throttle. 2 *stifle laughter*. check, control, curb, dampen, muffle, restrain, suppress, withhold. 3 *stifle free speech*. destroy, extinguish, quash, repress, silence, stamp out, stop.

stigma n blot, disgrace, dishonour, mark, shame, slur, stain, taint.

stigmatize v brand, condemn, denounce, label, mark, slander, vilify.

still adj at rest, calm, even, flat, hushed, immobile, inert, lifeless, motionless, noiseless, peaceful, placid, quiet, restful, serene, silent, smooth, soundless, static, stationary, tranquil, unmoving, unruffled, untroubled, windless. *Opp* ACTIVE, NOISY. • v allay, appease, assuage, calm, lull, pacify, quieten, settle, silence, soothe, subdue. *Opp* AGITATE.

stimulant n antidepressant, drug, *inf* pick-me-up, restorative, *inf* reviver, *inf* shot in the arm, tonic. ▷ STIMULUS.

stimulate v activate, arouse, awaken, encourage, excite, fan, fire, foment, galvanize, goad, incite, inflame, inspire, instigate, invigorate, kindle, motivate, prompt, provoke, quicken, rouse, spur, stir up, urge, whet. *Opp* DISCOURAGE.

stimulating adj arousing, challenging, exciting, exhilarating, inspiring, interesting, intoxicating, invigorating, provocative, rousing, stirring, thought-provoking. *Opp* UNINTERESTING.

stimulus n encouragement, fillip, goad, incentive, inducement, inspiration, provocation, spur, stimulant. *Opp* DISCOURAGEMENT.

sting n bite, prick, stab. ▷ PAIN. • v 1 bite, nip, prick, wound. 2 smart, tingle. ▷ HURT.

stingy adj 1 *inf* cheese-paring, close, close-fisted, mean, *inf* mingy, miserly, niggardly, parsimonious, penny-pinching, tight-fisted, ungenerous. 2 *stingy* helpings. insufficient, meagre, *inf* measly, scanty. ▷ SMALL. *Opp* GENEROUS.

stink n, v ▷ SMELL.

stipulate v demand, insist on, require, specify.

stipulation n condition, demand, prerequisite, proviso, requirement, specification.

stir n ▷ COMMOTION. • v 1 beat, blend, churn, mingle, mix, scramble, whisk. 2 *stir from sleep*. arise, bestir yourself, *inf* get a move on, *inf* get going, get up, move, rise, *inf* show signs of life. 3 *stir emotions*. activate, affect, arouse, awaken, electrify, excite, exhilarate, fire, impress, inspire, kindle, move, revive, rouse, stimulate, touch, upset.

stirring adj affecting, arousing, dramatic, electrifying, emotional, emotive, exciting, exhilarating, heady, impassioned, inspiring, interesting, intoxicating, invigorating, moving, provocative, rousing, spirited, stimulating, thought-provoking, thrilling. *Opp* UNEXCITING.

stitch v darn, mend, repair, sew, tack.

stock adj banal, clichéd, commonplace, conventional, customary, expected, hackneyed, ordinary, predictable, regular, routine, *inf* run-of-the-mill, set, standard, staple, stereotyped, *inf* tired, traditional, trite, usual. *Opp* UNEXPECTED. • n 1 cache, hoard, reserve, reservoir, stockpile, store, supply. 2 goods, merchandise, range, wares. 3 *farm stock*. animals, beasts, cattle, livestock. 4 *ancient stock*. ancestry, blood, breeding, descent, extraction, family, forebears, genealogy, line, lineage, parentage, pedigree. 5 *treasury stock*. ▷ CAPITAL. ● *v* carry, deal in, handle, have available, *inf* keep, keep in stock, offer, provide, sell, supply, trade in. **out of stock** sold out, unavailable. **take stock** ▷ REVIEW.

stockade *n* fence, paling, palisade, wall.

stockist *n* merchant, retailer, seller, shopkeeper, supplier.

stocky *adj* burly, dumpy, short, solid, stubby, sturdy, thickset. *Opp* TALL, THIN.

stodgy *adj* 1 filling, heavy, indigestible, solid, starchy. 2 *stodgy book*. boring, dull, ponderous, *inf* stuffy, tedious, tiresome, turgid, uninteresting. *Opp* LIVELY.

stoical *adj* calm, cool, impassive, imperturbable, long-suffering, patient, philosophical, phlegmatic, resigned, stolid, uncomplaining. *Opp* EXCITABLE.

stoke *v* fuel, keep burning, put fuel on, tend.

stole *n* cape, shawl, wrap.

stolid *adj* bovine, dull, heavy, impassive, phlegmatic, unemotional, unimaginative, wooden. ▷ STOICAL. *Opp* LIVELY.

stomach *n* abdomen, belly, *inf* guts, *inf* insides, *derog* paunch, *derog* pot, *inf* tummy. ● *v* ▷ TOLERATE.

stomach-ache *n* colic, *inf* gripes, *inf* tummy-ache.

stone *n* 1 boulder, cobble, *pl* gravel, pebble, *pl* scree. ▷ ROCK. 2 block, flagstone, slab. 3 *memorial stone*. gravestone, headstone, obelisk, tablet.

4 *precious stone*. ▷ JEWEL.
5 *peach stone*. pip, pit, seed.

stony *adj* 1 pebbly, rocky, rough, shingly. 2 *stony silence*. callous, chilly, cold, expressionless, hard, heartless, hostile, icy, indifferent, merciless, obdurate, pitiless, steely, unfeeling, unforgiving, unresponsive, unsympathetic.

stooge *n* butt, dupe, *inf* fall-guy, lackey, puppet.

stoop *v* 1 bend, bow, crouch, duck, hunch your shoulders, kneel, lean, squat. 2 condescend, degrade yourself, deign, humble yourself, lower yourself, sink.

stop *n* 1 ban, cessation, close, conclusion, end, finish, halt, pause, shut-down, standstill, stoppage, termination. 2 *bus stop*. station, stopping place, terminus. 3 *a stop at a hotel*. break, holiday, stay, vacation, visit. ● *v* 1 break off, call a halt to, cease, conclude, cut off, desist from, discontinue, end, finish, halt, *inf* knock off, leave off, *inf* pack in, pause, *inf* quit, refrain from, terminate. 2 bar, block, check, curb, delay, frustrate, halt, hamper, hinder, impede, intercept, interrupt, *inf* nip in the bud, obstruct, put a stop to, stanch, stem, suppress, thwart. 3 *stop in a hotel*. be a guest, have a holiday, spend time, stay, visit. 4 *stop a gap*. close, fill in, plug, seal. 5 *stop a thief*. arrest, capture, catch, detain, hold, seize. 6 *the rain stopped*. cease, come to an end, finish, peter out. 7 *the bus stopped*. come to rest, draw up, halt, pull up.

stopper *n* bung, cork, plug.

store *n* 1 accumulation, cache, fund, hoard, quantity, reserve,

reservoir, stock, stockpile, supply. ▷ STOREHOUSE.
2 *grocery store*. ▷ SHOP.
● *v* accumulate, deposit, hoard, keep, lay by, lay in, lay up, preserve, put away, reserve, save, set aside, *inf* stash away, stockpile, stock up, store away.

storehouse *n* armoury, arsenal, depository, depot, repository, store, storeroom, warehouse.

storey *n* deck, floor, level, stage, tier.

storm *n* **1** blizzard, cloudburst, cyclone, deluge, disturbance, dust-storm, electrical storm, gale, hailstorm, hurricane, monsoon, rainstorm, sandstorm, snowstorm, squall, tempest, thunderstorm, tornado, typhoon, turbulence, whirlwind. **2** *storm of protest*. ▷ CLAMOUR.
● *v* ▷ ATTACK.

stormy *adj* angry, blustery, choppy, fierce, furious, gusty, raging, rough, squally, tempestuous, thundery, tumultuous, turbulent, vehement, violent, wild, windy. *Opp* CALM.

story *n* **1** account, anecdote, chronicle, detective story, epic, fable, fairy tale, fiction, history, legend, myth, narrative, parable, plot, recital, romance, saga, tale, thriller, *inf* whodunit, yarn.
2 *story in newspaper*. article, exclusive, feature, news item, piece, report, scoop. **3** falsehood, *inf* fib, lie, tall story, untruth.

storyteller *n* author, narrator, raconteur, teller.

stout *adj* **1** beefy, chubby, corpulent, fleshy, heavy, *inf* hulking, overweight, plump, portly, solid, stocky, *inf* strapping, thickset, tubby, well-built. ▷ FAT. *Opp* THIN.

2 *stout rope*. durable, robust, sound, strong, sturdy, substantial, thick, tough. **3** *stout fighter*. bold, brave, courageous, fearless, gallant, heroic, intrepid, plucky, resolute, spirited, valiant. *Opp* WEAK.

stove *n* boiler, cooker, fire, furnace, heater, oven, range.

stow *v* load, pack, put away, *inf* stash away, store.

straggle *v* be scattered, dawdle, drift, fall behind, lag, loiter, meander, ramble, scatter, spread out, stray, trail, wander. **straggling** ▷ DISORGANIZED, LOOSE.

straight *adj* **1** direct, even, flat, horizontal, level, regular, smooth, true, unbending, undeviating, unswerving, vertical.
2 neat, orderly, organized, right, shipshape, spruce, tidy.
3 *straight sequence*. consecutive, continuous, non-stop, perfect, sustained, unbroken, uninterrupted. **4** ▷ STRAIGHTFORWARD. *Opp* CROOKED, INDIRECT, UNTIDY. **straight away** at once, directly, immediately, instantly, now, without delay.

straighten *v* disentangle, put straight, rearrange, sort out, tidy, unravel, untangle.

straightforward *adj* blunt, candid, direct, easy, forthright, frank, genuine, honest, intelligible, lucid, open, plain, simple, sincere, straight, truthful, uncomplicated. *Opp* DEVIOUS.

strain *n* **1** anxiety, difficulty, effort, exertion, hardship, pressure, stress, tension, worry.
2 *genetic strain*. ▷ ANCESTRY.
● *v* **1** haul, heave, pull, stretch, tug. **2** *strain to succeed*. endeavour, exert yourself, labour, make an effort, strive, struggle, toil,

try. 3 *strain yourself*. exhaust, overtax, *inf* push to the limit, stretch, tax, tire out, weaken, wear out. 4 *strain a muscle*. damage, hurt, injure, pull, sprain, tear, twist, wrench, 5 *strain liquid*. drain, draw off, filter, percolate, purify, riddle, separate, sieve, sift.

strained *adj* 1 artificial, awkward, false, forced, insincere, self-conscious, stiff, tense, uncomfortable, uneasy, unnatural. 2 *strained look*. drawn, tired, weary. 3 *strained interpretation*. far-fetched, incredible, laboured, unlikely.
Opp NATURAL, RELAXED.

strainer *n* colander, filter, riddle, sieve.

strand *n* fibre, filament, string, thread, wire. ● *v* 1 abandon, desert, forsake, maroon. 2 *strand a ship*. beach, ground, run aground, wreck. **stranded**
▷ AGROUND, HELPLESS.

strange *adj* 1 abnormal, astonishing, atypical, bizarre, curious, eerie, exceptional, extraordinary, fantastic, *inf* funny, irregular, odd, out of the ordinary, peculiar, quaint, queer, rare, remarkable, singular, surprising, surreal, uncommon, unexpected, unheard-of, unique, unnatural, untypical, unusual. 2 *strange neighbours*. *inf* cranky, eccentric, unconventional, weird. 3 *strange problem*. baffling, bewildering, inexplicable, mysterious, mystifying, perplexing, puzzling, unaccountable. 4 *strange places*. exotic, foreign, little-known, off the beaten track, outlandish, out-of-the-way, remote, unexplored. 5 *strange experience*. different, fresh, new,

novel, unaccustomed, unfamiliar. *Opp* FAMILIAR, ORDINARY.

strangeness *n* abnormality, bizarreness, eccentricity, eeriness, irregularity, mysteriousness, novelty, oddity, peculiarity, rarity, singularity, unfamiliarity.

stranger *n* alien, foreigner, newcomer, outsider, visitor.

strangle *v* 1 asphyxiate, choke, garrotte, smother, stifle, suffocate, throttle. 2 *strangle a cry*.
▷ SUPPRESS.

strangulation *n* asphyxiation, garrotting, suffocation.

strap *n* band, belt, thong, webbing. ● *v* ▷ FASTEN.

stratagem *n* device, *inf* dodge, manoeuvre, plan, ploy, ruse, scheme, subterfuge, tactic, trick.

strategic *adj* advantageous, critical, crucial, deliberate, key, politic, tactical, vital.

strategy *n* approach, design, manoeuvre, method, plan, plot, policy, procedure, programme, scheme, tactics.

stratum *n* layer, seam, sheet, thickness, vein.

stray *adj* 1 abandoned, homeless, lost, roaming, wandering. 2 *stray bullets*. accidental, chance, haphazard, occasional, odd, random. ● *v* 1 get lost, get separated, go astray, meander, ramble, range, roam, rove, straggle, wander. 2 *stray from the point*. deviate, digress, diverge, drift, get off the subject, go off at a tangent, veer.

streak *n* 1 band, bar, dash, line, mark, smear, stain, strip, stripe, vein. 2 *selfish streak*. element, strain, touch, trace. 3 *streak of good luck*. period, run, series, spate, spell, stretch, time.

● *v* 1 smear, smudge, stain.
2 *streak past.* dart, dash, flash,
fly, gallop, hurtle, move at
speed, rush, *inf* scoot, speed,
sprint, *inf* tear, *inf* whip, zoom.

streaky *adj* barred, lined,
smeary, smudged, streaked,
stripy, veined.

stream *n* 1 beck, brook, burn,
channel, *poet* rill, river, rivulet,
watercourse. 2 cascade, cataract,
current, deluge, flood, flow, fountain, gush, jet, outpouring, rush,
spate, spurt, surge, tide, torrent.
● *v* cascade, course, deluge,
flood, flow, gush, issue, pour,
run, spill, spout, spurt, squirt,
surge, well.

streamer *n* banner, flag,
pennant, pennon, ribbon.

streamlined *adj* 1 aerodynamic,
elegant, graceful, sleek, smooth.
2 ▷ EFFICIENT.

street *n* avenue, roadway,
terrace. ▷ ROAD.

strength *n* 1 brawn, capacity,
energy, fitness, force, health,
might, muscle, power, resilience, robustness, sinew, stamina, toughness, vigour.
2 *strength of purpose.* backbone,
commitment, courage, determination, firmness, *inf* grit, perseverance, persistence, resolution, resolve, spirit, tenacity.
Opp WEAKNESS.

strengthen *v* 1 bolster, boost,
brace, build up, buttress, encourage, fortify, harden, hearten,
increase, make stronger, prop
up, reinforce, stiffen, support,
tone up, toughen. 2 *strengthen
an argument.* back up, consolidate, corroborate, enhance, justify, substantiate. *Opp* WEAKEN.

strenuous *adj* 1 arduous,
back-breaking, burdensome,

demanding, difficult, exhausting,
gruelling, hard, laborious, punishing, stiff, taxing, tough,
uphill. *Opp* EASY. 2 *strenuous
efforts.* active, determined,
dogged, dynamic, eager, energetic, herculean, indefatigable,
spirited, strong, tenacious, tireless, unremitting, vigorous, zealous. *Opp* CASUAL.

stress *n* 1 anxiety, difficulty, distress, hardship, pressure, strain,
tension, trauma, worry.
2 accent, accentuation, beat,
emphasis, importance, urgency,
weight. ● *v* 1 accent, accentuate,
assert, draw attention to,
emphasize, feature, highlight,
insist on, lay stress on, mark,
repeat, spotlight, underline,
underscore. 2 *stressed by work.*
burden, overstrain, pressure,
pressurize, *inf* push to the limit,
tax, weigh down.

stressful *adj* anxious, difficult,
taxing, tense, traumatic, worrying. *Opp* RELAXED.

stretch *n* 1 period, spell, stint,
term, time, tour of duty.
2 *stretch of country.* area, distance, expanse, length, span,
spread, sweep, tract. ● *v* 1 crane
(*your neck*), dilate, distend, draw
out, elongate, expand, extend,
inflate, lengthen, open out, pull
out, spread out, swell, tauten,
tighten, widen. 2 *stretch into the
distance.* continue, disappear,
extend, go, reach out, spread.
3 *stretch resources.* overextend,
overtax, *inf* push to the limit,
strain, tax.

strew *v* disperse, distribute,
scatter, spread, sprinkle.

strict *adj* 1 austere, authoritarian, autocratic, firm, harsh, merciless, *inf* no-nonsense, rigorous,

severe, stern, stringent, tyrannical, uncompromising. Opp EASYGOING. **2** *strict rules.* absolute, binding, *inf* hard and fast, inflexible, precise, rigid, stringent, tight. Opp FLEXIBLE. **3** *strict truthfulness.* accurate, complete, correct, exact, perfect, precise, right, scrupulous.

stride *n* pace, step. ● *v* ▷ WALK.

strident *adj* clamorous, discordant, grating, harsh, jarring, loud, noisy, beat, raucous, screeching, shrill, unmusical. Opp SOFT.

strife *n* animosity, arguing, bickering, competition, discord, disharmony, dissension, enmity, friction, hostility, quarrelling, rivalry, unfriendliness. ▷ FIGHT. Opp COOPERATION.

strike *n* **1** go-slow, industrial action, stoppage, walk-out, withdrawal of labour. **2** assault, attack, bombardment. ● *v* **1** bang against, bang into, beat, collide with, hammer, knock, rap, run into, smack, smash into, thump, whack. ▷ ATTACK, HIT. **2** *strike a match.* ignite, light. **3** *The tragedy struck us deeply.* affect, afflict, *inf* come home to, *inf* impress. **4** *clock struck one.* chime, ring, sound. **5** *strike for more pay.* *inf* come out, *inf* down tools, stop work, take industrial action, withdraw labour, work to rule. **6** *strike a flag, tent.* dismantle, lower, pull down, remove, take down.

striking *adj* arresting, conspicuous, distinctive, extraordinary, glaring, impressive, memorable, noticeable, obvious, out of the ordinary, outstanding, prominent, showy, stunning, telling, unmistakable, unusual. Opp INCONSPICUOUS.

string *n* **1** cable, cord, fibre, line, rope, twine. **2** chain, file, line, procession, progression, queue, row, sequence, series, stream, succession, train. ● *v* *string together* connect, join, line up, link, thread.

stringy *adj* chewy, fibrous, gristly, sinewy, tough. Opp TENDER.

strip *n* band, belt, fillet, line, narrow piece, ribbon, shred, slat, sliver, stripe, swathe. ● *v* **1** bare, clear, defoliate, denude, divest, flay, lay bare, peel, remove the covering, remove the paint, remove the skin, skin, uncover. Opp COVER. **2** *strip to the waist.* bare yourself, disrobe, get undressed, uncover yourself. Opp DRESS. **strip down** ▷ DISMANTLE. **strip off** ▷ UNDRESS.

stripe *n* band, bar, chevron, line, ribbon, streak, strip.

striped *adj* banded, barred, lined, streaky, stripy.

strive *v* attempt, *inf* do your best, endeavour, make an effort, strain, struggle, try.

stroke *n* **1** blow, knock, move, swipe. ▷ HIT. **2** *stroke of the pen.* flourish, gesture, line, mark, movement, sweep. **3** [*medical*] attack, embolism, fit, seizure, spasm, thrombosis. ● *v* caress, fondle, massage, pat, pet, rub, soothe, touch.

stroll *n*, *v* amble, meander, saunter, wander. ▷ WALK.

strong *adj* **1** durable, hard, hardwearing, heavy-duty, impregnable, indestructible, permanent, reinforced, resilient, robust, sound, stout, substantial, thick, unbreakable, well-made. **2** *strong physique.* athletic, *inf* beefy, brawny, burly, fit, *inf* hale and hearty, hardy, *inf* hefty, mighty, muscular, powerful, robust, sinewy, stalwart, *inf* strapping, sturdy, tough, well-built, wiry. **3** *strong personality.* assertive, determined, dogmatic, domineering, dynamic, energetic, forceful, independent, reliable, resolute, stalwart, steadfast, strong-minded, strong-willed, tenacious, vigorous. ▷ STUBBORN. **4** *strong commitment.* active, assiduous, deep-rooted, deep-seated, eager, earnest, fervent, fierce, firm, genuine, intense, keen, loyal, passionate, positive, sedulous, staunch, true, vehement, zealous. **5** *strong government.* decisive, dependable, *derog* dictatorial, *derog* doctrinaire, firm, unswerving. **6** *strong measures.* aggressive, draconian, drastic, extreme, harsh, high-handed, ruthless, severe, tough, unflinching, violent. **7** *strong army.* formidable, invincible, large, numerous, powerful, unconquerable, well-equipped, well-trained. **8** *strong colour, light.* bright, brilliant, clear, dazzling, garish, glaring, vivid. **9** *strong taste, smell.* highly-flavoured, hot, intense, noticeable, obvious, overpowering, prominent, pronounced, pungent, sharp, spicy, unmistakable. **10** *strong evidence.* clear-cut, cogent, compelling, convincing, persuasive, plain, solid, telling, undisputed. **11** *strong drink.* alcoholic, concentrated, intoxicating, potent, undiluted. *Opp* WEAK.

stronghold *n* bastion, bulwark, castle, citadel, fort, fortification, fortress, garrison.

structure *n* **1** arrangement, composition, configuration, constitution, design, form, *inf* make-up, order, organization, plan, shape, system. **2** building, construction, edifice, fabric, framework, pile, superstructure. ● *v* arrange, build, construct, design, form, frame, give structure to, organize, shape, systematize.

struggle *n* **1** challenge, difficulty, effort, endeavour, exertion, labour, problem. **2** ▷ FIGHT. ● *v* **1** endeavour, exert yourself, labour, make an effort, strain, strive, toil, try, work hard, wrestle. **2** *struggle through mud.* flail, flounder, stumble, wallow. **3** ▷ FIGHT.

stub *n* butt, end, remains, remnant, stump. ● *v* ▷ HIT.

stubble *n* **1** stalks, straw. **2** beard, bristles, *inf* five-o'clock shadow, hair, roughness.

stubbly *adj* bristly, prickly, rough, unshaven.

stubborn *adj* defiant, determined, difficult, dogged, headstrong, inflexible, intractable, intransigent, *inf* mulish, obdurate, obstinate, persistent, pertinacious, *inf* pig-headed, recalcitrant, refractory, rigid, self-willed, tenacious, uncompromising, uncooperative, unmanageable, unreasonable, unyielding, wayward, wilful. *Opp* AMENABLE.

stuck *adj* **1** bogged down, cemented, fast, fastened, firm, fixed, glued, immovable. **2** baffled, beaten, *inf* stumped, *inf* stymied.

stuck-up *adj* arrogant, *inf* big-headed, bumptious, *inf* cocky, conceited, condescending, *inf* high-and-mighty, patronizing, proud, self-important, snobbish, *inf* snooty, supercilious, *inf* toffee-nosed. *Opp* MODEST.

student *n* apprentice, disciple, learner, postgraduate, pupil, scholar, schoolchild, trainee, undergraduate.

studied *adj* calculated, conscious, contrived, deliberate, intentional, planned, premeditated.

studious *adj* academic, assiduous, attentive, bookish, *inf* brainy, earnest, hardworking, intellectual, scholarly, serious-minded, thoughtful.

study *v* 1 analyse, consider, contemplate, enquire into, examine, give attention to, investigate, look closely at, peruse, pore over, read carefully, research, scrutinize, survey, think about. 2 *study for exams.* *inf* cram, learn, *inf* mug up, read, *inf* swot, work.

stuff *n* 1 ingredients, matter, substance. 2 cloth, fabric, material, textile. 3 *all sorts of stuff.* accoutrements, articles, belongings, *inf* bits and pieces, *inf* clobber, effects, *inf* gear, junk, objects, paraphernalia, possessions, *inf* tackle, things. ● *v* 1 compress, cram, crowd, force, jam, pack, press, push, ram, shove, squeeze, stow, thrust. 2 *stuff a cushion.* fill, pad. **stuff yourself** ▷ EAT.

stuffing *n* 1 filling, padding, quilting, wadding. 2 *stuffing in poultry.* forcemeat, seasoning.

stuffy *adj* 1 airless, close, fetid, fuggy, fusty, heavy, humid, muggy, musty, oppressive, stale, steamy, stifling, suffocating, sultry, unventilated, warm.

Opp AIRY. 2 [*inf*] *stuffy old bore.* boring, conventional, dreary, dull, formal, humourless, narrow-minded, old-fashioned, pompous, prim, staid, *inf* stodgy, strait-laced. *Opp* LIVELY.

stumble *v* 1 blunder, flounder, lurch, miss your footing, reel, slip, stagger, totter, trip, tumble. 2 *stumble through a speech.* become tongue-tied, falter, hesitate, stammer, stutter.

stumbling block *n* difficulty, hindrance, hurdle, impediment, obstacle, snag.

stump *v* baffle, bewilder, *inf* catch out, confound, confuse, defeat, *inf* flummox, mystify, outwit, perplex, puzzle, *inf* stymie. **stump up** ▷ PAY.

stun *v* 1 daze, knock out, knock senseless. 2 amaze, astonish, astound, bewilder, confound, confuse, dumbfound, flabbergast, numb, shock, stagger, stupefy. **stunning** ▷ BEAUTIFUL, STUPENDOUS.

stunt *n* exploit, feat, trick. ● *v* stunt growth. ▷ CHECK.

stupendous *adj* amazing, colossal, enormous, exceptional, extraordinary, huge, incredible, marvellous, miraculous, phenomenal, prodigious, remarkable, *inf* sensational, singular, special, staggering, stunning, tremendous, unbelievable, wonderful. *Opp* ORDINARY.

stupid *adj* [*Most synonyms derog*] 1 addled, bird-brained, boneheaded, bovine, brainless, clueless, dense, dim, doltish, dopey, drippy, dull, dumb, emptyheaded, feather-brained, feebleminded, foolish, gormless, halfwitted, idiotic, ignorant, imbecilic, lacking, mindless, moronic, naive, obtuse, puerile, senseless, silly, simple, simple-minded, slow, slow in the uptake, thick, thickheaded, thick-skulled, unintelligent, unthinking, unwise, vacuous, weak in the head, witless. 2 *It was a stupid thing to do.* absurd, asinine, barmy, crack-brained, crass, fatuous, futile, half-baked, hare-brained, ill-advised, inane, irrational, irresponsible, laughable, ludicrous, lunatic, mad, nonsensical, pointless, rash, reckless, ridiculous, scatterbrained, thoughtless. 3 *I had to read a pile of stupid books.* boring, dreary, dull, monotonous, tedious, tiresome, uninteresting. Opp INTELLIGENT. **stupid person** ▷ FOOL.

stupidity n absurdity, crassness, *inf* dumbness, fatuousness, folly, foolishness, futility, idiocy, ignorance, imbecility, lack of intelligence, lunacy, madness, mindlessness, naivety, pointlessness, recklessness, silliness, thoughtlessness. Opp INTELLIGENCE.

stupor n coma, daze, inertia, lassitude, lethargy, numbness, shock, state of insensibility, torpor, trance, unconsciousness.

sturdy adj 1 athletic, brawny, burly, hardy, healthy, hefty, muscular, powerful, robust, stalwart, stocky, *inf* strapping, vigorous, well-built. 2 *sturdy shoes.* durable, solid, substantial, tough, well-made. 3 *sturdy opposition.* determined, firm, indomitable, resolute, staunch, steadfast, vigorous. ▷ STRONG. Opp WEAK.

stutter v falter, hesitate, stammer, stumble.

style n 1 chic, dash, dress-sense, elegance, flair, flamboyance, panache, polish, refinement, smartness, sophistication, stylishness, taste. 2 *the latest style.* craze, fad, fashion, mode, look, trend, vogue. 3 *style of writing.* approach, manner, mode of expression, phraseology, phrasing, sentence structure, tenor, tone, wording. 4 *style of clothes.* cut, design, fashion, make, pattern, shape, type.

stylish adj chic, *inf* classy, contemporary, dapper, elegant, fashionable, modern, *inf* natty, *inf* posh, smart, *inf* snazzy, sophisticated, *inf* trendy, up-to-date. Opp OLD-FASHIONED.

subconscious adj deep-rooted, hidden, inner, intuitive, latent, repressed, subliminal, suppressed, unacknowledged, unconscious. Opp CONSCIOUS.

subdue v check, curb, hold back, moderate, quieten, repress, restrain, suppress, temper. ▷ SUBJUGATE.

subdued adj 1 chastened, crestfallen, depressed, downcast, grave, reflective, restrained, serious, silent, sober, solemn, thoughtful. ▷ SAD. Opp EXCITED. 2 *subdued music.* hushed, low, mellow, muted, peaceful, placid, quiet, soft, soothing, tranquil, unobtrusive.

subject adj 1 captive, dependent, enslaved, oppressed, ruled, subjugated. 2 *subject to interference.* exposed, liable, prone, susceptible, vulnerable. Opp FREE.
● n 1 citizen, dependant, national, passport-holder, taxpayer, voter. 2 *subject for discussion.* affair, business, issue, matter, point, proposition,

question, theme, thesis, topic.
3 *subject of study.* area, branch of knowledge, course, discipline, field. ● v **1** *subject a thing to scrutiny.* expose, lay open, submit. **2** ▷ SUBJUGATE.

subjective *adj* biased, emotional, *inf* gut (*reaction*), individual, instinctive, intuitive, personal, prejudiced. *Opp* OBJECTIVE.

subjugate *v* beat, conquer, control, crush, defeat, dominate, enslave, *inf* get the better of, master, oppress, overcome, overpower, put down, quash, quell, subdue, subject, tame, triumph over, vanquish.

sublimate *v* divert, idealize, purify, redirect, refine.

sublime *adj* ecstatic, elevated, exalted, heavenly, inspiring, lofty, noble, spiritual, splendid, transcendent. *Opp* BASE.

submerge *v* **1** cover with water, dip, drench, drown, dunk, engulf, flood, immerse, inundate, overwhelm, soak, swamp. **2** dive, go under, plummet, sink, subside.

submission *n* **1** acquiescence, capitulation, compliance, giving in, surrender, yielding.
▷ SUBMISSIVENESS.
2 contribution, entry, offering, presentation, tender. **3** *legal submission.* argument, claim, contention, idea, proposal, suggestion, theory.

submissive *adj* accommodating, acquiescent, amenable, biddable, *derog* boot-licking, compliant, deferential, docile, humble, meek, obedient, obsequious, passive, resigned, servile, sycophantic, tame, tractable, unas-

sertive, uncomplaining, weak, yielding. *Opp* ASSERTIVE.

submissiveness *n* acquiescence, compliance, deference, docility, humility, meekness, obedience, passivity, resignation, submission, subservience, tameness.

submit *v* **1** accede, bow, capitulate, concede, give in, *inf* knuckle under, succumb, surrender, yield. **2** *submit a proposal.* advance, enter, give in, hand in, offer, present, proffer, propose, propound, put forward, state, suggest. **submit to** ▷ ACCEPT, OBEY.

subordinate *adj* inferior, junior, lesser, lower, menial, minor, secondary, subservient, subsidiary. ● n aide, assistant, dependant, employee, inferior, junior, menial, *inf* underling.

subscribe *v* **subscribe to 1** contribute to, donate to, give to, patronize, sponsor, support. **2** *subscribe to a magazine.* buy regularly, pay a subscription to. **3** *subscribe to a theory.* advocate, agree with, approve of, *inf* back, believe in, condone, endorse, *inf* give your blessing to.

subscriber *n* patron, regular customer, sponsor, supporter.

subscription *n* fee, due, payment, regular contribution, remittance.

subsequent *adj* consequent, ensuing, following, future, later, next, resultant, resulting, succeeding. *Opp* PREVIOUS.

subside *v* **1** abate, decline, decrease, die down, diminish, dwindle, ebb, fall, lessen, melt away, moderate, quieten, recede, shrink, slacken, wear off. **2** *subside into a chair.* collapse, descend, lower yourself, settle, sink. *Opp* RISE.

subsidiary *adj* additional, ancillary, auxiliary, complementary, contributory, lesser, minor, secondary, subordinate.

subsidize *v* aid, back, finance, fund, maintain, promote, sponsor, support, underwrite.

subsidy *n* aid, backing, financial help, funding, grant, sponsorship, support.

substance *n* **1** actuality, body, corporeality, reality, solidity. **2** chemical, fabric, material, matter, stuff. **3** *substance of an argument.* core, essence, gist, import, meaning, significance, subject-matter, theme. **4** [*old use*] *person of substance.* ▷ WEALTH.

substandard *adj inf* below par, disappointing, inadequate, inferior, poor, shoddy.

substantial 1 durable, hefty, massive, solid, stout, strong, sturdy, well-built, well-made. **2** big, considerable, generous, great, large, significant, sizeable, worthwhile. *Opp* FLIMSY, SMALL.

substitute *adj* **1** acting, deputy, relief, reserve, stand-by, surrogate, temporary. **2** alternative, ersatz, imitation. ● *n* alternative, deputy, locum, proxy, relief, replacement, reserve, stand-in, stopgap, substitution, supply, surrogate, understudy.
● *v* **1** change, exchange, interchange, replace, *inf* swop, *inf* switch. **2** *substitute for an absentee.* cover, deputize, double, stand in, supplant, take the place of, understudy.

subtle *adj* **1** delicate, elusive, faint, fine, gentle, mild, slight, unobtrusive. **2** *subtle argument.* clever, indirect, ingenious,

refined, shrewd, sophisticated, tactful, understated. ▷ CUNNING. *Opp* OBVIOUS.

subtract *v* debit, deduct, remove, take away. *Opp* ADD.

suburban *adj* residential, outer, outlying.

suburbs *n* fringes, outer areas, outskirts, residential areas, suburbia.

subversive *adj* challenging, disruptive, questioning, radical, seditious, treacherous, unsettling. ▷ REVOLUTIONARY. *Opp* CONSERVATIVE, ORTHODOX.

subvert *v* challenge, corrupt, destroy, disrupt, overthrow, overturn, pervert, ruin, undermine, upset, wreck.

subway *n* tunnel, underpass.

succeed *v* **1** *inf* arrive, be a success, do well, flourish, *inf* get on, *inf* get to the top, *inf* make it, prosper, thrive. **2** be effective, *inf* catch on, produce results, work. **3** be successor to, come after, follow, inherit from, replace, take over from. *Opp* FAIL. **succeeding** ▷ SUBSEQUENT.

success *n* **1** fame, good fortune, prosperity, wealth. **2** *success of a plan.* accomplishment, achievement, attainment, completion, effectiveness, successful outcome. **3** *a great success. inf* hit, *inf* sensation, triumph, victory, *inf* winner. *Opp* FAILURE.

successful *adj* **1** booming, effective, flourishing, fruitful, lucrative, money-making, productive, profitable, profit-making, prosperous, thriving, useful, well-off. **2** best-selling, celebrated, famed, famous, leading, popular, top, unbeaten, victorious, well-

known, winning.
Opp UNSUCCESSFUL.

succession n chain, flow, line, procession, progression, run, sequence, series, string.

successive adj consecutive, continuous, in succession, uninterrupted.

successor n heir, inheritor, replacement.

succinct adj brief, compact, concise, condensed, epigrammatic, pithy, short, terse, to the point. Opp WORDY.

succulent adj fleshy, juicy, luscious, moist, mouthwatering, rich, tender.

succumb v accede, be overcome, capitulate, give in, give up, give way, submit, surrender, yield. Opp RESIST.

suck v suck up absorb, soak up. suck up to ▷ FLATTER.

sudden adj 1 abrupt, hasty, hurried, impetuous, impulsive, precipitate, quick, rash, inf snap, swift, unconsidered, unplanned, unpremeditated. Opp SLOW.
2 sudden shock. sharp, startling, surprising, unexpected, unforeseeable, unforeseen, unlooked-for. Opp PREDICTABLE.

suds n bubbles, foam, froth, lather, soapsuds.

sue v 1 indict, proceed against, prosecute, summons, take legal action against. 2 sue for peace. ▷ ENTREAT.

suffer v 1 bear, cope with, endure, experience, feel, go through, live through, put up with, stand, tolerate, undergo, withstand. 2 suffer from a wound. ache, agonize, hurt, smart. 3 suffer for a crime. be punished, make amends, pay.

suffice v answer, be sufficient, inf do, satisfy, serve.

sufficient adj adequate, enough, satisfactory. Opp INSUFFICIENT.

suffocate v asphyxiate, choke, smother, stifle, stop breathing, strangle, throttle.

sugary adj 1 glazed, iced, sugared, sweetened. ▷ SWEET.
2 sugary sentiments. cloying, sickly. ▷ SENTIMENTAL.

suggest v 1 advise, advocate, counsel, moot, move, propose, propound, put forward, raise, recommend, urge. 2 call to mind, evoke, hint, imply, indicate, insinuate, intimate, mean, signal.

suggestion n 1 advice, counsel, offer, plan, prompting, proposal, recommendation, urging.
2 breath, hint, idea, indication, intimation, notion, suspicion, touch, trace.

suggestive adj 1 evocative, expressive, indicative, reminiscent, thought-provoking.
2 ▷ INDECENT.

suicidal adj 1 hopeless, inf kamikaze, self-destructive.
2 ▷ DESOLATE.

suit n costume, dress, ensemble, outfit. • v 1 accommodate, be suitable for, conform to, fit in with, gratify, match, please, satisfy, tally with. Opp DISPLEASE.
2 That colour suits you. become, fit, look good on.

suitable adj acceptable, applicable, apposite, appropriate, apt, becoming, befitting, congenial, convenient, decorous, fit, fitting, handy, opportune, pertinent, proper, relevant, right, satisfactory, seemly, tasteful, timely, well-chosen, well-judged, well-timed. Opp UNSUITABLE.

sulk v be sullen, brood, mope.

sullen adj 1 antisocial, bad-tempered, brooding, crabby, cross, disgruntled, dour, glum, grudging, ill-humoured, lugubrious, moody, morose, inf out of sorts, pouting, resentful, silent, sour, stubborn, sulking, sulky, surly, uncommunicative, unforgiving, unfriendly, unhappy, unsociable. 2 *sullen sky*. dark, dismal, dull, gloomy, grey, leaden, sombre. Opp CHEERFUL.

sultry adj 1 close, hot, humid, muggy, oppressive, steamy, stifling, stuffy, warm. Opp COLD. 2 *sultry beauty*. erotic, provocative, seductive, sensual, sexy, voluptuous.

sum n aggregate, amount, number, quantity, reckoning, result, score, tally, total, whole.
● v **sum up** ▷ SUMMARIZE.

summarize v abridge, condense, encapsulate, give the gist, outline, précis, inf recap, recapitulate, reduce, review, shorten, simplify, sum up. Opp ELABORATE.

summary n abridgement, abstract, digest, gist, outline, précis, recapitulation, reduction, résumé, review, summation, summing-up, synopsis.

summery adj bright, sunny, warm. Opp WINTRY.

summit n 1 apex, crown, height, peak, pinnacle, point, top. Opp BASE. 2 *summit of success*. acme, climax, culmination, high point, zenith. Opp NADIR.

summon v 1 command, demand, invite, order, send for. 2 assemble, call, convene, convoke, gather together, muster, rally.

sunbathe v bake, bask, get a tan, sun yourself, tan.

sunburnt adj blistered, bronzed, brown, peeling, tanned, weather-beaten.

sundry adj assorted, different, miscellaneous, mixed, various.

sunken adj 1 submerged, underwater. 2 *sunken cheeks*. concave, haggard, drawn, hollow, hollowed.

sunless adj cheerless, cloudy, dark, dismal, dreary, dull, gloomy, grey, overcast, sombre. Opp SUNNY.

sunlight n daylight, sun, sunbeams, sunshine.

sunny adj 1 bright, clear, cloudless, fair, fine, summery, sunlit, sunshiny, unclouded. Opp SUNLESS. 2 ▷ CHEERFUL.

sunrise n dawn, daybreak.

sunset n dusk, evening, nightfall, sundown, twilight.

superannuated adj 1 discharged, inf pensioned off, inf put out to grass, old, retired. 2 discarded, disused, obsolete, thrown out, worn out. ▷ OLD.

superb adj admirable, excellent, fine, first-class, first-rate, impressive, marvellous, superior. ▷ SPLENDID. Opp INFERIOR.

superficial adj 1 cosmetic, external, exterior, on the surface, outward, shallow, skin-deep, slight, surface, unimportant. 2 careless, casual, cursory, desultory, facile, frivolous, hasty, hurried, lightweight, inf nodding (*acquaintance*), oversimplified, passing, perfunctory, simplistic, sweeping (*generalization*), trivial, unconvincing, uncritical, undiscriminating, unquestioning, unscholarly. *Opp* ANALYTICAL, DEEP.

superfluous *adj* excess, excessive, extra, needless, redundant, spare, surplus, unnecessary, unneeded, unwanted. *Opp* NECESSARY.

superhuman *adj* **1** herculean, heroic, phenomenal, prodigious. **2** *superhuman powers*. divine, higher, supernatural.

superimpose *v* overlay, place on top of.

superintend *v* administer, be in charge of, control, direct, look after, manage, organize, oversee, preside over, run, supervise, watch over.

superior *adj* **1** better, *inf* classier, greater, higher, loftier, more important, nobler, senior, up-market. **2** *superior quality*. choice, exclusive, fine, first-class, first-rate, select, top, unrivalled. **3** *superior attitude*. arrogant, condescending, contemptuous, disdainful, elitist, haughty, *inf* high-and-mighty, lofty, patronizing, self-important, smug, snobbish, *inf* snooty, *inf* stuck-up, supercilious. *Opp* INFERIOR.

superlative *adj* best, choicest, consummate, excellent, finest, first-rate, incomparable, matchless, peerless, *inf* tip-top, *inf* top-notch, unrivalled, unsurpassed. ▷ SUPREME.

supernatural *adj* abnormal, ghostly, inexplicable, magical, miraculous, mysterious, mystic, occult, other-worldly, paranormal, preternatural, psychic, spiritual, unearthly, unnatural, weird.

superstition *n* myth, *inf* old wives' tale, superstitious belief.

superstitious *adj* credulous, illusory, irrational, mythical, traditional, unfounded.

supervise *v* administer, be in charge of, conduct, control, direct, govern, invigilate (*an exam*), *inf* keep an eye on, lead, look after, manage, organize, oversee, preside over, run, superintend, watch over.

supervision *n* administration, conduct, control, direction, government, invigilation, management, organization, oversight, surveillance.

supervisor *n* administrator, chief, controller, director, foreman, *inf* gaffer, head, inspector, invigilator, leader, manager, organizer, overseer, superintendent.

supine *adj* **1** face upwards, flat on your back, prostrate, recumbent. *Opp* PRONE. **2** ▷ PASSIVE.

supplant *v* displace, dispossess, eject, expel, oust, replace, supersede, *inf* step into the shoes of, *inf* topple, unseat.

supple *adj* bending, *inf* bendy, elastic, flexible, graceful, limber, lithe, pliable, pliant, resilient, soft. *Opp* RIGID.

supplement *n* **1** additional payment, excess, surcharge. **2** *newspaper supplement, etc.* addendum, addition, appendix, codicil, continuation, endpiece, extra, insert, postscript, sequel. ● *v* add to, augment, boost, complement, extend, reinforce, *inf* top up.

supplementary *adj* accompanying, added, additional, ancillary, auxiliary, complementary, extra, further, new, spare.

supplication n appeal, entreaty, petition, plea, prayer, request, solicitation.

supplier n dealer, provider, purveyor, retailer, seller, shopkeeper, vendor, wholesaler.

supply n cache, hoard, quantity, reserve, reservoir, stock, stockpile, store. 2 [pl] equipment, food, necessities, provisions, rations, shopping. 3 regular supply. delivery, distribution, provision. • v cater to, contribute, deliver, distribute, donate, endow, equip, feed, furnish, give, produce, provide, purvey, sell, stock.

support n 1 aid, approval, assistance, backing, backup, contribution, cooperation, donation, encouragement, friendship, help, interest, loyalty, patronage, protection, reassurance, reinforcement, sponsorship, succour. 2 brace, bracket, buttress, crutch, foundation, frame, pillar, post, prop, sling, stay, strut, substructure, trestle, truss, underpinning. 3 financial support. funding, keep, maintenance, subsistence, upkeep. • v 1 bear, bolster, buoy up, buttress, carry, give strength to, hold up, keep up, prop up, provide a support for, reinforce, shore up, strengthen, underlie, underpin. 2 support someone in trouble. aid, assist, back, be faithful to, champion, comfort, defend, encourage, fight for, give support to, help, rally round, reassure, side with, speak up for, stand by, stand up for, inf stick up for, take someone's part. 3 support a family. bring up, feed, finance, fund, keep, look after, maintain, provide for, sustain. 4 support a charity. be a supporter of, contribute to, espouse (a cause), follow, give to, patronize, sponsor, subsidize, work for. 5 support a point of view. adhere to, advocate, agree with, argue for, confirm, corroborate, defend, endorse, justify, promote, ratify, substantiate, uphold, validate, verify. Opp SUBVERT, WEAKEN. **support yourself** lean, rest.

supporter n 1 adherent, admirer, advocate, aficionado, apologist, champion, defender, devotee, enthusiast, inf fan, fanatic, follower, seconder, upholder, voter. 2 ally, assistant, collaborator, helper, inf henchman, second.

supportive adj caring, concerned, encouraging, helpful, favourable, heartening, interested, kind, loyal, positive, reassuring, sustaining, sympathetic, understanding. Opp UNSYMPATHETIC.

suppose v 1 accept, assume, believe, conclude, conjecture, expect, guess, infer, judge, postulate, presume, presuppose, speculate, surmise, suspect, take for granted, think. 2 daydream, fancy, fantasize, hypothesize, imagine, pretend, theorize. **supposed** ▷ HYPOTHETICAL, PUTATIVE. **supposed to** expected to, meant to, required to.

supposition n assumption, belief, conjecture, fancy, guess, hypothesis, inference, notion, opinion, speculation, surmise, theory, thought.

suppress v 1 conquer, inf crack down on, crush, overcome, overthrow, put an end to, put down, quash, quell, stamp out, stop, subdue. 2 suppress emotion, the *facts.* bottle up, censor, choke back, conceal, cover up, hide, hush up, keep quiet about, keep secret, muffle, repress, restrain, silence, smother, stamp on, stifle, strangle.

supremacy *n* ascendancy, dominance, domination, dominion, lead, mastery, predominance, pre-eminence, sovereignty, superiority.

supreme *adj* best, choicest, consummate, crowning, culminating, finest, greatest, highest, incomparable, matchless, outstanding, paramount, peerless, predominant, pre-eminent, prime, principal, superlative, surpassing, *inf* tip-top, top, *inf* top-notch, ultimate, unbeatable, unbeaten, unparalleled, unrivalled unsurpassable, unsurpassed.

sure *adj* 1 assured, certain, confident, convinced, definite, persuaded, positive. 2 *sure to come.* bound, certain, obliged, required. 3 *sure fact.* accurate, clear, convincing, guaranteed, indisputable, inescapable, inevitable, infallible, proven, reliable, true, unchallenged, undeniable, undisputed, undoubted, verifiable. 4 *sure ally.* dependable, established, faithful, firm, infallible, loyal, reliable, resolute, safe, secure, solid, steadfast, steady, trustworthy, trusty, unerring, unfailing, unfaltering, unflinching, unswerving, unwavering. *Opp* UNCERTAIN.

surface *n* 1 coat, coating, covering, crust, exterior, façade, outside, shell, skin, veneer. 2 *cube has six surfaces.* face, facet, plane, side. 3 *working surface.* bench, table, top, worktop.

● *v* 1 appear, arise, *inf* come to light, come up, *inf* crop up, emerge, materialize, rise, *inf* pop up. 2 coat, cover, laminate.

surfeit *n* excess, flood, glut, overabundance, oversupply, plethora, superfluity, surplus.

surge *n* burst, gush, increase, onrush, outpouring, rush, upsurge. ▷ WAVE. ● *v* billow, eddy, flow, gush, heave, move irresistibly, push, roll, rush, stampede, stream, sweep, swirl, well up.

surgery *n* 1 biopsy, operation. 2 *doctor's surgery.* clinic, consulting room, health centre, infirmary, medical centre.

surly *adj* bad-tempered, boorish, cantankerous, churlish, crabby, cross, crotchety, crusty, curmudgeonly, dyspeptic, gruff, grumpy, ill-natured, irascible, miserable, morose, peevish, rude, sulky, sullen, testy, touchy, unfriendly, ungracious, unpleasant. *Opp* FRIENDLY.

surmise *v* assume, believe, conjecture, expect, fancy, gather, guess, hypothesize, imagine, infer, judge, postulate, presume, presuppose, sense, speculate, suppose, suspect, take for granted, think.

surpass *v* beat, better, eclipse, exceed, excel, go beyond, leave behind, *inf* leave standing, outclass, outdo, outshine, outstrip, overshadow, top, transcend, worst.

surplus *n* balance, excess, extra, glut, oversupply, remainder, residue, superfluity, surfeit.

surprise *n* 1 alarm, amazement, astonishment, consternation, incredulity, stupefaction, wonder. 2 *complete surprise.*

blow, *inf* bolt from the blue, *inf* bombshell, *inf* eye-opener, jolt, shock. ● v 1 alarm, amaze, astonish, astound, disconcert, dumbfound, flabbergast, nonplus, rock, shock, stagger, startle, stun, stupefy, take aback, *inf* throw. 2 capture, catch out, *inf* catch red-handed, come upon, detect, discover, take unawares.

surprised *adj* alarmed, amazed, astonished, astounded, disconcerted, dumbfounded, flabbergasted, incredulous, *inf* knocked for six, nonplussed, *inf* shattered, shocked, speechless, staggered, startled, struck dumb, stunned, taken aback, *inf* thrown, thunderstruck.

surprising *adj* alarming, amazing, astonishing, astounding, disconcerting, extraordinary, frightening, incredible, shocking, staggering, startling, stunning, sudden, unexpected, unforeseen, unlooked-for, unplanned, unpredictable. *Opp* PREDICTABLE.

surrender *n* capitulation, giving in, resignation, submission. ● v 1 acquiesce, capitulate, *inf* cave in, collapse, concede, fall, *inf* give in, give up, give way, give yourself up, resign, submit, succumb, *inf* throw in the towel, yield. 2 *surrender your ticket.* give up, hand over, part with, relinquish. 3 *surrender your rights.* abandon, cede, renounce, waive.

surreptitious *adj* clandestine, concealed, covert, crafty, disguised, furtive, hidden, private, secret, secretive, *inf* shifty, sly, sneaky, stealthy, underhand. *Opp* BLATANT.

surround *v* besiege, beset, cocoon, cordon off, encircle, enclose, encompass, engulf, hedge in, hem in, ring, skirt, trap, wrap.

surrounding *adj* adjacent, adjoining, bordering, local, nearby, neighbouring.

surroundings *pl n* area, background, context, environment, location, milieu, neighbourhood, setting, vicinity.

surveillance *n* check, observation, reconnaissance, scrutiny, supervision, vigilance, watch.

survey *n* appraisal, assessment, census, count, evaluation, examination, inquiry, inspection, investigation, review, scrutiny, study. ● v 1 appraise, assess, estimate, evaluate, examine, inspect, investigate, look over, review, scrutinize, study, view, weigh up. 2 do a survey of, map out, measure, plan out, plot, reconnoitre.

survival *n* continuance, continued existence, persistence.

survive *v* 1 *inf* bear up, carry on, continue, endure, keep going, last, live, persist, remain. 2 *survive disaster.* come through, live through, outlast, outlive, pull through, weather, withstand. *Opp* SUCCUMB.

susceptible *adj* affected (by), disposed, given, inclined, liable, open, predisposed, prone, responsive, sensitive, vulnerable. *Opp* RESISTANT.

suspect *adj* doubtful, dubious, questionable, *inf* shady, suspicious, unconvincing, unreliable, unsatisfactory, untrustworthy. ● v 1 call into question, disbelieve, distrust, doubt, have suspicions about, mistrust. 2 *suspect* *that she's lying.* believe, conjecture, consider, guess, imagine, infer, presume, speculate, suppose, surmise, think.

suspend v 1 dangle, hang, swing. 2 *suspend work.* adjourn, break off, defer, delay, discontinue, hold in abeyance, interrupt, postpone, put off, *inf* put on ice, shelve. 3 *suspend from duty.* debar, dismiss, exclude, expel, lay off, lock out.

suspense n anticipation, anxiety, apprehension, doubt, excitement, expectancy, expectation, insecurity, nervousness, not knowing, tension, uncertainty, waiting.

suspicion n 1 apprehension, caution, distrust, doubt, dubiousness, *inf* funny feeling, guess, hesitation, *inf* hunch, impression, misgiving, mistrust, presentiment, qualm, scepticism, uncertainty, wariness. 2 *suspicion of a smile.* glimmer, hint, inkling, shadow, suggestion, tinge, touch, trace.

suspicious adj 1 apprehensive, chary, disbelieving, distrustful, doubtful, dubious, incredulous, mistrustful, sceptical, uncertain, unconvinced, uneasy, wary. Opp TRUSTFUL. 2 *suspicious character.* disreputable, dubious, *inf* fishy, peculiar, questionable, *inf* shady, suspect, unreliable, untrustworthy. Opp TRUSTWORTHY.

sustain v 1 continue, develop, extend, keep alive, keep going, keep up, maintain, prolong. 2 ▷ SUPPORT.

sustenance n eatables, food, foodstuffs, nourishment, provisions, rations, *old use* victuals.

swag n booty, loot, plunder.

swagger v boast, brag, parade, strut.

swallow v consume, *inf* down, gulp down, guzzle, ingest. ▷ DRINK. EAT. **swallow up** absorb, assimilate, enclose, enfold. ▷ SWAMP.

swamp n bog, fen, marsh, marshland, morass, mud, mudflats, quagmire, quicksand, wetlands. ● v deluge, drench, engulf, envelop, flood, immerse, inundate, overcome, overwhelm, sink, submerge, swallow up.

swampy adj boggy, marshy, muddy, soft, soggy, waterlogged, wet. Opp DRY, FIRM.

swarm n cloud, crowd, horde, host, multitude. ▷ GROUP. ● v cluster, congregate, crowd, flock, gather, mass, throng. **swarm up** ▷ CLIMB. **swarm with** ▷ TEEM.

swarthy adj brown, dark, dark-skinned, dusky, tanned.

swashbuckling adj adventurous, bold, daredevil, daring, dashing, *inf* macho, swaggering. Opp TIMID.

sway v 1 bend, lean, lurch, oscillate, reel, rock, roll, swing, undulate, wave, wobble. 2 affect, bias, bring round, change (someone's mind), convert, convince, influence, persuade, win over. 3 *sway from a chosen path.* divert, go off course, swerve, veer, waver.

swear v 1 affirm, attest, avow, declare, give your word, insist, pledge, promise, state on oath, take an oath, testify, vouchsafe, vow. 2 blaspheme, curse, utter profanities.

swear word n curse, expletive, *inf* four-letter word, imprecation, oath, obscenity, profanity, swearing.

sweat v 1 *inf* glow, perspire, swelter. 2 ▷ WORK.

sweaty *adj* clammy, damp, humid, moist, perspiring, steamy, sticky, sweating.

sweep v brush, clean, clear, dust, tidy up. **sweep along** ▷ MOVE. **sweep away** ▷ REMOVE. **sweeping** ▷ GENERAL, SUPERFICIAL.

sweet *adj* 1 aromatic, fragrant, honeyed, luscious, mellow, perfumed, sweetened, sweet-smelling. 2 [*derog*] cloying, saccharine, sentimental, sickening, sickly, sugary, syrupy, treacly. 3 *sweet sounds.* dulcet, euphonious, harmonious, heavenly, mellifluous, melodious, musical, pleasant, silvery, soothing, tuneful. 4 *sweet nature.* affectionate, amiable, attractive, charming, dear, endearing, engaging, friendly, genial, gentle, gracious, lovable, lovely, nice, pretty, unselfish, winning. *Opp* ACID, BITTER, NASTY, SAVOURY. ● n 1 *inf* afters, dessert, pudding. 2 [*pl*] *Amer* candy, confectionery, *inf* sweeties.

sweeten v 1 make sweeter, sugar. 2 *sweeten your temper.* appease, assuage, calm, mellow, mollify, pacify, soothe.

swell v 1 balloon, billow, blow up, bulge, dilate, distend, enlarge, expand, fatten, fill out, grow, increase, inflate, mushroom, puff up, rise. 2 *swell numbers.* augment, boost, build up, increase, raise, step up. *Opp* SHRINK.

swelling n blister, boil, bulge, bump, distension, enlargement, excrescence, hump, inflammation, knob, lump, protuberance, protrusion, tumescence, tumour.

sweltering *adj* humid, muggy, oppressive, steamy, sticky, stifling, sultry. ▷ HOT.

swerve v change direction, deviate, dodge about, sheer off, swing, take avoiding action, turn aside, veer, wheel.

swift *adj* agile, brisk, fast, fleet-footed, hasty, hurried, nimble, *inf* nippy, prompt, quick, rapid, speedy, sudden. *Opp* SLOW.

swill v 1 bathe, clean, rinse, sponge down, wash. 2 ▷ DRINK.

swim v bathe, float, go swimming, *inf* take a dip.

swimming pool n baths, lido, swimming bath.

swimsuit n bathing costume, bathing suit, bikini, swimwear, trunks.

swindle n cheat, chicanery, *inf* con, confidence trick, deception, double-dealing, fraud, *inf* racket, *inf* rip-off, *inf* sharp practice, *inf* swizz, trickery. ● v *inf* bamboozle, cheat, *inf* con, deceive, defraud, *inf* diddle, *inf* do, double-cross, dupe, exploit, *inf* fiddle, fleece, fool, hoax, hoodwink, *inf* pull a fast one, *inf* take for a ride, trick, welsh (*on a bet*).

swindler n charlatan, cheat, *inf* con-man, counterfeiter, double-crosser, extortioner, forger, fraud, hoaxer, impostor, quack, racketeer, *inf* shark, trickster.

swing n change, fluctuation, movement, oscillation, shift, variation. ● v 1 be suspended, dangle, flap, fluctuate, move to and fro, oscillate, revolve, rock, sway, swivel, turn, twirl, wave about. 2 *swing opinion.* affect, bias, bring round, change (someone's mind), convert, con-

vince, influence, persuade, win
over. 3 *support swung to the
opposition*. change, move across,
shift, transfer. 4 *swing from a
path*. deviate, go off
course, swerve, veer, waver,
zigzag.

swipe *v* 1 lash out at, strike,
swing at. ▷ HIT. 2 ▷ STEAL.

swirl *v* boil, churn, curl, eddy,
move in circles, seethe, spin,
surge, twirl, twist, whirl.

switch *n* light-switch, power-
point. ● *v* change, divert,
exchange, replace, reverse, shift,
substitute, swap, transfer, turn.

swivel *v* gyrate, pirouette, pivot,
revolve, rotate, spin, swing,
turn, twirl, wheel.

swoop *v* descend, dive, drop, fall,
fly down, lunge, plunge, pounce.
swoop on ▷ RAID.

sword *n* blade, broadsword,
cutlass, dagger, rapier, sabre,
scimitar.

sycophantic *adj* flattering,
insincere, obsequious, servile,
inf smarmy, unctuous.

syllabus *n* course, curriculum,
outline, programme of study.

sylvan *adj* arboreal, leafy, tree-
covered, wooded.

symbol *n* badge, character,
cipher, crest, device, emblem,
figure, insignia, logo, mark,
motif, representation, sign,
token, trademark.

symbolic *adj* allegorical,
emblematic, figurative, meaningful, metaphorical, representative, symptomatic, token
(*gesture*).

symbolize *v* be a sign of,
betoken, connote, denote,
epitomize, imply, indicate,

mean, represent, signify,
stand for, suggest.

symmetrical *adj* balanced,
even, proportional, regular.
Opp ASYMMETRICAL.

sympathetic *adj* benevolent,
caring, charitable, comforting,
compassionate, concerned, con-
soling, friendly, humane, interested, kind-hearted, kindly, merciful, soft-hearted, sorry,
supportive, tender, tolerant,
understanding, warm.
Opp UNSYMPATHETIC.

sympathize *v inf* be on the same
wavelength, be sorry, be sympathetic, comfort, commiserate,
condole, console, empathize, feel
for, identify (with), pity,
respond, show sympathy,
understand.

sympathy *n* affinity, commiseration, compassion, concern, condolence, consideration, empathy,
feeling, fellow-feeling, kindness,
mercy, pity, rapport, tenderness,
understanding.

symptom *n* characteristic, evidence, feature, indication, manifestation, mark, marker, sign,
warning, warning-sign.

symptomatic *adj* characteristic,
indicative, representative, suggestive, typical.

synopsis *n* ▷ SUMMARY.

synthesis *n* amalgamation,
blend, combination, composite,
compound, fusion, integration,
union.

synthetic *adj* artificial, bogus,
concocted, counterfeit, ersatz,
fabricated, fake, *inf* made-up,
man-made, manufactured, mock,
inf phoney, simulated, spurious,
unnatural. *Opp* GENUINE,
NATURAL.

syringe *n* hypodermic, needle.

system *n* **1** network, organization, *inf* set-up, structure. **2** approach, arrangement, method, methodology, order, plan, practice, procedure, process, routine, rules, scheme, technique. **3** *system of government*. constitution, regime. **4** *system of knowledge*. classification, code, discipline, philosophy, science, set of principles, theory.

systematic *adj* businesslike, classified, coordinated, logical, methodical, neat, ordered, orderly, organized, planned, rational, routine, scientific, structured, tidy, well-arranged, well-organized, well-rehearsed, well-run. *Opp* UNSYSTEMATIC.

systematize *v* arrange, catalogue, categorize, classify, codify, organize, rationalize, standardize, tabulate.

T

table *n* **1** bench, board, counter, desk, worktop. **2** *table of information*. catalogue, chart, diagram, graph, index, inventory, list, register, schedule, tabulation, timetable. ● *v* lay on the table, offer, proffer, propose, submit.

tablet *n* **1** capsule, lozenge, medicine, pellet, pill. **2** *tablet of soap*. bar, block, chunk, piece, slab. **3** *tablet of stone*. gravestone, headstone, memorial, plaque, plate, tombstone.

taboo *adj* banned, censored, forbidden, off limits, out of bounds, prohibited, proscribed, rude, unacceptable, unmentionable, unthinkable. ● *n* anathema, ban, prohibition, proscription, taboo subject.

tabulate *v* arrange as a table, catalogue, list, set out in columns, systematize.

tacit *adj* implicit, implied, silent, undeclared, understood, unsaid, unspoken, unvoiced.

taciturn *adj* quiet, reserved, reticent, silent, tight-lipped, uncommunicative, unforthcoming. *Opp* TALKATIVE.

tack *n* **1** drawing-pin, nail, pin, tintack. **2** *the wrong tack*. approach, bearing, course, direction, line, policy, procedure, technique. ● *v* **1** nail, pin. ▷ FASTEN. **2** sew, stitch. **3** *tack in a yacht*. beat against the wind, change course, zigzag.

tack on ▷ ADD.

tackle *n* **1** accoutrements, apparatus, *inf* clobber, equipment, *inf* gear, implements, kit, outfit, paraphernalia, rig, tools. **2** *football tackle*. attack, block, challenge, interception, intervention. ● *v* **1** address (yourself to), apply yourself to, attempt, attend to, concentrate on, confront, cope with, deal with, face up to, focus on, get involved in, *inf* get to grips with, grapple with, handle, *inf* have a go at, manage, settle down to, sort out, take on, undertake. **2** *tackle an opponent*. attack, challenge, intercept, stop, take on.

tacky *adj* adhesive, gluey, *inf* gooey, gummy, sticky, viscous, wet. *Opp* DRY.

tact *n* adroitness, consideration, delicacy, diplomacy, discernment, discretion, finesse, judgement, perceptiveness, politeness, *Fr* savoir faire, sensitivity, tactfulness, thoughtfulness, understanding. *Opp* TACTLESSNESS.

tactful *adj* adroit, appropriate, considerate, courteous, delicate, diplomatic, discreet, judicious, perceptive, polite, sensitive, thoughtful, understanding. *Opp* TACTLESS.

tactical *adj* artful, calculated, clever, deliberate, planned, politic, prudent, shrewd, skilful, strategic.

tactics *pl n* approach, campaign, course of action, design, device, manoeuvre, manoeuvring, plan, ploy, policy, procedure, ruse, scheme, stratagem, strategy.

tactless *adj* blundering, blunt, clumsy, discourteous, gauche, heavy-handed, hurtful, impolite, impolitic, inappropriate, inconsiderate, indelicate, indiscreet, inept, insensitive, maladroit, misjudged, thoughtless, undiplomatic, unkind. ▷ RUDE. *Opp* TACTFUL.

tactlessness *n* clumsiness, gaucherie, indelicacy, indiscretion, ineptitude, insensitivity, lack of diplomacy, misjudgement, thoughtlessness. ▷ RUDENESS. *Opp* TACT.

tag *n* **1** docket, label, marker, name tag, price tag, slip, sticker, tab, ticket. **2** *a Latin tag.* ▷ SAYING. • *v* identify, label, mark, ticket. **tag along with** ▷ FOLLOW.

tail *n* appendage, back, brush (*of fox*), buttocks, end, extremity, rear, rump, scut (*of rabbit*), tail-end. • *v* dog, follow, hunt, pursue, shadow, stalk, track, trail. **tail off** ▷ DECLINE.

taint *v* **1** adulterate, contaminate, defile, dirty, infect, poison, pollute, soil. **2** *taint a reputation.* blacken, damage, dishonour, harm, ruin, smear, spoil, stain, tarnish.

take *v* **1** acquire, bring, carry away, *inf* cart off, clasp, fetch, gain, get, grab, grasp, grip, hold, pick up, pluck, seize, snatch. **2** *take prisoners.* abduct, arrest, capture, catch, detain, ensnare, secure. **3** *take property.* appropriate, pocket, remove. ▷ STEAL. **4** *take 2 from 4.* deduct, subtract, take away. **5** *I can take two passengers.* accommodate, carry, have room for, hold. **6** *I'll take you home.* accompany, conduct, convey, escort, ferry, guide, lead. **7** *take a taxi.* engage, hire, travel by, use. **8** *take a subject.* have lessons in, read, study. **9** *He can't take it any longer.* abide, bear, brook, endure, stand, stomach, suffer, tolerate, undergo, withstand. **10** *take food, drink.* consume, drink, eat, have, swallow. **11** *It takes courage to own up.* necessitate, need, require. **12** *take a new name.* adopt, assume, choose, select. **take aback** ▷ SURPRISE. **take after** ▷ RESEMBLE. **take against** ▷ DISLIKE. **take back** ▷ WITHDRAW. **take in** ▷ ACCOMMODATE, DECEIVE, UNDERSTAND. **take life** ▷ KILL. **take off** ▷ IMITATE. **take off, take out** ▷ REMOVE. **take on, take up** ▷ UNDERTAKE. **take over** ▷ USURP. **take part** ▷ PARTICIPATE. **take place** ▷ HAPPEN. **take to task** ▷ REPRIMAND. **take up** ▷ BEGIN, OCCUPY.

takeover *n* amalgamation, incorporation, merger.

takings *pl n* earnings, gains, gate, income, proceeds, profits, receipts, revenue.

tale *n* account, anecdote, chronicle, fable, legend, narration, narrative, report, saga, *sl* spiel, story, yarn.

talent *n* ability, accomplishment, aptitude, brilliance, capacity, expertise, facility, faculty, flair, genius, gift, knack, *inf* know-how, prowess, skill, versatility.

talented *adj* able, accomplished, artistic, brilliant, distinguished, expert, gifted, inspired, proficient, skilful, skilled, versatile. ▷ CLEVER. *Opp* UNSKILFUL.

talisman *n* amulet, charm, mascot.

talk *n* 1 baby-talk, *inf* blarney, *inf* chat, *inf* chin-wag, *inf* chit-chat, conference, conversation, dialogue, discourse, discussion, gossip, language, palaver, *inf* powwow, *inf* tattle, *inf* tittle-tattle, words. 2 *a public talk*. address, diatribe, exhortation, harangue, lecture, oration, *inf* pep talk, presentation, sermon, speech, tirade. ● *v* 1 address one another, commune, communicate, confer, converse, discourse, discuss, exchange views, have a conversation, *inf* hold forth, negotiate, *inf* pipe up, pontificate, speak, use your voice, utter, verbalize, vocalize. 2 *She never stops talking*. babble, *inf* chat, chatter, gabble, gossip, jabber, jaw, mumble, mutter, *inf* natter, prattle, *inf* rabbit on, *inf* rattle on, spout, whisper, *inf* witter. 3 *talk French*. communicate in, converse in, express yourself in, speak. 4 *get someone to talk*. confess, give information, *sl* grass,

inform, *inf* spill the beans, *inf* squeal, *inf* tell tales. 5 *talk to an audience*. deliver a speech, give an address, lecture, preach, sermonize. ▷ SAY, SPEAK. **talk about** ▷ DISCUSS. **talk to** ▷ ADDRESS.

talkative *adj* articulate, chatty, communicative, effusive, eloquent, expansive, garrulous, glib, gossipy, long-winded, loquacious, open, prolix, unstoppable, verbose, vocal, voluble, wordy. *Opp* TACITURN. **talkative person** chatterbox, *sl* gasbag, gossip, *inf* windbag.

tall *adj* colossal, giant, gigantic, high, lofty, soaring, towering. ▷ BIG. *Opp* SHORT.

tally *n* addition, count, reckoning, record, sum, total. ● *v* 1 accord, agree, coincide, concur, correspond, match up, square. 2 *tally up the bill*. add, calculate, compute, count, reckon, total, work out.

tame *adj* 1 amenable, biddable, compliant, docile, gentle, ineffectual, meek, mild, obedient, passive, subdued, submissive, tractable, unassertive. 2 *tame animals*. approachable, broken in, domesticated, fearless, friendly, harmless, house-trained, manageable, safe, sociable, tamed, trained, unafraid. 3 *Her life was very tame*. bland, boring, colourless, dull, feeble, flat, insipid, prosaic, tedious, unadventurous, unexciting, uninspiring, uninteresting, vapid, *inf* wishy-washy. *Opp* EXCITING, WILD. ● *v* break in, conquer, curb, discipline, domesticate, house-train, make tame, master, pacify, quell, repress, subdue, subjugate, suppress, temper, tone down, train.

tamper v **tamper with** alter, fiddle about with, interfere with, make adjustments to, meddle with, tinker with.

tan n sunburn, suntan.
● v bronze, brown, burn, colour, darken, get tanned.

tang n acidity, inf bite, inf nip, piquancy, pungency, savour, sharpness, spiciness, zest.

tangible adj actual, concrete, corporeal, definite, material, palpable, perceptible, physical, real, solid, substantial, tactile, touchable. Opp INTANGIBLE.

tangle n coil, complication, confusion, jumble, jungle, knot, labyrinth, mass, maze, mesh, mess, muddle, scramble, web.
● v 1 complicate, confuse, entangle, entwine, inf foul up, intertwine, interweave, muddle, scramble, inf snarl up, twist. 2 tangle fish in a net. catch, enmesh, ensnare, trap. Opp DISENTANGLE, FREE. 3 tangle with criminals. become involved with, confront, cross. **tangled** ▷ DISHEVELLED, INTRICATE.

tangy adj acid, appetizing, bitter, fresh, piquant, pungent, refreshing, sharp, spicy, strong, tart. Opp BLAND.

tank n 1 aquarium, basin, cistern, reservoir. 2 army tank. armoured vehicle.

tanned adj brown, sunburnt, suntanned, weather-beaten.

tantalize v entice, frustrate, inf keep on tenterhooks, lead on, provoke, taunt, tease, tempt, titillate, torment.

tap n 1 Amer faucet, spigot, stopcock, valve. 2 knock, rap.
● v 1 knock, rap, strike. ▷ HIT. 2 tap a savings account. drain, draw on, exploit, milk, utilize.

tape n 1 band, binding, braid, ribbon, strip. 2 audiotape, cassette, magnetic tape, tape recording, videotape. ● v 1 tape up a package. ▷ FASTEN. 2 tape a programme. ▷ record, tape-record, video.

taper n candle, lighter, spill.
● v attenuate, become narrower, narrow, thin. **taper off** ▷ DECLINE.

target n 1 aim, ambition, end, goal, hope, intention, objective, purpose. 2 target of attack. butt, object, quarry, victim.

tariff n 1 charges, menu, pricelist, schedule. 2 tariff on imports. customs, duty, excise, impost, levy, tax, toll.

tarnish v 1 blacken, corrode, dirty, discolour, soil, taint. 2 tarnish a reputation. blemish, blot, defame, denigrate, disgrace, dishonour, mar, ruin, spoil, stain, sully.

tarry v dawdle, hang about, linger, wait. ▷ DELAY.

tart adj 1 acid, acidic, astringent, biting, citrus, lemony, piquant, pungent, sharp, sour, tangy. 2 tart rejoinder. ▷ SHARP. Opp BLAND, SWEET. ● n 1 flan, pastry, pie, quiche, tartlet, turnover. 2 ▷ PROSTITUTE.

task n activity, assignment, business, charge, chore, duty, employment, enterprise, errand, job, mission, requirement, test, undertaking, work. **take to task** ▷ REPRIMAND.

taste n 1 character, flavour, relish, savour. 2 bit, bite, morsel, mouthful, nibble, piece, sample, titbit. **3** *acquired taste*. appetite, appreciation, choice, fondness, inclination, judgement, leaning, liking, partiality, preference. **4** *person of taste*. breeding, cultivation, culture, discernment, discretion, discrimination, education, elegance, fashion sense, finesse, good judgement, perception, polish, refinement, sensitivity, style. ● *v* nibble, relish, sample, savour, sip, test, try. **in bad taste** ▷ TASTELESS. **in good taste** ▷ TASTEFUL.

tasteful *adj* aesthetic, artistic, attractive, charming, cultivated, decorous, dignified, discerning, discreet, discriminating, elegant, fashionable, in good taste, judicious, *inf* nice, proper, refined, restrained, sensitive, smart, stylish, well-judged. *Opp* TASTELESS.

tasteless *adj* **1** cheap, coarse, crude, *inf* flashy, garish, gaudy, graceless, improper, in bad taste, indecorous, indelicate, inelegant, injudicious, in poor taste, *inf* kitsch, loud, ugly, unattractive, uncouth, undiscriminating, unfashionable, unimaginative, unpleasant, unrefined, unseemly, unstylish, vulgar. *Opp* TASTEFUL. **2** *tasteless food*. bland, flavourless, insipid, mild, watered-down, watery, weak, *inf* wishy-washy. *Opp* TASTY.

tasty *adj* appetizing, delectable, delicious, flavoursome, luscious, *inf* mouth-watering, *inf* nice, palatable, piquant, savoury, *inf* scrumptious, spicy, tangy, *sl* yummy. *Opp* TASTELESS.

tattered *adj* frayed, ragged, ripped, shredded, *inf* tatty,

threadbare, torn, worn out. *Opp* SMART.

tatters *pl n* bits, pieces, rags, ribbons, shreds, torn pieces.

tatty *adj* **1** frayed, old, patched, ragged, ripped, *inf* scruffy, shabby, tattered, torn, threadbare, untidy, worn out. **2** ▷ TAWDRY. *Opp* SMART.

taunt *v* annoy, goad, insult, jeer at, mock, tease, torment. ▷ RIDICULE.

taut *adj* firm, rigid, stiff, strained, stretched, tense, tight. *Opp* SLACK.

tautological *adj* long-winded, prolix, redundant, repetitious, repetitive, superfluous, tautologous, verbose, wordy. *Opp* CONCISE.

tautology *n* longwindedness, prolixity, repetition, verbiage, verbosity, wordiness.

tavern *n old use* alehouse, bar, hostelry, inn, *inf* local, pub, public house.

tawdry *adj* cheap, common, fancy, *inf* flashy, garish, gaudy, inferior, meretricious, poor quality, showy, tasteless, *inf* tatty, tinny, vulgar, worthless. *Opp* TASTEFUL.

tax *n* charge, customs, due, duty, excise, impost, income tax, levy, tariff, toll. ● *v* **1** assess, exact, impose a tax on, levy a tax on. **2** *tax someone's patience*. burden, exhaust, make heavy demands on, overwork, strain, try. ▷ TIRE. **tax with** accuse of, blame for, charge with, reproach for, reprove for.

taxi *n* cab, minicab, taxicab.

taxing *adj* arduous, demanding, exhausting, onerous, stressful, tiring. ▷ DIFFICULT.

teach *v* advise, coach, counsel, demonstrate to, discipline, drill, edify, educate, enlighten, familiarize with, give lessons in, ground in, guide, impart knowledge to, indoctrinate, inform, instruct, lecture, school, train, tutor.

teacher *n* adviser, coach, don, educator, governess, guide, guru, headteacher, instructor, lecturer, master, mentor, mistress, professor, schoolteacher, trainer, tutor.

teaching *n* **1** coaching, education, grounding, guidance, indoctrination, instruction, schooling, training, tuition. **2** *religious teaching*. doctrine, dogma, gospel, precept, principle, tenet.

team *n* club, crew, gang, *inf* line up, side. ▷ GROUP.

tear *n* **1** droplet, tear-drop. [*pl*] *inf* blubbering, crying, sobs, weeping. **2** cut, fissure, gash, hole, laceration, opening, rent, rip, slit, split. ● *v* **1** claw, gash, lacerate, mangle, rend, rip, rupture, scratch, sever, shred, slit, snag, split. **2** [*inf*] ▷ RUSH. **shed tears** ▷ WEEP.

tearful *adj inf* blubbering, crying, emotional, in tears, lachrymose, snivelling, sobbing, weeping, *inf* weepy, whimpering. ▷ SAD.

tease *v inf* aggravate, annoy, bait, chaff, goad, irritate, laugh at, make fun of, mock, *inf* needle, pester, plague, provoke, *inf* pull someone's leg, *inf* rib, tantalize, taunt, torment. ▷ RIDICULE.

teasing *n* badinage, banter, chaffing, joking, mockery, provocation, raillery, *inf* ribbing, ridicule, taunts.

technical *adj* **1** complicated, detailed, expert, professional, specialized. **2** *technical skill*. mechanical, scientific, technological.

technician *n* engineer, mechanic, skilled worker.

technique *n* **1** approach, knack, manner, means, method, mode, procedure, routine, system, trick, way. **2** *artist's technique*. art, artistry, craft, craftsmanship, expertise, facility, *inf* know-how, proficiency, skill, talent, workmanship.

technological *adj* automated, computerized, electronic, scientific.

tedious *adj* boring, dreary, *inf* dry as dust, dull, endless, humdrum, irksome, laborious, long-drawn-out, long-winded, monotonous, prolonged, repetitive, slow, soporific, tiresome, tiring, unexciting, uninteresting, wearing, wearisome, wearying. *Opp* INTERESTING.

tedium *n* boredom, dreariness, dullness, ennui, monotony, slowness, tediousness.

teem *v* **1** abound (in), be alive (with), be full (of), be infested, be overrun (by), *inf* bristle, *inf* crawl, proliferate, seethe, swarm with. **2** ▷ RAIN.

teenager *n* adolescent, boy, girl, juvenile, minor, youngster, youth.

teetotal *adj* abstemious, abstinent, *sl* on the wagon, self-disciplined, sober.

teetotaller *n* abstainer, nondrinker.

telegram *n* cable, cablegram, fax, telemessage, telex, wire.

telepathic adj clairvoyant, psychic.

telephone n inf blower, car-phone, handset, phone.
● v inf buzz, call, dial, inf give someone a buzz, inf give someone a call, phone, ring, ring up.

televise v broadcast, relay, send out, transmit.

television n inf the box, receiver, inf small screen, inf telly, inf TV, video.

tell v 1 acquaint with, advise, announce, assure, communicate, describe, disclose, divulge, explain, impart, inform, make known, narrate, notify, portray, promise, recite, recount, rehearse, relate, reveal, utter. ▷ SPEAK, TALK. 2 tell the difference. comprehend, discover, discriminate, distinguish, identify, notice, recognize, see. 3 tell me what to do. command, direct, instruct, order. **tell off** ▷ REPRIMAND.

teller n 1 author, narrator, raconteur, storyteller. 2 teller in a bank. bank clerk, cashier.

telling adj effective, influential, potent, powerful, significant, striking, weighty.

temper n 1 attitude, character, disposition, frame of mind, humour, inf make-up, mood, personality, state of mind, temperament. 2 Beware of his temper. anger, churlishness, fury, ill-humour, irascibility, irritability, peevishness, petulance, surliness, volatility, wrath. 3 She flew into a temper. fit of pique, inf paddy, passion, rage, tantrum. 4 Try to keep your temper. calmness, composure, sl cool, coolness, equanimity, sang-froid, self-control, self-possession.

● v 1 assuage, lessen, mitigate, moderate, modify, reduce, soften, soothe, tone down. 2 temper steel. harden, strengthen, toughen.

temperament n attitude, character, disposition, frame of mind, humour, inf make-up, mood, nature, personality, spirit, state of mind, temper.

temperamental adj 1 characteristic, constitutional, inherent, innate, natural. 2 temperamental moods. capricious, changeable, emotional, erratic, excitable, explosive, fickle, highly-strung, impatient, inconsistent, inconstant, irascible, irritable, mercurial, moody, neurotic, passionate, touchy, unpredictable, unreliable, inf up and down, variable, volatile.

temperance n abstemiousness, moderation, self-denial, self-discipline, self-restraint, sobriety, teetotalism.

temperate adj calm, mild, moderate, reasonable, restrained, self-possessed, sensible, sober, stable, steady. Opp EXTREME.

tempest n cyclone, gale, hurricane, tornado, tumult, typhoon, whirlwind. ▷ STORM.

tempestuous adj fierce, furious, tumultuous, turbulent, violent, wild. ▷ STORMY. Opp CALM.

temple n church, house of God, mosque, pagoda, place of worship, shrine, synagogue.

tempo n beat, pace, rate, rhythm, pulse, speed.

temporal adj earthly, fleshly, impermanent, material, mortal, mundane, non-religious, secular, terrestrial, transient, transitory, worldly. Opp SPIRITUAL.

temporary adj 1 brief, ephemeral, evanescent, fleeting, fugitive, impermanent, interim, makeshift, momentary, passing, provisional, short, short-lived, short-term, stopgap, transient, transitory. 2 temporary captain. acting. Opp PERMANENT.

tempt v allure, attract, bait, bribe, coax, decoy, entice, fascinate, inveigle, lure, offer incentives, persuade, seduce, tantalize, woo. **tempting** ▷ APPETIZING, ATTRACTIVE.

temptation n allure, appeal, attraction, cajolery, coaxing, draw, enticement, fascination, inducement, lure, persuasion, pull, seduction.

tenable adj believable, conceivable, credible, defensible, feasible, justifiable, legitimate, logical, plausible, rational, reasonable, sensible, sound, supportable, understandable, viable. Opp INDEFENSIBLE.

tenacious adj determined, dogged, firm, intransigent, obdurate, obstinate, persistent, pertinacious, resolute, single-minded, steadfast, strong, stubborn, tight, uncompromising, unfaltering, unshakeable, unswerving, unwavering, unyielding. Opp WEAK.

tenant n inhabitant, leaseholder, lodger, occupant, occupier, resident.

tend v 1 attend to, care for, cherish, cultivate, guard, keep, inf keep an eye on, look after, manage, mind, minister to, protect, take care of, watch. 2 tend the sick. nurse, treat. 3 tend to fall asleep. be disposed to, be inclined, be liable, be prone, have a tendency, incline.

tendency n bias, disposition, drift, inclination, instinct, leaning, liability, partiality, penchant, predilection, predisposition, proclivity, propensity, readiness, susceptibility, trend.

tender adj 1 dainty, delicate, fragile, frail, vulnerable, weak. 2 tender meat. chewable, eatable, edible, soft. 3 tender place. aching, inflamed, painful, sensitive, smarting, sore. 4 tender love-song. emotional, heartfelt, moving, poignant, romantic, sentimental, touching. 5 tender care. affectionate, amorous, caring, compassionate, concerned, considerate, fond, gentle, humane, kind, loving, merciful, pitying, soft-hearted, sympathetic, warm-hearted. 6 tender age. immature, inexperienced, young, youthful. Opp TOUGH, UNSYMPATHETIC.

tense adj 1 rigid, strained, stretched, taut, tight. 2 tense person. anxious, apprehensive, edgy, excited, fidgety, highly-strung, intense, inf jittery, jumpy, keyed up, nervous, on edge, inf on tenterhooks, overwrought, restless, strained, stressed, inf strung up, touchy, uneasy, inf uptight, worried. 3 tense situation. exciting, fraught, inf nail-biting, nerve-racking, stressful, worrying. Opp RELAXED.

tension n 1 pull, strain, tautness, tightness. 2 the tension of waiting. anxiety, apprehension, edginess, excitement, nervousness, stress, suspense, unease, worry. Opp RELAXATION.

tent n big-top, marquee, tepee, wigwam.

tentative adj cautious, diffident, doubtful, experimental, exploratory, half-hearted, hesitant, inconclusive, indecisive, indefinite, nervous, preliminary, provisional, shy, speculative, timid, uncertain, unsure. Opp DECISIVE.

tenuous adj attenuated, fine, flimsy, fragile, insubstantial, slender, slight, weak. ▷ THIN. Opp 3STRONG.

tepid adj 1 lukewarm, warm. 2 tepid response. ▷ APATHETIC.

term n 1 duration, period, season, span, spell, stretch, time. 2 school term. Amer semester, session. 3 technical terms. designation, expression, name, phrase, saying, title, word. **terms** 1 conditions, particulars, provisions, specifications, stipulations. 2 hotel's terms. charges, fees, prices, rates, tariff.

terminal adj deadly, fatal, final, incurable, killing, lethal, mortal. • n 1 keyboard, VDU, workstation. 2 passenger terminal. destination, terminus. 3 electric terminal. connection, connector, coupling.

terminate v bring to an end, cease, come to an end, discontinue, end, finish, inf pack in, phase out, stop, inf wind up. ▷ END. Opp BEGIN.

terminology n choice of words, jargon, language, nomenclature, phraseology, special terms, vocabulary.

terminus n destination, last stop, station, terminal.

terrain n country, ground, land, landscape, territory.

terrestrial adj earthly, mundane, ordinary.

terrible adj 1 acute, appalling, awful, beastly, distressing, dread-ful, fearful, fearsome, formidable, frightening, frightful, ghastly, grave, gruesome, harrowing, hideous, horrendous, horrible, horrific, horrifying, intolerable, loathsome, nasty, nauseating, outrageous, revolting, shocking, terrifying, unbearable, vile. 2 ▷ BAD.

terrific adj Terrific may mean causing terror (▷ TERRIBLE). It is more often used informally of anything which is extreme in its own way: a terrific problem ▷ EXTREME; terrific size ▷ BIG; a terrific party ▷ EXCELLENT; a terrific storm ▷ VIOLENT.

terrify v appal, dismay, horrify, inf make your blood run cold, petrify, shock, terrorize. ▷ FRIGHTEN. **terrified** ▷ FRIGHTENED. **terrifying** ▷ FRIGHTENING.

territory n area, colony, district, domain, dominion, enclave, jurisdiction, land, neighbourhood, precinct, preserve, province, region, sector, sphere, state, terrain, tract, zone. ▷ COUNTRY.

terror n alarm, awe, dismay, dread, fright, horror, panic, shock, trepidation. ▷ FEAR.

terrorist n assassin, bomber, guerilla, gunman, hijacker, revolutionary.

terrorize v browbeat, bully, coerce, cow, intimidate, menace, persecute, terrify, threaten, torment, tyrannize. ▷ FRIGHTEN.

terse adj abrupt, brief, brusque, concise, crisp, curt, epigrammatic, incisive, laconic, pithy, short, inf short and sweet, inf snappy, succinct, to the point. Opp VERBOSE.

test n analysis, appraisal, assessment, audition, inf check-over,

inf check-up, evaluation, examination, inspection, interrogation, investigation, quiz, screentest, trial, *inf* try-out.
● *v* analyse, appraise, assess, audition, check, evaluate, examine, experiment with, inspect, interrogate, investigate, probe, *inf* put someone through their paces, put to the test, question, quiz, screen, try out.

testify *v* affirm, attest, bear witness, declare, give evidence, proclaim, state on oath, swear, vouch, witness.

testimonial *n* character reference, commendation, recommendation, reference.

testimony *n* assertion, declaration, deposition, evidence, statement, submission.

tether *n* chain, cord, halter, lead, leash, restraint, rope. ● *v* chain up, fetter, keep on a tether, leash, restrain, rope, secure, tie up. ▷ FASTEN.

text *n* 1 argument, content, contents, matter, subject matter, wording. 2 *literary text.* book, textbook, work. 3 *text from scripture.* line, passage, quotation, sentence, theme, topic, verse.

textile *n* cloth, fabric, material, stuff.

texture *n* composition, consistency, feel, finish, grain, quality, surface, touch, weave.

thank *v* acknowledge, express thanks, say thank you, show gratitude.

thankful *adj* appreciative, contented, glad, grateful, happy, indebted, pleased, relieved. *Opp* UNGRATEFUL.

thankless *adj* bootless, futile, profitless, unappreciated,

unrecognized, unrewarded, unrewarding. *Opp* PROFITABLE.

thanks *pl n* acknowledgement, appreciation, gratitude, recognition, thanksgiving. **thanks to** as a result of, because of, owing to, through.

thaw *v* defrost, de-ice, heat up, melt, soften, unfreeze, warm up. *Opp* FREEZE.

theatre *n* 1 amphitheatre, auditorium, hall, opera house, playhouse. 2 acting, stagecraft. ▷ DRAMA. **the theatre** entertainment, show business, *inf* showbiz, the stage.

theatrical *adj* 1 *theatrical company.* dramatic, repertory, stage. 2 [*derog*] *theatrical behaviour.* affected, artificial, exaggerated, forced, *inf* hammy, melodramatic, ostentatious, overacted, overdone, *inf* over the top, showy, stagy, unnatural. *Opp* NATURAL.

theft *n* burglary, embezzlement, fraud, housebreaking, larceny, looting, pilfering, *inf* pinching, poaching, purloining, robbery, shoplifting, stealing, swindling, thieving.

theme *n* 1 argument, essence, gist, idea, issue, keynote, matter, subject, text, thesis, thread, topic. 2 *musical theme.* air, melody, motif, subject, tune.

theology *n* divinity, religion, religious studies.

theoretical *adj* abstract, academic, conjectural, doctrinaire, hypothetical, ideal, notional, pure (*science*), putative, speculative, suppositious, unproven, untested. *Opp* PRACTICAL, PROVEN.

theorize v conjecture, form a theory, guess, hypothesize, reason, speculate.

theory n 1 argument, assumption, belief, conjecture, explanation, guess, hypothesis, idea, notion, speculation, supposition, surmise, thesis, view. 2 *theory of a subject*. laws, principles, rules, science. Opp PRACTICE.

therapeutic adj beneficial, corrective, curative, healing, healthy, helpful, medicinal, remedial, restorative, salubrious. Opp HARMFUL.

therapist n analyst, counsellor, healer, physiotherapist, psychoanalyst, psychotherapist.

therapy n 1 cure, healing, remedy, tonic, treatment. 2 *therapy sessions*. analysis, group therapy, psychotherapy, psychoanalysis.

therefore adv accordingly, consequently, hence, so, thus.

thesis n 1 argument, assertion, contention, hypothesis, idea, opinion, postulate, premise, premiss, proposition, theory, view. 2 *research thesis*. dissertation, essay, paper, tract, treatise.

thick adj 1 broad, inf bulky, chunky, stout, sturdy, wide. ▷ FAT. 2 *thick layer, sweater*. deep, heavy, substantial, woolly. 3 *thick crowd*. dense, impenetrable, numerous, packed, solid. 4 *thick liquid*. clotted, coagulated, concentrated, condensed, firm, glutinous, heavy, sticky, stiff, viscous. 5 *thick growth*. abundant, bushy, luxuriant, plentiful. 6 *thick with visitors*. alive, bristling, inf chock-full, choked, covered, crammed, crawling, crowded, filled, full,

jammed, swarming, teeming. Opp THIN.

thicken v clot, coagulate, concentrate, condense, congeal, firm up, inf jell, reduce, solidify, stiffen.

thickness n 1 breadth, density, depth, viscosity, width. 2 *thickness of paint, rock*. coating, layer, seam, stratum.

thief n bandit, brigand, burglar, criminal, inf crook, embezzler, highwayman, housebreaker, kleptomaniac, looter, mugger, pickpocket, pilferer, pirate, plagiarist, poacher, purloiner, robber, safe-cracker, shoplifter, stealer, swindler.

thieving adj dishonest, light-fingered, rapacious.
● n ▷ THEFT.

thin adj 1 anorexic, attenuated, bony, cadaverous, emaciated, fine, gangling, gaunt, lanky, lean, narrow, pinched, rangy, scraggy, scrawny, skeletal, skinny, slender, slight, slim, small, spare, spindly, underfed, undernourished, underweight, wiry. Opp FAT. 2 *thin layer*. delicate, diaphanous, filmy, fine, flimsy, gauzy, insubstantial, light, inf see-through, shallow, sheer (*silk*), superficial, translucent, wispy. 3 *thin crowd*. meagre, scanty, scarce, scattered, sparse. 4 *thin liquid*. dilute, fluid, runny, sloppy, watery, weak. 5 *thin atmosphere*. rarefied. 6 *thin excuse*. feeble, implausible, tenuous, transparent, unconvincing. Opp DENSE, STRONG, THICK. ● v dilute, water down, weaken. **thin out** 1 decrease, diminish, disperse. 2 prune, reduce, trim, weed out.

thing n 1 apparatus, artefact, article, device, entity, gadget, implement, item, object, utensil. 2 affair, circumstance, deed, event, eventuality, happening, incident, occurrence, phenomenon. 3 *I need to mention one thing.* detail, fact, factor, feature, point, statement, subject, thought. 4 *the first thing to do.* act, action, chore, deed, job, responsibility, task. 5 [*inf*] *thing about snakes.* aversion, fixation, *inf* hang-up, mania, neurosis, obsession, passion, phobia, preoccupation. **things** 1 baggage, belongings, clothing, equipment, *inf* gear, luggage, possessions, *inf* stuff. 2 *How are things?* circumstances, conditions, life.

think v 1 attend, brood, chew things over, cogitate, concentrate, consider, contemplate, daydream, deliberate, dream, dwell (on), expect, fantasize, give thought (to), imagine, meditate, mull over, muse, ponder, *inf* rack your brains, reason, reflect, remind yourself of, reminisce, ruminate, work things out. 2 *Do you think it's true?* accept, admit, assume, believe, be under the impression, conclude, deem, estimate, feel, guess, imagine, judge, presume, reckon, suppose, surmise. **think better of** ▷ RECONSIDER. **thinking** ▷ INTELLIGENT, THOUGHTFUL. **think up** ▷ DEVISE.

thinker n *inf* brain, innovator, intellect, inventor, philosopher, sage, scholar.

thirst n 1 drought, dryness, thirstiness. 2 *thirst for knowledge.* appetite, craving, desire, eagerness, hunger, itch, longing, love (of), lust, passion, urge,

wish, yearning, *inf* yen. • v be thirsty, crave, have a thirst, hunger, long, strive (after), wish, yearn. **thirst for** ▷ WANT.

thirsty adj 1 arid, dehydrated, dry, *inf* gasping, panting, parched. 2 *thirsty for news.* avid, craving, desirous, eager, greedy, hankering, itching, longing, voracious, yearning.

thorn n barb, bristle, needle, prickle, spike, spine.

thorny adj 1 barbed, bristly, prickly, scratchy, sharp, spiky, spiny. 2 ▷ DIFFICULT.

thorough adj 1 assiduous, attentive, careful, comprehensive, conscientious, deep, detailed, diligent, efficient, exhaustive, extensive, full, *inf* in-depth, methodical, meticulous, minute, observant, orderly, organized, painstaking, scrupulous, searching, systematic, thoughtful, watchful. *Opp* SUPERFICIAL. 2 *thorough rascal.* absolute, complete, downright, out and out, perfect, proper, sheer, thoroughgoing, total, unmitigated, unmixed, unqualified, utter.

thought n 1 *inf* brainwork, brooding, *inf* brown study, cogitation, concentration, consideration, contemplation, daydreaming, deliberation, intelligence, introspection, meditation, musing, pensiveness, reason, reasoning, reflection, reverie, rumination, study, thinking, worrying. 2 *clever thought.* belief, concept, conception, conclusion, conjecture, conviction, idea, notion, observation, opinion. 3 *no thought of gain.* aim, design, dream, expectation, hope, intention, plan, prospect, purpose. 4 *kind thought.* compassion, concern, consideration, kindness, solicitude, thoughtfulness.

thoughtful *adj* 1 absorbed, abstracted, attentive, brooding, contemplative, dreamy, engrossed, grave, introspective, meditative, pensive, rapt, reflective, serious, solemn, studious, thinking, watchful. 2 *thoughtful work.* careful, conscientious, diligent, exhaustive, intelligent, methodical, meticulous, observant, orderly, organized, painstaking, rational, scrupulous, sensible, systematic, thorough. 3 *thoughtful behaviour.* caring, compassionate, concerned, considerate, good-natured, helpful, obliging, public-spirited, solicitous, unselfish. ▷ KIND.
Opp THOUGHTLESS.

thoughtless *adj* 1 absentminded, careless, hasty, heedless, ill-considered, impetuous, inadvertent, inattentive, injudicious, irresponsible, mindless, negligent, rash, reckless, scatterbrained, unobservant, unthinking. ▷ STUPID. 2 *thoughtless insult.* cruel, heartless, inconsiderate, insensitive, rude, selfish, tactless, undiplomatic, unfeeling. ▷ UNKIND.
Opp THOUGHTFUL.

thrash *v* beat, birch, cane, flay, flog, lash, scourge, whip.
▷ DEFEAT, HIT.

thread *n* 1 fibre, filament, hair, strand, string, twine, yarn. 2 *thread of a story.* argument, course, direction, drift, line of thought, plot, story line, theme. ● *v* put on a thread, string together. **thread your way** file, pass, pick your way, wind.

threadbare *adj* frayed, old, ragged, shabby, tattered, *inf* tatty, worn, worn-out.

threat *n* 1 danger, intimidation, menace, risk, warning. 2 *threat of rain.* foreboding, forewarning, intimation, omen, portent, presage.

threaten *v* 1 browbeat, bully, cow, intimidate, menace, pressurize, terrorize. ▷ FRIGHTEN. *Opp* REASSURE. 2 *clouds threaten rain.* forebode, foreshadow, portend, presage, warn of. 3 *the recession threatens jobs.* endanger, imperil, jeopardize, put at risk.

threatening *adj* forbidding, grim, impending, looming, menacing, ominous, portentous, sinister, stern, *inf* ugly, unfriendly, worrying.

three *n* threesome, triad, trio, triplet, triumvirate.

threshold *n* 1 doorstep, doorway, entrance, sill. 2 *threshold of a new era.* ▷ BEGINNING.

thrifty *adj* careful, *derog* close-fisted, economical, frugal, mean, *derog* niggardly, parsimonious, provident, prudent, skimping, sparing.
Opp EXTRAVAGANT.

thrill *n* adventure, *inf* buzz, excitement, frisson, *inf* kick, pleasure, sensation, shiver, suspense, tingle, titillation, tremor. ● *v* arouse, delight, electrify, excite, rouse, stimulate, stir, titillate. **thrilling** ▷ EXCITING.

thriller *n* crime story, detective story, mystery, *inf* whodunit.

thrive *v* be vigorous, bloom, boom, burgeon, *inf* come on, do well, expand, flourish, grow, increase, *inf* make strides, pros-

per, succeed. *Opp* DIE. **thriving**
▷ PROSPEROUS, VIGOROUS.

throat *n* gullet, neck,
oesophagus, windpipe.

throaty *adj* deep, gravelly, gruff,
guttural, hoarse, husky, rasping,
rough, thick.

throb *v* beat, palpitate, pound,
pulsate, pulse, vibrate.

throe *n* convulsion, fit, *pl* labour-
pains, pang, paroxysm, spasm.
▷ PAIN.

thrombosis *n* blood-clot, embolism, stroke.

throng *n* crowd, gathering,
horde, mass, mob, multitude,
swarm. ▷ GROUP. ● *v* ▷ GATHER.

throttle *v* asphyxiate, choke,
smother, stifle, strangle,
suffocate.

throw *v* 1 bowl, *inf* bung, cast,
inf chuck, fling, heave, hurl,
launch, lob, pelt, pitch, propel,
put (*the shot*), send, *inf* shy,
sling, toss. 2 *throw light.* cast,
project, shed. 3 *throw a rider.*
dislodge, floor, shake off, throw
down, throw off, unseat, upset.
4 ▷ DISCONCERT. **throw away**
▷ DISCARD. **throw out** ▷ EXPEL.
throw up ▷ PRODUCE, VOMIT.

throw-away *adj* 1 cheap,
disposable. 2 *throw-away*
remark. casual, offhand,
passing, unimportant.

thrust *v* butt, drive, elbow, force,
impel, jab, lunge, plunge, poke,
press, prod, propel, push, ram,
send, shoulder, shove, stab,
stick, urge.

thug *n* assassin, *inf* bully-boy,
delinquent, gangster, hoodlum,
hooligan, mugger, *inf* rough, ruffian, *inf* tough, troublemaker,
vandal, *inf* yob. ▷ CRIMINAL.

thunder *n* clap, crack, peal,
reverberation, roll, rumble.
● *v* ▷ REVERBERATE.

thunderous *adj* booming, deafening, reverberant, reverberating, roaring, rumbling.
▷ LOUD.

thus *adv* accordingly, consequently, for this reason,
hence, so, therefore.

thwart *v* baffle, foil, frustrate,
hinder, impede, obstruct, prevent, stand in the way of, stop,
inf stump.

ticket *n* 1 coupon, pass, permit,
token, voucher. 2 *price ticket.*
docket, label, marker, tab, tag.

ticklish *adj* 1 hypersensitive,
inf prickly, sensitive, touchy.
2 *ticklish situation.* awkward, delicate, difficult, precarious, risky,
tricky, uncertain.

tide *n* current, drift, ebb and
flow, movement, rise and fall.

tidiness *n* meticulousness, neatness, order, orderliness, organization, smartness, system.
Opp DISORDER.

tidy *adj* neat, orderly, presentable, shipshape, smart, *inf* spick
and span, spruce, straight, trim,
uncluttered, well-groomed, well-
kept. 2 *tidy habits.* businesslike,
careful, house-proud, methodical, meticulous, organized, systematic, well-organized.
Opp UNTIDY. ● *v* arrange, clean
up, groom, neaten, put in order,
rearrange, reorganize, set
straight, smarten, spruce up,
straighten. *Opp* MUDDLE.

tie *v* 1 bind, do up, hitch, join,
knot, lash, moor, rope, secure,
splice, tether, truss up.
▷ FASTEN. *Opp* UNTIE. 2 *tie in a*
race. be equal, be level, be neck
and neck, draw.

tier n layer, level, line, order, range, rank, row, stage, storey, stratum, terrace.

tight adj 1 close, fast, firm, fixed, immovable, secure, snug. 2 *tight lid*. airtight, close-fitting, hermetic, impermeable, impervious, leak-proof, sealed, waterproof, watertight. 3 *tight supervision*. inflexible, rigorous, severe, strict, stringent. 4 *tight ropes*. rigid, stiff, stretched, taut. 5 *tight space*. compact, constricted, crammed, cramped, crowded, inadequate, limited, packed, small. 6 ▷ DRUNK. 7 ▷ MISERLY. Opp FREE, LOOSE.

tighten v 1 clamp down, close, close up, constrict, harden, make tighter, squeeze, stiffen, tense. ▷ FASTEN. 2 *tighten ropes*. pull tighter, stretch, tauten. 3 *tighten screws*. give another turn to, screw up, secure. Opp LOOSEN.

till v cultivate, dig, farm, plough, work.

tilt v 1 angle, bank, incline, keel over, lean, list, slant, slope, tip. 2 *tilt with lances*. joust, thrust. ▷ FIGHT.

timber n 1 trees, forest, woodland. 2 beams, boards, hardwood, logs, lumber, planks, softwood. ▷ WOOD.

time n 1 date, hour, instant, juncture, moment, occasion, opportunity, point. 2 duration, interval, period, phase, season, Amer semester, session, spell, stretch, term, while. 3 *time of Queen Victoria*. age, days, epoch, era, period. 4 *time in music*. beat, measure, rhythm, tempo. ● v 1 choose a time for, estimate, fix a time for, judge, organize, plan, schedule, timetable. 2 *time a race*. clock, measure the time of.

timeless adj ageless, deathless, eternal, everlasting, immortal, immutable, unchanging, undying, unending.

timely adj appropriate, apt, fitting, suitable.

timepiece n chronometer, clock, hourglass, stopwatch, sundial, timer, watch, wrist-watch.

timetable n agenda, calendar, curriculum, diary, list, programme, rota, schedule.

timid adj afraid, apprehensive, bashful, cowardly, diffident, faint-hearted, fearful, modest, inf mousy, nervous, pusillanimous, reserved, retiring, scared, shrinking, shy, spineless, tentative, timorous, unadventurous, unheroic, inf wimpish. ▷ FRIGHTENED. Opp BOLD.

tingle n 1 itch, itching, pins and needles, prickling, stinging, throb, throbbing, tickle, tickling. 2 *tingle of excitement*. quiver, shiver, thrill. ● v itch, prickle, sting, tickle.

tinker v dabble, fiddle, fool about, interfere, meddle, inf mess about, inf play about, tamper, try to mend.

tinny adj cheap, flimsy, inferior, insubstantial, poor-quality, shoddy, tawdry.

tinsel n decoration, glitter, gloss, show, sparkle.

tint n colour, colouring, dye, hue, shade, stain, tincture, tinge, tone, wash.

tiny adj diminutive, dwarf, imperceptible, infinitesimal, insignificant, microscopic, inf mini, miniature, minuscule, minute, negligible, pygmy, *inf* teeny, unimportant, *inf* wee, *inf* weeny. ▷ SMALL. Opp BIG.

tip n 1 apex, cap, crown, end, extremity, head, nib, peak, pinnacle, point, sharp end, summit, top, vertex. 2 *tip for a waiter*. gift, gratuity, money, present, reward, service charge. 3 *useful tip*. advice, clue, forecast, hint, information, pointer, prediction, suggestion, tip-off, warning. 4 *rubbish tip*. dump, rubbish-heap. • v 1 incline, keel, lean, list, slant, slope, tilt. 2 drop off, dump, empty, pour out, spill, unload, upset. 3 *tip a waiter*. give a tip to, reward. **tip over** ▷ OVERTURN.

tire v 1 become bored, become tired, flag, grow weary. 2 debilitate, drain, enervate, exhaust, fatigue, *inf* finish, *sl* knacker, overtire, sap, *inf* shatter, *inf* take it out of, tax, wear out, weary. Opp REFRESH. **tired** ▷ WEARY. **tired of** bored with, *inf* fed up with, sick of. **tiring** ▷ EXHAUSTING.

tiredness n drowsiness, exhaustion, fatigue, inertia, jet-lag, lassitude, lethargy, listlessness, sleepiness, weariness.

tireless adj determined, diligent, dogged, dynamic, energetic, hard-working, indefatigable, persistent, pertinacious, resolute, sedulous, unceasing, unfaltering, unflagging, untiring, unwavering, vigorous. Opp LAZY.

tiresome adj 1 boring, dull, monotonous, tedious, tiring, unexciting, uninteresting, wearisome, wearying. Opp EXCITING. 2 *tiresome delays*. annoying, bothersome, exasperating, inconvenient, infuriating, irksome, irritat-

ing, maddening, troublesome, trying, unwelcome, upsetting, vexing.

tiring adj debilitating, demanding, difficult, exhausting, fatiguing, hard, laborious, strenuous, taxing, wearying. Opp REFRESHING.

tissue n 1 fabric, material, stuff, substance. 2 napkin, paper handkerchief, serviette.

title n 1 caption, heading, headline, inscription, name, rubric. 2 appellation, designation, form of address, office, position, rank, status. ▷ RANK. 3 *title to an inheritance*. claim, deed, entitlement, ownership, possession, prerogative, right. • v call, designate, entitle, give a title to, label, name, tag.

titled adj aristocratic, noble, upper-class.

titter v chortle, chuckle, giggle, laugh, snicker, snigger.

titular adj formal, nominal, official, *inf* so-called, theoretical, token. Opp ACTUAL.

toast v 1 brown, cook, grill. 2 *toast a guest*. drink a toast to, drink the health of, drink to, honour, pay tribute to, raise your glass to.

together adv all at once, at the same time, collectively, concurrently, hand in hand, in chorus, in unison, jointly, shoulder to shoulder, side by side, simultaneously.

toil n *inf* donkey work, drudgery, effort, exertion, industry, labour, work. • v drudge, exert yourself, grind away, *inf* keep at it, labour, *inf* plug away, *inf* slave away, struggle, sweat. ▷ WORK.

toilet n 1 convenience, ladies'
room, latrine, lavatory, inf loo,
men's room, urinal, WC. 2 [old
use] make your toilet. dressing,
grooming, making up.

token adj cosmetic, emblematic,
nominal, notional, perfunctory,
representative, superficial, symbolic. Opp GENUINE. ● n 1 badge,
emblem, evidence, indication,
mark, marker, proof, reminder,
sign, symbol. 2 token of affection.
keepsake, memento, reminder,
souvenir. 3 bus token. coin, counter, coupon, disc, voucher.

tolerable adj 1 acceptable, bearable, endurable, sufferable.
2 tolerable food. adequate, all
right, average, fair, mediocre,
middling, inf OK, ordinary,
passable, satisfactory.
Opp INTOLERABLE.

tolerance n 1 broad-mindedness,
charity, fairness, forbearance,
forgiveness, lenience, open-
mindedness, openness, patience,
permissiveness. 2 tolerance of
others. acceptance, sympathy
(towards), toleration, understanding. 3 tolerance in moving
parts. allowance, clearance,
play, variation.

tolerant adj big-hearted, broad-
minded, charitable, easygoing,
fair, forbearing, forgiving, generous, indulgent, lenient, liberal,
magnanimous, open-minded,
patient, permissive, derog soft,
sympathetic, understanding.
Opp INTOLERANT.

tolerate v abide, accept, admit,
bear, brook, condone, countenance, endure, inf lump (I'll have
to lump it!), make allowances
for, permit, put up with, sanction, inf stick, stand, stomach,

suffer, inf take, undergo,
inf wear, weather.

toll n charge, dues, duty, fee,
levy, payment, tariff, tax.
● v chime, peal, ring, sound.

tomb n burial chamber, burial
place, catacomb, crypt, grave,
last resting place, mausoleum,
memorial, monument, sepulchre, vault.

tone n 1 accent, expression,
inflection, intonation, manner,
modulation, note, phrasing,
pitch, quality, sound, timbre.
2 air, atmosphere, character,
effect, feel, mood, spirit, style,
temper, vein. 3 colour tone.
colour, hue, shade, tinge, tint.
tone down ▷ SOFTEN. **tone in**
▷ HARMONIZE. **tone up**
▷ STRENGTHEN.

tongue n dialect, idiom, language, parlance, patois, speech,
talk, vernacular.

tongue-tied adj dumbfounded,
inarticulate, inf lost for words,
mute, silent, speechless, struck
dumb.

tonic n boost, fillip, inf pick-
me-up, refresher, restorative,
stimulant.

tool n 1 apparatus, appliance,
contraption, contrivance, device,
gadget, hardware, implement,
instrument, invention, machine,
mechanism, utensil, weapon.
2 He was used as a tool. dupe,
puppet, stooge.

tooth n canine, eye-tooth, fang,
incisor, molar, tusk, wisdom
tooth. **false teeth** bridge, den-
ture, dentures, plate.

toothed adj jagged, ragged,
rough, serrated. Opp SMOOTH.

top adj inf ace, best, choicest,
finest, first, foremost, greatest,

highest, leading, maximum, most, pre-eminent, prime, principal, supreme, topmost, unequalled, winning. *n* 1 acme, apex, crest, crown, culmination, head, height, high point, peak, pinnacle, summit, tip, vertex, zenith. 2 *top of a table.* surface. 3 *top of a jar.* cap, cover, covering, lid, stopper. *Opp* BOTTOM. • *v* 1 complete, cover, decorate, finish off, garnish. 2 beat, better, cap, exceed, excel, outdo, outstrip, surpass, transcend.

topic *n* issue, matter, point, question, subject, talking point, text, theme, thesis.

topical *adj* contemporary, current, recent, timely, up-to-date.

topography *n* features, geography, *inf* lie of the land.

topple *v* 1 bring down, fell, knock down, overturn, tip over, upset. 2 collapse, fall, overbalance, totter, tumble. 3 *topple a rival.* overthrow, unseat.
▷ DEFEAT.

torment *n* affliction, agony, anguish, distress, harassment, misery, ordeal, persecution, plague, scourge, suffering, torture, vexation, woe, worry, wretchedness. ▷ PAIN. • *v* afflict, annoy, bait, bedevil, bother, bully, distress, harass, intimidate, nag, persecute, pester, plague, tease, torture, vex, victimize, worry. ▷ HURT.

torpid *adj* apathetic, dull, inactive, indolent, inert, languid, lethargic, lifeless, listless, passive, phlegmatic, slothful, slow, slow-moving, sluggish, somnolent, spiritless. *Opp* LIVELY.

torrent *n* cascade, cataract, deluge, downpour, flood, flow,

gush, inundation, outpouring, overflow, rush, spate, stream, tide.

torrential *adj* copious, heavy, relentless, soaking, teeming, violent.

tortuous *adj* bent, circuitous, complicated, contorted, convoluted, corkscrew, crooked, curling, curvy, devious, indirect, involved, labyrinthine, meandering, roundabout, serpentine, sinuous, turning, twisted, twisting, twisty, wandering, winding, zigzag. *Opp* DIRECT, STRAIGHT.

torture *n* 1 cruelty, degradation, humiliation, persecution, punishment, torment. 2 affliction, agony, anguish, distress, misery, pain, suffering. • *v* 1 be cruel to, brainwash, bully, degrade, dehumanize, humiliate, hurt, inflict pain on, intimidate, persecute, rack, torment, victimize.
2 *tortured by doubts.* afflict, agonize, bedevil, bother, distress, harass, pester, plague, vex, worry.

toss *v* 1 bowl, cast, *inf* chuck, fling, flip, heave, hurl, lob, pitch, shy, sling, throw. 2 *toss about in a storm.* bob, dip, flounder, lurch, pitch, plunge, reel, rock, roll, twist and turn, wallow, welter, writhe.

total *adj* 1 complete, comprehensive, entire, full, gross, overall, whole. 2 *total disaster.* absolute, downright, out and out, outright, perfect, sheer, thorough, thoroughgoing, unalloyed, unmitigated, unqualified, utter. • *n* aggregate, amount, answer, lot, sum, whole. • *v* 1 add up to, amount to, come to, make. 2 add up, calculate, compute, count, reckon up, *inf* tot up, work out.

totalitarian *adj* absolute, authoritarian, autocratic, despotic, dictatorial, fascist, one-party, oppressive, tyrannous, undemocratic. *Opp* DEMOCRATIC.

totter *v* dodder, falter, reel, rock, stagger, stumble, teeter, topple, tremble, waver, wobble.

touch *n* 1 feel, feeling, texture. 2 brush, caress, contact, pat, stroke, tap. 3 *expert's touch*. ability, capability, experience, expertise, facility, flair, gift, knack, manner, sensitivity, skill, style, technique, understanding, way. 4 *touch of salt*. bit, dash, drop, hint, intimation, suggestion, suspicion, taste, tinge, trace. • *v* 1 be in contact with, brush, caress, embrace, feel, finger, fondle, graze, handle, kiss, lay a hand on, lean against, nuzzle, pat, paw, pet, push, rub, stroke, tap. 2 *touch the emotions*. affect, arouse, awaken, disturb, impress, influence, inspire, move, stimulate, stir, upset. 3 *touch 100 m.p.h.* attain, reach, rise to. 4 *No-one can touch him*. be in the same league as, come near, *inf* come up to, compare with, equal, match, parallel, rival.

touched ▷ EMOTIONAL, MAD.

touching ▷ EMOTIONAL.

touch off ▷ BEGIN, IGNITE.

touch on ▷ MENTION.

touch up ▷ IMPROVE.

touchy *adj* edgy, highly-strung, hypersensitive, irascible, irritable, *inf* jittery, jumpy, oversensitive, peevish, querulous, quick-tempered, sensitive, short-tempered, snappy, tempera-

mental, testy, tetchy, thin-skinned, waspish.

tough *adj* 1 durable, hard-wearing, indestructible, lasting, rugged, stout, strong, substantial, unbreakable, well-built, well-made. 2 *tough physique*. *inf* beefy, brawny, burly, hardy, muscular, robust, stalwart, strong, sturdy. 3 *tough man to work for*. cold, cool, hard, *inf* hard-boiled, *inf* hard-nosed, obstinate, resolute, ruthless, severe, stern, stony, stubborn, unsentimental, unsympathetic, unyielding. 4 *tough meat*. chewy, hard, gristly, inedible, leathery, rubbery. 5 *tough job*. arduous, demanding, difficult, exacting, exhausting, gruelling, hard, laborious, strenuous, taxing, troublesome. 6 *tough questions*. baffling, *inf* knotty, mystifying, perplexing, puzzling, *inf* thorny. *Opp* EASY, TENDER, WEAK.

toughen *v* harden, make tougher, reinforce, strengthen.

tour *n* drive, excursion, expedition, jaunt, journey, outing, ride, trip. • *v* do the rounds of, go round, make a tour of, visit. ▷ TRAVEL.

tourist *n* day-tripper, holidaymaker, sightseer, traveller, tripper, visitor.

tournament *n* championship, competition, contest, event, match, meeting, series.

tow *v* drag, draw, haul, lug, pull, trail, tug.

tower *n* belfry, bell-tower, minaret, skyscraper, spire, steeple, turret. • *v* loom, rear, rise, soar, stand out, stick up.

towering *adj* 1 colossal, gigantic, high, huge, imposing, lofty, mighty, soaring. ▷ TALL.

2 *towering rage.* extreme, fiery, intense, overpowering, passionate, unrestrained, vehement, violent.

town *n* borough, city, community, conurbation, municipality, settlement, township, village.

toxic *adj* dangerous, deadly, harmful, lethal, noxious, poisonous. *Opp* HARMLESS.

trace *n* 1 clue, evidence, footprint, *inf* give-away, hint, indication, intimation, mark, remains, sign, spoor, token, track, trail, vestige. 2 ▷ BIT. ● *v* 1 detect, discover, find, recover, retrieve, seek out, track down. 2 chart, copy, draw, map, mark out, outline, sketch. **kick over the traces** ▷ REBEL.

track *n* 1 footmark, footprint, mark, scent, spoor, trace, trail, wake (*of ship*). 2 *farm track.* bridle path, bridleway, footpath, path, road, route, trail, way. 3 *racing track.* circuit, course, dirt track, racetrack. 4 *railway track.* branch, branch line, line, rails, railway, route, tramway. ● *v* chase, dog, follow, hound, hunt, pursue, shadow, stalk, *inf* tail, trace, trail. **make tracks** ▷ DEPART. **track down** ▷ TRACE.

tract *n* 1 *tract of land.* area, expanse, region, stretch, territory. 2 *political tract.* ▷ TREATISE.

trade *n* 1 barter, business, buying and selling, commerce, dealing, exchange, marketing, merchandising, trading, traffic, transactions. 2 *skilled trade.* calling, career, craft, employment, job, *inf* line, occupation, profession, pursuit, work. ● *v* buy and sell, do business, have dealings,

market goods, merchandise, retail, sell, traffic (in). **trade in** ▷ EXCHANGE. **trade on** ▷ EXPLOIT.

trader *n* broker, buyer, dealer, merchant, retailer, salesman, seller, shopkeeper, stockist, supplier, tradesman, trafficker (*in illegal goods*), vendor.

tradition *n* 1 convention, custom, habit, institution, practice, ritual, routine, usage. 2 *popular tradition.* belief, folklore.

traditional *adj* 1 accustomed, conventional, customary, established, familiar, habitual, historic, normal, orthodox, regular, time-honoured, typical, usual. *Opp* UNCONVENTIONAL. 2 *traditional stories.* folk, handed down, old, oral, popular, unwritten. *Opp* MODERN.

traffic *n* conveyance, movements, shipping, trade, transport, transportation. ● *v* ▷ TRADE.

tragedy *n* adversity, affliction, *inf* blow, calamity, catastrophe, disaster, misfortune.

tragic *adj* 1 appalling, awful, calamitous, catastrophic, dire, disastrous, dreadful, fatal, fearful, hapless, ill-fated, ill-omened, ill-starred, inauspicious, lamentable, terrible, unfortunate, unlucky. 2 *tragic expression.* bereft, distressed, grief-stricken, hurt, pathetic, piteous, pitiful, sorrowful, woeful, wretched. *Opp* COMIC.

trail *n* 1 evidence, footmarks, footprints, marks, scent, signs, spoor, traces, wake (*of ship*). 2 path, pathway, route, track. ● *v* 1 dangle, drag, draw, pull, tow. 2 chase, follow, hunt, pursue, shadow, stalk, *inf* tail, trace, track. 3 ▷ DAWDLE.

train n 1 carriage, coach, diesel, electric train, express, intercity, local train, railcar, steam train. 2 *train of servants*. cortège, entourage, escort, followers, retainers, retinue, staff, suite. 3 *train of events*. ▷ SEQUENCE. • v 1 coach, discipline, drill, educate, instruct, prepare, school, teach, tutor. 2 exercise, *inf* get fit, practise, prepare yourself, rehearse, *inf* work out. 3 *train a gun*. ▷ AIM.

trainee n apprentice, beginner, cadet, learner, *inf* L-driver, novice, pupil, starter, student.

trainer n coach, instructor, teacher, tutor.

training n discipline, education, instruction, practice, teaching, tuition.

trait n attribute, characteristic, feature, idiosyncrasy, peculiarity, property, quality, quirk.

traitor n betrayer, blackleg, collaborator, defector, deserter, double-crosser, informer, *inf* Judas, quisling, renegade, turncoat.

tramp n 1 hike, march, trek, trudge, walk. 2 beggar, destitute person, *inf* dosser, *inf* down and out, drifter, homeless person, rover, traveller, vagabond, vagrant, wanderer. • v *inf* footslog, hike, march, plod, stride, toil, traipse, trek, trudge.

trample v crush, flatten, squash, *inf* squish, stamp on, step on, tread on, walk over.

trance n *inf* brown study, daydream, daze, dream, hypnotic state, reverie, semiconsciousness, spell, stupor.

tranquil adj 1 calm, halcyon (*days*), peaceful, placid, quiet, restful, serene, still, undisturbed, unruffled. *Opp* STORMY. 2 *tranquil mood*. collected, composed, dispassionate, *inf* laid-back, sedate, sober, untroubled. *Opp* EXCITED.

tranquillizer n barbiturate, narcotic, opiate, sedative.

transaction n agreement, bargain, business, contract, deal, negotiation, proceeding.

transcend v beat, exceed, excel, outdo, outstrip, rise above, surpass, top.

transcribe v copy out, render, reproduce, take down, translate, write out.

transfer v bring, carry, change, convey, deliver, displace, ferry, hand over, make over, move, pass on, relocate, remove, shift, sign over, take, transplant, transport, transpose.

transform v adapt, alter, change, convert, improve, metamorphose, modify, rebuild, reconstruct, remodel, revolutionize, transfigure, translate, transmute, turn.

transformation n adaptation, alteration, change, conversion, improvement, metamorphosis, modification, mutation, reconstruction, revolution, transfiguration, transition, *inf* turnabout.

transgression n crime, error, fault, lapse, misdeed, misdemeanour, offence, sin, wickedness, wrongdoing.

transient adj brief, ephemeral, evanescent, fleeting, fugitive, impermanent, momentary, passing, quick, short, short-lived,

temporary, transitory.
Opp PERMANENT.

transit *n* conveyance, journey, movement, moving, passage, progress, shipment, transfer, transportation, travel.

transition *n* alteration, change, change-over, conversion, development, evolution, modification, progression, shift, transformation, transit.

translate *v* change, convert, decode, elucidate, explain, interpret, paraphrase, render, reword, transcribe.
▷ TRANSFORM.

translation *n* interpretation, paraphrase, rendering, transcription, version.

translator *n* interpreter, linguist.

transmission *n* 1 broadcast, communication, diffusion, dissemination, relaying, sending out. 2 *transmission of goods.* carriage, conveyance, dispatch, shipment, transfer, transport, transportation.

transmit *v* 1 convey, dispatch, disseminate, forward, pass on, post, send, transfer, transport. 2 *transmit a message.* broadcast, cable, communicate, emit, fax, phone, radio, relay, telephone, telex, wire. *Opp* RECEIVE.

transparent *adj* 1 clear, crystalline, diaphanous, filmy, gauzy, limpid, pellucid, *inf* see-through, sheer, translucent. 2 *transparent honesty.* ▷ CANDID.

transpire *v* ▷ HAPPEN.

transplant *v* displace, move, relocate, reposition, resettle, shift, transfer, uproot.

transport *n* 1 carrier, conveyance, haulage, removal, ship-

ment, shipping, transportation. 2 ▷ VEHICLE. ● *v* 1 bear, carry, convey, fetch, haul, move, remove, send, shift, ship, take, transfer. 2 ▷ DEPORT.

transpose *v* change, exchange, interchange, move round, rearrange, reverse, substitute, swap, switch, transfer.

transverse *adj* crosswise, diagonal, oblique.

trap *n* ambush, booby-trap, net, noose, pitfall, ploy, snare, trick. ● *v* ambush, capture, catch, catch out, corner, deceive, dupe, ensnare, entrap, inveigle, net, snare, trick.

trappings *pl n* accessories, accoutrements, adornments, decorations, equipment, finery, fittings, furnishings, *inf* gear, ornaments, paraphernalia, *inf* things, trimmings.

trash *n* 1 debris, garbage, junk, litter, refuse, rubbish, sweepings, waste. 2 ▷ NONSENSE.

trauma *n* ▷ SHOCK.

travel *n* globe-trotting, moving around, touring, tourism, travelling. **travels** excursions, expeditions, holidays, journeys, outings, pilgrimages, tours, treks, trips, voyages, wanderings. ● *v* 1 *inf* gad about, *inf* gallivant, journey, make a trip, proceed, progress, roam, rove, voyage, wander. 2 commute, cruise, cycle, drive, fly, hitchhike, navigate, ride, sail, tour, trek. ▷ GO.

traveller *n* 1 astronaut, aviator, commuter, cosmonaut, cyclist, driver, flyer, motorcyclist, motorist, passenger, pedestrian, sailor, voyager, walker. 2 *company traveller.* *inf* rep, representative, salesman, saleswoman. 3 *overseas traveller.*

explorer, globe-trotter, hiker, hitchhiker, holidaymaker, pilgrim, rambler, stowaway, tourist, tripper, wanderer, wayfarer. **4** *live as a traveller*. gypsy, itinerant, nomad, tramp.

travelling *adj* itinerant, migrant, migratory, nomadic, peripatetic, restless, roaming, roving, touring, wandering.

treacherous *adj* **1** deceitful, disloyal, double-crossing, double-dealing, duplicitous, faithless, false, perfidious, sneaky, unfaithful, untrustworthy. **2** *treacherous conditions*. dangerous, deceptive, hazardous, perilous, risky, unreliable, unsafe, unstable.
Opp LOYAL, RELIABLE.

treachery *n* betrayal, dishonesty, disloyalty, double-dealing, duplicity, faithlessness, infidelity, perfidy. ▷ TREASON.
Opp LOYALTY.

tread *v* tread on crush, squash underfoot, stamp on, step on, trample, walk on.

treason *n* betrayal, high treason, mutiny, rebellion, sedition.
▷ TREACHERY.

treasure *n* cache, fortune, gold, hoard, jewels, riches, treasure trove, valuables, wealth.
● *v* adore, appreciate, cherish, esteem, guard, keep safe, love, prize, rate highly, value, worship.

treasury *n* bank, exchequer, treasure-house, vault.

treat *n* entertainment, gift, outing, pleasure, surprise.
● *v* **1** attend to, behave towards, care for, look after, use. **2** *treat a topic*. consider, deal with, discuss, tackle. **3** *treat a patient, wound*. cure, dress, give treatment to, heal, nurse, prescribe

medicine for, tend. **4** *treat food*. process. **5** *I'll treat you to lunch*. entertain, pay for, regale.

treatise *n* dissertation, essay, monograph, pamphlet, paper, thesis, tract.

treatment *n* **1** care, conduct, dealing (with), handling, management, organization, reception, usage, use. **2** *treatment of illness*. cure, first aid, healing, medicine, nursing, remedy, therapy.

treaty *n* agreement, alliance, armistice, concordat, contract, convention, covenant, *inf* deal, entente, pact, peace, settlement, truce, understanding.

tree *n* bush, deciduous tree, conifer, evergreen, sapling.

tremble *v* quail, quake, quaver, quiver, shake, shiver, shudder, vibrate, waver.

tremendous *adj* alarming, appalling, awe-inspiring, fearsome, frightening, horrifying, overpowering, terrible. ▷ BIG, EXCELLENT, REMARKABLE.

tremor *n* **1** quiver, shaking, trembling, vibration. **2** earthquake.

tremulous *adj* **1** agitated, anxious, excited, frightened, *inf* jittery, jumpy, nervous, timid. *Opp* CALM. **2** quivering, shaking, shivering, trembling. *Opp* STEADY.

trend *n* **1** direction, drift, inclination, leaning, movement, shift, tendency. **2** *latest trend*. craze, fad, fashion, style, *inf* thing, vogue.

trendy *adj inf* all the rage, fashionable, *inf* in, latest, modern, stylish, up-to-date. *Opp* OLD-FASHIONED.

trespass *v* encroach, enter illegally, intrude, invade.

trial n **1** case, court martial, enquiry, examination, hearing, judicial proceeding, tribunal. **2** attempt, *inf* dry run, experiment, rehearsal, test, trial run, *inf* try-out. **3** affliction, difficulty, hardship, nuisance, ordeal, *sl* pain in the neck, *inf* pest, tribulation, trouble, worry.

triangular adj three-cornered, three-sided.

tribe n clan, dynasty, family, group, people, race, stock, strain.

tribute n accolade, commendation, compliment, eulogy, homage, honour, panegyric, praise, respect. **pay tribute to** ▷ HONOUR.

trick n **1** illusion, magic, sleight of hand. **2** *deceitful trick.* cheat, *inf* con, deceit, deception, fraud, hoax, joke, *inf* leg-pull, ploy, practical joke, prank, pretence, ruse, scheme, stratagem, stunt, subterfuge, swindle, trap, trickery, wile. **3** *useful trick.* art, craft, knack, *inf* know-how, secret, skill, technique. **4** *trick of speech.* characteristic, habit, idiosyncrasy, mannerism, peculiarity, way. ● v *inf* bamboozle, catch out, cheat, *inf* con, *inf* diddle, dupe, fool, hoax, hoodwink, *inf* kid, mislead, outwit, *inf* pull your leg, swindle, take in.

trickery n bluffing, cheating, deceit, deception, dishonesty, double-dealing, duplicity, fraud, *inf* funny business, guile, *inf* hocus-pocus, *inf* skulduggery, swindling, trick.

trickle v dribble, drip, drizzle, drop, exude, leak, ooze, run, seep. *Opp* GUSH.

trifle v dabble, fiddle, play about.

trifling ▷ TRIVIAL.

trill v sing, warble, whistle.

trim adj compact, neat, orderly, shipshape, smart, spruce, tidy, well-groomed, well-kept. *Opp* UNTIDY. ● v clip, crop, cut, pare down, prune, shape, shear, shorten, snip, tidy.

trip n day out, drive, excursion, expedition, holiday, jaunt, journey, outing, ride, tour, visit, voyage. ● v **1** fall, stumble, totter, tumble. **2** *trip along.* caper, dance, frisk, gambol, run, skip. **make a trip** ▷ TRAVEL.

trite adj banal, commonplace, ordinary, pedestrian, predictable, uninspired, uninteresting.

triumph n **1** accomplishment, achievement, conquest, coup, *inf* hit, knockout, master-stroke, success, victory, *inf* walk-over, win. **2** *return in triumph.* elation, exultation, joy, jubilation. ● v be victorious, carry the day, prevail, succeed, win. **triumph over** ▷ DEFEAT.

triumphant adj **1** conquering, dominant, successful, victorious, winning. *Opp* UNSUCCESSFUL. **2** *inf* cocky, elated, exultant, gleeful, gloating, joyful, jubilant, proud.

trivial adj frivolous, inconsequential, inconsiderable, inessential, insignificant, little, meaningless, minor, negligible, paltry, petty, *inf* piddling, slight, small, superficial, trifling, trite, unimportant, worthless. *Opp* IMPORTANT.

trophy n **1** [*pl*] booty, loot, souvenirs, spoils. **2** *sporting trophy.* award, cup, medal, prize.

trouble n **1** adversity, affliction, anxiety, burden, difficulty, distress, grief, hardship, inconvenience, misfortune, problem, sadness, sorrow, suffering, trial, tribulation, unhappiness, vexation, worry. **2** *crowd trouble.* commotion, conflict, discontent, disorder, dissatisfaction, disturbance, fighting, fuss, misconduct, *inf* row, strife, turmoil, unpleasantness, unrest, violence. **3** *stomach trouble.* ▷ ILLNESS. **4** *took the trouble to get it right.* care, concern, effort, exertion, pains, struggle. ● *v* afflict, agitate, alarm, annoy, bother, concern, distress, disturb, exasperate, harass, *inf* hassle, impose on, inconvenience, interfere with, irk, irritate, molest, nag, pain, perturb, pester, plague, put out, ruffle, threaten, torment, upset, vex, worry. **troubled** ▷ WORRIED.

troublemaker *n* agitator, culprit, delinquent, hooligan, mischief-maker, offender, rabble-rouser, rascal, ringleader, *inf* stirrer, vandal.

troublesome *adj* annoying, bothersome, disobedient, disorderly, distressing, inconvenient, irksome, irritating, naughty, tiresome, trying, uncooperative, unruly, upsetting, vexatious, vexing, wearisome, worrying. *Opp* HELPFUL.

truancy *n* absenteeism, malingering, *sl* skiving.

truant *n* absentee, malingerer, runaway, shirker, *sl* skiver. **play truant** be absent, malinger, *sl* skive, stay away.

truce *n* armistice, ceasefire, pact, peace, suspension of hostilities, treaty.

true *adj* **1** accurate, actual, authentic, correct, exact, factual, faithful, genuine, literal, proper, real, realistic, right, veracious, verified. *Opp* FALSE. **2** *true*

friend. constant, dependable, devoted, faithful, firm, honest, honourable, loyal, reliable, sincere, staunch, steadfast, trustworthy. **3** *the true owner.* authorized, legitimate, rightful, valid. **4** *true aim.* accurate, exact, perfect, precise, *inf* spot-on, unerring. *Opp* INACCURATE.

truncheon *n* ▷ BATON.

trunk *n* **1** shaft, stalk, stem. **2** body, frame, torso. **3** proboscis, snout. **4** box, case, casket, chest, coffer, crate, suitcase.

trust *n* **1** belief, certainty, confidence, conviction, credence, faith, reliance. **2** *position of trust.* duty, responsibility. ● *v* **1** *inf* bank on, believe in, be sure of, confide in, count on, depend on, have confidence in, have faith in, rely on. **2** assume, expect, hope, imagine, presume, suppose. *Opp* DOUBT.

trustful *adj* credulous, gullible, innocent, trusting, unquestioning, unsuspecting. *Opp* DISTRUSTFUL.

trustworthy *adj* constant, dependable, ethical, faithful, honest, honourable, loyal, moral, *inf* on the level, reliable, responsible, *inf* safe, sincere, steadfast, true, truthful, upright. *Opp* DECEITFUL.

truth *n* **1** facts, reality. *Opp* LIE. **2** accuracy, authenticity, correctness, exactness, integrity, reliability, truthfulness, validity, veracity. **3** *an accepted truth.* axiom, fact, maxim, truism.

truthful *adj* accurate, candid, correct, credible, factual, faithful, forthright, frank, honest, realistic, reliable, right, sincere, straight, true, trustworthy, vera-

cious, unvarnished.
Opp DISHONEST.

try *n* attempt, *inf* bash, effort,
endeavour, *inf* go, *inf* shot,
inf stab, test, trial. • *v* 1 aim,
attempt, endeavour, make an
effort, strain, strive, struggle.
2 *try something new. inf* check
out, evaluate, examine, experiment with, *inf* have a go at,
inf have a stab at, investigate,
test, try out. **trying**
▷ ANNOYING, TIRESOME. **try
someone's patience** ▷ ANNOY.

tub *n* barrel, bath, butt, cask,
drum, keg, pot, vat.

tube *n* capillary, cylinder, duct,
hose, pipe, tubing.

tuck *v* insert, push, shove, stuff.
tuck in ▷ EAT.

tuft *n* bunch, clump, tussock.

tug *v* drag, draw, haul, heave,
jerk, lug, pluck, pull, tow,
twitch, wrench, *inf* yank.

tumble *v* collapse, drop, fall,
flop, pitch, roll, stumble, topple,
trip up.

tumbledown *adj* broken down,
crumbling, decrepit, derelict,
dilapidated, ramshackle, rickety.

tumult *n* ado, agitation, commotion, excitement, fracas, hubbub,
upheaval. ▷ UPROAR.

tumultuous *adj* agitated, confused, excited, frenzied, hectic,
passionate, stormy, tempestuous, turbulent, unruly, violent,
wild. *Opp* CALM.

tune *n* air, melody, song, strain.
• *v* adjust, regulate, set.

tuneful *adj inf* catchy, euphonious, mellifluous, melodious,
musical, pleasant, sweetsounding. *Opp* TUNELESS.

tuneless *adj* cacophonous,
discordant, dissonant, harsh,
unmusical. *Opp* TUNEFUL.

tunnel *n* burrow, gallery, hole,
mine, passage, passageway,
shaft, subway. • *v* burrow, dig,
excavate, mine.

turbulent *adj* 1 agitated, confused, disordered, excited,
hectic, passionate, restless,
seething, violent, volatile, wild.
2 *turbulent crowd.* disorderly,
lawless, obstreperous, riotous,
rowdy, undisciplined, unruly.
3 *turbulent weather.* blustery,
choppy (*sea*), rough, stormy, tempestuous, violent, wild, windy.
Opp CALM.

turf *n* grass, green, lawn. • *v* **turf
out** ▷ EVICT.

turgid *adj* bombastic, grandiose,
high-flown, pompous, stilted,
wordy.

turmoil *n* bedlam, chaos, commotion, confusion, disturbance, ferment, hubbub, hullabaloo, riot,
inf row, *inf* rumpus, tumult,
unrest, upheaval, uproar.
Opp CALM.

turn *n* 1 coil, cycle, loop, pirouette, revolution, rotation, spin,
twirl, twist, whirl. 2 angle, bend,
change of direction, corner,
curve, detour, dogleg, hairpin
bend, junction, shift, turning
point, U-turn, zigzag. 3 *It's my
turn.* chance, *inf* go, innings,
opportunity, shot. 4 *comic turn.*
▷ PERFORMANCE. 5 *gave me a
turn.* ▷ SHOCK. • *v* 1 circle,
gyrate, loop, orbit, pivot,
revolve, roll, rotate, spin, spiral,
swivel, twirl, twist, whirl, wind.
2 bend, change direction, go
round a corner, swerve, veer,
wheel. 3 *turn a book into a film.*
adapt, alter, change, convert,

make, modify, transform. **4** *turn to and fro.* squirm, twist, wriggle, writhe. **turn aside** ▷ DEVIATE. **turn down** ▷ REJECT. **turn into** ▷ BECOME. **turn off** ▷ DEVIATE, DISCONNECT, REPEL. **turn on** ▷ ATTRACT, CONNECT. **turn out** ▷ EXPEL, HAPPEN, PRODUCE. **turn over** ▷ CONSIDER, OVERTURN. **turn tail** ▷ ESCAPE. **turn up** ▷ ARRIVE, DISCOVER.

turning point *n* crisis, crossroads, new direction, watershed.

turnover *n* efficiency, output, production, productivity, profits, yield.

twiddle *v* fiddle with, fidget with, twirl, twist.

twig *n* branch, offshoot, shoot, spray, sprig, stalk, stem, stick, tendril.

twilight *n* dusk, evening, gloaming, gloom, nightfall, sundown, sunset.

twin *adj* corresponding, duplicate, identical, indistinguishable, matching, paired, similar, symmetrical. ● *n* clone, double, duplicate, *inf* look-alike, match, pair, *inf* spitting image.

twirl *v* gyrate, pirouette, revolve, rotate, spin, turn, twist, wheel, whirl.

twist *n* **1** bend, coil, curl, kink, knot, loop, tangle, turn, zigzag. **2** *twist to a story.* revelation, surprise ending. ● *v* **1** bend, coil, corkscrew, curl, curve, loop, rotate, spin, spiral, turn, weave, wind, wreathe, wriggle, writhe, zigzag. **2** *twist ropes.* entangle, entwine, tangle. **3** *twist a lid.* turn, wrench. **4** *twist out of shape.* buckle, contort, crumple, distort, warp. **5** *twist meaning.* alter, change, falsify, misquote,

misrepresent. **twisted**
▷ CONFUSED, PERVERTED, TWISTY.

twisty *adj* bending, *inf* bendy, crooked, curving, *inf* in and out, indirect, meandering, rambling, roundabout, serpentine, twisted, twisting, *inf* twisting and turning, winding, zigzag. *Opp* STRAIGHT.

twitch *n* blink, convulsion, flutter, jerk, jump, spasm, tic, tremor. ● *v* fidget, flutter, jerk, jump, start, tremble.

type *n* **1** category, class, classification, designation, form, genre, group, kind, sort, species, variety. **2** *the very type of evil.* embodiment, epitome, model, pattern, personification. **3** *large type.* characters, lettering, letters, print, typeface.

typical *adj* **1** characteristic, distinctive, particular, representative. **2** *typical day.* average, conventional, normal, ordinary, standard, stock, unsurprising, usual. *Opp* UNUSUAL.

tyrannical *adj* authoritarian, autocratic, *inf* bossy, cruel, despotic, dictatorial, domineering, harsh, high-handed, imperious, oppressive, overbearing, ruthless, severe, totalitarian, undemocratic, unjust. *Opp* DEMOCRATIC.

tyrant *n* autocrat, despot, dictator, *inf* hard taskmaster, slave-driver.

U

ugly *adj* **1** deformed, disfigured, disgusting, frightful, ghastly, grisly, grotesque, gruesome, hideous, horrible, misshapen, monstrous, offensive, repulsive, revolting, shocking, sickening, terrible, vile. 2 *ugly furniture.* inelegant, plain, tasteless, unattractive, unprepossessing, unsightly. 3 *ugly mood, weather.* angry, dangerous, hostile, menacing, ominous, sinister, unfriendly. *Opp* BEAUTIFUL.

ulterior *adj* concealed, covert, hidden, secret, undeclared, undisclosed. *Opp* OVERT.

ultimate *adj* 1 closing, concluding, eventual, extreme, final, last. 2 *ultimate truth.* basic, fundamental.

umpire *n* arbiter, arbitrator, judge, official, *inf* ref, referee.

unable *adj* impotent, incapable, powerless, unfit, unprepared, unqualified. *Opp* ABLE.

unacceptable *adj* distasteful, inadmissible, inappropriate, inexcusable, invalid, objectionable, unpalatable, unsatisfactory. *Opp* ACCEPTABLE.

unaccompanied *adj* alone, lone, single-handed, unaided.

unadventurous *adj* cautious, conventional, diffident, quiet, tame, timid, unimaginative. *Opp* ADVENTUROUS.

unalterable *adj* ▷ IMMUTABLE.

unambiguous *adj* ▷ DEFINITE.

unanimous *adj* ▷ UNITED.

unassuming *adj* ▷ MODEST.

unattached *adj inf* available, free, independent, separate, single, uncommitted, unmarried.

unattractive *adj* colourless, dowdy, dull, nasty, objectionable, *inf* off-putting, plain, repulsive, tasteless, uninviting, unpleasant, unprepossessing,

unsightly. ▷ UGLY.
Opp ATTRACTIVE.

unauthorized *adj* illegal, illicit, irregular, unlawful, unofficial. *Opp* OFFICIAL.

unavoidable *adj* certain, compulsory, destined, fated, fixed, inescapable, inevitable, inexorable, mandatory, necessary, obligatory, required, unalterable.

unaware *adj* ▷ IGNORANT.

unbalanced *adj* 1 asymmetrical, irregular, lopsided, off-centre, shaky, uneven, unstable, wobbly. 2 *unbalanced mind.* ▷ MAD.

unbearable *adj* insufferable, insupportable, intolerable, unacceptable, unendurable. *Opp* TOLERABLE.

unbeatable *adj* ▷ INVINCIBLE.

unbecoming *adj* inappropriate, indecorous, indelicate, offensive, tasteless, unattractive, undignified, ungentlemanly, unladylike, unseemly, unsuitable. *Opp* DECOROUS.

unbelievable *adj* ▷ INCREDIBLE.

unbend *v* 1 straighten. 2 [*inf*] loosen up, relax, rest, unwind.

unbending *adj* ▷ INFLEXIBLE.

unbiased *adj* balanced, disinterested, even-handed, fair, impartial, independent, just, neutral, non-partisan, objective, openminded, reasonable, straight, unprejudiced. *Opp* BIASED.

unbroken *adj* ▷ CONTINUOUS, WHOLE.

uncalled-for
adj ▷ UNNECESSARY.

uncaring *adj* ▷ CALLOUS.

unceasing *adj* ▷ CONTINUOUS.

uncertain *adj* 1 ambiguous, arguable, *inf* chancy, conjectural, *inf* iffy, inconclusive, indefinite, indeterminate, questionable, risky, speculative, *inf* touch and go, unclear, unconvincing, undetermined, unforeseeable, unknown, unresolved, woolly. **2** *uncertain what to believe.* ambivalent, doubtful, dubious, equivocal, *inf* in two minds, unconvinced, undecided, unsure, vague, wavering. **3** *uncertain climate.* changeable, erratic, precarious, unpredictable, unreliable, unsettled, variable. *Opp* CERTAIN.

unchanging *adj* ▷ CONSTANT.

uncharitable *adj* ▷ UNKIND.

uncivilized *adj* **1** primitive, savage, wild. **2** antisocial, coarse, crude, philistine, rough, uncultured, uneducated, unsophisticated. *Opp* CIVILIZED.

unclean *adj* ▷ DIRTY.

unclear *adj* ▷ UNCERTAIN.

uncomfortable *adj* **1** cramped, formal, hard, lumpy, painful, restrictive, tight, tight-fitting. **2** *uncomfortable silence.* awkward, distressing, embarrassing, nervous, restless, troubled, uneasy, worried. *Opp* COMFORTABLE.

uncommon *adj* ▷ UNUSUAL.

uncommunicative *adj* ▷ TACITURN.

uncomplimentary *adj* censorious, critical, derogatory, disparaging, pejorative, scathing, slighting, unfavourable, unflattering. ▷ RUDE. *Opp* COMPLIMENTARY.

uncompromising *adj* ▷ INFLEXIBLE.

unconcealed *adj* ▷ OBVIOUS.

unconditional *adj* absolute, categorical, complete, full, outright, total, unequivocal, unlimited, unqualified, unreserved, unrestricted, wholehearted, *inf* with no strings attached. *Opp* CONDITIONAL.

uncongenial *adj* disagreeable, incompatible, unfriendly, unpleasant, unsympathetic. *Opp* CONGENIAL.

unconscious *adj* **1** anaesthetized, comatose, concussed, *inf* dead to the world, insensible, *inf* out for the count, sleeping. **2** ignorant, oblivious, unaware. **3** *unconscious humour.* accidental, inadvertent, unintentional, unwitting. **4** *unconscious reaction.* automatic, instinctive, involuntary, reflex, unthinking. **5** *unconscious desire.* repressed, subconscious, subliminal, suppressed. *Opp* CONSCIOUS.

unconsciousness *n* blackout, coma, faint, oblivion, sleep.

uncontrollable *adj* ▷ UNDISCIPLINED.

unconventional *adj* abnormal, different, eccentric, exotic, independent, odd, off-beat, original, peculiar, strange, surprising, unorthodox, unusual, *inf* way-out, weird. *Opp* CONVENTIONAL.

unconvincing *adj* implausible, improbable, incredible, unbelievable, unlikely. *Opp* PERSUASIVE.

uncooperative *adj* awkward, difficult, obstructive, stubborn, unhelpful. *Opp* COOPERATIVE.

uncover *v* bare, come across, detect, dig up, disclose, discover, expose, reveal, strip, unearth, unmask, unveil, unwrap. *Opp* COVER.

undamaged *adj* ▷ PERFECT.

undefended *adj* defenceless, exposed, insecure, unprotected, vulnerable.

undemanding *adj* ▷ EASY.

undemonstrative *adj* ▷ ALOOF.

underclothes *pl n* lingerie, *inf* smalls, underwear, *inf* undies.

undercurrent *n* atmosphere, feeling, hint, sense, suggestion, trace, undertone.

underestimate *v* belittle, minimize, miscalculate, misjudge, underrate, undervalue. *Opp* EXAGGERATE.

undergo *v* bear, endure, experience, go through, put up with, stand, suffer, withstand.

underground *adj* 1 buried, subterranean. 2 clandestine, hidden, revolutionary, secret, subversive, unofficial.

undergrowth *n* brush, bushes, ground cover, vegetation.

undermine *v* 1 erode, excavate, mine under, tunnel under. 2 destroy, ruin, sap, spoil, subvert, weaken.

underprivileged *adj* deprived, disadvantaged, impoverished, needy. ▷ POOR. *Opp* PRIVILEGED.

understand *v* 1 appreciate, be conversant with, *inf* catch on, comprehend, decipher, fathom, figure out, follow, gather, *inf* get, grasp, know, learn, make out, make sense of, master, perceive, realize, recognize, see, take in, *inf* twig. 2 be in sympathy with, empathize with, sympathize with.

understanding *n* 1 ability, acumen, brains, cleverness, discernment, insight, intellect, intelligence, judgement, penetration, perceptiveness, sense,

wisdom. 2 *understanding of a problem.* appreciation, awareness, comprehension, grasp, knowledge. 3 *understanding between people.* accord, consensus, empathy, fellow feeling, harmony, sympathy, tolerance. 4 *formal understanding.* arrangement, bargain, contract, deal, pact, settlement, treaty.

understate *v* belittle, *inf* make light of, minimize, *inf* play down. *Opp* EXAGGERATE.

undertake *v* 1 agree, consent, guarantee, pledge, promise, try. 2 *undertake a task.* accept responsibility for, address, approach, attend to, begin, commence, commit yourself to, embark on, manage, tackle, take on.

undertaking *n* 1 affair, business, enterprise, project, task, venture. 2 ▷ PROMISE.

undervalue *v* ▷ UNDERESTIMATE.

underwater *adj* submarine, sunken, undersea.

undeserved *adj* unfair, unjustified, unwarranted.

undesirable *adj* ▷ OBJECTIONABLE.

undisciplined *adj* anarchic, chaotic, disobedient, disorderly, disorganized, intractable, rebellious, uncontrollable, unmanageable, unruly, wild, wilful. *Opp* OBEDIENT.

undisguised *adj* ▷ OBVIOUS.

undistinguished *adj* ▷ ORDINARY.

undo *v* 1 detach, disconnect, loosen, open, unchain, unfasten, unhook, unleash, unlock, unpick, unscrew, untie, unwrap, unzip. **2** *undo someone's good work.* cancel out, destroy, nullify, reverse, ruin, spoil, undermine, vitiate, wipe out, wreck.

undoubted *adj* ▷ INDISPUTABLE.

undoubtedly *adv* certainly, definitely, of course, surely, undeniably, unquestionably.

undress *v* disrobe, *inf* peel off, shed your clothes, strip off.
undressed ▷ NAKED.

undue *adj* ▷ EXCESSIVE.

undying *adj* ▷ ETERNAL.

uneasy *adj* anxious, apprehensive, awkward, distressed, disturbed, edgy, fearful, insecure, *inf* jittery, nervous, restless, tense, troubled, uncomfortable, unsettled, worried.

uneducated *adj* ▷ IGNORANT.

unemotional *adj* apathetic, clinical, cold, cool, dispassionate, frigid, hard-hearted, heartless, impassive, indifferent, objective, unfeeling, unmoved, unresponsive. *Opp* EMOTIONAL.

unemployed *adj* jobless, laid off, on the dole, out of work, redundant, unwaged. *Opp* IDLE.

unenthusiastic *adj* ▷ APATHETIC, UNINTERESTED.

unequal *adj* **1** different, differing, disparate, dissimilar, varying. **2** *unequal treatment.* biased, prejudiced, unjust. **3** *unequal contest.* one-sided, unbalanced, uneven, unfair. *Opp* EQUAL, FAIR.

unequalled *adj* incomparable, inimitable, matchless, peerless, supreme, unparalleled, unsurpassed.

unethical *adj* ▷ IMMORAL.

uneven *adj* **1** broken, bumpy, irregular, jagged, pitted, rough, rutted. **2** *uneven rhythm.* erratic,

fitful, fluctuating, inconsistent, jerky, spasmodic, unpredictable. **3** *uneven load.* lopsided, unsteady. **4** *uneven contest.* one-sided, unbalanced, unequal, unfair. *Opp* EVEN.

uneventful *adj* ▷ UNEXCITING.

unexciting *adj* boring, dull, monotonous, predictable, routine, tedious, trite, uneventful, uninspiring, vapid, wearisome. ▷ ORDINARY. *Opp* EXCITING.

unexpected *adj* accidental, chance, fortuitous, sudden, surprising, unforeseen, unlooked-for, unplanned, unpredictable, unusual. ▷ PREDICTABLE.

unfair *adj* ▷ UNJUST.

unfaithful *adj* disloyal, duplicitous, faithless, false, fickle, inconstant, perfidious, traitorous, treacherous, untrustworthy. *Opp* FAITHFUL.

unfaithfulness *n* **1** duplicity, perfidy, treachery. **2** adultery, infidelity.

unfamiliar *adj* ▷ STRANGE.

unfashionable *adj* dated, old-fashioned, *inf* passé, unstylish. *Opp* FASHIONABLE.

unfasten *v* ▷ UNDO.

unfavourable *adj* adverse, bad, critical, disapproving, discouraging, hostile, ill-disposed, negative, uncomplimentary, unfriendly, unkind. **2** *unfavourable conditions.* inauspicious, unpromising, unpropitious. *Opp* FAVOURABLE.

unfeeling *adj* ▷ CALLOUS.

unfinished *adj* imperfect, incomplete, rough, sketchy. *Opp* PERFECT.

unfit *adj* **1** inadequate, incapable, incompetent, unsatisfactory, useless. **2** *unfit for family viewing.*

inappropriate, unsuitable, unsuited. **3** out of condition, unhealthy. ▷ ILL. *Opp* FIT.

unflagging *adj* ▷ TIRELESS.

unforeseen *adj* ▷ UNEXPECTED.

unforgettable
adj ▷ MEMORABLE.

unforgivable *adj* inexcusable, mortal (*sin*), shameful, unjustifiable, unpardonable.
Opp FORGIVABLE.

unfortunate *adj* ▷ UNLUCKY.

unfriendly *adj* aloof, antagonistic, antisocial, cold, cool, detached, disagreeable, distant, forbidding, hostile, ill-disposed, impersonal, inhospitable, quarrelsome, remote, reserved, rude, sour, standoffish, *inf* starchy, sullen, threatening, unapproachable, uncivil, uncongenial, unforthcoming, unkind, unresponsive, unsociable, unsympathetic, unwelcoming.
Opp FRIENDLY.

ungainly *adj* ▷ AWKWARD.

ungodly *adj* ▷ IRRELIGIOUS.

ungrateful *adj* ill-mannered, rude, unappreciative.
Opp GRATEFUL.

unhappy *adj* **1** dejected, depressed, dispirited, discontented, disgruntled, dissatisfied, down, downcast, gloomy, fed up, miserable, mournful, sorrowful. ▷ SAD. **2** *unhappy coincidence*. ill-fated, unlucky. **3** *unhappy choice*. inappropriate, unfortunate, unsuitable.

unhealthy *adj* **1** ailing, delicate, diseased, feeble, frail, infected, infirm, *inf* poorly, sick, sickly, unwell, weak. ▷ ILL. **2** *unhealthy conditions*. dirty, harmful, insalubrious, insanitary, noxious,

polluted, unhygienic, unwholesome. *Opp* HEALTHY.

unheard-of *adj* ▷ UNUSUAL.

unhelpful *adj* difficult, disobliging, inconsiderate, uncooperative. *Opp* HELPFUL.

unidentifiable *adj* camouflaged, disguised, hidden, unknown, unrecognizable.
Opp IDENTIFIABLE.

unidentified *adj* anonymous, incognito, nameless, unknown, unmarked, unnamed, unrecognized, unspecified. *Opp* SPECIFIC.

uniform *adj* consistent, even, homogeneous, invariable, regular, same, similar, smooth, steady, unbroken, unvarying.
Opp DIFFERENT. ● *n* costume, livery, outfit.

unify *v* amalgamate, bring together, combine, consolidate, fuse, integrate, join, merge, unite. *Opp* SEPARATE.

unimaginative *adj* banal, boring, conventional, derivative, dull, hackneyed, obvious, ordinary, prosaic, stale, trite, uninspired, uninteresting, unoriginal. *Opp* IMAGINATIVE.

unimportant *adj* forgettable, immaterial, inessential, insignificant, irrelevant, minor, negligible, peripheral, petty, secondary, slight, trifling, trivial, worthless. ▷ SMALL.
Opp IMPORTANT.

uninhabited *adj* abandoned, deserted, desolate, empty, unoccupied, vacant.

uninhibited *adj* candid, easygoing, frank, natural, open, outgoing, outspoken, relaxed, spontaneous, unconstrained, unreserved, unrestrained, unselfconscious, wild. *Opp* REPRESSED.

unintelligent *adj* ▷ STUPID.

unintelligible
adj ▷ INCOMPREHENSIBLE.

unintentional *adj* accidental, fortuitous, inadvertent, involuntary, unconscious, unwitting. *Opp* INTENTIONAL.

uninterested *adj* apathetic, bored, indifferent, passive, phlegmatic, unconcerned, unenthusiastic, uninvolved, unresponsive. *Opp* INTERESTED.

uninteresting *adj* boring, dreary, dry, dull, flat, monotonous, predictable, tedious, uninspiring. ▷ ORDINARY. *Opp* INTERESTING.

uninterrupted
adj ▷ CONTINUOUS.

uninvited *adj* unasked, unbidden, unwelcome.

uninviting
adj ▷ UNATTRACTIVE.

union *n* 1 alliance, amalgamation, association, coalition, confederation, federation, integration, joining together, merger, unification, unity. 2 blend, combination, compound, fusion, mixture, synthesis. 3 marriage, matrimony, partnership, wedlock.

unique *adj* distinctive, incomparable, *inf* one-off, peerless, *inf* second to none, single, singular, unequalled, unparalleled, unrepeatable.

unit *n* component, constituent, element, entity, item, module, part, piece, portion, section, segment, whole.

unite *v* ally, amalgamate, associate, blend, bring together, collaborate, combine, connect, consolidate, cooperate, couple, fuse, go into partnership, incorporate, integrate, join, join forces, link, merge, mingle, mix, tie up, unify. *Opp* SEPARATE.

united *adj* agreed, allied, collective, common, concerted, corporate, harmonious, integrated, joint, like-minded, *inf* of one mind, shared, unanimous, undivided. *Opp* DISUNITED. **be united** ▷ AGREE.

unity *n* accord, agreement, concord, consensus, harmony, integrity, oneness, rapport, solidarity, unanimity, wholeness. *Opp* DISUNITY.

universal *adj* all-embracing, all-round, common, comprehensive, general, global, international, prevailing, prevalent, total, ubiquitous, unlimited, widespread, worldwide.

universe *n* cosmos, creation, the heavens.

unjust *adj* biased, bigoted, indefensible, one-sided, partisan, prejudiced, undeserved, unfair, unreasonable, unwarranted, wrong, wrongful. *Opp* JUST.

unjustifiable *adj* excessive, indefensible, inexcusable, unacceptable, unforgivable, unwarranted. *Opp* JUSTIFIABLE.

unkind *adj* abrasive, *inf* beastly, callous, hard, hard-hearted, harsh, heartless, hurtful, ill-natured, inconsiderate, inhumane, insensitive, malicious, mean, nasty, rough, ruthless, selfish, severe, sharp, spiteful, tactless, thoughtless, uncaring, uncharitable, unfeeling, unfriendly, unpleasant, unsympathetic. ▷ CRITICAL, CRUEL. *Opp* KIND.

unknown *adj* 1 anonymous, disguised, incognito, mysterious, strange, unidentified, unnamed, unrecognized. **2** *unknown country*. alien, foreign, uncharted, unexplored, unfamiliar. **3** *unknown actor*. little-known, obscure, undistinguished. *Opp* FAMOUS.

unlawful *adj* ▷ ILLEGAL.

unlikely *adj* **1** doubtful, dubious, faint, improbable, remote, slight. **2** far-fetched, implausible, incredible, unconvincing. *Opp* LIKELY.

unlimited *adj* ▷ BOUNDLESS.

unload *v* discharge, drop off, *inf* dump, empty, offload, unpack. *Opp* LOAD.

unloved *adj* abandoned, forsaken, loveless, neglected, rejected, spurned, uncared-for, unwanted. *Opp* LOVED.

unlucky *adj* **1** accidental, calamitous, chance, tragic, unfortunate, untimely. **2** *unlucky person*. *inf* accident-prone, hapless, luckless, unhappy, unsuccessful. **3** *unlucky number*. cursed, ill-fated, ill-omened, ill-starred, inauspicious, jinxed, unfavourable. *Opp* LUCKY.

unmanageable *adj* ▷ UNDISCIPLINED.

unmarried *adj inf* available, *inf* free, single, unwed. **unmarried person** bachelor, spinster.

unmentionable *adj* ▷ TABOO.

unmistakable *adj* ▷ DEFINITE, OBVIOUS.

unnamed *adj* ▷ UNIDENTIFIED.

unnatural *adj* **1** abnormal, bizarre, eerie, extraordinary, fantastic, freak, freakish, inexplicable, magic, magical, odd, outlandish, queer, strange, supernatural, unaccountable, uncanny, unusual, weird. **2** *unnatural feelings*. callous, cold-blooded, heartless, inhuman, inhumane, monstrous, perverse, perverted, sadistic. **3** *unnatural behaviour*. affected, contrived, fake, feigned, forced, insincere, laboured, mannered, *inf* out of character, *inf* phoney, pretended, *inf* pseudo, *inf* put on, self-conscious, stagey, stiff, stilted, theatrical, uncharacteristic. **4** *unnatural materials*. ▷ MAN-MADE. *Opp* NATURAL.

unnecessary *adj* dispensable, excessive, expendable, extra, inessential, needless, non-essential, redundant, superfluous, surplus, uncalled-for, unjustified, useless. *Opp* NECESSARY.

unobtrusive *adj* ▷ INCONSPICUOUS.

unofficial *adj* informal, *inf* off the record, unconfirmed. *Opp* OFFICIAL.

unorthodox *adj* ▷ UNCONVENTIONAL.

unpaid *adj* due, outstanding, owing, payable, unsettled.

unpalatable *adj* disgusting, inedible, nauseating, *inf* off, rancid, sour, unacceptable, unappetizing, uneatable, unpleasant. *Opp* PALATABLE.

unparalleled *adj* ▷ UNEQUALLED.

unplanned *adj* ▷ SPONTANEOUS.

unpleasant *adj* disagreeable, disgusting, displeasing, distasteful, foul, ghastly, grim, hateful, horrible, *inf* horrid, nasty, objectionable, obnoxious, offensive, *inf* off-putting, repulsive, sordid, squalid, unattractive, undesirable, unfriendly, unkind, unsavoury, unwelcome, upsetting. ▷ BAD. *Opp* PLEASANT.

unpopular *adj* disliked, friendless, ignored, out of favour, rejected, shunned, unfashionable, unloved, unwanted. *Opp* POPULAR.

unpredictable *adj* changeable, erratic, uncertain, unexpected, unforeseeable, variable. *Opp* PREDICTABLE.

unprejudiced *adj* ▷ UNBIASED.

unprepared *adj* caught napping, caught out, ill-equipped, taken off-guard, unready.

unpretentious *adj* humble, modest, plain, simple, unaffected, unassuming, unsophisticated. *Opp* PRETENTIOUS.

unproductive *adj* 1 ineffective, fruitless, futile, pointless, unprofitable, unrewarding, useless, worthless. 2 *unproductive land*. arid, barren, infertile, sterile, unfruitful. *Opp* PRODUCTIVE.

unprofessional *adj* amateurish, incompetent, inefficient, negligent, shoddy, *inf* sloppy, unethical, unseemly, unskilful, unskilled. *Opp* PROFESSIONAL.

unprofitable *adj* futile, loss-making, uneconomic, unproductive, unremunerative, unrewarding, worthless. *Opp* PROFITABLE.

unpunctual *adj* belated, delayed, late, overdue, tardy, unreliable. *Opp* PUNCTUAL.

unravel *v* disentangle, solve, straighten out, undo, untangle.

unreal *adj* false, fanciful, illusory, imaginary, imagined, make-believe, non-existent, *inf* pretend, *inf* pseudo, sham. *Opp* REAL.

unrealistic *adj* 1 inaccurate, unconvincing, unnatural, unrecognizable. 2 *unrealistic ideas*. fanciful, idealistic, impossible,

impracticable, impractical, over-ambitious, quixotic, romantic, silly, visionary, unworkable. 3 *unrealistic prices*. ▷ EXCESSIVE. *Opp* REALISTIC.

unreasonable *adj* ▷ IRRATIONAL.

unrelated *adj* 1 different, independent, unconnected. 2 ▷ IRRELEVANT. *Opp* RELATED.

unreliable *adj* 1 deceptive, false, flimsy, inaccurate, misleading, suspect, unconvincing. 2 *unreliable friends*. changeable, fallible, fickle, inconsistent, irresponsible, unpredictable, unstable, untrustworthy. *Opp* RELIABLE.

unrepentant *adj* brazen, confirmed, hardened, impenitent, incorrigible, incurable, inveterate, irredeemable, shameless, unashamed. *Opp* REPENTANT.

unripe *adj* green, immature, sour, unready. *Opp* RIPE.

unrivalled *adj* ▷ UNEQUALLED.

unruly *adj* ▷ UNDISCIPLINED.

unsafe *adj* ▷ DANGEROUS.

unsatisfactory *adj* defective, deficient, disappointing, displeasing, faulty, frustrating, imperfect, inadequate, incompetent, inefficient, inferior, insufficient, lacking, poor, *inf* sad, unacceptable, unhappy, *inf* wretched. *Opp* SATISFACTORY.

unscrupulous *adj* amoral, corrupt, *inf* crooked, cunning, dishonest, dishonourable, immoral, improper, shameless, slippery, unethical, untrustworthy. *Opp* SCRUPULOUS.

unseemly *adj* ▷ UNBECOMING.

unselfish *adj* altruistic, caring, charitable, considerate, generous, humanitarian, kind, magnanimous, open-handed, philanthropic, public-spirited, self-effacing, selfless, self-sacrificing, thoughtful. *Opp* SELFISH.

unsightly *adj* ▷ UGLY.

unskilful *adj* amateurish, bungled, clumsy, crude, incompetent, inept, inexpert, maladroit, shoddy, unprofessional. *Opp* SKILFUL.

unskilled *adj* inexperienced, unqualified, untrained. *Opp* SKILLED.

unsociable *adj* ▷ UNFRIENDLY.

unsophisticated *adj* artless, childlike, guileless, ingenuous, innocent, lowbrow, naive, plain, simple, straightforward, unaffected, unpretentious, unrefined, unworldly. *Opp* SOPHISTICATED.

unspeakable *adj* dreadful, indescribable, inexpressible, nameless, unutterable.

unstable *adj* ▷ CHANGEABLE, UNSTEADY.

unsteady *adj* **1** flimsy, frail, insecure, precarious, rickety, *inf* rocky, shaky, tottering, unbalanced, unsafe, unstable, wobbly. **2** erratic, inconstant, intermittent, irregular, variable. **3** *unsteady light.* flickering, fluctuating, quivering. *Opp* STEADY.

unsuccessful *adj* **1** abortive, failed, fruitless, futile, ill-fated, ineffective, loss-making, unavailing, unlucky, unproductive, unprofitable, unsatisfactory, useless, vain, worthless. **2** *unsuccessful contestants.* beaten, defeated, losing, vanquished. *Opp* SUCCESSFUL.

unsuitable *adj* ill-chosen, ill-judged, ill-timed, inapposite, inappropriate, inapt, unbecoming, unfitting, unhappy, unsatisfactory, unseemly, untimely. *Opp* SUITABLE.

unsure *adj* ▷ UNCERTAIN.

unsurpassed *adj* ▷ UNEQUALLED.

unsuspecting *adj* ▷ CREDULOUS.

unsympathetic *adj* callous, dispassionate, hard-hearted, heartless, indifferent, insensitive, pitiless, ruthless, stony, unaffected, uncaring, uncharitable, unconcerned, unfeeling, unkind, unmoved, unresponsive. *Opp* SYMPATHETIC.

unsystematic *adj* chaotic, confused, disorganized, haphazard, jumbled, muddled, random, *inf* shambolic, *inf* sloppy, unmethodical, unstructured, untidy. *Opp* SYSTEMATIC.

unthinkable *adj* ▷ INCONCEIVABLE.

unthinking *adj* ▷ THOUGHTLESS.

untidy *adj* careless, chaotic, cluttered, disorderly, disorganized, haphazard, *inf* higgledy-piggledy, in disarray, jumbled, messy, muddled, *inf* shambolic, slapdash, *inf* sloppy, slovenly, *inf* topsy-turvy, unsystematic, upside-down. **2** bedraggled, dishevelled, disordered, rumpled, *inf* scruffy, shabby, tangled, tousled, uncombed, unkempt. *Opp* TIDY.

untie *v* cast off (*boat*), disentangle, free, loosen, release, undo, unfasten.

untried *adj* experimental, innovatory, new, novel, unproved, untested. *Opp* ESTABLISHED.

untroubled adj carefree, peaceful, quiet, relaxed, undisturbed, unruffled.

untrue adj ▷ FALSE.

untrustworthy adj ▷ DISHONEST.

untruthful adj ▷ LYING.

unused adj blank, clean, fresh, intact, mint (condition), new, pristine, untouched. Opp USED.

unusual adj abnormal, atypical, curious, different, exceptional, extraordinary, inf funny, irregular, odd, out of the ordinary, peculiar, queer, rare, remarkable, singular, strange, surprising, uncommon, unconventional, unexpected, unfamiliar, unheard-of, inf unique, unnatural, untypical. Opp USUAL.

unwanted adj ▷ UNNECESSARY.

unwarranted adj ▷ UNJUSTIFIABLE.

unwavering adj ▷ RESOLUTE.

unwelcome adj disagreeable, undesirable, uninvited, unwanted. Opp WELCOME.

unwell adj ▷ ILL.

unwholesome adj ▷ UNHEALTHY.

unwieldy adj awkward, bulky, cumbersome, unmanageable. Opp HANDY, PORTABLE.

unwilling adj averse, disinclined, grudging, half-hearted, hesitant, lazy, loath, reluctant, uncooperative, unenthusiastic, unhelpful. Opp WILLING.

unwise adj inf daft, foolhardy, foolish, ill-advised, ill-judged, imprudent, inadvisable, indiscreet, injudicious, irresponsible, misguided, rash, reckless, senseless, short-sighted, silly, stupid, thoughtless. Opp WISE.

unworthy adj contemptible, despicable, discreditable, dishonourable, disreputable, ignoble, shameful, substandard, undeserving, unsuitable. Opp WORTHY.

unwritten adj oral, spoken, verbal. Opp WRITTEN.

unyielding adj ▷ INFLEXIBLE.

upbringing n care, education, instruction, nurture, raising, rearing, teaching, training.

update v bring up to date, correct, modernize, revise.

upgrade v enhance, expand, improve, promote.

upheaval n chaos, commotion, confusion, disruption, disturbance, inf to-do, turmoil.

uphill adj arduous, difficult, exhausting, gruelling, hard, laborious, strenuous, taxing, tough.

uphold v back, champion, defend, endorse, maintain, preserve, promote, stand by, support, sustain.

upkeep n care, conservation, keep, maintenance, operation, preservation, running, support.

uplifting adj edifying, enlightening, enriching, exhilarating, spiritual.

upper adj elevated, higher, raised, superior, upstairs.

uppermost adj dominant, highest, supreme, top.

upright adj 1 erect, on end, perpendicular, vertical. 2 conscientious, fair, highminded, honest, honourable, incorruptible, just, moral, principled, righteous, inf straight, true, upstanding, virtuous. ● n column, pole, post, vertical.

uproar *n* bedlam, chaos, clamour, commotion, confusion, din, disorder, disturbance, furore, hubbub, hullabaloo, noise, outcry, pandemonium, racket, riot, *inf* row, *inf* ructions, *inf* rumpus, tumult, turmoil.

uproot *v* eliminate, eradicate, get rid of, pull up, remove, tear up, weed out.

upset *v* 1 capsize, overturn, spill, tip over, topple. 2 *upset a plan.* alter, change, disrupt, hinder, interfere with, interrupt, jeopardize, spoil. 3 *upset someone's feelings.* agitate, annoy, disconcert, dismay, distress, disturb, fluster, grieve, irritate, offend, perturb, *inf* rub up the wrong way, ruffle.

upside-down *adj inf* topsy-turvy, upturned, wrong way up.

upstart *n* arriviste, nobody, *Fr* nouveau riche, social climber.

up-to-date *adj* contemporary, current, fashionable, *inf* in, modern, new, *inf* trendy. *Opp* OLD-FASHIONED.

upward *adj* ascending, going up, rising, uphill. *Opp* DOWNWARD.

urban *adj* built-up, metropolitan, suburban. *Opp* RURAL.

urge *n* compulsion, craving, desire, drive, hunger, impetus, impulse, itch, longing, pressure, thirst, yearning, *inf* yen.
• *v* advise, advocate, appeal to, beg, beseech, chivvy, compel, counsel, drive, egg on, encourage, entreat, exhort, goad, impel, implore, importune, incite, induce, nag, persuade, plead with, press, prod, prompt, propel, push, recommend, spur. *Opp* DISCOURAGE.

urgent *adj* 1 acute, compelling, essential, high-priority, immediate, imperative, important, necessary, pressing, top-priority, unavoidable. 2 *urgent request.* earnest, importunate, insistent, persistent.

usable *adj* fit to use, functioning, operational, serviceable, valid, working.

use *n* advantage, application, benefit, employment, *inf* point, purpose, usefulness, utility, value, worth. • *v* 1 administer, apply, employ, exercise, exploit, handle, make use of, manage, operate, put to use, utilize, work. 2 consume, exhaust, expend, spend, use up, waste.

used *adj* cast-off, *inf* hand-me-down, second-hand.

useful *adj* 1 advantageous, beneficial, constructive, good, helpful, invaluable, positive, profitable, salutary, valuable, worthwhile. 2 *useful tool.* convenient, effective, efficient, handy, practical, utilitarian. 3 *useful player.* capable, competent, proficient, skilful, talented. *Opp* USELESS.

useless *adj* 1 fruitless, futile, hopeless, pointless, unavailing, unprofitable, unsuccessful, vain, worthless. 2 *inf* broken down, faulty, unusable. 3 *useless player.* incapable, incompetent, unhelpful, unskilful, untalented. *Opp* USEFUL.

usual *adj* accustomed, average, common, conventional, customary, everyday, expected, familiar, general, habitual, natural, normal, ordinary, orthodox, predictable, prevalent, recognized, regular, routine, standard, stock, traditional, typical, unsurpris-

ing, well-known, widespread,
wonted. *Opp* UNUSUAL.

usurp *v* appropriate, commandeer, seize, take over.

utensil *n* ▷ TOOL.

utter *v* articulate, *inf* come out
with, express, pronounce, voice.
▷ SPEAK, TALK.

V

vacancy *n* job, opening, place,
position, post, situation.

vacant *adj* 1 available, clear,
empty, free, open, unfilled, void.
2 abandoned, deserted, uninhabited, unoccupied. 3 *vacant look.*
absent-minded, abstracted,
blank, dreamy, expressionless,
far-away, inattentive, vacuous.
Opp BUSY.

vacate *v* abandon, desert, evacuate, get out of, give up, leave,
quit.

vacuous *adj* blank, emptyheaded, inane, mindless, uncomprehending, vacant. ▷ STUPID.
Opp ALERT.

vacuum *n* emptiness, space,
void.

vagary *n* caprice, fluctuation,
quirk, uncertainty, whim.

vagrant *n* beggar, *inf* downand-out, homeless person,
itinerant, tramp, traveller.

vague *adj* 1 ambiguous, diffuse,
equivocal, evasive, general, generalized, imprecise, indefinite,
inexact, loose, nebulous, uncertain, unclear, undefined,
unspecific, unsure, *inf* woolly.
2 amorphous, blurred, dim,

hazy, ill-defined, indistinct,
misty, shadowy, unrecognizable.
3 absent-minded, disorganized,
forgetful, inattentive, scatterbrained. *Opp* DEFINITE.

vain *adj* 1 arrogant, *inf* bigheaded, boastful, *inf* cocky,
conceited, egotistical,
narcissistic, proud, selfimportant, self-satisfied.
Opp MODEST. 2 *vain attempt.*
abortive, fruitless, futile, ineffective, pointless, senseless,
unproductive, unsuccessful,
useless. *Opp* SUCCESSFUL.

valiant *adj* courageous, gallant,
heroic. ▷ BRAVE.
Opp COWARDLY.

valid *adj* authentic, authorized,
bona fide, current, genuine,
lawful, legal, legitimate, official,
permissible, ratified, rightful,
usable. *Opp* INVALID.

validate *v* authenticate, authorize, certify, endorse, legalize,
legitimize, ratify.

valley *n* canyon, dale, dell,
dingle, glen, gorge, gully,
hollow, pass, ravine, vale.

valour *n* bravery, courage.

valuable *adj* 1 expensive, irreplaceable, precious, priceless,
prized, treasured. 2 *valuable
advice.* advantageous, beneficial,
constructive, helpful, invaluable,
profitable, useful, worthwhile.
Opp WORTHLESS.

value *n* 1 cost, price, worth.
2 advantage, benefit, importance, merit, significance, use,
usefulness. ● *v* 1 assess, evaluate, price, *inf* put a figure on.
2 appreciate, care for, cherish,
esteem, *inf* hold dear, love, prize,
respect, treasure.

vandal *n* delinquent, hooligan,
thug, troublemaker.

vanish v disappear, disperse, dissolve, evaporate, fade, melt away, pass. *Opp* APPEAR.

vanity n arrogance, conceit, egotism, narcissism, pride, self-esteem.

vapour n fog, fumes, gas, haze, miasma, mist, smoke, steam.

variable adj capricious, changeable, erratic, fitful, fluctuating, fluid, inconsistent, inconstant, mercurial, mutable, protean, shifting, uncertain, unpredictable, unreliable, unstable, unsteady, *inf* up-and-down, varying, volatile. *Opp* INVARIABLE.

variation n alteration, change, deviation, difference, discrepancy, elaboration, modification, permutation.

variety n 1 change, difference, diversity, variation. 2 array, assortment, blend, collection, combination, medley, miscellany, mixture, multiplicity. 3 brand, breed, category, class, kind, make, sort, species, strain, type.

various adj assorted, different, differing, dissimilar, diverse, heterogeneous, miscellaneous, mixed, *inf* motley, multifarious, several, sundry, varied, varying.

vary v 1 change, deviate, differ, fluctuate. 2 *vary your speed*. adapt, adjust, alter, modify, regulate. *Opp* STABILIZE. **varied**, **varying** ▷ VARIOUS.

vast adj boundless, broad, colossal, enormous, extensive, gigantic, great, huge, immeasurable, immense, infinite, limitless, massive, monumental, sweeping, tremendous, unbounded, unlimited, voluminous, wide. ▷ BIG. *Opp* SMALL.

vault n basement, cavern, cellar, crypt, strongroom. ● v bound over, clear, hurdle, jump, leap, spring over.

veer v change direction, dodge, swerve, turn, wheel.

vegetable adj growing, organic.

vegetate v do nothing, *inf* go to seed, idle, stagnate.

vegetation n foliage, greenery, plants, undergrowth, weeds.

vehement adj ardent, eager, emphatic, enthusiastic, fervent, fierce, forceful, heated, impassioned, intense, passionate, strong, urgent, vigorous, violent. *Opp* APATHETIC.

vehicle n bus, car, coach, conveyance, lorry, means of transport, minibus, taxi, van, *inf* wheels.

veil v cloak, conceal, cover, disguise, hide, mask, shroud.

vein n 1 artery, blood vessel, capillary. 2 *mineral vein*. bed, course, deposit, line, lode, seam, stratum. 3 ▷ MOOD.

veneer n covering, layer, surface. ● v ▷ COVER.

venerable adj august, esteemed, estimable, honourable, honoured, old, respectable, respected, revered, sedate.

venerate v esteem, hero-worship, honour, idolize, look up to, pay homage to, respect, revere, worship.

vengeance n reprisal, retaliation, retribution, revenge.

vengeful adj avenging, bitter, spiteful, unforgiving, vindictive. *Opp* FORGIVING.

venom n poison, toxin.

venomous adj deadly, lethal, poisonous, toxic.

vent n aperture, duct, gap, hole, opening, outlet, passage, slit.
● v articulate, express, give vent to, voice. ▷ SPEAK.

ventilate v aerate, air, freshen.

venture n ▷ ENTERPRISE.
● v 1 bet, chance, gamble, put forward, risk, speculate, stake, wager. 2 *venture out*. dare to go, risk going.

venturesome
adj ▷ ADVENTUROUS.

venue n meeting place, location.

verbal adj oral, spoken, unwritten, vocal, word-of-mouth.
Opp WRITTEN.

verbatim adj exact, faithful, literal, precise, word for word.

verbose adj long-winded, rambling, repetitious. ▷ WORDY.
Opp CONCISE.

verbosity n long-windedness, prolixity, verbiage, wordiness.

verdict n assessment, conclusion, decision, finding, judgement, opinion, sentence.

verge n bank, brim, brink, edge, hard shoulder, kerb, lip, margin, roadside, side.

verifiable adj demonstrable, provable.

verify v affirm, ascertain, attest to, authenticate, inf check out, confirm, corroborate, establish, prove, show the truth of, substantiate, support, uphold, validate, vouch for.

verisimilitude n authenticity, realism.

vermin pl n parasites, pests.

vernacular adj indigenous, local, native, ordinary, popular.

versatile adj adaptable, all-round, multi-purpose, resourceful, skilful, talented.

verse n lines, metre, poem, rhyme, stanza.

versed adj accomplished, competent, experienced, expert, practised, proficient, skilled, trained.

version n 1 account, description, portrayal, report, story. 2 adaptation, interpretation, rendering, translation. 3 design, kind, model, style, type, variant.

vertical adj erect, perpendicular, sheer, upright.
Opp HORIZONTAL.

vertigo n dizziness, giddiness.

very adv acutely, enormously, especially, exceedingly, extremely, greatly, highly, noticeably, outstandingly, particularly, really, remarkably, inf terribly, unusually.

vessel n 1 ▷ CONTAINER. 2 boat, craft, ship.

vet v inf check out, examine, investigate, review, scrutinize.

veteran adj experienced, mature, old, practised.
● n experienced soldier, old hand, inf old soldier, survivor, inf vet.

veto n ban, embargo, prohibition, refusal, rejection, inf thumbs down. ● v ban, bar, block, disallow, forbid, prohibit, quash, refuse, reject, rule out, say no to, turn down, vote against. Opp APPROVE.

vex v inf aggravate, annoy, bother, displease, exasperate, harass, irritate, provoke, put out, trouble, upset, worry.
▷ ANGER.

viable adj achievable, feasible, possible, practicable, practical, realistic, reasonable, workable.
Opp IMPRACTICAL.

vibrant *adj* alive, animated, dynamic, electric, energetic, lively, pulsating, quivering, resonant, spirited, vivacious. *Opp* LIFELESS.

vibrate *v* judder, pulsate, quiver, rattle, reverberate, shake, shiver, shudder, throb, wobble.

vibration *n* juddering, pulsation, quivering, rattling, reverberation, shaking, shivering, shuddering, throbbing, tremor.

vicarious *adj* indirect, secondhand, surrogate.

vice *n* 1 corruption, depravity, evil, immorality, iniquity, sin, villainy, wickedness, wrongdoing. 2 bad habit, defect, failing, fault, flaw, foible, imperfection, shortcoming, weakness.

vicinity *n* area, district, environs, locale, locality, neighbourhood, proximity, region, surroundings, zone.

vicious *adj* 1 atrocious, barbaric, bloodthirsty, brutal, callous, cruel, diabolical, fiendish, heinous, hurtful, inhuman, merciless, monstrous, murderous, pitiless, ruthless, sadistic, savage, violent. 2 *vicious character*. depraved, evil, heartless, immoral, malicious, mean, perverted, rancorous, sinful, spiteful, venomous, villainous, vindictive, vitriolic, wicked. 3 *vicious animals*. aggressive, dangerous, ferocious, fierce. 4 *vicious wind*. cutting, severe, sharp. *Opp* GENTLE.

vicissitude *n* change, flux, mutability, unpredictability.

victim *n* casualty, fatality, injured person, martyr, scapegoat, sufferer.

victimize *v* bully, discriminate against, exploit, intimidate,

oppress, persecute, *inf* pick on, take advantage of, terrorize, torment. ▷ CHEAT.

victor *n* champion, conqueror, winner. *Opp* LOSER.

victorious *adj* champion, conquering, first, leading, successful, top, triumphant, winning. *Opp* UNSUCCESSFUL.

victory *n* conquest, success, superiority, supremacy, triumph, *inf* walk-over, win. *Opp* DEFEAT.

vie *v* compete, contend, strive.

view *n* 1 aspect, outlook, panorama, picture, prospect, scene, scenery, vista. 2 perspective, sight, vision. 3 *political views*. attitude, belief, conviction, idea, notion, opinion, perception, position, thought. ● *v* 1 behold, contemplate, examine, eye, gaze at, inspect, observe, regard, scan, survey, witness. 2 *view TV*. look at, watch.

viewer *n pl* audience, observer, onlooker, spectator, watcher.

viewpoint *n* angle, perspective, point of view, position, slant, standpoint.

vigilant *adj* alert, attentive, awake, careful, eagle-eyed, observant, on your guard, *inf* on your toes, wary, watchful, wide awake. *Opp* NEGLIGENT.

vigorous *adj* active, alive, animated, brisk, dynamic, energetic, flourishing, forceful, *inf* full of beans, healthy, lively, potent, robust, spirited, strenuous, strong, thriving, virile, vivacious, zestful. *Opp* FEEBLE.

vigour *n* animation, dynamism, energy, force, gusto, health, life, liveliness, might, potency, power, robustness, spirit, stamina, strength, verve, virility, vitality, zeal, zest.

vile *adj* base, contemptible, degenerate, depraved, despicable, disgusting, evil, execrable, filthy, foul, hateful, horrible, loathsome, nauseating, obnoxious, odious, offensive, perverted, repellent, repugnant, repulsive, revolting, sickening, ugly, vicious, wicked.

vilify *v* abuse, denigrate, insult. ▷ SLANDER.

villain *n* criminal, evil-doer, malefactor, mischief-maker, miscreant, reprobate, rogue, scoundrel, sinner.

villainous *adj* bad, corrupt, criminal, dishonest, evil, sinful, treacherous, vile. ▷ WICKED.

vindictive *adj* malicious, nasty, rancorous, spiteful, unforgiving, vengeful, vicious. *Opp* FORGIVING.

vintage *adj* choice, classic, fine, good, high-quality, mature, mellowed, old, seasoned.

violate *v* 1 breach, break, contravene, defy, disobey, disregard, flout, ignore, infringe, transgress. 2 *violate someone's privacy.* abuse, disturb, invade. 3 *[of men] violate a woman.* assault, attack, force yourself on, rape.

violation *n* breach, contravention, defiance, flouting, infringement, invasion, offence (against), transgression.

violent *adj* 1 acute, damaging, dangerous, destructive, devastating, explosive, ferocious, fierce, furious, hard, intense, powerful, rough, savage, severe, strong, swingeing, tempestuous, turbulent, uncontrollable, vehement. 2 *violent behaviour.* brutal, cruel, desperate, frenzied, homicidal, murderous, riotous, rowdy, ruthless, uncontrolled, unruly, vehement, vicious, wild. *Opp* GENTLE.

VIP *n* celebrity, dignitary, important person.

virile *adj derog* macho, manly, masculine, potent, vigorous.

virtue *n* 1 decency, fairness, goodness, high-mindedness, honesty, honour, integrity, morality, nobility, principle, rectitude, respectability, righteousness, sincerity, uprightness, worthiness. 2 advantage, asset, good point, merit, *inf* redeeming feature, strength. 3 *sexual virtue.* chastity, innocence, purity, virginity. *Opp* VICE.

virtuoso *n* expert, genius, maestro, prodigy, *inf* wizard.

virtuous *adj* blameless, chaste, decent, ethical, exemplary, fair, God-fearing, good, high-minded, honest, honourable, innocent, irreproachable, just, law-abiding, moral, noble, principled, praiseworthy, pure, respectable, righteous, sincere, *derog* smug, spotless, uncorrupted, unsullied, upright, virginal, worthy. *Opp* WICKED.

virulent *adj* 1 deadly, lethal, life-threatening, noxious, poisonous, toxic. 2 *virulent abuse.* acrimonious, bitter, hostile, malicious, nasty, spiteful, vicious, vitriolic.

viscous *adj* gluey, sticky, syrupy, thick. *Opp* RUNNY.

visible *adj* apparent, clear, conspicuous, detectable, discernible, distinct, evident, manifest, noticeable, obvious, open, perceptible, plain, recognizable, unconcealed, undisguised, unmistakable. *Opp* INVISIBLE.

vision n 1 eyesight, perception, sight. 2 apparition, chimera, daydream, delusion, fantasy, ghost, hallucination, mirage, phantasm, phantom, spectre, spirit. 3 *man of vision.* foresight, imagination, insight, understanding.

visionary adj dreamy, fanciful, far-sighted, idealistic, imaginative, mystical, prophetic, quixotic, romantic, speculative, unrealistic, Utopian.
● n dreamer, idealist, mystic, prophet, seer.

visit n 1 call, stay, stop, visitation. 2 excursion, outing, trip.
● v call on, *inf* descend on, *inf* drop in on, *inf* look up, pay a call on, stay with. **visit regularly** ▷ HAUNT.

visitor n 1 caller, *pl* company, guest. 2 foreigner, holidaymaker, sightseer, tourist, traveller, tripper.

vista n landscape, outlook, panorama, prospect, scene, scenery, seascape, view.

visualize v conceive, dream up, envisage, imagine, picture.

vital adj 1 alive, animate, animated, dynamic, energetic, exuberant, life-giving, live, lively, living, spirited, vigorous, vivacious, zestful. *Opp* LIFELESS. 2 crucial, essential, fundamental, imperative, important, indispensable, mandatory, necessary, relevant, requisite. *Opp* INESSENTIAL.

vitality n animation, dynamism, energy, exuberance, *inf* go, life, liveliness, *inf* sparkle, spirit, stamina, strength, vigour, vivacity, zest.

vitriolic adj biting, bitter, caustic, cruel, hostile, hurtful, malicious, savage, scathing, vicious, virulent.

vituperate v ▷ ABUSE.

vivacious adj animated, bubbly, cheerful, ebullient, energetic, high-spirited, light-hearted, lively, merry, spirited, sprightly. *Opp* LETHARGIC.

vivid adj 1 bright, brilliant, colourful, dazzling, fresh, *derog* gaudy, glowing, intense, rich, shining, strong, vibrant. 2 *vivid description.* clear, detailed, graphic, imaginative, lifelike, memorable, powerful, realistic, striking. *Opp* LIFELESS.

vocabulary n 1 diction, words. 2 dictionary, glossary, lexicon, word-list.

vocal adj 1 oral, said, spoken, sung, voiced. 2 communicative, loquacious, outspoken, talkative, vociferous. *Opp* TACITURN.

vocation n ▷ CALLING.

vogue n craze, fad, fashion, *inf* latest thing, rage, style, taste, trend. **in vogue** ▷ FASHIONABLE.

voice n articulation, expression, speech, utterance, words.
● v ▷ SPEAK.

void adj 1 blank, empty, unoccupied, vacant. 2 cancelled, invalid, not binding, useless.
● n emptiness, nothingness, space, vacancy, vacuum.

volatile adj 1 explosive, unstable. 2 *volatile moods.* changeable, erratic, fickle, flighty, inconstant, mercurial, temperamental, unpredictable, *inf* up and down. *Opp* STABLE.

volley n barrage, bombardment, burst, cannonade, fusillade, salvo, shower.

voluble adj chatty, fluent, garrulous, glib, loquacious, talkative.
▷ WORDY.

volume n 1 book, publication, tome. 2 amount, bulk, capacity, dimensions, mass, quantity, size.

voluminous adj ample, billowing, bulky, capacious, enormous, extensive, immense, large, roomy, spacious, vast. ▷ BIG. Opp SMALL.

voluntary adj 1 free, gratuitous, optional, spontaneous, unpaid, willing. Opp COMPULSORY. 2 voluntary act. ▷ CONSCIOUS. Opp INVOLUNTARY.

volunteer v 1 be willing, offer, put yourself forward. 2 ▷ ENLIST.

voluptuous adj 1 voluptuous pleasures. ▷ HEDONISTIC. 2 voluptuous figure. buxom, inf curvaceous, desirable, erotic, sensual, sexy, shapely, inf well-endowed.

vomit v be sick, inf bring up, disgorge, inf heave up, regurgitate, retch, inf throw up.

voracious adj avid, eager, gluttonous, greedy, hungry, insatiable, ravenous.

vortex n eddy, spiral, whirlpool, whirlwind.

vote n ballot, election, plebiscite, poll, referendum, show of hands. ● v cast your vote. **vote for** choose, nominate, opt for, pick, return, select.

vouch v **vouch for** answer for, guarantee, speak for, sponsor, support.

voucher n coupon, ticket, token.

vow n assurance, guarantee, oath, pledge, promise, undertaking, word of honour. ● v declare, give your word, guarantee, pledge, promise, swear, take an oath.

voyage n cruise, journey, passage. ● v cruise, sail, travel.

vulgar adj 1 coarse, common, crude, foul, gross, ill-bred, impolite, improper, indecent, indecorous, offensive, rude, uncouth. ▷ OBSCENE. Opp POLITE. 2 vulgar colour scheme. crude, gaudy, in bad taste, tasteless, tawdry, unsophisticated. Opp TASTEFUL.

vulnerable adj 1 at risk, defenceless, exposed, helpless, unguarded, unprotected, weak, wide open. 2 sensitive, thin-skinned. Opp RESILIENT.

W

wad n bundle, lump, mass, pack, pad, plug, roll.

wadding n filling, lining, packing, padding, stuffing.

wade v ford, paddle, splash.

waffle n evasiveness, padding, verbiage, wordiness. ● v inf beat about the bush, hedge, prattle.

waft v 1 drift, float, travel. 2 bear, carry, convey, transport.

wag v bob, flap, move to and fro, nod, oscillate, rock, shake, sway, undulate, inf waggle, wave, inf wiggle.

wage n earnings, income, pay, pay packet, remuneration, reward, salary, stipend. ● v carry on, conduct, engage in, undertake.

wager n, v ▷ BET.

wail v caterwaul, complain, cry, howl, lament, moan, shriek, weep, inf sing.

waist n middle, waistline.

wait n delay, halt, hesitation, hiatus, inf hold-up, interval, pause, postponement, rest, stay, stop, stoppage. ● v 1 delay, halt, inf hang on, hesitate, hold back, keep still, linger, mark time, pause, remain, rest, stand by, stay, stop. 2 wait at table. serve.

waive v abandon, disclaim, dispense with, forgo, give up, relinquish, renounce, resign, sign away, surrender.

wake n 1 funeral, vigil, watch. 2 ship's wake. path, track, trail, wash. ● v 1 awaken, call, disturb, rouse, stimulate, stir, waken. 2 bestir yourself, inf come to life, get up, rise, inf stir, wake up. **wake up to** ▷ REALIZE. **waking** ▷ CONSCIOUS.

wakeful adj alert, awake, insomniac, restless, sleepless.

walk n 1 carriage, gait, stride. 2 constitutional, hike, promenade, ramble, saunter, stroll, traipse, tramp, trek, trudge, inf turn. 3 paved walk. aisle, alley, path, pathway, pavement. ● v advance, amble, go, march, move, pace, promenade, ramble, saunter, step, stride, stroll, tramp, traipse, trek, trudge. **walk away with** ▷ WIN. **walk off with** ▷ STEAL. **walk out** ▷ QUIT. **walk out on** ▷ DESERT.

walker n hiker, pedestrian, rambler.

wall n barricade, barrier, dam, divider, embankment, fence, obstacle, parapet, partition, rampart, screen, stockade. **wall in** ▷ ENCLOSE.

wallet n notecase, pocketbook, pouch, purse.

wallow v 1 flounder, roll about, stagger about, tumble. 2 wallow in luxury. glory, indulge yourself, luxuriate, revel, take delight.

wan adj anaemic, ashen, colourless, feeble, livid, pale, pallid, pasty, sickly.

wand n baton, rod, staff, stick.

wander v 1 drift, meander, ramble, range, roam, rove, stray, stroll, travel about, walk. 2 wander off course. deviate, digress, drift, go off at a tangent, stray, swerve, turn, twist, veer, zigzag. **wandering** ▷ INATTENTIVE, NOMADIC.

wane v decline, decrease, dim, diminish, dwindle, ebb, fade, fail, inf fall off, lessen, peter out, shrink, subside, taper off, weaken. Opp STRENGTHEN.

want n 1 demand, desire, need, requirement, wish. 2 want of ready cash. absence, lack, shortage. 3 war against want. famine, hunger, penury, poverty, privation. ● v 1 aspire to, covet, crave, demand, desire, fancy, hanker after, inf have a yen for, hunger for, itch for, long for, miss, pine for, inf set your heart on, thirst for, wish for, yearn for. 2 want manners. be short of, lack, need, require.

war n battle, campaign, conflict, crusade, fighting, hostilities, military action, strife, warfare. **wage war** ▷ FIGHT.

ward n charge, dependant, minor. ● v **ward off** avert, beat off, chase away, deflect, fend off, forestall, parry, repel, repulse, stave off, thwart.

warder n gaoler, guard, jailer, keeper, prison officer.

warehouse n depository, depot, store, storehouse.

wares pl n commodities, goods, merchandise, produce, stock, supplies.

warlike adj aggressive, bellicose, belligerent, hawkish, hostile, militant, militaristic, pugnacious, warmongering.

warm adj 1 close, hot, subtropical, sultry, summery, temperate, tepid. 2 warm clothes. cosy, thick, woolly. 3 warm welcome. affable, affectionate, cordial, emotional, enthusiastic, fervent, friendly, genial, kind, loving, sympathetic, warm-hearted. Opp COLD, UNFRIENDLY. ● v heat, melt, thaw, thaw out. Opp COOL.

warn v advise, alert, caution, counsel, give notice, inform, notify, raise the alarm, remind, tip off.

warning n 1 advance notice, augury, forewarning, hint, indication, notice, notification, omen, portent, premonition, presage, prophecy, reminder, sign, signal, threat, tip-off, inf word to the wise. 2 let off with a warning. admonition, reprimand. ▷ CAUTION.

warp v bend, buckle, contort, deform, distort, kink, twist.

warrant n authority, authorization, guarantee, licence, permit, pledge, sanction, search-warrant, warranty.
● v ▷ JUSTIFY.

wary adj alert, apprehensive, careful, chary, cautious, circumspect, distrustful, heedful, observant, on your guard, suspicious, vigilant, watchful. Opp RECKLESS.

wash n joc ablutions, bath, rinse, shampoo, shower. ● v 1 clean, cleanse, flush, launder, mop, rinse, scrub, shampoo, sluice, sponge down, swill, wipe. 2 bath, bathe, joc perform your ablutions, shower. 3 The sea washes against the cliff. dash, flow, pound, roll, splash. **wash your hands of** ▷ ABANDON.

washout n debacle, disappointment, disaster, failure, inf flop.

waste adj 1 discarded, extra, superfluous, unusable, unused, unwanted, worthless. 2 waste land. bare, barren, derelict, empty, overgrown, run-down, undeveloped. ● n 1 debris, dregs, effluent, excess, garbage, junk, leavings, leftovers, litter, offcuts, refuse, remnants, rubbish, scrap, scraps, trash, wastage. 2 extravagance, prodigality, wastefulness. ● v be wasteful with, dissipate, fritter, misspend, misuse, inf splurge, squander, use up. Opp CONSERVE. **waste away** become thin, mope, pine, weaken.

wasteful adj excessive, extravagant, improvident, imprudent, lavish, needless, prodigal, profligate, reckless, spendthrift, uneconomical. Opp ECONOMICAL. **wasteful person** ▷ SPENDTHRIFT.

watch n chronometer, clock, digital watch, stopwatch, timepiece, timer, wrist-watch.
● v 1 attend, concentrate, contemplate, eye, gaze, heed, keep your eyes on, look at, mark, note, observe, pay attention, regard, see, stare, take notice, view. 2 care for, chaperon, defend, guard, keep an eye on, look

after, mind, protect, superintend, supervise, take charge of, tend. **keep watch** ▷ GUARD. **on the watch** ▷ WATCHFUL. **watch your step** ▷ BEWARE.

watcher n pl audience, observer, onlooker, spectator, viewer, witness.

watchful adj attentive, eagle-eyed, heedful, observant, inf on the lookout, sharp-eyed, vigilant. ▷ ALERT. Opp INATTENTIVE.

watchman n caretaker, custodian, night-watchman, security guard. ▷ GUARD.

water n 1 brine, distilled water, drinking water, mineral water, rainwater, sea water, spring water, tap water. 2 lake, lido, ocean, pond, pool, river, sea. ▷ STREAM. ● v dampen, douse, drench, flood, hose, irrigate, moisten, saturate, soak, spray, sprinkle, wet. **water down** ▷ DILUTE.

waterfall n cascade, cataract, chute, rapids, torrent.

waterlogged adj full of water, saturated, soaked.

waterproof adj damp-proof, impermeable, impervious, water-resistant, watertight, weatherproof. Opp LEAKY. ● n cape, inf mac, mackintosh, sou'wester.

watertight adj hermetic, sealed, sound. ▷ WATERPROOF.

watery adj 1 aqueous, diluted, fluid, liquid, inf runny, inf sloppy, tasteless, thin, watered-down, weak, inf wishy-washy. 2 watery eyes. damp, moist, tearful, inf weepy.

wave n 1 billow, breaker, crest, ridge, ripple, roller, surf, swell, tidal wave, undulation, wavelet,

inf white horse. 2 flourish, gesticulation, gesture, shake, sign, signal. 3 wave of enthusiasm. current, flood, ground swell, outbreak, surge, tide, upsurge. 4 a new wave. advance, tendency, trend. ● v 1 billow, brandish, flap, flourish, fluctuate, flutter, move to and fro, ripple, shake, sway, swing, twirl, undulate, waft, wag, zigzag. 2 gesticulate, gesture, indicate, sign, signal. **wave aside** ▷ DISMISS.

wavelength n channel, station.

waver v be in two minds, dither, falter, flicker, hesitate, quaver, quiver, shake, sway, teeter, totter, tremble, vacillate, wobble.

wavy adj curly, curving, rippling, rolling, sinuous, undulating, up and down, winding, zigzag. Opp STRAIGHT.

way n 1 course, direction, journey, path, progress, road, route. 2 distance, length, stretch. 3 way to do something. approach, fashion, knack, manner, means, method, mode, procedure, process, system, technique. 4 foreign ways. custom, fashion, habit, practice, routine, style, tradition. 5 funny ways. characteristic, idiosyncrasy, peculiarity. 6 in some ways. aspect, detail, feature, particular, respect.

waylay v accost, ambush, buttonhole, detain, intercept, lie in wait for, surprise.

wayward adj disobedient, headstrong, obstinate, self-willed, stubborn, wilful. ▷ NAUGHTY. Opp COOPERATIVE.

weak adj 1 breakable, brittle, flimsy, fragile, frail, frangible, inadequate, insubstantial, rickety, shaky, slight, substandard, unsafe, unsound, unsteady. **2** *weak in health.* anaemic, debilitated, delicate, exhausted, feeble, frail, helpless, ill, infirm, listless, *inf* low, poorly, puny, sickly, *derog* weedy. **3** *weak character.* cowardly, fearful, impotent, indecisive, ineffective, ineffectual, powerless, pusillanimous, spineless, timid, unassertive, *inf* wimpish. **4** *weak position.* ▷ DEFENCELESS. **5** *weak excuses.* hollow, lame, *inf* pathetic, shallow, unconvincing. **6** *weak light.* dim, fading, faint, indistinct, pale, poor. **7** *weak tea.* diluted, tasteless, thin, watery. *Opp* STRONG.

weaken *v* **1** debilitate, destroy, dilute, diminish, emasculate, enervate, erode, exhaust, impair, lessen, lower, reduce, ruin, sap, soften, thin down, undermine, *inf* water down. **2** abate, decline, decrease, dwindle, ebb, fade, flag, give in, give way, sag, wane, yield. *Opp* STRENGTHEN.

weakling *n* coward, *inf* pushover, *inf* runt, weak person, *inf* weed, *inf* wimp.

weakness *n* **1** *inf* Achilles' heel, defect, failing, fault, flaw, flimsiness, fragility, frailty, imperfection, inadequacy, instability, shortcoming, *inf* weak spot. **2** debility, decrepitude, delicacy, feebleness, impotence, incapacity, infirmity, lassitude, vulnerability. ▷ ILLNESS. **3** affection, fancy, fondness, inclination, liking, partiality, penchant, predilection, *inf* soft spot, taste. *Opp* STRENGTH.

wealth *n* **1** affluence, assets, capital, fortune, means, money, opulence, possessions, property, prosperity, riches, *old use* substance. *Opp* POVERTY. **2** *wealth of information.* abundance, copiousness, cornucopia, mine, plenty, profusion, store. *Opp* SCARCITY.

wealthy *adj* affluent, *inf* flush, *inf* loaded, moneyed, opulent, privileged, prosperous, rich, *inf* well-heeled, well-off, well-to-do. *Opp* POOR. **wealthy person** billionaire, capitalist, millionaire, tycoon.

weapon *n* bomb, gun, missile. **weapons** armaments, armoury, arms, arsenal, magazine, munitions, ordnance, small arms, weaponry.

wear *v* **1** be dressed in, clothe yourself in, don, dress in, have on, put on, wrap up in. **2** *wear a smile.* adopt, assume, display. **3** *wears the carpet.* damage, fray, wear away, weaken. **4** *wear well.* endure, last, *inf* stand the test of time, survive. **wear away** ▷ ERODE. **wear off** ▷ SUBSIDE. **wear out** ▷ WEARY.

wearisome *adj* boring, dreary, exhausting, monotonous, repetitive, tedious, tiring, wearying. ▷ TROUBLESOME. *Opp* STIMULATING.

weary *adj* *inf* dead beat, *inf* dog-tired, *inf* done in, drained, enervated, exhausted, fatigued, fed up, flagging, footsore, jaded, *inf* jet-lagged, listless, *inf* shattered, *inf* sick (of), sleepy, spent, tired out, *inf* whacked, worn out. *Opp* FRESH, LIVELY.
● *v* **1** debilitate, drain, enervate, exhaust, fatigue, sap, *inf* shatter, tax, tire, wear out. *Opp* REFRESH. **2** become bored, become tired, flag, grow weary.

weather *n* climate, the elements, meteorological conditions.
● *v* ▷ SURVIVE. **under the weather** ▷ ILL.

weave *v* 1 braid, criss-cross, entwine, interlace, intertwine, interweave, knit, plait. 2 *weave a story*. compose, create, put together. 3 *weave your way*. dodge, *inf* twist and turn, wind, zigzag.

web *n* criss-cross, lattice, mesh, net, network.

wedding *n* marriage, nuptials, union.

wedge *v* cram, force, jam, pack, squeeze, stick.

weep *v* bawl, *inf* blub, blubber, cry, *inf* grizzle, lament, mewl, moan, shed tears, snivel, sob, wail, whimper, whine.

weigh *v* 1 measure the weight of. 2 assess, consider, contemplate, evaluate, judge, ponder, reflect on, think about, weigh up. 3 be important, carry weight, *inf* cut ice, count, matter. **weigh down** ▷ BURDEN. **weigh up** ▷ EVALUATE.

weight *n* 1 avoirdupois, burden, heaviness, load, mass, pressure, strain, tonnage. 2 *His voice had some weight*. authority, emphasis, force, gravity, importance, power, seriousness, substance. ● *v* hold down, load, make heavy, weigh down.

weird *adj* 1 creepy, eerie, ghostly, mysterious, *inf* scary, *inf* spooky, supernatural, uncanny, unearthly, unnatural. 2 *weird clothes*. abnormal, bizarre, curious, eccentric, *inf* funny, grotesque, odd, outlandish, peculiar, queer, strange, unconventional, unusual,

inf way-out. *Opp* CONVENTIONAL, NATURAL.

welcome *adj* acceptable, accepted, agreeable, appreciated, gratifying, much-needed, *inf* nice, pleasant, pleasing, pleasurable. *Opp* UNWELCOME.
● *n* greeting, hospitality, reception, salutation. ● *v* 1 greet, hail, receive. 2 *They welcome comments*. accept, appreciate, delight in, like, want.

weld *v* bond, cement, fuse, join, solder, unite.

welfare *n* advantage, benefit, felicity, good, happiness, health, interest, prosperity, well-being.

well *adj* 1 fit, healthy, hearty, *inf* in fine fettle, lively, robust, sound, strong, thriving, vigorous. 2 *All is well*. fine, *inf* OK, satisfactory. ● *n* fountain, source, spring, waterhole.

well-behaved *adj* cooperative, dutiful, good, law-abiding, manageable, polite, quiet, well-trained. ▷ OBEDIENT. *Opp* NAUGHTY.

well-bred *adj* courteous, cultured, genteel, polite, proper, refined, sophisticated, urbane, well-mannered. *Opp* RUDE.

well-built *adj* athletic, burly, muscular, powerful, stocky, *inf* strapping, strong, sturdy.

well-known *adj* celebrated, eminent, familiar, famous, illustrious, noted, *derog* notorious, prominent, renowned. *Opp* UNKNOWN.

well-meaning *adj* good-natured, obliging, sincere, well-intentioned, well-meant. ▷ KIND. *Opp* UNKIND.

well-off *adj* affluent, comfortable, moneyed, prosperous, rich, *inf* well-heeled, well-to-do. *Opp* POOR.

well-spoken *adj* articulate, educated, polite, *inf* posh, refined.

wet *adj* 1 awash, bedraggled, clammy, damp, dank, dewy, drenched, dripping, moist, saturated, soaked, soaking, sodden, soggy, sopping, waterlogged, wringing. 2 *wet weather*. drizzly, misty, pouring, rainy, showery, teeming. 3 *wet paint*. runny, sticky, tacky. ● *n* dampness, dew, drizzle, humidity, moisture, rain. ● *v* dampen, douse, drench, irrigate, moisten, saturate, soak, spray, sprinkle, steep, water. *Opp* DRY.

wheel *n* circle, disc, hoop, ring. ● *v* change direction, circle, gyrate, pivot, spin, swerve, swing round, swivel, turn, veer, whirl.

wheeze *v* breathe noisily, cough, gasp, pant, puff.

whereabouts *n* ▷ LOCATION.

whiff *n* breath, hint, puff, smell.

whim *n* caprice, desire, fancy, impulse, quirk, urge.

whine *v* complain, cry, *inf* grizzle, moan, wail, whimper, *inf* whinge.

whip *n* birch, cane, cat-o'-nine-tails, crop, lash, scourge, switch. ● *v* 1 beat, birch, cane, flog, lash, scourge, *sl* tan, thrash. ▷ HIT. 2 beat, stir vigorously, whisk.

whirl *v* circle, gyrate, pirouette, reel, revolve, rotate, spin, swivel, turn, twirl, wheel.

whirlpool *n* eddy, maelstrom, swirl, vortex, whirl.

whirlwind *n* cyclone, hurricane, tornado, typhoon, vortex.

whisk *n* beater, mixer. ● *v* beat, mix, stir, whip.

whiskers *pl n* bristles, hairs, moustache.

whisper *n* 1 murmur, undertone. 2 *whisper of scandal*. hint, rumour, suspicion, whiff. ● *v* breathe, hiss, murmur, mutter. ▷ TALK.

whistle *n* hooter, pipe, siren. ● *v* blow, pipe.

white *adj* chalky, ivory, milky, off-white, snow-white, snowy, spotless. ▷ PALE.

whiten *v* blanch, bleach, fade, lighten, pale.

whole *adj* coherent, complete, entire, full, in one piece, intact, perfect, sound, total, unabridged, unbroken, uncut, undamaged, undivided, unedited, unexpurgated, unscathed. *Opp* FRAGMENTARY, INCOMPLETE.

wholesale *adj* comprehensive, extensive, general, global, indiscriminate, mass, total, universal, widespread. *Opp* LIMITED.

wholesome *adj* beneficial, good, health-giving, healthy, hygienic, nourishing, nutritious, salubrious. *Opp* UNHEALTHY.

wicked *adj* abominable, *inf* awful, bad, base, beastly, corrupt, criminal, depraved, diabolical, dissolute, evil, foul, guilty, heinous, immoral, impious, incorrigible, indefensible, iniquitous, insupportable, intolerable, irresponsible, lawless, lost (*soul*), machiavellian, malevolent, malicious, mischievous, murderous, naughty, nefarious, offensive, perverted, scandalous, shameful, sinful, sinister, spiteful, *inf* terrible, ungodly, unprincipled, unrighteous, unscrupulous, vicious, vile, villainous, wrong. *Opp* MORAL. **wicked person** ▷ VILLAIN.

wickedness *n* depravity, guilt, immorality, infamy, iniquity, malice, misconduct, sin, sinfulness, spite, turpitude, vice, villainy, wrongdoing. ▷ EVIL.

wide *adj* **1** ample, broad, expansive, extensive, large, panoramic, spacious, vast, yawning. **2** *wide sympathies*. all-embracing, broad-minded, catholic, comprehensive, eclectic, inclusive, wide-ranging. **3** *arms open wide*. extended, outspread, outstretched. **4** *a wide shot*. off-course, off-target. *Opp* NARROW.

widen *v* augment, broaden, dilate, distend, enlarge, expand, extend, flare, increase, open out, spread, stretch.

widespread *adj* common, extensive, far-reaching, general, global, pervasive, prevalent, rife, universal, wholesale. *Opp* RARE.

width *n* beam (*of ship*), breadth, compass, diameter, distance across, extent, girth, range, scope, span, thickness.

wield *v* **1** brandish, flourish, handle, hold, ply, wave. **2** *wield power*. exercise, exert, possess, use.

wild *adj* **1** *wild animals*. free, undomesticated, untamed. **2** *wild country*. deserted, desolate, god-forsaken, overgrown, remote, rough, rugged, uncultivated, uninhabited, waste. **3** *wild people*. ferocious, fierce, savage, uncivilized. **4** *wild behaviour*. aggressive, boisterous, disorderly, hysterical, noisy, obstreperous, on the rampage, out of control, reckless, riotous, rowdy, uncontrollable, uncontrolled, undisciplined, unmanageable, unrestrained, unruly, uproarious, violent. **4** *wild weather*. blustery, stormy, tempestuous, turbulent, violent, windy. **5** *wild enthusiasm*. eager, excited, passionate, unrestrained. **6** *wild notions*. crazy, fantastic, irrational, silly, unreasonable. **7** *wild guess*. impetuous, inaccurate, random. *Opp* CALM, CULTIVATED, TAME.

wilderness *n* desert, jungle, waste, wasteland, wilds.

wile *n* artifice, machination, manoeuvre, plot, ploy, ruse, stratagem, subterfuge, trick.

wilful *adj* **1** calculated, conscious, deliberate, intended, intentional, premeditated, purposeful, voluntary. *Opp* ACCIDENTAL. **2** *wilful child*. *inf* bloody-minded, determined, headstrong, obstinate, perverse, refractory, self-willed, stubborn, unyielding, wayward. *Opp* AMENABLE.

will *n* aim, commitment, desire, determination, disposition, inclination, intention, purpose, resolution, resolve, volition, will-power, wish. ● *v* **1** encourage, influence, inspire, persuade. **2** bequeath, hand down, leave, pass on, settle on.

willing *adj* acquiescent, agreeable, amenable, complaisant, compliant, cooperative, disposed, docile, *inf* game, happy, helpful, inclined, pleased, prepared, obliging, ready, well-disposed. ▷ EAGER. *Opp* UNWILLING.

wilt *v* become limp, droop, fade, flag, flop, languish, sag, shrivel, weaken, wither. *Opp* THRIVE.

wily *adj* artful, astute, canny, clever, crafty, cunning, deceptive, designing, devious, disingenuous, guileful, scheming, *inf* shifty, shrewd, sly, underhand. ▷ DISHONEST.
Opp STRAIGHTFORWARD.

win *v* 1 be victorious, carry the day, come first, conquer, overcome, prevail, succeed, triumph. 2 *win a prize.* achieve, *inf* carry off, collect, earn, gain, get, obtain, *inf* pick up, receive, secure, *inf* walk away with. *Opp* LOSE.

wind *n* 1 air current, blast, breath, breeze, current of air, cyclone, draught, gale, gust, hurricane, puff, tornado, whirlwind. 2 *wind in the stomach.* flatulence, gas. ● *v* bend, coil, curl, curve, furl, loop, meander, ramble, roll, snake, spiral, turn, twine, twist, *inf* twist and turn, veer, wreathe, zigzag. **winding** ▷ TORTUOUS. **wind up** ▷ FINISH.

windswept *adj* bare, bleak, desolate, exposed. ▷ WINDY.

windy *adj* blowy, blustery, breezy, draughty, fresh, gusty, squally, stormy, tempestuous, windswept. *Opp* CALM.

wink *v* 1 bat (*eyelid*), blink, flutter. 2 flash, flicker, sparkle, twinkle.

winner *n inf* champ, champion, conqueror, medallist, prize-winner, title-holder, victor. *Opp* LOSER.

winning *adj* 1 champion, conquering, first, successful, top, top-scoring, triumphant, undefeated, victorious. *Opp* UNSUCCESSFUL. 2 *winning smile.* ▷ ATTRACTIVE.

wintry *adj* arctic, icy, snowy. ▷ COLD. *Opp* SUMMERY.

wipe *v* clean, cleanse, dry, mop, polish, rub, scour, sponge, swab, wash. **wipe out** ▷ DESTROY.

wire *n* 1 cable, flex, lead, wiring. 2 cablegram, telegram.

wiry *adj* lean, muscular, sinewy, strong, thin, tough.

wisdom *n* astuteness, common sense, discernment, discrimination, good sense, insight, judgement, penetration, perceptiveness, perspicacity, prudence, reason, sagacity, sense, understanding. ▷ INTELLIGENCE.

wise *adj* 1 astute, discerning, enlightened, erudite, fair, just, knowledgeable, perceptive, philosophical, sagacious, sage, sensible, shrewd, sound, thoughtful, understanding, well-informed. ▷ INTELLIGENT. 2 *wise decision.* advisable, considered, diplomatic, expedient, informed, judicious, politic, proper, prudent, rational, reasonable, right. *Opp* UNWISE. **wise person** philosopher, pundit, sage.

wish *n* aim, ambition, appetite, aspiration, craving, desire, fancy, hankering, hope, inclination, itch, keenness, longing, request, urge, want, yearning, *inf* yen. ● *v* ask, bid, desire, request, want. **wish for** ▷ WANT.

wisp *n* shred, strand, streak.

wispy *adj* flimsy, fragile, gossamer, insubstantial, light, thin. *Opp* SUBSTANTIAL.

wistful *adj* disconsolate, forlorn, melancholy, mournful, nostalgic, regretful, yearning. ▷ SAD.

wit *n* 1 banter, cleverness, comedy, facetiousness, humour,

ingenuity, repartee, witticisms, wordplay. ▷ INTELLIGENCE.
2 comedian, comic, humorist, joker, wag.

witch *n* enchantress, gorgon, hag, sibyl, sorceress, *pl* weird sisters.

witchcraft *n* black magic, charms, enchantment, magic, *inf* mumbo-jumbo, necromancy, the occult, sorcery, spells, voodoo, wizardry.

withdraw *v* 1 call back, cancel, *inf* go back on, recall, rescind, retract, take back. 2 *withdraw from the fight*. back away, back out, *inf* chicken out, *inf* opt off, draw back, drop out, move back, pull out, quit, recoil, retire, retreat, run away. ▷ LEAVE. *Opp* ADVANCE, ENTER.
3 *withdraw teeth*. extract, pull out, remove, take out.

withdrawn *adj* bashful, diffident, distant, introverted, private, quiet, reclusive, remote, reserved, retiring, shy, silent, solitary, taciturn, timid, uncommunicative. *Opp* SOCIABLE.

wither *v* become limp, dehydrate, droop, dry up, fail, flag, flop, sag, shrink, shrivel, waste away, wilt. ▷ THRIVE.

withhold *v* conceal, hide, hold back, keep secret, repress, retain, suppress. ▷ GIVE.

withstand *v* bear, confront, cope with, defy, endure, fight, grapple with, hold out against, oppose, put up with, resist, stand up to, *inf* stick, survive, take, weather (*storm*). *Opp* SURRENDER.

witness *n* bystander, eyewitness, looker-on, observer, onlooker, spectator, viewer, watcher.
● *v* be present at, notice, observe,

see, view, watch. **bear witness** ▷ TESTIFY.

witty *adj* amusing, clever, comic, droll, facetious, funny, humorous, ingenious, intelligent, jocular, waggish.

wizard *n* enchanter, magician, magus, sorcerer, *old use* warlock, witch-doctor.

wobble *v* be unsteady, move unsteadily, quake, quiver, rock, shake, sway, teeter, totter, vibrate, waver.

wobbly *adj* loose, rickety, rocky, shaky, teetering, tottering, unsafe, unstable, unsteady. *Opp* STEADY.

woe *n* affliction, anguish, dejection, despair, distress, grief, heartache, melancholy, misery, misfortune, sadness, suffering, trouble, unhappiness, wretchedness. ▷ SORROW. *Opp* HAPPINESS.

woebegone *adj* crestfallen, dejected, downhearted, forlorn, gloomy, melancholy, miserable, woeful, wretched. ▷ SAD. *Opp* CHEERFUL.

woman *n* bride, daughter, dowager, female, girl, girlfriend, housewife, lady, lass, madam, maid, *old use* maiden, matriarch, matron, mistress, mother, virgin, widow, wife.

wonder *n* 1 admiration, amazement, astonishment, awe, bewilderment, curiosity, fascination, respect, reverence, stupefaction, surprise. 2 *wonder of science*. marvel, miracle, phenomenon.
● *v* ask yourself, be curious, conjecture, marvel, ponder, speculate. ▷ THINK. **wonder at** ▷ ADMIRE.

wonderful *adj* amazing, astonishing, astounding, awe-inspiring, extraordinary, impressive, incredible, marvellous, miraculous, phenomenal, remarkable, surprising, unexpected. *Opp* ORDINARY.

woo *v* 1 *sl* chat up, court. 2 *woo custom*. attract, cultivate, persuade, pursue, seek, tempt.

wood *n* 1 afforestation, coppice, copse, forest, grove, jungle, orchard, plantation, spinney, thicket, trees, woodland, woods. 2 chipboard, deal, hardwood, lumber, planks, plywood, softwood, timber.

wooded *adj* afforested, *poet* bosky, forested, sylvan, timbered, tree-covered, woody.

wooden *adj* 1 timber, wood. 2 *wooden acting*. dead, emotionless, expressionless, lifeless, rigid, stiff, stilted, unnatural. *Opp* LIVELY.

woodwork *n* carpentry, joinery.

woody *adj* fibrous, hard, tough, wooden.

woolly *adj* 1 wool, woollen. 2 *woolly toy*. cuddly, fleecy, furry, fuzzy, shaggy, soft. 3 *woolly ideas*. confused, hazy, ill-defined, indefinite, uncertain, unclear, unfocused, vague.

word *n* 1 expression, name, term. 2 ▷ NEWS. 3 ▷ PROMISE. ● *v* articulate, express, phrase. **word for word** ▷ VERBATIM.

wording *n* choice of words, expression, language, phraseology, phrasing, style, terminology.

wordy *adj* diffuse, digressive, discursive, garrulous, long-winded, loquacious, prolix, rambling, repetitious, talkative, unstoppable, verbose, voluble. *Opp* CONCISE.

work *n* 1 *inf* donkey work, drudgery, effort, exertion, *inf* fag, *inf* graft, *inf* grind, industry, labour, *inf* slog, *inf* spadework, strain, struggle, *inf* sweat, toil. 2 *work to be done*. assignment, chore, commission, duty, errand, job, mission, project, responsibility, task, undertaking. 3 *regular work*. business, calling, career, employment, job, livelihood, living, métier, occupation, post, profession, situation, trade. ● *v* 1 *inf* beaver away, drudge, exert yourself, *inf* grind away, *inf* keep your nose to the grindstone, labour, *inf* plug away, *inf* slave, *inf* slog away, strain, strive, struggle, sweat, toil. 2 be effective, function, go, operate, perform, run, succeed, thrive. 3 *work employees hard*. drive, use, utilize. **working** ▷ EMPLOYED, OPERATIONAL. **work out** ▷ CALCULATE. **work up** ▷ DEVELOP, EXCITE.

worker *n* artisan, breadwinner, craftsman, employee, *old use* hand, labourer, member of staff, navvy, operative, operator, tradesman, wage-earner, workman.

workforce *n* employees, staff, workers.

workmanship *n* art, artistry, craft, craftsmanship, expertise, handiwork, skill, technique.

workshop *n* factory, mill, studio, workroom.

world *n* 1 earth, globe, planet. 2 *the art world*. domain, field, milieu, sphere.

worldly *adj* 1 earthly, human, mundane, physical, secular, temporal. 2 cosmopolitan, urbane, sophisticated. **3** covetous, greedy, materialistic, selfish.

worm v crawl, creep, slither, squirm, wriggle. writhe.

worn adj **1** frayed, moth-eaten, old, ragged, inf scruffy, shabby, tattered, inf tatty, thin, thread-bare. **2** worn out. ▷ WEARY.

worried adj afraid, agitated, alarmed, anxious, apprehensive, bothered, concerned, distraught, distressed, disturbed, edgy, fearful, inf fraught, fretful, insecure, nervous, obsessed (by), on edge, overwrought, perplexed, perturbed, tense, troubled, uncertain, uneasy, unhappy, upset.

worry n **1** agitation, anxiety, apprehension, disquiet, distress, fear, perplexity, tension, unease, uneasiness. **2** affliction, bother, burden, care, concern, misgiving, problem, pl trials and tribulations, trouble. ● v **1** agitate, annoy, badger, bother, disquiet, distress, disturb, inf hassle, irritate, nag, perplex, perturb, pester, plague, torment, trouble, upset. Opp REASSURE. **2** worry about money. agonize, be anxious, brood, exercise yourself, feel uneasy, fret.

worsen v **1** aggravate, exacerbate, intensify, make worse. **2** His health worsened. decline, degenerate, deteriorate, get worse, inf go downhill. Opp IMPROVE.

worship n adoration, devotion, glorification, homage, love, praise, reverence, veneration. ● v admire, adore, be devoted to, dote on, exalt, glorify, hero-worship, idolize, lionize, laud, look up to, love, pay homage to, praise, pray to, inf put on a pedestal, revere, venerate.

worth n benefit, cost, good, importance, merit, quality, significance, use, usefulness, utility, value. be worth be priced at, cost, have a value of.

worthless adj dispensable, disposable, futile, inf good-for-nothing, hollow, insignificant, meaningless, meretricious, paltry, pointless, poor, inf rubbishy, inf trashy, trifling, trivial, unimportant, unprofitable, useless, vain, valueless. Opp WORTHWHILE.

worthwhile adj advantageous, beneficial, considerable, fruitful, gratifying, helpful, important, invaluable, meaningful, noticeable, productive, profitable, remunerative, rewarding, satisfying, significant, sizeable, substantial, useful, valuable. ▷ WORTHY. Opp WORTHLESS.

worthy adj admirable, commendable, creditable, decent, deserving, estimable, good, honest, honourable, laudable, meritorious, praiseworthy, reputable, respectable, worthwhile. Opp UNWORTHY.

wound n **1** bite, bruise, burn, contusion, cut, damage, gash, graze, injury, laceration, scar, scratch. **2** distress, grief, hurt, insult, pain, trauma. ● v **1** bite, bruise, cut, damage, harm, hurt, gore, graze, injure, lacerate, lash, maul, scratch, shoot, stab. **2** cause pain to, distress, grieve, offend, shock, traumatize. Opp HEAL, MEND.

wrap n cape, cloak, mantle, poncho, shawl, stole. ● v bundle up, cloak, cocoon, conceal, cover, encase, enclose, enfold, envelop, hide, insulate, lag, muffle, pack, package, shroud, surround, swathe.

wreathe v adorn, decorate, encircle, festoon, intertwine, interweave, twist, weave.

wreck n 1 hulk, shipwreck. ▷ WRECKAGE. 2 *wreck of all my hopes.* demolition, destruction, devastation, loss, obliteration, overthrow, ruin, undoing. ● v 1 annihilate, break up, crush, dash to pieces, demolish, destroy, devastate, ruin, shatter, smash, spoil, *inf* write off. 2 *wreck a ship.* capsize, founder, scuttle, sink, shipwreck.

wreckage n debris, flotsam and jetsam, fragments, pieces, remains, rubble, ruins.

wrench v force, jerk, lever, prize, pull, rip, strain, tear, tug, twist, wrest, wring, *inf* yank.

wrestle v grapple, strive, struggle, tussle. ▷ FIGHT.

wretch n 1 miserable person, poor devil, unfortunate. 2 rascal, rogue, scoundrel, villain.

wretched adj 1 dejected, depressed, dispirited, downhearted, hapless, melancholy, miserable, pitiful, unfortunate. ▷ SAD. 2 ▷ UNSATISFACTORY.

wriggle v crawl, snake, squirm, twist, worm, writhe.

wring v 1 clasp, crush, grip, shake, squeeze, twist, wrench, wrest. 2 coerce, extort, extract, force.

wrinkle n corrugation, crease, crinkle, *pl* crow's feet, fold, furrow, gather, line, pleat, pucker, ridge, ripple. ● v corrugate, crease, crinkle, crumple, fold, furrow, gather, pleat, pucker up, ridge, ripple, rumple, screw up.

wrinkled adj corrugated, creased, crinkly, crumpled, furrowed, lined, pleated, ridged, rumpled, screwed up, shrivelled, wizened, wrinkly. *Opp* SMOOTH.

write v compile, compose, copy, correspond, draft, draw up, inscribe, jot, note, pen, print, put in writing, record, scrawl, scribble, take down, transcribe.

write off ▷ CANCEL, DESTROY.

writer n author, columnist, composer, contributor, correspondent, dramatist, essayist, *derog* hack, journalist, novelist, *derog* pen-pusher, playwright, poet, reporter, scribe, scriptwriter.

writhe v coil, contort, squirm, struggle, thrash about, twist, wriggle.

writing n 1 calligraphy, characters, copperplate, handwriting, hieroglyphics, inscription, longhand, penmanship, scrawl, screed, scribble, script. 2 literature, letters. 3 [*often pl*] article, book, column, composition, correspondence, diary, document, editorial, essay, fiction, manuscript, non-fiction, novel, play, poem, poetry, prose, opus, publication, review, text, treatise, typescript, work.

written adj documentary, *inf* in black and white, inscribed, in writing, set down, transcribed, typewritten. *Opp* SPOKEN.

wrong adj 1 base, corrupt, criminal, *inf* crooked, deceitful, dishonest, dishonourable, evil, illegal, illegitimate, illicit, immoral, iniquitous, irresponsible, misleading, reprehensible, sinful, specious, unethical, unjustifiable, unlawful, unprincipled, unscrupulous, vicious, villainous, wicked. *Opp* 2 *wrong*

answers. erroneous, false, imprecise, inaccurate, incorrect, misleading, mistaken, wide of the mark. **3** *wrong decision, idea*. illadvised, ill-considered, illjudged, impolitic, imprudent, injudicious, misguided, misjudged, unfair, unfounded, unjust, untrue, unwise, wrongful. **4** *He saw nothing wrong in his behaviour*. improper, inappropriate, incongruous, unacceptable, undesirable, unseemly, unsuitable, **5** *Something's wrong*. amiss, defective, faulty, out of order, the matter. *Opp* RIGHT.
● *v* abuse, cheat, do an injustice to, harm, hurt, injure, malign, misrepresent, mistreat, treat unfairly. **do wrong**
▷ MISBEHAVE.

wrongdoer *n* convict, criminal, *inf* crook, culprit, delinquent, evil-doer, law-breaker, malefactor, mischief-maker, miscreant, offender, sinner, transgressor.

wrongdoing *n* crime, delinquency, disobedience, evil, iniquity, malpractice, misbehaviour, mischief, naughtiness, offence, sin, wickedness.

wry *adj* **1** askew, awry, crooked, lopsided, twisted, uneven. **2** *wry sense of humour*. droll, dry, ironic, mocking, sardonic.

yawning *adj* gaping, open, wide.

yearly *adj* annual, perennial.

yearn *v* ache, hanker, hunger, itch, long, pine. ▷ WANT.

yellow *adj* blond(e), gold, golden, tawny.

yield *n* **1** crop, harvest, output, product. **2** earnings, gain, income, interest, proceeds, profit, return, revenue.
● *v* **1** acquiesce, assent, bow, capitulate, *inf* cave in, comply, concede, defer, give in, give way, submit, succumb, surrender, *inf* throw in the towel. **2** *yield interest*. bear, earn, generate, pay out, produce, provide, return, supply. **yielding**
▷ FLEXIBLE, SUBMISSIVE.

young *adj* baby, early, growing, immature, new-born, undeveloped. **2** *young people*. adolescent, juvenile, pubescent, teenage, underage, youthful. **3** *young for your age*. babyish, boyish, childish, girlish, *inf* green, immature, infantile, juvenile, naive, puerile. ● *n* brood, family, issue, litter, offspring, progeny.

youth *n* **1** adolescence, boyhood, childhood, girlhood, infancy, minority, puberty, *inf* salad days, *inf* teens. **2** adolescent, boy, juvenile, *inf* kid, lad, minor, teenager, youngster.

youthful *adj* fresh, lively, sprightly, vigorous, wellpreserved. ▷ YOUNG.

Y

yard *n* court, courtyard, enclosure, garden.

yarn *n* **1** fibre, thread. **2** anecdote, narrative, story, tale.

Z

zany *adj* absurd, eccentric, *inf* mad, madcap, ridiculous.

zeal *n derog* bigotry, enthusiasm, fanaticism, fervour, partisanship.

zealot *n* bigot, extremist, fanatic, radical.

zealous *adj* eager, earnest, enthusiastic, fanatical, fervent, keen, militant, obsessive, partisan, passionate. *Opp* APATHETIC.

zenith *n* acme, apex, height, highest point, peak, pinnacle, summit, top. *Opp* NADIR.

zero *n* nil, nothing, nought, *sl* zilch. **zero in on** ▷ AIM.

zest *n* appetite, eagerness, energy, enjoyment, enthusiasm, gusto, passion, relish, zeal.

zigzag *adj inf* bendy, *inf* in and out, indirect, meandering, serpentine, twisting, winding.
● *v* bend, curve, meander, snake, tack, twist, wind.

zone *n* area, belt, district, locality, neighbourhood, quarter, region, sector, sphere, territory, vicinity.

zoom *v* career, dart, dash, hurry, hurtle, race, rush, shoot, speed, *inf* whiz, *inf* zip.